# University Textbook Series
## Especially Designed for Collateral Reading
### HARRY W. JONES
**Directing Editor**
Professor of Law, Columbia University

---

**ADMIRALTY**
Grant Gilmore, Professor of Law, University of Chicago.
Charles L. Black, Jr., Professor of Law, Yale University.

**ADMIRALTY AND FEDERALISM**
David W. Robertson, Professor of Law, University of Texas.

**CIVIL PROCEDURE, BASIC**
Milton D. Green, Professor of Law, University of California, Hastings College of the Law.

**COMMERCIAL TRANSACTIONS—Selected Statutes, Fourth Edition**
Robert Braucher, Professor of Law, Harvard University.
Arthur E. Sutherland, Jr., Professor of Law, Harvard University.

**CONFLICT OF LAWS, Third Edition**
The late George W. Stumberg, Professor of Law, University of Texas.

**CONFLICT OF LAWS, COMMENTARY ON THE**
Russell J. Weintraub, Professor of Law, University of Texas.

**CORPORATIONS, Second Edition**
Norman D. Lattin, Professor of Law, University of California, Hastings College of the Law.

**CRIMINAL LAW, Second Edition**
Rollin M. Perkins, Professor of Law, University of California, Hastings College of the Law.

**ESTATES IN LAND & FUTURE INTERESTS, PREFACE TO**
Thomas F. Bergin, Professor of Law, University of Virginia.
Paul G. Haskell, Professor of Law, Case Western Reserve University.

**EVIDENCE: COMMON SENSE AND COMMON LAW**
John M. Maguire, Professor of Law, Harvard University.

**EVIDENCE, STUDENTS' TEXT ON THE LAW OF**
John Henry Wigmore.

**JURISPRUDENCE: MEN AND IDEAS OF THE LAW**
The late Edwin W. Patterson, Cardozo Professor of Jurisprudence, Columbia University.

**LEGAL RESEARCH, FUNDAMENTALS OF, Fourth Edition, with 1973 Assignments Pamphlet**
J. Myron Jacobstein, Professor of Law, Law Librarian, Stanford University.
Roy M. Mersky, Professor of Law, Director of Research, University of Texas.

**THE PROFESSION OF LAW**
L. Ray Patterson, Professor of Law, Vanderbilt University.
Elliott E. Cheatham, Professor of Law, Vanderbilt University.

**PROPERTY**
John E. Cribbet, Dean of the Law School, University of Illinois.

**TORTS**
Clarence Morris, Professor of Law, University of Pennsylvania.

**TRUSTS, Second Edition**
Ralph A. Newman, Professor of Law, University of California, Hastings College of the Law.

**TRUSTS AND WILLS, THE PLANNING AND DRAFTING OF**
Thomas L. Shaffer, Dean of the Law School, University of Notre Dame.

ERVIN H. POLLACK'S

# FUNDAMENTALS

OF

# LEGAL RESEARCH

FOURTH EDITION

By

**J. MYRON JACOBSTEIN**

Professor of Law and Law Librarian
Stanford University

and

**ROY M. MERSKY**

Director of Research and Professor of Law
University of Texas, Austin

Mineola, N. Y.
THE FOUNDATION PRESS, INC.
1973

To our Families

He Who Cites His Source, Brings Deliverance to the World.

*Mishnah, Avot. VI*

# FOREWORD

This fourth edition of *Fundamentals of Legal Research* is presented by the new editors as a tribute and in memory of Ervin H. Pollack.

When the gravestone of Sir William Blackstone was erected, it contained the following tribute:

> "He's gone, whose talents charmed the wise,
> Who rescued law from pedant phrase,
> Who cleared the student's clouded eyes,
> And led him through the legal maze."

Since 1956 countless students of legal research have seen through the legal maze with less clouded eyes because of the first three editions of this work by Ervin Harold Pollack. The design and structure of the volume were innovative and evidenced the pioneering labors in the field of teaching legal research. But he would have been the first to admit that the result was not perfect. Twice in his lifetime he strove to improve his endeavor. In 1962 and 1967 he published up-dated versions of the original manuscript. It is fitting that a further revision be published as a memorial of his achievements.

As a teacher and librarian he was not unmindful of the complexities of legal research. At Ohio State he taught courses on legal process and legal research and writing. As administrator of the law library there, he provided both the required resources and an ease in using them. During twenty-five years as law librarian, he strove for excellence in building his collection until, at his death, the library was the sixth largest academic law library in the country. He instituted innovations which allowed a facility of access often found only in personal libraries. It was this proficiency at home which provoked the calls for help from others.

He founded the Ohio Association of Law Libraries, served the American Association of Law Libraries as President, and sat as Trustee of the Ohio Legal Center Foundation. His reputation extended beyond the United States, and he was invited to assist the Organization of Central American States as economic consultant. They gave him their Certificate of Merit and dedicated to him their Central American Economic Integration Law.

At home and abroad he was recognized as a legal scholar. But those who knew him for his professional expertise were aware of only one side of the man. It is for his friends to reflect on the joy of having known him while he lived and to remember with pleasure the companionship which he offered. They tell us that as a librarian he was imaginative, alert, resilient, accommodating, gifted in administration with an open-minded interest and a sense of community responsibility. As a man: kind, gentle, and understanding.

To read his words again is to provide a reminder of the achievement that he gained. The revisions in this edition are offered as a reminder of the effort which he made to improve the ease and facility of research for those whose clouded eyes still peer through the legal maze.

There is little need to say that the value of this publication rests with the original scholarship; there is need to aver that any present shortcomings spring from the actions of the current collaborators.

J. MYRON JACOBSTEIN
ROY M. MERSKY

# PREFACE

Authors of books on legal research have always faced the dilema of reconciling the desire for completeness with the realization that their work is intended primarily for students beginning the study of law.  In preparing this new edition we have consciously kept in mind that the book is not intended to be a definitive source for legal bibliography, but rather an aid to students who are learning how to do legal research.

It is intended that both the text and the illustrations in each chapter should be studied for a proper understanding of the format and use of the legal materials described.  Only the summary and citation sections of the chapters are intended primarily for reference purposes.

As most law students begin the study of law with the reading of court decisions, it is the Editors' belief that it is easier to begin the study of legal research with case law.  The organization, however, of the chapters is such that instruction may conveniently begin with any part of the book.

We wish to express our deep appreciation to all members of our libraries' staff who contributed to the preparation of this edition.  In particular, we wish to thank the following: Gwyn Anderson, Lance Dickson, Yi-Ning (Frank) Liu, Harry S. Martin, Beth Mobley, Catherine Porter, and Leslie Sheridan, of the Tarlton Law Library of The University of Texas at Austin; and Adrienne Adan, Howard Sugarman, and George Torzsay-Biber, of the Stanford University Law Library.

J. MYRON JACOBSTEIN
ROY M. MERSKY

May, 1973

\*

# SUMMARY OF CONTENTS

## APPENDICES

\*

# TABLE OF CONTENTS

## TABLE OF CONTENTS

## TABLE OF CONTENTS

# GLOSSARY OF TERMS USED
# IN LEGAL RESEARCH

This glossary of terms is limited in scope and the definitions of words are restricted in meaning to their legal or legal research context. Words whose meanings conform to general usage and are obvious are omitted from the list, e. g., Index.

### ACT

Is an alternative name for statutory law. When introduced into the first house of the legislature, a piece of proposed legislation is known as a bill. When passed to the next house, it may then be referred to as an act. After enactment the terms "law" and "act" may be used interchangeably. An act has the same legislative force as a joint resolution but is technically distinguishable, being of a different form and introduced with the words "Be it enacted" instead of "Be it resolved."

### ADVANCE SHEETS

Are current pamphlets containing the most recently reported opinions of a court or the courts of several jurisdictions. The volume and page numbers usually are the same as in the subsequently bound volumes of the series, which cover several numbers of the advance sheets.

### ADVISORY OPINION

May be rendered by a court at the request of the government or an interested party indicating how the court would rule on a matter should adversary litigation develop. An advisory opinion is thus an interpretation of the law without binding effect. The International Court of Justice and some state courts will render advisory opinions; the United States Supreme Court will not.

### AMICUS CURIAE

Means, literally, friend of the court. A party with strong interest in or views on the subject matter of the dispute will petition the court for permission to file a brief, ostensibly on behalf of a party but actually to suggest a rationale consistent with its own views.

### ANALYSIS

Generally follows the scope-note, giving a conceptual breakdown of the topic into main and subordinate categories.

### ANNOTATIONS

Are: (1) Statutory: brief summaries of the law and facts of cases interpreting statutes passed by Congress or state legislatures which are included in codes, or (2) Textual: expository essays of varying length on significant legal topics chosen from selected cases published with the essays.

## ANSWER

Is the pleading filed by the defendant in response to plaintiff's complaint.

## APPEAL PAPERS

Are briefs and transcripts of records on appeal filed by attorneys with courts in connection with litigation. A brief consists of a summary of the facts and circumstances or legal propositions as presented by a party to a pending action.

## ATTORNEY GENERAL OPINIONS

Are issued by the government's chief counsel at the request of some governmental body and interpret the law for the requesting agency in the same manner as a private attorney would for his client. The opinions are not binding on the courts but are usually accorded some degree of persuasive authority.

## AUTHORITY

Refers to the precedential value to be accorded an opinion of a judicial or administrative body. A court's opinion is binding authority on other courts directly below it in the judicial hierarchy. Opinions of lower courts or of courts outside the hierarchy are governed by the degree to which it adheres to the doctrine of stare decisis. See: Stare decisis.

Authority may also be either primary or secondary. Statute law, administrative regulations issued pursuant to enabling legislation, and case law are primary authority and if applicable will usually determine the outcome of a case. Other statements of or about law are considered secondary authority, and thus not binding.

## BILL

Refers to a legislative proposal introduced in the legislature. The term distinguishes unfinished legislation from directly enacted law.

## BRIEFS AND RECORDS

See: Appeal Papers.

## CALENDAR

Can mean the order in which cases are to be heard during a term of court. *Martindale-Hubbel Law Directory* contains calendars for state and federal courts, and includes the name of the court, the name of the judge, and the date of the term's beginning.

## CERTIORARI

Is a Latin term meaning to be informed of. Most of the cases determined by the United States Supreme Court reach the Court on writs of certiorari. Granting this writ is discretionary with the Court, a fact which allows it some control over its burgeoning docket.

## CITATION

Is the reference to authority necessary to substantiate the validity of one's argument or position. Citation to authority and supporting references is both important and extensive in any form of legal writing. Citation form is also given emphasis in legal writing, and early familiarity with *A Uniform System of Citation* will stand the law student in good stead.

## CITATORS

Provide, through letter-form abbreviations or words, judicial history and interpretation of reported decisions, and information as to cases and legislative enactments construing, applying or affecting statutes.

## CITED CASE

Is a case which is treated by other cases.

## CITING CASE

Is the case which operates on the cited case.

## CODE

By popular usage means a compilation or a revised statute. Technically, however, in it the laws in force are rewritten and arranged in classified order, with the addition of material having the force of law taken from judicial decrees. The repealed and temporary acts are eliminated and the revision is re-enacted.

## COMMON LAW

Is the origin of the Anglo-American legal systems. English common law was largely customary law and unwritten, until discovered, applied, and reported by the courts of law. In theory, the common law courts did not create law but rather discovered it in the customs and habits of the English people. The strength of the judicial system in pre-parliamentary days is one reason for the continued emphasis in common law systems on case law. In a narrow sense, common law is the phrase still used to distinguish case law from statutory law.

## COMPILED STATUTES

By popular usage means a code. Technically, however, it prints acts verbatim as originally enacted but in a new classified order. The text is not modified; however, the repealed and temporary acts are omitted.

## COMPLAINT

Is the plaintiff's initial pleading and, according to the Federal Rules of Civil Procedure, is no longer full of the technicalities demanded by the common law. A complaint need only contain a short and plain statement of the claim upon which relief is sought, an indication of the type of relief requested, and an indication that the court has jurisdiction to hear the case.

### CONCURRING OPINION

Is an opinion of a judge which agrees with the decision of the majority but disagrees with the reasoning.

### CONGRESSIONAL DOCUMENTS

Are important sources for legislative histories, which are often necessary for proper interpretation of statute law. Congressional documents are most accessible through specialized indexes and include hearings before Congressional committees, reports by or to House or Senate committees, and special studies conducted under Congressional authority.

### CONSOLIDATED STATUTES

By popular usage means a code. Technically, however, in it the text of the acts are rewritten, arranged in classified order and re-enacted. The repealed and temporary acts are eliminated.

### CONSTITUTION

Contains the fundamental law of any organization possessing one. Most national constitutions are written; the English and Israeli constitutions are unwritten.

### COURT DECISION

Is the disposition of the case by the court. See: Court Opinion.

### COURT OPINION

Is an explanation of the court's decision. Often, however, the term is used interchangeably, but inaccurately, with Court Decision.

### DECREE

Is a special type of court order, most often used in divorce actions where the court sets out the details of alimony, custody, support and visitation rights. Before certain administrative agencies, consent decrees are awarded where a corporation agrees to act in a certain matter and thus ends litigation against it.

### DICTUM

See: Obiter Dictum.

### DIGEST

Is an index to reported cases, providing brief, unconnected statements of court holdings or facts of cases, which is arranged by subject and subdivided by jurisdiction and courts.

### DISSENTING OPINION

Expresses disagreement of one or more judges of a court with a decision in a case rendered by the majority.

## EN BANC

Refers to a session where the entire bench of the court will participate in the decision rather than the regular quorum. In other countries, it is common for a court to have more members than are usually necessary to hear an appeal. In the United States, the Circuit Courts of Appeal usually sit in groups of three judges but for important cases may expand the bench to nine members, when they are said to be sitting *en banc*.

## ENCYCLOPEDIA

Contains expository statements on principles of law, topically arranged, with supporting footnote references to cases in point.

## EXECUTIVE AGREEMENT

Is an international agreement, not a treaty, concluded by the President without senatorial consent on his authority as Commander-in-Chief and director of foreign relations. The distinction between treaty and executive agreement is complicated and often of questionable constitutionalities, but the import of such agreements as that of Yalta or Potsdam is unquestionably great.

## EXECUTIVE ORDERS

Are issued by the President under specific authority granted to him by Congress. There is no precise distinction between presidential proclamations and executive orders; however, proclamations generally cover matters of widespread interest, and executive orders often relate to the conduct of government business or to organization of the executive departments. Every act of the President authorizing or directing the performance of an act, in its general context, is an executive order. See: Presidential Proclamations.

## FORMS OF ACTION

Governed common law pleading and were the procedural devices used to give expression to the theories of liability recognized by the common law. Failure to analyze the cause of action properly, to select the proper theory of liability and to choose the appropriate procedural mechanism or forms of action could easily result in being thrown out of court. A plaintiff had to elect his remedy in advance and could not subsequently amend his pleadings to conform to his proof or to the court's choice of another theory of liability. According to the relief sought, actions have been divided into three categories: real actions were brought for the recovery of real property; mixed actions were brought to recover real property and damages for injury to it; personal actions were brought to recover debts or personal property, or for injuries to personal, property, or contractual rights. The common law actions are usually considered to be eleven in number: trespass, trespass on the case, trover, ejectment, detinue, replevin, debt, covenant, account, special assumpsit, and general assumpsit.

**FORM–BOOKS**

Include sample instruments which are helpful in drafting legal documents.

**HEADNOTE**

Is a brief summary of a legal rule or significant facts in a case, which, among other headnotes applicable to the case, precedes the printed opinion in reports.

**HEARINGS**

Are extensively employed by both legislative and administrative agencies and can be adjudicative or merely investigatory. Adjudicative hearings can be appealed in a court of law. Congressional committees often hold hearings prior to enactment of legislation; these hearings are then important sources of legislative history.

**HOLDING**

Is the declaration of the conclusion of law reached by the court as to the legal effect of the facts of the case.

**HORNBOOK**

Is the popular reference to a series of textbooks published by West Publishing Company which reviews a certain field of law in summary, textual form, as opposed to a casebook which is designed as a teaching tool and includes many reprints of court opinions.

**LEGISLATIVE HISTORY**

Provides the meanings and interpretations of a statute (intent) as embodied in legislative documents. Also, citations and dates to legislative enactments, amendments and repeals of statutes are sometimes imprecisely identified as legislative histories. More accurate designations of these citations of legislative changes, as included in codes, are historical notes or amendatory histories.

**LOOSE–LEAF SERVICES AND REPORTERS**

Contain federal and state administrative regulations and decisions and applicable statutes. They consist of separate, perforated leaves in special binders, simplifying frequent substitution and insertion of new leaves.

**MEMORANDUM OPINION**

Is a brief holding of the whole court in which the opinion is very concise or totally absent.

**MODEL CODES**

Are formulated by various groups or institutions to serve as model laws for legislatures, and may be intended as improvements over existing laws or as sources of unification of diverse state legislation.

**MOOT**

Points are no longer subjects of contention and are raised only for purposes of discussion or hypothesis. Many law schools have moot courts where students gain practice by arguing hypothetical or moot cases.

**NISI PRIUS**

Generally refers to a court where a case is first tried, as distinguished from an appellate court.

**NOTER–UP**

Is the term used in the British Commonwealth countries for a citator.

**OBITER DICTUM**

Is an official, incidental comment, not necessary to the formulation of the decision, made by the judge in his opinion which is not binding as precedent.

**OFFICIAL REPORTS**

Are court reports directed by statute.

**OPINION**

See: Court Opinion.

**ORDINANCE**

Is the equivalent of a municipal statute, passed by the city council and governing matters not already covered by federal or state law.

**PARALLEL CITATION**

Is a citation reference to the same case printed in two or more different reports.

**PER CURIAM OPINION**

Is an opinion of the whole court as distinguished from an opinion written by a specific judge.

**PERMANENT LAW**

Is an act which continues in force for an indefinite time.

**PETITION**

Is an application to a court requesting relief or some action of judicial authority.

**PLEADINGS**

Are the technical means by which parties to a dispute frame the issue for the court. The plaintiff's complaint or declaration is all followed by the defendant's answer; subsequent papers may be filed as needed.

## POCKET SUPPLEMENT

Is a paper-back supplement to a book, inserted in the book through a slit in its back cover. Depending on the type of publication, it may have textual, case or statutory references keyed to the original publication.

## PRECEDENT

See: Stare Decisis.

## PRESIDENTIAL PROCLAMATIONS

Are issued under specific authority granted to the President by Congress. Generally, they relate to matters of widespread interest. Some proclamations have no legal effect but merely are appeals to the public, e. g., the observance of American Education Week. See: Executive Orders.

## PRIMARY AUTHORITY

Judicial precedent or legislative enactment which is cited as first or mandatory authority.

## PRIVATE LAW

Is an act which relates to a specific person.

## PUBLIC LAW

Is an act which relates to the public as a whole. It may be (1) general (applies to all persons within the jurisdiction), (2) local (applies to a geographical area), or (3) special (relates to an organization which is charged with a public interest).

## RATIO DECIDENDI

Is the point in a case which determines the result—the basis of the decision.

## RECORDS AND BRIEFS

See: Appeal Papers.

## REGULATIONS

Are issued by various governmental departments to carry out the intent of the law. Agencies issue regulations to guide the activity of their employees and to ensure uniform application of the law. Regulations are not the work of the legislature and do not have the effect of law in theory. In practice, however, because of the intricacies of judicial review of administrative action, regulations can have an important effect in determining the outcome of cases involving regulatory activity. United States Government regulations appear first in the *Federal Register*, published five days a week, and are subsequently arranged by subject in the *Code of Federal Regulations*.

## REPORTS

Are (1) (court reports) published judicial cases arranged according to some grouping, such as jurisdiction, court, period of time, subject matter or case significance, (2) (administrative reports or decisions) published decisions of an administrative agency, (3) annual statements of progress, activities or policy issued by an administrative agency or an association.

## RESTATEMENTS OF THE LAW

Have been published covering several major subjects. In 1923 the American Law Institute was formed by leading American lawyers to help combat the growing uncertainty and undue complexity of American case law. The purpose of the Institute was to restate "the existing common law as developed by the courts with such care and accuracy that courts and lawyers may rely upon the Restatement as a correct statement of the law as it now stands." The Restatements lack legislative sanction and are not critically evaluative, but are considered an important source of secondary authority.

## REVISED STATUTES

By popular usage means a code. Technically, however, it identifies a compilation of statutes in the identical order as originally passed by the legislature with the temporary and repealed acts eliminated.

## RULES OF COURT

Regulate practice and procedure before the various courts. In most jurisdictions, these rules are issued by the court itself, or by the highest court in that jurisdiction.

## SCOPE–NOTE

Delimits and identifies the content of a topic and appears below the topic's heading in a publication.

## SECONDARY AUTHORITY

Are sources of the law which have only persuasive and no mandatory authority, e. g., encyclopedia.

## SECTION LINE

Is preceded by the Key-number, indicating the subject of the key-number.

## SESSION LAWS

Are published laws of a state enacted by each assembly and separately bound for the session and for extra sessions. The session laws are published in bound or pamphlet volumes after adjournment of the legislatures for the regular or special sessions.

**SHEPARDIZING**

Is a term which is the trade-mark property of Shepard's Citations, Inc. and is descriptive of the general use of its publications.

**"SLIP" LAW**

Is a legislative enactment which is separately and promptly published in pamphlet or in single sheet format after its passage.

**"SLIP" OPINION**

Is an individual court decision published separately soon after it is rendered.

**STAR–PAGINATION**

Is a scheme in reprint editions of Court reports, showing on its pages where the text of the pages of the official edition begins and ends.

**STARE DECISIS**

Is the doctrine of English and American law which states that when a court has formulated a principle of law as applicable to a given set of facts, it will follow that principle and apply it in future cases where the facts are substantially the same. It connotes the decision of present cases on the basis of past precedent.

**STATUS TABLE**

Gives the current status of a bill or court decision.

**STATUTES**

Are acts of a legislature. Depending upon its context in usage, a statute may mean a single act of a legislature or a body of acts which are collected and arranged according to a scheme or for a session of a legislature or Parliament.

**STATUTES AT LARGE**

Is the official compilation of acts passed by the Congress. The arrangement is chronological, not topical as is the United States Code. The Code may be cited as the official source for laws which it contains, but since not all laws are reprinted in the Code, the Statutes at Large represents the only complete source of federal legislation.

**STATUTORY INSTRUMENTS**

Are English administrative regulations and orders. The term applies especially to the administrative rules published since 1939, supplementing the English administrative code, Statutory Rules and Orders . . .

**STATUTORY RULES AND ORDERS**

Are English administrative regulations and orders.

**SUPERSEDE**

Is to displace or to supplant one publication or its segment with another.

**SYLLABUS**

See: Headnote.

**TABLE OF CASES**

Is a list of cases, arranged alphabetically by case names, with citations and references to the body of the publication where the cases are treated.

**TEMPORARY LAW**

Is an act which continues in force for a specific period of time.

**TERM OF COURT**

Signifies the space of time prescribed by law during which a court holds session. The court's session may actually extend beyond the term. The October Term of the United States Supreme Court is now the only term during which the Court sits, and lasts from October to June.

**TRANSCRIPT OF RECORD**

Refers to the printed record as made up in each case of the proceedings and pleadings necessary for the appellate court to review the history of the case.

**TREATISE**

Is an exposition, which may be critical, evaluative, interpretative, or informative, on case law or legislation. Usually it is more exhaustive than an encyclopedia but less detailed or critical than a periodical article.

**TREATY**

Is an agreement between two or more sovereign nations.

**UNIFORM LAWS**

On various subjects have been drafted. A considerable number have been approved by the National Conference of Commissioners on Uniform State Laws, and may have been adopted in one or more jurisdictions in the United States and its possessions. The Uniform Commercial Code is now the law in all fifty states.

**UNOFFICIAL REPORTS**

Are court reports published without statutory direction. They are not distinguished from official reports on grounds of varying quality or accuracy of reporting.

**WRIT**

Of which there are many types, is a written order, issued by a court and directed to an official or party, commanding the performance of some act.

# FUNDAMENTALS OF LEGAL RESEARCH

## Chapter 1

## THE LEGAL PROCESS

### SECTION A. SOURCES OF THE LAW

### 1. Introduction

The American legal system, as that of most English-speaking countries, is part of the common law tradition. The term "common law" is used here in the sense that distinguishes it from Roman law, modern civil law, canon law, and other systems of law. The common law has been defined as:

> " * * * [T]hat body of law and juristic theory which was originated, developed, and formulated and is administered in England, and has obtained among most of the states and peoples of Anglo-American stock." [1]

In the early history of English law, the custom developed of considering the decision of the courts as precedents. This was interpreted as "furnishing an example or authority for an identical or similar case afterwards arising or for a similar question of law." [2] This, in turn, led to the development of the doctrine of *stare decisis* which has been defined as:

> " * * * [T]hat when [a] court has once laid down a principle of law as applicable to a certain state of facts, it will adhere to that principle, and apply it to all future cases where facts are substantially the same." [3]

---

[1] Lux v. Huggin, 69 Cal. 255, 10 Pac. 674 (1886).

[2] Black's Law Dictionary. Rev. 4th Ed. (1968). For a succinct and scholarly treatment of the development of case law, see Dawson, The Oracles of the Law 1–80 (1968).

[3] Moore v. City of Albany, 98 N.Y. 396, 410 (1895).

Under the doctrine of *stare decisis* the law became embodied in the written decisions of the English courts and was to be found in the decisions of the courts rather than in a codified body of law as in other countries of Europe with legal systems based on the Roman law. It is in this sense that the common law became known as the "unwritten" law. The doctrines of *precedent* and *stare decisis* necessarily require access to the decisions of the courts and resulted in their publication under the generic term of *law reports*. To "find the law," then, a lawyer has to search the law reports for opinions of the courts that arose from a similar fact situation to the one at hand and then determine if the cases located can serve as a precedent for the present case.

While the development of case law was predominant, the place of statutes cannot be ignored. The earliest statutes were enacted by the King with the concurrence of his Council, and then gradually the role of statute-making was assumed by Parliament. It was not until after the passage of the *Reform Act of 1832* that statutes played a significant role in the English legal system. The real growth of statutory law reflected the impact of the industrial revolution on society as it became apparent that a jurisprudence based only on judicial decisions could not meet the needs of a growing dynamic society. Situations soon developed where answers were needed that were not found in the court reports, or the answers found no longer met current needs, or resulted in actions that were felt to be unjust. To remedy this, Parliament began to pass statutes which changed the prior rules for circumstances not found in any decisions of the court. A statute has been defined as:

> "An act of the legislature declaring, commanding, or prohibiting something; a particular law established by the will of the legislative department of government . . . according to the forms necessary to constitute it the law of the state." [4]

> "The word is used to designate the written law in contradistinction to the unwritten law." [5]

The sources of law, then, in common law jurisdictions derive from the enactments of their legislative bodies and from the decisions of their courts.[6] The authorities of law in all common law jurisdictions are separated into two divisions—primary and secondary. Primary law is that found in the enactments of the legislature (and in

---

[4] Federal Trust Co. v. East Hartford Fire Dept., 283 Fed. 95 (C.C.Conn.) (1922).

[5] Foster v. Brown, 199 Ga. 444, 34 S.E.2d 530, 535 (1945).

[6] For a more detailed discussion of the sources of the common law, see Jackson, The Machinery of Justice in England 10–18 6th ed. (1972).

some jurisdictions, that adopted through vote of the electorate) and the body of law found in the written opinions of the courts. In form of publication, the former are found in statute books, and the latter in sets of court reports. All other written expressions of the law are known as secondary authorities.

The term "sources of the law" has been variously defined. In relation to legal research, the phrase is employed to denote: (1) the literature of the law, (2) the authoritative organ of the state which formulates the legal rules or (3) the derivation of the concepts or ideas expressed in the body of the law. These meanings do not exhaust the definitions of the term; however, the present discussion will be limited to the concepts they impart.

## 2. The Literature of the Law

It is axiomatic to describe the law libraries as containing the literature of the law. This material includes statutes, administrative rules, judicial decisions, digests of case law, treatises, encyclopedias and other publications.

American law libraries contain large, diffused collections, since pursuant to the common law, much of our law is "found" or "made" by judicial decisions. Under the doctrine of *stare decisis* or precedent when a court has laid down a principle of law as applicable to a given set of facts, it, and other courts under it, will adhere to that principle and apply it similarly in future cases where the facts are substantially the same. Determining the decision of present cases on the basis of past precedent results in the literature of the law accumulating and assuming large proportions.

Another factor which has added to the extensiveness of American legal collections is the multiple systems of state and federal laws.

## 3. The Authoritative Organ of the State

The officials or bodies of officials whose acts give validity to the law are descriptive of another meaning of its source. In the democratic countries, there are two types of officials with such authority. They are legislators and judges. The latter group includes ordinary judges and administrative hearing officials. The former covers legislators and administrative rule-makers. These officials produce two authoritative forms of law: legislation and case law.

## 4. The Derivation of Legal Concepts

The third meaning given to the sources of the law relates to the derivation of its preceptual contents. Thus, the modern law of vicarious liability is considered by some as having its origin in the slave laws of the Romans.[7]  The famous article by Warren and Brandeis was a source of the American law of the right to privacy.[8]  The writings of Blackstone, Kent and Story contributed significantly to the early development of American law.

---

## SECTION B.  THE LEGAL SYSTEM OF THE UNITED STATES

As a result of our federal system, any particular legal transaction may be governed solely by state law, or solely by federal law, or perhaps both.  Although the question of determination of jurisdiction is beyond the scope of this book, its significance, however, cannot be overlooked in determining the answer to a legal question and knowledge is needed of both federal and state law.

As previously indicated, the United States is a common law jurisdiction.  The federal system of government in this country, however, has made its legal system extremely complex.  Under our federal constitution, each state, except for those powers delegated to the federal government, is a sovereign state.  This means that, in fact, there is not one legal system in this country, but fifty-one.

1.  **States:** The primary sources for each of the fifty states are found in each state's constitution as adopted by the people, the enactments of the legislature (and those initiated and enacted directly by the electorate) and the written decisions of its highest court of appeal, and in the law of England as delineated in its reception statute.[9]

2.  **Federal Government:** The primary sources of the United States Government are found in its Constitution, the Acts of Congress, and the interpretations of the Constitution and Acts of Congress by the United States Supreme Court and inferior federal courts.

[7] Holmes, Common Law 16–17 (1881).

[8] Warren and Brandeis, The Right to Privacy, 4 Harv.L.Rev. 193 (1890).

[9] Most states (except Louisiana, whose legal system is based on the civil law) have adopted a statute incorporating (with certain exceptions) the common law of England as part of their laws.  E. g., Va.Code 1–11 (1950); West's Ann.Calif. Civ.Code § 22.2.  A few states have recognized the role of the English common law by court decisions.  See 1 Powell on Real Property § 45 et seq. (1969).

## SECTION C. THE LEGAL SYSTEMS OF OTHER COUNTRIES

The doctrine of judicial precedent is not recognized by the European countries,[10] whose legal systems are derived from the Roman law, to the degree followed by common-law countries. Justinian, in codifying the law for the Roman state, declared that his code was to be the exclusive source of the law "on penalty of forgery," [11] thus attempting to discourage reference to earlier sources. Codification as a legal instrument was later adopted by the countries which followed the Roman law. However, in recent years, on the continent of Europe, judicial decisions are assuming a more significant authoritative role, claiming recognition with commentaries in interpreting the civil law. Modern European codes also recognize that no codification scheme can be all-inclusive and complete; thus, courts may be required to go outside the code, when its text is silent, obscure or deficient, for the solution to controversies.

The Latin American courts have followed a modified procedure. If a rule has been applied several times in different cases by the highest court, it is considered as binding. The French practice is also a compromise between the rule of *stare decisis* and the civil-law concept. A single decision by a court is not binding on it or on subordinate courts. While another lower court in a comparable case is not bound to follow the highest court's twice-told precedent, in practice the lower courts are prone to follow the precedent. Further, a uniform pattern of decisions is considered as binding in all courts in a manner similar to that of the highest courts in the United States.[12]

## SECTION D. LEGAL RESEARCH

The short summary so far presented on the structure of the legal system must be understood before one can approach the methods of doing legal research. What is involved in this process is a search for authorities. When engaged in legal research (more properly, le-

---

[10] For articles on judicial precedent in Europe see: Von Mehren, Judicial Process: A Comparative Analysis, 5 Am.J.Compar.L. 197 (1956); Dietze, Judicial Review in Europe, 55 Mich.L.Rev. 539 (1957).

[11] Kocurek, An Introduction to the Science of Law 162 (1930).

[12] Goodhart, Precedents in English and Continental Law, 50 Law Q.Rev. 40 (1934). See also: Dawson, op. cit. supra note 2 at 100 et seq.; Merryman, The Civil Law Tradition: An Introduction to the Legal Systems of Western Europe and Latin America. 1969.

gal search) a lawyer is seeking to find those authorities in the primary sources of the law that are applicable to a particular legal situation. In short, he is seeking to find the applicable statutes or court decisions (or both)[13] from the particular jurisdiction wherein the legal situation has occurred or will occur. The search is always first for mandatory primary sources, that is, constitutional or statutory provisions of the legislature, and court decisions of the jurisdiction involved. If these cannot be located, then the search focuses on locating persuasive primary authorities, that is, decisions from courts of other common law jurisdictions. Statutes are never considered persuasive authority. When in the legal search process primary authorities cannot be located, the searcher will seek for secondary authorities. These usually are considered to be the writings of lawyers as found in treatises or law reviews, or the publications of law reform organizations such as the American Law Institute and the law revision commissions of the various states.

This conglomerate mass and the diffusion of secondary American legal publications bespeak the need for the organized study of the use of legal materials in our law schools. In addition, the systematized study of legal research reflects an increasing emphasis in law school curricula on training students in the professional crafts. But this is not suggestive of a pedagogical deemphasis of legal evaluation and theory. On the contrary, the modern curriculum also attempts to impart to the student the reasonings, the insights and the principles which characterize the law. Without instruction in legal analysis and policy insights and training in legal skills, the modern lawyer is ill-prepared to meet the responsibilities of his profession.

To engage in an effective legal search, one must have an understanding not only of the organization of the legal system, but also of how law books are published and organized.

In the American Colonial period, law books were extremely scarce. At the time of the Revolution, only about thirty of the one hundred and fifty English reports were generally accessible in the Colonies. There were even fewer treatises in use. Law books were not found in the colleges for, at that time, the law was not an integrated academic study. The most extensive law collections of attorneys numbered from fifty to one hundred volumes.[14]

This situation did not prevail for long. As the economy of the country changed from an agrarian to an industrial society and greater demands were made upon the courts and the legislatures, the repos-

---

[13] The place of administrative regulations and ruling will be covered in Chapter XI.

[14] Harno, Legal Education in the United States 19 (1953).

itories of the law proportionately grew. In 1850, there were 80,000 reported American judicial decisions but today they total more than three million. Currently, courts of last resort annually report over 30,000 decisions. Congress and state legislatures produce about 9,-000 pages of statutory law per year, and the Federal Register annually publishes about 10,000 pages of federal administrative regulations.[15]

A search may involve using the statutes of the various states and court reports of the fifty states as well as countless numbers of secondary sources.

--------

### SECTION E.  SUMMARY

The sources of American law are found in the Constitution and statutes of the Congress and the states, and in the appellate court decisions of the court. Statutes and court decisions are primary authority. Other law books are secondary sources of the law and may be categorized into two types.

#### Books of Search

Books of search may be subdivided into the following groups:

> Annotated Reports and Annotated Statutes, with the annotations being secondary authority.
>
> Encyclopedias.
>
> Loose-Leaf Services and Reporters.

Books of search are cited as persuasive authority, for they serve in collating, describing and explaining the law.

#### Books of Index

This category includes the following types of legal publications:

> Books of Definition, such as dictionaries.
>
> Citators.
>
> Digests.
>
> Form-Books.
>
> Indexes.
>
> Tables.

Books of index serve primarily as aids in obtaining information. Most of these aids are not cited as persuasive authority. Thus, a

--------

[15] Kelso, Does the Law Need a Technological Revolution?  18 Rocky Mt.L.Rev. 378, 379 (1946).

dictionary, in certain circumstances, will be cited, but digests and citators are never cited as sources of the law.

The remaining chapters of this book will be devoted to charting a path through the law publications which must be used in finding the law.

# Chapter 2

# PRELIMINARY PROCEDURE IN LEGAL RESEARCH

Let us begin our study by surveying the procedure which is preliminary to the actual use of research publications. This entails three steps: Step 1, The determination and integration of facts. Step 2, The determination of the legal issues. Step 3, The procedure to be applied in searching for the law. Now we will consider each of these steps in this order.

## SECTION A.  THE DETERMINATION AND INTEGRATION OF FACTS

A clear understanding of a legal problem, relating either to litigation or to counselling, requires a careful screening and ascertaining of the relevant facts. The application of various fact-situations may result in different conclusions although the principle of law remains the same. Since the facts are determinative of the results, their derivation through circumspective interrogation and resourceful investigation assumes paramount importance and may mean the difference between success or failure.

After the facts are assembled, the mass of information must be screened, integrated and evaluated. Although screening, integrating and evaluating the facts are not necessarily distinct, separate processes, each possesses sufficiently distinguishable characteristics to be identifiable. Thus, screening entails the eliminating of nonessential facts; integration is the process of assembling the pertinent data; and evaluation gives direction to the research.

The process of factual appraisal of litigious or nonlitigious issues calls for recognizing and weighing of the following four factors:

T—Thing or subject matter

A—Cause of action or ground of defense

R—Relief sought    -

P—Persons or parties involved

This analysis can be quickly learned as the TARP rule, and the process embodies these considerations:

1. *Thing or subject matter.* The place or property involved in a problem or controversy may be a significant element. Thus, where

a passenger is injured in a skidding automobile, the personal property, the automobile, becomes an essential factor in the dispute.

2. *Cause of action or ground of defense.* A claim is asserted or a defense is made. The action centers around a point of controversy or a circumstance relating to the problem. The cause of action may be a breach of contract, negligence or some other claim.

3. *Object or relief sought.* This relates to the purpose of the lawsuit or the claim. It may be a civil suit for damages, an equity matter seeking affirmative or injunctive relief or a criminal action being brought by the state.

4. *Parties to the suit or the persons involved in the problem; their factual and legal status and relationship to each other.* The parties or persons may fit within a group or class which is salient to the solution of the problem or the outcome of the lawsuit. Thus, infancy or insanity may have an important bearing on a result.

The commercial or professional activities of the parties or persons may be significant. For example, banking or medicine.

The relationship between the parties or persons may be of special import, such as exists between a husband and wife or an employer and an employee.

An analysis of the facts in a problem, through the use of the TARP rule, should provide suggestive headings to be examined in an index of a publication, e. g., the descriptive-word index of a digest, or the table of contents. References to the applicable sections of the publication may be found under the appropriate headings.

---

## SECTION B.  THE DETERMINATION OF THE LEGAL ISSUES

When the facts have been determined and integrated, the legal issues should then be ascertained. Legal controversies frequently involve more than one point of law. In such cases, the issues should be interrelated, not merged, and should be given unital treatment.

If introductory, general information is required to orient the researcher to the topic, some secondary sources are helpful at this stage. They include treatises, periodical articles, general and local encyclopedias.

As the methods of research vary greatly with the problems and the subject matter, no single example can illustrate adequately all phases of research methodology. However, to facilitate the present study and to illustrate the handling of a problem, an example case is analyzed below:

## Example Case

A built a new home in Anycity, Iowa, and rented it to B for a period of three years. B personally arranged for the water service with the Acme Water Company, a privately owned local corporation. B moved out when his lease (containing no provision as to water supply) expired and left unpaid a six-months water bill of $30.00. A moved into the house and had the account changed to his own name. Now, six months after A moved in, the Acme Company is threatening that unless A pays the delinquent account of $30.00, it will discontinue the supply of water to the house. A, feeling that he should not have to pay the bill, seeks to have the threatened shut-off enjoined.

First, let us analyze the case for A.

(1) *Subject matter.* Here the subject matter is the water supply. Or it might be expanded to include all utilities. (A case similar to our example case but involving the supply of gas would certainly help in the solution.) But when the elements are thus expanded, caution must be used to avoid changing the issues.

(2) *Parties concerned.* There does not seem to be any particular class or group that includes A, except that he is now a consumer and was the owner and landlord at the time B consumed the water.

The Acme Company's status here is very important. It is a public utility and, of course, a water-works or water supply company. A further distinguishing feature is that it is a private rather than a governmental utility.

(3) *Cause of action.* The suit here is based on the threat to turn off the water, which would cause property damage as well as personal inconvenience, discomfort and injury. The defense would be non-payment of bills.

(4) *Object—Injunction.* In this particular case, it would be dangerous to discard immediately any of the related elements as being unimportant. Perhaps, after further study as to B, we might discard one or more of them without adverse effect.

The next question is: What is the primary law on the subject and where can it be found? You, no doubt, have assumed that this is essentially a problem on the state or local level, but it is not safe to disregard completely the federal legislation on the subject without some thought. Apparently, the Acme Company is doing business only in Anycity; hence, it would not be subject to the Congressional authority over interstate commerce. Therefore, in our particular example case, it is fairly safe to proceed to the state and local levels, for the company is private and is not subject to the Fourteenth Amendment.

After this analysis, we are now ready to proceed in the search for the law.   At this point, the decision must be made on whether to start the search in Books of Search or Books of Index, as described in Chapter One.   The descriptions and illustrations of different sets of law books which can be used in searching for and locating relevant court decisions and controlling statutes will be discussed in the remaining chapters.

# Chapter 3

# COURT REPORTS

## SECTION A.  THE REPORTING OF COURT DECISIONS

### 1.  Introduction

The editing and publishing of court decisions have assumed special characteristics in American law.  These manifestations were influenced significantly by the doctrine of judicial precedent or *stare decisis*.  Since past decisions play such an important role in our law, the tremendous growth and inclusiveness of court reports are quite understandable.  However, this extensive development in turn has created problems for the legal profession—problems relating to the informational content of case law, publication costs, absorption of office space and related issues.

There are over 3,000,000 reported judicial opinions in the United States, and over 30,000 American cases are published each year.  These include decisions of federal and state appellate courts and some trial courts or courts of original jurisdiction.  Although most reporting covers appellate decisions, some lower court cases are published.  It does not follow, however, that all appellate opinions are reported.  But it should be noted that notwithstanding this selectivity of appellate and trial cases, far too many opinions are written and reported which do not merit the treatment of permanent publication.

The point is that a significant number of reported decisions relate merely to prosaic problems and make no doctrinal advancements.  Although these cases are of value in resolving individual controversies, they add little or nothing to existing law.  However, where the facts of cases are distinguishable, their precedential value is ascertainable.  Therefore, the extensive publication of judicial decisions is a culmination of doctrinal development and fact differentiation.

But the problem which extensive case reporting presents is not serious.  It has been reduced significantly through the availability of secondary sources.  Also, as an ancillary matter, earlier decisions chiefly perform a historical function.  As Holmes observed, "It is a great mistake to be frightened by the ever-increasing number of reports.  The reports of a given jurisdiction in the course of a generation take up pretty much the whole body of the law, and restate it from the present point of view. We could reconstruct the corpus from them if all that went before were burned.  The use of the earlier reports is mainly historical  *   *   * " [1]

[1] Holmes, The Path of the Law in Collected Legal Papers 167, 169 (1921).

See also "Unreported Decisions in the United States Courts of Appeals" Cornell Law Review 63:128-148 (Fall 1977) for a view of the federal treatment of this problem.

### 2.   Court Organization

Each jurisdiction has its own system of court organization, and although there may be differences in detail, the general structure is the same.  In general, there are trial courts and appellate courts.  The former are the courts where the trial is first held (courts of the first instance).  It is here where the parties appear, witnesses testify, and the evidence is presented.  The trial court usually determines any questions of fact that may be in dispute and then applies the applicable rules of law.

Once the trial court reaches its decision, the losing party has a right of appeal to an appellate court.  Generally, the appellate court can only decide questions of law and its decision in each case is based on the record made below.  Appellate courts do not receive new testimony or decide questions of fact and in most jurisdictions only the appellate courts issue written opinions.  Each state has a final court of appeal (usually called the Supreme Court) and some states have intermediate courts of appeal.  [see Illustration 1]

### 3.   Methods of Court Reporting

When a case has been appealed to an appellate court, both parties submit written briefs which contain a summary of the facts and arguments on the points of law involved, and the court may hear oral arguments by the attorneys.  The court then writes an opinion in which it states the reasons for its decision.  Technically speaking, the decision of a court only indicates the action of the court and is indicated by the words *Affirmed,* or *Reversed,* or *Remanded,* or similar words and phrases.  The reasons for this action are then stated in the opinion of the court.  However, in actual practice, the use of *opinion* and *decision* has become interchangeable and the word *decision* herein will be used to describe both.

----

### SECTION B.   THE ELEMENTS OF COURT DECISIONS

The elements of an American court decision are as follows:

### 1.   Name or Title of the Case

Cases generally are identified by the names of the parties to a lawsuit:

*Payne* v. *Green*—in table of cases as *Payne* v. *Green.*

*In re Payne*—in table of cases as *Payne, In re.*  Judicial proceedings in which there are no adversary parties.  Such designations usually denote a bankruptcy case, a probate case, a guardianship matter, a contempt case, a disbarment, or a habeas corpus case.

*Ex parte Payne*—in tables of cases as *Payne, Ex parte*—This is a special proceeding.

*State on the relation of Payne* v. *Green*—in tables of cases as *State ex rel. Payne* v. *Green*. These cases involve the extraordinary legal remedies, viz.: Mandamus, prohibition, certiorari, quo warranto, or habeas corpus.

*State* v. *Payne*—in tables of cases as *State* v. *Payne*. Suit by the state in its collective capacity as the party wronged by a criminal deed. In some sets the criminal cases are arranged in alphabetical order under the names of the respective states. "People" or "Commonwealth" are used in some states instead of "State."

In maritime law, a suit may be brought against the ship, e. g., The Caledonia.

Cases involving the seizure of commodities are brought in their names, e. g., *United States* v. *45 Barrels of Whisky*.

Usually, the plaintiff-defendant names remain in that order when cases are appealed by a defendant; however, in some states, they are reversed and the defendant on appeal becomes the plaintiff in error.

## 2. Docket Number

A docket number is the numerical designation assigned to each case by a court. It is the means of identifying the case as the suit progresses. Also, it is a convenient method for filing briefs in cases in libraries.

## 3. Date of Decision

This is the date on which the decision was rendered, and generally it appears after the docket number in the reported case.

## 4. Prefatory Statement

The prefatory statement explains the nature of the case, its disposition in the lower court, the name of the lower court and sometimes its judge, and the disposition of the case in the appellate court as being affirmed or reversed.

## 5. Syllabus or Headnote

In most court reports, the headnotes or syllabi, which are brief summaries of the legal rules or significant facts in a case, are drafted by the editors; however, in some jurisdictions, they are prepared by the judges who rendered the decisions. In the latter cases, the syllabi of the judges are printed in the official reports and reprinted in the unofficial publications which reprint the decisions. The syllabi are intended merely as indexes to the points of law in the opinions and that is equally true where the judges write them. It has been held, in the latter instances, that, when the syllabus conflicts with the opinion, the latter shall control. The United States Supreme Court has stated, "We look to the opinion for the original and authentic statement of the grounds of decision."[2]  In view of this, the headnotes should be used merely as indexes to the law stated in the opinions of the cases and not as the law itself.[3]

To the extent that the syllabus culls the rule of law from the opinion, it is useful. Unfortunately, too often its use has been extended to give to the common law an unrealistic measure of certitude. This, in part, is an attempt to "bring certainty and order out of the wilderness of precedent."[4]

Admittedly, there is great value to certainty in a legal system. This principle applies with equal vigor to American law and is underscored by the demands of our legal practice. The practicing lawyer is frequently called upon to act as a forecaster of the law. Mr. Justice Holmes took special notice of this when he observed that the lawyer often prophesies as to the future decisions of courts on specific sets of facts. But, as the legal realists have convincingly demonstrated, the stating of legal rules alone is inconclusive of the judicial results. Judge Jerome Frank has elaborated at length upon this point, contending that the failure of the legal rules to perform their principal function—to guide and predict the decisions of the courts— is due primarily to the uncertainty as to which facts were applied to the rules by the judges in reaching their decisions. Since the inclusion or exclusion of certain facts materially affects the results in a case, the mere exposition of the applicable rule is inconclusive. This proposition can be stated another way: the operative facts may influence the judicial result in favor of one party or the other, so the stating of a rule of law alone is indeterminative of the judicial findings in specific cases. This point was forcefully made by Holmes when he said, "General propositions do not decide concrete cases,"[5] for a judge could

[2] Burbank v. Ernst, 232 U.S. 162, 34 S.Ct. 299, 58 L.Ed. 551 (1914).

[3] The Ohio Supreme Court has gone farther than most courts in that it gives to the syllabus a special status in relation to the law. Rule VI of the Court has been interpreted to mean that the syllabus and not the opinion is the law of the case. State ex rel. Donahey v. Edmondson, 89 Ohio St. 93, 105 N.E. 269 (1913). However, this ruling has been broadened by the Ohio Supreme Court to mean that the syllabus must be read in the light of the facts of the specific case, thus demonstrating an awareness as to the importance of the facts in controversies. In re Poage, 87 Ohio St. 72, 100 N.E. 125 (1912).

See Fenneberg, The Rule of the Syllabus in Ohio, 31 Ohio Bar 1105 (1958).

[4] Cardozo, The Growth of the Law 1 (1927); Selected Writings of Benjamin Nathan Cardozo 186 (ed. Hall, 1947). Mr. Justice Cardozo used the phrase here in relation to the need of some restatement of the common law.

[5] Lochner v. N. Y., 198 U.S. 45, 76, 25 S.Ct. 539, 547, 49 L.Ed. 937, 949 (1905).

admit any general rule that anyone might lay down and decide the case either way.[6]

Obviously, therefore, the use of the syllabus should be restricted merely to its identifying and indexing functions.

The number of headnotes to a case is determined by the variety of legal propositions and factual statements it embodies, each of which is individually digested.

### 6.   Names of Counsel

The names of counsel for both parties to a suit precede the opinion of the court.

### 7.   Synopsis of Briefs of Counsel

In the early period of reporting American cases, summaries of the briefs of counsel were given with almost all cases reported. This aided researchers in locating cases in point and revealed the theories of law followed by counsel in support of their arguments. With the increased volume of cases and the introduction of secondary aids, e. g., encyclopedias, digests, citators, annotated reports and text books, this practice has diminished. However, some reports continue to provide abridged statements of the briefs of counsel, e. g., *United States Supreme Court Reports* (Lawyers' Edition), *New York Court of Appeals Reports*, etc.

### 8.   Statement of Facts

A statement of the facts in the case usually follows the briefs of counsel.

### 9.   Opinion of the Court

The opinion of the court is the explanation of the court's decision, the latter being the conclusion or result in a controversy. The opinion is written by one member of the court after the majority has agreed to a decision. A member of the majority, while agreeing with a decision, may disagree with its reasoning; he then may write a concurring opinion which gives his reasons for the decision. The views of the minority generally are expressed by a dissenting opinion which is written by one of the dissenting judges. An opinion, in accord with the dissent, may be written by a dissenting judge when he agrees with the conclusions and result of the dissent but disagrees with its reasoning. Or several dissenting opinions may be rendered independently by the judges, each expressing different views. A *per curiam* opinion is an opinion of the whole court as distinguished from an opinion written by a specific judge. It may present a lengthy or a brief

---

[6] 1 Holmes—Laski Letters 390 (1953).

discussion of the issues in the case, e. g., New York Court of Appeals. In some courts, it may only give the conclusion without any reasoning, e. g., United States Supreme Court. A memorandum opinion is a brief holding of the whole court in which the opinion is limited or omitted.

Dissenting opinions are not the law in a case; nor are they binding as precedent. They assume the characteristics of *dicta* and serve merely as secondary authority. However, not infrequently the controlling opinion may later be overruled and the dissenting opinion is then accepted as the correct statement of the law.[7]

There are two additional elements of a case which merit brief attention. The first is the *ratio decidendi*, or the point in a case which determines the result. In other words, it is the basis of the decision, explicitly or implicitly, stated in the opinion. The second is *obiter dictum*. The latter is a collateral statement contained in the opinion which does not relate directly to the issues raised in the case. *Dictum*, therefore, is an official, incidental comment, not necessary to the formulation of the decision, made by the judge in his opinion which is not binding as precedent.

### 10.  Decision, with Judgment or Decree

This refers to the actual disposition of the case by the court. Thus, a decision is noted by such terms as "affirmed," "reversed," "modified," etc. Often the words "decision" and "judgment" are synonymously used. However, a judgment upon the verdict of a jury is the most common of the judgments upon facts found, and is for the party, i. e., plaintiff or defendant, obtaining the verdict.

---

### SECTION C.  OFFICIAL AND UNOFFICIAL REPORTS

If the publication of the court reports is directed by statute, they are called "official reports." Those published without such authority are referred to as "unofficial reports," i. e., commercial or private publications. Neither term relates to quality or accuracy. The opinions in the unofficial reports have the same origins as those in the official reports; i. e., the clerks and the judges.

---

[7] E. g., In FTC v. R. F. Keppel & Bro., Inc., 291 U.S. 304 (1934), the United States Supreme Court adopted the dissenting opinion of Mr. Justice Brandeis in FTC v. Gratz, 253 U.S. 421, 429 (1920) as to the broad powers of FTC to declare trade practices unfair under Section 5 of the Federal Trade Commission Act. In FTC v. Brown Shoe Co., 384 U.S. 316 (1966), Mr. Justice Black, speaking for an undivided Supreme Court, again rejected the Gratz case as a precedent, indicating that the case had been decided shortly after the FTC Act was passed and that the view of the Court is now in line with Brandeis' dissent in Gratz.

See Illustrations 3 and 4 for an example of the same case as reported in an official and unofficial set of reports.

The success of unofficial reporting in the United States is due materially to the frequency and speed of those publications.

### 1.    Unofficially Reported Cases as Authority

The plethora of reported judicial decisions has been the object of concern in some quarters. The judges or court clerks generally select the cases for publication; however, attempts directed at their voluntarily reducing either the judicial output or the number of published decisions have met with failure. Regardless of the reasons for the continued stream of reported cases, the fact remains that this judicial mill has produced a bulky, unattractive and inferior product, with the duplication of reports by commercial publishers adding needlessly to this grist.

The legislatures have also been challenged by this problem, but their efforts likewise have gone for naught. It is not inconceivable that these failures were inevitable since the problem was attacked procedurally, avoiding the central issue—the nature of our judicial process and, conjointly, the accumulation of decisions inspired by the doctrine of *stare decisis*, the methods of judicial selection and tenure, and related questions.

A method of legislative attack upon this problem is to declare that cases not properly selected by a court for publication shall not be recognized and receive the official sanction of any court.[8] However, courts and attorneys have continued to cite such improperly reported cases, and at times those decisions have been given equal recognition by the courts.[9]

Apart from the judicial latitude practiced in interpreting such legislation, it presents a vexing issue as to the correctness of legislative restriction on the judicial doctrine of *stare decisis*. Since the unreported cases were decided by courts of proper jurisdiction, the persuasive argument is that they should be given equal weight as other cases handed down by the same courts, and the absence of authorized publication should not negate the precedential value of those decisions. Further, the significance of unreported opinions is demonstrated in some state contested proceedings. This view is supported by the Bar which has favorably subscribed to and received the unofficial, commercial publication of unauthorized cases.

Under such statutes a doubtful choice is given between the legislative restriction of judicial precedents and the reduction in the num-

---

[8] E. g., Ohio Revised Code 2503.20 and California Supreme Court Rule 976 (1972).

[9] See Gustin v. Sun Life Assur. Co. of Canada, 154 F.2d 961 (6th Cir. 1946).

ber of reported decisions. So long as precedent plays a dominant role in American law, it is unrealistic to expect any appreciable reduction in the volume of case law unless the judges themselves initiate a plan whereby the writing of opinions in cases under certain conditions is circumscribed.

---

### SECTION D. THE ELEMENTS OF JUDICIAL REPORTING

Several techniques are used in publishing court cases. Generally, the order of their release is determined by their decision dates and not by a logical arrangement, such as subject. Some decisions are published individually, when rendered by a court, and are called "slip" opinions. Usually, the "slip" opinions do not contain syllabi, nor are they indexed.

"Advance sheets" contain the decisions of a court or the courts of several jurisdictions decided just prior to publication. Their format is that of a periodical pamphlet, and the emphasis is on speed of publication. The paging of the "advance sheets" ordinarily is the same as the bound volumes which the latter eventually cumulate. This permits quick, permanent citations to cases. The features of the cases in the "advance sheets" are identical with those included in the bound volumes. Some jurisdictions do not publish "advance sheets."

### 1. Features of Bound Volumes of Reports

As indicated above, the cases are finally cumulated in bound volumes. The bound volumes include most of the following significant features:

a. A table of cases contained in the volume.

b. A table of statutes interpreted by the decisions reported.

c. The opinions are cumulated from advance sheets and have the same volume and page numbers as the advance sheets.

d. The types of opinions are (1) written by a judge (majority, dissenting or concurring), (2) *per curiam* and (3) memorandum.

e. Subject index or digest of the cases reported.

f. Judicial definition of words and phrases used in the cases reported.

g. Court rules.

h. The various volumes of unofficial reports generally contain cross reference tables to the official reports.

## SECTION E.   ORGANIZATION OF COURT REPORTS

Court reports are organized (1) jurisdictionally, (2) geographically and (3) selectedly.   They are published in series and the bound volumes and advance sheets are consecutively numbered.   E. g., Federal Reporter and Federal Reporter, Second Series.

### 1.   Jurisdictional Reports

The decisions of a specific court or several courts within a system may be published in a set of volumes and kept current by advance sheets and new bound volumes.

EXAMPLES are:

United States Supreme Court Reports

Minnesota Reports (reports cases of the Minnesota Supreme Court)

California Appellate Reports (reports cases of the District Courts of Appeals of California)

### 2.   Geographical Reports

Cases covering several courts of a state may be published in a reporter.

Examples:

New York Miscellaneous Reports

Ohio Opinions

Also, the decisions of small numbers of states, divided into geographical regions, are grouped together and published as units.   This grouping is called the National Reporter System.

EXAMPLES:

North Western Reporter (includes cases from Iowa, Michigan, Minnesota, Nebraska, North Dakota, South Dakota and Wisconsin)

South Western Reporter (includes cases from Arkansas, Kentucky, Missouri, Tennessee and Texas)

### 3.   Special Reports

Another method of reporting is that of the special reports which are collections of decisions, some with notes and annotations, on specific legal subjects, e. g., criminal law, negligence, etc.   These cases are mostly reprinted (with some exceptions) from the reports of the various federal and state courts and administrative bodies.

This feature has also been adopted by a number of the loose-leaf services. A few examples of current special reports are:

a. Commerce Clearing House, Trade Regulation Reporter (Trade Cases).

b. Negligence and Compensation Cases, Annotated.

c. Prentice-Hall, Tax Court Memorandum Decisions.

d. Public Utilities Reports.

e. U. S. Patents Quarterly.

# SECTION F.  ILLUSTRATIONS

1. Court Organization Chart

2. Statutory Provisions for the Publication of Court Decisions

3. A Typical Case as Reported in an Official Set of Court Reports

4. The Same Case as Reported in an Unofficial Set of Court Reports

## [Illustration 1]
## COURT ORGANIZATION CHART

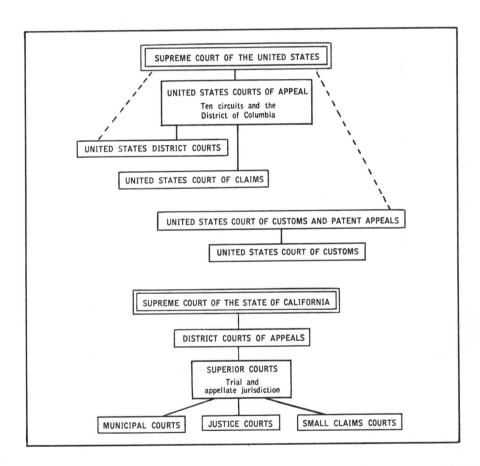

**[Illustration 2]**

## TYPICAL STATUTORY PROVISIONS FOR PUBLICATION
## OF COURT REPORTS

**Excerpt from West's Ann.Calif. Gov't Code**

**§ 68902. Publication of reports: Supervision by Supreme Court.**

Such opinions of the Supreme Court, of the courts of appeal, and of the appellate departments of the superior courts as the Supreme Court may deem expedient shall be published in the official reports. The reports shall be published under the general supervision of the Supreme Court.

**Excerpts from McKinney Consol.Laws of N.Y. Judiciary Law**

**§ 430. Law reporting bureau; state reporter**

There is hereby created and established the law reporting bureau of the state of New York. The bureau shall be under the direction and control of a state reporter, who shall be appointed and be removable by the court of appeals by an order entered in its minutes. The state reporter shall be assisted by a first deputy state reporter and such other deputy state reporters and such staff as may be necessary, all of whom shall be appointed and be removable by the court of appeals.

**§ 431. Causes to be reported**

The law reporting bureau shall report every cause determined in the court of appeals and every cause determined in the appellate divisions of the supreme court, unless otherwise directed by the court deciding the cause; and, in addition, any cause determined in any other court which the state reporter, with the approval of the court of appeals, considers worthy of being reported because of its usefulness as a precedent or its importance as a matter of public interest.

Each reported decision shall be published as soon as practicable after it is rendered. Added L.1938, c. 494, § 1, eff. July 1, 1938.

**Excerpt from Vernon's Ann.Mo.Stat.**

**§ 447,231. Designation of private publication as official reports**

The supreme court may declare the published volumes of the decisions of the supreme court as the same are published by any person, firm or corporation, to be official reports of the decisions of the supreme court, and the courts of appeals may jointly make a similar declaration with respect to published volumes of the opinions of the courts of appeals. Any publication so designated as the official reports may include both the opinions of the supreme court and the courts of appeals in the same volume.

[Illustration 3]

## A TYPICAL CASE AS REPORTED IN AN OFFICIAL SET OF COURT REPORTS

(438 Pa. 468, 1971)

> All written decisions of the Pennsylvania Supreme Court are published in the Official Pennsylvania Reports.
>
> The headnotes or syllabus is prepared by the court reporter from the written opinion.

completed by another were unauthorized, but this civil standard of proof is not governing in a criminal prosecution.

### Argo *v.* Goodstein, Appellant.

*Negligence—Possessor of property—Business visitor—Definition—Duty of possessor—Unilateral lessening of standard of care—Restatement 2d, Torts, §343—Charge to jury—Injury to blind man.*

1. A business visitor is a person who is invited or permitted to enter or remain on land in the possession of another for a purpose directly or indirectly connected with business dealings between them. [472]

2. The class of persons qualifying as business visitors is not limited to those coming upon the land for a purpose directly or indirectly connected with the business conducted thereon by the possessor, but includes as well those coming upon the land for a purpose connected with their own business which itself is directly or indirectly connected with a purpose for which the possessor uses the land. [472]

3. Where the relationship of possessor of land and business visitor has existed in the past, and the possessor of land has given the visitor no indication that the relationship between the parties has changed, the possessor of land cannot lessen the standard of care owing to the business visitor by unilaterally removing him from the class of business visitors. [474]

[Illustration 3–a]

## SAMPLE PAGE FROM 438 Pa. 468

---

470                    ARGO *v.* GOODSTEIN, Appellant.

Syllabus—Opinion of the Court.                    [438 Pa.

from which the jury could determine whether there was contributory negligence; the trial judge was correct in charging that on this issue defendant had the burden of proof.

> The name of the judge writing the opinion is always given. All matter preceding this is editorial and not part of the opinion. It usually consists of (1) headnotes (2) summary of facts and judgment of court (indication, when appropriate, of concurring or dissenting opinion (3) Names of attorneys.

Mr. Justice JONES and Mr. Justice COHEN dissented.

Argued January 12, 1970. Before BELL, C. J., JONES, COHEN, EAGEN, O'BRIEN, ROBERTS and POMEROY, JJ.

Appeal, No. 30, Jan. T., 1970, from judgment of Court of Common Pleas of Delaware County, March T., 1962, No. 1621, in case of James Argo v. Sidney Goodstein. Judgment affirmed.

Trespass for personal injuries. Before DIGGINS, J.

Verdict for plaintiff, and judgment thereon. Defendant appealed.

*Robert B. Surrick,* with him *Cramp & D'Iorio,* for appellant.

*Garland D. Cherry,* with him *Kassab, Cherry, Curran & Archbold,* for appellee.

OPINION BY MR. JUSTICE O'BRIEN, May 27, 1970:

Appellee, James Argo, blind since birth, was a door-to-door peddler of brooms, brushes and dusters. For some ten to twelve years, on the occasion of every three

[Illustration 3–b]
## SAMPLE PAGE FROM 438 Pa. 468

---

ARGO *v.* GOODSTEIN, Appellant.       471

468, (1970).]         Opinion of the Court.

to four months, appellee had visited each and every store in the 6700 block of Market Street in Upper Darby, Delaware County, a business section of town, including the premises owned by the Good Company, whose president was Sidney Goodstein, the appellant. On July 11, 1960, at approximately 11:30 a.m., appellee approached the door to the premises in question, heavily laden with his wares. Pushing open the unlocked door, he felt with his cane (apparently striking on the foundation wall or threshold area). Then, holding open the door with his right shoulder, he grabbed his brooms and stepped quickly so as not to be hit by

> A page from the opinion. A decision may vary from one page to several hundred.

brought in trespass against Good Company, Inc., the owner of the premises, and against its President, Sidney Goodstein, as the general contractor in charge of the construction work being done on the premises.

Initially, the case was tried in May, 1964, and a jury verdict totalling $27,500 was rendered in favor of the appellee against both defendants. The defendants appealed from the judgment entered on the verdict after the denial of their motions for judgment n.o.v., and for a new trial. We affirmed the judgment in an opinion by Mr. Justice MUSMANNO.

However, the appellants filed a petition for reargument concerning a communication between the trial judge and the jury in the absence of counsel. After reargument, based on the aforesaid communication, we withdrew our previously rendered opinion and ordered a new trial.

## [Illustration 4]

## A TYPICAL CASE AS REPORTED IN A SET OF UNOFFICIAL REPORTS

### (265 A.2d 783, 1971)

ARGO v. GOODSTEIN                    Pa.    **783**

Cite as 265 A.2d 783

438 Pa. 468

**James ARGO**

v.

**Sidney GOODSTEIN, Appellant.**

Supreme Court of Pennsylvania.

May 27, 1970.

Action by blind door-to-door salesman for injuries sustained when he opened door of defendant's premises, where he had previously done business, entered, and fell in area where there was no floor since premises were being remodeled. The Common Pleas Court, Delaware County, at No. 1621 March Term, 1962, John V. Diggins, J., rendered judgment for plaintiff, and the defendant appealed. The Supreme Court, at No. 30 January Term, 1970, O'Brien, J., held that evidence supported finding that plaintiff was a business visitor and that defendant had been negligent in failing to lock door.

Affirmed.

Jones and Cohen, JJ., dissented.

**1. Negligence ⬉134(3)**

Evidence in action by blind door-to-door salesman for injuries sustained when he entered defendant's premises and stepped into floorless area sustained finding that

mony of other persons but may be impeached by its own inconsistencies or by such intrinsic improbability or obvious falsity as to stamp it as unworthy of credit.

**4. Evidence ⬉591**

Plaintiff was not bound by defendant's testimony given as on cross-examination where there were numerous inconsistencies in testimony.

**5. Negligence ⬉32(2.8)**

Owner of premises who is not interested in talking to salesman, even though he has dealt with him in past and even though he has given salesman no indication that relations have changed, may not unilaterally remove salesman from class of business visitors, thereby lessening standard of care owed to him.

**6. Trial ⬉312(2)**

That trial judge in action involving plaintiff's status as business visitor responded to jury's question by stating definition of business visitor, without reading remainder of trial guide provision, was not error where judge had fully covered applicable law in great detail and additional instructions were adequate to resolve jury's doubts.

**7. Negligence ⬉134(8)**

---

This is the same case as shown in Illustration 3 as it appears in the Atlantic Reporter, an unofficial set of court reports. The headnotes are prepared by the Publisher's Editorial staff. Note how they differ from the headnotes for this case in the Pennsylvania Reports. (Illus. 3)

---

**3. Evidence ⬉591**

**Witnesses ⬉400(2)**

Where litigant calls his adversary on cross-examination he is bound by testimony, but rule is limited by principle that testimony adduced as on cross-examination may not only be contradicted by direct testi-

Blind door-to-door salesman, who had previously done business in defendant's store, was not contributorily negligent as matter of law for failing to use his cane to determine change of level, resulting in his fall when he entered area which was floorless since premises were being remodeled.

## [Illustration 4–a]
## SAMPLE PAGE FROM 265 A.2d 783

**784**    Pa.        **265 ATLANTIC REPORTER, 2d SERIES**

**9. Trial ⬅═296(4)**

Refusal to instruct that plaintiff could not recover if he showed contributory negligence in his own case, while instructing that contributory negligence was affirmative defense on which defendant had burden of proof, was not error where other instructions made it clear that plaintiff's own testimony was part of evidence from which jury could determine whether there was contributory negligence.

> **While the material printed preceding the Opinion of the Court varies in the unofficial reports from the official reports, the text of the opinion is exactly the same.**

relation between plaintiff's negligence and resulting harm as between defendant's negligence and resulting harm.

**12. Appeal and Error ⬅═882(12)**

Defendant who, by means of request for specific instruction, injected element of proximate cause into charge was without standing to complain of charge that plaintiff's conduct must be proximate cause of happening of injury to bar recovery.

**13. Witnesses ⬅═216**

State Department of Health records were privileged under statutes and regulations. 62 P.S. §§ 403, 404; 65 P.S. § 66.1 (2).

**14. Appeal and Error ⬅═1047(5)**

Any error in ruling that Department of Health records were privileged was harmless to defendant where defendant was able to use records extensively on cross-examination with understanding that plaintiff on redirect could rebut inference that plaintiff was receiving pension. 62 P.S. §§ 403, 404; 65 P.S. § 66.1(2).

Robert B. Surrick, Cramp & D'Iorio, Media, for appellant.

Garland D. Cherry, Kassab, Cherry, Curran & Archbold, Chester, for appellee.

Before BELL, C. J., and JONES, COHEN, EAGEN O'BRIEN, ROBERTS and POMEROY, JJ.

OPINION OF THE COURT

O'BRIEN, Justice.

Appellee, James Argo, blind since birth, was a door-to-door peddler of brooms, brushes and dusters. For some ten to twelve years, on the occasion of every three to four months, appellee had visited each and every store in the 6700 block of Market Street in Upper Darby, Delaware County, a business section of town, including the premises owned by the Good Company, whose president was Sidney Goodstein, the appellant. On July 11, 1960, at approximately 11:30 a. m., appellee approached the door to the premises in question, heavily laden with his wares. Pushing open the unlocked door, he felt with his cane (apparently striking on the foundation wall or threshold area). Then, holding open the door with his right shoulder, he grabbed his brooms and stepped quickly so as not to be hit by the door. The first step he took was within the range of his cane and brought his foot onto a solid surface. Unfortunately, as he entered he stepped into a floorless area and fell 8 feet 8 inches onto the basement floor below, as a result of which he sustained serious personal injuries.

As appellee later discovered, the Good Company was expanding and remodeling. Two companion suits were brought in trespass against Good Company, Inc., the owner of the premises, and against its President, Sidney Goodstein, as the general contractor in charge of the construction work being done on the premises.

Initially, the case was tried in May, 1964, and a jury verdict totalling $27,500 was

## [Illustration 4–b]
## SAMPLE PAGE FROM 265 A.2d 783

ARGO v. GOODSTEIN    Pa.    **785**

Cite as 265 A.2d 783

rendered in favor of the appellee against both defendants. The defendants appealed from the judgment entered on the verdict after the denial of their motions for judgment n. o. v., and for a new trial. We affirmed the judgment in an opinion by Mr. Justice Musmanno.

However, the appellants filed a petition for reargument concerning a communication between the trial judge and the jury in the absence of counsel. After reargument, based on the aforesaid communication, we withdrew our previously rendered opinion and ordered a new trial.

A second trial was held on February 13,

Furthermore, "the class of persons qualifying as business visitors is not limited to those coming upon the land for a purpose directly or indirectly connected with the business conducted thereon by the possessor, but includes as well, those coming upon the land for a purpose connected with their own business which itself is directly or indirectly connected with a purpose for which the possessor uses the land." Straight v. B. F. Goodrich Co., 354 Pa. 391, 47 A.2d 605 (1946), citing 332(a) of the Restatement of Torts.

[2] Appellee's purpose on the premises was to sell his brooms, brushes, and dusters.

---

The difference between the official and unofficial reports and other features of court reports will be discussed in Chapters 4, 5 and 6.

---

trial, is whether there was sufficient evidence of negligence to allow submission of the case to the jury.

The standard of care required of appellant towards appellee, the breach of which would be negligence, depends on appellee's status on the premises, i. e., whether he was a trespasser (voluntary or involuntary), a licensee, or a business visitor. By a special finding of fact, the jury found that appellee was a business visitor.

[1] We are of the opinion that sufficient evidence was present in the record to sustain this finding. "A business visitor is a person who is invited or permitted to enter or remain on land in possession of another for a purpose directly or indirectly connected with business dealings between them." Kimble v. Mackintosh Hemphill Co., 359 Pa. 461, 59 A.2d 68 (1948), citing Sec. 332 of Restatement of Torts.

265 A.2d—50

[3] In challenging the jury's finding that appellee was a business visitor, appellant argues that appellee was bound by the conclusion to which appellant testified, i. e., that the premises were no longer a store, but were instead a construction site; since appellant was called as for cross-examination. However, the rule that where a litigant calls his adversary on cross-examination he is bound by the testimony is limited by the principle that "the testimony adduced as on cross-examination may not only be contradicted by the direct testimony of other persons but may be impeached by its own inconsistencies or by such intrinsic improbability or obvious falsity as to stamp it as unworthy of credit." Bogdanoff v. Manis, 346 Pa. 243, 30 A.2d 321 (1943).

[4] As the court below points out, there were at least nine inconsistencies in appel-

## SECTION G.  ABBREVIATIONS AND CITATIONS OF COURT REPORTS

### 1.  Abbreviations

The first American decisions were reported by private reporters. The first American report published was Kirby's Connecticut Reports in 1789.  Harris and McHenry's Maryland Reports contains the first American reported decision, dated 1658.

The early English and American reports were cited by the names of the reporters, such as Bunbury (English) and Cranch (American). The current policy is to cite reports by reference to the name of the set and not to the name of the reporter who edited the publication.

In judicial opinions, briefs, treatises and other legal publications the names of reporters and the reports are abbreviated in the citations.  E. g., "Rich." for Richardson's Equity (S.C.) ; "Nev." for Nevada.  A Table of Abbreviations, with references to the full names of reporters and reports, is given in Appendix B, below.

### 2.  Methods of Citation

The objective of citations is to facilitate research through ready recourse to publications.  The importance of accuracy, consistency and clarity in the citation of legal sources has increased with the steady flow of materials and the pressing need for brevity.  From these demands certain standard forms and practices have evolved in citing legal publications.

The essence of legal citation is embodied in logical brevity and clear abbreviation.  It avoids the brevity which confuses or misinforms and the minutia which embellishes and protracts.

Good form in a legal document is important not only for its communicative value but also for the favorable impression it creates in the mind of the reader, whether he be a judge, a lawyer or a teacher. As in other professions, the quality of the workmanship of an attorney inures to his reputation and influences eventual success or failure. It behooves the young lawyer, therefore, to form work-habits early in his career, as manifested in his legal writing, which will redound to his credit and help to enhance his reputation.

The more general criteria on systematic citation of court reports is given below.  Details as to citation of federal, state and selected reports will be furnished in the following chapters.

a.   Only so much of the case name is given as is needed to avoid confusion.  Therefore, Laura M. Jackson v. Richard A. Mermis is identified as Jackson v. Mermis.

b.    The following phrases, among others, are omitted from case names: "et al.," "et ux.," "appellees," "respondent," "decedent," "executor," and "administrator."   The following references are included in case names: "In re," "In the matter of," "ex rel.," and "ex parte."

c.    When a change in name order occurred on appeal or certiorari granted, cite as follows: U. S. Fire Escape Counterbalance Co. v. Joseph Halsted Co., 246 Fed. 947 (N.D.Ill.1917), mod. and aff'd sub nom.   Joseph Halsted Co. v. U. S. Fire Escape Counterbalance Co., 257 Fed. 95 (7th Cir. 1919).

d.    The disposition of a case on appeal is generally indicated as follows:   188 F.2d 423 (5th Cir. 1951), cert. denied, 342 U.S. 835 (1951).

Urie v. Thompson, 352 Mo. 211, 176 S.W.2d 471 (1943), rev'd 337 U.S. 163 (1948).

------

### SECTION H.   SUMMARY

To facilitate learning the essential features of the significant publications described in the chapters, a summary of them is provided towards the end of the various chapters.   The summaries are generally arranged with the following categories in mind:  (1) scope—indicating coverage by subject matter and chronology, if any;  (2) arrangement—for example, alphabetically by subject, by names or titles, or by chronology (following a time sequence);  (3) index;  and  (4) supplementation.

1.   **Elements of a Court Decision**

a.    Name of the case.

b.    Docket number.

c.    Date of decision.

d.    Synopsis, or Summary, of case.

e.    Syllabus or headnote—brief summary of the legal rule or significant facts in a case.

f.    Names of counsel.

g.    Synopsis of briefs of counsel.

h.    Statement of facts.

i.    Opinion of the court—explanation of the court's decision.

Concurring opinion—opinion of a judge which agrees with the decision of the majority but disagrees with the reasoning.

Dissenting opinion—expressed disagreement of one or more judges of a court with the decision reached by the majority in a case before them.

*Per curiam* opinion—opinion of the whole court as distinguished from an opinion written by a specific judge.

Memorandum opinion—is a brief holding of the whole court in which the opinion (explanation) is very concise or totally absent.

*Ratio decidendi*—the point in a case which determines the result.

*Obiter dictum*—official, incidental comment, not necessary to the formulation of the decision, made by the judge in his opinion which is not binding as precedent.

    j.   Decision of the court—disposition of the case by the court.

## 2. Official and Unofficial Reports

    a.   Official reports—court reports directed by statute.

    b.   Unofficial reports—court reports published without statutory direction.

## 3. Elements of Judicial Reporting

    a.   "Slip" opinion—is an individual court decision published separately soon after it is rendered.

    b.   Advance sheets—contain the decisions of a court or the courts of several jurisdictions decided just prior to publication and is in pamphlet format.

    c.   Order of release of cases is determined by their decision dates and not by a logical arrangement, such as subject.

    d.   A bound volume includes:

    (1)  Table of cases contained in the volume.

    (2)  Table of statutes interpreted by the decisions reported.

    (3) Opinions (comprising of cases from preceding advance sheets)—written, *per curiam* or memorandum.

    (4)  Subject index or digest of the cases reported.

    (5)  Judicial definitions of words and phrases used in the cases reported.

    (6)  Court rules.

    (7)  Unofficial reports generally contain cross reference tables to the official reports.

## 4. Organization of Court Reports

    a.   Jurisdictional reports—decisions of a specific court or several courts within a system.

    b.   Geographical reports:

    (1)  Cases from several courts of a state.

    (2)  Regional reporters.

# Chapter 4

## FEDERAL COURT DECISIONS

For present purposes, the federal court system can be described as consisting of three main divisions: The Supreme Court of the United States (the highest court), the Courts of Appeals (intermediate appellate courts), and the district courts (courts of original jurisdiction.)[1]

All written opinions of the Supreme Court are published in the official and unofficial reports. Most *per curiam* decisions also are reported. All written decisions of the Courts of Appeals and special courts are unofficially published. As for the district court decisions, only selected opinions of those courts are unofficially reported. Typewritten unreported cases of the district courts generally are available through the court clerks.

## SECTION A.   UNITED STATES SUPREME COURT REPORTS

The decisions of the United States Supreme Court are published in five current reports:

1. United States Reports (official edition), cited "U. S."
2. United States Supreme Court Reports (Lawyers Cooperative Pub. Co.), cited "L.Ed." and "L.Ed.2d".
3. Supreme Court Reporter (West Publishing Co.), cited "Sup.Ct." or "S.Ct."
4. United States Law Week (Bureau of National Affairs), cited "U.S.L.W." or "U.S.L. Week."
5. Commerce Clearing House, United States Supreme Court Bulletin.

### 1.   United States Reports (Official Ed.)

Prior to 1817, the United States Reports were published by private reporters. Since that date they have been published by official reporters. The reports were cited by the name of the reporters from

[1] For a more detailed description of the federal court system, see U.S. Congress. House Committee on the Judiciary. The United States Courts: Their Jurisdiction and Work. 1971 (Committee Print).

Dallas through Wallace.  The seven early reporters, with their abbreviations, are as follows:

| Dallas (Dall.) | 4 v. | v. 1– 4 U.S. (1789–1800) |
| Cranch (Cranch) | 9 v. | v. 5–13 U.S. (1801–1815) |
| Wheaton (Wheat.) | 12 v. | v. 14–25 U.S. (1816–1827) |
| Peters (Peters) | 16 v. | v. 26–41 U.S. (1828–1842) |
| Howard (How.) | 24 v. | v. 42–65 U.S. (1843–1860) |
| Black (Black) | 2 v. | v. 66–67 U.S. (1861–1862) |
| Wallace (Wall.) | 23 v. | v. 68–90 U.S. (1863–1874) |

The first ninety volumes, from Dallas through Wallace, were later numbered consecutively and beginning with volume 91 (1875) this method of numbering was adopted.  1 Dallas, although a volume of the U. S. Reports, contains only Pennsylvania decisions.  The other volumes of Dallas contain U. S. Supreme Court and Pennsylvania decisions.

Generally, three or four bound volumes of the official edition are published each term of the U. S. Supreme Court.  The bound volumes are preceded by advance sheets and the advance sheets have the same volume and page numbers as the subsequent volumes.

The decisions of the Supreme Court are initially printed separately as "slip" opinions when they are rendered by the Court.  The "slip" opinions are not headnoted or indexed.  They appear prior to the advance sheets.  See Illustrations 5 and 6.

## 2.   United States Supreme Court Reports (Lawyers' Edition)

This reprint-edition of the United States Supreme Court opinions prints three or more volumes of a term of the official reports in one or two of its volumes.  The books are consecutively numbered in two series and the edition contains all decisions included in the official set.

Thumb indexes or Reference Tables separate or index the single official volumes included in each book since volume 15 of the Lawyers' Edition.  The Reference Tables, beginning with volume 15, cross reference from the pages of the official edition to the pages where the same text is located in the Lawyers' Edition.  The official pagination is also given on each Lawyers' Edition page.

The text of the decisions is given in full.  Case summaries precede the headnotes.  The headnotes of the cases are prepared by the editors.  Briefs of counsel are summarized and the annotations, which are included in increasing number in each volume since volume 92, 1st series, are also written by the editors.  The annotations are articles or essays on significant legal issues in the reported cases and each appears after the related decision. The annotations and briefs in the second series appear in a separate section of each volume.

A *Later Case Service* for the Second Series of the *U. S. Supreme Court Reports* serves as a means to keep the Annotations that appear in this set current. This volume is keyed to the volumes of the *Lawyers Edition* 2nd and serves as a supplement to its annotations. It is kept up to date by an annual cumulative pocket supplement.

*The Supreme Court Reports Index to Annotations* (1972) is a subject index to the annotations in the *Lawyer's Edition* and in *A. L.R. Fed.* (Discussed in Chapter 7). Current annotations are indexed in the cumulative annual pocket supplement to the *Index*. References to the annotations also are included in the body of the *U. S. Supreme Court Reports Digest,* thereby providing the user with two sources of entry to *Lawyers' Edition* annotations. This *Index* supersedes the *Index to Annotations* formerly published in volume 14 of the *Digest*.

The *Index to Annotations* should be consulted first on any topic which may have been the subject of a Supreme Court decision.

Annotations which cite words and phrases judicially defined are listed in the *Index to Annotations*. The words and phrases are arranged alphabetically under the heading "Words and Phrases."

The Lawyers' Edition has advance sheets which are published biweekly during the term of the Court. The table of cases listed in each advance sheet is cumulated. See Illustration 8.

### 3.  Supreme Court Reporter (West Edition)

This publication is a unit of the *National Reporter System* which is published by the West Publishing Co. The opinions in the set are therefore *key-numbered.* In Chapter 6 we will consider the key-numbering system.

This edition begins with volume 106 (1882) of the official set; therefore, it does not contain the cases reported in volumes 1–105 of the official reports.

Each volume of the West Edition, prior to the 1959 Term (Vol. 80), contains the several volumes of the official reports published in a term. Beginning with volume 80, the cases per term are published in two volumes. E. g., volumes 80 and 80A. This modification conforms with a similar publication change in the Lawyers' Edition.

The full text of the decisions, edited headnotes and other features of reports are included in the *Supreme Court Reporter;* however, it does not contain summaries of the arguments of counsel.

As in the case of the *Lawyers' Edition*, the paging of the West Edition does not correspond with the paging of the official edition. In order that the original page references can be cited from the reprint, the reprint pages show, in relation to the text, where the pages of the official edition begin. This is called "star-pagination." (See Illustration 9. Also, observe that the *Supreme Court Reporter* page number on that page is at the upper left-hand corner and the volume number is noted in the center. The duplicate official (U.S.) citation is given in the upper right-hand corner.)

The advance sheets of the *Supreme Court Reporter* also contain cumulative lists of cases or references to them.

Preceding the general table of cases in each bound volume since volume 47 is a cross reference table from the official *U. S. Reports* citations to the volumes and pages of the *Supreme Court Reporter*. These tables appear in the backs of volumes 43–46. Prior to volume 43 there are no cross reference tables. See Illustration 7.

### 4. Other Publications

Two speedy, current services, which report the texts of the Supreme Court decisions, are the *United States Law Week* and *Commerce Clearing House, United States Supreme Court Bulletin*. These are loose-leaf publications.

The *United States Law Week* is a two-volume service, published weekly, consisting of two sections: (1) Supreme Court sections and (2) General Law Sections. The Supreme Court Sections give the complete texts of the United States Supreme Court opinions, a topical index and a journal and calendar of the Supreme Court cases. The *Law Week* reproduces the full texts of all Supreme Court opinions within twenty-four hours after they are rendered. The General Law Sections include the more important current federal statutes, a summary and analysis of federal legal trends, some federal agency rulings and significant new court decisions not yet reported in general or regional law reports. A general topical index to the Sections is also provided.

The *Commerce Clearing House, United States Supreme Court Bulletin* is a loose-leaf publication which gives the docket of the Supreme Court cases and the full texts of all the opinions. The opinions are reproduced by photo-offset from the official "slip" opinions immediately after they are handed down. This is also an "overnight" service.

These two sets are most useful to locate decisions of the Supreme Court for the current term. For older decisions it is preferable to use one of the three other sets discussed *supra*.

### SECTION B. LOWER FEDERAL COURT REPORTS

There have been numerous editions of the early official lower federal court reports. The official appellate and district courts reports have been discontinued and their current opinions are available, for the most part, only in unofficial publications. However, it should be noted that the appellate courts publish "slip" opinions for interim use. These may be obtained from the clerks of courts. The early United States circuit courts and district courts reports were published by private reporters and are generally cited by the name of the reporter.

However, there are several official, special lower federal court reports, currently published. They are:

Cases decided in the Court of Claims. Washington, Government Printing Office, 1863 to date. v. 1 et seq.

U. S. Court of Customs Appeals and U. S. Court of Customs and Patent Appeals. Reports. Washington, Government Printing Office, 1911 to date. v. 1 et seq. (Customs). 1929 to date, v. 1 et seq. (Patents).

U. S. Customs Court. Reports. Washington, Government Printing Office, July 1938 to date. v. 1 et seq.

Tax Court of the United States. Reports. Washington, Government Printing Office, Oct. 1942 to date. v. 1 et seq.

### 1. Privately Published Editions of Lower Federal Court Reports

#### a. *Federal Cases*

*Federal Cases* is an annotated report of all available U. S. Circuit and District Courts decisions, 1789–1879, in 31 volumes. It contains approximately 18,000 cases and is arranged alphabetically by names of cases and the cases are consecutively numbered. The decisions are generally cited by number. The annotations are brief notes to the cases. The Digest volume, volume 31, includes Blue Tables which cross reference from the citation of the original report to the Federal Cases Number. This reprint of the decisions for that period is a very useful annotated reference and includes cases from reports, periodicals and other sources.

#### b. *Federal Reporter and Federal Supplement*

From 1879 to date the lower federal court decisions are printed in the *Federal Reporter*, the *Federal Supplement* and the *Federal Rules Decisions*. These three sets are part of the *National Reporter System*, the other units of which will be discussed in Chapter 5. The

*Federal Rules Decisions* will be considered later in Chapter 12, Court Procedure.

The *Federal Reporter* consists of two series. The First Series stopped with volume 300, and the Second Series started numbering anew from volume 1. This series scheme was instituted to avoid the reports ever having long unmanageable numbers. In October 1932, the *Federal Supplement* was introduced. This current set contains the opinions of the U. S. District Courts, the District Court of the U. S. for the District of Columbia, and (since volume 135) the U. S. Customs Court. With volume 182, the *Federal Supplement* discontinued publishing the Court of Claims cases. Beginning with volume 276 2d, the Court of Claims cases are included in the *Federal Reporter*.

The *Federal Reporter* now includes the opinions of the U. S. Courts of Appeals, the Court of Customs and Patent Appeals and the Court of Claims.

The *Federal Reporter* and the *Federal Supplement* are unofficial publications, there being no current official reports for the decisions of the U. S. Courts of Appeals and the District Courts.

The cases are first reported in advance sheets, are key-numbered and subsequently appear in the uniformly bound volumes of the sets. The decisions appearing in the bound volumes have the same volume and page numbers which they had in the advance sheets.

These sets contain only those federal cases which are designated for publication by the courts. All written appellate opinions are published. Some District opinions are omitted and remain unreported.[2] Typed copies of unreported District Court cases can be obtained from the clerks of the District Courts.

2 For full discussion of Federal Court reporting, see articles by Vestal, 4 Houston L.Rev. 185 (1966); 52 Iowa L.Rev. 379 (1966); 39 So.Calif.L.Rev. 608 (1966); 17 Loyola L.Rev. 373 (1970–71).

tion B(e). Special Federal Courts.

For additional information, see M. Fisher, Research Tools in Custom Law. 33 Bus. Law 89 (1977).

## SECTION C.  ILLUSTRATIONS

The opinion of *Healy v. James* [408 U.S. 169, 92 S.Ct. 2338, 33 L.Ed.2d 260] as it is published in:

5.  **Slip opinion**—U.S. Supreme Court

6.  **Advance Sheets to the U.S. Reports (Official)**

7.  **Advance Sheets to the Supreme Court Reporter.**  (West Publishing Co.)

8.  **Advance Sheets to the Lawyers Edition of the United States Supreme Court Reports.**  (Lawyers Co-operative Publishing Co.)

9.  **Sample page from Supreme Court Reporter illustrating "star" paging.**

10.  **Title page—Federal Reporter**

11.  **Title page—Federal Supplement**

## [Illustration 5]

## HEALY v. JAMES AS REPORTED IN A SLIP DECISION OF THE UNITED STATES SUPREME COURT

NOTICE : This opinion is subject to formal revision before publication in the preliminary print of the United States Reports. Readers are requested to notify the Reporter of Decisions, Supreme Court of the United States, Washington, D.C. 20543, of any typographical or other formal errors, in order that corrections may be made before the preliminary print goes to press.

## SUPREME COURT OF THE UNITED STATES

### No. 71–452

| | |
|---|---|
| Catherine J. Healy et al., Petitioners,<br>*v.*<br>F. Don James et al. | On Writ of Certiorari to the United States Court of Appeals for the Second Circuit. |

[June 26, 1972]

MR. JUSTICE POWELL delivered the opinion of the Court.

This case, arising out of a denial by a state college of official recognition to a group of students who desired to form a local chapter of Students for a Democratic Society (SDS), presents this Court with questions requiring the application of well-established First Amendment principles. While the factual background of this particular case raises these constitutional issues in a manner not heretofore passed on by the Court, and only infrequently presented to lower federal courts, our decision today is governed by existing precedent.

> A typical slip opinion of a decision of the U. S. Supreme Court. Note that the only information given is (1) Docket Number (2) Names of Parties (3) Date of Opinion and (4) Name of Justice who wrote the Opinion.

interests appear to compete the First Amendment, made binding on the States by the Fourteenth Amendment, strikes the required balance.

[Illustration 6]

## HEALY v. JAMES AS REPORTED IN THE ADVANCE SHEETS OF 408 U.S. 169

---

HEALY *v.* JAMES           169

Syllabus

## HEALY ET AL. *v.* JAMES ET AL.

**CERTIORARI TO THE UNITED STATES COURT OF APPEALS FOR THE SECOND CIRCUIT**

No. 71–452.   Argued March 28, 1972—Decided June 26, 1972

Petitioners, seeking to form a local chapter of Students for a Democratic Society (SDS) at a state-supported college, were denied recognition as a campus organization. Recognition would have entitled petitioners to use campus facilities for meetings and to use of the campus bulletin board and school newspaper. The college president denied recognition because he was not satisfied that petitioners' group was independent of the national SDS, which he concluded has a philosophy of disruption and violence in conflict with

---

The first page of the *Healy* case as it appeared in the advance sheets to the *U. S. Reports.*

Note how the Reporter of Decisions has added a summary of the case and headnotes.

---

that petitioners had failed to avail themselves of the due process accorded to them and to meet their burden of complying with the prevailing standards for recognition. *Held:*

1. The courts erred in (1) discounting the cognizable First Amendment associational interest that petitioners had in furthering their personal beliefs and (2) assuming that the burden was on petitioners to show entitlement to recognition by the college rather than on the college to justify its nonrecognition of the group, once petitioners had made application conformably to college requirements. Pp. 180–185.

2. Insofar as the denial of recognition to petitioners' group was based on an assumed relationship with the national SDS, or was a result of disagreement with the group's philosophy, or was a consequence of a fear of disruption, for which there was no support in the record, the college's decision violated the petitioners' First Amendment rights. A proper basis for nonrecognition might have

[Illustration 6–a]

## SAMPLE PAGE FROM HEALY v. JAMES, 408 U.S. 169

170　　　　　　OCTOBER TERM, 1971

Opinion of the Court　　　　　408 U. S.

> **This is the second page of the *Healy* opinion in the *U. S. Reports*. Note how names of the attorneys for both parties were added.**

REHNQUIST, J., filed a statement concurring in the result, *post*, p. 201.

*Melvin L. Wulf* argued the cause for petitioners. With him on the brief were *Eugene Z. DuBose, Jr., Alvin Pudlin,* and *Sanford Jay Rosen.*

*F. Michael Ahern,* Assistant Attorney General of Connecticut, argued the cause for respondents. With him on the brief was *Robert K. Killian,* Attorney General.

Briefs of *amici curiae* urging affirmance were filed by *Evelle J. Younger,* Attorney General of California, and *Donald B. Day,* Deputy Attorney General, for the Board of Trustees of California State Colleges; by *Frank G. Carrington, Jr.,* and *Alan S. Ganz* for Americans for Effective Law Enforcement, Inc.; and by *Morris I. Leibman* and *Philip B. Kurland* for the American Association of Presidents of Independent Colleges and Universities.

MR. JUSTICE POWELL delivered the opinion of the Court.

This case, arising out of a denial by a state college of official recognition to a group of students who desired to form a local chapter of Students for a Democratic Society (SDS), presents this Court with questions requiring the application of well-established First Amendment principles. While the factual background of this

## [Illustration 7]
## HEALY v. JAMES AS REPORTED IN 92 S.Ct. 2338

---

**2338**      92 **SUPREME COURT REPORTER**

other civilians. The case is therefore ripe for adjudication. Because the evil alleged in the Army intelligence system is that of overbreadth, *i. e.*, the collection of information not reasonably relevant to the Army's mission to suppress civil disorder, and because there is no indication that a bet-

> The first page of the *Healy* opinion as it appears in the Advance Sheets of the *Supreme Court Reporter*. An unofficial set published by the West Publishing Co. The summary is prepared by its Editors.

cannot agree. If the Army's system does indeed derogate First Amendment values, the [respondents] are persons who are sufficiently affected to permit their complaint to be heard. The record shows that most if not all of the [respondents] and/or the organizations of which they are members have been the subject of Army surveillance reports and their names have appeared in the Army's records. Since this is precisely the injury of which [respondents] complain, they have standing to seek redress for that alleged injury in court and will provide the necessary adversary interest that is required by the standing doctrine, on the issue of whether the actions complained of do in fact inhibit the exercise of First Amendment rights. Nor should the fact that these particular persons are sufficiently uninhibited to bring this suit be any ground for objecting to their standing." *Id.*, at 954, n. 17.

Respondents may or may not be able to prove the case they allege. But I agree with the Court of Appeals that they are entitled to try. I would therefore affirm the remand to the District Court for a trial and determination of the issues specified by the Court of Appeals.

Catherine J. **HEALY** et al., Petitioners,

v.

F. Don **JAMES** et al.

No. 71–452.

Argued March 28, 1972.

Decided June 26, 1972.

After evidentiary hearing was ordered, 311 F.Supp. 1275, plaintiffs' application requesting official campus recognition of organization was denied by college president and plaintiffs sought equitable relief affording them right to form group with official campus recognition. The United States District Court for the District of Connecticut, 319 F.Supp. 113, dismissed the action and plaintiffs appealed. The Court of Appeals, 445 F.2d 1122, affirmed and certiorari was granted. The Supreme Court, Mr. Justice Powell, held that once college students filed application for recognition of student organization in conformity with requirements, burden was on college administration to justify rejection, and that local group's assumed relationship with national organization, disagreement with group's philosophy, unsupported fear of disruption were insufficient to warrant denial of official recognition but such denial would be authorized on showing that group refused to comply with rule requiring them to abide by reasonable campus regulations.

Reversed and remanded.

Mr. Chief Justice Burger filed concurring opinion.

Mr. Justice Douglas concurred and filed opinion.

Mr. Justice Rehnquist filed statement concurring in result.

**1. Constitutional Law ⊜82**

Colleges and universities are not enclaves immune from sweep of First Amendment. U.S.C.A.Const. Amend. 1.

[Illustration 7–a]

## SAMPLE PAGE FROM 92 S.Ct. 2340

---

**2340**                    **92 SUPREME COURT REPORTER**

**16. Colleges and Universities ⬅︎10**

Evidence in action by students seeking to obtain official recognition for proposed local chapter identified with campus bulletin board and school newspaper. The college president denied recognition because he was not satisfied that petitioners' group was independent

> Note how 21 headnotes have been assigned. These differ from the headnotes in the *U. S. Reports* and *L.Ed. Reports.*
>
> Note also how syllabus as it appeared in the U. S. Reports is also printed in this set.

Critical line for First Amendment purposes must be drawn between advocacy, which is entitled to full protection, and action, which is not. U.S.C.A.Const. Amend. 1.

**18. Colleges and Universities ⬅︎9**

College students may preach propriety of amending or even doing away with any or all campus regulations but may not undertake to flout those rules.

**19. Colleges and Universities ⬅︎9**

Reasonable regulations with respect to time, place, and manner in which student groups conduct their speech-related activities must be respected.

**20. Colleges and Universities ⬅︎7**

College administration may impose requirement that group seeking official recognition affirm in advance its willingness to adhere to reasonable campus law.

**21. Colleges and Universities ⬅︎9**

Recognition once accorded student organization may be withdrawn or suspended if campus laws are not respected.

*Syllabus* *

Petitioners, seeking to form a local chapter of Students for a Democratic Society (SDS) at a state-supported college, were denied recognition as a campus organization. Recognition would have entitled petitioners to use campus facilities for meetings and to use of the

Approving the president's judgment, the District Court held that petitioners had failed to show that they could function free from the national SDS and that the college's refusal to approve the group, which the court found "likely to cause violent acts of disruption," did not violate petitioners' associational rights. The Court of Appeals, purporting not to reach the First Amendment issues, affirmed on the ground that petitioners had failed to avail themselves of the due process accorded to them and to meet their burden of complying with the prevailing standards for recognition. *Held:*

1.  The courts erred in (1) discounting the cognizable First Amendment associational interest that petitioners had in furthering their personal beliefs and (2) in assuming that the burden was on petitioners to show entitlement to recognition by the college rather than on the college to justify its nonrecognition of the group, once petitioners had made application conformably to college requirements. Pp. 2345–2348.

2.  Insofar as the denial of recognition to petitioners' group was based on an assumed relationship with the national SDS, or was a result of disagreement with the group's philosophy, or was a consequence of a fear of disruption, for which there was no support in the record, the college's decision violated the petitioners' First Amendment rights. A

---

* The syllabus constitutes no part of the opinion of the Court but has been prepared by the Reporter of Decisions for the convenience of the reader. See United States v. Detroit Timber & Lumber Co., 200 U.S. 321, 337, 26 S.Ct. 282, 287, 50 L.Ed. 499.

[Illustration 7–b]

## SAMPLE PAGE FROM 92 S.Ct. 2341

**HEALY v. JAMES**      **2341**
Cite as 92 S.Ct. 2338 (1972)

proper basis for nonrecognition might have been afforded, however, by a showing that the group refused to comply with a rule requiring them to abide by reasonable campus regulations. Since the record is not clear whether the college has such a rule and, if so, whether petitioners intend to observe it, these issues remain to be resolved.

2 Cir., 445 F.2d 1122, reversed and remanded.

———

Melvin L. Wulf, New York City, for petitioners.

F. Michael Ahern, Hartford, Conn., for respondents.

Mr. Justice POWELL delivered the opinion of the Court.

This case, arising out of a denial by a state college of official recognition to a group of students who desired to form a local chapter of Students for a Democratic Society (SDS), presents this Court with questions requiring the application of well-established First Amendment principles. While the factual background of this particular case raises these constitutional issues in a manner not heretofore passed on by the Court, and only infrequently presented to lower federal courts, our decision today is governed by existing precedent.

As the case involves delicate issues concerning the academic community, we approach our task with special caution, recognizing the mutual interest of students, faculty members, and administrators in an environment free from disruptive interference with the educational process. We also are mindful of the equally significant interest in the widest latitude for free expression and debate consonant with the maintenance of order. Where these interests appear to compete, the First Amendment, made binding on the States by the Fourteenth Amendment, strikes the required balance.

I

We mention briefly at the outset the setting in 1969–1970. A climate of unrest prevailed on many college campuses in this country. There had been widespread civil disobedience on some campuses, accompanied by the seizure of buildings, vandalism, and arson. Some colleges had been shut down altogether, while at others files were looted and manuscripts destroyed. SDS chapters on some of those campuses had been a catalytic force during this period.[1] Although the causes of campus disruption were many and complex, one of the

> Opinion of the Court printed exactly the same as in the official *U. S. Reports*.

Fortunately, with the passage of time, a calmer atmosphere and greater maturity now pervade our campuses. Yet, it was in this climate of earlier unrest that this case arose.

Petitioners are students attending Central Connecticut State College (CCSC), a state-supported institution of higher learning. In September 1969 they undertook to organize what they then referred to as a "local chapter" of Students for a Democratic Society (SDS). Pursuant to procedures established by the College, petitioners filed a request for official recognition as a campus organization with the Student Affairs Committee, a committee composed of four students, three faculty members and the Dean of Student Affairs. The request specified three purposes for the proposed organization's existence. It would provide "a forum of discussion and self-education for students developing an analysis of American society"; it would serve as "an agency for integrating thought with action so as to bring about constructive changes"; and it would endeavor to pro-

---

1. See Report of the President's Comm'n on Campus Unrest (1970); Report of

the ABA Comm'n on Campus Gov't and Student Dissent (1970).

[Illustration 8]

## HEALY v. JAMES AS REPORTED IN 33 L.Ed.2d 266

266         U. S. SUPREME COURT REPORTS         33 L Ed 2d

CATHERINE J. HEALY et al., Petitioners,

v

F. DON JAMES et al.

— US —, 33 L Ed 2d 266; 92 S Ct —

[No. 71–452]

Argued March 28, 1972. Decided June 26, 1972.

### SUMMARY

The petitioners, a group of college students, organized what they called a "local chapter" of Students for a Democratic Society (SDS), and filed a request for official recognition as a campus organization. Following a hearing at which representatives of the group stated that they would not affiliate with the national SDS and that the group would remain "completely independent," the Student Affairs Committee of the college ap-

First page of the *Healy* opinion as it appears in the Advance Sheets of *L.Ed.2d* Summary has been prepared by the Editors of the Lawyers Co-operative Publishing Co.

This is an unofficial edition of the Supreme Court reports.

sion on conclusions drawn from materials outside the record, the District Court ordered the college administration to hold another hearing to clarify several ambiguities surrounding the president's decision. The hearing was held, during which the petitioners, though reaffirming that they would have no connection whatsoever with the national SDS, equivocated when asked whether they might respond to "issues of violence" in the same manner as other SDS chapters had responded, and whether they could envision situations where they might advocate interrupting classes. Upon reviewing the hearing transcript and exhibits, the president reaffirmed his prior decision to reject the application, stating that the group would be a disruptive influence at the college and that recognition would be

[Illustration 8–a]

## SAMPLE PAGE FROM 33 L.Ed.2d 267

HEALY v JAMES                              **267**
33 L Ed 2d 266

contrary to the orderly process of change on the campus. The case was subsequently returned to the District Court, where it was ordered dismissed (319 F Supp 113). The United States Court of Appeals for the Second Circuit affirmed on the theory that the petitioners had failed to avail themselves of the due process accorded them by the hearings and the court proceedings, and had failed to meet their burden of complying with the prevailing standards at the college for recognition of "campus organizations" (445 F2d 1122).

On certiorari, the United States Supreme Court reversed and remanded. In an opinion by POWELL, J., expressing the views of eight members of the court, it was held that (1) it is perfectly proper for a college administration to prohibit activities by students or by groups of students which infringe reasonable campus rules, interrupt classes, or substantially interfere with the opportunity of other students to obtain an education, (2) it is also proper for a college administration to inflict discipline for the violation of reasonable campus rules, to protect itself and its property, and to require that its students adhere to generally accepted standards of

cond                                                             icial
colle;                                                           able
camɪ   ┌─────────────────────────────────────────┐              luct,
(4) :  │    Second page of *Healy* opinion.  Note how Sum-      │  ı, to
colle; │  mary is much longer than that prepared by the Re-     │  ider
the I  │  porter of Decisions in the Official *U. S. Reports*.   │  iate
with   └─────────────────────────────────────────┘              itify
their                                                          n to

justify any decision it might make rejecting such an application, (6) justification for nonrecognition may not be based on a mere disagreement with the philosophy of a group of persons, or even upon the mere expression of views condoning violence and disruption, but nonrecognition may be based upon a group's unlawful or disruptive activities, or upon its advocacy of views directed to inciting or producing imminent lawless action and likely to incite or produce such action, and recognition may be denied to any group that reserves the right to violate any valid campus rules with which it disagrees, and (7) because it was impossible to tell from the record whether the student group in the instant case was willing to acknowledge its obligation to abide by reasonable campus regulations, the case should be remanded for such a determination.

BURGER, Ch. J., concurring, added that the academic community should solve such problems, that courts should become involved in them only as a last resort, and that the "Statement of Rights, Freedoms and Responsibilities of Students," in effect on the college campus, reflected a rational adjustment of the competing interests of college administrators and students, but that it was impossible from the record to tell whether the student group was willing to abide by such a statement.

DOUGLAS, J., joined in the court's opinion, but added that the fact that the case had to come to the Supreme Court for ultimate resolution indicated the sickness of the academic world, and that in order to achieve an integrated, adult society, rather than a stubborn status quo society

## [Illustration 8–b]
## SAMPLE PAGE FROM 33 L.Ed.2d 268

**268**  U. S. SUPREME COURT REPORTS  33 L Ed 2d

oppos[...] [...]erests
in wł

RE  Note references to the other related publica-  ⹁f the
langu  tions of the Publisher. These will be discussed in  ⹁ween
the li  later chapters.  ⹁rcing
its cr  as an
empl⹁

### TOTAL CLIENT-SERVICE LIBRARY® REFERENCES

15 AM JUR 2d, Colleges and Universities §§ 22, 25–27; 16 AM JUR 2d, Constitutional Law §§ 341–355

4 AM JUR LEGAL FORMS 2d, Colleges and Universities §§ 60:71–60:125

US L ED DIGEST, Colleges and Universities § 1; Constitutional Law §§ 925, 940

ALR DIGESTS, Colleges and Universities §§ 1–3; Constitutional Law §§ 791, 803

L ED INDEX TO ANNO (Rev), Colleges and Universities; Constitutional Law; Schools

ALR QUICK INDEX, Colleges and Universities; Constitutional Law; Freedom of Assembly; Freedom of Speech and Press; Schools

FEDERAL QUICK INDEX, Colleges and Universities; Constitutional Law; Freedom of Assembly and Petition; Freedom of Speech and Press; Schools and School Districts

### ANNOTATION REFERENCES

Student organization registration statement, filed with public school or state university or college, as open to inspection by public. 37 ALR3d 1311.

Participation of student in demonstration on or near campus as warranting expulsion or suspension from school or college. 32 ALR3d 864.

Participation of student in demonstration on or near campus as warranting imposition of criminal liability for breach of peace, disorderly conduct, trespass, unlawful assembly, or similar offense. 32 ALR3d 551.

Regulations as to fraternities and similar associations connected with educational institution. 10 ALR3d 389.

[Illustration 8–c]

## SAMPLE PAGE FROM 33 L.Ed.2d 269

HEALY v JAMES 269
33 L Ed 2d 266

### HEADNOTES

Classified to U. S. Supreme Court Digest, Annotated

**Colleges and Universities § 1; Constitutional Law §§ 925.5, 925.8 — academic environment — disruptive interferences — free expression**

1. Where the mutual interest of students, faculty members, and administrators in having in an academic community an environment free from disruptive interference with the educational process, appears to conflict with the equally significant interest in affording the widest latitude for free expression and debate consonant with the maintenance of order, the First Amendment to the United States Constitution, made binding on the states by the Fourteenth Amendment, strikes the required balance.

**Colleges and Universities § 1; Constitutional Law § 925 — state colleges — freedom of speech**

2. State colleges and universities are not enclaves immune from the sweep of the First Amendment, and neither s[...]their con[...]of speech[...]house gat[...]

Constitut[...]ity — [...]

3. First Amendment rights must always be applied in light of the special characteristics of the environment in each particular case.

**Colleges and Universities § 1 — state-operated institutions — officials — prescribing conduct**

4. Where state-operated educational institutions are involved, the states and the officials of the schools have a comprehensive authority, consistent with fundamental constitutional safeguards, to prescribe and control conduct in the schools.

**Colleges and Universities § 1; Constitutional Law §§ 925, 940 — state institutions — need for order — constitutional freedoms**

5. Although there is an acknowl-

edged need for order at state-operated educational institutions, it is not the case that First Amendment protections should apply with less force on college campuses than in the community at large; quite to the contrary, the vigilant protection of constitutional freedoms is nowhere more vital than in the community of American schools.

**Constitutional Law § 940 — right of association — implicit nature**

6. Among the rights protected by the First Amendment is the right of individuals to associate to further their personal beliefs; and while the freedom of association is not explicitly set out in the First Amendment, it is implicit in the freedoms of speech, assembly, and petition.

**Colleges and Universities § 1; Constitutional Law § 940 — denying official recognition — abridging right of association**

[...]ognition,[...]ge organ-[...]the right[...]ociate to[...]iefs, the[...]right be-ing the denial of the right to use campus facilities, for meetings and for other appropriate purposes.

**Constitutional Law § 940 — right of association**

8. The Constitution's protection of the right to associate freely is not limited to direct interference with fundamental rights.

**Colleges and Universities § 1 — official recognition — off-campus existence — disabilities**

9. The consequences of not extending official recognition to a group of college students seeking recognition from a college administration as a "campus organization" is not limited to a mere denial of the stamp of official college respectability; and the fact

*The headnotes are prepared by the publisher's editorial staff. They differ from the headnotes in the other two sets of U. S. Supreme Court Reports.*

[Illustration 8–d]

## SAMPLE PAGE FROM 33 L.Ed.2d 272

---

**272**      **U. S. SUPREME COURT REPORTS**      **33 L Ed 2d**

students adhere to generally accepted standards of conduct.

**Colleges and Universities § 1; Constitutional Law §§ 928, 940 — student groups — regulations — associational rights and freedoms**

26. Just as in the community at large, a college administration may impose reasonable regulations with respect to the time, the place, and the manner in which student groups may conduct their speech-related activities, and it may also impose a requirement

> Note how this opinion was assigned 30 headnotes. The number vary from case to case.
>
> Also note how this unofficial edition reprints the Syllabus from the official *U. S. Reports.*

seeking the privilege of official recognition.

**Colleges and Universities § 1 — student group — denial of participation**

27. The benefits of participation in the internal life of a college community may be denied to any student group that reserves the right to violate any valid campus rules with which it disagrees.

**Colleges and Universities § 1 — rulemaking authority — student groups — withdrawal of recognition**

28. In addition to a college administration's broad rulemaking power to assure that the traditional academic

atmosphere is safeguarded, it may also impose sanctions on those students or groups which violate such rules; and official recognition of a "campus organization" formed by a group of students, once accorded, may be withdrawn or suspended if the organization's members fail to respect campus law.

**Appeal and Error § 1698 — college students — reasonable regulations**

29. Where the record does not disclose whether a group of college students, seeking official recognition as a campus organization" from their college for a group they wish to form, such recognition has been denied by the college's president, are willing to abide by reasonable campus rules and regulations, the United States Supreme Court will remand the action for such a determination to be made.

**Constitutional Law §§ 925, 940 — rights of expression and association — wide latitude — dedication to principles**

30. The wide latitude accorded by the Constitution to the freedoms of expression and association is not without its cost in terms of the risk to the maintenance of civility and an ordered society, and this latitude often has resulted, on the college campus and elsewhere, in the infringement of the rights of others; however, though the tendency of some to abuse the very constitutional privileges they invoke is to be deplored, and though the infringement of the rights of others is not to be tolerated, the United States Supreme Court nevertheless is dedicated to the principles of the Constitution's Bill of Rights upon which the vigorous and free society of the United States is founded.

### SYLLABUS BY REPORTER OF DECISIONS

Petitioners, seeking to form a local chapter of Students for a Democratic Society (SDS) at a state-supported college, were denied recognition as a campus organization. Recognition would have entitled petitioners to use campus facilities for meetings and to use of the campus bulletin board and school newspaper. The college president denied recognition because he was not satisfied that petitioners' group was independent of the national

[Illustration 8–e]

## SAMPLE PAGE FROM 33 L.Ed.2d 273

HEALY v JAMES                                273
33 L Ed 2d 266

SDS, which he concluded has a philosophy of disruption and violence in conflict with the college's declaration of student rights. Petitioners thereupon brought this action for declaratory and injunctive relief. The District Court first ordered a further administrative hearing, after which the president reaffirmed his prior decision. Approving the president's judgment, the District Court held that petitioners had failed to show that they could function free from the national SDS and that the college's refusal to approve the group, which the court found "likely to cause violent acts of disruption," did not violate petitioners' associational rights. The Court of Appeals, purporting not to reach the First Amendment issues, affirmed on the ground that petitioners had failed to avail themselves of the due process accorded to them and to meet their burden

tify its nonrecognition of the group, once petitioners had made application conformably to college requirements.

2. Insofar as the denial of recognition to petitioners' group was based on an assumed relationship with the national SDS, or was a result of disagreement with the group's philosophy, or was a consequence of a fear of disruption, for which there was no support in the record, the college's decision violated the petitioners' First Amendment rights. A proper basis for nonrecognition might have been afforded, however, by a showing that the group refused to comply with a rule requiring them to abide by reasonable campus regulations. Since the record is not clear whether the college has such a rule and, if so, whether petitioners intend to observe it, these issues remain to be resolved.

ing sta
1. Tl
ing the
associa
had in
liefs a

**Starting with the opinion of the court, the text of the opinion is exactly the same as in the official reports.**

anded.
ion of
J., and
White,
joined.
g opin-
e opin-

burden was on petitioners to show entitlement to recognition by the college rather than on the college to jus-

ion. Rehnquist, J., filed a statement concurring in the result.

### APPEARANCES OF COUNSEL

**Melvin L. Wulf** argued the cause for petitioners.
**F. Michael Ahern** argued the cause for respondents.

### OPINION OF THE COURT

Mr. Justice **Powell** delivered the opinion of the Court.

This case, arising out of a denial by a state college of official recognition to a group of students who desired to form a local chapter of Students for a Democratic Society (SDS), presents this Court with questions requiring the application of well-established First Amendment principles. While the factual background of this particular case raises these constitutional issues in a man-

[33 L Ed 2d]—18

ner not heretofore passed on by the Court, and only infrequently presented to lower federal courts, our decision today is governed by existing precedent.

[1] As the case involves delicate issues concerning the academic community, we approach our task with special caution, recognizing the mutual interest of students, faculty members, and administrators in an environment free from disruptive interference with the educational proc-

## [Illustration 9]

## SAMPLE PAGE FROM 80 SUPREME COURT REPORTER 175

---

**361 U.S. 110**    **SENTILLES v. INTER–CARIBBEAN SHIPPING CORP.**     **175**
Cite as 80 S.Ct. 175

was submitted to a jury in the District Court, where a verdict was returned for the petitioner, and judgment entered thereon.

\*   \*   \*   \*   \*

The Court of Appeals agreed with the respondent's contention and reversed, 5 Cir., 256 F.2d 156. We granted certiorari on a petition in which it was asserted that the Court of Appeals had applied an improper standard in reviewing the medical evidence and in examining the judgment rendered on the jury's verdict. 359 U.S. 923, 79 S.Ct. 604, 3 L.Ed.2d 627.

There was evidence that petitioner (whose medical history was an active one) had been examined several times by his regular physician in the year preceding the accident, as recently as two months before it, with no appearance of tuberculosis being then noted. During the petitioner's acute tuberculosis subsequent to the accident, a specialist re-examined X-ray pictures taken in the years preceding the accident, and concluded that

<sub>109</sub>
they did in fact reveal a pulmonary lesion, at first involving a "small scarred inactive area." "In retrospect," the specialist felt that the lesion had been tubercular. In response to a hypothetical question as to the effect of an accident like petitioner's on the aggravation or activation of a pre-existing, dormant tubercular condition, the specialist gave an opinion that "acute dissemination of the tuberculosis" might be a consequence of the accident. Another specialist, who had treated petitioner during his hospitalization after

the accident, posited the trauma and petitioner's pre-existing diabetic condition as the most likely causes of the aggravation of the tuberculosis, though he was not

his condition," though he would not say definitely: "We don't ever select one item and say that is the cause of any particular aggravation."

[2–6] The jury's power to draw the inference that the aggravation of petitioner's tubercular condition, evident so shortly after the accident, was in fact caused by that accident, was not impaired by the failure of any medical witness to testify that it was in fact the cause. Neither can it be impaired by the lack of medical unanimity as to the respective likelihood of the potential causes of the aggravation, or by the fact that other potential causes of the aggravation existed and were not conclusively negated by the proofs. The matter does not turn on the use of a particular form of words by the physicians in giving their testimony. The members of the jury, not the medical witnesses, were sworn to make a legal determination of the question of causation.[2] They were entitled

<sub>110</sub>
to take all the circumstances, including the medical testimony into consideration. See Sullivan v. Boston Elevated R. Co., 185 Mass. 602, 71 N.E. 90; Miami Coal Co. v. Luce, 76 Ind.App. 245, 131 N.E. 824.[3] Though this case involves a medical issue, it is no exception to the admonition that, "It is not the function of a court to search the record for conflicting circumstantial evidence in order to take the case away from the jury on a theory that

---

2. For a discussion of the reluctance of medical opinion to assign trauma as the cause of disease, and of the varying medical and legal concepts of causation, see Small, Gaffing at a Thing Called Cause: Medico-Legal Conflicts in the Concept of Causation, 31 Tex.L.Rev. 630.

3. The medical testimony in the case last cited moved the court to say: "Indeed, if it were not for the saving grace of what we call common sense, justice would be defeated in almost every case where opinion evidence is admitted." Id., 76 Ind. App. at page 249, 131 N.E. at page 826.

---

### ILLUSTRATION

A page from the Supreme Court Reporter showing how pagination is cross-referenced to the official *U. S. Reports.*

A similar system is used in the *L.Ed.* set of *Supreme Court Reports.*

[Illustration 10]
TITLE PAGE FROM A VOLUME OF THE FEDERAL
REPORTER

# FEDERAL REPORTER

*Second Series*

## Volume 446 F.2d

*Cases Argued and Determined*
*in the*

**UNITED STATES COURTS OF APPEALS**

**UNITED STATES COURT OF CLAIMS**

**AND**

**UNITED STATES COURT OF CUSTOMS**
**AND PATENT APPEALS**

ST. PAUL, MINN.

WEST PUBLISHING CO.

1972

[Illustration 11]
TITLE PAGE FROM A VOLUME OF THE FEDERAL SUPPLEMENT

# FEDERAL SUPPLEMENT

## Volume 331

*Cases Argued and Determined*

*in the*

**UNITED STATES DISTRICT COURTS**

**UNITED STATES CUSTOMS COURT**

*and Rulings of the*

**JUDICIAL PANEL ON MULTIDISTRICT LITIGATION**

ST. PAUL, MINN.

WEST PUBLISHING CO.

1972

## SECTION D.   METHODS OF CITATION

### 1.   Supreme Court of the United States

a.   United States Supreme Court cases may be cited by reference only to the official reports.   An example follows:

International Shoe Co. v. Washington, 326 U.S. 310 (1945).

A case so cited can be readily found in other reports of Supreme Court opinions, which carry volume and page numbers of the U. S. Reports in addition to their own.   For convenience, however, these other reports may also be cited as follows:

International Shoe Co. v. Washington, 326 U.S. 310, 66 S.Ct.
154, 90 L.Ed. 95 (1945).

b.   The first 90 volumes of the *U. S. Reports* are cited by the names of their reporters.

Leary v. United States, 14 Wall. 607 (U.S.1871).

or

81 U.S. (14 Wall.) 607 (1871).

### 2.   Appellate Decisions

a.   Indicate the circuit number in the citation of United States Court of Appeals decisions.   A distinction between United States Circuit Court of Appeals decisions (rendered prior to August 31, 1948) and later United States Court of Appeals cases appears unnecessary.

Westchester Fire Insurance Co. v. Bringle, 86 F.2d 262 (6th
Cir. 1936).

b.   Cases from the Court of Appeals for the District of Columbia may be cited as follows:

Barker v. Albright, 86 F.2d 852 (D.C.Cir. 1936).

c.   Cite decisions in the *Federal Cases* (covering federal judicial opinions prior to 1880) as follows:

Dike v. Kuhns, 7 Fed.Cas. 696, No. 3907 (C.C.W.D.Pa.1857).

d.   The old circuit courts, abolished on January 1, 1912, are cited by reference to the district.

Thayer v. Hart, 24 Fed. 558 (C.C.S.D.N.Y.1885).

### 3.   District Court Decisions

a.   A district court case from a state with only one district may be cited:

United States v. McCrillis, 104 F.Supp. 183 (D.C.R.I.1952).

b. A district court case from a state with more than one district may be cited:

Alstead Coal Co. v. Yoke, 104 F.Supp. 606 (N.D.W.Va.1952).

The divisions within a district, as in this illustration, Fairmont Division, are *not* cited.

c. A district court case of the District of Columbia may be cited:

Haberle v. Reconstruction Finance Corp., 104 F.Supp. 636 (D.D.C.1951).

d. A district court case in *Federal Cases* may be cited:

Grey v. Thomas, 11 Fed.Cas. 1, No. 5806 (D.C.N.J.1878).

---

### SECTION E.  SUMMARY

**1.  United States Supreme Court Reports**

a. United States Reports (Official Ed.).

(1) Text of all Supreme Court cases.

(2) First ninety volumes are cited frequently by reporter, for, originally, they were not consecutively numbered.

(3) Bound volumes and advance sheets have same volume and page numbers.

(4) "Slip" opinions are initially printed.

(5) No summaries of briefs of counsel; other standard reporting features are included.

b. United States Supreme Court Reports (Lawyers' Edition).

(1) Reprint of all Supreme Court cases—two series.

(2) Bound volume combines several volumes of official edition.

(3) Advance sheets and bound volumes have same volume and page numbers.

(4) Reference table appears at the beginning of each volume unit which cross references from the official citations to Lawyers' Edition pages.

(5) Briefs of counsel are summarized.

(6) Annotations in increasing number since volume 92, 1st series.

(7) *Index to Annotations*—subject index to annotations in Lawyers' Edition.

(8) Star-pagination.

(9) Standard reporting features are included.

c.   Supreme Court Reporter (West Edition).

(1) Part of the National Reporter System; key-numbered sections of headnotes.

(2) Begins with volume 106 of the official set.

(3) Each volume contains several volumes of the official reports.

(4) Advance sheets and bound volumes have same volume and page numbers.

(5) Cross reference table from the official citations to the *Supreme Court Reporter* volume and pages.

(6) Star-pagination.

(7) No summaries of briefs of counsel; other standard reporting features are included.

d.   United States Law Week.

(1) Supreme Court Sections—speedy publication of Supreme Court decisions and journal of cases.

(2) General Law Sections—include more important current federal statutes, summary of federal legal trends, some federal agency rulings and the texts of significant new court decisions; general topical index.

e.   Commerce Clearing House, U. S. Supreme Court Bulletin.

(1) Loose-leaf reporter of current Supreme Court decisions; provides fast service.

(2) Docket of Supreme Court cases.

## 2.   Federal Cases

a.   Reprinted reports of all available U. S. Circuit and District Courts decisions, 1789–1879.

b.   Cases are arranged alphabetically by case names and consecutively numbered.

c.   Cases are cited by number.

d.   Annotations are brief notes to the cases.

e.   Digest volume, volume 31, includes Blue Tables which cross-reference from the original reporter citations to the *Federal Cases* Numbers.

## 3.   Federal Reporter

a.   Part of *National Reporter System;* key-numbered sections of headnotes.

b.   Only current reporter for federal appellate cases.

    c.   Reporter from 1879 to date.

    d.   Prior to 1932 included District Court decisions.

    e.   Now reports cases of the Courts of Appeals, the U. S. Court of Customs and Patent Appeals and the Court of Claims (Court of Claims since 1960).

    f.   Includes *all* appellate cases.

    g.   Advance sheets and bound volumes have same volume and page numbers.

    h.   No summaries of briefs of counsel; other standard reporting features are included.

### 4. Federal Supplement

    a.   Part of *National Reporter System;* key-numbered sections of headnotes.

    b.   Only current reporter of lower federal court cases.

    c.   Reporter since 1932.

    d.   Now includes cases of the District Courts and the U. S. Customs Court (U. S. Customs Court since 1949).

    e.   From 1932 to 1960, included the Court of Claims cases.

    f.   Includes *selected* District Courts cases.

    g.   Advance sheets and bound volumes have same volume and page numbers.

    h.   No summaries of briefs of counsel; other standard reporting features are included.

# Chapter 5

# STATE COURT DECISIONS AND THE
# NATIONAL REPORTER SYSTEM

## SECTION A.  STATE COURT REPORTS

As has been indicated previously, the laws of the several states generally provide the method of publishing state court decisions. Opinions published in accordance with such legislation are called "official" reports.  Private companies also publish judicial decisions, with or without legislative directives.  The private publications that are not legislatively endorsed are called "unofficial" reports, though no less accurate than the official reports.  The unofficial reports may duplicate official reports or may be the only source of case publication.  The unofficial opinions comprise three categories: (1) the *National Reporter System* and other private publications of similar coverage (2) the annotated reports and (3) the special reports.  The latter two will be described in later chapters.

Most states officially publish their judicial decisions in bound volumes.  The decisions of the highest court, generally called the Supreme Court, are published chronologically by the terms of the court, and the volumes are consecutively numbered.  As in the case of the United States Supreme Court, the early state reports are frequently cited by the names of reporters, e. g., Binney's Reports, Pennsylvania, cited "Binn."

The intermediate appellate court decisions of a number of states also are published in bound volumes.[1]  An example is the *Indiana Appellate Court Reports*.

Trial court opinions are less frequently published by the states; however, when published, they are selected cases.  The *New York Miscellaneous Reports* contains selected decisions decided in the courts of New York State other than the Court of Appeals and the Appellate Division of the Supreme Court.

In some states the printing of opinions is privately contracted by the government.  An increasing number of states are discontinuing

---

[1] The following states have intermediate courts of appeal: Alabama, Arizona, California, Colorado, Delaware, Georgia, Illinois, Indiana, Louisiana, Maryland, Massachusetts, Michigan, Missouri, New Mexico, North Carolina, New York, Ohio, Oklahoma, Oregon, Pennsylvania, Tennessee and Washington.

the publication of their judicial opinions and are relying solely on the *National Reporter System.*[2]

Advance sheets or slip opinions precede the publication of the official reports in several states. The unofficial publications generally include advance sheets for the state cases.

A court or its reporter may have the power to select the decisions for publication in the official state reports. In the exercise of that power some less important cases may be eliminated from the official reports, e. g., *New York Miscellaneous Reports.* However, these unreported decisions sometimes are unofficially compiled by private publishers, e. g., *California Unreported Cases.*

In a general survey, such as this, it would be inappropriate to present a detailed study of the reporting systems of each state. It is sufficient to note that the Table of Abbreviations in Appendix B is adequate to direct the researcher to the specific unfamiliar publications for the occasional use which he will make of them.

---

## SECTION B.  NATIONAL REPORTER SYSTEM

The *National Reporter System,* published by the West Publishing Company consists of two main divisions: (1) opinions of the state appellate and trial courts and (2) opinions of the federal courts. This system of state court reporting was initiated in 1879 with the *North Western Reporter.* The state reporting units consist of seven regional reporters arranged roughly by geographical divisions. The four federal units cover the various federal courts. There are also two state reports which are part of the *National Reporter System;* namely, *New York Supplement* and *California Reporter.* The entire system, with its coverage, is outlined below:

|  | Began in | Coverage |
|---|---|---|
| **Atlantic Reporter** | 1885 | Conn., Dela., Maine, Maryland, N. H., N. J., Penna., R. I., Vermont, and District of Columbia Municipal Court of Appeals. |
| **North Eastern Reporter** | 1885 | Ill., Ind., Mass., N. Y., and Ohio |

[2] About one third of the states no longer publish their own official reports and either have officially adopted or rely on the decisions as reported in the regional reporters of the National Reporter System. These states are listed at Section 1.2.4. of the Uniform System of Citations. 11th ed.

|  | Began in | Coverage |
|---|---|---|
| **North Western Reporter** | 1879 | Ia., Mich., Minn., Nebr., N. D., S. D., and Wisc. |
| **Pacific Reporter** | 1883 | Alaska, Ariz., Calif. to 1960, Calif. S.Ct. since 1960, Colo., Hawaii, Idaho, Kan., Mont., Nev., N. M., Okla., Ore., Utah, Wash., and Wyo. |
| **South Eastern Reporter** | 1887 | Ga., N. C., S. C., Va., and W. Va. |
| **South Western Reporter** | 1886 | Ark., Ky., Indian Territory, Mo., Tenn., and Tex. |
| **Southern Reporter** | 1887 | Ala., Fla., La., and Miss. |
| **Supreme Court Reporter** | 1882 | U. S. Supreme Court. |
| **Federal Reporter** | 1880 | From 1880 to 1932: Circuit Courts of Appeals and District Courts of the U. S., U. S. Court of Customs and Patent Appeals, Court of Claims of the U. S., and Court of Appeals of the District of Columbia. From 1932 to date: U. S. Courts of Appeals, and U. S. Court of Customs and Patent Appeals. From 1942 to 1961: U. S. Emergency Court of Appeals. Since 1960: U. S. Court of Claims. |
| **Federal Supplement** | 1932 | U. S. District Courts, Court of Claims to 1960, U. S. Customs Court since Vol. 135 (1949). |
| **Federal Rules Decisions** | 1940 | District Courts of the U. S. |
| **New York Supplement** | 1888 | N. Y. (all state courts). Since 1932, the N. Y. Court of Appeals opinions are published here as well as in the North Eastern Reporter. |
| **California Reporter** | Dec. 1959 | Calif.S.Ct., District Courts of Appeal and Appellate Dept. Superior Court. |

The full text of the decisions of the courts are provided by this service. The editors usually prepare the headnotes and digest the briefs of counsel when they are given. The syllabi are numbered and are key-numbered to the American Digest classification system. This is a very significant and helpful feature, the nature of which is described in Chapter 6. However, cases in the early volumes of the units of the *National Reporter System*, although headnoted, are not integrated into the key-number system which was developed at the turn of the century.

The cumulation of decisions from several states promotes speedier publication of state cases by *Regional Reporters*.

The opinions first appear in advance sheets. The advance sheets are very useful for providing the text of recent opinions which have not yet been published in the official state reports. The pagination of the opinions is the same in the bound volumes as in the advance sheets.

The *National Reporters* list words and phrases as defined by judicial opinions. These definitions cover both legal and nonlegal words and phrases. Except for the *Supreme Court Reporter*, each bound volume provides two tables of cases: (1) a single alphabetical listing of all cases in the volume and (2) separate alphabetical listings of the cases by states or courts. The tables of cases in the advance sheets of the *Regional Reporters* are alphabetically arranged under the names of the states. Another significant feature is the Tables of Statutes Construed included in the bound volumes and the advance sheets. These lists cite the reported cases which interpret statutory law (including cases reported in other *Reporter* units covering the same period) and are cumulated into some West's state digests. The *Reporter* units now publish the current revisions and amendments to appropriate court rules. Each advance sheet and bound volume includes a digest section comprising the key-numbered headnotes of the cases covered.

The publishers claim that the *National Reporter System* contains over 90,000 cases which are not in the official state reports.

The decisions of some but not all state intermediate appellate courts are included in the *National Reporter System*. Further, as to each intermediate court, the inclusion of its cases in the *Reporter System* began at different times. For example, Missouri appellate cases are included in the *South Western Reporter*, beginning with 93 Mo.App. (1902); Illinois appellate decisions are contained in the *North Eastern Reporter*, beginning with 284 Ill.App. (1936). Variations also exist between the *Reporters* as to general inclusion of state trial court cases, and the trial courts which are covered have different starting dates in each set. Thus, since 1887, nearly all reported court decisions are available in the seven regional reporters and the four sets of federal reporters that comprise the *National Reporter System*. This becomes significant in legal research as it provides a common editorial treatment to the syllabi which become the basis of locating court decisions through the use of the *American Digest System* which will be discussed in the next chapter.

———

## SECTION C.   CROSS REFERENCE TABLES

1.   To find the *National Reporter System* citation, when you have the official citation, refer to one of the following:

  a.   *National Reporter Blue Book.*   These tables refer the user from the official citation to the unofficial Reporter citation.   [Illustration 13]

  b.   *Shepard's Citations* for the state.

  c.   Table of Cases of the state digest.

2.   To locate the official citation, when given the *National Reporter System* citation, refer to one of the following:

  a.   *State Blue and White Book.*[3]   Consult the White Tables which cross-reference from the unofficial Reporter citation.   [Illustration 14]

  b.   *Shepard's Citations* for the Reporter.

  c.   Table of Cases of the state digest.

The *American Digest System, Shepard's Citations* and state digests, which are listed above, will be discussed in greater detail in later chapters.

[3] Law libraries generally only have the *Blue and White Book* for the state in which they are located.

# SECTION D.  ILLUSTRATIONS

[Illustration 12]

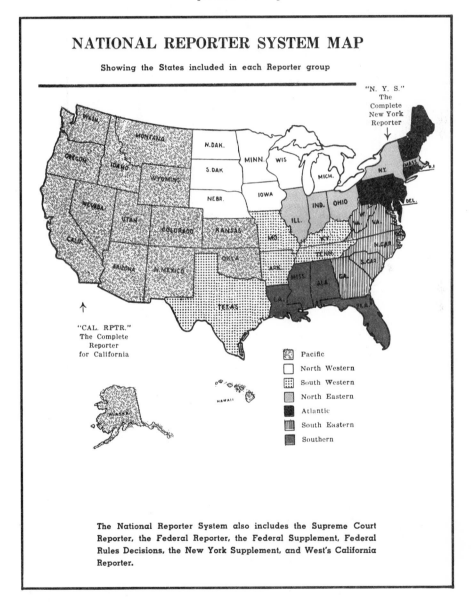

NATIONAL REPORTER SYSTEM MAP

Showing the States included in each Reporter group

"N. Y. S."
The Complete New York Reporter

"CAL. RPTR."
The Complete Reporter for California

Pacific
North Western
South Western
North Eastern
Atlantic
South Eastern
Southern

The National Reporter System also includes the Supreme Court Reporter, the Federal Reporter, the Federal Supplement, Federal Rules Decisions, the New York Supplement, and West's California Reporter.

[Illustration 13]

## AN EXCERPT FROM A CROSS REFERENCE PAGE OF NATIONAL REPORTER BLUE BOOK

### (265 Alabama Reports)

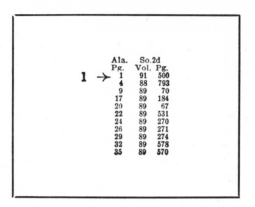

**Note to Illustration 13:**

(The *Blue Book* cross references from an official citation to the *National Reporter* citation.)

1.   The case beginning on page 1 of Vol. 265 Ala. Reports is reprinted in Vol. 91, beginning on page 500 of the Southern Reporter, 2d Series.

[Illustration 14]

## AN EXCERPT FROM THE WHITE TABLES IN OHIO BLUE AND WHITE BOOK

(Ohio References for North Eastern Cases)

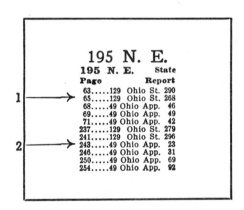

**Notes to Illustration 14:**

(The White Tables cross-reference from a *National Reporter* citation to the official citation.)

1. 195 N.E. 65 appears at 129 Ohio State Reports 268.

2. 195 N.E. 243 appears at 49 Ohio Appellate Reports 23.

---

## SECTION E.  METHODS OF CITATION

### 1.  State Decisions

a.  Parallel Citations

Parallel citations to the official and the unofficial state reports are commonly provided in federal and state court briefs, treatises and periodical articles. This practice is frequently modified by some state court briefs where the parallel citations are given for all state court reports except the forum, in which cases only the official citations are provided.

Oliver v. Robnett, 190 Cal. 51, 210 P. 408 (1922).

State ex rel. Fire District of Lemay v. Smith, 353 Mo. 807, 184 S.W.2d 593 (1945).

Standard v. Orleans Flour Co., 93 Neb. 389, 140 N.W. 636 (1913).

The abbreviations of the Regional Reporters are:

Atlantic Reporter cited "Atl." or "A." and "A.2d"

North Eastern Reporter cited "N.E." and "N.E.2d"

North Western Reporter cited "N.W." and "N.W.2d"

Pacific Reporter cited "Pac." or "P." and "P.2d"

South Eastern Reporter cited "S.E." and "S.E.2d"

South Western Reporter cited "S.W." and "S.W.2d"

Southern Reporter cited "So." and "So.2d"

New York Supplement cited "N.Y.Supp." or "N.Y.S." and "N.Y.S.2d"

California Reporter cited "Cal.Rptr."

b.   Complete Citation

The state, the court and the date are explicitly or implicitly given. Some information is clearly understood from the official citation and should not be repeated.   When the court is not identified by the citation, the assumption is that it is a case reported by the highest court. Thus, in the examples noted above, the cases cover supreme court decisions.

c.   Early State Reporters

Where the name of a reporter is used in citing an early state report, the favored practice is to indicate the state and the date.

Da Costa v. Shrewsbury, 1 Bay 211 (S.C.1791).

d.   Recent Decisions

If the official report has not yet been published, cite the unofficial report, such as the *National Reporter System,* and indicate the jurisdiction and date.

Corsair v. Dempsey, 218 A.2d 478 (R.I.1966).

e.   National Reporter Reprint of State Cases

In the absence of an official state report, the reprints of cases of a state from the *National Reporter System* are cited by volume and page of the unit of the *National Reporter.*   The state and court are explicitly or implicitly given with the date.

Arch Sellery, Inc. v. Simpson, 346 P.2d 1068 (Wyo.1959).

f.   Several Courts Included in a Report

If the decisions of several courts are included in a single report, the court rendering the decision and the date should be noted.

Kuebler v. Cleveland Short Line Ry., 10 Ohio N.P. (N.S.) 385 (C.P.1910).

## SECTION F. SUMMARY

**1. State Court Reports**

a. Official reports are court reports directed by statute.

b. Unofficial reports are court reports published without statutory direction.

c. Advance sheets and slip opinions are published in several states—most states rely on unofficial advance sheets, e. g., *National Reporter System* or other private publication.

**2. National Reporter System—see Section B, above**

a. Opinions of state appellate and trial courts—7 regional reporters arranged roughly by geographical divisions and two state reporters.

b. Opinions of the federal courts.

**3. Cross Reference Tables**

a. *National Reporter Blue Book* refers the user from the official citation to the unofficial *National Reporter* citation.

b. White Tables in *State Blue and White Book* refers the user from the unofficial *National Reporter* citation to the official citation.

# Chapter 6

# DIGESTS FOR COURT DECISIONS

Since our system of law follows the doctrine of *stare decisis*, the location of past cases in the reports, which we have just studied, is an essential requirement. We learned that the cases in the reports are published as rendered and follow no subject or systematic arrangement. It is compelling, therefore, that logical organization be applied to the search for the law in the cases. Otherwise, case law would be unwieldly and unmanageable. For this reason, index books serve an important function in analyzing, synthesizing and indexing the law.

The digest is an index book, which is closely allied to the encyclopedia, the latter being a search book. A search book may be cited as persuasive authority, for it not only collates, but it also describes and explains the law. On the other hand, the digest is a case finder or an index to the law. Hence, a digest is never cited as legal authority. It is used only to find the law.

An encyclopedia presents, alphabetically by topics, a narrative statement of the law with footnote references to cases in point. A digest is an index to case law, giving brief, unconnected statements of court holdings or facts of cases, and is classified by subject.

The scope of the various digests embodies: (1) all courts, federal and state, (2) a region, a group of neighboring states, (3) an individual state or (4) a specific court or court system, e. g., the federal courts. In a broader sense, digests are of a general or a special nature, with the general digest covering all courts and the special digests encompassing the others.

## SECTION A. THE AMERICAN DIGEST SYSTEM

### 1. Key Number System

The *American Digest System* is a subject classification scheme whereby decisions that were reported chronologically in the various units of the *National Reporter System* are rearranged by subject, bringing together all cases on a similar point of law. Instead, however, of rearranging complete decisions, it rearranges digests (abstracts) of decisions. The West Publishing Co. has developed its own classification of law and classifies the digests of all cases to its system of classification. The system divides the subject of law into seven main classes. Each class is then divided into sub-classes and then each sub-class into topics. There are over 435 topics, each of which corresponds to a legal concept. [See Illustration 15] The topics are then divided into subdivisions of the topic and each subdivision is given a paragraph number called a "Key Number." The Key Numbers vary from topic to topic from a few to many hundred.

With this outline in mind, it is then necessary to examine the actual steps involved in the making of the *American Digest System.* Basically, it all starts with a slip decision. After a decision is written, a copy of it goes to the West Publishing Company and is assigned to an editor. Keep in mind that all he has is the decision with no other information than the name of the case, the name of the judge who wrote it, and the name of the court. The editor reads the case and determines the headnotes. In theory, each headnote represents a particular point of law. The editor takes each point of law which he is about to make into a headnote and assigns to it a Topic and Key Number. He decides that a particular paragraph deals with, for example, negligence, and then turning to the *Table of Key Numbers* [Illustration 16] under *Negligence*, further decides that it specifically is involved with Business Visitors in Stores and thus gives it the Topic and Key Number *Negligence* 32 (2.8). Frequently a paragraph will deal with two points of law and will then get two Topics and Key Numbers.

Consequently, when the editor is finished with a case, all of the points of law covered in the case will be made into headnotes and placed at the beginning of the case, with each headnote assigned a Topic and Key Number. [See Illustration 4] This procedure is followed for each case reported in the *National Reporter System.* The next step in the construction of the digest begins with each advance sheet. In the front of each advance sheet, all of the headnotes for all of the decisions reported are brought together in the *Key Number Digest.* In it, they are arranged alphabetically by Topic and then under each Topic, numerically by Key Number. Thus, through the *Key Number Digest* all decisions in an advance sheet pamphlet dealing with the same topic of law can be located.

## 2.   Units of the American Digest System

The next step is found in a publication called the *General Digest.* This is first issued monthly in *pamphlet* form. The January issue, for example, will consist of *all* the headnotes taken from *all* of the units of the *National Reporter System.* These again are arranged alphabetically by Topic and then numerically by Key Number under Topic. Thus, in the January issue of the *General Digest,* by looking under a particular Topic and Key Number, digests of all cases that dealt with that particular point of law reported in the January issue can be located.

From now on, the digest building becomes mechanical. The monthly issues of the *General Digest* are cumulated every three months into bound volumes. This process has now been going on since 1886. If no further cumulation had taken place, digests of all the cases, arranged topically, would be in all of the bound volumes of the *General Digest*. In order to find all the cases dealing with a particular topic, it would be necessary to examine each one of hundreds of bound volumes. As this was not practical, the publishers in 1906 cumulated all the topics from all of the volumes from 1896 to 1906 into one alphabet. This is called the First *Decennial*. Now, by examining the volume containing a particular Topic and Key Number, all of the cases decided on that point during the years 1896–1906 may be located. This process has taken place since 1896 with a new *Decennial* every ten years. The latest one is the *Seventh*, covering the years 1956–66. All of the cases since 1966 are in the *General Digest*, 4th Series. Thus, given a Topic and Key Number, one can start with the First *Decennial* and then proceed through the Seventh *Decennial* and then examine the individual bound volumes of the General Digest, and then the monthly issues and thereby locate all cases on a point of law under a particular Key Number from 1896 to approximately six weeks ago. [See Illustration 18]

It is actually possible to find all cases from 1658 as cases from 1658–1896 are in the *Century Digest*. However, the *Century Digest* did not use Key Numbers. This means that the numbering system in the *Century* is different than that of the *Decennials*. For example, Key Number *Negligence* 32 (2.8) in the *Decennials* stands for Business Visitors and Store and Restaurant Patrons, whereas in the *Century*, *Negligence* 32 stands for "Blasting" and cases dealing with Business Visitors are digested under *Negligence* 43 in the *Century*.

Thus, it is necessary when researching with a Key Number to translate this to the equivalent number in the *Century Digest*. This, however, is a simple matter. In both the First and Second *Decennials*, at the beginning of each Key Number, reference is made to where that Key Number is located in the *Century*. [See Illustration 18–f]

Should the search be started in the *Century Digest* under *Negligence 43*, a means of transfer from the *Century* paragraph number to the equivalent Key Number is needed. This is accomplished by using the *Table of Key Numbers Section for Century Digest*, located in the Table of Cases volume to the First and Second *Decennials*.

Law, of course, is constantly expanding. It is obvious that when the original classification was made in 1896 no provision was made for cases dealing with damages resulting from a jet plane breaking the sound barrier or cases subsequently to be decided under the *Labor Relations Management Act of 1937*. Consequently, in order to keep abreast of the law, new topics have to be added and old ones expanded. Thus, in the Sixth *Decennial* the following new titles were added: *Aviation, Labor Relations, Mental Health, Social Security,* and *Telecommunication*. Also, the titles of *Discovery* and *Divorce* had additional Key Numbers added to them. In the Seventh *Decennial* additional new titles were also added.

When a new title is added, all cases previously digested under another title are re-digested under the new classification. Thus, for example, the *Labor Relations* topic in the Sixth *Decennial* digests *all* cases on that topic and not merely those for the years 1946–56.

The *American Digest System* consists of the following sets:

| | Chronological Coverage | No. of Vols. |
|---|---|---|
| Century Digest | 1658–1896 | 50 vols. |
| First Decennial | 1897–1906 | 25 vols. |
| Second Decennial | 1907–1916 | 24 vols. |
| Third Decennial | 1916–1926 | 29 vols. |
| Fourth Decennial | 1926–1936 | 34 vols. |
| Fifth Decennial | 1936–1946 | 49 vols. |
| Sixth Decennial | 1946–1956 | 36 vols. |
| Seventh Decennial | 1956–1966 | 38 vols. |
| General Digest (4th Series) | 1966 to date | |

From two to four bound volumes of the *General Digest* are published each year. They are preceded by unbound monthly supplements. A new Decennial appears each ten years and supersedes the *General Digest* for that period. Thus, the *Seventh Decennial* takes the place of the *General Digest*, 3d series, and covers the period 1956–1966. The *General Digest*, 4th series, will span the ten-year period, 1966–1976, and eventually will be superseded by the *Eighth Decennial*.

### 3. Finding the Key Number

The *American Digest System* as classified to the *Key Number System* provides a means to locate all decisions on the same point of law. Once it is determined to what Topic and Key Number a particular point of law has been classified, searching for cases can commence in the various units of the *American Digest System.*

The important matter is to learn how to find the Topic and Key Number. There are three common methods provided for within the *American Digest System.*

### a.    The Descriptive-Word Index to the American Digest System

The TARP rule as explained in Chapter 2, applies to the initial analysis of a problem in this situation, as in others. After the TARP rule brings the facts and issues in focus, the *Descriptive-Word Index* to the *American Digest System* may be consulted to obtain digest-references to applicable cases. It is a convenient aid to the Index Method of searching for court decisions.

The *Descriptive-Word Index* is arranged alphabetically and includes: (1) all topics of the digest classification, (2) all key-number section lines and editorial reference lines in the *Decennial Digests* and (3) "catch" words or descriptive words relating to parties to the suits who are members of a class, occupation or legal relation; place names and physical objects; questions of law; constitutional and legislative provisions; and legal principles which relate to the subject matter of the suit.

In the *Descriptive-Word Index*, reference is made to topics and key-numbers under the "catch" words or other entries. After locating the appropriate key-number in the index, refer to the Digest volumes under the key-number designations.

There is a separate *Descriptive-Word Index* to each of the *Decennial* units as well as to the *General Digest.*

Let us examine a problem to see how the *Descriptive-Word Index* to the *Decennials* units of the *American Digest System* may be used to locate a Topic and Key Number. Assume this problem.

A, accompanied by her grandmother, was shopping in a supermarket. As A was waiting at the check-out counter, she suddenly remembered that she needed a pound of butter. She asked her grandmother to go to the dairy department for it. As the grandmother was returning to the check-out counter, she slipped, fell to the floor, and broke her hip. While A was assisting her grandmother, she noticed a piece of lettuce was attached to her grandmother's shoe.

The grandmother brings suit against the supermarket.

Using the TARP method as described in Chapter Two, this problem may be analyzed as follows:

T (Thing or subject          Supermarket or Store
    matter)

A (Cause of action          Negligence; duty
    or grounds for              of care of defendant
    defense)                     to plaintiff.

R (Relief sought)           Money damages for
                                    injury suffered.

P (Parties—legal            Status of plaintiff
    status to each              to store owner.
    other)

In starting the search, it is best to start with the *Descriptive-Word Index* to the *General Digest*, or the latest *Decennial* unit. When using the index method, the first entry looked under should be the *least common denominator* to the problem being researched. In this instance, it may be *vegetable* or *lettuce;* if no suitable index entry is found, then try *stores* or *supermarket;* if still no entry is located, then broaden the search and if necessary use legal concepts such as *personal injuries* or *negligence.* Illustration 19 demonstrates the use of the *Descriptive Word Index* method. After the Topic and Key Number is located, the digest paragraphs under it should then be consulted to locate those cases analogous to the problem being searched.

### b.   Analysis or Topic Approach

As the *American Digest System* is based on a classification system, it is possible to analyze a fact situation and to determine from this analysis what Topic and Key Number would cover the point of law. In the problem used to illustrate the *Descriptive-Word Index* approach, *supra,* one could determine that the topic of law involved is *Negligence* and then check the *Analysis and Outline* that appears immediately after the Topic *Negligence* in the Seventh *Decennial* and then locate Key Number 32 (2.8). [Illustration 16–16–a]

This method requires a certain amount of legal sophistication and should not be used without having a fairly good knowledge of law. Moreover, there is always the danger inherent in this approach that the researcher may arrive at one analysis which leads to a specific Topic and Key Number, whereas the Editors in their analysis assigned a different Topic and Key Number. Hence, it is recommended that this method be used with care and only after one has had considerable experience in legal research.

## c.  Table of Cases Method

Each *Decennial* unit and each volume of the *General Digest* as well as the ten volume Cumulative Index volumes of the *General Digest* have an alphabetical table of cases by plaintiff.  Each case listed gives its citation and what Topics and Key Numbers the case has been digested under.  Thus, if one knew, for example, that *McKenney v. Quality Foods* dealt with the question of care due to a business visitor, by consulting the Table of Cases volumes of the Seventh *Decennial* the citation and Topics and Key Numbers can easily be located.  [Illustration 20.]

## d.  Table of Cases by Popular Names

When only the popular name of a case is known, such as the *Dred Scott case* the best sources to use to find the actual citation are:

(1) *Shepard's Federal and State Acts and Cases by Popular Name.* [See Illustration 22]

(2) The Sixth *Decennial* of the *American Digest System* contains a cumulative *List of Popular Name Titles* in the *American Digest System*.  This feature has been discontinued in the Seventh *Decennial*.

(3) Most special digests contain a Table of Cases by Popular Name.

---

## SECTION B.  SPECIAL DIGESTS

As the *American Digest System* with its Key Number classification is made up from the *National Reporter System*, it is all-inclusive and most useful when one is interested in locating decisions from all American jurisdictions.  Frequently, however, when engaged in legal research, one is primarily interested in locating decisions from a particular state or region or only those decisions from the Federal Courts.

The West Publishing Company publishes Key Number digests that are less inclusive than the *American Digest System*.  As these are published in one alphabet (rather than chronologically as in the *American Digest System*) and they are kept up-to-date by pocket supplements, it is frequently easier to start the search in one of the following.  Each has its own *Descriptive-Word Index* and Table of Cases volumes.  Once a Topic and Key Number is located in a Key Number Digest, search for decisions can proceed in any other Key Number Digest.

**1. U. S. Supreme Court Digest** (West Pub. Co.)

This 17-volume digest (20 physical volumes) of all the Supreme Court decisions is classified under the *Key-Number System,* and duplicates the Supreme Court cases in the *American Digest System.* It is kept up-to-date by cumulative annual pocket supplements and includes the following:

(1) Volume 1 of the Digest comprises the Descriptive-Word Index.

(2) Volume 14, Table of Cases.

a. U. S. Supreme Court Reports Digest (Lawyers Co-op. Pub. Co.).

This is an 18-volume digest (19 physical volumes), with cumulative annual pocket supplements, to all U. S. Supreme Court decisions. It is arranged under a special subject classification and contains the various features of a digest.

(1) Volume 16 is the Word Index, used in the first instance when applying the Index Method.

(2) Volumes 15 and 15A include the Table of Cases.

(3) Volumes 17 and 18 cover Court Rules (to be discussed in Chapter 12, Court Procedure).

(4) Volume 17 contains the text of the U. S. Constitution, with references to topics in the *U. S. Supreme Court Reports Digest* (Lawyers Co-op.) covering the subject matter.

(5) Volume 14 of the *Digest* includes: (a) a *Table of Statutes, Constitutions, Proclamations and Treaties Cited and Construed;* it covers the U. S. Constitution, federal statutes, state constitutions, state statutes, proclamations, treaties and foreign laws construed by the Supreme Court; (b) a *Table of Adjudicated Supreme Court Cases;* (c) a *Table of all Federal and State Decisions* which have been heard by the Supreme Court; (d) a *Table of Statutes by Popular Name;* and other tables. The *Index to Annotations,* included in volume 14, has been superseded by a separate volume, *Index to Annotations* in the U. S. Supreme Court Reports (L.Ed.).

**2. Modern Federal Practice Digest and Federal Digest**

The *Federal Digest* was published originally in 1940 and for twenty years served as a basic source in locating federal court cases. Since its publication, however, significant changes in statutory and case law and federal court rules of procedure have occurred. New Titles 18 and 28 to the *U. S. Code,* a reemphasis on state law by *Erie R. Co. v. Tompkins,*[1] and the adoption of the present Rules of

---

[1] 304 U.S. 64, 58 S.Ct. 817, 82 L.Ed. 1188 (1937).

Federal Procedure, Civil and Criminal, prompted the West Publishing Co. to publish a new federal courts digest, *Modern Federal Practice Digest*, thus separating modern federal practice from the old federal case law.   In this manner, the *Federal Digest* is retained as the permanent index to federal case law for the years prior to 1939, and the *Modern Federal Practice Digest* covers the "Modern Era" since 1939.

a.   Modern Federal Practice Digest.

(1) This digest contains 58 numbered volumes and four unnumbered (Descriptive-Word Index) volumes.

(2) It is kept up-to-date by cumulative annual pocket supplements and subsequent pamphlet supplements.   Periodically, replacement volumes are substituted for present volumes and supplements.

(3) Covers U. S. Supreme Court decisions, the *Federal Reporter, 2d Series*, the *Federal Supplement* and the *Federal Rules Decisions* since 1939.

(4) Classified under the *Key-Number System*.

(5) A *Descriptive-Word Index* of four unnumbered volumes covers *all* federal case law in the *Federal Digest* and the *Modern Federal Practice Digest*.

(6) *A Table of Cases* is in volumes 53 and 54.

(7) A *Defendant-Plaintiff Table* is included in volumes 55 and 56.

(8) Volumes 57 and 58 alphabetically list words and phrases judicially defined by the federal courts since 1939.

(9) Case history—the *Digest* paragraphs include information as to whether a case has been affirmed, reversed or modified.

(10) "Library references" note other general secondary sources in point, e. g., *Corpus Juris Secundum, Davis, Administrative Law*.

(11) The cases are arranged in this order:  (1) Supreme Court, (2) Courts of Appeal, arranged alphabetically by jurisdiction and (3) District Courts, arranged alphabetically by jurisdiction.   The cases of a jurisdiction, which are digested under the same key-number, are listed chronologically, beginning with the latest case.

(12) A complete numerical listing of all patents adjudicated by the courts since 1939 is included under the topic "Patents"  ☞328.

(13) An alphabetical table of all *Trade-Marks and Trade-Names Adjudicated* from the earliest times to date is included in volume 48 under the topic "Trade Regulation," Division I Trade-Marks and Trade-Names and Unfair Competition, Subdivision H.

b.   Federal Digest (West Pub. Co.).

Under the new arrangement with the *Modern Federal Practice Digest*, the *Federal Digest* indexes federal case law of historical significance, some of which is no longer controlling, from the foundation of the Government to 1939. The features of the *Federal Digest* are:

(1) Consists of 72 volumes, covering *Federal Cases*, the U. S. Supreme Court decisions, the *Federal Reporter* and the *Federal Supplement* from the earliest times to 1939.

(2) Classified under the *Key-Number System*.

(3) The *Descriptive-Word Index* to the *Modern Federal Practice Digest* covers the *Federal Digest* and the *Modern Federal Practice Digest*.

(4) A *Table of Cases* is included in volumes 66 through 68.

(5) Volumes 69 and 70 contain a *Defendant-Plaintiff Table of Cases*.

(6) *Words and Phrases* judicially defined in federal decisions is a feature of volumes 71 and 72.

(7) Volume 72 also has a *Table of Popular Name Titles*, covering cases in this *Digest*.

(8) A complete numerical listing of all patents adjudicated by the courts, covered by the set, is included under the topic "Patents" ⬤➾328.

(9) Although the federal procedure cases in the *Federal Digest* are no longer controlling, the *Digest's* decisions have a bearing on other federal law which has not significantly changed or which, though changed, is still germane, as patent law and constitutional law.

## 3. Regional Digests (West Pub. Co.)

The units of the *National Reporter System* have separate digests. These digests presently follow the *Key-Number* classification and cover all the reports of each state in the regions. Each regional digest includes a *Descriptive-Word Index*. The digest paragraphs under the key-numbers are arranged alphabetically by states. The publishers in recent years have expanded some of the reporter digests to include synopses of the early court decisions not covered by the *National Re-*

~~porter System.~~ These expanded services are the *North Western Di-*

Add 3(A).

West's Federal Cases. The West Publishing Co. has added a new tool to aid the users of its National Reporter System. West's Federal Case News is issued weekly, and provides a short summary of all federal cases received by West in the preceding week. The summaries are arranged by level of federal court and by subject. This means that the researcher will become aware of the case weeks before the appropriate advance sheet arrives. Since its contents are accessible through case name, court and topic tables, it is an excellent current awareness tool.

## 4.  State Digests

Digests to the court decisions of the several states have been published by the West Publishing Co. and other publishers.  The West's state digests follow the *Key-Number* scheme.  In fact, the various digests published by the West Publishing Co. are segments of the *American Digest System* with divisions into the *Federal* and *regional digests* and further subdivision of these units, with some minor variances, into the *U. S. Supreme Court* and *state digests*.  This can be illustrated by the following chart:

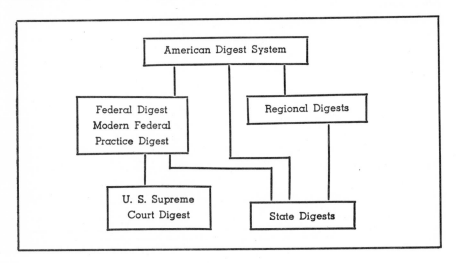

### Features Common to Most
### State Digests

As with other legal publications, the characteristics common to most state digests [2] may be surveyed in relation to their: (1) scope, (2) arrangement, (3) special features and (4) supplementation.

The state digests usually cover all reported state decisions and the U. S. Supreme Court and other federal cases arising in each state or applying state law, from the earliest period to date.  The digests are arranged by a subject classification, with titles, sections, scope-notes and analyses.  The most common additional features are: (1) a descriptive-word and topical index, (2) a table of the digested cases and (3) words and phrases judicially defined by the digested cases.  The state digests are kept up-to-date by replacement volumes and cumulative periodic pocket and pamphlet supplements.

---

[2] The West Publishing Co., publishes Key-Number Digests for nearly every state and for the District of Columbia.  Some states also have state digests of other publishers.  Although not Key-Number Digests, the method of use is similar.

The characteristics of the various state digests, regardless of the publishers, are sufficiently uniform to make the methods of use of one generally applicable to the others. But each state digest should be examined for any special features. Thus, the *Massachusetts Digest Annotated* contains a "Table of Statutes Construed." In the *West's Indiana Digest* and *Callaghan's Illinois Digest*, a number of cases may be grouped under a single digest paragraph, where the same proposition of law has been stated. The "Table of Cases Judicially Noticed" (CJN) in *Page's Ohio Digest* lists all cases which have been considered by more than one court with the specific history of the action taken by courts. This table functions as a case citator. Some state digests provide additional research aid by references to A.L.R. annotations, encyclopedias, local treatises, forms, etc., e. g., *Mississippi Digest* and *Callaghan's Illinois Digest*.

## SECTION C. WORDS AND PHRASES AS AIDS IN THE USE OF THE DEFINITION METHOD

We have observed that at times the meaning or definition of a legal or non-legal word or phrase plays a significant role in the solution to a problem. Occasionally, the English language dictionaries are helpful in providing definitions of words whose interpretations and meanings influence the results in decisions. Legal dictionaries are also useful aids in providing informational content to the meaning of words.

The need extended to include the meaning given words and phrases by judges. This resulted in specialized publications devoted to words and phrases judicially defined.

Further, by using the Definition Method in research it became possible to deconceptualize problems and depart from subject fields in eliciting word meanings. Thus, a definition of a word framed in a negligence case could be applied with equal significance to a contracts problem where it was correspondingly applicable. To have limited the search for the definition of the word to the confines of the subject matter, contracts, would have eliminated the possibility of locating its definition in a different area, torts. The advantage of this extensive approach to definition research is obvious. To illustrate, "good faith" is defined in bankruptcy, corporation, landlord and tenant and family law.[3]

The most significant set for use in this technique is:

### 1. Words and Phrases

The West Publishing Co. has compiled words and phrases which have been defined judicially by federal and state courts in a compre-

---

[3] See Fenneberg, A Short Cut in Legal Research, 29 Ohio Bar 523 (1956).

hensive publication called *"Words and Phrases"* (Permanent edition). This 46-volume set includes over 350,000 court definitions of *legal* and *non-legal* terms, arranged alphabetically by the words or phrases. When there are numerous definitions under a word or a phrase, they are arranged and subdivided by topics. The publication is kept up-to-date by cumulative annual pocket supplements and replacement volumes. To obtain supplemental down-to-the-minute definitions, consult the Tables of Words and Phrases in the current volumes and advance sheets of the *National Reporter System*. The back of the title page of each pocket supplement to *Words and Phrases* indicates the volumes of the *Reporter System* covered by the set. See Illustration 21.

## SECTION D.  ILLUSTRATIONS

[Illustration 15]

## SAMPLE PAGE FROM ALPHABETICAL LIST OF DIGEST TOPICS USED IN KEY NUMBER SYSTEM

### DIGEST TOPICS

| | | |
|---|---|---|
| Navigable Waters | Quo Warranto | Subscriptions |
| Ne Excat | Railroads | Suicide |
| Negligence | Rape | Sunday |
| Neutrality Laws | Real Actions | Supersedeas |
| Newspapers | Receivers | Taxation |
| New Trial | Receiving Stolen Goods | Telecommunications |
| Notaries | Recognizances | Tenancy in Common |
| Notice | Records | Tender |
| Novation | Reference | Territories |
| Nuisance | Reformation of Instruments | Theaters and Shows |
| Oath | Reformatories | Threats |
| Obscenity | | |
| Obstructing Justice | | |
| Officers | | |
| Pardon and Parole | | |
| Parent and Child | | There are over 435 Topics in the *American Digest System.* Each Topic is subdivided into "Key-Numbers". See next Illustration. |
| Parliamentary Law | | |
| Parties | | |
| Partition | | |
| Partnership | | |
| Party Walls | | |
| Patents | Rewards | Trespass to Try Title |
| Paupers | Riot | Trial |
| Pawnbrokers and Money Lenders | Robbery | Trover and Conversion |
| | Sales | Trusts |
| Payment | Salvage | Turnpikes and Toll Roads |
| Penalties | Schools and School Districts | Undertakings |
| Pensions | Scire Facias | United States |
| Perjury | Seals | United States Commissioners |
| Perpetuities | Seamen | United States Marshals |
| Physicians and Surgeons | Searches and Seizures | Unlawful Assembly |
| Pilots | Seduction | Use and Occupation |
| Piracy | Sequestration | Usury |
| Pleading | Set-Off and Counterclaim | Vagrancy |
| Pledges | Sheriffs and Constables | Vendor and Purchaser |
| Poisons | Shipping | Venue |
| Possessory Warrant | Signatures | War and National Defense |
| Post Office | Slaves | Warehousemen |
| Powers | Social Security and Public Welfare | Waste |
| Principal and Agent | | Waters and Water Courses |
| Principal and Surety | Sodomy | Weapons |
| Prisons | Specific Performance | Weights and Measures |
| Private Roads | Spendthrifts | Wharves |
| Prize Fighting | States | Wills |
| Process | | |

[Illustration 16]

## FIRST PAGE OF TOPIC NEGLIGENCE FROM SEVENTH DECENNIAL DIGEST

# NEGLIGENCE

### SUBJECTS INCLUDED

Failure to use due care, either in respect of acts or of omissions, in performance or observance of a duty not founded on contract, which failure is the proximate cause of unintended injury to the person to whom such duty is owing

Nature and extent of liability for such injuries in general

Nature and effect of negligence or other fault on the part of the person injured contributing to his injury

> In each unit of the Decennial and General digests, each topic has a list of subjects included and excluded and of the Key-Number classification for the Topic.

### SUBJECTS EXCLUDED AND COVERED BY OTHER TOPICS

Death, actions for damages for, see DEATH

Manslaughter by negligence, see AUTOMOBILES, HOMICIDE

Particular kinds of property, negligence in care and use of, see MINES AND MINERALS, WATERS AND WATER COURSES, ANIMALS, SHIPPING, COLLISION, and other specific topics

Particular kinds of works, public improvements, etc., negligence in construction and use of, see RAILROADS, BRIDGES, HIGHWAYS, MUNICIPAL CORPORATIONS, and other specific topics

Particular personal relations, occupations, employments, contracts, etc., negligence in respect of duties incident to, see ATTORNEY AND CLIENT, MASTER AND SERVANT, PHYSICIANS AND SURGEONS, CARRIERS, LANDLORD AND TENANT, BAILMENT, and other specific topics

**For detailed references to other topics, see Descriptive-Word Index**

---

*Analysis.*

I. ACTS OR OMISSIONS CONSTITUTING NEGLIGENCE, ☞1–55.
    A. PERSONAL CONDUCT IN GENERAL, ☞1–15.
    B. DANGEROUS SUBSTANCES, MACHINERY, AND OTHER INSTRUMENTALITIES, ☞16–27.
    C. CONDITION AND USE OF LAND, BUILDINGS, AND OTHER STRUCTURES, ☞28–55.

[Illustration 16–a]

## SAMPLE PAGE OF TOPIC NEGLIGENCE—Cont'd

---

## NEGLIGENCE

I. **ACTS OR OMISSIONS CONSTITUTING NEGLIGENCE**—Continued.

    C. **Condition and Use of Land, Buildings, and Other Structures.**

        ☞28. Care required in general.
        29. Duty to use care.
        30. Customary methods and acts.
        31. Requirements of statutes or ordinances.
        32. Care as to licensees or persons invited.
            (1). In general.
            (2). Who are licensees, and status of person going on land of another in general.
            (2.1). Classes of licensees, and distinction between them in general.
            (2.2). Bare licensees.
            (2.3). Invitees in general.
            (2.4). Implied invitation in general.
            (2.5). Automobile service stations and parking service.
            (2.6). Bill collectors.
            (2.7). Buildings in process of construction, alteration, or demolition.
       → (2.8). Business visitors, and store and restaurant patrons.
            (2.9). Deliverymen and haulers.
            (2.10). Employees and contractors.
            (2.11). Frequenters.
            (2.12). Gratuitous licensees.
            (2.13). Guests in private homes.
            (2.14). Meter readers.
            (2.15). Persons accompanying invitees.
            (2.16). Postmen.
            (2.17). Public officials in general.

---

      **Immediately following the summary and analysis, there appears a detailed listing of the Key-Numbers, each representing a minute point of law. Each time a headnote deals with business visitors in a store or restaurant and involves negligence it will receive the Topic Negligence and Key-Number 32(2.8)**

---

        35. Care as to persons on adjacent highway.
        36. Private grounds in general.
        37. Places open to public.
        38. Places abutting on or near highways.
        39. Places attractive to children.
        41. Streams, ponds, and wells.
        42. Excavations.
        43. Embankments and piling of materials.
        44. Buildings and other structures.
        45. Elevators, hoistways, and shafts.
        46. Use of property.
        47. Traps, pitfalls, and harmful devices.
        48. Knowledge of defect or danger.
        49. Precautions against injury.
        50. —— In general.

## [Illustration 17]
## SAMPLE PAGE FROM THE PACIFIC REPORTER

---

**450**    Cal.        **319 PACIFIC REPORTER, 2d SERIES**

his failure to exercise ordinary care in remedying the defect after he has discovered it or as a man of ordinary prudence should have discovered it."

[4–7] As to the first issue, it is conceded that here the plaintiff was a business invitee and to whom the defendant owed a duty to exercise reasonable care in keeping the premises safe. Oldenburg v. Sears, Roebuck & Co., 152 Cal.App.2d ——, 314 P. 2d 33; Raber v. Tumin, 36 Cal.2d 654, 226 P.2d 574. Plaintiff in order to recover must establish that the defendant breached that duty and that such breach was the proximate cause of the injury. Palmer v. Crafts, 16 Cal.App.2d 370, 60 P.2d 533. The burden is on the plaintiff to prove every essential fact on which she relies. McKellar v. Pendergast, 68 Cal.App.2d 485, 156 P.2d 950. As no inference of negligence arises based simply upon proof of a fall on the owner's floor (Vaughn v. Montgomery Ward & Co., 95 Cal.App.2d 553, 213 P.2d 417; Thomas v. Moore, 146 Cal.App. 2d 59, 303 P.2d 624), we must turn to the record to discover if there are any facts from which the inference may be drawn that defendant was responsible for the presence of the lettuce on the floor.

The record reveals that defendant's market is one of several businesses occupying a common building and served with a common terrazzo corridor. Defendant is the only tenant of the building who sells vegetables. While all of the tenants participated in the cleaning of the corridor, defendant had assumed the duty of removing vegetable and other matter which fell thereon from the checkstands, a portion of which extended to the corridor.

Before entering defendant's market plaintiff and her companions had not been in the other area where vegetables were sold. They did not enter defendant's vegetable department. Plaintiff went through defendant's usual checking-out procedure which is as follows: the customer places his purchases on the revolving package platform extending beyond the entrance to the checkstand; the customer has nothing further to do with the

handling of his purchases until the attendant has completely packaged them and handed them to the customer at the far end of the checkstand.

On the date in question, defendant carried five or more types of lettuce, of which only the Los Angeles head lettuce was sold in a sealed cellophane bag. The other kinds of lettuce were sold in bulk tied with a flexible wire band. There was some evidence that the piece of vegetable matter found on plaintiff's shoe may have been of the Los Angeles type. The packaging and handling of the lettuce was done in defendant's basement. It was the custom of defendant's checkstand operators to remove

> This is a typical page from a case reported in the National Reporter System. It illustrates how headnotes are developed. The bracketed numbers are inserted by the editors. Each number has been rewritten into a headnote. See next Illustration.

its employees at the checkstand would fall from the counter to the floor, and therefore instructed its checkers that spilled greens were to be cleaned immediately after they fell and to inspect and sweep customers' aisles and the common corridor whenever necessary. Brooms and dustpans for this purpose were located between checkstands numbers 5 and 6. Defendant's janitor was employed only until 12:00 noon. After the janitor left, it was the duty of the checkers and baggers to sweep if they had the time.

Defendant's manager had no personal knowledge whether the area in question had been swept in the three hours preceding the fall but had inspected the area about fifteen minutes before the accident and had seen no lettuce leaves. Defendant's assistant manager had been delegated the duty of seeing that the corridors and aisle walk by the checkstands were clean but had not inspected the area in question for several hours before the fall. One of

[Illustration 17–a]

## SAMPLE PAGE FROM THE PACIFIC REPORTER

448   Cal.          319 **PACIFIC REPORTER**, 2d SERIES

**Beryl McKENNEY, Plaintiff and Respondent,**

v.

**QUALITY FOODS, Inc., a corporation, et al., Defendant and Appellant.**

Civ. 17528.

District Court of Appeal, First District, Division 2, California.

Dec. 26, 1957.

Action for customer's personal injuries allegedly resulting from fall in defendant's supermarket. The jury returned a verdict for plaintiff. The Superior Court, City and County of San Francisco, Edward Molken-buhr, J., rendered judgment, and defendant appealed. The District Court of Appeal, Kaufman, P. J., held that evidence raised questions for jury as to whether defendant was responsible for vegetable matter on floor and whether fall was caused by slipping on such matter and whether defendant had actual or constructive notice of the presence of vegetable matter on the floor.

Affirmed.

**1. Appeal and Error ⏗930(1)**

On appeal from judgment on verdict for plaintiff, the District Court of Appeal was required to accept the evidence most favorable to plaintiff.

**2. Negligence ⏗136(22, 25)**

In action for injuries sustained by customer who fell in defendant's super-market, evidence raised question for jury as to whether defendant was responsible for vegetable matter on floor and whether fall was caused by slipping on such matter.

**3. Negligence ⏗136(16)**

In action for injuries sustained by customer who fell in defendant's supermarket, evidence raised question for jury as to whether defendant had actual or constructive notice of presence of vegetable matter on floor.

**4. Negligence ⏗32(2.8)**

Customer in defendant's supermarket was a business invitee to whom defendant owed duty to exercise reasonable care in keeping the premises safe.

**5. Negligence ⏗121(1, 5)**

Customer suing for injuries sustained when she fell in defendant's supermarket must establish that defendant breached duty to exercise reasonable care in keeping premises clean and that such breach was proximate cause of injury.

**6. Negligence ⏗121(1)**

In personal injury action, burden is on plaintiff to prove every essential fact on which she relies.

**7. Negligence ⏗121(3)**

No inference of negligence of store-keeper arises based simply on proof of fall of customer on the storekeeper's floor.

**8. Negligence ⏗3**

The quantum of care which the law

> **Note how the wording of the headnotes are paraphrased from the opinion. See Illustration 17.**

**10. Trial ⏗260(1)**

The refusal of proposed instruction was not error where other instructions covered the matter adequately.

**11. Appeal and Error ⏗1067**

In action for injuries sustained by customer who allegedly fell in defendant's supermarket when she slipped on vegetable matter on the floor, the refusal to instruct on unavoidable accident was not prejudicial.

———————

Hadsell, Murman & Bishop, San Francisco, for appellant.

Hoberg & Finger, L. Chas. Gay, San Francisco, for respondent.

KAUFMAN, Presiding Justice.

Plaintiff brought this action to recover for personal injuries resulting from a fall in defendant's grocery store. The cause was tried before a jury which returned a

[Illustration 18]

## SAMPLE PAGE FROM GENERAL DIGEST, FOURTH SERIES

---

# NEGLIGENCE ⊂⇒32(2.13)

owes duty to avoid willfully, intentionally or recklessly injuring him.—Id.

**N.Y.A.D. 1969.** School district employee

> V. 12. *General Digest 4th* (1970). **This volume contains digests of all cases for a 3 month period arranged under topic and key-numbers. Note how under each key-number, decisions are arranged alphabetically by jurisdiction, with Federal courts listed first. In 1977, all of the volumes of the** *General Digest* 4th **will be cumulated into the** *Eighth Decennial Digest.*

status, whether that of a trespasser, a licensee, a social guest, or a mere passerby only duty to avoid willfully, intentionally or recklessly injuring him.—Lemon v. Busey, 461 P. 2d 145.

An "invitee" on premises to whom owner owes duty to exercise ordinary care for his safety is either a public invitee or a business visitor.—Id.

A "public invitee" to whom owner of property owes duty to exercise ordinary care for his safety is person who is invited to enter or remain on land as member of public for purpose for which land is held open to public.—Id.

Fact that someone is invited to visit does not make him a "public invitee" to whom owner of land owes duty to exercise ordinary care for his safety; rather purpose of his visit determines his status.—Id.

Meaning of "invitee" to whom owner of property owes duty to exercise ordinary care for his safety is more limited than meaning of term "invitation" in popular sense and not all of those who are invited to enter on land are invitees.—Id.

Place and purpose of visit determine whether person on premises is invitee to whom owner owes duty to exercise ordinary care for his safety or merely licensee to whom owner owes duty to avoid willfully, intentionally or recklessly injuring him.—Id.

**Miss. 1969.** Lady who paid admission charge to go upon historical site controlled and maintained by county historical society was "public invitee", toward whom society owed duty of reasonable care including reasonable inspection to discover actual condition of premises and any latent defects, followed by such repairs as might be reasonably necessary for protection under circumstances.—Alexan-

der v. Jackson County Historical Soc., Inc., 227 So.2d 291.

### ⊂⇒32(2.8). Business visitors, and store and restaurant patrons

**Kan. 1969.** A "business visitor" to whom owner of property owes duty to exercise ordinary care for his safety is a person who is invited to enter or remain on land for purpose directly or indirectly connected with business dealings with possessor of land.—Lemon v. Busey, 461 P.2d 145.

**Minn. 1969.** A "business visitor" is a person who is invited or permitted to enter or remain on land in possession of another for a purpose directly or indirectly connected with business dealings between them.—Berry v. Haertel, 170 N.W.2d 558.

Where city employees had entered garden-supply dealer's building to help load hay used by city on municipal projects and none of city's employees had ever been instructed or warned not to enter building, employee, who entered building for purpose of loading hay and sustained injury when board gave way and he slipped into hole up to his hip, was a business visitor as a matter of law.—Id.

### ⊂⇒32(2.10). Employees and contractors

**C.A.Miss. 1969.** The United States, which engaged independent contractor to remove debris from lake and against which suit was brought to recover for death of contractor's employee who, while returning by boat from work to base camp, struck submerged highway bridge turntable located in center of lake and suffered fatal heart attack in attempting to rescue coemployee who was thrown overboard by impact, owed the contractor-invitee, under Mississippi law, a duty to (1) use ordinary care to have the premises in reasonably safe condition for uses consistent with the snagging operations, (2) not expose the contractor to unreasonable risks, and (3) give the contractor adequate notice of latent perils known to the United States.—Market' Ins. Co. v. U. S., 415 F.2d 459.

### ⊂⇒32(2.13). Guests in private homes

**Ala. 1969.** Where mother went to home of her son at invitation of son's wife, mother was a mere social guest and son and remodeling contractor owed her only the duty to refrain from putting traps in her way and were under no duty to take affirmative care to prepare premises for her reception and were not liable for injuries she sustained when wooden block, serving as temporary step, turned over under her weight with result that she fell and suffered fracture.—Deese v. Espy, 226 So.2d 332.

**Ill.App. 1969.** Care owed a business invitee by owner of a private home is less than that required by owner of a business establishment.—Hunter v. Alfina, 251 N.E.2d 303.

**Kan. 1969.** An owner of property owes an invitee a duty to exercise ordinary care for his safety but owes a person having any other status, whether that of a trespasser, a licensee, a social guest, or a mere passerby only duty to avoid willfully, intentionally or recklessly injuring him.—Lemon v. Busey, 461 P. 2d 145.

**N.J.Super.A.D. 1969.** At time niece and her husband were in process of proceeding from

[Illustration 18–a]

## SAMPLE PAGE FROM THE SEVENTH DECENNIAL DIGEST

### NEGLIGENCE  ⬤⟹32(2.8)

tempted to descend after finishing playing.—West v. Shizuko Tan, 208 F.Supp. 708.

**D.C.La. 1962.** Generally, one who is on premises in the performance of his duty occupies the status of an invitee or a business visitor with respect to degree of care owed by him to owner or person in charge.—Hurst v. Point Landing, Inc., 212 F.Supp. 160, quoting 65 C.J.S. Negligence § 43(4).

**D.C.S.C. 1964.** Relationship between storekeeper and customer is that of invitor and invitee.—Rikard v. J. C. Penny Co., Columbia Division, 233 F.Supp. 133.

**Cal.App.** Customer in defendant's supermarket was a business invitee to whom defendant owed duty to exercise reasonable care in keeping the premises safe.—McKenney v. Quality Foods, Inc., 319 P.2d 448.

**Cal.App.** A patron of a tavern is a business invitee and proprietors thereof owe patron a duty of exercising ordinary care to keep premises in a safe condition.—Shaw v. Colonial Room, 1 Cal.Rptr. 28.

**Cal.App.** Adult accompanying friend into store where friend intended to make purchase was an invitee rather than a mere licensee.—Farrier v. Levin, 1 Cal.Rptr. 742.

**Cal.App.** Customer in a store was an invitee to whom the store owed the duty to exercise ordinary care to keep the premises in reasonably safe condition or to warn of danger, and duty was not limited to conditions actually known to be dangerous but extended also to conditions which might have been found dangerous by reasonable care.—Iloff v. Purity Stores, Limited, 2 Cal.Rptr. 735.

**Cal.App.** In order to be an invitee or business visitor, it is not necessary that visitor should himself be on land for purpose of possessor's business, but it is sufficient that he be on premises for convenience or necessity of one who is on land for such purpose.—Beeston v. Lampasona, 6 Cal.Rptr. 531.

**Cal.App. 1962.** Store patron was business invitee while walking on parking lot adjacent to store as well as while in store itself, and storekeeper owed invitee duty of exercising ordinary care to avoid injury to her.—Perez v. Ow, 19 Cal.Rptr. 372.

**Cal.App. 1963.** Generally, "invitee" or "business visitor" is person who is invited or permitted to enter or remain on land in possession of another for a purpose directly or indirectly connected with business dealings between them.—Clawson v. Stockton Golf and Country Club, 34 Cal.Rptr. 184.

Invitation to an invitee or business visitor may be implied from such circumstances as conduct of possessor, arrangement of premises, or local custom.—Id.

**Colo. 1964.** Plaintiff's driver while on shipper's premises in connection with plaintiff's business was an invitee.—Colorado-Wyoming Ry. Co. v. Wheelock Bros. Inc., 395 P.2d 1.

**Del.** A storekeeper is not an insurer of his patrons, and has only duty to exercise same standard of care reasonably prudent storekeepers would exercise under like circumstances to keep premises in reasonably safe condition for customers' use.—Robelen Piano Co. v. Di Fonzo, 169 A.2d 240.

**D.C.Mun.App.** An adult daughter who accompanied her mother who desired to purchase a rake needed in house where daughter lived with her mother was an "invitee" of store from the time she entered store because she was a potential customer.—Sears, Roebuck & Co. v. Donovan, 137 A.2d 716.

Under Maryland law an adult daughter who accompanied her mother for purpose of buy-

ing a rake was "invitee" of store notwithstand-

> *Seventh Decennial Digest* **covers cases reported from 1956–1966.**

from father, and, who, after returning to shop shirts which father, who was corporation's employee, had forgotten to return to shop after having taken them home to work on them in evening, tripped and fell on worn carpet while attempting to go to rest room in shop, was, at time of her injury, a "licensee", not a "business invitee".—Eisen v. Sportogs, Inc., 87 So. 2d 44.

**Fla.App.** A customer who walked across service station premises for purpose of paying a bill for oil previously purchased was a "business invitee", and persons in control of premises had duty to exercise ordinary care for customer's safety and to warn customer of latent or concealed defects which should have been known to such persons; however, the persons in control had no duty to warn customer against patent or obvious conditions which were not dangerous per se.—Andrews v. Goetz, 104 So.2d 653.

**Fla.App.** Incidental motives of the visit of a social guest, other than purely social, or minor services performed by guest for host during visit will not be sufficient to change status of visitor from licensee to invitee or business visitor.—Cochran v. Abercrombie, 118 So.2d 636.

**Fla.App.** In absence of showing of reason why can fell from shelf and struck patron on leg and foot, patron could not recover for her injuries from store owners.—Food Fair Stores, Palm Beach, Inc. v. Spinelli, 122 So.2d 41.

**Fla.App. 1962.** An "invitee" is normally considered to be one who enters upon premises of another for purposes connected with business of owner or occupant of premises.—North Broward Hospital Dist. v. Adams, 143 So.2d 355.

**Fla.App. 1964.** Plaintiff who was injured when sacks of cow feed stacked in defendants' barn struck plaintiff on the back and head at a time when he was engaged, with permission of defendants, in removing bags of feed from their barn to plaintiff's truck for transportation to ranch on which he worked for another, was, while he was in the barn, a "licensee."—Jerrell v. Whitehurst, 164 So.2d 875.

**Fla.App. 1966.** Plaintiffs, as customers of defendants' cocktail lounge, were invitees of defendants' place of business.—Carter v. Parker, 183 So.2d 3.

**Ga.App.** While there must be at least some mutuality of interest in the subject matter to which the visitor's business relates, the particular subject of the visit need not be for the benefit or the profit of the occupant.—Knudsen v. Duffee-Freeman, Inc., 109 S.E.2d 339.

A mere permissive use of premises is sufficient to raise an implied invitation to those having business with the permittee to come upon the premises and the existence of the relation of landlord and tenant as between the owner and the person visited is not essential to the owner's liability.—Id.

[Illustration 18–b]

## SAMPLE PAGE FROM THE SIXTH DECENNIAL DIGEST

---

**32(2.4) NEGLIGENCE**      23–6th D—898

premises and those adjacent thereto, petitioner was deviating from driveway for his own purposes and could not recover for injuries.—Walters v. Markwardt, 237 S.W.2d 177.

**N.C.** Not every accident is in the category of actionable negligence, and keeper of a store or service station cannot be made insurer of safety of his customers.—Mills v. Waters, 70 S.E.2d 11, 235 N.C. 424.

**Ohio App.** One injured in fall from automobile parking floor to ground below while seeking shelter from rain after searching unsuccessfully for one who had offered to drive him home in pro-

> *Sixth Decennial Digest* **covers cases reported from 1946–1956.**

ployee who did not have either express or implied authority to invite friends into garage for purpose of "showing them around", and she was injured while using escalator, plaintiff was at best a "bare licensee" to whom the defendant owed no duty to exercise due care.—Akerson v. D. C. Bates & Sons, 174 P.2d 953, 180 Or. 224.

**Pa.Com.Pl.** Where the evidence indicates that defendant's parking lot remained covered with snow and ice in mounds and ridges three to four inches in height three days later and that the defendant had made faulty or ineffectual efforts to clear the lot, a jury may reasonably and properly conclude that the defendant had failed to exercise reasonable care and to keep the lot in a reasonably safe condition thus breeching its duty to the plaintiff.—Morris v. Atlantic and Pacific Tea Co., 42 Del.Co. 366, affirmed 121 A.2d 135, 384 Pa. 464.

In such case where the testimony shows that many persons had been and were using defendant's lot on the day of the accident and prior thereto, it is not for the court, but for the jury, to determine whether the plaintiff performed the duty of reasonable care required of him under the circumstances.—Morris v Atlantic and Pacific Tea Co., 42 Del.Co. 366, affirmed 121 A.2d 135, 384 Pa. 464.

**Pa.Com.Pl.** A person entering upon land occupied as a gasoline station for the purpose of patronizing the business of the operator is a business visitor.—Egan v. Bradican, 51 Lack.Jur. 173.

**Tex.Civ.App.** A person who stops at gasoline filling station to buy gasoline is an invitee, but he is not an invitee if he stops to obtain information about where he might find a trailer camp.—Dofner v. Branard, 236 S.W.2d 544, ref. n. r. e.

**32(2.6). Bill collectors**

**N.J.Super.A.D.** Where collector was requested to call at residence and two weeks later called, and collector, who knew that defendants lived in second floor apartment, entered stairway to cellar without announcing her presence or requesting admittance, after she was informed that owner was in cellar, status of collector was not that of invitee, but rather that of "licensee."—Tomsky v. Kaczka, 85 A.2d 809, 17 N.J.Super. 211.

**32(2.7). Buildings in process of construction, alteration, or demolition**

**Ohio App.** Where watchman entered leased portion of premises to lead

plumber to source of water leak, but watchman was not doing so to prevent waste and hence was a licensee, duty of company remodeling leased portion was not to willfully cause watchman injury.—Helvich v. George A. Rutherford Co., 114 N.E.2d 514, 96 Ohio App. 367, appeal dismissed Helvich v. Eastman Kodak Stores, Inc., 117 N.E.2d 439, 160 Ohio St. 571.

**32(2.8). Business visitors, and store and restaurant patrons**

**C.A.2.** One who is in possession of realty owes to a "business guest" or "invited person" no greater duty than to advise him of any dangers which reasonable prudence would foresee and correct.—Slattery v. Marra Bros., 186 F.2d 134, certiorari denied Marra Bros. v. Slattery, 71 S.Ct. 736, 341 U.S. 915, 95 L.Ed. 1351.

**C.A.Ga.** Purchaser of surplus goods stored in Government warehouse was an invitee upon the premises of the Government for purpose of loading the goods purchased, and Government was under a duty to exercise ordinary care in keeping the premises, approaches and instrumentalities to be used, for such purpose, in a safe condition.—U. S. v. Adams, 212 F.2d 912.

**C.A.Ill.** A storekeeper is not liable as an insurer to his customers, but may only be held liable for injuries caused by his negligence.—Ernst v. Jewel Tea Co., 197 F.2d 881, certiorari denied 73 S.Ct. 346, 344 U.S. 918, 97 L.Ed. —.

**C.A.Kan.** Under Kansas law, a merchant owes to his patrons and invitees the duty to maintain his premises in a reasonably safe condition, and his failure to do so constitutes negligence.—Parks v. Montgomery Ward & Co., 198 F.2d 772.

A merchant has the general duty to exercise the degree of care that an ordinarily cautious and prudent storekeeper would exercise under the same or similar circumstances to protect his customers and invitees from danger.—Parks v. Montgomery Ward & Co., 198 F.2d 772.

**C.C.A.N.Y.** Owner of automobile and his guests who went to garage to get automobile were "business visitors" to whom garage owner owed duty to maintain garage in a safe condition within the area of the business invitation.—Bollinger v. Gotham Garage Co., 155 F.2d 326, certiorari denied 67 S.Ct. 95, 329 U.S. 733, 91 L.Ed. 633.

**C.A.N.Y.** Owner owes duty to business visitor to exercise reasonable care to make the premises safe.—Stoffel v. New York, N. H. & H. R. Co., 205 F.2d 411, certiorari denied 74 S.Ct. 222, 346 U.S. 898, 98 L.Ed. 399.

**C.A.Pa.** A possessor of land is subject to liability to business visitors for personal injuries to them by artificial conditions on premises only if possessor knew, or by exercise of reasonable care could discover, condition which he should realize as involving unreasonable risk to invitees, and if possessor has no reason to believe that visitors will discover condition of realized risk involved, and he invites or permits them to enter or remain upon premises without exercising reasonable care to make conditions safe or give adequate warning to visitors.—Wild v. Atlantic Refining Co., 195 F.2d 151, certiorari denied 73 S.Ct. 92, 344 U.S. 857, 97 L.Ed. —.

**C.A.Tenn.** A person, to become a business invitee on another's premises, need not be expressly invited by owner to enter premises for purpose of doing business with him, but such invitation is implied from owner's acts leading visitor to believe that his use of premises is in accordance with design for which they are adapted and allowed

[Illustration 18–c]

## SAMPLE PAGE FROM THE FIFTH DECENNIAL DIGEST

⚖️32(2.5)          NEGLIGENCE          34–5th D—1172

**Tex.Civ.App.** 1937. One injured by fall in ... ng st ... e ov ...

> *Fifth Decennial Digest* covers cases reported from 1936–1946.

n- au ... r, bu ... e v. ... d Gulf Refining Co. v. Beane, 127 S.W.2d 169, 133 Tex. 157.

**W.Va.** 1938. A member of the family, or an invited guest of a motorist who goes to gasoline filling station as a customer, is an "invitee" of the operator of the station, and may recover for injuries sustained at station because of unsafe condition of premises.—Wingrove v. Home Land Co., 196 S.E. 563, 120 W.Va. 100, 116 A.L.R. 1197.

⚖️**32(2.6). Bill collectors.**

**Kan.** 1939. A collector who was on partnership premises for purpose of making collections from partner on account with partner's son was at least a "licensee" as respects right of licensee to recover against partnership for injuries received on premises.—Montague v. Burgerhoff, 92 P.2d 98, 150 Kan. 217.

⚖️**32(2.7). Buildings in process of construction, alteration, or demolition.**

**C.C.A.N.Y.** 1939. A woman, reasonably believing from condition of post office building being demolished that post office business was still being conducted therein when she mounted steps to enter building for purpose of mailing letter, was not a "trespasser," but gratuitous "licensee" or "business visitor."—Lewis-Kures v. Edward R. Walsh & Co., 102 F.2d 42, certiorari denied 60 S.Ct. 132, 308 U.S. 596, 84 L.Ed. 499.

**C.C.A.Va.** 1940. Where plaintiff who was member of building committee of board of trustees of town library and who had undertaken active supervision of building of library was injured by falling of defective scaffold while plaintiff was upon town property while contractors were constructing library thereon, formal or written authority from town or board of trustees was not necessary to clothe plaintiff with status of an "invitee," in determining contractors' liability for injuries, irrespective of whether plaintiff was authorized representative of town or board.—Robey v. Keller, 114 F.2d 790.

**Cal.App.** 1939. Corporation for which building was being constructed was "invitor" of employee of a subcontractor, and by exercising ordinary care in its conduct, discharged obligation, as an invitor, to the employee.—Hayden v. Paramount Productions, 91 P.2d 231, 33 Cal.App.2d 287.

Contractor and subcontractor were "invitees" of corporation for which they were constructing building, but as between each

other contractor and subcontractor were strangers, owing to employees of each other the same duty of exercising ordinary care for their safety during progress of work as contactor and subcontractor owed to the public generally.—Hayden v. Paramount Productions, 91 P.2d 231, 33 Cal.App.2d 287.

⟶ ⚖️**32(2.8). Business visitors, and store and restaurant patrons.**

**C.C.A.Idaho** 1944. A patron who entered a store for purpose of purchasing merchandise was an "invitee" to whom store owner owed duty of maintaining its premises in reasonably safe condition and exercising reasonable care to protect patrons from injury and store owner was negligent if it violated that duty.—Montgomery Ward & Co. v. Lamberson, 144 F.2d 97.

A store owner's duty to patron was not that of an insurer but was merely that of maintaining his premises in a reasonably safe condition and of exercising reasonable care to protect patron from injury.—Montgomery Ward & Co. v. Lamberson, 144 F.2d 97.

**C.C.A.Minn.** 1939. A department store patron was on steps in store at implied invitation of owner, and was entitled to protection afforded by ordinance requiring handrails on both sides of department store "stairways."—Montgomery Ward & Co. v. Snuggins, 103 F.2d 458.

**C.C.A.N.Y.** 1938. The "business visitor" relation with its resulting duty arises only when person who enters premises does so in the interest of the owner, or upon some business of his own, of which the owner has notice and to an entry in pursuit of which he consents, directly or indirectly.—Gunnarson v. Robert Jacob, Inc., 94 F.2d 170, certiorari denied Robert Jacob, Inc., v. Gunnarson, 58 S.Ct. 764, 303 U.S. 660, 82 L.Ed. 1119, rehearing denied 58 S.Ct. 948, 304 U.S. 588, 82 L.Ed. 1548.

**C.C.A.N.C.** 1938. A customer who after having made purchases and left store, returned merely to recover pocketbook which she had left by mistake was nevertheless an invitee to whom store owed ordinary care, rather than a mere licensee, especially in view of store rule requiring customers to go to the office to recover lost articles.—H. L. Green Co. v. Bobbitt, 99 F.2d 281.

**C.C.A.N.C.** 1939. While a storekeeper is not an insurer of safety of customers, customers are "invitees" and he owes them the duty of keeping his premises in a reasonably safe condition and must use ordinary care to avoid accidents or injuries.—Baskin v. Montgomery Ward & Co., 104 F.2d 531.

**C.C.A.Va.** 1940. A "business visitor" is a person who is invited or permitted to cater or remain on land in possession of another for a purpose directly or indirectly connect-

## [Illustration 18–d]

## SAMPLE PAGE FROM THE FOURTH DECENNIAL DIGEST

---

24–4th D—171　　　　　　　　NEGLIGENCE　　　　　　　　☞32(2)

**Wis. 1934.** Employer must make premises safe for performance by frequenters of acts which he knows or reasonably should know are going to be performed there. St.1929, § 101.-06.—Neitzke v. Kraft-Phenix Dairies, 253 N.W. 579, 214 Wis. 441.

Where employees or frequenters are injured as result of unsafe condition of place to work against which employer could reasonably have protected them, employer is liable where injured persons had exercised ordinary care. St.1929, § 101.06.—Neitzke v. Kraft-Phenix Dairies, 253 N.W. 579, 214 Wis. 441.

**Wyo. 1927.** Garage proprietor *held* required to exercise reasonable care to protect customer's agent from danger; "invitee."—Loney v. Laramie Auto Co., 255 P. 350, 36 Wyo. 339, 53 A.L.R. 73.

Garage keeper's duty to protect invitee is coextensive with invitation limited by character and purpose of visit.—Loney v. Laramie Auto Co., 255 P. 350, 36 Wyo. 339, 53 A.L.R. 73.

➡️ ☞**32 (2). Who are licensees, and status of persons going on land of another.**

**C.C.A.Cal. 1928.** Owner has duty to refrain from subjecting to unnecessary peril employee of contractor working on unfinished building.—McCready v. Southern Pac. Co., 26 F.2d 569.

**C.C.A.Ill. 1926.** Person injured considered invitee rather than licensee, when on premises for mutual benefit of parties.—Fleischmann Malting Co. v. Mrkacek, 14 F.2d 602.

Person injured *held* invitee in going on premises with permission of foreman in immediate control.—Fleischmann Malting Co. v. Mrkacek, 14 F.2d 602.

**C.C.A.Md. 1931.** One who, considering nature of shop and use made of it by public, feels reasonably free to enter by implied invitation, is invitee.—Elkton Auto Sales Corporation v. State of Maryland, to Use of Ferry, 53 F.2d 8.

**C.C.A.Mass. 1932.** One entering restaurant and falling on floor was "invitee" to whom proprietor owed duty to maintain premises in reasonably safe condition.—Holmes v. Ginter Restaurant Co., 54 F.2d 876.

**C.C.A.N.Y. 1932.** Applicants for work in construction gang, while in temporary building of contractor, were invitees, entitled to reasonably safe place for their entertainment.—Mideastern Contracting Corporation v. O'Toole, 55 F.2d 909.

**C.C.A.N.Y. 1934.** "Invited person" is one entering another's premises not only for his own purposes, but in interest of owner aware that mutual interest of both may lead to such entry.—Radoslovich v. Navigazione Libera Triestina, S. A., 72 F.2d 367.

**C.C.A.Tenn. 1931.** One entering storage building in search of work, who was told to see man in rear thereof, was not invitee when injured.—American Ry. Express Co. v. Gilbreath, 48 F.2d 809.

**D.C.N.Y. 1928.** Repair company permitting ship's employees to use its gangway, must use ordinary care to keep gangway in proper condition; owner's employees being invitees.—Standard Oil Co., N.J., v. Robbins Dry Dock &

Repair Co., 25 F.2d 339, affirmed, C.C.A., Standard Oil Co. v. Robins Dry Dock & Repair Co., 32 F.2d 182.

**D.C.Pa. 1933.** Customer, in using pay telephone maintained by storekeeper for customers' use, *held* invitee, not mere licensee, as respects storekeeper's liability for negligence.—Randolph v. Great Atlantic & Pacific Tea Co., 2 F.Supp. 462, affirmed, C.C.A., Great Atlantic & Pacific Tea Co. v. Randolph, 64 F.2d 247.

**Ala. 1927.** Customer using toilet *held* "invitee," to whom storekeeper owed duty to use ordinary care.—McClusky v. Duncan, 113 So. 250, 216 Ala. 388.

**Ala. 1928.** Boy on employer's premises at invitation of employee for whom he was working for purpose of receiving pay *held* an "invitee."—Stephens v. Walker, 117 So. 22, 217 Ala. 466.

**Ala. 1928.** Plaintiff carrying cotton into public warehouse must have been in warehouse

> *Fourth Decennial Digest* covers cases reported from 1926–1936. Note that key-number 32 (2) is not subdivided into 32 (2.8) as in later Decennials. Starting with the Fifth *Decennial* this key-number was expanded and further sub-divided to accommodate the growing number of cases on this point of law.

**Ark. 1933.** Invitation to come upon premises will not be implied ordinarily from fact that owner or occupant has acquiesced in or tolerated trespasses thereon.—Missouri Pac. R. Co. v. English, 61 S.W.2d 445, 187 Ark. 557.

Owner or occupant who has permitted persons generally to use or establish way under such circumstances as to induce belief that it is public in character, owes to persons availing themselves thereof duty due to those who come upon premises by invitation.—Missouri Pac. R. Co. v. English, 61 S.W.2d 445, 187 Ark. 557.

**Cal. 1931.** One having business in office building and, while searching for washroom, stepping through open door into totally dark space and falling down air shaft, *held* not then invitee.—Medcraft v. Merchants' Exchange, 295 P. 822, 211 Cal. 404.

Person may be invitee in one portion of building and not in others.—Medcraft v. Merchants' Exchange, 295 P. 822, 211 Cal. 404.

**Cal. 1933.** One taking possession of stall in newly completed produce building occupied status of tenant, though rent payments had not started, and subcontractor constructing doors owed such occupant duty of due care.—Hall v. Barber Door Co., 23 P.2d 279, 218 Cal. 412.

**Cal. 1935.** Where defendant did not expressly consent to plaintiff being in place where plaintiff was at time of injury and plaintiff was there for personal reasons having no connec-

## [Illustration 18–e]

## SAMPLE PAGE FROM THE THIRD DECENNIAL DIGEST

21—3d Dec.Dig.,Page 129 NEGLIGENCE ⚿32(2)

(Pa.1924) Where defendant company permitted persons to use its passageway, it was defendant's duty to use reasonable care either to keep the way free from obstruction, or to give reasonable notice to persons using the way of existing danger.—John v. Reick-McJunkin Dairy Co., 127 A. 143, 281 Pa. 543.

(Pa.1925) One inviting another to his place of business assumes toward him certain duties, and is liable if he negligently permits a danger of any kind to exist which results in injury to person invited without negligence on his part.—Fredericks v. Atlantic Refining Co., 127 A. 615, 282 Pa. 8, 38 A. L. R. 666.

(S.C.1921) Where defendant's own requested charge conceded that plaintiff was a licensee, it was proper to modify that portion of the charge which stated that defendant's only duty was not to willfully or wantonly injure him, and impose on defendant the duty of reasonable

*Third Decennial Digest* **covering cases reported from 1916–1926.**

(Vt.1916) An owner does not owe to a person employed on his premises in the service of an independent contractor any duty to furnish a safe working place, yet as such employé is on the premises by invitation, the owner if retaining control must exercise reasonable care to see that the premises are safe.—Richards v. Consolidated Lighting Co., 99 A. 241, 90 Vt. 552.

(Va.1919) An occupant of land is charged with knowledge of the use of his premises by a licensee, and while not chargeable with the duty of provision or preparation for the safety of the licensee, he is chargeable with the duty of lookout.—John P. Pettyjohn & Sons v. Basham, 100 S. E. 813, 126 Va. 72.

An occupant of land owes to an invitee, to the extent of the invitation, the duty of prevision, preparation, and lookout, and must use ordinary care to see that his premises are in a reasonably safe condition.—Id.

(Va.1924) Employer of independent contractor engaged to paint skylight *held* not liable for injuries to contractor's employés who fell when light collapsed with his and a helper's weight, though such employé be deemed while on skylight to have been an invitee, in absence of showing of employer's negligence.—Davis Bakery v. Dozier, 124 S. E. 411, 139 Va. 628.

(Wash.1919) The duty of care which the owner of a building owes to invitees differs from the duty of care he owes to a mere licensee, the duty to an invitee being to keep the ways reasonably safe for him and open to entry at all reasonable hours, and the duty to a licensee being only the negative one of not wantonly injuring him.—Konick v. Champneys, 183 P. 75, 108 Wash. 35, 6 A. L. R. 459.

(Wash.1921) All persons having occasion to enter an office building on legitimate business have an implied invitation from the owner of the building for that purpose, and such owner owes a duty to all such persons to exercise reasonable care to provide a reasonably safe entrance, and such entrance, or the approach thereto, must be so constructed and maintained that visitors will not be liable to step into dangerous pitfalls by reason of misleading doors or deceptive landings.—Johnson v. Smith, 194 P. 997, 114 Wash. 311.

v.21,3d Dec.Dig.—9

(Wash.1925) An owner or occupier of realty is not obliged to make it safe, or to keep it in any particular condition for benefit of trespassers, intruders, mere volunteers or bare licensees.—Bolden v. Independent Order of Odd Fellows, 233 P. 273, 133 Wash. 293.

(W.Va.1918) One using premises of another by owner's invitation has right to assume that such premises are reasonably safe for purpose for which he is invited thereon.—Starcher v. South Penn Oil Co., 95 S. E. 28, 81 W. Va. 587.

(Wis.1921) In cases of invitor and invitee, where the invitor is sought to be made liable for failure to exercise ordinary care to keep and maintain the premises in a safe condition, there must be some mutuality of interest or benefit in order to render the invitor liable.—Greenfield v. Miller, 180 N. W. 834, 173 Wis. 184, 12 A. L. R. 982.

Ordinarily there is no liability on the part of a licensor for injuries sustained by those coming on the premises as mere licensees, unless there is something on the premises in the nature of a trap or the licensor was guilty of active negligence.—Id.

The owner of a house is not liable to a guest for injuries sustained when the guest slipped on an unfastened oriental rug on a polished hardwood floor; the guest being a mere licensee, and it not appearing that the floor and rug constituted any trap.—Id.

**⚿32 (2). Who are licensees, and status of persons going on land of another.**

See Automobiles, ⚿155; Electricity, ⚿15 (1).
Burden of proof, see post, ⚿121(1).
Employé of contractor to repair, see Municipal Corporations, ⚿848.
Licensees on master's premises, see Master and Servant, ⚿302(1).
Wharf, see Wharves, ⚿21.

To come under an implied invitation, as distinguished from a mere license, the visitor must come for a purpose connected with the occupant's business, and there must be some mutuality of interest to which the visitor's business relates.

—(Cal.App.1923) Bush v. Weed Lumber Co., 218 P. 618, 63 Cal. App. 426;

(Me.1918) Kidder v. Sadler, 103 A. 159, 117 Me. 194;

(N.Y.App.Div.1922) Brister v. Flatbush Leasing Corporation, 195 N. Y. S. 424, 202 App. Div. 294;

(Vt.1921) Coburn v. Village of Swanton, 115 A. 153, 95 Vt. 320;

(Wash.1916) Gasch v. Rounds, 160 P. 962, 93 Wash. 317.

One who during business hours lawfully enters a store to purchase goods does so at the implied invitation of the owner upon whom the law imposes the duty of exercising ordinary care.

—(Cal.App.1921) Brinkworth v. Sam Seelig Co., 197 P. 427, 51 Cal. App. 668;

(Iowa,1922) Keeran v. Spurgeon Mercantile Co., 191 N. W. 99, 194 Iowa, 1240, 27 A. L. R. 579;

(N.Y.App.Div.1923) Tryon v. Chalmers, 200 N. Y. S. 362, 205 App. Div. 816, appeal dismissed (1925) 148 N. E. 713, 240 N. Y. 580.

If purpose of persons going on premises of another is common interest or mutual advantage of parties, implied invitation may be inferred, making it duty of owner or occupier to maintain premises in a reasonably safe condition.

—(Iowa,1925) Printy v. Reimbold, 202 N. W. 122, 200 Iowa, 541, 41 A. L. R. 1423, peti-

[Illustration 18–f]

## SAMPLE PAGE FROM THE SECOND DECENNIAL DIGEST

⬅32(1)               NEGLIGENCE           [17—2d Dec.Dig.,Page 56]

I. Acts or Omissions Constituting Negligence. (C) Condition and Use of Land, Buildings, and
Other Structures.

*Second Decennial Digest* covers
all reported cases from 1906–
1916. Note reference to *Century Digest.*

its telegraph offices a front room in a small
building, access to which room from the street
was by a hall running along the side of the room.
The hall could be lighted by opening a shutter.
The public transacted its business with the company through a window in the partition between
the hall and the front room. Between this
window and the door to the back room there
was a trap in the floor of the hall leading to the
cellar. Defendant had no control over the
cellar nor the door to the trap. Plaintiff went
to the defendant's office about 10 o'clock in
the morning to deliver a telegraph message.
She entered the hall, found the window closed,
and, not receiving any answer to her knock,
she started along the hall to enter the back
room in order to secure attention. As she did
so she fell into the trap, the door of which had
been left open by a plumber employed by the
owner of the house, a few minutes before.
*Held,* that there was no negligence of defendant, except that it had failed to open the shutter by which the hall could have been adequately lighted.—Donohue v. Western Union
Telegraph Co., 57 Pa. Super. Ct. 251.

A telegraph company is not bound to supply
its patrons a safe place to do business, but only
a reasonably safe place.—Id.

(**Tex.**1910) Invitation, license, or allurement of others to come on premises may give
rise to responsibility on the part of the owner
which, without it, would not exist, for injuries
sustained by them from dangerous things there
on against which he has not exercised ordinary
care to guard them.—Stamford Oil Mill Co. v.
Barnes, 128 S. W. 375, 103 Tex. 409, 31 L. R.
A. (N. S.) 1218, Ann. Cas. 1913A, 111, reversing judgment (Civ. App. 1909) 119 S. W. 871.

(**Tex.Civ.App.**1907) Where a railway track is
constructed and used through a smelter company's premises by its permission and for its
benefit, it is the duty of the smelter company to
exercise ordinary care to avoid injury to the
employés of the railway company rightfully upon its premises in the discharge of their duties.
—Consolidated Kansas City Smelting & Refining Co. v. Binkley, 99 S. W. 181, 45 Tex. Civ.
App. 100.

(**Tex.Civ.App.**1907) Defendant owed a customer's employé on its premises the legal
duty to exercise at least ordinary care to protect him from injury.—Waters-Pierce Oil Co.
v. Snell, 106 S. W. 170, 47 Tex. Civ. App. 413.

(**Utah,**1912) A gas company maintaining an
office for the payment of gas bills *held* only
bound to exercise ordinary care to provide a
reasonably safe place for customers.—Quinn v.
Utah Gas & Coke Co., 129 P. 362, 42 Utah,
113, 43 L. R. A. (N. S.) 328.

(**Wash.**1911) Defendant engaged in removing
a rock bluff, incident to the construction of its
railroad, contracted with plaintiff to drive a
tunnel in the face of the bluff in which to explode powder. A heavy blast in another tunnel, for the purpose of loosening part of the
face of the bluff, brought down a quantity of
rock immediately in front of plaintiff's tunnel,
blocking the entrance to it. Plaintiff, at
the direction of defendant's foreman, commenced to remove the débris, but being alarmed by
the fall of a rock, ceased work, and reported

fall to defendant's foreman who said he
d make the bluff safe. Plaintiff did not
n to work till the next morning, after
oreman had assured him that he had caus-
ie wall and slope to be made safe. *Held*
even if plaintiff was an independent con-
or, and not an employé, defendant having
him the wall would be made safe, and as-
l him that this had been done, owed him
luty of making it safe, in so far as this
be done by inspection and barring down
ose rock; so that, plaintiff having a right
ly on the assurance that it had been made
defendant was liable for injury to him
through the falling of a rock, caused by negligence in not making the place safe.—Gibson v.
Chicago, M. & P. S. Ry. Co., 112 P. 919, 61
Wash. 639.

(**Wash.**1914) Where defendant's servant,
dropped the skip of a derrick on deceased, who
was on defendant's premises after refusal of
employment, *held* that defendant was not liable.
—Kroeger v. Grays Harbor Const. Co., 145 P.
63, 83 Wash. 68.

(**W.Va.**1914) A property owner owes a higher degree of care in keeping the premises reasonably safe, to persons entering by his inducement or by his invitation, than to persons
who are mere licensees.—Smith v. Sunday Creek
Co., 82 S. E. 608, 74 W. Va. 606.

(**Wis.**1911) Maintenance of an open stairway
in part of a store not intended for use by customers, but merely for storage, is not negligence, so as to create a liability to a customer
falling down the stairway, unless he was expressly or impliedly invited there.—Lehman v.
Amsterdam Coffee Co., 131 N. W. 362, 146 Wis.
213.

(**Wis.**1913) A manufacturing company maintaining in its yard a switch track owes the
duty to the members of a railroad switching
crew, switching on the track, of removing obstructions on the track.—Landry v. Great
Northern Ry. Co., 140 N. W. 75, 152 Wis. 379.

⬅32(2). *Who are licensees, and status of persons going on land of another.*

See 37 Cent. Dig. Neglig. § 43.

(**U.S.C.C.A.Ga.**1914) One who goes on the
premises of another for the benefit, real or
supposed, of the owner or occupant, or in a
matter of mutual interest, or in the ordinary
course of their business, or for the performance of some duty, is an invitee.—Middleton v.
P. Sanford Ross, 213 F. 6, 129 C. C. A. 622,
reversing order (D. C. 1913) 202 F. 799.

The rule that an owner or occupant of premises is required to use ordinary care to keep
them in safe condition for invitees' use is applicable to a servant of an independent contractor.—Id.

(**U.S.C.C.A.Neb.**1913) Plaintiff accompanying
a friend owning an automobile to defendant's
garage, where he was injured by falling down
a cellar stairway, *held* a mere licensee for
whose injury defendant was not liable, where
the place was lighted, with a door at the head
of the stairway.—Rhode v. Duff, 208 F. 115, 125
C. C. A. 343.

(**U.S.C.C.A.N.Y.**1914) Employé of seller of
oil, who went upon buyer's tank to measure
the oil therein before and after delivery, *held*
an invitee, and it was the buyer's duty to exercise ordinary care to keep the premises in
a safe condition.—New York Lubricating Oil
Co. v. Pusey, 211 F. 622, 129 C. C. A. 88.

(**U.S.C.C.A.Pa.**1908) Where defendant had
consented to the use of a crane runway in defendant's mill by plaintiff, a servant of an independent contractor, in moving scaffolding
from one truss in an addition to the mill to
another, plaintiff in so using the runway was
not a trespasser, but was within the class of
persons present in dangerous premises by the

## [Illustration 18–g]

# SAMPLE PAGE FROM THE FIRST DECENNIAL DIGEST

§ 32 (1)     [15 Dec. Dig. '06—Page 133]   NEGLIGENCE.                                § 32 (2)

I. Acts or Omissions Constituting Negligence.  (C) Condition and Use of Land, Buildings,
and Other Structures.

and thereafter in getting them falls through a trapdoor, shut at the time when the packages were placed there, but left open by the negligence of the merchant, he is liable for resulting injuries.—League v. Stradley, 47 S. E. 975, 68 S. C. 515.

> *First Decennial Digest* **covers all cases reported from 1897–1906.**

care was the care of a prudent man under like circumstances.—Hoadley v. International Paper Co., 47 A. 169, 72 Vt. 79.

[zz]   (W. Va. 1902)
The owner of property owes to an independent contractor going upon the premises to do work under a contract with the owner the duty of reasonable care to have the premises in safe condition for the work, unless the defects be known to the contractor.—Sesler v. Rolfe Coal & Coke Co., 41 S. E. 216, 51 W. Va. 318.

§ 32 (2).   *Who are licensees, and status of persons going on land of another.*

Burden of proof, see post, § 121 (1).

[a]   (U. S. C. C. A., Colo., 1902)
A mining corporation which erects dwelling houses on a tract of land owned by it, and operated for mining purposes, extends an implied invitation to the public to treat the tract as a residence tract, and to enter and depart therefrom for all proper purposes incident to its use as such, and must therefore exercise reasonable care to have the premises in safe condition; and where it omits to open streets or highways, but requires persons desiring to visit the residences to cross the tract "at any point most convenient," and leaves unguarded a deep and abandoned shaft alongside one of the paths leading thereto, into which a person returning from one of the residences falls and is injured, it is guilty of negligence; the injured party not being, in such case, a mere trespasser or licensee.—Foster v. Portland Gold Min. Co., 114 F. 613, 52 C. C. A. 393.

[b]   (Ill. 1899)
Defendant's lumber was being unloaded from a vessel into defendant's dock. Defendant's yard men were piling up the lumber after it was passed out of the boat by another set of men, who were employed by H., who had a contract with defendant to unload the lumber. Plaintiff, belonging to the latter set, was injured, by the falling of a pile of lumber, while he was passing from the vessel to a watercloset maintained by defendant on its docks for the men then engaged. *Held*, that defendant was bound to exercise reasonable care for plaintiff's safety, as plaintiff was not a mere licensee. Judgment (1899) 80 Ill. App. 394, affirmed.—John Spry Lumber Co. v. Duggan, 54 N. E. 1002, 182 Ill. 218.

[c]   (Ill. App. 1903)
An invitation to come on the premises of an owner exists, where some benefit accrues or is supposed to accrue to the one who extends the invitation.—Northwestern Elevated R. Co. v. O'Malley, 107 Ill. App. 599.

[d]   (Ind. 1893)
The owner of a building in a populous city does not owe it as a duty at common law, independent of any statute or ordinance, to keep such building safe for firemen or other officers, who in a contingency may enter the same without a license. It seems to be settled, however, that such duty may be imposed by statute or by an ordinance adopted for that purpose.—Woodruff v. Bowen, 34 N. E. 1113, 136 Ind. 431, 22 L. R. A. 198.

[e]   (Ind. App. 1893)
It is not necessary that the invitation to enter premises should be special or even direct, as it may be implied from the circumstances and facts of the particular case.—Howe v. Ohmart, 33 N. E. 466, 7 Ind. App. 32.

[f]   (Ind. App. 1900)
Where the jury found that defendants owned and operated the factory in which decedent received his injuries, and that M., one of the owners, had authority to manage and look after its business, and that at the time of the accident M. was showing decedent through the factory, with the intention of hiring him as watchman, it cannot be contended that decedent was a mere licensee, since he was viewing the premises on invitation of M.—Warner v. Mier Carriage & Buggy Co., 58 N. E. 554, 59 N. E. 873, 26 Ind. App. 350.

[g]   (Ind. App. 1906)
Where the contract between a telephone company and the proprietor of a building in which a telephone was located required the company to keep it in order, and on receipt of a request from the building for the repair of the telephone, plaintiff, a servant of the company, was sent to repair it, and while in the elevator shaft making the repairs he was injured through the negligence of defendant's servant in operating the elevator, the facts warranted a finding that the servant was injured in repairing the telephone upon the invitation of defendant, who owed the servant protection.—Rink v. Lowry, 77 N. E. 967, 38 Ind. App. 132.

[h]   (Ky. 1898)
A United States revenue storekeeper on duty at a private distillery, and required to daily inspect all parts of it, is present at the implied invitation of the distiller, and is not a mere licensee.—Anderson & Nelson Distilling Co. v. Hair, 44 S. W. 658, 19 Ky. Law Rep. 1822, 103 Ky. 196.

[i]   (Ky. 1904)
Where the acting superintendent on defendant's premises saw plaintiff come up on the elevator, and allowed him to get on to go down again, it could not be said that plaintiff was using the elevator without defendant's consent.—Kentucky Distilleries & Warehouse Co. v. Leonard, 79 S. W. 281, 25 Ky. Law Rep. 2046.

[j]   (Me. 1902)
The owners of a steamer, desiring to make repairs on her, contracted with the owners of the marine railway to take the steamer out of the water for the purpose of repairs; the owners of the steamer to have the use of the railway, and to employ their own men on the repairs and furnish their own material, paying a certain sum per day for the use of the railway. *Held*, that the relation of the parties was that of licensor and licensee.—Moore v. Stetson, 52 A. 767, 96 Me. 197.

[k]   (Me. 1903)
Persons going on the property on the business of the owner are deemed to do so by the implied invitation of the property owner, who owes him the duty of keeping the premises reasonably safe, and giving warning of their dangerous condition.—Dixon v. Swift, 56 A. 761, 98 Me. 207.

[l]   (Me. 1903)
Where plaintiff's intestate, who lost his life by falling into a tank on defendants' premises left open by the negligence of servants, went upon the premises not on any business connected with defendants, but had a gratuitous message to deliver to an employé there, having no relation to the business conducted there, and was indulging his curiosity to look over the place, he was a mere licensee, and defendants owed him no duty except that they should not wantonly injure him.—Dixon v. Swift, 56 A. 761, 98 Me. 207.

**For later cases in Am. Digest 1907A and continuations, see same topic and section NUMBER.**

[Illustration 18–h]

## SAMPLE PAGE FROM THE CENTURY EDITION DIGEST

377 (§ 42)　　　　　　　　NEGLIGENCE.　　　　　　　　(§ 43)　378
Cent. Ed.] I. Acts or Omissions Constituting Negligence. (C) Condition and Use of Land, Buildings, and Other Structures. 1. In General.

[p] (N. J. 1871) It is well settled that the mere permission to pass over lands which are dangerous, either naturally or by reason of the use which is made of them, imposes no duty or obligation upon the owner of such lands, except to refrain from acts which are willfully injurious or knowingly in the nature of a trap, and except, also, where there are hidden dangers, the concealment of which would be in the nature of a fraud. He who enjoys the permission or passive license is only relieved from the responsibility of being a trespasser, and must assume all the ordinary risk attached to the nature of the place or the business carried on there.—Vanderbeck v. Hendry, 34 N. J. Law (5 Vroom) 467.

> *Century Digest* **covers all reported cases from 1658–1896.**
>
> **Note this is not a "key-number" digest and classifications differ from the** *Decennial Digests.*

who unnecessarily follows a clerk to that part of the store, and in so doing stumbles over the truck.—Hart v. Grennell, 122 N. Y. 371, 25 N. E. 354.

[s] (N. Y. 1892) While plaintiff was on premises adjoining her own, seeking her children, who were accustomed to play there, she was injured by the breaking of a decayed stairway. *Held*, that she could not recover from the owner of such premises on the ground that he negligently permitted the stairs to remain in an unsafe condition, because, she being on the premises without invitation and as a mere licensee, the owner owed her no duty of protection.—Sterger v. Vansiclen, 132 N. Y. 499, 30 N. E. 987, 28 Am. St. Rep. 594, 16 L. R. A. 640, affirming (1890) 55 Hun, 605, 7 N. Y. Supp. 805.

[t] (Ohio, 1884) Where a lot is left unfenced, a person who goes upon it by bare permission, because there is no obstruction to keep him off, goes at his own risk; and the owner is not liable for injuries resulting to him from the unsafe or dangerous condition of the lot.—Kelley v. City of Columbus, 41 Ohio St. 263.

[u] (S. C. 1873) The plaintiff was in the store of the defendant as a customer. A clerk invited her to walk into a dark part of the store, in which there was an open trapdoor, through which she, without negligence on her part, fell and broke her arm. *Held*, that the defendant was liable.—Freer v. Cameron, 4 Rich. Law, 228, 55 Am. Dec. 663.

[v] (Vt. 1875) Plaintiff went to defendant late in the evening to buy oats. Defendant had no oats to sell, but, yielding to plaintiff's importunity, he consented to sell him the oats, to accommodate him. Defendant always kept his granary locked, but he obtained the key by sending some distance for it, and went with plaintiff to the upper floor of the granary, where the oats were, and, while defendant stepped back to get a measure, plaintiff walked about the floor in the dark, and fell through an aperture therein, and was injured. *Held*, defendant was not liable for the injury.—Pierce v. Whitcomb, 48 Vt. 127, 21 Am. Rep. 120.

[w] (Wis. 1895) Plaintiff alleged that his intestate was invited by defendant into an uncompleted building, to make certain estimates. At the head of the stairs there was a hallway, in which there was a partially open window. Deceased followed defendant up the stairs, thrust his head through the window, without knowledge that the window was part of the

elevator shaft, and was struck by the descending elevator. *Held*, that defendant was not guilty of any breach of duty to the deceased, and therefore the facts alleged did not constitute a cause of action.—Peake v. Buell, 90 Wis. 508, 63 N. W. 1053, 48 Am. St. Rep. 946.

§ 43. —— Who are licensees.

*Places open to public, see post, § 53 [b].*

[a] (Ill. 1892) A person who breaks into a building to protect property from fire is a mere licensee, to whom the owner owes no duty to keep the premises in safe repair.—Gibson v. Leonard, 143 Ill. 182, 32 N. E. 182, 36 Am. St. Rep. 376, 17 L. R. A. 588, affirming (1890) 37 Ill. App. 344.

[b] (Ind. 1893) In an action for personal injuries caused by falling through an open cellarway in a college building, there was evidence that plaintiff was a visitor, but had previously been a student; that he was in attendance at a literary society at the invitation of a student; that circulars had been prepared, advertising the society as a feature of the college; that the students were authorized to send out the circulars; that plaintiff received one by mail; and that he was personally asked by the superintendent to visit the building. *Held*, that plaintiff was in the building at the invitation of the college authorities.—Howe v. Ohmart, 7 Ind. App. 32, 33 N. E. 466.

[c] (Ind. 1893) Where plaintiff came into defendant's store without invitation on part of defendant, and solely on plaintiff's own business, and fell into an elevator shaft in a part of the store unfrequented by visitors, whereby he sustained injuries, defendant cannot be held liable for negligence, as plaintiff can only be regarded as a licensee.—Faris v. Hoberg, 134 Ind. 269, 33 N. E. 1028, 39 Am. St. Rep. 261.

[d] (Ind. 1893) A fireman in the course of his duty goes on the roof of a building on fire as a mere licensee, and not as of right or by invitation of the owner.—Woodruff v. Bowen, 136 Ind. 431, 34 N. E. 1113, 22 L. R. A. 198.

[e] (Mass. 1880) If a religious society gives notice of a meeting to be held at its house of worship, and invites the members of other societies to attend, a member of a church so invited, while on the land of the society, is not a mere licensee, and may maintain an action against the society for a personal injury sustained, while in the exercise of due care, from the dangerous condition of the defendant's premises.—Davis v. Central Congregational Soc., 129 Mass. 367, 37 Am. Rep. 368.

[f] (Mass. 1892) A person who enters a building containing offices, to inquire about a servant of the occupier of one of the offices, who keeps no servant's registry and who has no connection with such business, the building not being used or designed in any part for such purpose, is a mere licensee therein; and the owner is not liable for injuries received by her through the unsafe condition of the building.—Plummer v. Dill, 156 Mass. 426, 31 N. E. 128, 32 Am. St. Rep. 463.

[g] (Mich. 1893) A teamster, after delivering merchandise at the back door of a store, started towards the desk for a receipt, and fell through an open trapdoor. *Held*, that the proprietor was not liable for the injuries; it not appearing that there had been any express or implied invitation to the teamster to pass to the desk, but that it was the custom of truckmen to make their presence known by calling, when no one was at the door.—Pelton v. Schmidt, 97 Mich. 231, 56 N. W. 689.

[h] (N. Y. 1890) Plaintiff having gone, in the course of his business, to defendant's factory, to find an employé of defendant who usually attended to the business, went, through a passageway not generally used for that purpose,

[Illustration 19]

## SAMPLE PAGE FROM THE DESCRIPTIVE WORD INDEX TO THE SEVENTH DECENNIAL DIGEST

**NEGLIGENCE**          36-7th D—294

**NEGLIGENCE—Cont'd**
Product liability—Cont'd
  Wheel chair, defective fork stem.
    **Torts 1**
  Wooden box—
    **Neglig 136(18)**
    **Sales 445(1)**
Propane gas—
  Explosion. **Gas 17, 20(4)**
  Heater installation. **Gas 17**
Questions for jury—
  Injury from escape or explosion of
    gas. **Gas 20(4)**
  Parking truck hitting lessee's wall—
    Fall on pedestrian on sidewalk.
      **Land & Ten 169(11)**
  Personal injuries on pier. **Wharves
    21**
  Statutory violations, evidence of
    negligence. **Neglig 6**
  Town's negligence. **Towns 45**
Reformation of instruments relief as
  barred by. **Ref of Inst 25**
Religious organizations and societies—
  Abolishing immunity. **Relig Soc 3**
Religious society's employees injuring
  patrons, liability of society. **Relig
  Soc 30**
Repudiation, absolute liability rule.
  **Torts 1**
Rescue doctrine. **Neglig 74**
  Conduct constituting negligence.
    **Neglig 74**
  Overturned vehicle, injuries warn-
    ing overtaking vehicles, action
    against overturned driver. **Autos
    246(33)**
Safety inspections, workmen's compen-
  sation insurance carrier. **Neglig 2**
Safety pilot valve, gas water heater,
  malfunction—
    **Gas 16, 20(2, 5)**
    **Neglig 27**
School districts, softball playing during
  recess. **Schools 5**
Secured transactions—
  Secured party. **Sec Tran 165**
Servant's injuries, liability of employer
  for latent defect. **Mast & S 123**
Sewing machines, spraying oil into
  eyes of operator. **Neglig 134(11)**
Ships and shipping, firemen, duty of
  care. **Ship 80, 86(2½)**
Skating rinks, ice. **Theaters 6(26)**
Skidding of automobile, evidence.
  **Autos 168(1), 244(35)**
Ski
ri
Sm
st
Sov

Sov
S
Sta
s
Sta
States 112
Statutory requirements—
  Violation as negligence, automobile
    speed limit, negligence per se.
    **Autos 168(2)**
  Violation of requirements as negli-
    gence—
      Questions for jury. **Neglig 6**
      Safety standards. **Neglig 6**
Statutory standard of care. **Neglig 6**
Stevedores, breach of warranty of
  workmanlike service—
  Recovery over from vessel from
    stevedore for liability to injured
    longshoreman. **Ship 84(6)**
Stopping motor vehicle without warn-
  ing. **Autos 158, 169**
Storekeeper, accumulation of slush.
  **Neglig 134(5)**
Stores and storekeepers, injury to pa-
  tron, attractive display doctrine.
  **Neglig 67**
Subrogation, automobile accident, ac-
  crual of right, time. **Subrog 35**
Sudden emergency rule. **Neglig 12, 72**
Suntan lotion, skin irritation. **Neglig
27**

**NEGLIGENCE—Cont'd**
Superseding cause, defined. **Neglig 62
(3)**
Surgical nail becoming stuck in leg
  during operation, liability for mis-
  branding. **Drug 9**
Swimming pool operated by city. **Mun
  Corp 747(2)**
Swimming pools, municipal corporation
  operating. **Mun Corp 734**
Taxicabs, inference or presumption from
  happening of accident. **Carr 316(4)**
Teachers—
  Personal liability for injuries to
    pupils. **Schools 147**
Third person—
  Insulating negligence of third per-
    son. **Neglig 62(3)**
Tools, defective and dangerous tools—
  Product liability. **Neglig 27**
Tractor-trailer, test. **Autos 146**
Trees, low hanging branches, infants.
  **Neglig 32(4)**
Unavoidable accident, instruction to
  jury. **Neglig 140**
United States, weapons, reckless use on
  United States property, tort liability.
  **U S 78(15)**
University employee causing injury to
  patron, liability of university. **Col-
  leges 5**
Violation of law—
  Causal connection, violation and in-
    jury. **Neglig 136(25)**
  Negligence per se. **Neglig 6**
Visible and obvious hazards, duty to
  warn. **Neglig 52**
Voluntary violation of standards of
  due care. **Neglig 138(1), 145(4)**
Volunteer. **Neglig 2**
  Firemen, fire district liability. **Au-
    tos 187**
  Standard of care. **Neglig 2**
Warnings—
  Door, resistance opening, reducing,
    social guest. **Neglig 44, 47**
  Golfers. **Neglig 25**
Water heaters, gas, safety pilot valve,
  malfunction—
    **Gas 16, 20(2, 5)**
    **Neglig 27**
Weapons, sale to infants. **Weap 18(1)**
Welding. **Neglig 135(4), 136(17)**
Wrecking company—
  Pedestrian's death, claim for reim-
    bursement, building owners. In-

Previous charge of conviction, evidence
  in homicide case. **Crim Law 369(3)**

**NEGLIGENT INTERRUPTION OF
BUSINESS**
Action against United States. **U S 78
(14)**

**NEGLIGENCE PER SE**
Speed of automobiles in municipality.
  **Autos 168(1), 246(56)**

**NEGLIGENT HOMICIDE**
Burden of proving affirmative defense.
  **Autos 353**

**NEGOTIABLE INSTRUMENTS**
Assignment to secure money, usury,
  evidence. **Usury 117**
Attachment, jurisdiction of court. **At-
  tach 62**
Certificate of savings account in savings
  and loan association. **B & L Assoc
  40**
Chattel mortgages providing for maturity without notice on customer's default as not negotiable. **Chat Mtg 203**
Corporations, dissolution of. **Corp 617
(2)**

**NEGOTIABLE INSTRUMENTS—C't'd**
Cross-action for rescission, summary
  judgment. **Judgm 181(10)**
Divorce, award of homestead. **Divorce
  249(6)**
Income tax—
  Capital gains, new note for old.
    **Int Rev 410.1**
Judgment, setting aside, authority of
  trial court. **Judgm 67(2)**
Pawn ticket as not. **Pawnb 5**
Reformation, third party rights. **Ref
  of Inst 6**
Summary judgment, reversible error in
  changing cause from one on nego-
  tiable instrument to one based
  upon quantum meruit—
    **App & E 1073(1)**
    **Judgm 186**
Trade acceptances, non-licensed foreign
  corporation payee—
  Assignee as holder in due course,
    jury question. **Bills & N 537(6)**
  Enforcement. **Corp 657(7)**
Trading stamps, negotiable character.
  **Insurance 508.5**
United States bonds. **U S 91**

**NEGOTIATIONS**
Enticement of nonresident into jurisdiction for service of process. **Proc
  65**

**NEGRO CANDIDATES**
Race designation, discrimination. **Const
  Law 215**

**NEGROES**
Adoption of children—
  Negro by white parents, application,
    mandamus to compel acceptance.
    **Mand 168(4)**
Airports—
  Preliminary injunction against ex-
    clusion from waiting room. **Inj
    136(3)**
  Regulation and use in general.
    **Aviation 224**
  Separate facilities for whites and
    Negroes—
    **Aviation 224**
    **Commerce 62**
Amusement parks—
  Refusal to leave park which did
    not admit Negroes—
    Arrest and convicting defend-
      ants as violative of equal pro-
      tection. **Const Law 217**
    Disorderly conduct. **Disorderly
      C 9**
  Right to entry or tickets—
    **Const Law 217**
    **Theaters 4**
Amusement places—
  Denial of admission, damages—
    **Civil R 4, 6**
    **Inj 7**
  Picket lines, segregation. **Inj 128**
Anti-miscegenation statutes, constitu-
  tionality—
    **Const Law 250, 258**
    **Misceg 1**
Apartment houses—
  Civil rights, entrapment. **Civil R 1**
  Discrimination. **Civil R 3**
Appeal, order directing board of edu-
  cation to submit desegregation plan.
  **Courts 405(12.1, 12.23)**
Appeal to race prejudice by district at-
  torney in argument to jury. **Crim
  Law 723(5), 1171(1)**
Appeal to racial prejudice in criminal
  prosecution. **Crim Law 723(5), 730
  (14)**
Apprentices—
  Aptitude test. **Civil R 1**
  Qualifications. **Civil R 1**
Apprenticeship classes, union discrimi-
  nation. **Civil R 1**
Arguments and conduct of counsel—
  Retaliatory statement of prosecutor
    elicited by defense counsel's re-
    marks. **Crim Law 726**
Assault with automobile, asserting civil
  rights, federal court pendent juris-
  diction. **Courts 263**

> If the search is started under *negligence*, it quickly becomes apparent that this entry is too broad to locate a specific topic and key-number applicable to the problem being researched.

[Illustration 19–a]

## EXCERPTS FROM THE DESCRIPTIVE WORD INDEX TO THE SEVENTH DECENNIAL DIGEST

**STORES AND STOREKEEPERS—C't'd**

Customers—
  Assault and battery by employee—
    Course of employment. **Mast & S 302(3)**
    Pleading. **Mast & S 329**
  Class suit, recovery, tax collections by retailer. **Parties 10**
  Falling on onion stalk on floor. **Neglig 134(7)**
  Friend as invitee of licensee. **Neglig 32(2.8)**
  Injuries, falling over stock truck in aisle, questions for jury, sufficiency of evidence. **Neglig 136(22)**
  Invitees. **Neglig 32(2.8)**
  Use of reasonable care. **Neglig 67, 80**
Damages for loss of view by extension of building over sidewalk area. **Mun Corp 671(4)**

**35–7th D—1221**

**INVITATION**
Assumption, normal or obvious risks. **Neglig 105**
Assumption of risk, invitee. **Neglig 105**
Care as to invited person in respect to condition and use of land, buildings or other structures—
  Knowledge of dangerous condition. **Neglig 48**
  Pupils, private school. **Schools 5**
  Slipping on waxed floor. **Neglig 121(3)**
Church premises, member of public injured on portion of premises to which not invited, jury question. **Relig Soc 30(6)**
Clinic door identical to basement door, invitee falling **Neglig 50**
Contributory negligence of invitee. **Neglig 65**
Custom concerning movement of motor vehicles—
  Duty of invitee to inform self concerning custom. **Autos 152**
  Effect of custom on invitee's liability for another's injuries in collision. **Autos 170(3)**
→ Customer's friend as invitee of licensee. **Neglig 32(2.8)**
Docks—

---

This illustrates how by looking under either *Stores and Storekeepers* or *INVITATION* subentries will lead to Topic *Negligence* and Key-Number 32(2.8) which stands for "Business Visitor, and Store and Restaurant Patron". While not shown in illustrations, this Topic and Key-Number could also have been located in the *Descriptive Word Digest* index to the *Seventh Decennial* under the entries: *Business Invitee; Fall,* or *Floors.* After locating the Topic and Key-Number the next step is to search all units of the *American Digest System* under Negligence 32(2.8) as shown in Illustrations 18 to 18–h.

[Illustration 20]

## SAMPLE PAGE FROM TABLE OF CASES VOLUME OF THE SEVENTH DECENNIAL DIGEST

**McKENNEY**                                                    38—7th D—38

References are to Digest Topics and Key Numbers

McKenney v. Buel, Or, 329 P2d 664—Account 3; Action 6; App & E 781 (1); Judgm 829(3).
McKenney v. F C C, CADC, 324 F2d 444—Tel 398.
McKenney v. McKenney, Md, 135 A2d 423—Equity 219; Ex & Ad 43, 85 (1); Ten in C 11; Wills 627(3), 741.
McKenney v. Oregon Am Lumber Co, Or, 304 P2d 426—App & E 78(3, 4), 103, 870(5); Judgm 196.
McKenney v. Quality Foods, Inc, Cal App, 319 P2d 448—App & E 930(1), 1067; Neglig 3, 32(2.8), 121(1, 3, 5), 136(16, 22, 25, 26); Trial 260 (1).
McKenney Logging Co v. Buffelen Mfg Co, CAOr, 232 F2d 5. See McKenney v. Buffelen Mfg Co.
McKennon v. Anderson, Wash, 298 P 2d 492—App & E 766; Evid 384, 417(7), 455, 461(1); Frds St of 129 (6); Land & Ten 24(1), 25(1), 31, 180(4); Licens 44(2).
Mackensworth v. Mathiasen's Tanker Industries, Inc, DCPa, 203 FSupp 316—Adm 82; Seamen 12, 26, 30.
Mackenzie, Application of, Sup, 164 NYS2d 319, aff In re Mackenzie, 170 NYS2d 987, appeal den 178 NYS 2d 594, motion dism 179 NYS2d 857, 154 NE2d 137—Trusts 272(3).
McKenzie v. Albaeck, CalApp, 32 Cal Rptr 762—App & E 948, 962; Dismissal 60(1, 2).
McKenzie v. Arthur T McIntosh & Co, IllApp, 200 NE2d 138—App & E 714 (5); Const Law 70(1); Counties 21¼; Offic 103; Plead 360(10).
McKenzie v. Atlantic Manor, Inc, Fla App, 181 So2d 554—Land & Ten 150 (1), 152(3), 169(11); Trial 178.
McKenzie v. Brixite Mfg Co, NJ, 166 A2d 753—Work Comp 673, 1983.
McKenzie v. Brixite Mfg Co, NJSuper AD, 161 A2d 276, rev 166 A2d 753 —Work Comp 51, 230, 673, 676, 1357, 1562.
McKenzie v. Campbell & Dann Mfg Co, Tenn, 354 SW2d 440—Evid 501 (2); Work Comp 546, 836, 854, 862, 1336, 1638, 1643, 1644, 1855.
McKenzie v. Carte, TexCivApp, 385 SW2d 520, ref n r e—App & E 758 (1), 1175(7); Contracts 141(1); Elect of Rem 1, 7(1); Land & Ten 48(2), 105, 180(1, 3, 4, 6); Plead 427; Trial 392(1), 404(1).
McKenzie v. City of Florence, SC, 108 SE2d 825—Mun Corp 54, 57, 59, 189(1), 723, 724, 745½, 747(3); Princ & S 66(1).
McKenzie v. Com for Use and Benefit of Hicks, Ky, 373 SW2d 595—Bankr 198, 216; Execution 110, 116; Interest 39(3); Sheriffs 120½, 138 (3).
McKenzie v. Cutter, Wis, 117 NW2d 249. See Schmitz' Estate, In re.
MacKenzie v. Fritzinger, Mich, 121 NW2d 410—Trusts 103(3), 107, 110.
McKenzie v. International Ladies Garment Worker's Union, AFL-CIO, SC, 141 SE2d 834. See Bouchette v. International Ladies Garment Worker's Union, AFL-CIO, Local No 371.
McKenzie v. Kirkpatrick, DCCal, 141 FSupp 49—Armed S 3; Courts 265; Decl Judgm 272.
McKenzie v. McKenzie, FlaApp, 105 So2d 614—Divorce 227(1), 312.4.
McKenzie v. McKenzie, Mich, 84 NW 2d 333—Divorce 246.
MacKenzie v. MacKenzie, Mich, 115 NW2d 326—Divorce 27(18), 49(2), 50, 135.
McKenzie v. McKenzie, Mich, 132 NW 2d 73—App & E 927(7); Autos 245 (24).
McKenzie v. McKenzie, MoApp, 306 SW2d 588—Contin 22; Divorce 1, 164, 172, 179, 225, 255, 298(3, 4); Infants 19.2(2); Parent & C 2 (3.2, 3.3).
McKenzie v. Nelson, Mich, 91 NW2d 1—Autos 244(6, 36), 245(72); Judgm 199(3.2); Neglig 136(26); Trial 178.

Mackenzie v. Newton, TexCivApp, 341 SW2d 498, ref n r e—Licens 39.45; Trial 350(3).
McKenzie v. North River Ins Co, Ala, 58 So2d 581—Insurance 599.3.
McKenzie v. Ohio State Racing Commission, Ohio, 215 NE2d 397—Admin Law 676; App & E 2; Theaters 3.
McKenzie v. Ohio State Racing Commission, Ohio App, 204 NE2d 569, rev 215 NE2d 397—Admin Law 676; Theaters 2.
McKenzie v. Pacific Gas & Elec Co, CalApp, 19 CalRptr 628—App & E 927(3), 989; Electricity 14(1, 2), 19(3, 5, 9, 10, 12); Neglig 10, 121 (2); Torts 1.
McKenzie v. Porter, Idaho, 386 P2d 363—Joint Adv 5(2).
McKenzie v. Racing Commission, Ohio App, 204 NE2d 569, rev 215 NE2d 397.
MacKenzie v. Reesey, Md, 201 A2d 848—Autos 160(1), 217(3), 227(3); Neglig 65, 83.1.

A page from the Table of Cases volume of the Seventh Decennial.

When a case is known to deal with a topic of law, Key-Number can be located by the use of a Table of Cases.

Mackenzie v. Soden Mineral Springs Co 27 AbbNC 402, 18 NYS 240—Trade Reg 436.
McKenzie v. State, AlaApp, 177 So2d 110—Crim Law 1076(5), 1081, 1099 (6), 1106(1), 1109(1), 1182.
McKenzie v. State, Md, 187 A2d 885—Crim Law 260(11), 566, 901, 1044.
McKenzie v. State, Md, 204 A2d 678 —Const Law 250, 257; Crim Law 511(1), 586, 589(1), 590(2), 594(3), 595(4), 627.5(2), 742(1), 747, 1171 (1); Sod 6.
McKenzie v. State, Miss, 101 So2d 651—Const Law 268(3); Crim Law 641(1), 641.6(3), 641.12(1, 2), 1163 (2).
MacKenzie v. State, CtCl, 166 NYS2d 408—Em Dom 136, 149; States 184.- 5; Stip 14(11).
McKenzie v. State, TexCrApp, 383 S W2d 177—Crim Law 13, 739(1), 814(8), 1036(1), 1038(3); Poisons 4, 9.
McKenzie v. State, TexCrApp, 390 SW 2d 281—Crim Law 1028, 1170½(2); Poisons 9.
MacKenzie v. Sullivan 40 Erie 216—Land & Ten 167(2), 168(1), 169 (11); Neglig 67.
Mackenzie v. Sun Choo Choi, Hawaii, 387 P2d 475—App & E 78(7), 801 (1); Dismissal 24, 42.
MacKenzie v. Town Planning and Zoning Commission of Town of Trumbull, Conn, 183 A2d 619—Const Law 93(1); Evid 43(3); Int Liq 46½, 59(1), 75(7); Statut 265; Zoning 324.
McKenzie v. U S, DCMunApp, 158 A2d 912—Weap 11(1).
McKenzie v. U S, CAOkl, 266 F2d 524 —Crim Law 452(2), 456, 493, 570 (2), 740, 753(2).
MacKenzie v. U S, CAOr, 244 F2d 712, rev Simpson v. U S, 78 SCt 14 —Crim Law 1134(3); Witn 297 (8).
McKenzie v. Western Greenbrier Bank, Va, 124 SE2d 234—App & E 1062(1); Fixt 7, 14; Land & Ten 37, 152(3), 154(3), 160(2).
McKenzie Const Co v. Pittman, Tex CivApp, 288 SW2d 527, error dism—Venue 7.
McKenzie Const Co v. U S, DCTex, 214 FSupp 738—Int Rev 550.
McKenzie Elec Co-op, Inc v. Eklund Bros Transport, Inc, DCND, 225 F

Supp 940. See White v. McKenzie Elec Co-op, Inc.
McKenzie Mach Shop v. Western Fire Ins Co, DCMinn, 161 FSupp 115. See Richard v. Western Fire Ins Co.
MacKenzie Sand & Gravel Co v. State, CtCl, 166 NYS2d 408. See MacKenzie v. State.
McKenzie's Estate, In re, CalApp, 18 CalRptr 680—Ex & Ad 497, 501, 502, 506(3), 507(1), 510(4), 10), 513(9); Wills 728, 734(1), 753.
McKenzie's Estate, In re, CalApp, 38 CalRptr 496—Char 1, 10, 18, 21(1); Perp 8(1, 8); Trusts 160(2).
Mackenzie's Estate, In re, Sur, 230 NYS2d 63—Corp 123(10).
McKenzie's Estate, In re, Ohio Prob, 139 NE2d 505—Des & Dist 76; Ex & Ad 3(1), 7, 43.
McKenzie, State ex rel, v. La Driere, MoApp, 294 SW2d 610. See State ex rel McKenzie v. La Driere.
Mackenzie's Will, In re, Sur, 227 NYS2d 561, adhered to In re Mac-

Estop 72; Ex & Ad 456(1).
McKeon v. Goldstein, Del, 164 A2d 260—Land & Ten 169(11); Neglig 56(1), 60, 62(1), 136(25).
McKeon v. Highway Truck Drivers and Helpers Local 107, of Intern Broth of Teamsters, Chauffeurs, Warehousemen and Helpers of America, DCDel, 223 FSupp 341—Courts 289; Labor 123, 140.
McKeon v. Highway Truck Drivers and Helpers, Local 107, of Intern Broth of Teamsters, Chauffeurs, Warehousemen and Helpers of America, DCDel, 28 FRD 592—Fed Civ Proc 1275, 1483, 1512.
McKeon v. Northeast Service Corp, Mass, 166 NE2d 733—App & E 1064 (1); Death 58(1); Trial 295(6).
McKeon v. Santa Claus of Cal, Inc, CalApp, 41 CalRptr 43—App & E 882(9), 1010(1); Equity 38; Evid 448, 450(5), 455; Spec Perf 28(1), 121(9), 126(3); Trial 404 (5), 413.
McKeon v. State for Use of Conrad, Md, 127 A2d 635—Death 9, 18(3), 58(1); Statut 181(1), 235.
McKeon v. Unemployment Compensation Bd of Review 195 PaSuper 69, 169 A2d 332—Social S 388, 399.
McKeon v. U S, DCNJ, 152 FSupp 427. See Gordon v. U S.
McKeon's Estate, In re, Sur, 199 NYS 2d 158—Des & Dist 43.
McKeon Unemployment Compensation Case 195 PaSuper 69, 169 A2d 332. See McKeon v. Unemployment Compensation Bd of Review.
McKeone, Appeal of, IllApp, 204 NE 2d 611. See Rakus v. Black.
Mackerman, Ex parte, TexCrApp, 376 SW2d 350—Evid 590; Extrad 36; Hab Corp 85.8(1).
McKernan v. Mutual of Omaha 31 LehLJ 201—Insurance 536, 583(1), 583.1.
McKeough v. Witman, OhiSuper, 127 A2d 234—Autos 245(40, 72); Judgm 181(2); Neglig 122(1).
McKeown v. Wheat, CAGa, 231 F2d 640—Courts 359; Judgm 664(2), 675(1), 678(2), 828(3.32), 3.32).
McKeown's Estate, In re 394 Pa 186, 147 A2d 331—App & E 1008(1); Infants 83.
McKerley v. U S Fidelity & Guaranty Co, GaApp, 101 SE2d 103—Work Comp 1433, 1939.

[Illustration 21]

## SAMPLE PAGE FROM VOLUME OF WORDS AND PHRASES

### BUSINESS INVITEE

Corp. v. Morse, D.C.Minn., 222 F.Supp. 645, 652.

"Store patron" was a "business invitee". Stewart v. George B. Peck Co., 135 S.W.2d 405, 408, 234 Mo.App. 864.

Independent contractor employed to put a new surface on roof was on the premises as a "business invitee." U. S. Steel v. Warner, C.A.Utah, 378 F.2d 995, 997.

Paying patron of skating rink was a "business invitee". Noble v. Park Enterprise, 47 N.E.2d 947, 949, 313 Mass. 454.

One who enters retail store for purpose of making a purchase is a "business invitee". Little v. Butner, 348 P.2d 1022, 1028, 186 Kan. 75.

A member of crew of fishing trawler whose owner paid wharfage for right to unload vessels was "business invitee" of pier operator. Hayes v. Boston Fish Market Corp., 66 N.E.2d 713, 715, 319 Mass. 556.

Where plaintiff's intestate went to defendants' funeral home to attend wake of his father, intestate was a "business invitee". Watts v. Rhodes, 91 N.E.2d 925, 926, 325 Mass. 697.

A master pilot who was assigned to take charge of shifting of steamship was a "business invitee". Mason v. U. S., D.C.N.Y., 77 F.Supp. 921, 922.

A registered guest of a hotel is a "business ... of c... Irwi...

...latio... party... is im... "busi...

S. F. R. Co., 392 P.2d 873, 876, 193 Kan. 223.

One entering strafing range at army camp pursuant to contract with the United States for recovery of scrap metal from range was a "business invitee". White v. U. S., D.C.Cal., 97 F.Supp. 12, 13, 14.

A minor child, accompanying mother, when she went to store, on business errand, was "business invitee". Takashi Kataoka v. May Dept. Stores Co., 140 P.2d 467, 470, 60 Cal.App.2d 177.

Truck driver, delivering lumber for his employer to lumber yard of buyers, was a "business invitee" of lumber yard operators. Nowell v. Harris, 68 So.2d 464, 467, 219 Miss. 363.

Where United States as owner of vessel contracted with engineering company for removal of contents of life boats, rigger employed by company was a 'business invitee'. Mack v. U. S., D.C.Mass., 105 F.Supp. 149, 152.

A motel guest is a "business invitee" to whom operator of motel owes a duty to use ordinary or reasonable care to provide the guest with reasonably safe premises. Winer v. Walo, Inc., Fla.App., 105 So.2d 376, 377.

Woman attending evening bingo games at incorporated school was "business invitee" of school and was entitled to protection accorded such invitees. Garofoli v. Salesianum School, Inc., Del.Super., 208 A.2d 308, 310.

Society newspaper reporter, who was given complimentary membership by country club was its "business invitee" so that club owed her duty to keep its premises in reasonably safe condition. Country Club of Coral Gables v. McHale, Fla.App., 188 So.2d 405, 407.

Bowler at bowling alley was "business invitee" or proprietors, and they owed him duty to use ordinary care to keep bowling alley reasonably safe for his use. Guidani v. Cumerlato, 207 N.E.2d 1, 6, 59 Ill.App.2d 13.

... was ...l but ...ation ...s in- ...ity & ...So.2d

...erat- ing elevator in building under control of landlord during evening after landlord's regular operator had left was a "business invitee" of tenant. Peay v. Reidy, 73 N.E.2d 737, 738, 321 Mass. 455.

Painters on service station premises with permission of operator and for purpose in which he had beneficial interest would be his "business invitees" even though they were not under contract with him or in his employ. Bates v. Callahan, 198 N.E.2d 644, 646, 347 Mass. 772.

A page from *Words & Phrases*. The paragraphs are essentially the same as they appeared as headnotes in the volumes of the *National Reporter System*. The pocket supplement of the volumes of *Words & Phrases* should always be checked.

[Illustration 22]

## AN EXCERPT FROM A PAGE OF SHEPARD'S FEDERAL AND STATE CASES BY POPULAR NAMES

**D-E     TABLE OF CASES CITED BY POPULAR NAMES**

302 US 134, 82 LE 155, 58 SC 208;
114 F2d 242; 312 US 678, 85 LE
1117, 61 SC 450; 312 US 714, 85
LE 1144, 61 SC 620

1→ **Dred Scott Case**
60 US 393, 15 LE 691

**Drive-It-Yourself Case**
144 Md 223, 125 At 69

**Driven-Well Cases**
8 Fed 269
15 Fed 109; 122 US 40, 30 LE 1064,
  7 SC 1073

2→
16 Fed 387; 123 US 267, 31 LE 160,
  8 SC 101; 124 US 694, 31 LE 557,
  8 SC 676
FC No. 371

**Driver's License Revocation Case**
(Cal) 187 P2d 421; 32 Cal2d 226, 195
  P2d 792

**Drover's Pass Cases**
84 US 357, 21 LE 627
95 US 655, 24 LE 535
67 Fed 209, 14 CCA 368
73 Fed 519, 19 CCA 551
200 Fed 197, 118 CCA 383
40 Ark 298
6 Del 469
160 Ill 40, 43 NE 809; 57 IllApp 538
174 Ill 13, 50 NE 1019; 69 IllApp 363
184 Ill 294, 56 NE 331; 81 IllApp 137
47 Ind 471
71 Ind 271

**Drummer Cases—Cont'd**
102 Ark 314, 144 SW 211; 227 US 401,
  57 LE 569, 33 SC 298
57 Md 251; 120 US 502, 30 LE 699,
  7 SC 655
167 Mich 417, 132 NW 1071; 232 US
  665, 58 LE 786, 34 SC 476
127 NC 521, 37 SE 138; 187 US 622,
  47 LE 336, 23 SC 229
143 PaSt 642, 22 At 893; 153 US 289,
  38 LE 719, 14 SC 829
81 Tenn 303; 120 US 489, 30 LE 694,
  7 SC 592
105 Tenn 412, 58 SW 1061; 185 US 27,
  46 LE 785, 22 SC 576
23 TexCrim 662, 5 SW 91; 128 US 129,
  32 LE 368, 9 SC 1
113 Va 562, 75 SE 1135; 236 US 697,
  59 LE 795, 35 SC 479

**Dry Ice Case**
25 F2d 730; 38 F2d 62; 281 US 711,
  74 LE 1133, 50 SC 347; 283 US
  27, 75 LE 819, 51 SC 334; 283
  US 794, 75 LE 1419, 51 SC 483;
  283 US 420, 75 LE 1153, 51 SC
  496

**Duck Lake Case**
223 La 47, 64 So2d 839

**Dud Fireworks Bomb Case**
273 AppDiv 939, 78 NYSupp2d 4; 298
  NY 409, 84 NE2d 38

---

**Notes to Illustration 22:**

1. Popular name of case.
2. Several different cases may go by the same popular name.

---

**Drowned Child Liability Case**
(Tex) 200 SW2d 699; 146 Tex 434,
  208 SW2d 843

**Druggists Cases**
85 Tenn 449, 3 SW 490

**Drugless Healer Case**
36 Wash2d 482, 219 P2d 79; 340 US
  892, 95 LE 646, 71 SC 208

**Drummer Cases**
16 DC 489; 129 US 141, 32 LE 637,
  9 SC 256
95 Ark 464, 130 SW 569; 227 US 389,
  57 LE 565, 33 SC 294

58 SC 300

**Dulles Case**
123 Fed 371, 59 CCA 499; 139 Fed
  510; 139 Fed 513, 71 CCA 500

**Duncan Iron Works Case**
136 PaSt 478, 20 At 647

**Duplex Case**
247 Fed 192; 252 Fed 722, 164 CCA
  562; 254 US 443, 65 LE 349, 41
  SC 172

**Du Pont Trust Case**
188 Fed 127; 273 Fed 869

### SECTION E.   CITING DIGESTS

Digests are *indexes* to cases and indexes, as such, are never cited. Therefore, *do not cite* digests.

In connection with the use of digests, a further caveat is appropriate at this time.   Do not rely on the text of the digest-paragraphs for the essence or the theory of a case.   They are intended to serve merely as guide-posts and not as edifices.   Since the paragraphs are necessarily brief, they can be misleading, can fail to suggest a nuance or shading of the case or can omit an element which may have specific bearing on your problem.   Thus, the digest is not the final repository of the law, and when research is important, it should not be the singular source of research.   Such perfunctory practice, in matters requiring deliberateness, could be embarrassing to you and catastrophic to your client.

---

### SECTION F.   SUMMARY

**1.   Index books—digests**

   a.   Digest—is an index to case law, giving brief, unconnected statements of court holdings or facts of cases, and is classified by subject.

**2.   Types of Digests**

   a.   All courts, federal and state.

   b.   A region, a group of neighboring states.

   c.   A state.

   d.   A specific court or court system.

**3.   American Digest System**

   a.   Scope.

   (1)   Digest which purports to cover every reported case, federal, state or local, from 1658 to date.

   (2)   Consists of a *Century Digest* (1658–1896), seven *Decennial Digests* (1897–1906, 1907–1916, 1916–1926, 1926–1936, 1936–1946, 1946–1956, and 1956–1966), and the *General Digest, 4th Series* (1966 to date).

   b.   Arrangement.

   (1)   Key-Number System—(topic and number) subject classification, e. g., Corporations ⊶343.

(2) Corresponding key-numbers used in all *Decennial Digests, General Digest* and other West digests.

(3) Scope-note (delimits and identifies the content of a topic).

(4) Analysis (conceptual breakdown of a topic).

(5) Section lines, preceded by the key-numbers, indicate the content of each key-number under a topic.

(6) Digest-paragraphs arranged under key-numbers by: U. S. Supreme Court, other federal courts, and state cases listed alphabetically by names of states. The name and citation of each case follows the digest-paragraph.

(7) Expanded topics are periodically added, e. g., Trade Regulation.

c. Century Digest (1658–1896).

(1) Not classified by Key-Number System.

(2) To refer from *Century Edition* to the *Decennials,* use the pink reference table in volume 21 of the *First Decennial.*

(3) When a key-number is known and one wishes to locate the corresponding section in the *Century Edition,* refer to the cross reference included in the *First* or *Second Decennials* under the appropriate key-number. The references in the *Second Decennial* are more complete.

d. Use of the Index Method with the *American Digest System.*

(1) Each Decennial and the *General Digest* have a *Descriptive-Word Index.*

(2) Since recent cases are preferred, begin research with the latest Decennial's *Descriptive-Word Index.* After locating a key-number, check it in all Decennials and the *General Digest* for cases in point. Then consult the cross reference under the key-number to the *Second Decennial* to identify the corresponding section in the *Century Edition.* Examine the *Century Edition,* under that section number, for early cases. This research will disclose cases in point from 1658 to date.

e. Using the Topic Method with the *American Digest System.*

(1) Avoids use of the *Descriptive-Word Index.*

(2) Examine the scope-note and analysis under the appropriate title. Select the key-number and proceed as above.

**3a. U. S. Supreme Court Reports Digests** (see Section B2 *supra*)

### 4. Modern Federal Practice Digest

    a.  Scope.

    (1) Index to modern federal practice cases since 1939.

    (2) Covers U. S. Supreme Court decisions, the *Federal Reporter, 2d Series*, the *Federal Supplement* and the *Federal Rules Decisions*.

    b.  Arrangement.

    (1) Under the Key-Number System.

    (2) Descriptive-Word Index to *Federal Digest* and to *Modern Federal Practice Digest*.

    (3) Tables of Cases in volumes 53 and 54.

    (4) Words and Phrases in volumes 57 and 58.

    (5) Case history.

    (6) Library references.

    (7) The cases of a jurisdiction, which are digested under a key-number, are listed chronologically, beginning with the latest case.

    (8) Cumulative annual pocket and pamphlet supplements keep the *Digest* current.

### 5. Federal Digest

    a.  Scope.

    (1) Indexes federal case law of historical significance, some of which is no longer controlling, from the foundation of the Government to 1939.

    (2) Covers *Federal Cases*, the U. S. Supreme Court decisions, the *Federal Reporter* and the *Federal Supplement*.

    b.  Arrangement.

    (1) By the Key-Number System.

    (2) Descriptive-Word Index to the *Modern Federal Practice Digest* also covers the *Federal Digest*.

    (3) Tables of Cases in volumes 66–68.

    (4) Words and Phrases in volumes 71 and 72.

    (5) Volume 72 has a *Table of Popular Name Titles*, covering cases in the *Digest*.

### 6. Regional Digests

    a.  Segments of the *American Digest System*, arranged by states which form the units of the *National Reporter System*.

    b.  Some *Regional Digests* do not include cases prior to the unit of the *National Reporter*.

c.   Classified under the Key-Number System.

d.   Contain standard digest features, e. g., Descriptive-Word Index, Table of Cases, etc.

## 7.   State Digests

a.   West state digests follow the Key-Number System and are fragments of the *American Digest System*.

b.   Standard features common to many state digests:

(1) Cover all reported state decisions and federal cases arising in each state or applying state law from the earliest period to date.

(2) Classified by subject, with titles, sections, scope-notes and analyses.

(3) Descriptive-Word Index.

(4) Table of Cases.

(5) Words and phrases judicially defined by the digested cases.

(6) Kept up-to-date by replacement volumes and cumulative pocket and pamphlet supplements.

# Chapter 7

# ANNOTATED LAW REPORTS

The *National Reporter System* with its *Key-Number Digest System* provides for the comprehensive reporting of all reported decisions. Another private publishing company, the Lawyers Co-operative Publishing Co. (and its related company, the Bancroft-Whitney Co.) publish court reports on a selective basis. Their theory is that only a small portion of the total number of cases handed down each year is of interest to most lawyers, as most cases deal with either strictly local matters, or cover an area of law so well settled that they add very little to an understanding of the law. What would serve lawyers better, they claim, is reporting only significant court decisions, those that deal with points of law not previously decided, or that indicate a change in the law, or indicate a new trend in legal thinking. By this manner of selective reporting a lawyer could have all important decisions and not have to burden his bookshelves with thousands of cases that really add nothing to the corpus of the law.

Although selective law reporting was the basis for their first venture in publishing court reports, they realized that lawyers would have to be able also to locate other decisions not reported in their publication and also have a method of locating current decisions. To provide this service they began to publish auxiliary sets, all related to each other, and all aimed to assist the lawyer in finding answers to all of his legal questions through the use of their publications. These sets gradually grew into what they now call *The Total Client Service Library*,[1] which consists of seven distinctive sets of law books. This chapter will discuss its annotated law reports.

## SECTION A.  AMERICAN LAW REPORTS (A.L.R.)

The *American Law Reports* is a selective reporter of appellate court decisions. Its editors scan all current decisions and select those that in their opinion are or will become "leading" cases. There are no advance sheets to this set and several volumes are published each

[1] The Total Client Service Library consists of: American Law Reports Annotated, U. S. Supreme Court Reports, Annotated, Lawyers Edition, American Jurisprudence, American Jurisprudence Legal Forms, American Jurisprudence Pleading and Practice Forms, American Jurisprudence Proof of Facts, American Jurisprudence Trials, United States Code Service.

year.  *A.L.R.*, however, is significant not for the decisions it reports
but for the editorial service that follows each reported decision, or for
what the publishers call *Annotations*.  These are expository encyclopedic essays of varying length on the significant legal topics embodied in the reprinted cases with each case followed by an annotation.  *A.L.R.* annotations contain: (1) statements and reasons for
general rules; (2) discussion of supposedly all cases on the point annotated, with jurisdictional analyses and emphases; (3) consideration of the application of rules to specific facts, as well as distinctions, differentiations and commentaries; and (4) definitions of
words and phrases.

The annotations are very helpful in providing discussions on detailed points of law, thus obviating exploratory research in locating
and analyzing cases.  Annotations may also cover topics of such cur-
rency as not to be found in encyclopedias, treatises or periodical literature.  The annotations on overriding cases add to the usefulness
of the set.  The manner in which *A.L.R.* is published and the role of
annotations can be made clear by example.

In 1956 a decision was handed down by the Vermont Supreme
Court *(Ferris v. Patch)* which involved a collision of a truck backing
out of a driveway into an automobile driving along the street.  The
plaintiff, the driver of the auto, sued the defendant, the truck driver,
for damages, alleging negligence on his part.  The editors of *A.L.R.*
decided that this decision was suitable for publication in *A.L.R.* but
in terms of legal research this is not significant, as this decision will
also be published in the official *Vermont Reports* and in the *Atlantic
Reporter*.  What is significant is what *A.L.R.* furnishes *in addition to*
the decision, which is a 143 page annotation that immediately follows
this decision in the *A.L.R.* volume.  In legal research, *A.L.R.* is used
not for the reported decisions, but for the annotations that follow.
The decision is merely a basis for an annotation on a particular point
of law.  The case of *Ferris v. Patch*, as in nearly any reported case,
involves more than one point of law.  This case, for instance, dealt
with the issues of negligence in motor vehicle collisions, rules of evidence, and instructions to juries.  It was chosen by *A.L.R.* because
it dealt with an aspect of negligence law and it uses this issue for the
subsequent annotation.  The point of law in a case reported in *A.L.R.*
and chosen for the annotation is then generalized into a legal topic.
Thus, the annotation following the *Patch* decision is entitled:

> Liability for injury occasioned by backing of motor vehicle
> from private premises into public street or highway.

The annotation is then written on this generalized topic and the
editor assigned to it researches this area and locates all previous decisions from all jurisdictions that dealt with this topic.  It cites and

summarizes the facts and holdings of every reported case in point and presents an analysis and synthesis of the cases. In short, what *A.L.R.* designates as an "Annotation" is in fact a legal memorandum on a particular topic of law which covers all sides of every question, presents general principles deduced from the cases, and gives their exceptions, qualifications, distinctions, and applications.

The usefulness of locating an *A.L.R.* annotation should be evident, since it presents in an organized fashion a commentary and discussion of all previously reported decisions and saves the searcher the task of locating the cases and then analyzing and synthesizing them.

*A.L.R.*, in summary, consists of bound volumes containing selected appellate decisions, each of which has an annotation on a point of law decided in the case. An annotation may vary from one page to over a hundred. See Illustration 25 for example of a typical *A.L.R.* Annotation.

### 1. A.L.R. Series.

*The American Law Reports* are published in four series.[2]

First Series (cited *"A.L.R."*) 1919–1948, 175 v.

Second Series (cited *"A.L.R.2d"*) 1948–1965, 100 v.

Third Series (cited *"A.L.R.3d"*) 1965 to date.

Federal (cited *"A.L.R.*Fed."*) 1969 to date.

The latter set started in 1969 and includes only court decisions from the federal courts. As mentioned in Chapter 3, the Lawyers Cooperative Publishing Company publishes an annotated set of the U. S. Reports. Although decisions from the Federal Court of Appeals previously have appeared in *A.L.R.* litigation has, however, been increasing in both amount and importance and the publishers felt that federal cases now deserved special treatment.

*A.L.R.-Fed.* is published in a format similar to *A.L.R.* Leading decisions of the federal courts are published followed by an annotation in the same manner as described *supra*.

### 2. A.L.R. Upkeep Service.

Once an *A.L.R.* annotation has been found in a volume, further steps must be taken to determine cases subsequent to those found in the *A.L.R.* annotation. For example, after Volume 1 of *A.L.R.* was published in 1919, the publishers were immediately faced with the problem of providing their subscribers with a means of alerting them to cases that were handed down after Volume 1 was published and

---

[2] The American Law Reports replaced the Lawyers Reports Annotated (L.R.A.) For a description of the set and other earlier sets of annotated reports, see Pollack, Fundamentals of Legal Research. 3d ed. 116 (1967).

that related to the annotations in it and would have been cited had they been handed down before Volume 1 had been published. They accomplished this by providing their subscribers a supplementary set to *A.L.R.* Each of the *A.L.R.* Series is now supplemented as follows.

(a) *A.L.R.* (First). Volume 1 of *A.L.R.* was published in 1919. The publishers then started a companion set to *A.L.R.*, which they called the *A.L.R. Blue Book of Supplemental Decisions.* This service is correlated to *A.L.R.* annotation and lists citations to all decisions on the same topic as the annotation. Thus, if one located an Annotation in 117 *A.L.R.* 606–639, all that is necessary is to turn to that citation in *A.L.R. Blue Book of Supplemental Decisions* and find citations to all cases on that topic handed down after the Annotation in 117 *A.L.R.* 606–639 was written. The *A.L.R. Blue Book of Supplemental Decisions* is now in four volumes and is kept current by a semi-annual cumulative pamphlet. [See Illustration 28]

(b) *A.L.R.*2d. After the publication of 175 *A.L.R.* in 1948, the publishers decided to stop this series and the next volume published was 1 *A.L.R.*2d, being the second series of the *American Law Reports.* Actually, each volume of the second series appears nearly the same as the first series. The most fundamental change was in the method of keeping annotations published in *A.L.R.*2d up-to-date. For this purpose it abandoned the use of the *A.L.R. Blue Book of Supplemental Decisions* (although still publishing it for use with *A.L.R.* [first series]). In its place, a new set called *A.L.R.2d Later Case Service* was started. This provides the same service for *A.L.R.*2d that *A.L.R. Blue Book of Supplemental Decisions* does for the first series, but instead of merely listing citations to later cases, it provides digests of these cases and then keys them directly to each section of the *A.L.R.* 2d annotations. In using *A.L.R.*2d then, after the annotation has been read, the set of *A.L.R.2d Later Case Service* must be consulted. [See Illustration 27]

(c) *A.L.R.3d.* After 100 volumes of *A.L.R.2d* were published, the publishers again decided to change the method of up-keep. In 1965, *A.L.R.*3d started and the most significant difference from the previous two series is that it is no longer necessary to examine an auxiliary set, such as the *A.L.R. Blue Book of Supplemental Decisions,* or *A.L.R.2d Later Case Service.* Rather, each volume of *A.L.R.* 3d has an annual cumulative pocket supplement. When using *A.L.R.* 3d and after reading the annotations, it is only necessary to check the pocket supplement to locate later cases. [See Illustration 26]

(d) *A.L.R.*Fed. This is kept up-to-date by pocket supplements the same as *A.L.R.*3d.

### 3. Supplementing and Superseding Annotations.

Frequently after an annotation on a particular topic has been published, the law outlined in the annotation undergoes rapid development and the number of subsequent decisions become quite substantial. In such instances, one of two methods are utilized.

(a) Supplementing annotations. This is accomplished by taking all of the cases in point and handed down since the original annotation was written and writing a new annotation. This supplementary annotation is to be read in connection with the original annotation. The original and supplementing annotation are kept up-to-date in the appropriate up-keep service only under the citation to the supplementing annotation.

(b) Superseding annotations. There are times when the topic of law covered in an *A.L.R.* annotation is subsequently completely changed. For example, an annotation in an early volume of *A.L.R.* may have dealt with the right to recover damages for emotional distress when there was no physical impact. Subsequently, this rule is changed by the courts and they start allowing damages in such instances. The editors of *A.L.R.* may decide that the current status of law on a topic covered in an earlier annotation is such that it is better to rewrite the annotation completely. This is known as a *superseding annotation*.

Thus, any *A.L.R.* annotation may subsequently be *supplemented* or *superseded*. In the former instance, the supplemented and supplementing annotations must be read; in the latter, only the superseding annotation has to be read.

(c) Two means are used to alert users of *A.L.R.* to the fact that an annotation has been either supplemented or superseded. One is notation of this in the appropriate up-keep service. The other is through a *Historical Table* which appears in the back of the *Quick Index* to *A.L.R.*3d. Its use may best be described graphically:

Assume that one has a reference to an annotation to 12 *A.L.R.* 111–144, this citation is then checked in the *Historical Table*. As the illustration below indicates, the annotation at 12 *A.L.R.* 111–144 is now supplemented in 37 *A.L.R.*2d 453.

## HISTORICAL TABLE

| 10 ALR 321–336 | 11 ALR 1325–1328 | 13 ALR 151–156 |
|---|---|---|
| Superseded 75 ALR2d 633 | Superseded 50 ALR2d 143 | Superseded 46 ALR2d 1227 |
| 10 ALR 409–410 | 11 ALR 1401–1402 | 13 ALR 225–247 |
| Superseded 84 ALR2d 1017 | Superseded 24 ALR2d 194 | Supplemented 43 ALR2d 1291 |
| 10 ALR 429–435 | 11 ALR 1405–1407 | 13 ALR 324–340 |
| Superseded 17 ALR3d 705 | Superseded 20 ALR2d 1053 | Superseded 8 ALR3d 235 |
| 10 ALR 488–494 | 12 ALR 111–144 | 13 ALR 346–355 |
| Superseded 92 ALR2d 570 | Supplemented 37 ALR2d 453 | Superseded 19 ALR3d 1227 |
| 10 ALR 783–809 | 12 ALR 333 | 13 ALR 372–383 |
| Supplemented 40 ALR2d 1407 | Superseded 7 ALR2d 226 | Superseded 35 ALR2d 124 |

This means that 12 *A.L.R.* 111–140 and 37 *A.L.R.*2d 453 should be read together as if it were a single annotation, and then searching for later decisions as previously outlined in *A.L.R.2d Later Case Service.*

Assuming, however, that the reference was to 15 *A.L.R.* 244–245 instead of 12 *A.L.R.* 111–144, as in our first assumption. When this citation is checked in the *Historical Table* we note that 15 *A.L.R.* 244–45 has been superseded by an annotation in 32 *A.L.R.*3d 589, as indicated below.

## HISTORICAL TABLE

| 13 ALR 1414–1419 | 14 ALR 1300–1328· | 16 ALR 984–996 |
|---|---|---|
| Superseded 41 ALR2d 329 | Supplemented 26 ALR2d 1139 | Superseded 87 ALR2d 407 |
| 14 ALR 240–249 | 14 ALR 1350–1352 | 16 ALR 1162–1165 |
| Superseded 51 ALR2d 331 | Superseded 6 ALR3d 297 | Superseded 91 ALR2d 618 |
| 14 ALR 316–318 | 15 ALR 244–245 | 16 ALR 1273–1286 |
| Superseded 11 ALR3d 1074 | Superseded 32 ALR3d 589 | Supplemented 24 ALR2d 1161 |
| 14 ALR 344–347 | 15 ALR 437–446 | 16 ALR 1316–1322 |
| Superseded 77 ALR2d 1307 | Superseded 2 ALR3d 1151 | Superseded 31 ALR2d 713 |
| 14 ALR 409–411 | 15 ALR 569–575 | 17 ALR 170–179 |
| Superseded 33 ALR2d 145 | Superseded 69 ALR2d 203 (civil liability) and 73 ALR2d 960 (criminal liability) | Superseded 39 ALR2d 209 |

This means that the Annotation in 15 *A.L.R.* 244 should be ignored and only the annotation in 32 *A.L.R.* 589 has to be read, and its pocket supplement checked for later cases.

## SECTION B.   FINDING A.L.R.   ANNOTATIONS

### 1.   Index Method.

Each of the four sets has a one-volume index entitled *Quick Index*. These are alphabetically arranged indexes to the annotations in the *A.L.R.* volumes, and are subdivided by topics and facts, and the annotations are listed by their titles.   Presently, the indexes available are as follows:

*Quick Index* to *A.L.R.* (1st Ser.) (1 vol.)

*Quick Index* to *A.L.R.*2d (1 vol.)

*Quick Index* to *A.L.R.*3d (presently kept inside front cover to
    *A.L.R.*2d *Quick Index* volume)

*Quick Index* to *A.L.R.*Fed. (1 vol.)[3]

The use of these indexes is shown in Illustration 23.

### 2.   Table of Cases.

An alphabetical listing of all cases reported in *A.L.R.* may be found in volume 12 of *A.L.R.* Permanent Digest and volume 7 of the *A.L.R.*2d Digest.   For *A.L.R.*3d and *A.L.R.*Fed. a cumulative List of Cases appears in the latest pocket supplement to the *Quick Index* for each set.

### 3.   Digest Method.

*A.L.R.* and *A.L.R.*2d were both provided with additional sets entitled *A.L.R.* Digests.   This is no longer provided for *A.L.R.*3d.   For use of *A.L.R.* Digests, see Pollack, Fundamentals of Legal Research. 3d ed. 1967 p. 132, *et seq.*

---

[3] This index is called Federal Quick Index to Total Client Service Library.   It indexes *A.L.R.*Fed. as well as all matter on federal law in the other sets of the Total Client Service Library.

## SECTION C. ILLUSTRATIONS

**Illustrative Problem on Use of A.L.R.**

Assume the following problem.

A, in walking to a supermarket enters its parking lot to reach the entrance. There had been considerable snow the previous week and the movement of automobiles in and out of the parking lot had created icy ruts on the ground. A slips on the ice and injures himself. He brings an action against the supermarket. Find A.L.R. annotation covering this fact situation.

### Illustrations

23. Quick Index.

24. Historical Table.

25. An A.L.R. Annotation.

26. A.L.R.3d Supplement.

27. A.L.R.2d Later Case Service.

28. A.L.R. (First) Blue Book of Supplemental Decisions.

## [Illustration 23]

## SAMPLE PAGE FROM AN A.L.R. QUICK INDEX

**Parent and Child**                                                        ALR2d

Will contest: authority of parent to make     Judicial notice of matters relating to public

W

> **NOTES:**
> 1. Cross reference to main index heading.
> 2. *Quick index* indexes under specific facts and under topic.
> 3. Under Main Index entry, title of annotation is given.

or operator for injury or death of patron, 67 ALR2d 965

#### PARENT CORPORATION

Income of subsidiary as taxable to it or to parent corporation, 10 ALR2d 576

#### PARI DELICTO

Purchaser's right to set up invalidity of contract because of violation of state securities regulation as affected by doctrines of estoppel or pari delicto, 84 ALR2d 479

#### 2. PARKING

Automobiles, see **Automobiles and Highway Traffic**

#### PARKING METERS

Installation or operation of parking meters as within governmental immunity from tort liability, 33 ALR2d 761

Permissible use of funds from parking meters, 83 ALR2d 625

Pledging parking-meter revenues as unlawful relinquishment of governmental power, 83 ALR2d 649

#### 1. PARKING STATIONS OR LOTS

See **Garages, Liveries, Parking and Filling Stations**

#### PARKS AND PLAYGROUNDS

Access: power of park commission to directly regulate or prohibit abutter's access to street or highway, 73 ALR2d 671

Baseball: liability of owner or operator of park or other premises on which baseball or other game is played, for injuries by ball to person on nearby street, sidewalk, or premises, 16 ALR2d 1458

Estate conveyed by deed for park or playground purposes, nature of, 15 ALR2d 975

#### PARKWAYS

Relative rights and liabilities of abutting owners and public authorities in parkways in center of street, 81 ALR2d 1436

#### PAROCHIAL SCHOOLS

See **Religion and Religious Matters**

#### 3. PAROL ACCEPTANCE

Statute of frauds, oral acceptance of written offer by party sought to be charged as satisfying, 30 ALR2d 972

#### PAROL CONTRACTS

Bids: rights of parties under oral agreement to buy or bid in land for another, 27 ALR2d 1285

Broker's right to commission where customer repudiates or fails to complete contract or promise which is oral or not specifically enforceable, 12 ALR2d 1410

Employment: admissibility of oral agreement respecting duration of employment or agency where written contract is silent, 85 ALR2d 1331

Question, as one of law for court or of fact for jury, whether oral promise was an original one or was a collateral promise to answer for the debt, default, or miscarriage of another, 20 ALR2d 246

Statute of frauds, see **Frauds, Statute of**

Time: admissibility of oral agreement as to specific time for performance where written contract is silent, 85 ALR2d 1269

Will: validity of oral promise or agreement not to revoke will, 29 ALR2d 1229

#### PAROLE

See **Pardon, Parole, or Probation**

544                    Consult POCKET PART for ALR3d annotations

[Illustration 23–a]

## SAMPLE PAGE FROM A.L.R. QUICK INDEX

---

Gambling                                                              ALR2d

---

> NOTES:
> 1. Under Main entry, annotations arranged by specific sub-
>    ject within entry.  Annotations for topic being searched will
>    be found under § 3.

---

Defense of person or property, right to kill game in, 93 ALR2d 1366

Entrapment with respect to violation of game laws, 75 ALR2d 709

Fish, see **Fish and Fisheries**

Forfeiture of property for unlawful use in violation of game laws, before trial of individual offender, 3 ALR2d 745

Possession of game, or of specified hunting equipment, prima facie evidence of viola-tion, 81 ALR2d 1093

Private grant or reservation to hunt on an-other's land, 49 ALR2d 1395

### GAMES

Generally, see **Amusements, Exhibitions, Shows, and Resorts**

Liability of employer for injury resulting from games or other recreational or social activities, 18 ALR2d 1372

### GARAGES, LIVERIES, PARKING AND FILLING STATIONS

1.
§ 1. Generally
§ 2. Compensation and charges and lien therefor
§ 3. Liability for injury, loss, or damage

---

### § 1. Generally.

Church parking lots as entitled to tax exemp-tions, 75 ALR2d 1106

Insurance—
automobile insurance, omnibus clause ex-ception relating to public garages, sales agencies, service stations, and the like, 47 ALR2d 556
construction and effect of clause in li-ability policy voiding policy while in-sured vehicles are being used more than a specified distance from principal garage, 29 ALR2d 514

Nuisances—
lights of gasoline stations or parking lots as actionable wrong to persons annoyed by, 5 ALR2d 710
parking lot or place as nuisance, 82 ALR 2d 413

Off-street public parking facilities, 8 ALR2d 373

Restrictive agreements or covenants—
purchase or handling of petroleum prod-ucts by operator of filling station, 26 ALR2d 219
use of premises for parking place as vio-lation of restrictive covenant, 80 ALR 2d 1258

Towing: regulation of vehicle wrecker or towing service business, 42 ALR2d 1208

Warranties in connection with leasing or hiring of motor vehicles, 68 ALR2d 850

Zoning, see **Zoning**

### § 2. Compensation and charges and lien therefor.

Price: validity and construction of statute or ordinance requiring or prohibiting post-ing or other publication of price of com-modity or services by automobile dealer or gasoline station or parking lot operator, 89 ALR2d 914, 949, 951

Priority as between lien for repairs and the like, and right of seller under conditional sales contract, 36 ALR2d 198

Storage: lien for storage of motor vehicle, 48 ALR2d 894

### § 3. Liability for injury, loss, or damage.

Attractive nuisance, filling and service sta-tion as, 23 ALR2d 1160

Bailment: liability of bailee for hire of au-tomobile for loss of, or damage to, con-tents, 27 ALR2d 796

---

**386**          Consult POCKET PART for ALR3d annotations

[Illustration 23–b]

## SAMPLE PAGE FROM A.L.R. QUICK INDEX

QUICK INDEX                                              **Gas**

Fire, liability of garageman, service or repair station, or filling station operator for destruction or damage of motor vehicle by, 16 ALR2d 799

Overhead door, liability of garage operator for injury to patron from, 83 ALR2d 750

Owner of motor vehicle as liable for negligence of garageman or mechanic, 35 ALR 2d 804

→Parking lot or station—
duty and liability of vehicle drivers within parking lot, 62 ALR2d 288

→liability of owner or operator of parking lot or station for personal injuries, 14 ALR2d 780

Proximate cause as affecting liability of garageman to one ordering repair of motor vehicle, for defective work, 93 ALR2d 1423

Repairs: liability of garageman to one ordering repair of motor vehicle for defective work, 92 ALR2d 1408

Servicing vehicle: liability of filling station operator, garageman, or the like, in connection with servicing vehicle with lubricants or fuel, 38 ALR2d 1453

Theft—
liability of garageman for theft or unauthorized use of motor vehicle, 43 ALR 2d 403
tort liability of garage keeper for theft by servant, 15 ALR2d 856

### GARBAGE

Regulation and licensing of private garage or rubbish removal services, 83 ALR2d 799

### "GARDEN-TYPE APARTMENTS"

Validity, construction, and effect of a zoning

Drilling or mining operations and leases, see **Mines and Minerals**

Natural gas: rights and liabilities with respect to natural gas reduced to possession and subsequently stored in natural reservoir, 94 ALR2d 543

Public utilities, generally, see **Public Utilities**

Special requirements of consumer as giving rise to implied contract by public utility to furnish particular amount of electricity, gas, or water, 13 ALR2d 1233

### § 2. Liability for injury or damage.

Attractive nuisance, gas tanks, pipes and pipelines, and apparatus and accessories thereof as constituting, 23 ALR2d 1157

Defects in service lines on consumer's premises, liability of gas company for injury or damage due to, 26 ALR2d 136

Discontinuing service to premises, duty of gas company as regards precautions to be taken upon or after, 13 ALR2d 1396

Escaping gas: liability of gas company for personal injury or property damage caused by gas escaping from mains in street, 96 ALR2d 1007

Excavator's liability for injury or damage resulting from explosion or fire caused by his damaging of gas mains and pipes, 53 ALR2d 1083

Exhaust fumes, see **Exhaust Fumes**

Exterminator's liability for personal injury or death as affected by contributory negligence, 73 ALR2d 1155

Landowner's or occupant's liability in damages for escape, without negligence, of harmful gases or fumes from premises, 54 ALR2d 764

Liquid or bottled gas, liability of one selling or distributing, for personal injury, death

NOTES:

Sub-entry under the main index terms leads to an annotation published in 14 ALR 2d 780 that appears to cover the topic being researched.

The next step before examining that volume is to check to see if this annotation has been supplemented or superseded.

See next Illustration.

## [Illustration 24]
## PAGE FROM A.L.R. HISTORICAL TABLE

### ALR3d

| | | |
|---|---|---|
| **2 ALR2d 1196–1227**<br>Supplemented 13 ALR2d 642 | **10 ALR2d 1059–1072**<br>Superseded 40 ALR3d 1222 | **17 ALR2d 1003–1007**<br>Superseded 43 ALR3d 699 |

> Illustration 23–b indicated that an Annotation on the subject under research can be located in 14 A.L.R.2d 780.
>
> The next step is to check this in the Historical Table which appears in the back of the Quick Index to A.L.R.3d.
>
> This refers to a superseding Annotation. It is now only necessary to read 38 A.L.R.3d 10.

| | | |
|---|---|---|
| **4 ALR2d 1253–1264**<br>Superseded 45 ALR3d 658 | **13 ALR2d 191–252**<br>Supplemented 58 ALR2d 865 | **19 ALR2d 1274–1297**<br>Superseded 40 ALR3d 864 |
| **5 ALR2d 1239–1247**<br>Supplemented 10 ALR2d 932 | **14 ALR2d 353–371 § 6**<br>Superseded 41 ALR3d 1021 | **20 ALR2d 95–111**<br>Superseded 38 ALR3d 363 |
| **6 ALR2d 492–503**<br>Superseded 92 ALR2d 598 | **14 ALR2d 750–774**<br>§ 14 superseded 23 ALR3d 865<br>§ 20 superseded 11 ALR3d 1296 | **20 ALR2d 235–240**<br>Superseded 39 ALR3d 1332 |
| **6 ALR2d 1367–1395**<br>Supplemented 26 ALR2d 1376 | ⟶ **14 ALR2d 780–806**<br>Superseded 38 ALR3d 10 and 38<br>⟶ ALR3d 138 | **21 ALR2d 220–238**<br>Superseded 12 ALR3d 56 |
| **7 ALR2d 276–288**<br>Superseded 46 ALR3d 7 | | **21 ALR2d 369–373**<br>Superseded 36 ALR3d 630 |
| **7 ALR2d 1074–1078**<br>Superseded 22 ALR3d 8 | **15 ALR2d 762–777**<br>Superseded 92 ALR2d 1180 | **22 ALR2d 1248–1260**<br>Superseded 96 ALR2d 973 |
| **8 ALR2d 433–435**<br>Superseded 30 ALR2d 366 | **16 ALR2d 3–390**<br>Superseded 11 ALR3d 9; 11 ALR3d<br>370; 12 ALR3d 117; 12 ALR3d 475 | **23 ALR2d 1105–1114**<br>Superseded 43 ALR3d 1120 |
| **8 ALR2d 614–617**<br>Superseded 12 ALR3d 56 | **16 ALR2d 393–458**<br>Superseded 11 ALR3d 9; 11 ALR3d<br>370; 12 ALR3d 117; 12 ALR3d 475 | **23 ALR2d 1378–1397**<br>Superseded 36 ALR3d 900 |
| **8 ALR2d 772–781**<br>Superseded 37 ALR3d 420 | **16 ALR2d 979–1014**<br>§ 8 superseded 43 ALR3d 930 | **24 ALR2d 579–611**<br>Superseded 46 ALR3d 578 |
| **8 ALR2d 862–878**<br>Superseded 46 ALR3d 801 | **16 ALR2d 1322–1328**<br>Superseded 24 ALR3d 1261 | **24 ALR2d 850–864**<br>Superseded 37 ALR3d 645 |
| **9 ALR2d 320–324**<br>Superseded 63 ALR2d 1393 | **17 ALR2d 888–895**<br>Superseded 41 ALR3d 782 | **25 ALR2d 1029–1030**<br>Superseded 29 ALR3d 766 |
| **10 ALR2d 214–216**<br>Superseded 13 ALR2d 713 | **17 ALR2d 913–922**<br>Superseded 44 ALR3d 862 | **25 ALR2d 1070–1071**<br>Superseded 93 ALR2d 1319 |
| **10 ALR2d 639–641**<br>Superseded 15 ALR3d 992 | **17 ALR2d 948–963**<br>Superseded by 44 ALR3d 555, 44<br>ALR3d 760 and 44 ALR3d 1243 | **27 ALR2d 946–948**<br>Superseded 40 ALR3d 1012 |

402

[Illustration 25]

## FIRST PAGE OF ANNOTATION OF 38 A.L.R.3d 10

> This is the first page of the Annotation for 38 A.L.R.3d 10.
> After the title of the Annotation, a detailed analysis of it is given.

### ANNOTATION

### LIABILITY OF OWNER OR OPERATOR OF PARKING LOT FOR PERSONAL INJURIES ALLEGEDLY RESULTING FROM CONDITION OF PREMISES

*by*

*Wade R. Habeeb, LL.B.*

### TOTAL CLIENT-SERVICE LIBRARY® REFERENCES

38 Am Jur 2d Garages, and Filling and Parking Stations §§ 81–107

9 Am Jur Pl & Pr Forms Garages, Parking Stations, and Filling Stations, Form 9:835.5

10 Am Jur Trials 255, Premises Liability—Trip and Fall

ALR Digests, Automobiles and Highway Traffic § 232

ALR Quick Index, Garages, Liveries, Parking and Filling Stations

**Consult POCKET PART in this volume for later case service**

[Illustration 25–a]

## PAGE FROM 38 A.L.R.3d—ANALYSIS OF ANNOTATION

> **Cases dealing with snow causing falls on parking lots are discussed at Paragraph 7 of the Annotation.**

## [Illustration 25-b]

## PAGE FROM 38 A.L.R.3d 10: INDEX TO ANNOTATION

---

38 ALR3d　　Negligence—Parking Lot—Conditions　　13
38 ALR3d 10

Boxes, fall over, § 10[a]

Bumpers, falls over, §§ 4[b], 13, 14, 20[a], 25

Business invitee or visitor, duty to, generally, §§ 3, 4

Canopy as contributing to snow and ice accumulation, § 7[b]

Cellar, fall into, §§ 11[a], 19[a]

Chain, fall over, §§ 5, 13[a], 20[b]

Children as invitees, § 4[b]

Cinder, fall on, § 10[a]

City, liability of, §§ 3[a], 11[a], 12[b]

Climate as factor, §§ 7[a], 15[a]

Collapse of sidewalk, § 6[b]

Color of obstruction as factor, §§ 9, 13[a], 20[a], 25[a]

Companions of invitee, status of and duty to, §§ 3-5, 7[c], 15[a]

Consortium, action for loss of, § 9[a]

Contest, injury to observer of, §§ 15[a], 26[a]

Contributory negligence, generally, §§ 17-26

Credibility, § 13[b]

Creek, drowning of boy in, §§ 3[b], 15[a]

Crowd and crowded condition as factor, §§ 4[a], 15[a], 25[a], 26[a]

Curb, fall over, §§ 4[a], 13[a], 20[a], 24[a], 25[a, b]

Dangerous or hazardous condition—
　injured party, knowledge or notice by, §§ 4[a], 7[a], 13[b], 15[b], 20[a], 26

Embankment, fall down, § 11[a]

Employee as invitee, § 4[a]

Experiment conducted by trial court during jury view, effect of, § 25[c]

Expert witnesses, §§ 13[a], 15[a]

→Falls, generally, §§ 7-26

Familiarity with premises as factor, §§ 19[a], 20[a], 25[b, c]

Family relationship as factor in status of companion to invitee, §§ 4[b], 7[c]

Federal Tort Claims Act, action under, § 7[c]

Fence.　Barriers, guard railings or fences, supra

Foot injury.　Leg or foot injury, infra

Foreseeability or probability of harm, §§ 7[a], 11[b], 13[a], 15[a]

Geographical extent of duty to invitee, § 3[b]

Glare of light as factor, § 25[b]

Golf shoes, injury incurred while wearing, §§ 15[a], 26[a]

Grass and weeds as affecting notice of danger, §§ 11[a], 20[a], 24[a]

Grating, injury due to stepping upon, § 26[a]

Gravel as cause of fall, §§ 6, 13[b], 23[a]

Grease or oil, fall due to, §§ 5, 6[b], 9, 10[a], 23[a]

Grease pit, fall into, §§ 3[c], 11[a], 19

Guards or attendants, absence of, §§ 11[a],

---

**Immediately following the Analysis there is a detailed subject index of all specific facts and topics covered by the Annotation.**

---

Debris or other foreign material, falls caused by, generally, §§ 9, 10, 18, 23

Depressions.　Holes, pits, excavations or dropoffs, infra

Dirt fill, injury due to, §§ 11[a], 12[b]

Dividers, ties or bumpers, falls over, §§ 4[b], 13, 14, 20[a], 25

Dog, tavern patron attacked by, § 3[c]

Door, fall over, § 25[a]

Downspout as cause of dangerous condition, §§ 7[b, c], 8[b]

Drainage pattern as factor, § 8[b]

Driveway, fall on, §§ 7[a], 11[a], 22[a]

Drowning, death by, §§ 3[b], 15[a]

Economic benefit theory, invitee under, § 4[a]

13[a]

Holes, pits, excavations or dropoffs—
　adjacent sidewalk, duty to persons on, § 6[b]
　falls, § 11
　　contributory negligence, §§ 19, 24
　　notice of condition by owner or operator, § 12
　invitees, duty to, §§ 3[c], 4[a]
　motor vehicle backing into, § 11[b]
　size as factor, § 12[b]

Hotel, fall by guest in, § 15[a]

Hydrant, ice accumulation due to leak in, § 6[a]

Ice cream, slipping on, § 10[a]

Illumination as factor, generally, §§ 17-21

[Illustration 25–c]

## FIRST PAGE OF TEXT OF ANNOTATION AT 38 A.L.R.3d 10

---

16               NEGLIGENCE—PARKING LOT—CONDITIONS               38 ALR3d
§ 1[a]                              38 ALR3d 10

| | |
|---|---|
| Or ------- §§ 7[a], 11[a], 22[a] | Utah ----- §§ 15[a], 16[a], 21, 22[a] |
| Pa ------- §§ 3[a, b], 4[b], 5, 7[c], 8 | Vt ------- § 3[c] |
|        [a, b], 11[a], 12[a], 13[a], | Va ------- §§ 3[a], 4[a], 7[c], 11[a], 12 |
|        15[a], 19[a], 20[a, b], 21, 22 |        [b], 13[a], 14[b], 20[a] |
|        [a], 26[a] | Wash ---- §§ 6[b], 13[b], 15[a], 23[a], 25 |
| RI ------- §§ 12[a], 13[a, b], 25[a] |        [c], 26[a] |
| SC ------- §§ 11[a], 12[b], 13[a, b], 20 | W Va ---- § 9[a] |
|        [a], 24[a] | Wis ------- §§ 3[b], 7[a–c], 8[a, b], 17[a], |
| Tenn ---- §§ 6[a], 11[a], 12[b], 24[a, b] |        22[c] |
| Tex ------ §§ 3[b], 4[b], 8[a], 10[a], 13 | Wyo ----- § 7[b] |
|        [a], 14[a], 15[a–c], 16[a] | |

---

### I. Introduction

### § 1. Prefatory matters

**[a] Scope**

This annotation[1] considers the nature and extent of the liability of the owner or operator[2] of a parking lot[3] to customers[4] or other members of the general public negligently[5] injured as the result of the condition of the premises.[6] The matter of contributory negligence and assumption of risk on the part of a person so injured is also treated.

Beyond the scope of the annotation is the liability, to employees, of owners or operators of facilities of the kind here considered, for personal injury on the premises,[7] as well as the liability of lessors to employees or business patrons of the tenant operator.[8]

---

1. It is no longer necessary to consult the annotation in 14 ALR2d 780 for cases within the scope of the present subject of annotation.

2. For purposes of this annotation it is assumed that the person against whom liability is asserted is the owner or operator of the parking lot involved. Cases involving merely a determination as to who is an owner or operator or who else may be liable are not included.

with a theater are included, cases involving drive-in theaters are excluded herefrom.

4. Liability of municipalities is covered only insofar as the ordinary rules of negligence are applicable, to the exclusion of questions of municipal tort immunity. In this regard, see the annotation in 8 ALR2d 373, entitled "Municipal establishment or operation of off-street public parking facilities."

5. Not considered are cases of intentional

---

Immediately preceding the beginning of the Annotation there is a Table listing all jurisdictions for which there have been cited cases within the Annotation. E. g., Rhode Island cases will be found cited at §§ 12a, 13a, b, 25a.

Also note how § 1 of the Annotation always outlines its scope.

---

Further, this annotation does not consider parking lots operated primarily for the benefit of a private business enterprise, such as the parking lot of a bus company or of a trucking company.

Although cases involving injuries sustained on a parking lot maintained in connection

7. See, in general, 53 Am Jur 2d, Master and Servant §§ 187 et seq.

8. See, in general, 49 Am Jur 2d, Landlord and Tenant § 780.

Landlord's liability to tenant's business

## [Illustration 25–d]

## SECOND PAGE OF TEXT OF ANNOTATION AT 38 A.L.R.3d 10

38 ALR3d     Negligence—Parking Lot—Conditions     17

38 ALR3d 10        § 2[a]

Further, this annotation does not purport to discuss liability for injury incurred on public sidewalks, public roadways, or other adjoining premises, except where those constituted joint approaches to the parking lot.

Statutory provisions affecting the subject matter of this annotation are treated herein only insofar as they are discussed in the reported cases, and this annotation does not purport to reflect the current statutory law of any jurisdiction. The reader is advised always to consult the statute of the jurisdiction in which he is interested.

#### [b] Related matters

Liability of owner or operator of parking lot for personal injuries caused by movement of vehicles. 38 ALR3d 138.

Premises liability: proceeding in the dark across exterior premises as contributory negligence. 23 ALR3d 441.

Premises liability: proceeding in the dark along outside path or walkway as contributory negligence. 22 ALR3d 599.

Premises liability: proceeding in the dark as contributory negligence. 22 ALR3d 286 (comment note).

Landlord's liability to tenant's business patron injured as a result of defective condition of premises. 17 ALR3d 422.

Liability of owner or operator of garage or gasoline filling station for bodily injury to nonemployees on premises. 8 ALR3d 6.

Liability for loss of or damage to automobile left in parking lot or garage. 7 ALR3d 927.

Liability of owner or operator of interior parking facility for bodily injuries to nonemployees on premises. 4 ALR3d 938.

Liability of owner or operator of shop-

ping center to patrons for injuries from defects or conditions in sidewalks, walks, or pedestrian passageways. 95 ALR2d 1341.

> § 1 also always indicates related Annotations.
>
> § 2 always gives a summary of the contents of the Annotation.

Liability of private owner or operator of picnic ground for injury or death of patron. 67 ALR2d 965.

Duty and liability of vehicle drivers within parking lot. 62 ALR2d 288.

Duty of a possessor of land to warn adult licensees of danger. 55 ALR2d 525 (comment note).

Child accompanying business visitor to store, shop, or the like, as invitee or licensee. 44 ALR2d 1319.

Status of injured party; modern status of rules conditioning owner's liability upon status of injured party as invitee, licensee, or trespasser. 32 ALR3d 508.

Liability of owner or operator of public gasoline filling station for injury to person or damage to property. 116 ALR 1205.

Cases from these earlier annotations which fall within the scope of the present annotation have been repeated herein.

#### § 2. Summary and comments

#### [a] Generally

It is a broad principle of the common law that as a general rule there is no liability for unintentional bodily injury unless it results from the breach of a duty owed to the person injured. The duty owed is recognized by the law as an obligation to comply with the particular standards of conduct toward the other person that the duty of due care imposes. In a given case, the nature of the standard of conduct thus required

patrons injured as a result of defective condition of premises. 17 ALR3d 422.

**[38 ALR3d]—2**

## [Illustration 25–e]

## PAGE FROM ANNOTATION OF 38 A.L.R.3d 10

---

38 ALR3d      Negligence—Parking Lot—Conditions     19
                        38 ALR3d 10              § 2[b]

tive" negligence.[20] In short, the operator

> **Practice Pointers is a new service that was started with A.L.R.3d. Its purpose is to alert the user to the procedural aspects involved in case.**
>
> **Note footnote references to the other sets of the Publishers.**

the business.[2]

The question whether particular acts or circumstances constitute negligence rendering the owner or operator of a parking lot liable to one injured as a result thereof has generally been held to be a fact question, except in those situations where the evidence is so strong one way or the other that a reasonable man could reach only one conclusion. And the same may be said as to the existence of contributory negligence.[3]

An issue of considerable importance in determining liability for injuries resulting from the condition of the premises is the question of notice, actual or constructive, since the owner or operator is liable for a condition arising without his fault only where he knew, or should have known, of it in time to take steps to protect his invitees, either by warning them or by correcting the condition.

Where constructive notice is relied upon, the question has frequently been held to be one of fact, the principal factors justifying a finding of constructive notice being the time the condition existed and its nature.[4]

### [b] Practice pointers

After having interviewed the client who was injured because of the condition of the parking lot and after having received from him all relevant information,[5] it is advisable for counsel to make, as soon as possible, a detailed examination of the scene of the accident[6] and to draw a diagram of the locality, with particular emphasis upon the exact place of the accident.[7] Not only will such a diagram, which, if possible, should be drawn to scale by a professional and qualified expert,[8] prove extremely useful for purposes of comparing and orienting the accounts of various witnesses and of revealing discrepancies or inaccuracies in their statements, but such diagram, after a proper foundation has been laid, may be used at the start of a witness' testimony to illustrate and explain the subject matter that might not otherwise be conveniently described.[9] Equally important as the making of a diagram as a part of the investigation of the accident is the taking of photographs of the place of the accident. It is advisable

---

20. § 5, infra.

1. § 5, infra.
Generally, regarding the duty of an owner or occupant of land as to licensees, see Am Jur, Negligence (1st ed § 104).

2. § 6, infra.

3. §§ 7 et seq., infra.

4. §§ 8, 10, 12, 14, 16, infra.

5. As to interviewing the client generally, see 1 Am Jur Trials 1, Interviewing the Client §§ 1 et seq.

6. As to visiting the scene of the injury in premises liability cases generally, see 10 Am Jur Trials 255, Premises Liability—Trip and Fall.

7. As to diagrams and drawings generally, see 29 Am Jur 2d, Evidence §§ 802 et seq. and see also 7 Am Jur Proof of Facts 601, Maps, Diagrams, and Models, Proofs 1 and 2.

8. 2 Am Jur Trials 293, Locating Scientific and Technical Experts.

9. Admissibility of maps, plats, or other drawings to illustrate verbal testimony. 9 ALR2d 1044.
As to proof of foundation for admission of a map or diagram, see 7 Am Jur Proof of Facts 601, Maps, Diagrams, and Models, Proof 1.

## [Illustration 25–f]

## PAGE FROM ANNOTATION AT 38 A.L.R.3d 10

36            NEGLIGENCE—PARKING LOT—CONDITIONS            38 ALR3d
§ 7[a]                  38 ALR3d 10

fendant's negligence was for the jury. The court stated that an abutting owner may become liable for injury to a pedestrian caused by a defect in the sidewalk, where he created the defective condition or where the manner in which the sidewalk was used for his own business or special purpose produced the

---

**The beginning of para. 7 wherein cases on "Falls caused by snow and ice" begin.**

**This Annotation contains 115 pages. The full Annotation should be examined in 38 A.L.R. 3d 10.**

**An Annotation may vary from one page to several hundred.**

---

ing a verdict against the lessor, but not the operator of the parking lot. Stating that the owner of property creating a potentially dangerous condition was liable to pedestrians injured as a result thereof, as would be a lessee taking possession and continuing the condition with notice thereof, the court sustained the verdict, adding that the lessor, as a joint tortfeasor, had no cause to complain because of the failure to find the lessee liable.

In James v Burchett (1942) 15 **Wash** 2d 119, 129 P2d 790, it was held that where the operators of a used-car lot used the abutting sidewalk as a driveway, the special use, though lawful, carried with it the duty to use reasonable care to see that the use did not create conditions rendering it unsafe for the passing thereon of pedestrians, so that a pedestrian who had been injured due to the presence of gravel from the lot on the sidewalk was entitled to recover against the defendants.

### III. What constitutes breach of duty with respect to particular causes of injury

### § 7. Falls caused by snow or ice

**[a] Finding of negligence held supported or supportable**

Where invitees sustained injuries as a result of falls caused by ice or snow on a parking lot, courts in a number of cases have determined the evidence to be sufficient to take to the jury the issue of the negligence of the owner or occupant, or to support findings of such negligence.[6]

In Kremer v Carr's Food Center, Inc. (1969, **Alaska**) 462 P2d 747, 38 ALR3d 1, it appeared that shortly before midnight the 66-year-old plaintiff walked to the defendant supermarket to purchase food; that in attempting to traverse the defendant's parking lot, he noticed an approaching vehicle and worried that the driver would not see him and stop; that the vehicle did stop and at approximately the same time the plaintiff slipped on an icy rut apparently created by the action of automobile tires on the ice during the day when the ice was in a melted condition; that the rut was 6 inches deep and was located about 10 feet from the main entrance to the supermarket; that the parking lot was not scraped, salted, or sanded; that the surface of the lot was "extremely slick" and at least one employee of the defendant had slipped on it that day; and that the plaintiff testified that he could distinguish the surface conditions of the lot because the area was lit, and that he knew the surface was icy but he had not seen the ruts in the ice before falling. Holding that the trial court erred in directing a verdict in favor of the defendant, the court stated that § 343 of the Restatement of Torts 2d was determinative, and that the jury could have

---

6. As to the condition of the adjacent sidewalk as negligence, resulting in injury to passers-by or persons casually thereon, see the cases discussed in § 6, supra.

[Illustration 25–g]

## PAGE FROM ANNOTATION AT 38 A.L.R.3d 10

38 ALR3d     Negligence—Parking Lot—Conditions     37
38 ALR3d 10     § 7[a]

found that the defendant possessed the parking lot and knew the conditions, that the defendant should have realized that this condition involved an unreasonable risk of harm to its business invitees, that the defendant should have expected that its business invitees would not discover or realize the danger, or should have anticipated that they would fail to protect themselves against a danger they did discover or realize, or should otherwise have anticipated harm to invitees despite the fact that the danger was known or obvious to them, and that the defendant failed to exercise reasonable care to protect business invitees from the dangerous surface conditions in the parking lot. Rejecting the contention that no cause of action could be maintained by a business invitee against a landowner for injury resulting from a slip and fall occasioned by natural accumulations of ice and snow, and the contention that the duty owed by the possessor to a business invitee was discharged by the invitee's knowledge of the dangerous condition, the court pointed out that the natural-unnatural accumulation of ice and snow rule has been limited to cases involving the duty owed by municipalities to licensees who, as a class, must take the condition of the land as the

despite the latter's personal knowledge of the dangerous snow and ice conditions or the general obviousness of such conditions.

In Palmer Park Gardens, Inc. v Potter (1967) 162 Colo 178, 425 P2d 268, where the plaintiff, intending to visit a tenant of an apartment house, parked her car in the apartment house parking lot, which was intended for the use of both the tenants and their guests, and in order to avoid alighting in slush or water due to an accumulation of snow on the driver's side, she got out of her automobile on the passenger side, where it was only 2 or 3 inches deep, and after taking a few steps she slipped and fell and was injured, and there was testimony that it had snowed a few days before the accident and that the sidewalks were cleared by the landlord's maintenance men, but they failed to clear the parking lot of snow on this occasion, although they customarily did so, it was held that the trial court did not err in submitting the issues to the jury, which found in favor of the plaintiff, in view of the fact that there was competent evidence substantiating the essential allegations of the complaint that the defendant had negligently and carelessly permitted ice and snow to accumulate

Continuation of Para. 7 of Annotation

vailed for many months throughout various locations in Alaska was not in and of itself sufficient rationale for the insulation of the possessor from liability to his business invitee; and that such climatic conditions did not negate the possibility that the possessor should have anticipated harm to the business invitee

the landlord-invitee relationship than on a municipal corporation with reference to the common use of its sidewalks, and that the landlord was subject to liability for harm to an invitee caused by the natural or artificial condition of his premises, if he knew or by the exercise of reasonable care should have known of

[Illustration 26]
TITLE PAGE TO SUPPLEMENT TO 38 A.L.R.3d

AMERICAN LAW REPORTS

# ALR 3d

· 1972

# SUPPLEMENT

---

### INSERT IN BACK OF VOLUME

## 38

ALR3d

---

> After reading the Annotation, a check should be made for later cases. When using A.L.R.3d, this is done by checking in the annual cumulative pocket supplement in the back of the volume. See next Illustration.

1972

THE LAWYERS CO-OPERATIVE PUBLISHING CO.
Rochester, New York 14603

BANCROFT-WHITNEY CO.
San Francisco, California 94107

[Illustration 26–a]

## PAGE FROM SUPPLEMENT TO 38 A.L.R.3d

# AMERICAN
# LAW REPORTS

### THIRD SERIES

#### 1972 Supplement

## VOLUME 38 ALR3d

### 38 ALR3d 10–124

§ 11   [38 ALR3d 59]

**[a] Finding of negligence held supported or supportable**

Jury could properly be permitted to find actionable negligence against parking lot owner for maintaining lot with deep hole which was filled or covered by natural accumulation of snow. Mikula v Tailors, 24 **Ohio** St 2d 48, 53 Ohio Ops 2d 40, 263 NE2d 316.

§ 15   [38 ALR3d 88]

**[a] Finding of negligence held supported or supportable**

Summary judgment should not have been granted in favor of city, owner of parking lot, since city could have been found guilty of actionable negligence in omitting danger signs and guardrails to warn of edge of lot near dropoff of several feet, in action by 74-year-old patron of lot. Harrigan v Reno, 86 **Nev** 678, 475 P2d 94.

§ 26   [38 ALR3d 122]

**[a] Finding of no contributory negligence or assumption of risk supported or supportable**

Summary judgment should not have been granted in favor of city, owner of parking lot, where question of fact existed with respect to alleged contributory negligence of 74-year-old patron who was blown from dropoff near edge of lot by high wind while attempting to retrieve parking ticket. Harrigan v Reno, 86 **Nev** 678, 475 P2d 94.

### 38 ALR3d 272–314

§ 15   [38 ALR3d 305]

**[a] Held relevant**

Allegations against doctor in malpractice suit, charging negligence as result of his having

> Note how the pocket supplement is keyed to the paragraph numbers of the main annotation.

prior action by purchaser under contract for sale of land, all damages growing out of seller's breach of contract were litigable in that action, and separate subsequent action to recover damages in nature of rent for period during which seller denied purchaser possession could not be maintained. Sechovec v Harms, 187 **Neb** 70, 187 NW2d 296.

### 38 ALR3d 363–411

§ 4   [38 ALR3d 373]

**[b] Plaintiff's own act as intervening cause**

Where 6-year-old boy tripped and fell into stacked beer cases in center of supermarket aisle, causing them to fall and injure him, and admitted that cases were not falling or moving before he ran into them, boy's collision with cases was proximate cause of his own injuries. Melton v Allied Supermarkets, Inc. **(Mo** App) 456 SW2d 644 (citing annotation).

§ 7   [38 ALR3d 392]

**[b] No negligence found**

Supermarket owner was not negligent, and directed verdict was properly granted in his favor, where he stacked 5 cases of bottled beer in center of aisle, in plain view, in abundance of light, leaving passageway of over 4 feet on either side, where stack was caused to fall by 6-year-old boy who tripped and fell into stack. Melton v Allied Supermarkets, Inc. **(Mo** App) 456 SW2d 644 (citing annotation).

Verdict was properly directed in favor of

3

## [Illustration 27]

# PAGE FROM A.L.R.2d LATER CASE SERVICE

543        LATER CASE SERVICE      **63 ALR2d 108–175**

### 63 ALR2d 108–175

*Liability for injury occasioned by backing of motor vehicle from private premises into public street or highway.*

**§ 1. Scope, p. 114.**

3 Am Jur Pl & Pr Forms, Automobiles and Highway Traffic, Forms 480, 481.

extremely careful, and if he is backing onto highway he must use an even higher degree of care. Morgan v Southern Farm Bureau Casualty Ins. Co. (DC La) 223 F Supp 996, affd (CA5) 339 F2d 755 (applying Louisiana law).

**[b] Right of way and lookout.**

Also recognizing duties of backing drivers:

**Iowa.**—Sayre v Andrews (Iowa) 146 NW2d 336 (duty to exercise high degree of care, keep proper lookout, stop, and yield right of way to approaching vehicles).

**La.**—State Farm Mut. Auto. Ins. Co. v C. & C. Oil Field Servicing Co. (La App) 168 So 2d 918 (statutory duty to yield right of way, and duty to exercise unusual degree of care); Deville v Aetna Ins. Co. (La App) 191 So 2d 324 (duty to exercise high degree of care, stop at curb or sidewalk, and yield right of way), writ refused 250 La 13, 193 So 2d 527.

**Miss.**—Baxter v Rounsaville (Miss) 193 So 2d 735 (statutory duty to yield right of way).

**Okla.**—Turner v Gallagher (Okla) 371 P2d 733 (duty to keep proper lookout while

**§ 3. Generally; lookout and right of way, p. 116.**

**[a] Generally.**

Automobile operator who drives from private driveway onto highway must be imposed upon backing motorist; remaining half of duty is to maintain proper lookout during continuing maneuver. Smith v Hearn (La App) 181 So 2d 433.

**§ 4. Warning signals; lights, p. 120.**

Also recognizing duty to signal or to warn of presence:

**Ky.**—Nolan v Nally (Ky) 342 SW2d 400 (duty to warn that truck backed across highway at night near curve was blocking road).

**§ 5. In general; action against owner or operator of backing vehicle, p. 122.**

**[b] Questions of negligence of one responsible for backing automobile.**

In action for injuries to plaintiff when car she was driving was struck by defendant's car, being backed from private driveway into street, evidence supported finding that defendant's negligence proximately caused accident, and that plaintiff was not contributorily negligent. Alessi v Farkas (Fla App) 118 So 2d 658.

Where plaintiffs, motorist and passenger, testified that defendant backing from driveway at night had stopped car with its

When using an Annotation in A.L.R.2d a different method of locating later cases must be used as A.L.R.2d did not use pocket supplements. Rather, a separate 11 volume set called *A.L.R.2d Later Case Service* is provided. The citation of the A.L.R.2d Annotation should be checked in this set. While not shown in this Illustration, the pocket supplement to *A.L.R.2d Later Case Service* must also be checked.

**[Illustration 28]**

## EXCERPTS FROM A.L.R. BLUE BOOK OF SUPPLEMENTAL
## DECISIONS

| VOL. 1 | VOL. 3 | LATEST PAM. SUPPL. |
|---|---|---|
| **117 A.L.R. 606–639.**<br>Richardson v. D. (Ala.) 187 So. 176.<br>Norgard v. N. 54 CalApp(2d) 82, 128 P(2d) 566.<br>Morrison v. N. 311 IllApp 411, 36 NE(2d) 581.<br>Loeser v. S. (Ind) 39 NE(2d) 945.<br>Re Gollobit (Iowa) 3 NW(2d) 191.<br>Crawford v. C. (Iowa) 15 NW (2d) 633.<br>Re Stephenson (Iowa) 14 NW (2d) 684.<br>Simpson v. S. 276 Ky. 223, 123 S.W.(2d) 816.<br>Leitner v. G. (Ky) 177 SW (2d) 903.<br>Re Boese (Minn) 7 NW(2d) 355. | **117 ALR 583–599**<br>General Motors Acceptance Corp. v M. (Kan) 311 P2d 339.<br><br>**117 ALR 606–639**<br>Berendsen v. Mcl. 126 Cal App2d 347, 272 P2d 76.<br>Seeba v. B. (Fla) 86 So2d 432.<br>Fuller v F. (Ga) 97 SE2d 306.<br>Hays v I. I. H. (Ill) 147 NE2d 287.<br>Re Guardianship of Anderson (Iowa) 78 NW2d 788.<br>Reidinger v. A. (Mo) 266 SW2d 610.<br>Grimm v G. (Mo) 303 SW2d 43.<br>Ellison v. S. (ND) 62 NW2d 95.<br>Theadgill v A. (Okla) 303 P2d 297.<br>Chandler v W. (Tex) 294 SW2d 801.<br>Leach v C. E. (Tex Civ App) 279 SW2d 630.<br>Chandler v W. (Tex Civ App) 282 SW2d 940<br>Chamberlain v R. (Tex Civ App) 305 SW2d 817. | **117 ALR 470–484**<br>Supplemented 168 ALR 581+<br><br>**117 ALR 496–498**<br>Superseded 95 ALR2d 585+<br><br>**117 ALR 522–538**<br>Mo.—Swiastyn v S. J. L. & P. Co. (App) 459 SW2d 24 (citing anno)<br><br>**117 ALR 563–565**<br>Superseded 53 ALR2d 224+<br><br>**117 ALR 571–572**<br>U. S.—Doyle v N. J. Const. Co. (CA Wis) 382 F2d 735<br><br>**117 ALR 606–639**<br>Fla.—Roberts v B. (App) 201 So 2d 811<br>S. C.—Havird v S. 166 SE2d 801<br>Tex.—Gibson v A. (Civ App) 463 SW2d 277 |

| VOL. 2 | VOL. 4 | |
|---|---|---|
| **117 ALR 606–639**<br>Livingston v. P. (Ala) 57 So2d 521.<br>Cross v. P. (Ark) 221 SW2d 24.<br>Guyot v. F. (Ark) 243 SW2d 639.<br>Black v. B. 91 Cal App2d 328, 204 P2d 950<br>Johnson v. B. (Ga App) 67 SE2d 189.<br>Re Conner's Estate (Iowa) 36 NW2d 833.<br>Boggess v. C. E. (Mo App) 207 SW2d 814.<br>Re Haas' Estate, 10 NJ Super 581, 77 A2d 523.<br>Santos v. M. (Tex Civ App) 195 SW2d 927.<br>Logan v. T. (Tex Civ App) 199 SW2d 210. error granted. | **117 ALR 606–639**<br>Ala.—Taylor v F. N. B. 189 So 2d 141<br>Alaska—Re Hewett's Estate. 358 P2d 579<br>Ky.—Cook v B. 346 SW2d 725<br>Neb.—Olsen v B. 92 NW2d 531<br>N. J.—Moss v G. (Co) 146 A2d 227 .<br>N. Y.—Lindsay v L. 22 Misc 2d 1071, 203 NYS2d 705<br>Tex.—Connor v P. (Civ App) 360 SW2d 438<br><br>**117 ALR 649**<br>Superseded 130 ALR 272+ | Note how A.L.R. Blue Book of Supplemental Decisions also indicates when an Annotation has been supplemented or superseded. It is simpler to use the *Historical Table*. |

After using an Annotation in A.L.R. (First Series), later cases may be found in the A.L.R. Blue Book of Supplemental Decisions. There are four Blue Books that contain references decided after the original annotation was written. Vol. 1 covers 1919–46; Vol. 2, 1946–52; Vol. 3, 1953–58; Vol. 4, 1959–67. A semi-annual pamphlet lists citations since 1967.

## SECTION D.  METHODS OF CITATIONS

The *American Law Reports* are generally not cited as parallel citations of case reports.  However, when cited for that purpose, the form and the order of citation are as follows:

New Mexico v. Martinez, 48 N.M. 232, 149 P.2d 124, 155 *A.L.R.* 811 (1944)

Hardy v. Plaisted, 109 N.H. 428, 456 A.2d 642, 38 *A.L.R.*3d 799 (1971)

The annotated reports are more often cited for their annotations than for their case reports.  Then the citation is to the page where the annotation begins and possibly to an appropriate page reference in the annotation.

Hardy v. Plaisted, 109 N.H. 428, 256 A.2d 642 (1971)
See Annotation, 38 A.L.R.3d 799 (1971)

---

## SECTION E.  SUMMARY

*A.L.R.* may be used to locate court decisions on a topic of law. If, through its indexes, an *A.L.R.* annotation is located, it will cite all previous court decisions on the topic, and the up-keep services provided will locate cases subsequent in time to the writing of the *A.L.R.* annotation.

It is important to keep in mind that *A.L.R.* is primarily a *case finding tool* and all decisions located through its use should be read.

### Summary of Finding A.L.R. Annotations

Step 1.  Start search in *Quick Index* to A.L.R.3d.

(a.)  If reference in index to an appropriate annotation is located, proceed to Step 2; if not:

(1)  search *Quick Index* to A.L.R.2d; if reference located, proceed to Step 2, if not,

(2)  search Index to *A.L.R.* (1st); if applicable reference found, proceed to Step 2, if not:

(a)  subject being researched probably not covered by *A.L.R.*; start search for cases using other techniques outlined in Ch. 21.

**Step 2.** Check *Historical Table* in Pocket *Supplement in Quick Index to A.L.R.*2d to determine if annotation(s) located through Step 1 have been *superseded* or *supplemented*:

  (a) If superseded, note superseding annotation, ignore original, and proceed to Step 3;

  (b) if supplemented, note supplementary annotation and proceed to Step 3;

  (c) if annotation not listed in *Historical Table,* proceed to Step 3.

**Step 3.** Read annotation(s) found through Steps 1 and 2.

  After reading annotation(s) check for later cases in:

  (a) if *A.L.R.* (1st) annotation in *A.L.R. Blue Book of Supplemental Decisions;*

  (b) If *A.L.R.*2d annotation in *Later Case Service to A.L.R.*2d;

  (c) if *A.L.R.*3d annotation in pocket supplement to *A.L.R.*3d volume.

Other methods of locating *A.L.R.* annotations will be discussed in Chapters 14 and 15.

# Chapter 8

# CONSTITUTIONS

A study of American legal sources emphasizes the constitutions of the federal and state governments since they, as law, are supreme.

## SECTION A.  FEDERAL CONSTITUTION: RESEARCH PUBLICATIONS

### 1.  The Federal Constitution

Our federal organic system stems from the Declaration of Independence.  It can be located in numerous publications.  Generally, it is included in all federal and state codes, most municipal codes and in many treatises and pamphlets.

The Articles of Confederation followed in 1777.  It usually is found with the Declaration of Independence and the Constitution.

The third federal document of note is the Ordinance of 1787: the Northwest Territorial Government.  The Ordinance is located with the preceding documents.

Finally, on September 17, 1787, the Constitution of the United States as engrossed and agreed upon was signed by a majority of the members of the Convention.  March 4, 1789, was the day which had been set for beginning the operations of the Government under the new Constitution, after ratification by the states.  The text of the Constitution can be found in the various federal, state and city codes, treatises, pamphlets and other publications.

These official documents, for the most part, are included in the following basic sources:

United States Code.

United States Code Annotated.

United States Code Service-F.C.A.

United States Supreme Court Reports Digest.  (Lawyers Co-op Pub. Co.)

Library of Congress, Constitution of the United States of America (1964).

## 2. The Interpretation of the Constitution: Historical Sources

It is the interpretation of the Constitution which gives rise to most of the problems concerning it. Since the formation of our government many opinions as to the meaning of the provisions of the Constitution have been rendered. Our chief concern, therefore, is to become familiar with the sources of those interpretations. This may be done in three ways: (1) study the historical sources or the background and the records of the Constitutional Convention, (2) study the interpretations of the Constitutional provisions by the courts and (3) study the textbooks, commentaries, periodical literature and encyclopedias.

As to the historical method, the source material may be found in the following:

a. *Madison, James. The papers of James Madison,* being his correspondence and reports of debates during the Congress of the Federation and his reports of debates in the Federal Convention. Now published from the original manuscripts deposited in the Department of State, by direction of the Joint Library Committee of Congress, under the superintendence of Henry D. Gilpin. Washington, Langtree and O'Sullivan, 1840. 2 vols.

b. *Elliott, Jonathan. The debates in the several State conventions on the adoption of the Federal Constitution together with the journal of the Federal convention.* Philadelphia, J. B. Lippincott Co., 1937. 4 vols. Supplement, vol. 5: Debates on the adoption of the Federal constitution in the convention held at Philadelphia in 1787. Philadelphia, J. B. Lippincott Co., 1937. (Pages 123–565, Madison papers revised and newly arranged.)

c. *The Federalist:* a commentary on the Constitution of the United States, by Alexander Hamilton, James Madison and John Jay. Edited by Paul Leicester Ford. New York, H. Holt and Co., 1898. 793 p. (This is one of several editions.)

d. *U. S. Bureau of Rolls and Library of the Department of State. Documentary history of the Constitution of the United States of America, 1786–1870.* Derived from the records, manuscripts and rolls deposited in the Bureau of Rolls and Library, Washington, Gov't Printing Office, 1894–1905. 5 vols.

e. *Farrand, Max. The records of the Federal convention of 1787.* New Haven, Yale University Press, 1934–1937, 4 vols.

f. *U. S. Library of Congress. Legislative Reference Service. Documents illustrative of the formation of the union of the American states,* Washington, Gov't Printing Office, 1927, 1115 p. (House Doc. 398, 69th Cong., 1st Sess.)

Although no official records were taken at the Constitutional Convention and the sessions were secret, James Madison's notes of the Convention were copious and the most accurate of all the recordings.

### 3. Judicial Interpretation: Annotated Editions of the Federal Constitution

The second method which may be used to determine the meaning of the United States Constitution, requires a search for the interpretations of constitutional provisions by the courts.

One source is the annotated constitution. An annotated constitution refers to the publication of the constitution with notes following each clause and section making specific reference to citations of court decisions in point. Some annotations give brief digest paragraphs, thus noting the nature of the decisions. Others merely provide the citations to the cases which interpret the provisions.

### a. United States Code Annotated. Constitution of the United States

This separate unit of the *United States Code Annotated* consists of ten unnumbered volumes, including a separate index to the Constitution. The annotations cover federal and state court decisions and opinions of the Attorney General which have interpreted the constitutional provisions, and the volumes are kept current by pocket and pamphlet supplements. The topical headings in the index (do not confuse the index to the Constitution with the general index to the statutes in U.S.C.A.) relate to the text of the Constitution and do not cover the substance of the cases. However, subject analyses, preceding the digests of cases under the provisions, relate to the decisions and are provided when the cases are numerous.

The Index and Topic Methods may be used in examining the annotated constitutions. This can be illustrated by a simple problem. Does a state have authority to seize property of a foreign power as a pledge (letters of marque)?

To use the Index Method, consult the index to the Constitution in U.S.C.A. under:

**Letters**

Marque and reprisal

      *   *   *

    States, prohibited from issuing, Art. 1, § 10, cl. 1

The index reference is to the applicable provision of the Constitution. Refer to the appropriate constitution volume, under art. 1, sec. 10, cl. 1. The "Notes of Decisions," following the text of the section of the Constitution, should then be consulted, for the index only covers the text of the Constitution and does not analyze case interpretations. The pertinent note is "2. Letters of marque and reprisal." A digested case in point appears under this heading. (See Illustration 29, below.)

The Topic Method applies the same procedure as above except for the use of the index. Under the Topic Method, the researcher must be sufficiently familiar with the Constitution to consult its text directly without the aid of an index.

b. Federal Code Annotated.[1] Constitution

The Constitution and annotations are included in two unnumbered volumes of this set which are kept up-to-date by pocket and pamphlet supplements. The annotations, as in the case of the U.S. C.A., relate to decisions of the federal and state tribunals and opinions of the Attorney General. Preceding the annotations, under each extensively interpreted clause or section, is a subject analysis to aid in the use of the annotations. The index is to the provisions of the Constitution and does not cover the substance of the cases which interpret the document. The index to the Constitution is printed at the end of each volume of the Constitution.

The letters of marque problem, discussed in connection with the use of the Constitution volumes of U.S.C.A., can be approached in a similar manner through the *Federal Code Annotated.* [See illustration 30]

c. Library of Congress. Constitution of the United States of America (1964)

This edition,[2] edited by the Library of Congress, was preceded by several earlier publications. As a one-volume edition, it attempts the difficult task of balancing an adequate annotated coverage against the desire for a compact ready-reference manual. To achieve this objective, the annotations relate to only selected decisions of the Supreme Court of the United States. But to give fuller understanding to the document, proceedings of the Convention which framed the Constitution, the views of dissenting Justices and those of writers, other documents and commentary are included. The annotations

---

[1] The F.C.A. was previously published by the Bobbs-Merrill Company. It has recently been taken over by the Lawyers Cooperative Publishing Co. They are now in the process of issuing revised volumes, but it will be several years before this is completed. As new volumes are issued, they are called United States Code Service (U.S.C.S.).

[2] In 1970 Congress passed Public Law 91–589, which directs the preparation of a new edition of the Constitution of the United States of America: Analysis and Interpretation. The Library of the Congress has announced that this new edition will be available from the United States Government Printing Office during 1973.

cover only significant Supreme Court cases, omitting those which merely support the main decisions and do not contain doctrinal novelties. A table of contents precedes each article and amendment of the Constitution. The index to this edition partially retains the earlier desirable feature of analyzing the subject matter of the annotated materials as well as the Constitution. No provision is made for keeping this publication up-to-date. The annotations are to cases decided by the Supreme Court to June 22, 1964.

The volume contains the following useful lists:

(1) Proposed amendments not ratified by the States.

(2) Acts of Congress held unconstitutional in whole or in part by the Supreme Court of the United States.

(3) State constitutional and statutory provisions and municipal ordinances held unconstitutional on their face or as administered.

(4) Supreme Court decisions overruled by subsequent decision.

d. United States Supreme Court Reports Digest (Lawyers Co-op. Pub. Co.)

Volume 17 of this digest, covering the Constitution and court rules, gives the text of the Constitution and references under its provisions to related sections in the Digest. A Table of Constitutional Provisions with citations to decisions of the Supreme Court of the United States which construe them is published in volume 14 of the Digest. These volumes are kept current by pocket supplements.

e. Digests

The following digests of federal cases provide additional judicial interpretations to the Constitution. These publications are discussed in detail in Chapter 6.

United States Supreme Court Reports Digest (Lawyers Co-op. Pub. Co.).

United States Supreme Court Digest (West Pub. Co.).

Federal Digest and Modern Federal Practice Digest.

f. Encyclopedias

The general legal encyclopedias *(American Jurisprudence 2d* or *Corpus Juris Secundum)* may treat the topic and provide references to pertinent cases. This is frequently a good starting point. The use of encyclopedias is described in Chapter 13.

g. Annotations

The annotations in the *American Law Reports* and the *U. S. Supreme Court Reports (L.Ed.)* may contain discussion, with case analysis, on a phase of the Constitution which is being studied.

## 4. Treatises and Periodical Literature

The third method of finding interpretations to the provisions of the Constitution is through the commentaries of legal writers in treatises and periodicals. A listing of such publications here would be disproportionately long and would have little immediate value. However, a few of the more significant books in the field, including several recent publications which have generated more than the usual comments, are given below. However, an acknowledged weakness of the treatise in constitutional law is the amorphous and fluid nature of the subject matter. This evanescent character is irreconcilable with the fixity of formalized textual projection.

Antieau, Chester J. Modern constitutions. 1969. 2 vols.

Cooley, Thomas M. Constitutional Limitations. 8th ed. 1927. 2 vols.

Crosskey, William W. Politics and the Constitution in the History of the United States. 1953. 2 vols.

Forkosch, Morris D. Constitutional Law. 1963. 1 vol.

Schwartz, Bernard. A Commentary on the Constitution of the United States. 1963–68. 5 vols.

Story, Joseph. Commentaries on the Constitution. 5th ed. 1891. 2 vols.

For more detailed listings of treatises see:

New York University School of Law Library, *A Catalogue of the Law Collection at New York University (1953).*

Jacobstein and Pimsleur, *Law Books in Print,* and *Association of American Law Schools, Law Books Recommended for Libraries.* v. 2. *Constitutional Law.* 1968.

For periodical articles on constitutional law, consult the *Index to Legal Periodicals.* (See Chapter 16). An annual publication of note, devoted primarily to the topic, is *The Supreme Court Review.*

## 5. Amending the Federal Constitution

Amendments to the Constitution may be proposed: (1) on the initiative of Congress by two-thirds vote in each house, or (2) by convention on application of two-thirds of the state legislatures.

The 26 amendments, thus far adopted, originated with Congress. The text of the amendments, except for the earlier adoptions, were published in the *Statutes at Large* after passage by the two Houses. At the discretion of Congress, ratification may be by the legislatures or conventions in three-fourths of the states. Only the 21st Amendment, repealing the prohibition amendment, was ratified by state conventions. After ratification by three-fourths of the states, the General Services Administrator, pursuant to Reorganization Plan No. 20 (1950), publishes a certification to that effect in the Federal Register.

Two government publications provide information as to unratified and proposed amendments to the Constitution. They are:

    a.  The United States Constitution; text with analytical index; unratified amendments. Washington, Government Printing Office, 1972. 91st Cong., 2nd Sess. House Doc. No. 92–157.)

    b.  United States Congress. Senate Library. Proposed Amendments to the Constitution * * * 69th Congress, 2d Session through the 87th Congress, 2d Session, December 6, 1926 to January 3, 1963. Washington, Government Printing Office, 1963. (87th Cong., 2d Sess., Senate Doc. No. 163.)

It lists the proposed amendments to the Federal Constitution, 1926–1963, by Congresses and item numbers, with the Senate Joint Resolutions, preceding those of the House. The pamphlet contains a brief discussion of each of the five amendments which have not been ratified by the required three-fourths of the states (Appendix B). The action on the bills or resolutions by either or both Houses is noted in the legislative histories listed in Appendix C. It has author and subject indexes.

This has been supplemented by S. Doc. 91–38 (1969) and covers the period January 9, 1965, through January 3, 1969.

    c.  Library of Congress. Constitution of the United States of America (1964).

This publication contains a list of proposed amendments not ratified by the States.

    d.  Since 1950, the Senate Committee on the Judiciary has issued a report each year by its Subcommittee on Constitutional Amendments which is authorized to make a complete study of any and all matters pertaining to Constitutional Amendments pending before Congress during the year. See, e. g., Sen.Rep. No. 92–501.

## 6. Popular Names

Popular names by which provisions of the United States Constitution have been referred to are noted in *Shepard's Federal and State Acts and Cases by Popular Names, 1968.* It is kept up-to-date by a cumulative pamphlet supplement.

## SECTION B.  ILLUSTRATIONS

**29.  Page from United States Code Annotated.**

**30.  Page from United States Code Service, F.C.A. Edition.**

[Illustration 29]

### EXCERPTS FROM A PAGE OF THE CONSTITUTION OF THE U.S. ANNOTATED U.S.C.A.

TREATIES, LETTERS OF MARQUE AND REPRISAL    Art. 1, § 10

### ARTICLE I—THE CONGRESS

Sections 1–9.  See volume containing Art. 1, § 1 et seq.

Section 10.  [1] No State shall enter into any Treaty, Alliance, or Confederation; grant Letters of Marque and Reprisal; coin Money; ←1 emit Bills of Credit; make any Thing but gold and silver Coin a Tender in Payment of Debts; pass any Bill of Attainder, ex post facto Law, or Law impairing the Obligation of Contracts, or grant any Title of Nobility.

[2] No State shall, without the Consent of the Congress, lay any Imposts or Duties on Imports or Exports, except what may be absolutely

\* \* \*

Section 10.  Treaties, letters of marque and reprisal

[1] No State shall enter into any Treaty, Alliance, or Confederation; ←1 grant Letters of Marque and Reprisal; \* \* \*

#### Notes of Decisions

Confederate States  4, 5
  Obligations as unlawful  5
2 →Letters of marque and reprisal  2
Power of Congress, generally  1
State laws, city ordinances, effect  6
Treaties  3

Congress.  Barron v. Baltimore, Md.1833, 7 Pet. 249, 8 L.Ed. 672.

**3.  Treaties**

No power under the government can make "any treaty, alliance, or confederation," entered into by a state, valid, or dispense with the constitutional prohibi-

1.  Complete text of Section.
2.  Topic analysis of cases.
3.  Relevant cases digested under Topic.

treatment.  Howell v. Port of New York Authority, D.C.N.J.1940, 34 F.Supp. 797.

3 →2.  Letters of marque and reprisal

To grant letters of marque and reprisal would lead directly to war, the power of declaring which is expressly given to

stitutions are in express terms subordinated.  In re Tiburcio Parrott, C.C. Cal.1880, 1 F. 481, 501.

**4.  Confederate States**

By reason of this clause the confederation formed by Virginia and other states,

3

[Illustration 30]

## EXCERPTS FROM THE CONSTITUTION OF THE U. S. ANNOTATED F. C. A.

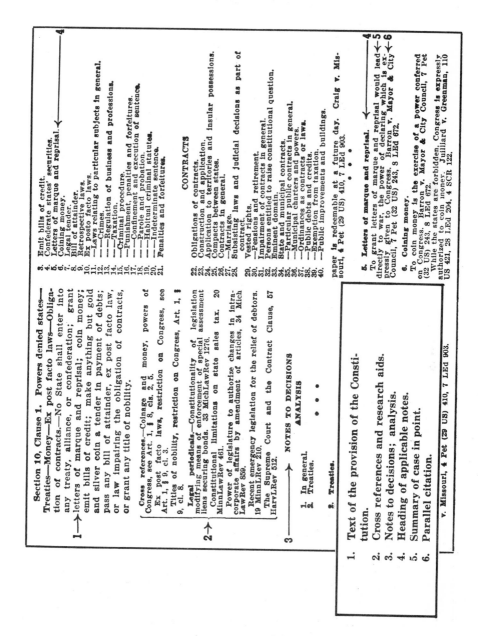

Section 10, Clause 1. Powers denied states—Treaties—Money—Ex post facto laws—Obligation of contracts.—No State shall enter into any treaty, alliance, or confederation; grant letters of marque and reprisal; coin money; emit bills of credit; make anything but gold and silver coin a tender in payment of debts; pass any bill of attainder, ex post facto law, or law impairing the obligation of contracts, or grant any title of nobility.

Cross references.—Coinage and money, powers of Congress, see Art. 1, § 8, cls. 2, 5.
Ex post facto laws, restriction on Congress, see Art. 1, § 9, cl. 3.
Titles of nobility, restriction on Congress, Art. 1, § 9, cl. 8.

Legal periodicals.—Constitutionality of legislation modifying means of enforcement of special assessment liens securing bonds. 33 MichLawRev 1276.
Constitutional limitations on state sales tax. 20 MinnLawRev 461.
Power of legislature to authorize changes in intra-corporate affairs by amendment of articles, 34 Mich LawRev 859.
Recent emergency legislation for the relief of debtors. 19 MinnLRev 210.
The Supreme Court and the Contract Clause, 57 HarvLRev 512.

NOTES TO DECISIONS

ANALYSIS

* * *

1. In general.
2. Treaties.

* * *

3. Treaties.

v. Missouri, 4 Pet (29 US) 410, 7 LEd 903.

3. Emit bills of credit.
4. Confederate states' securities.
5. Letters of marque and reprisal.
6. Coining money.
7. Legal tender.
8. Bill of attainder.
9. Retrospective laws.
10. Ex post facto laws.
11. —Laws relating to particular subjects in general.
12. —Crimes.
13. —Regulation of business and professions.
14. —Taxation.
15. —Criminal procedure.
16. —Punishment, penalties and forfeitures.
17. —Confinement and execution of sentence.
18. —Parole and probation.
19. —Habitual criminal statutes.
20. —Indeterminate sentence.
21. Penalties and forfeitures.

CONTRACTS

22. Obligations of contracts.
23. Construction and application.
24. Application to territories and insular possessions.
25. Compacts between states.
26. Contracts in general.
27. —Marriage.
28. Subsisting laws and judicial decisions as part of contract.
29. Vested rights.
30. —Pensions and retirement.
31. Impairment of contracts in general.
32. Persons entitled to raise constitutional question.
33. Eminent domain.
34. State and municipal contracts.
35. —Particular public contracts in general.
36. —Municipal charters and powers.
37. —Ordinances as contracts or laws.
38. —Public debts and credits.
39. —Exemption from taxation.
40. —Public improvements and buildings.

paper is redeemable at a future day. Craig v. Missouri, 4 Pet (29 US) 410, 7 LEd 903.

* * *

5. Letters of marque and reprisal.
To grant letters of marque and reprisal would lead directly to war, the power of declaring which is expressly given to Congress. Barron v. Mayor & City Council, 7 Pet (32 US) 243, 8 LEd 672.

6. Coining money.
To coin money is the exercise of a power conferred on Congress. Barron v. Mayor & City Council, 7 Pet (32 US) 243, 8 LEd 672.
While the states are forbidden, Congress is expressly authorized to coin money. Juilliard v. Greenman, 110 US 421, 28 LEd 204, 4 SCR 122.

1. Text of the provision of the Constitution.
2. Cross references and research aids.
3. Notes to decisions; analysis.
4. Heading of applicable notes.
5. Summary of case in point.
6. Parallel citation.

## SECTION C. FEDERAL CONSTITUTION: RESEARCH PROCEDURE FOR JUDICIAL INTERPRETATIONS

1. Treatises and legal encyclopedias *(Corpus Juris Secundum or American Jurisprudence 2d)*[3] may be consulted early in the research for general discussions on the subject. The periodical literature[4] provides more detailed subject studies. The *Index to Legal Periodicals* should be checked for appropriate articles. These discussions may also reveal cases in point or a useful theory applicable to the problem under consideration.

2. An applicable annotation may be included in the *American Law Reports* or the *U. S. Supreme Court Reports (L.Ed.)*.

A convenient ready-reference to A.L.R. annotations and to periodical articles relating to the Federal Constitution may be found in the *Michigan Statutes Annotated*, 1965 Revision of Volume 1. These annotations and periodical articles follow the text of the articles and sections of the Constitution.

3. The *United States Code Annotated* and the *United States Code Service-F.C.A. Edition* are most frequently consulted for the text and the judicial interpretations to the Constitution. Refer to the pocket and pamphlet supplements for recent material. The *Library of Congress Edition* may also be consulted.

Since the indexes to the annotated Constitutions do not provide comprehensive fact-analyses of cases, a modified topic or analytic method is generally used to ascertain cases in point for the indexes are consulted topically rather than factually.

The analyses preceding the Notes to Decisions to the Constitution in U.S.C.A. and F.C.A. are helpful in locating judicial interpretations.

4. Check the following digests, using the Index, Topic or Case Methods:

U. S. Supreme Court Reports Digest (Lawyers Co-op. Pub. Co.). If the specific provision of the Constitution is known, consult the Constitution Volume (Vol. 17) of the Digest for references under that provision to the related section of the Digest.

U. S. Supreme Court Digest (West Pub. Co.).

Federal Digest and Modern Federal Practice Digest.

[3] Chapter 15.

[4] Chapter 16.

5.   The Constitution Table in volume 14 of the *U. S. Supreme Court Reports Digest* (Lawyers Co-op. Pub. Co.) provides citations to the Supreme Court decisions under the sections of the Constitution.

6.   Shepardize[5] the provision of the Constitution, using *Shepard's United States Citations* and *Shepard's state citations*. Shepardize cases in point, after they have been located, in the *Shepard's United States Citations, Shepard's Federal Reporter Citations* and appropriate *state citations*.

---

## SECTION D.   STATE CONSTITUTIONS: RESEARCH PUBLICATIONS

The state constitutions are published with the state codes, in pamphlets and in appropriate local treatises. The usual source to locate a state constitution is the code or compilation of statutes for a specific state. Such publications generally include the text of the state constitution and annotations to it. As in the case of the Federal Constitution, they are separately indexed. However, the general indexes of some state codes also cover the state constitution. The indexes are generally topically arranged without factual analyses. Thus, a modified topic method is frequently used to ascertain cases in point, for the index must be topically analyzed. In some state publications, subdivision analyses precede the annotations. A few of the state codes include not only annotated state constitutions but also the Federal Constitution with annotations. An example of the latter is the *Iowa Code Annotated*, volume 2. Examples of annotated state constitutions are:

Florida Statutes Annotated, vols. 25, 26 and 26A.

Michigan Statutes Annotated, vol. 1 (1965 Revision).

New Jersey Statutes Annotated, Constitution vol.

Vernon's Annotated Texas Constitution, 3 vols.

The records, journals, proceedings and other documents relating to the state constitutional conventions provide valuable source data on the intended meanings and interpretations given to the state constitutions, as amended, by their framers. An array of these publications are available for the several states. Consult your library catalog for its holdings for your state.

Popular names by which provisions of individual state constitutions have been referred are indicated in *Shepard's Federal and State Acts and Cases by Popular Names, 1968*. Its cumulative pamphlet supplement keeps it current.

5 Chapter 14.

## SECTION E.   STATE CONSTITUTIONS: RESEARCH PROCEDURE

1.   For the meanings of the provisions of the state constitutions as given by the framers, see the documents (journals, proceedings, etc.) relating to the constitutional conventions.

2.   A local legal encyclopedia (e. g., *California Jurisprudence 2d* or *Michigan Law and Practice*) and periodical articles may be consulted for discussions relating to the state constitution.   The general encyclopedias *(American Jurisprudence 2d* or *Corpus Juris Secundum)* are less specific in their treatment but may have discussions helpful in orienting the researcher to the problem.

3.   Digests of the judicial interpretations to the state constitutions are included in the annotations to the constitutions as published in the *state codes*.   Refer to the pocket and pamphlet supplements for recent constitutional changes and cases in point.

4.   The *American Law Reports* may contain annotations on the topic covering the law for the several states.

5.   Consult the *state digest*.   The Index, Topic or Case Methods can be used.   The state digests are discussed in Chapter 6.

6.   Shepardize the provision of the state constitution in *Shepard's State Citations* (e. g., *Shepard's Minnesota Citations*).   Cases in point may also be Shepardized in the state citations.   *Shepard's Citations* are considered in Chapter 14.

---

## SECTION F.   SOURCES OF COMPARATIVE INFORMATION ABOUT STATE AND FEDERAL CONSTITUTIONS

In the absence of judicial interpretations of a constitutional provision or to support a theory favorable to a client's position, interpretations of similar measures of other states may provide useful supporting argument.   This comparative method should be used after the historical and other sources relating to the specific constitution have been examined.

The annotations in the *American Law Reports* and the *U. S. Supreme Court Reports (L.Ed.)* generally include comparative information as to the laws of the several states.

Also, there are other sources for comparative evaluation of state and federal constitutions.   Although these publications use the historical approach, they, nevertheless, may suggest a theory or present a clue not found elsewhere. These historical studies are:

Thorpe.    Constitutions and Organic Acts.   7 vols. 1909.

Poore.    Charters and Constitutions.   2 vols. 1877.

Stimson.    Federal and State Constitutions.   1918.

Kettleborough.    State Constitutions.   1918.

Constitutions of the States and the United States.   1938.

Index Digest of State Constitutions.   2d ed. 1959.

Although *Thorpe's* and *Poore's* are out of date, they are significant historical and parallelistic studies of state constitutions. Thorpe contains copies of all the constitutions of each state.

*Stimson* is another very good source for the comparative study of state constitutions. Its strength is in its treatment of the origin of constitutional provisions.

*Kettleborough* contains a compilation of the various state constitutions in force at that time. It can, therefore, be used as a supplement to Thorpe.

*The Constitutions of the States and the United States* (1938) is the product of the 1938 New York Constitutional Convention Commission. It includes the texts of the constitutions of all the states and the United States. The volume contains an index to the constitutions, and is useful for comparative study of constitutional provisions of the states and the United States. However, it is not up-to-date.

The *Index Digest of State Constitutions*, 2d edition, 1959, is a revision of the 1915 edition prepared by the Legislative Drafting Research Fund of Columbia University. The 1915 edition also was edited by the Fund for the use of the New York State Constitutional Convention of that year. The revised index is a "comparative statement of the provisions of all the (state) constitutions arranged by subject." It covers all fifty state constitutions. Analysis is not evaluative and is limited to the terms of the constitutional provisions. No attempt is made to reflect judicial interpretation or legislative implementation. Nor is there any exposition as to invalidity or other delimitations of the provisions. Thus, the editorial work is restricted to comparative reporting of paraphrased provisions followed by references, alphabetically arranged by states, to the articles and sections of applicable state constitutions. This is the most recent comprehensive, comparative study of the constitutional provisions of the states. It is kept reasonably current by a pocket supplement.

Having the citation to a similar constitutional provision of another jurisdiction, the researcher may check that constitution for judicial and other interpretations.

*Constitutions of the United States: National and State*, published in 1962, is a two-volume loose-leaf edition prepared by the Columbia University Legislative Drafting Research Fund. It collects the texts of the constitutions of the United States and the 50 states, and is kept current by loose-leaf releases. Thus, it is a companion publication to the *Index Digest* discussed above in that it provides the texts of the constitutions which the *Index Digest* analyzes.

----

## SECTION G.  FOREIGN CONSTITUTIONS

There are occasions when it is necessary to locate the constitutions of foreign countries. A recent publication has now made research in this area relatively simple. This is:

Blaustein, A. P. and Flanz, C. H. (eds.)  *Constitution of the Countries of the World*.  Permanent Edition.  Dobbs Ferry, N. Y., Oceana Publications, Inc., (1971) (to be completed in 12 volumes)

This set is published in loose-leaf format, with a separate pamphlet for each country. For those countries where there is not an official English version an English translation is provided. The constitutions for each country are preceded by a constitutional chronology and followed by an annotated bibliography.

Periodically supplements are issued keeping each constitution up-to-date.

The Introduction in Chapter One should be consulted for bibliographical references to previous compilations of constitutions.

----

## SECTION H.  METHODS OF CITATION

Constitutions are cited by reference to article, section and clause. A date is used with a state constitution only to indicate one which is not in force. The date of the Constitution of the United States is not given in a citation.

1. **Text Citations (Examples)**

   Article I, section 7, clause 1 of the Constitution of the United States.

   Article II, section 4 of the Constitution of New York.

   the fifth amendment of the Constitution ordains

   the fifth amendment ordains.

2. **Footnote Citations (Examples)**
    U.S.Const. art. I, § 7 cl. 1.
    U.S.Const. amend. V.
    Mass.Const. art. IV.
    Pa.Const. art. V, § 6.

---

### SECTION I.   SUMMARY

1. **Federal Constitution**
    a.   Text in:
        (1)  *United States Code.*
        (2)  *United States Code Annotated.*
        (3)  *United States Code Service-F.C.A. Edition.*
        (4)  *U. S. Supreme Court Reports Digest* (Lawyers Co-op.).
        (5)  *Library of Congress, Constitution of the United States of America* (1964).
    b.   Interpretation.
        (1)  Historical (see list of historical sources in Section A1, above).
        (2)  Judicial.
            (a)  U.S.C.A.:  (i) index is to the text of the Constitution;  does not cover interpretative cases;  (ii) topic analysis precedes digests of cases;  (iii) digests of interpretative federal and state cases and Attorneys General opinions under constitutional provisions, subdivided by topic analysis (Notes to Decisions) ;  (iv) parallel citation; and (v) cumulative annual pocket and subsequent pamphlet supplements.
            (b)  F.C.A.:  (i) index is to the text of the Constitution; does not cover interpretative cases;  (ii) topic analysis precedes digests of cases;  (iii) digests of interpretative federal and state cases and Attorneys General opinions under constitutional provisions, subdivided by topic analysis (Notes to Decisions) ;  (iv) parallel citation; and (v) cumulative annual pocket and later pamphlet supplements.
            (c)  *Library of Congress.   Constitution of the United States of America* (1964):  (i) partially indexes cases as well as the text of the Constitution;  (ii) discussion of selected cases of the Supreme Court of the United States;  documents;  views of writers; (iii) no provision is made for keeping this publication up-to-date.
            (d)  *U. S. Supreme Court Reports Digest:*  (i) volume 17 provides text and references to sections of the *Digest* covering the

Constitution and (ii) volume 14 contains a Table of Constitutional Provisions with citations to U. S. Supreme Court decisions which construe them.

> (e) Digests (see Section A3e), above.

> (f) Encyclopedias: Am.Jur.2d and C.J.S. may treat the topic.

> (g) Annotations: A.L.R. and the *U. S. Supreme Court Reports (L.Ed.)* may discuss the problem.

> (h) Shepard's Citations: (i) *U. S. Citations* for federal court cases and (ii) *State Citations* for state cases interpreting U. S. Constitution. Also Shepardize cases.

c. Treatises and periodical literature (see Section A1c, above).

## 2. Amending the Federal Constitution

a. *U. S. Constitution * * * unratified amendments. 1972.*

b. *U. S. Congress. Senate Library. Proposed Amendments to the Constitution * * * 69th Congress, 2d Sess. through 87th Congress, 2d Sess., 1926–1963; 1965–1969.*

## 3. State Constitutions

a. Published with state code.

b. Separate indexes and general indexes which are topically and not factually analyzed.

c. Annotated.

## 4. Sources of Comparative Information about State and Federal Constitutions

a. See Section F, above.

b. *Index Digest of State Constitutions*, 2d ed., 1959.

> (1) Comparative statement of the provisions of all state constitutions arranged by subject.

> (2) Analysis is not evaluative and is limited to the terms of the provisions.

> (3) Most recent comprehensive, comparative study of constitutional provisions.

> (4) Pocket supplement.

c. *Constitutions of the United States: National and State.*

> (1) Loose-leaf edition.

> (2) Texts of the constitutions of the U. S. and the 50 states.

> (3) Companion publication to the *Index Digest.*

# Chapter 9

# FEDERAL LEGISLATION

Article I, Section 8, of the United States Constitution enumerates the powers of Congress, and provides the authority for Congress to make all laws necessary and proper for carrying into execution the enumerated powers, as well as other powers vested in the Congress.

A Congress meets in two year periods with each such period known as a *Congress*. The period in which Congress met, for example, during the years 1971–72, is known as the 92nd Congress, the First Congress being 1789–91. Under the Constitution, Congress must meet at least once a year.

## SECTION A. THE ENACTMENT OF FEDERAL LAWS

Before we consider the source books relating to federal legislation, let us first review generally the method of enacting federal laws.[1]

Step 1. A bill [2] is introduced in a house and is assigned a number. Numbers are assigned consecutively in each house. A House of Representatives bill is designated as "H.R. ——"; a Senate bill is identified as "S. ——."

Bills do not carry over from one Congress to another; they must be re-introduced in the new Congress where they receive new numbers.

Each bill is separately printed in its several stages of progress through both houses.

Step 2. The bill is then assigned to the appropriate committee of the house where it was introduced. If the bill is acted upon favor-

---

[1] For more detailed statements on the enactment of federal laws see: United States, Congress. House of Representatives. How our Laws are Made, by Joseph Fischer, 1971. (H.Doc. 144, 92d Cong.) See also: Congressional Quarterly Service. Congressional Quarterly's Guide to the Congress of the United States; Origins, History and Procedure. 1971.

[2] A *bill* is the form used for most legislation. *Joint Resolutions* may also be used, but there is no practical difference between the two and the two forms are used indiscriminately. *Concurrent resolutions* are used for matters affecting both Houses, but are not legislative. Simple resolutions are used for matters concerning the operation of either house. The first three forms are published in the *Statutes at Large*. The latter in the *Congressional Record*. Fischer, op. cit. at 6.

ably by the committee, it is "reported out of committee." Significant and controversial bills are generally supported by hearings held by the committee to determine the views of the public on the subject and to obtain expert testimony. A committee report, which accompanies a reported out bill, is printed. The reports are numbered consecutively for each Congress and are identified as "H.R.Rep.No. ——" or "S.Rep.No. ——." The hearings may or may not be printed.

Step 3. The bill is reported out when the chairman of the committee, which considered it, reintroduces it in his house with the committee recommendations.

Step 4. The bill is debated in the house. The debates appear in the *Congressional Record.* Then the house votes on it; if the bill passes a house, it is sent to the other house [3] where it proceeds through a similar channel. If the second house passes the bill with amendments, it is returned to the first house for its further action. If the first house does not accept the amended bill, a conference committee consisting of members of both houses is appointed. If the conferees agree to a compromise bill, they report the bill out of conference. The report of the conference committee is printed. The conference bill is then voted on in both houses.

Step 5. If the bill passes both houses, it is enrolled and submitted to the President for signature and approval. It becomes law if the President signs the bill. If vetoed by the President, it must be passed by a two-thirds vote in both houses to become law. After a law has been passed by Congress, and signed by the President (or enacted over his veto) it is classified [4] as either a *public law* or a *private law.* The former is one that is of general applicability and applies to all within its scope, e. g., a tax law, or a law prohibiting certain activities. The latter applies only to those specifically designated in the law. An example of this would be a law providing for compensation to an individual for damages caused by an action of a federal employee.

The first law to pass a Congress is designated either Public Law No. 1 or Private Law No. 1. Each succeeding law is then numbered in numerical sequence throughout the two-year life of a Congress.

[3] Frequently the other house has a similarly worded bill before it known as a "companion bill". Sometimes it may substitute the first house's bill in place of its own.

[4] This is done by the Office of the Federal Register, General Services Administration. Letter from Fred J. Emery, Office of the Federal Register, to J. M. Jacobstein.

## 1. Current Laws

During a session of Congress, each law as passed is first issued by the U. S. Government Printing Office in *slip* law form. See Illustration 31. This means that each law is separately published and a particular law may be one page in length or several hundred. There are four sources commonly consulted for the text of current laws.

a   *Slip* laws. These are available at all libraries that are depositories for the publications of the U. S. Government Printing Office [5] and in certain law libraries.

b   *U. S. Code Congressional and Administrative News Service.* This set is published by the West Publishing Co. in connection with the *United States Code Annotated.* During each session of Congress it is issued monthly in pamphlet form and prints in full text all of the public laws. Each issue contains a cumulative subject index and a cumulative *Table of Laws Enacted.* After each session of Congress the pamphlets are re-issued in bound volumes.

c   *Current Public Laws and Administrative Service.* This set is published by the Lawyers Co-operative Publishing Company in connection with the *United States Code Service-F.C.A.* It contains similar information as that described in b *supra.*

d   *U. S. Law Week.* This is a weekly loose-leaf service which includes the text of the more important laws passed during the previous week.

## 2. U.S. Statutes at Large

At the end of each session of Congress all of the slip laws are published in numerical order as a volume of the set called the *Statutes at Large.* Thus all of the laws enacted since 1789 are contained in the many volumes of this set.[6]

It is important to keep in mind that the laws are arranged in the *Statutes-at-Large* in chronological order rather than by subject. Moreover, amendments to a previously passed law will appear in different volumes from the law being amended. As an example, a law passed in 1900 is in volume 31 of the *Statutes-at-Large.* If Congress amended it in 1905, the text of the amendment is in volume 33. Some laws have been amended many, many times and to obtain the full and current text of such a law, the *Statutes-at-Large* volume containing the

---

[5] A list of such libraries is published each year in the September issue of the Monthly Catalog of Government Publications. Each Government Documents depository collection may be consulted by the public.

[6] Until 1936, each volume of the Statutes at Large covered a two year period.

law as first passed must be examined in context with each subsequent volume in which an amendment to the law appears.

Each volume of the *Statutes-at-Large* has its own subject index and contains tables listing how each public law in it affects previous public laws.

---

## SECTION B. CODIFICATION OF FEDERAL LAWS

The method of publication of Congressional laws chronologically created obvious problems for the process of determining the statutory provisions on any given subject. In order to better accomplish this, the laws passed by Congress have to be rearranged in a manner that will do three things: (1) collate the original law with all subsequently passed amendments with the deletion or addition of language changed by the amendments; (2) bring all laws on the same subject or topic together, and (3) eliminate all repealed, superseded, or expired laws. This process is called codification.

Before considering the types of compilations of federal legislation, we should outline the general classification of the acts of legislatures, federal and state. We have already discussed the difference between a *public law* and a *private law*; another important distinction is between permanent and temporary laws. A *permanent law* continues for an indefinite period. A *temporary law* continues in force for a specific period of time.

### 1. United States Revised Statutes

The first codification [7] of the *Statutes-at-Large* was authorized by the Congress in 1866 and resulted in the publication of the *Revised Statutes of 1875*.

The Commissioners authorized by Congress to prepare this revision proceeded by extracting from the volumes of the *Statutes-at-Large* all public laws that met the following two criteria: (1) they were still in force, and (2) they were of a general and permanent nature. This eliminated all appropriation laws and those that did not have general applicability. The next step was to take each public law and all its amendments and rewrite the law in one sequence by incorporating amending language and eliminating deleting language. All of the laws on one topic were then arranged in a chapter. Chapter 35, for example, contained all legislation passed by Congress, and still in force, on taxation; Chapter 70 all legislation in force on criminal law. All of the chapters were then bound in one volume, a subject index prepared, and issued as the *Revised Statutes of 1875*.

---

[7] Feidler, The Federal Statutes, their history and use. 22 Minn.L.Rev. 1008 (1938).

This volume as prepared by the Commissioners was then submitted to Congress and introduced as a bill and went through the legislative process of becoming a public law. Within the bill before Congress there was a section specifically repealing each previously passed public law that had been incorporated into the *Revised Statutes of 1875*. Thus when it passed Congress and was signed by the President, all of the laws passed since 1789, in force and of a general and public nature, were codified in the *Revised Statutes of 1875*. Moreover, as the act of codification repealed all the previous Statutes at Large citations, the *Revised Statutes of 1875* became *positive law* and it was no longer necessary to refer back to the *Statutes at large* volumes.

Unfortunately, this volume, known as the first edition, was subsequently discovered to contain many inaccuracies and unauthorized changes in the law.[8] In 1878, a second edition of the *Revised Statutes* was authorized to be published which would include legislation passed and delete sections that were repealed since 1873 and would also correct the errors that had inadvertently been incorporated into the first edition.

The second edition indicated changes to the text of the first edition by the use of brackets and italics. It is important to note, however, that the second edition of the *Revised Statutes* was never re-enacted by Congress and all changes indicated in it are only *prima facie* evidence of the law. There were no further codification of federal laws until 1926.

## 2.   United States Code

Prior to 1926, the positive law for federal legislation was contained in the one volume of the *Revised Statutes of 1875* and then in each subsequent volume of the *Statutes at Large*. In 1925, Congress authorized the preparation of the *United States Code*. This was prepared by a Revisor of Statutes appointed by Congress, who extracted all sections of the *Revised Statutes of 1875* that had not been repealed and then all of the public and general laws from the *Statutes at Large* since 1873 that were still in force. These were then rearranged in fifty titles and published in 1926 as the *United States Code*, 1926 ed., in four volumes. Each year thereafter a cumulative supplement containing the laws passed since 1926 was published. In 1932 a new edition was issued incorporating the cumulated supplement into the 1926 edition and this became the *United States Code*, 1932 ed. Every six years a new edition of the *U.S.Code* is published with cumulative supplement volumes being issued during the intervening years.

---

8 *Ibid.*

The *United States Code* differs from the *Revised Statutes of 1875* in one important aspect. It was never submitted to Congress and re-enacted as a whole. Thus, the *United States Code* is *prima facie* evidence of the law rather than positive evidence. This means that should there be a conflict between the wording in the *United States Code* and the wording in the *Statutes at Large*, the latter will govern.[9]

Congress has, however, been re-enacting the separate titles of the *United States Code* on an individual basis. The nineteen titles already enacted into positive law are enumerated at 1 *U.S.C.* § 204(e) note.

### 3. Annotated Editions of the U.S. Code

The *United States Code* is designated as the official edition, and is printed and sold by U. S. Government Printing Office. As is frequently the case with such publications, it is slow in being published, particularly in the issuance of the supplements, which are seldom available until several months after a session of Congress is over. Furthermore, the meaning of a law passed by a legislative body is not always clear and the intent of the language used frequently must be interpreted by a court. Consequently, access to the court decisions interpreting statutes is frequently as important as the text of the statute itself. This has led to the publication of annotated codes where digests of court decisions interpreting a code section are given. There are two privately published annotated editions of the *United States Code*.

a    *United States Code Annotated (U.S.C.A.)*    This set is published by the West Publishing Co. and offers several advantages over the official set. Each of the fifty titles is published in separate volumes, and is kept up-to-date with annual cumulative pocket supplements. It also provides a quarterly pamphlet service supplementing the annual pocket supplements. In organization it follows exactly the arrangement of the *United States Code* and contains exactly the same text. In addition to the means of supplementation, the fundamental difference between the *United States Code* and the *United States Code Annotated* is its annotations. As previously pointed out,

---

[9] 1 U.S.C. § 204(a) (1970 ed.) provides that: "The matter set forth in the edition of the Code of Laws of the United States current at any time shall, together with the then current supplement, if any, establish prima facie the laws of the United States, general and permanent in their nature, in force on the day preceding the commencement of the session following the last session the legislation of which is included: Provided, however, that whenever titles of such Code shall have been enacted into positive law the text thereof shall be legal evidence of the laws therein contained in all the courts of the United States, the several States, and the Territories and insular possessions of the United States." See also *U. S. v. Welden,* 377 U.S. 95 (1963).

the *United States Code* is arranged in fifty titles, each on a specific subject. Each title is divided into sections. After each section, the *United States Code Annotated* has digest paragraphs (headnotes) from each decision that interpreted a particular code section. Once a code section has been located in the *United States Code Annotated* the exact text will be found with digests of all court decisions relevant to that section. Thus, an annotated code not only gives the provisions of a law but its interpretations by the courts.

The *United States Code Annotated* has a four-volume index to the entire set. Each title in addition has its own index.

b   *Federal Code Annotated (F.C.A.)-United States Code Service (U.S.C.S.)*. Another annotated set of the *United States Code* is the *Federal Code Annotated*. This set is similar in format to the *U.S.C.A.* but published by the Bobbs-Merrill Company. It is in 44 volumes, and each *United States Code* is followed by annotations of decisions as prepared by the publisher.

The *Federal Code Annotated* was recently purchased by the Lawyers Co-operative Publishing Co.—Bancroft-Whitney Co. They are now in the process of reissuing new volumes, title by title. Each newly reissued title is called *United States Code Service, Lawyers Edition*, which will then be the name of the set when all of the fifty titles of the *United States Code* have been published by them. The *United States Code Service* will become an integral part of their Total Client-Service Library as described in Chapter IV and will include references to all of the other units of this service.

[Illustrations 33–37 show the use of the various editions of the United States Code].

---

### SECTION C.   POPULAR NAMES OF FEDERAL ACTS

It is common practice to refer to a federal act by a popular name. Generally, this is the name which the public gives the statute and it may describe its subject matter or refer to its authors. The *Gold Clause Act* and the *Taft-Hartley Act* are examples of each type.

The tables of popular names of federal acts are designed to provide the citations to acts when only the popular names are known.

There are a number of such tables. They are:

1.   *Shepard's Federal and State Acts and Cases by Popular Names*, Vol. 1, 1968, and Cumulative Supplement. See Illustration 39.

2.   *United States Code Annotated* contains a table of acts cited by popular name in volume 5 of the Index and in its pocket supplement. See Illustration 38.

3. The popular names for federal acts are also listed in their alphabetical order in the general indexes to the *United States Code Annotated* and the *Federal Code Annotated.*

4. *The United States Code,* 1970 edition, in the General Index volume and supplements.

5. *Federal Code Annotated,* Tables volumes.

6. *U. S. Supreme Court Reports Digest* (Lawyers Co-op. Pub. Co.), volume 14.

7. *U. S. Code Congressional and Administrative News* provides *Tables of Popular Name Acts* for each session of Congress, beginning with the 77th Congress, 2d Session, 1942. These tables are for each session, are not cumulated, and cite the acts in the pages of the *News.*

The Tables in *Shepard's,* the *United States Code,* the *United States Code Annotated* and the *U. S. Supreme Court Reports Digest* give the date of enactment and the *Statutes at Large* and the *United States Code* citations following the popular name. For example, the U.S.C.A. reference is:

Export Trade Act

Apr. 10, 1918, ch. 50, 40 Stat. 516 (Title 15, §§ 61–65)

The F.C.A. Table does not include the *Statutes at Large* citation. The entry of the same act in the F.C.A. Table is:

Export Trade Act

Apr. 10, 1918, 15 §§ 61–65

------

## SECTION D.   TABLES OF FEDERAL STATUTES

Tables, providing cross reference and other information, are published with the current federal codes to facilitate their use. These tables are in the *United States Code* (Tables volume and Supplements), the *United States Code Annotated* (Tables volume) and the *Federal Code Annotated* (2 Tables volumes). The Tables provide such information as references from the *Revised Statutes* or *Statutes at Large* citations to the corresponding sections in the specific code, parallel tables from former Title 18 U.S.C. (Criminal Code) to the new section numbers, parallel tables from former Title 28 U.S.C. (Judicial Code) to the new section numbers, and tables of statutes repealed or eliminated. See Illustration 32.

U.S.C.A. and F.C.A. also show the disposition of all sections of former Titles by tables in the annotated titles volumes.

The basic Tables volume (vol. 11) of the *United States Code* contains the following tables:

1.   Table I—Revised Titles; these tables show where former sections of titles of the *United States Code*, which have been revised, are incorporated in U.S.C.

2.   Table II—*Revised Statutes 1878*; this table shows where sections of the *Revised Statutes of 1878* are found in U.S.C.

3.   Table III—*Statutes at Large*; this table shows where the Acts of Congress are found in U.S.C.

4.   Table IV—Executive Orders; this table lists the **Executive** Orders "that implement general and permanent law as contained in U.S.C."

5.   Table V—Proclamations; this table lists the Proclamations that are cited in U.S.C.

6.   Reorganization Plans; this table lists the Reorganization Plans that are provided in U.S.C.

The tables in U.S.C.A. and F.C.A. cover relatively the same materials as listed above for U.S.C.

## SECTION E.   ILLUSTRATIONS

31.   A public law in "slip" form.

32.   A page from U.S.C.A. showing conversion of Statute at Large Citation to U.S. Code Citation.

33.   A page from the Index Volume to the U.S.C.A.

34.   A page from the U.S. Code, 1952 ed.

35.   A page from Volume 73, Statutes at Large.

36.   A page from the U.S. Code, 1972 ed.

37.   Pages from Title 31, U.S.C.A., Pocket Supplement.

38.   A page from the Popular Name Table—U.S.C.A.

39.   A page from Shepard's Federal and State Acts by Popular Name.

## [Illustration 31]

## SLIP LAW—91 CONGRESS, FIRST SESSION

**Public Law 91-270**
**91st Congress,** H. R. 780 ←— **1.**
**May 28, 1970**

### An Act

**2.→** 84 STAT. 273

To authorize the Secretary of the Interior to construct, operate, and maintain the Merlin division, Rogue River Basin project, Oregon, and for other purposes.

*Be it enacted by the Senate and House of Representatives of the United States of America in Congress assembled,* That, for the purposes of providing irrigation water for approximately nine thousand three hundred acres, flood control, area redevelopment, and providing municipal and industrial water supply, fish and wildlife enhancement, and recreation benefits, the Secretary of the Interior, acting pursuant to the Federal reclamation laws (Act of June 17, 1902 (32 Stat. 388), and Act amendatory thereof or supplementary thereto), is authorized to construct, operate, and maintain the Merlin division, Rogue River Basin project, Oregon. The principal works of the division shall consist of Sexton Dam and Reservoir, diversion and distribution facilities, and drainage facilities.

> Rogue River Basin project, Ore. Merlin division, authorization.
>
> 43 USC 371 note, 391 note.

SEC. 2. Irrigation repayment contracts shall provide with respect to any contract unit, for repayment of the irrigation construction costs assigned for repayment to the irrigators over a period of not more than fifty years, exclusive of any development period authorized by law. Irrigation repayment contracts shall further provide for the assessment and collection of a service charge of not less than $40 per annum for each identifiable ownership receiving irrigation service from and through the works of the Merlin division, such charge to be in addition to the repayment capacity of the lands as determined by the Secretary on the basis of studies of the value of water for full-time family-size farm operations. Construction costs allocated to irrigation beyond the ability of irrigators to repay shall be charged to and returned to the reclamation fund in accordance with the provisions of section 2 of the Act of June 14, 1966 (80 Stat. 200), as amended by section 6 of the Act of September 7, 1966 (80 Stat. 707).

> Irrigation, repayment period.
>
> Service charge.
>
> Construction costs.
>
> 16 USC 835j-835m and notes.

SEC. 3. The conservation and development of the fish and wildlife resources and the enhancement of recreation opportunities in connection with the Merlin division shall be in accordance with the pro-

> Recreation; fish and wildlife enhance-
>
> 12
>
> ns.

---

> This is a typical "slip" law. At the end of the first session of the 91st Congress, all of the slip laws are published in a bound volume of the Statutes at Large.
>
> Marginal notes are not part of the law but editorial aids. The code citations in the margin indicate where the Statute at Large citations in the text are found in the U. S. Code.
>
> Notes: 1. Bill number in House of Representatives.
> 2. Statute at Large Citation.

---

SEC. 6. For a period of ten years from the date of enactment of this Act, no water from the project authorized by this Act shall be delivered to any water user for the production on newly irrigated lands of any basic agricultural commodity, as defined in the Agricultural Act of 1949, or any amendment thereof, if the total supply of such commodity for the marketing year in which the bulk of the crop would normally be marketed is in excess of the normal supply as

> Newly irrigated lands, use restriction.
>
> 63 Stat. 1051.
> 7 USC 1421 note, 1428.

[Illustration 32]

## TABLE FROM U.S.C.A. SHOWING CONVERSION OF STATUTE AT LARGE CITATION TO U.S.C. CITATION

**1970**           STATUTES AT LARGE

| 1970—91st Cong.—84 Stat. | | | | USCA | | |
|---|---|---|---|---|---|---|
| May P.L. | Sec. | Page | Tit. | Sec. | | Status |
| 21 .... 91-258..........207(d) (1).... | 248.....26........... | 874, 6201 | | | | |
| 207(d) (2).... | 248.....26................6201 | | | | | |
| 207(d) (3).... | 248.....26................6206 | | | | | |
| 207(d) (4)–(7).... | 248, 249 26................6416 | | | | | |
| 207(d) (8).... | 249.....26................6675 | | | | | |
| 207(d) (9)..... | 249.....26...... 7210, 7603–7605 | | | | | |
| 207(d) (10).... | 249.....26..........prec. 31 | | | | | |
| 207(d) (11).... | 249.....26..........prec. 6201 | | | | | |
| 207(d) (12).... | 249.....26..........prec. 6411 | | | | | |
| 207(d) (13).... | 249.....26..........prec. 6671 | | | | | |
| 207(e).... | 249.....23................120 nt | | | | | |
| 208..... | 250.....49................1742 | | | | | |
| | 23................120 nt | | | | | |
| 209..... | 252.....49................1742 nt | | | | | |
| 210..... | 253.... 4................104 nt | | | | | |
| 211..... | 253.....26................4041 nt | | | | | |
| 91-259................ 1.... | 253.....25................1191 | | | | | |
| 2.... | 254.....25................1192 | | | | | |
| 3.... | 254.....25................1193 | | | | | |
| 4.... | 254.....25................1194 | | | | | |
| 5.... | 254.....25................1195 | | | | | |
| 91-260................ —.... | 254.....20................635 | | | | | |
| 91-262................ 1.... | 256.....38................101 | | | | | |
| 2.... | 256.....38................413 | | | | | |
| 3.... | 256.....38................414 | | | | | |
| 4.... | 256.....38................413 nt | | | | | |
| 22 .... 91-264................ 1.... | 260.....25................641 | | | | | |
| 2.... | 260.....25................642 | | | | | |
| 3.... | 261.....25................643 | | | | | |
| 4.... | 261.....25................644 | | | | | |
| 5.... | 261.....25................645 | | | | | |
| 6.... | 261.....25................646 | | | | | |
| 91-265................ 1.... | 262.....15................1409 | | | | | |
| 2.... | 262.....15................1391 | | | | | |
| 3.... | 262.....15................1401 | | | | | |
| 4(a)–(c).... | 262.....15................1402 | | | | | |
| 4(d).... | 263.....15................1402 nt | | | | | |
| 5.... | 263.....15................1408 | | | | | |
| 6.... | 263.....15................1426 | | | | | |
| 7.... | 263.....15................1431 | | | | | |
| 8.... | 264.....15................1381 | | | | | |
| 27 .... 91-269................ 1.... | 271.....22................2801 | | | | | |
| 2.... | 271.....22................2802 | | | | | |
| 3.... | 272.....22................2803 | | | | | |
| 4.... | 272.....22................2804 | | | | | |
| 5.... | 272.....22................2805 | | | | | |
| 6.... | 272.....22................2806 | | | | | |
| 8.... | 272.....22................2807 | | | | | |
| 28 .... 91-270................ 1.... | 273.....43..........616mmmm | | | | | |
| 2.... | 273.....43..........616nnnn | | | | | |
| 3.... | 273.....43..........616oooo | | | | | |
| 4.... | 273.....43..........616pppp | | | | | |
| 5.... | 273.....43..........616qqqq | | | | | |
| 6.... | 273.....43..........616rrrr | | | | | |
| 7.... | 274.....43..........616ssss | | | | | |
| June 2 .... 91-271................101..... | 274.....28................1541 nt | | | | | |

> This exhibit is from the Tables volume of the U.S.C.A. These Tables indicate where each section of a Public Law has been modified in the *U.S.C.* Thus, section 2 of P.L. 91-270 (previous exhibit) is found at (Title) 2 U.S.C. 616nnnn.

[Illustration 33]

## PAGE FROM THE INDEX VOLUME TO THE U.S.C.A.

**TAXATION** 726

FINDING A FEDERAL STATUTE

Problem: Are stocks and bonds issued by the United States Government exempt from taxation by the states?

Step 1. Check index volumes to U.S.C., U.S.C.A., or U.S. C.S.–F.C.A.

This will indicate that there is a code section covering this topic at Title 31, § 742.

District of Columbia, this index
Employment Taxes, generally, this index
Escrows for future payments, exemption from computing finance charge, Truth in Lending Act, 15 § 1605
Estate Tax, generally, this index
Evasion. Internal Revenue, this index
Examination, deposit of fee before, 21 § 46a
Excess Profits, generally, this index
Exchanges of United States obligations. 26 § 1037
→ Exemption from taxation,
American Historical Association, real property, 36 § 20 **note**
American War Mothers' property or income, 36 § 96
Annuity or pension under Railroad Retirement Act. 45 § 228*l*
Armed forces,
Immunity on sale or transfer of arms and ammunition, Coast Guard, 14 § 655
Sale or transfer of arms and ammunition, 10 § 2385
Armed services housing,
Mortgage insurance debentures, 12 § 1748b
Realty acquired by Secretary of Housing and Urban Development, 12 § 1748h–3
Banks for cooperatives, 12 § 1138c
Central Bank for Cooperatives, 12 § 1138c
Certificates of indebtedness, 31 §§ 755, 769
Commodity Credit Corporation, obligations of, 15 § 713a–5
Consols of 1930, 31 § 751
Cotton Futures Tax, this index
Debentures issued,
To acquire rental project, 12 § 1747g
Under War Housing Insurance Law, 12 § 1739
Excess Profits, this index
Federal credit unions, 12 § 1768
Federal Crop Insurance Corporation, 7 § 1511
Federal Deposit Insurance Corporation, notes, bonds or other obligations of, 12 § 1825
Federal home loan banks, 12 § 1433
Federal Home Loan Mortgage Corporation, 12 § 1452
Federal intermediate credit banks, 12 § 1111
Federal land banks, 12 § 931
Federal National Mortgage Association, 12 § 1723a(c)
Federal Reserve banks, 12 § 531
First Liberty bonds, 31 § 746
Gifts to Congressional Library, 2 § 161
→ Government obligations, 31 § 742
Homestead of Indians, 25 § 412a
Housing project, 42 § 1410
Income Tax, this index
Indians, this index
Inter-American Social Development Institute, 22 § 290f
Interest on obligations of United States or agency or instrumentality thereof, 31 § 742a
Internal Revenue, this index

## [Illustration 34]
## PAGE FROM U.S. CODE, 1952 EDITION

**§ 741a. Sale and disposition of bonds, notes, and other securities.**

(a) Notwithstanding the provisions of section 302 of Title 40, the Secretary of the Treasury is authorized to sell, exchange, or otherwise dispose of any bonds, notes, or other securities, acquired by him on behalf of the United States under judicial process or otherwise, or delivered to him by an executive department or agency of the United States for disposal, or to enter into arrangements for the extension of the maturity thereof, in such manner, in such amounts, at such prices, for cash, securities, or other property, or any combination thereof, and upon such terms and conditions as he may deem advisable and in the public interest. No such bonds, notes, or other securities of any single issuer having at the date of disposal an aggregate face or par value, or in the case of no-par stock an aggregate stated or book value, in excess of $1,000,000, which may be held by the Secretary of the Treasury at any one time, shall be sold or otherwise disposed of under the authority of this section.

(b) Nothing contained in this section shall be construed to supersede or impair any authority otherwise granted to any officer or executive department or agency of the United States to sell, exchange, or otherwise dispose of any bonds, notes, or other securities, acquired by the United States under judicial process or otherwise. (Apr. 3, 1945, ch. 51, § 5, 59 Stat. 48.)

REFERENCES IN TEXT

Section 302 of Title 40, referred to in the text, was repealed by act Oct. 31, 1951, ch. 654, § 1 (95), 65 Stat. 705, and is now covered by sections 483 and 484 of Title 40, Public Buildings, Property and Works.

**§ 742. Exemption from taxation.**

Except as otherwise provided by law, all stocks, bonds, Treasury notes, and other obligations of the United States, shall be exempt from taxation by or under State or municipal or local authority. (R. S. § 3701.)

DERIVATION

Act Feb. 25, 1862, ch. 38, § 2, 12 Stat. 346; act Mar. 3, 1863, ch. 73, § 1, 12 Stat. 710; act Mar. 3, 1864, ch. 17, § 1, 13 Stat. 13; act June 30, 1864, ch. 172, § 1, 13 Stat. 218; act Jan. 28, 1865, ch. 22, § 1, 13 Stat. 425; act Mar. 3, 1865, ch. 77, § 2, 13 Stat. 469; act July 14, 1870, ch. 256, § 1, 16 Stat. 272.

CROSS REFERENCES

United States obligations and evidences of ownership issued after March 27, 1942, as subject to Federal taxation, see section 742a of this title.

---

This is a page from the United States Code 1952 edition. Ordinarily one would use the latest edition of the U.S.C., or one of the two annotated editions which are kept current by pocket supplements.

This edition is shown to illustrate how this section of the Code appeared before it was amended.

---

Note the reference to the *Revised Statutes.* All sections of the *Revised Statutes* not repealed are still in force.

After each code section, citation is given either to the *Revised Statutes* or the *Statutes at Large* where the section first appeared as passed by Congress.

## [Illustration 35]

## PAGE FROM VOLUME 73 OF THE STATUTES AT LARGE

---

622        **PUBLIC LAW 86-346—SEPT. 22, 1959**     [73 STAT.

bond shall be includible in gross income in the taxable year in which the obligation is finally redeemed or in the taxable year of final maturity, whichever is earlier."

Paying agents. Relief from liability. 57 Stat. 63.    SEC. 103. Subsection (i) of section 22 of the Second Liberty Bond Act, as amended (31 U.S.C., sec. 757c(i)), is amended by inserting after the third sentence thereof the following: "Relief from liability shall be granted in all cases where the Secretary of the Treasury shall determine, under regulations prescribed by him, that written notice of liability or potential liability has not been given by the United States, within ten years from the date of the erroneous payment, to any of the foregoing agents or agencies whose liability is to be determined: *Provided*, That no relief shall be granted in any case in which a qualified paying agent has assumed unconditional liability to the United States."

SEC. 104. The following provisions of law are amended by striking out the words "on original issue at par" and inserting in lieu thereof the words "on original issue at the issue price":

(1) Section 6(g)(5) of the Act of March 24, 1934, as amended
53 Stat. 1226.    (22 U.S.C., sec. 1393 (g)(5)), relating to the trust account for

---

R.S. 3701 (31 U.S.C. 742) was amended in 1959. Frequently, as in this instance, a public law amends many different sections of the U.S. Code.

---

(4) Section 15(b) of the Railroad Retirement Act of 1937 (45 U.S.C., sec. 228o(b)), relating to the Railroad Retirement Account.

70 Stat. 397.    (5) Section 209(e)(2) of the Highway Revenue Act of 1956
23 USC 120 note.   (23 U.S.C., sec. 173(e)(2)), relating to the Highway Trust Fund.
Tax exemption.   SEC. 105. (a) Section 3701 of the Revised Statutes (31 U.S.C., sec. 742) is amended by adding at the end thereof the following: "This exemption extends to every form of taxation that would require that either the obligations or the interest thereon, or both, be considered, directly or indirectly, in the computation of the tax, except nondiscriminatory franchise or other nonproperty taxes in lieu thereof imposed on corporations and except estate taxes or inheritance taxes."

Repeals.    (b) The following provisions of the Second Liberty Bond Act, as amended, relating to the tax-exempt status of obligations of the United States, are repealed, without changing the status of any outstanding obligation:

46 Stat. 19, 775.    (1) Subsections (b) and (d) of section 5 (31 U.S.C., sec. 754 (b) and (d));

40 Stat. 291, 1309.    (2) The second and third sentences of section 7 (31 U.S.C., sec. 747);

(3) Subsection (b) of section 18 (31 U.S.C., sec. 753(b));
55 Stat. 7.    (4) The first sentence of subsection (d) of section 22 (31 U.S.C., sec. 757c(d)).

## TITLE II—INCOME TAX TREATMENT OF CERTAIN EXCHANGES OF UNITED STATES OBLIGATIONS

68A Stat. 302. 26 USC 1031- 1036.    SEC. 201. (a) Part III of subchapter O of chapter 1 of the Internal Revenue Code of 1954 (relating to common nontaxable exchanges) is amended by adding at the end thereof the following new section:

## [Illustration 36]

## PAGE FROM U.S. CODE, 1970 EDITION

§ 742      TITLE 31.—MONEY AND FINANCE      Page 8428

any bonds, notes, or other securities, acquired by him on behalf of the United States under judicial process or otherwise, or delivered to him by an executive department or agency of the United States for disposal, or to enter into arrangements for the extension of the maturity thereof, in such manner, in such amounts, at such prices, for cash, securities, or other property, or any combination thereof, and upon such terms and conditions as he may deem advisable and in the public interest. No such bonds, notes, or other securities of any single issuer having at the date of disposal an aggregate face or par value, or in the case of no-par stock an aggregate stated or book value, in excess of $1,000,000, which may be held by the Secretary of the Treasury at any one time, shall be sold or otherwise disposed of under the authority of this section.

(b) Nothing contained in this section shall be construed to supersede or impair any authority otherwise granted to any officer or executive department or agency of the United States to sell, exchange, or otherwise dispose of any bonds, notes, or other securities, acquired by the United States under judicial process or otherwise. (Apr. 3, 1945, ch. 51, § 5, 59 Stat. 48.)

#### REFERENCES IN TEXT

Section 302 of Title 40, referred to in the text, was repealed by act Oct. 31, 1951, ch. 654, § 1 (95), 65 Stat. 705, and is now covered by sections 483 and 484 of Title 40, Public Buildings, Property and Works.

### § 742. Exemption from taxation.

Except as otherwise provided by law, all stocks, bonds, Treasury notes, and other obligations of the United States, shall be exempt from taxation by or under State or municipal or local authority. This exemption extends to every form of taxation that would require that either the obligations or the interest thereon, or both, be considered, directly or indirectly, in the computation of the tax, except nondiscriminatory franchise or other nonproperty taxes in lieu thereof imposed on corporations and except estate taxes or inheritance taxes. (R.S. § 3701; Sept. 22, 1959, Pub. L. 86–346, title I, § 105 (a), 73 Stat. 622.)

#### DERIVATION

Acts Feb. 25, 1862, ch. 33, § 2, 12 Stat. 346; Mar. 3, 1863, ch. 73, § 1, 12 Stat. 710; Mar. 3, 1864, ch. 17, § 1, 13 Stat. 13; June 30, 1864, ch. 172, § 1, 13 Stat. 218; Jan. 28, 1865, ch. 22, § 1, 13 Stat. 425; Mar. 3, 1865, ch. 77, § 2, 13 Stat. 469; July 14, 1870, ch. 256, § 1, 16 Stat. 272.

#### AMENDMENTS

1959—Pub. L. 86–346 added second sentence.

#### CROSS REFERENCES

United States obligations and evidences of ownership issued after March 27, 1942, as subject to Federal taxation, see section 742a of this title.

### § 742a. Same; by Federal tax Acts.

(a) Interest upon obligations, and dividends, earnings, or other income from shares, certificates, stock, or other evidences of ownership, and gain from the sale or other disposition of such obligations and evidences of ownership issued on or after March 28, 1942, by the United States or any agency or instrumentality thereof shall not have any exemption, as such, and loss from the sale or other disposition of such obligations or evidences of ownership shall not have any special treatment, as such, except as pro-

vided under the Internal Revenue Code of 1954; except that any such obligations which the United States Maritime Commission or the Federal Housing Administration had, prior to March 1, 1941, contracted to issue at a future date, shall when issued bear such tax-exemption privileges as were, at the time of such contract, provided in the law authorizing their issuance. For the purposes of this subsection a Territory, a possession of the United States, and the District of Columbia, and any political subdivision thereof, and any agency or instrumentality of any one or more of the foregoing, shall not be considered as an agency or instrumentality of the United States.

(b) The provisions of this section shall, with respect to such obligations and evidences of ownership, be considered as amendatory of and supplementary to the respective Acts or parts of Acts authorizing the issuance of such obligations and evidences of ownership, as amended and supplemented.

(c) Nothing contained herein shall be construed to amend or repeal sections 114 and 115 of the

> Here is 31 U.S.C. 742 as amended.
>
> Note how citation is given to original R.S. citation and amending public law.

(1), respectively, of Title 26, Internal Revenue Code of 1939, and were repealed by section 7851 of Title 26, Internal Revenue Code of 1954.

Sections 42 and 117 were repealed by section 7851 of Title 26, I. R. C. 1954. Section 42 is now covered by sections 451 and 454 of Title 26, I. R. C. 1954. Section 117 is now covered by sections 1221 and 1222 of Title 26, I. R. C. 1954. For provision deeming a reference in other laws to a provision of I. R. C. 1939, also as a reference to corresponding provision of I. R. C. 1954, see section 7852 (b) of Title 26.

#### AMENDMENTS

1959—Subsec. (a). Pub. L. 86–346 substituted "except as provided under the Internal Revenue Code of 1954" for "under the Internal Revenue Code, or laws amendatory or supplementary thereto."

1947—Subsec. (a). Act June 25, 1947, substituted "the

> Effect of amendment stated.

#### EFFECTIVE DATE OF 1959 AMENDMENT

Amendment of section by Pub. L. 86–346 effective for taxable years ending after Sept. 22, 1959, see section 203 of Pub. L. 86–346, set out as a note under section 1037 of Title 26, Internal Revenue Code.

#### ABOLISHMENT OF COMMISSION AND TRANSFER OF FUNCTIONS

The United States Maritime Commission was abolished by 1950 Reorg. Plan No. 21, eff. May 24, 1950, 15 F. R. 3178, 64 Stat. 1273, set out in the Appendix to Title 5, Government Organization and Employees, which transferred part of its functions and part of the functions of its Chairman to the Federal Maritime Board and the Chairman thereof, the Board having been created by that Plan as an agency within the Department of Commerce with an independent status in some respects, and transferred the remainder of the Commission's functions and the functions of its Chairman to the Secretary of Commerce, with power vested in the Secretary to authorize their performance by the Mari-

## [Illustration 37]

## PAGE FROM TITLE 31, U.S.C.A. POCKET SUPPLEMENT

---

MONEY AND FINANCE      **31 § 742**

#### Conditions for relief

(c) No relief shall be granted on account of interest coupons claimed to have been attached to a security unless the Secretary is satisfied that such coupons have not been paid and are in fact destroyed or will not become the basis of a valid claim against the United States.

#### Definition of "security"

(d) The term "security" means any direct obligation of the United States issued pursuant to law for valuable consideration, including bonds, notes, certificates of indebtedness, and Treasury bills, and interim certificates issued for any such security.

As amended May 27, 1971, Pub.L. 92–19, 85 Stat. 74.

**1971 Amendment.** Subsec. (a). Pub.L. 92–19, in revising the provisions, substituted former subsec. (d) provisions em- / or official, State or local government, Federal Government corporation, foreign government, or Federal Reserve bank.

This is the text of 31 U.S.C. 742 in an annotated code. Note how the text and notes are the same as in the U.S.C.

The difference is the case annotations that are added. They start immediately after the notes.

See next Illustration.

sec. (c) of this section.

Subsec. (b). Pub.L. 92–19, in revising the provisions, made it clear that indemnity bond is required whether relief is provided before, at, or after maturity, and deleted provision excepting certain classes of cases from the requirement of an indemnity bond where not essential in public interest, namely, where loss, theft, destruction, etc. occurred without fault of owner; where substantially entire security is surrendered and any missing portion is insufficient to form basis of a valid claim against the United States; where the security is transferable only by operation of law; and where owner of the security is the Federal Government

security and also meaning any bond issued under section 780 of Title 26, I.R.C. 1939, provision now covered in subsec. (d) of this section.

Subsec. (d). Pub.L. 92–19 substituted definition of "security", formerly included in former subsec. (c) defining "interest-bearing security of the United States" or "security" for former provision empowering Secretary of Treasury to make rules and regulations for administration of section, now incorporated in subsec. (a) of this section.

**Legislative History.** For legislative history and purpose of Pub.L. 92–19, see 1971 U.S.Code Cong. and Adm.News. p. ——.

→ **§ 742. Exemption from taxation** ←

Except as otherwise provided by law, all stocks, bonds, Treasury notes, and other obligations of the United States, shall be exempt from taxation by or under State or municipal or local authority. This exemption extends to every form of taxation that would require that either the obligations or the interest thereon, or both, be considered, directly or indirectly, in the computation of the tax, except nondiscriminatory franchise or other nonproperty taxes in lieu thereof imposed on corporations and except estate taxes or inheritance taxes. As amended Sept. 22, 1959, Pub.L. 86–346, Title I, § 105(a), 73 Stat. 622.

**1959 Amendment.** Pub.L. 86–346 amended section to add second sentence.

**Legislative History:** For legislative history and purpose of Pub.L. 86–346, see 1959 U.S.Code Cong. and Adm.News, p. 2769.

**Supplementary Index to Notes**

Generally **4a**
Mortgages **18**

**Library references**

Municipal Corporations ⟜956(1).
Taxation ⟜7.
C.J.S. Municipal Corporations § 1978 et seq.
C.J.S. Taxation § 209.

**4a. Generally**

Obligations of federal government cannot be taxed, either directly or indirectly, by state, municipal or local authorities. Peter Kiewit Sons' Co. v. Douglas County, 1955, 72 N.W.2d 415, 161 Neb. 93.

[Illustration 37–a]

## PAGE FROM TITLE 31, U.S.C.A.

**31 § 742**　　　MONEY AND FINANCE

**5. "Other obligation"**

Principle that obligations of federal government are immune from state taxation embraces indirect taxation of such obligations through their inclusion in tax imposed on all property of a taxpayer, and it is quite immaterial that state tax does not discriminate against the federal obligations. Society for Savings in City of Cleveland, Ohio, v. Bowers, Ohio 1955, 75 S.Ct. 607, 349 U.S. 143, 99 L.Ed. 950.

Mortgages, executed by mortgagors who were lessees of federal land to be used for construction of military housing projects, though guaranteed by United States, did not constitute direct obligations of United States within provisions of this section exempting from state or local taxation, except as otherwise provided by law, all stocks, bonds, treasury notes, and other obligations of United States. Application of S. S. Silberblatt, Inc., 1958, 180 N.Y.S.2d 210, 6 A.D.2d 693.

**6. Stocks and securities**

Federal securities owned by corporation for profit were properly included in franchise tax base in determining franchise taxes notwithstanding this section exempting federal securities from taxation. Raymond Bag Co. v. Bowers, 1955, 126 N.E.2d 321, 163 Ohio St. 275, appeal dismissed 76 S.Ct. 648, 350 U.S. 1003, 100 L.Ed. 866, rehearing denied 76 S.Ct. 777, 351 U.S. 928, 100 L.Ed. 1457.

**10. Franchise tax**

New Jersey statute imposing on each domestic corporation an annual franchise tax measured by corporation's net worth, which is defined as sum of corporation's issued and outstanding capital stock, paid-in or capital surplus, earned surplus and undivided profits, other surplus accounts, which will accrue to shareholders, not including depreciation reserves, and debts owed to shareholders owning 10 per cent or more of corporation's stock, is valid despite the inclusion of tax-exempt federal bonds in the determination of net worth. Werner Mach. Co. v. Director of Division of Taxation, Dept of Treasury, State of N. J., N.J.1956, 76 S.Ct. 534, 350 U.S. 492, 100 L Ed. 634.

**12. National bank notes**

As exception to general rule of immunity of federal government obligations from property taxation by states, tax may be levied upon shareholders of state or national banks though tax is meas-

ured by corporate assets which include federal obligations and though payment of tax by corporation as collecting agent is required. Society for Savings in City of Cleveland, Ohio v. Bowers, Ohio 1955, 75 S.Ct. 607, 349 U.S. 143, 99 L.Ed. 950.

**18. Mortgages**

Arrangement, whereby successful bidder on military housing project became sole stockholder of corporations which obtained leases of federal land and gave mortgages under National Housing Act, section 1748–1748h of Title 12 in order to procure necessary private financing for construction of project with payment of mortgages guaranteed by United States, was designed to relieve government of obligation to provide housing for its military personnel and at same time avoid increasing the national debt, government did not pledge its credit in the usual sense and mortgages were not exempt from mortgage recording tax under this section exempting stocks, bonds, treasury notes and all other obligations of the United States from local taxation. S. S. Silberblatt, Inc. v. Tax Commission of State of N. Y., 1959, 159 N.E.2d 195, 5 N.Y.2d 635, 186 N.Y.S.2d 646, certiorari denied 80 S.Ct. 253, 361 U.S. 912, 4 L. Ed.2d 183.

Where contractor, who was successful bidder on military housing project, was sole stockholder of corporations which obtained leases of federal land and gave mortgages under National Housing Act, section 1748–1748h of Title 12 in order to procure necessary private financing for construction of project with mortgage payments guaranteed by United States, it would not be assumed, in absence of statute, that the government function was involved, so as to exempt mortgages from New York mortgage recording tax. Id.

Where contractor, who was successful bidder on military housing project, was sole stockholder of corporations which obtained leases of federal land and gave mortgages under National Housing Act section 1748–1748h of Title 12 in order to procure necessary private financing for construction of project with mortgage payments guaranteed by United States, contractor and corporate mortgagors were not exempt from state and local taxation or state mortgage recording tax as instrumentalities of federal government or its agencies, notwithstanding fact that all of capital stock of each corporation would ultimately be owned by federal government. Id.

> Every time a court cites or interprets a code section, a digest of the case appears in the annotations.

cept as provided under the Internal Revenue Code of 1954; except that any such obligations which the United States Maritime Commission or the Federal Housing Administration had, prior to March 1, 1941, contracted to issue at a future date, shall when issued bear such tax-exemption privileges as were, at the time of such contract, provided in the law authorizing their issuance. For the purposes of this subsection a Territory, a possession of the United States, and the District of Columbia, and any political subdivision thereof, and any agency or instrumentality of any one or more of the foregoing, shall not be considered as an agency or

## [Illustration 38]

## PAGE FROM THE POPULAR NAME TABLE U.S.C.A.

**POPULAR NAME TABLE**                              **616**

**Legislative Reorganization Act of 1970**
Pub.L. 91–510, Oct. 26, 1970, 84 Stat. 1140 (**Title 2, §§ 28, 29, 60–1, 61–1, 72a, 88b–1, 166, 190a–190d, 190f, 190h–190k, 198, 281–281b, 282–282e, 331–336, 411–417, 2107, 8332; Title 5, §§ 2107, 5533, 8332; Title 8. § 1106 note; Title 31, §§ 11, 1151–1157, 1171–1176; Title 40, §§ 166 note, 166b–1a–166b–1f, 184a, 193m–1, 851**)
Pub.L. 91–522, § 1(1), (3)–(5), Dec. 16, 1970, 84 Stat. 1440

**Leprosy Act**
Mar. 3, 1905, ch. 1443, 33 Stat. 1009

**Lesinski Pension Increase Act**
June 6, 1940, ch. 246, 54 Stat. 237

**Lever Act (Food Control)**
Aug. 10, 1917, ch. 53, 40 Stat. 276
Oct. 22, 1919, ch. 80, 41 Stat. 297

**Liberty Loan Acts**
(First)
Apr. 24, 1917, ch. 4, 40 Stat. 35 (**Title 31, §§ 745, 746, 755, 755a, 759, 764, 768, 774, 804**)
(Second)
Sept. 24, 1917, ch. 56, 40 Stat. 288 (**Title 31, §§ 745, 747, 752–754b, 757, 757b–757e, 758, 760, 764–766, 769, 771, 773, 774, 801**)
(Third)
Apr. 4, 1918, ch. 44, 40 Stat. 502 (**Title 31, §§ 752, 752a, 754, 765, 766, 771, 774**)
(Fourth)
July 9, 1918, ch. 142, 40 Stat. 844 (**Title 31, §§ 750, 752, 772, 774**)
(Supplement to Second)
Sept. 24, 1918, ch. 176, 40 Stat. 965 (**Title 12, §§ 84, 95a; Title 31, §§ 757, 774; Title 50 App., § 5**)
(Victory)
Mar. 3, 1919, ch. 100, 40 Stat. 1309 (**Title 31, §§ 750, 753, 754, 763, 767, 774, 802, 803**)
Mar. 2, 1923, ch. 179, 42 Stat. 1427 (**Title 31, § 767**)

**Library of Congress Police Act**
Aug. 4, 1950, ch. 561, §§ 1 to 11, 64 Stat. 411 (**Title 2, §§ 167 to 167j**)
June 17, 1970, Pub.L. 91–281, 84 Stat. 309 (**Title 2, § 167j**)

**Library of Congress Trust Fund Board Act**
Mar. 3, 1925, ch. 423, 43 Stat. 1107 (**Title 2, §§ 154–163**)

**Library Services Act**

> **This Table of Popular Name Table is from the *U.S.C.A.***
>
> **There is a similar Table in the *U.S.C.***

Pub.L. 89–511, §§ 2–10, 12(a), (b), July 19, 1966, 80 Stat. 313 (**Title 20, §§ 351–353, 355–355b, 355e to 355e–3, 355f to 355f–7, 356–358**)
Pub.L. 90–154, § 1, Nov. 24, 1967, 81 Stat. 509 (**Title 20, §§ 355e–2, 355f–2, 355f–3, 355f–6, 355f–7, 358**)
Pub.L. 91–600, § 2(b), Dec. 30, 1970, 84 Stat. 1660–1669 (**Title 20, §§ 351–354, 355a–355c, 355e to 355e–2**)

**Library Services and Construction Act Amendments of 1966**
Pub.L. 89–511, July 19, 1966, 80 Stat. 313 (**Title 20, §§ 351–353, 355–355b, 355e to 355e–3, 355f to 355f–7, 356–358**)

**Library Services and Construction Amendments of 1970**
Pub.L. 91–600, Dec. 30, 1970, 84 Stat. 1660 (**Title 20, §§ 351–354, 355a–355c, 355e to 355e–2, 1204, 1211**)

## [Illustration 39]

## PAGE FROM SHEPARD'S FEDERAL AND STATE ACTS CITED BY POPULAR NAME

FEDERAL AND STATE ACTS CITED BY POPULAR NAMES     Bon

**Bond Act of 1915 (Improvement Bonds)**
Cal. Streets and Highways Code §8500 et seq.

**Bond Act of 1918**
N. J. Rev. Stat. 1937, 2:60-207 to 2:60-211

**Bond Act of 1935 (Revenue)**
N. C. Public Laws 1935, Ch. 473

**Bond Act of 1938 (Revenue)**
N. C. Gen. Stat. 1943, §160-413 et seq.

**Bond Act of 1946 (Veterans)**

> All laws are listed in this volume by popular name.

**Bond Act of 1951 (Veterans)**
Cal. Military and Veterans Code §996 et seq.

**Bond Act of 1962 (State Construction Program)**
Cal. Statutes 1962, 1st Ex. Sess., Ch. 23, p. 193

**Bond Act of 1962 (State School Building Aid)**
Cal. Education Code 1959, §19891 et seq.

**Bond Act of 1962 (Veterans)**
Cal. Military and Veterans Code §996.87 et seq.

**Bond and Coupon Collection Law**
Cal. Government Code §16311

**Bond and Coupon Registration Law**
Cal. Statutes 1935, p. 994

**Bond and License Act (Citrus Fruits)**
Fla. Stat. 1965, 601.55 et seq.

**Bond and Lien Collateral Act of 1949**
Az. Rev. Stat. 1956, §30-191 et seq.

**Bond and Mortgage Act**
N. J. Rev. Stat. 1937, 2A:50-1 et seq.

**Bond and Warrant Acts**
N. J. Rev. Stat. 1937, 2:27-266 to 2:27-277, 22: 1-13
Tex. Rev. Civ. Stat. 1948, Art. 2368a

**Bond Assumption Acts (Highways)**
Tex. Rev. Civ. Stat. 1948, Arts. 6674q-1 to 6674q-11a

**Bond Certification Law**
Cal. Water Code §20000 et seq.

**Bond Compromise Law (Municipal)**
Cal. Statutes 1903, p. 164

**Bond Curative Act (Municipalities)**
Wis. Stat. 1965, 67.02

**Bond for Deed Act**
La. Rev. Stat. 1950, 9:2941 et seq.

**Bond Guarantors Protection Law**
Cal. Government Code §5100 et seq.

**Bond Investment Act**
Ohio Rev. Code 1953, 3949.01 et seq.

**Bond Issue Acts (Roads)**
Ill. Rev. Stat. 1965, Ch. 121, §6-510 et seq.

**Bond Limitation Act**
U. S. Code 1964 Title 31, §757b
May 26, 1938, c. 285, 52 Stat. 447
Kan. Stat. Anno. 10-301 et seq.

**Bond Plan Enabling Act (Industrial Locations)**
Ala. Code 1958, Title 37, §511(20)

**Bond Purchase Act**
U. S. Code 1964 Title 31, §741
Mar. 3, 1881, c. 133, §2, 21 Stat. 435

**Bond Refinancing Act (Revenue)**
W. Va. Code 1931, Ch. 13, Art. 2A, §1 et seq.

**Bond Refinancing Act of 1937**
Ark. Stat. 1947, 19-4301 et seq.

**Bond Refunding Act**
Ark. Pope's Digest 1937, §§11237-11367

**Bond Refunding Act (Municipal)**
Mich. Comp. Laws 1948, 136.1 et seq.

**Bond Refunding and Special Assessment Law of 1939**
Cal. Government Code §59100 et seq.

**Bond Registration Act**
Mo. Rev. Stat. 1959, 108.240 et seq.

**Bond Registration Act (Municipal)**
Kan. Stat. Anno. 10-601 et seq.
N. C. Gen. Stat. 1943, §160-406 et seq.

**Bond Retirement Fund Act**
Okla. Stat. 1961, Title 62, §217.1 et seq.

**Bond Sinking Fund Law of 1943**
Cal. Statutes 1943, Ch. 611, p. 2225

**Bond Surrender Act**
Okla. Stat. 1961, Title 62, §341 et seq.

**Bond Trust Fund Act**
Nev. Rev. Stat. 1957, 282.230 et seq.

**Bond Validating Acts**
Fla. Stat. 1965, 75.01 et seq.
Ida. Laws 1935, First Extra Session, Ch. 3
Ida. Laws 1937, Ch. 232
*Continued*

## SECTION F.   ADDITIONAL SOURCES OF INTERPRETATION OF FEDERAL STATUTES

### 1.   Current Statutes

a.   *Shepard's United States Citations.*

This publication is discussed in detail on Chapter 14.

b.   *U. S. Supreme Court Reports Digest* (Lawyers Co-operative Publishing Co.).

Volume 14 of this digest provides citations to Supreme Court decisions which have construed federal acts.   The table of Laws Cited and Construed is divided according to:  (1) Statutes at Large, (2) United States Revised Statutes, and (3) United States Code Citations. The Supreme Court case references are given under the appropriate statutory designations.

c.   U. S. Supreme Court Digest.

d.   *Modern Federal Practice Digest* and *Federal Digest.*

e.   The Table of Statutes cited in each volume of *Am.Jur.2d* indicates where provisions of the *United States Code* are cited in articles in each volume.

f.   Texts, *A.L.R.* annotations, and encyclopedias provide expository discussion on federal statutory law.

g.   Periodical articles treat federal statutory law analytically and with some detail.

### 2.   Early Federal Statutes

The following selected compilations of earlier federal laws, since superseded, have been published.   They are useful historical sources.

a.   *Laws of the United States, 1789–1815.*   Fowell edition.   12 vols.   Chronological compilation.

b.   *Laws of the United States, 1785–1839.*   Bioren and Duane edition.   10 vols.   Chronological compilation.

c.   *Public and General Statutes,* 1789–1827 (1st ed.), 1789–1836 (2d ed.), 1789–1847 (3d ed.).   Story and Sharswood editions.   Chronological compilations.

d.   *United States Compiled Statutes* (West Pub. Co.) 1789–1901. (1st ed.) 3 vols. Unannotated.   (2d ed.), 1916 and two cumulative supplements, 1919 and 1923.   12 vols. + 4 vols. Annotated. This publication is arranged like the *Revised Statutes.*

e.   *Federal Statutes Annotated* (Edw. Thompson Co.).   (1st ed.), 1906.   10 vols. (2d ed.), 1916.   12 vols. with annual supplements. The arrangement is encyclopedic by topics.

f. *Barnes' Federal Code* (Bobbs-Merrill Co.). Published in 1919 with a 1925 cumulative supplement. Its arrangement is similar to the *Revised Statutes.*

g. *Mason's United States Code Annotated.* Published in 1926. 3 vols. with supplements. It is arranged like the *United States Code.*

---

## SECTION G.  INDEXES TO FEDERAL STATUTES

Several indexes to federal statutes of current utility, including obsolete and superseded laws, have been published. Of course, the standard indexes which are part of the current *United States Code Annotated, Federal Code Annotated* and *United States Code* provide access to the public, permanent laws in force. However, the indexes listed here cover *all* public, permanent laws (*operative* and *inoperative*) as of the dates of publication.

1. *Index Analysis of Federal Statutes* (Beaman and McNamara, ed., 1789–1873).

This index to the *Revised Statutes* and the *Statutes at Large,* for the period from 1789 to 1873, was published in 1911. Although covering an earlier period, it supplemented *Scott and Beaman's Index Analysis of the Federal Statutes,* 1873–1907 (since superseded). The Beaman and McNamara edition indexes the federal public, permanent laws for 1789 to 1873 and includes laws enacted which were inoperative when the *Revised Statutes* became law.

2. *Index to the Federal Statutes, 1874–1931,* compiled by Mc-Clenon and Gilbert.

This is a revision of the early *Scott and Beaman, Index Analysis of the Federal Statutes,* 1873–1907. The *Index* includes references to public, permanent laws, which were operative and inoperative, appearing in the *Revised Statutes, Statutes at Large* and the *United States Code* for 1874–1931. It contains a list of statutory definitions and a list of treaties and conventions.

Obsolete provisions (expressly repealed or otherwise superseded) are cited in italics. Where all the provisions cited for an entry appear to be obsolete, a * has been placed at the beginning of the entry. Where a provision appears to be amended, or superseded in part, by subsequent legislation, this is identified by a note (a) following the citation. Provisions which have become obsolete through the lapse of time, in the absence of specific superseding legislation, are assigned the designation (b).

The *Index* also includes a Table of Repeals and Amendments of Statutory Provisions Indexed. The Table lists the provisions by their

Revised Statutes section numbers or Statutes at Large citations with references and explanations to the amending or superseding Statutes at Large provisions.

---

## SECTION H. FEDERAL LEGISLATION: RESEARCH PROCEDURE

### Operative Federal Law

If the problem involves a federal act which is in effect, refer to the *United States Code Annotated* or the *Federal Code Annotated* for the text of the law, its history and digests of the cases interpreting it. The *United States Code* also provides the text of current federal laws; however, it is not annotated by digests of cases interpreting the legislation. The *Statutes at Large* is another available source for the text of the acts. The encyclopedias include discussion of Federal legislation. Treatises, A.L.R. annotations and periodical articles also give textual treatment and are good sources for expository and analytical evaluation of statutory law.

To trace the origin of an act and its amendments, consult the parenthetical references following the code section in the *United States Code Annotated* and the *Federal Code Annotated*. Reference also should be made to the historical notes which follow the parenthetical references.

If the *Statutes at Large* citation is given, an act can be located in a code by using the Tables Volume. Check the Parallel Tables from the *Statutes at Large* citation to the code title and sections.

The titles and section numbers of the *United States Code*, the *United States Code Annotated* and the *Federal Code Annotated* are the same; therefore, if a searcher has the citation to an act in one set, he can locate it equally well in the others by the use of the same reference.

To determine whether the act has recently been amended or repealed, check the pocket and pamphlet supplements to the *United States Code Annotated* or the *Federal Code Annotated*. This should be the standard procedure followed in using all legal publications with supplementary parts. *Shepard's United States Citations* also provides a history of the act with citations to the latest changes.

For additional cases interpreting the act, consult the *Shepard's United States Citations*. Volume 14 of the *U. S. Supreme Court Reports Digest* (Lawyers Co-op. Pub. Co.) also provides citations to Supreme Court decisions which have construed federal acts. The U. S. Supreme Court digests, *Federal Digest* and *Modern Federal Practice Digest* cover operative federal legislation cases.

The Statutes Tables in U.S.C.A. and F.C.A. also give the history of all acts passed (operative and inoperative) since the *Revised Statutes (1875)*.

## Search Methods

To determine the existence of federal legislation on a given point, the following procedure may be used:

(1) *The Index Method.* Analyze the facts and the law. Check the general index or the title or volume index (if one exists) to a current federal code, using a fact or topical analysis. Consult the general index pocket part for the latest information, for it supplements the general index and the title or volume index.

(2) *The Topic or Analytic Method.* The federal law is divided into fifty titles which are alphabetically arranged in codes. Select the appropriate topic. Then consult the analysis of the topic to locate the specific section number. The Table of Titles is useful to locate the proper topic if one is unfamiliar with the title designations. For an analysis of the cases interpreting the section, refer to the Subdivision Index (U.S.C.A.) or Analysis (F.C.A.) which follows the text of the law and precedes the notes to decisions. The figures following the headings in the Subdivision Index refer to case and note numbers.

(3) *The Definition Method.* If the definition of a word is in point, consult the general index to the code under the heading, "Definitions." The defined words are listed alphabetically under "Definitions." Reference is given to the title and section of the code which defines the word as used in the statute. Words are also defined under the subjects in the indexes.

## Inoperative Federal Law

To locate an act no longer in force, passed between 1874 and 1931, consult the *Index to Federal Statutes.* For acts in force prior to 1873, and inoperative when the *Revised Statutes* was enacted, refer to the *Index Analysis of the Federal Statutes* (Beaman and McNamara, ed. 1789–1873).

The *Revised Statutes*, an earlier edition to the *United States Code* or *a superseded code* (see Section F2 above) may provide the text to a law which is no longer in effect. Each has an index.

The Statutes Tables in U.S.C.A. and F.C.A. give the history of all acts passed since the *Revised Statutes (1875)*.

For notes to cases interpreting acts repealed prior to the compilation of the *Federal Code Annotated*, consult the Uncodified Laws volume of the *Federal Code Annotated*.

## Private, Temporary and Local Laws

The preceding sections relate to search for permanent, public, general laws. Less frequently, the lawyer is confronted with the problem of locating a private, temporary or local law which is not included in the codes or indexes previously discussed. The latter federal laws are published in the *Statutes at Large*. If the date is known, the law can be located easily in the *Statutes at Large*. However, if the date of enactment is not known, the act cannot be readily found. The *Consolidated Index to the Statutes at Large*, covering the period 1789 to 1903, should be consulted for acts passed during those dates. After that period, each volume of the *Statutes at Large* must individually be checked. Public temporary and local laws are published in the *United States Code Congressional and Administrative News*. Public temporary laws are sometimes included in the *United States Code Annotated*, the *Federal Code Annotated* and the *United States Code*, e. g., price control legislation. Some special, local and temporary public laws and appropriation acts are included in *F.C.A. Public Laws and Administrative Material* annual volumes and current pamphlet supplements.

For annotations to private, special and temporary acts, refer to the *Federal Code Annotated*, Uncodified Laws volume.

## Popular Names of Federal Acts

When the popular name of a federal act is known, one of the following publications can be consulted to ascertain its citation:

a. *Shepard's Federal Acts by Popular Names.*

b. *United States Code Annotated*, Table of Acts cited by popular names in volume (5) of its index and pocket supplement.

c. The popular names for federal acts are also listed in their alphabetical order in the general indexes to the *United States Code Annotated* and the *Federal Code Annotated*.

d. *United States Code*, 1970 edition, and Supplements.

e. *Federal Code Annotated*, Tables volumes.

f. *U. S. Supreme Court Reports Digest* (Lawyers Co-op. Pub. Co.), volume 14.

g. *U. S. Code Congressional and Administrative News.*

The preceding lists (paragraphs a–f, above) are cumulated. The Tables in the *News* appear in the annual volumes published for each session of Congress and are not cumulated.

## Use of Tables

Tables in the *United States Code* (Tables volume and Supplements), the *United States Code Annotated* (Tables volume) and the *Federal Code Annotated* (Tables volumes) provide useful parallel information. They can be consulted for the following significant, as well as other, purposes:

To refer from the *Revised Statutes* or *Statutes at Large* citations to the corresponding sections in the code.

To cross-reference from former Title 18 U.S.C. (Criminal Code) to the new section numbers.

To cross-reference from former Title 28 U.S.C. (Judicial Code) to the new section numbers.

To locate sections of the Bankruptcy Act of 1898, as amended in the code.

To refer from provisions of Title 26 of the *United States Code,* 1925 and 1934 editions, to Title 26, Internal Revenue Code.

To locate sections of the Interstate Commerce Act of 1887, as amended in Title 49 of the code.

To locate statutes repealed and eliminated.

## Public Law Citations

When only the public law number is known, consult the Statutes at Large Tables in U.S.C.A. or F.C.A. to obtain the citation to an act (from 32 Statutes at Large, 1902 to date). The List of Public Laws in each volume of the *Statutes at Large* also cross-references to the *Statutes at Large* citations. The *United States Code Congressional and Administrative News* is another source of obtaining statutory citations when only the public law numbers are known (consult the Table of Public Laws).

---

## SECTION I. METHODS OF CITATION

### 1. Current Federal Statutes

Current statutes which have not yet been published in the *Statutes at Large* are cited:

Pub.L. 89–531 (Aug. 11, 1966).

When a current statute has been published in the *United States Code Congressional and Administrative News,* cite it as follows:

Pub.L. 89–429 (May 24, 1966), U.S.Code Cong. & Ad.News 1478 (1966).

A law which has been published in the *Statutes at Large* should not be cited by Public or Private Law designation.

## 2.   Statutes at Large

An act appearing in the *Statutes at Large* and the *United States Code* is cited:

52 Stat. 851 (1938), 11 U.S.C. § 35 (1958).

## 3.   Revised Statutes

Laws in the *Revised Statutes of 1875* should be cited to it rather than to the *Statutes at Large*.  The "U.S." reference is omitted; however, the *United States Code* citation is included.

Rev.Stat. (or R.S.) § 1708 (1875), 22 U.S.C. § 1174 (1958).

When citing the second edition of 1878 to the *Revised Statutes*, note it as follows:

Rev.Stat. (or R.S.) § 1708 (2d ed. 1878), 22 U.S.C. § 1174 (1958).

## 4.   In General

References to other federal statutes should include the volume, page number and year of the *Statutes at Large* and the title, section and edition date of the *United States Code*.

60 Stat. 999 (1946), 22 U.S.C. § 801 (1958).

The title or date of enactment of an act may be cited when such information has research significance:

Foreign Service Act of 1946, 60 Stat. 999, 22 U.S.C. § 801 (1958).

Act of Aug. 13, 1946, 60 Stat. 999, 22 U.S.C. § 801 (1958).

## 5.   Amended Statutes

An amended statute may be cited as follows:
36 Stat. 914 (1911), as amended, 45 U.S.C. § 26 (1952).

## 6.   Internal Revenue Code

The *Internal Revenue Code* is cited:

Int.Rev.Code of 1954, § 564.

---

## SECTION J.   SUMMARY

## 1.   Statutes at Large

   a.   Published after each session of Congress.

   b.   Arrangement—by chapters and chronologically by date of passage of act.

c. Grouped into public and private laws.

d. Volumes 1–8 were published some time after the acts were passed.

(1) Volumes 1–5 contain public laws and are arranged in chronological order.

(2) Volume 6 consists of private laws.

(3) Volume 7 relates to Indian treaties.

(4) Volume 8 contains foreign treaties.

e. For various periods Public and Private Laws were published in two parts. Part two covered Private laws and resolutions, concurrent resolutions, treaties and proclamations. Since 1959, they are published in a single volume after each session of Congress.

f. Since 1950, treaties are not published as a part of the *Statutes at Large*.

g. Marginal notes since Volume 33 give House or Senate bill number, Public Law number and date.

h. Each volume includes a chronological and numerical list of laws and a very complete subject index.

2. **U.S. Code Congressional and Administrative News**

a. Biweekly or monthly pamphlet and cumulative annual volumes.

b. Full text of current federal public laws.

c. Cumulative index to public slip laws of the session of Congress.

d. Selected legislative histories relating to significant public acts.

e. Executive Orders and Proclamations of the President.

f. Pamphlets and cumulative annual volume of Federal Tax Regulations.

3. **Methods of Codification (see Section B, above)**

4. **Features Common to Codes**

a. Constitutions.

b. Text of statutes.

c. Historical notes.

d. Annotations.

e. Tables.

f. Indexes.

g. Popular names of acts.

h. Pocket and pamphlet supplementation.

### 5. United States Revised Statutes

    a.  1875 edition—rewritten and reenacted, with inaccuracies and unauthorized changes.

    b.  1878 edition—evidence of the law to December 1, 1873.

        (1) Rewritten and classified.

        (2) Some case annotations and marginal notes.

### 6. United States Code, 1970 Ed.

    a.  Current official code.

    b.  Covers public and permanent laws in force.

    c.  Arranged alphabetically under 50 titles.

    d.  Periodically supplemented by bound volumes.

    e.  Complete index.

    f.  Many tables.

    g.  *Prima facie* evidence of law; is a recompilation of the law and not a reenactment.

    h.  A number of titles has been revised and enacted. They are evidence of the law.

### 7. United States Code Annotated

    a.  Text of public, permanent laws in force.

    b.  Arranged under the 50 titles of U.S.C.

    c.  Annotations are complete, covering federal and state court decisions and Attorney General opinions.

    d.  Historical notes.

    e.  About 135 volumes with one or more separate volumes for each code title.

    f.  Kept current by cumulative pocket and pamphlet supplements and replacement volumes.

    g.  Five-volume Index and title indexes in recompiled volumes.

    h.  Tables.

    i.  Volume (5) of the Index includes a Table of Acts by Popular Names.

    j.  Federal court rules.

### 8. Federal Code Annotated

    a.  Compact publication of about 40 volumes, with several sequential titles bound together in a volume whenever feasible.

    b.  Covers public and permanent laws in force.

    c.  Annotations include federal and state court decisions and Attorney General's opinions.

    d.   Historical notes.

    e.   Volume of Uncodified Laws.

    f.   Two Tables volumes.

    g.   General Index and each individual volume also has an index covering its subject matter.

    h.   Research aid references.

    i.   Being replaced by United States Code Service.

    j.   Federal acts by popular names.

    k.   Kept up-to-date by cumulative annual pocket and pamphlet supplements and replacement volumes.

    *l.*   Federal court rules.

    m.   *Public Laws and Administrative Materials,* current pamphlet material cumulated into a bound annual volume.

**9.  Additional Sources of Interpretation of Federal Statutes (see Section F, above)**

**10.  Early Federal Statutes (see Section F2, above)**

**11.  Indexes to Federal Statutes**

    a.   Beaman and McNamara, Index Analysis of Federal Statutes, 1789–1873.

        (1)  Public and permanent laws.

        (2)  Includes obsolete and superseded laws.

    b.   Index to the Federal Statutes, 1874–1931 (ed. McClenon and Gilbert).

        (1)  Public and permanent laws.

        (2)  Includes operative and inoperative laws.

**12.  Popular Names of Federal Acts Tables**

    a.   *Shepard's Federal Acts by Popular Names or Short Titles.* Supplemented by the paper-covered cumulative supplement to *Shepard's United States Citations* (Statutes and Dept. Reps.).

    b.   *United States Code Annotated;* Table in volume (5) of the General Index.

    c.   *Federal Code Annotated,* Tables volumes.

    d.   The popular names for federal acts also are listed in the general indexes to U.S.C.A. and F.C.A.

    e.   *United States Code,* 1964 edition; in first General Index volume (vol. 12) and Supplements.

    f.   *U. S. Supreme Court Reports Digest* (Law. Co-op.), vol. 14.

    g.   *U. S. Code Congressional and Administrative News.*

### 13.  Functions of Tables of Federal Statutes

    a.   Refer from *Revised Statutes* and *Statutes at Large* to specific code; also give history of acts.

    b.   Parallel tables from former Title to current sections.

    c.   Lists of Executive Orders and Proclamations that implement or cite federal laws.

# Chapter 10

## FEDERAL LEGISLATIVE HISTORIES

### SECTION A.  LEGISLATIVE HISTORIES IN LEGAL RESEARCH

A law is the means by which a legislative body expressed its intent to declare, command, or prohibit some action.  A legislative history is the term used to designate the documents that contain the information considered by the legislature prior to reaching its decision to enact a law.  A legislative history of a statute is consulted in order to better understand the reasons for the enactment of the statute.  As an act of the legislature is prospective, and it is not always drafted with the most precise language, courts constantly look to extrinsic aids in determining the intent of a legislative body.  This intent may be found in the language of the bill introduced into the legislature, the subsequent amendments to the bill, the reports of legislative committees to which the bill was assigned, and other legislative documents issued in consideration of the submitted bill.

In more recent years, great weight has been given to legislative documents to determine the purpose of a statute when the act itself omits a clear intent or a plain meaning.  There have been some differences of opinion among judges as to the extent to which legislative histories should be used to determine the meaning of legislation.  But this conflict of opinion is more academic than it is practical, for the use of legislative histories is a very essential technique of contemporary federal litigation.[1]

Despite their popularity, the criticisms of their use should be noted.  Mr. Justice Jackson, holding the more circumspect view, rea-

---

[1] An illustration is Steiner v. Mitchell, 350 U.S. 247, 76 S.Ct. 330, 100 L.Ed. 267 (1956), in which the Supreme Court of the United States relied upon the legislative history of the Portal-to-Portal Act to reach its conclusion.  In fact, Mr. Chief Justice Warren, who wrote the opinion, attaches such significance to the legislative history as to include a colloquy from the Congressional Record as an Appendix to the Opinion of the Court, id. at 256.

See:  A Decade of Legislative History in the Supreme Court:  1950–1959, 46 Va. L.Rev. 1408 (1960).

Pro:  Finley, Crystal Gazing:  The Problem of Legislative History, 45 A.B.A.J. 1281 (1959).

Contra:  Stringham, Crystal Gazing:  Legislative History in Action, 47 A.B.A.J. 466 (1961).

See also:  Folson, Legislative History;  Research for Interpretation of Laws. 1972.

soned that "Resort to legislative history is only justified where the face of the Act is inescapably ambiguous, and then I think we should not go beyond Committee reports, which presumably are well considered and carefully prepared. \* \* \* But to select casual statements from floor debates, not always distinguished for candor or accuracy, as a basis for making up our minds what law Congress intended to enact is to substitute ourselves for the Congress in one of its important functions. \* \* \* Moreover, it is only the words of the bill that have presidential approval, where that approval is given. It is not to be supposed that, in signing a bill, the President endorses the whole Congressional Record. For us to undertake to reconstruct an enactment from legislative history is merely to involve the Court in political controversies which are quite proper in the enactment of a bill but should have no place in its interpretation." [2]

On another occasion Mr. Justice Jackson made the revealing point: "It is a poor cause that cannot find some plausible support in legislative history, which often includes tentative rather than final views of legislators or leaves misinterpretation unanswered lest more definite statements imperil the chance of passage." [3]

To many authorities, such legislative explorations are conceived to be hazardous. Supporting this view is the long-standing rule followed by the English courts which denies recognition to legislative statements in ascertaining the meaning of a statute.[4] Holmes shared the same opinion: "We do not inquire what the legislature meant, we ask only what the statute means."

Despite these emphatic viewpoints, Jackson and other judges, admittedly, have often resorted to legislative histories as guides to the meaning of statutes.[5] Therefore, it is well for the researcher to be aware of the value of legislative history in fortifying an argument. In this regard, a knowledge of the source materials, whence an interpretative theory is developed, or disproved, is most advantageous.

[2] Schwegmann Bros. v. Calvert Corp., 341 U.S. 384, 395–396, 71 S.Ct. 745, 751, 95 L.Ed. 1035, 1048–1049 (1950).

[3] Jackson, The Meaning of Statutes: What Congress Says or What the Court Says, 34 A.B.A.J. 535, 538 (1948).

[4] Holdsworth, Some Makers of English Law 294–296 (1938).

[5] Schwegmann Bros. v. Calvert Corp., op. cit. note 2 at 396. See also Jackson, op. cit. note 3 at 537.

## SECTION B.  THE ELEMENTS OF A FEDERAL LEGISLATIVE HISTORY

A legislative history consists of the following materials:

*Bill and Amendments.*  The bill and amendments as introduced, reported and passed by the two houses.

*Committee Hearings.*   The transcript of hearings before the Senate and House Committees on the bill containing the testimony of expert witnesses.

*Committee Reports.*  Individual reports, explaining the purpose of the bill, are prepared by the Committees when reported back to each house.  They may include majority and minority Committee reports.

*Congressional Debates.*  The floor debates on the bill appear in the *Congressional Record.*

*Conference Reports.*  When the bills passed by both houses differ substantively, a Conference Committee, comprised of members of the Senate and the House, may report back an agreed compromise.

### 1.   Bill and Amendments

Congressional bills are numbered consecutively for a Congress. This number identifies the bill and relates it to the reports, hearings and debates on it.  When finally enacted into law, the bill number is noted in the published slip law and in the *Statutes at Large.*

### 2.   Committee Hearings

The primary function of hearings is to provide members of Congress with information which may be useful in the preparation of legislation.  However, hearings are held in connection with some, but not all, bills.  Interested persons, experts and others may be given an opportunity or asked to express themselves at hearings on pending legislation.  The statements may be carefully prepared or impromptu, exhaustive or cursory, objective or biased.  Although some statements uttered by persons who support a special interest may be discounted, the objective opinions of experts carry significant weight in the formulation or modification of legislation.

Not all hearings are published.  The existence of printed hearings may be determined by consulting the table "History of Bills Enacted Into Public Law" in the appropriate annual *Daily Digest* of the *Congressional Record* or several other sources which will be subsequently discussed.

Hearings are not published as a part of an overall series; however, some committees have conveniently serialized their publications.

The absence of general uniformity in designating hearings is reflected in their numerical or alphabetical arrangements. A committee series may continue through a session, through a Congress or indefinitely. Specific details on hearings are furnished on the title pages. Frequently, the title pages provide only the subject and not the applicable bill number. On the other hand, the title pages of some hearings list the numbers of several bills on the same subject.

### 3. Committee Reports

Justice Jackson suggested that resort to legislative history "should not go beyond Committee reports, which presumably are well considered and carefully prepared." [6]

Each committee report is identified by a number of a specific Congress, e. g., Senate Report No. 105 of the 80th Congress, 1st Session is cited S.Rep.No.105, 80th Cong., 1st Sess. The committee reports are designated and located by the assigned numbers. The reports first appear in individual pamphlets and these are published each year in the Congressional serial set. When a minority report is made, it also is published.

### 4. Congressional Debates

Some authorities view Congressional floor debates as casual statements, lacking in candor or accuracy, and not as integrated parts of bills which the President signs. To reconstruct a law from such legislative history is seen by them as involving the courts in legislative polemics, a proper function of the legislature but inappropriate for judicial interpretation. Notwithstanding these objections, clarifying and explanatory statements are made by bill sponsors in floor debates, which are helpful in understanding and interpreting legislation; therefore, the verbatim debates in Congress, as published in the *Congressional Record*, assume an important role in the reconstruction of legislative histories.

The *Congressional Record* first appears as a daily publication (Monday through Friday, with a minor exception). Each issue includes a *Daily Digest* of House and Senate activity of the preceding day. The *Daily Digest* lists chamber action, committee meetings, bills introduced and passed, and other activity bearing on Congressional business. The *Digest* is cumulated annually. The bound annual index also contains a Table of Bills Enacted into Public Law and a History of Bills Enacted into Public Law. The Table of Bills Enacted into Public Law is arranged by Bill numbers and furnishes the corresponding Public Law numbers. After obtaining the Public Law

6 Id. at 395.

7 Id. at 396.

number, the researcher can more easily use the Table of History of Bills Enacted into Public Law. The latter table provides a checklist of legislative histories for a session of Congress, noting the title of a Bill, reports numbers, page of *Congressional Record* of passage, and Public Law number.

The *Congressional Record's Index* appears twice per month, and at the end of each session of Congress an annual bound *Index* is published. The *Index* is divided into (1) a consolidated general index, with topics and names of Congressmen and Senators arranged under one alphabet and (2) a history of Senate and House bills and resolutions separately given. The History serves as a status table.

## 5. Conference Reports

Conference reports are issued as House Reports.

--------

## SECTION C. THE SOURCES OF LEGISLATIVE HISTORIES

Rarely does one find bound volumes containing all of the documents pertaining to the passage of a particular law.[8] Rather, a legislative history has to be compiled from various sets containing different types of Government documents as listed below.

### 1. Bills

    a.   The bill as originally introduced in the House or Senate.

    b.   The bill as amended.

    c.   The bill as it passed in the originating body and as introduced into the other. (At this point, it is called an "act").

    d.   The "act" as amended.

    e.   The "act" as amended by Joint Conference Committee of the House and Senate.

### 2. Reports

    a.   The report of the committee to which the bill was assigned.

---

[8] Occasionally a compilation of a legislative history is published. But in most instances researchers have to compile their own. An example of a compiled legislative history is the following published by the Government Printing Office. *Legislative History: Federal Coal Health and Safety Act.* 1970. 1151 p.

The NCR company also has published in microform a Legislative History Service for Selected Acts of Congress, 82d Congress to date. NCR has also published, in microform, the Legislative Histories of Internal Revenue Acts, 1909–1950.

Many law libraries subscribe to both of these sets.

b.   The report of the committee to which the "act" was assigned.

c.   The report of the Joint Conference Committee of the House and Senate.   This is issued as a House report.

**3.   Debates**

The debates, if any, on the floor of Congress that appear in the *Congressional Record.*

**4.   Hearings**

The hearings, if any, held by the committees to which the bill or "act" had been assigned.

**5.**   The Public Law resulting from all of the above.

---

### SECTION D.   HOW TO COMPILE A LEGISLATIVE HISTORY

The compilation of a legislative history for a public law is a two step process which involves first locating citations to the documents listed in Section B, *supra,* and then locating the documents in the various sets referred to in the citations.

**1.   Locating Legislative Histories for Public Laws.**

a.   To locate bill number under which a law was introduced into Congress, check one of these three sources:

(1) *Daily Digest.*   This appears in each issue of the *Congressional Record* and highlights the daily activity of Congress.   The digest is cumulated annually.   The annual cumulation contains a History of Bills Enacted into Public Law, arranged by Public Law number.

(2) *Guide to Legislative History of Bills Enacted into Public Law.*   Beginning with Volume 77, 1963, each volume of the *Statutes at Large* contain this guide.   It is similar to the History of Bills described in (1) *supra.*

(3) *CCH Congressional Index.*   This is a privately published loose-leaf service, which issues weekly supplements and covers the legislative work of Congress.   New volumes are issued for each Congress.   It lists all bills introduced; and contains a table of the History of Senate and House Bills Approved.   It also contains a subject index to all bills introduced in Congress.

(4) *Digest and Public General Bills.*   This digest, published by the Library of Congress, contains brief summaries of public bills and resolutions as introduced and changed and more complete

synopses of reported materials. The *Digest* is normally published during each session of Congress in five cumulative issues, with biweekly supplements when necessary. Each cumulation is divided into seven parts: (1) Status of Measures Receiving Action, (2) Public Law Listing, (3) Digests of General Bills and Resolutions, (4) Sponsor Index, (5) Subject Index, (6) Specific Title Index, and (7) Identical Bill Index. The *Digest* is a useful source of information as to the status of proposed federal legislation.

b.   To locate citations to committee reports check:

(1) *Daily Digest,* History of Bills Enacted into Public Law (Annual Cumulation), or CCH *Congressional Record*—Tables of History of Senate and House Bills Approved.

c.   To determine if Hearings have been printed check (a) *CCH Congressional Index, supra,* or (b) U. S. Senate, Library, Cumulative Index of Committee Hearings,[9] 1959–

d.   For citations to transcripts of debates on the floor of Congress, check History of Bills and Resolutions Table in Annual Index volume of the *Congressional Record.*

2.  **Compiling Legislative Histories for Bills not Enacted into Public Law.**

a.   Locate bill number through subject index to *Annual Index to Congressional Record,* or subject index to *CCH Congressional Record,* or subject index to *Digest of Public General Bills.*

b.   Check Status Tables of Senate and House Bills in *CCH Congressional Index* or History of Bills and Resolutions Table in Annual Index volume of the *Congressional Record.*

3.  **Compiling Legislative Histories Using the Congressional Information Index.   (C.I.S.)**

This is a new service that simplifies the compiling of legislative histories for public laws passed during 1970 or later. The *CIS* indexes and abstracts nearly all Congressional publications. It is issued monthly and at the end of the year is cumulated into two bound volumes: [v. 1] *Abstracts of Congressional Publications* and [v. 2] *Legislative Histories and Index to Congressional Publications and Public Laws.*

The first bound volume contains a numerical list of all Public Laws passed during the year with citations to the abstracts within *CIS* of all the reports, hearings, and other documents. If the Public

---

[9] For a checklist of Hearings prior to 1959, see Pollack, Fundamentals of Legal Research, 3d ed. 1967.  p. 279.

Law number is not known, it can be located through the use of the *CIS* Index volume.

---

## SECTION E.  HOW TO OBTAIN ACCESS TO THE DOCUMENTS OF LEGISLATIVE HISTORY

After using the indexes as described *supra*, the actual documents have to be obtained.  Each Congressional District has at least one depository library [10] which receives nearly all the publications of the U. S. Government Printing Office.

1.  Bills.  These are usually kept together by Congress with each Bill, in all of its different stages, collated together.

2.  House and Senate reports are included as part of the *Serial Set*, and assistance from the library staff is usually needed to locate these.  Some law libraries maintain these reports as separate series.

3.  Transcripts of debates on the floor of Congress are found in the *Congressional Record* at the pages indicated in the *History of Bills Table*.

4.  Hearings are usually shelved according to the Government Printing Office classification scheme.  This number is always given in the *Monthly Catalog of Government Publications*.  In some law libraries, Hearings are cataloged separately.

5.  *U. S. Code Congressional and Administrative Service*.  This service [see Chapter 9, § A1(b)] prints committee reports for many Public Laws.  It is available in most law libraries and is most convenient to use when only seeking the committee reports for a public law.

The next Section illustrates how a legislative history can be compiled for a federal law.

[10] See Chapter 9, footnote 5.

## SECTION F.   ILLUSTRATIONS

The illustrations in this section demonstrate the two steps ordinarily required to compile a legislative history.   Step one involves using index volumes to obtain citation to documents.   Step 2 requires the obtaining of the documents from various sets of government documents.

For purposes of demonstration, the steps required to compile the legislative history for the *Interest Equalization Tax Extension Act of 1965* are shown.

## 1.   Indexes to Consult in Compiling a Legislative History

### Illustrations

40.   Daily Digest—Annual Cumulation—Congressional Record for 1965.

41.   Table of House Bills in Annual Index Volume, Congressional Record, 1965.

42.   Page from CCH Congressional Index for 1965.

## 2.   Locating documents cited in Indexes

### Illustrations

43.   First page of Public Law 89–243.

44.   First page of H.R. 4750.

45.   First page of House Hearings on H.R. 4750.

46.   First page of H.Rep. 602, on H.R. 4750.

47.   Excerpt the Congressional Record.

48.   First page of H.R. 4750 as amended by the House Committee.

49.   First page of H.R. 4750 as an "Act" in the Senate.

50.   First page of Sen.Rep. 621 on H.R. 4750.

51.   First page of H.R. 4750 as amended by Senate Committee.

52.   Excerpt from Congressional Record.

53.   First page of H.R. 4750 as amended by the Senate.

54.   First page of Conference report on H.R. 4750.

55.   Page from Congressional Information Service.

[Illustration 40]

## PAGE FROM DAILY DIGEST. ANNUAL CUMULATION VOLUME, CONGRESSIONAL RECORD. 1965

*October 22, 1965*      **CONGRESSIONAL RECORD — DAILY DIGEST**      **D639**

> The Daily Digest cumulative volume for the 1965 Congressional Record has Table listing all laws passed for this session. This indicates that P.L. 89-243 was introduced as H.R. 4750.

| Subject | Bill No. | Committee | Approved | P.L. No. |
|---|---|---|---|---|
| Authorizing acquisition of certain lands within the Uinta National Forest, Utah, by the Secretary of Agriculture. | S. 1764 | Com | Oct. 1 | 89-226 |
| To convey to the State of Maryland certain land located on the campus of the University of Maryland. | S. 1975 (H.R. 9734) | PW / Jud | Oct. 1 | 89-227 |
| Conveying certain lands in Oregon to the city of Roseburg. | S.J. Res. 98 | Jud | Oct. 1 | 89-228 |
| Extending period for existing suspension of duties on certain classes of yarn of silk. | | | Oct. 1 | 89-229 |
| Authorizing contribution by the U.S. to the International Committee of the Red Cross. | H.R. 2580 | Jud | Oct. 1 | 89-230 |
| Removing certain restrictions on the American Hospital of Paris. | H.R. 4152 | Agr | Oct. 1 | 89-231 |
| Authorizing funds for a continued study of effects of insecticides and other pesticides upon fish and wildlife. | | | Oct. 1 | 89-232 |
| To authorize certain facilities for the International Pacific Halibut Commission. | H.R. 5842 | IIA / IFC | Oct. 1 | 89-233 |
| Water Quality Act of 1965. | S. 596 (H.R. 3140) | | Oct. 2 | 89-234 |
| Requesting President to extend through 1966 his proclamation of a period to "See the U.S." | | | Oct. 2 | 89-235 |
| Proposing various amendments to the immigration and nationality laws. | S. 1766 (H.R. 10232) | Agr | Oct. 3 | 89-236 |
| To provide for loans to production credit associations by Federal intermediate credit banks without the necessity of collateral. | H.R. 7969 | Fin | Oct. 4 | 89-237 |
| To extend the Lead-Zinc Small Producers Stabilization Act. | S. 1620 | Jud | Oct. 7,6 | 89-238 |
| Authorizing funds for combating heart disease, cancer, stroke, and other major diseases. | | | Oct. 7 | 89-239 |
| Authorizing Secretary of Agriculture to make loans to public agencies and nonprofit corporations for the development of water systems serving rural areas. | | Fin / IIA | Oct. 7 | 89-240 |
| To amend and correct certain provisions of the tariff schedules of the U.S. | | | Oct. 7 | 89-241 |
| Consolidating two judicial districts in South Carolina into a single judicial district. | | | Oct. 7 | 89-242 |
| Interest Equalization Tax Extension Act. | H.R. 4750 | | Oct. 9 | 89-243 |
| | H.R. 8035 | IIA | Oct. 9 | 89-244 |
| Authorizing acceptance of a donation of certain property in Suffolk County, N.Y., for addition to the Fire Island National Seashore. | H.R. 10516 | AS | Oct. 9 | 89-245 |
| Authorizing disposal of vegetable tannin extract from the national stockpile. | H.R. 10714 | AS | Oct. 9 | 89-246 |
| Authorizing disposal of colemanite from the supplemental stockpile. | H.R. 10715 | AS | Oct. 9 | 89-247 |
| Authorizing disposal of chemical grade chromite from the supplemental stockpile. | H.J. Res. 309 | HA | Oct. 9 | 89-248 |
| Increasing the number of electric typewriters which may be furnished to Members of the House of Representatives. | H.R. 2091 | IIA | Oct. 9 | 89-249 |
| Relating to the establishment of concession policies in areas administered by the National Park Service. | H.R. 9417 | IIA / AS | Oct. 9 | 89-250 |
| To revise the boundary of Jewel Cave National Monument, S. Dak. | H.R. 10748 | | Oct. 9 | 89-251 |
| Authorizing transfer of copper from the national stockpile to the Bureau of the Mint. | H.J. Res. 330 | AS | Oct. 9 | 89-252 |
| Authorizing disposal of chromium metal acid grade fluorspar and silicon carbide from the supplemental stockpile. | H.R. 8283 | EdL / MMF | Oct. 9 | 89-253 |
| Economic Opportunity Act Amendments. | H.R. 728 (S. 2069) | | Oct. 10 | 89-254 |
| To broaden the vessel exchange provisions of section 510(i) of the Merchant Marine Act and to extend such provisions for 5 years. | H.R. 1065 (H.R. 9515) | IIA | Oct. 10 | 89-255 |
| Authorizing acquisition of certain property for the administration in connection with the George Washington Memorial Parkway. | H.J. Res. 695 | App | Oct. 15 | 89-256 |
| Making continuing appropriations for fiscal year 1966 through Oct. 23. | H.R. 3045 | AS | Oct. 19 | 89-257 |
| Authorizing military personnel who have served in Vietnam since 1961 to accept decorations from the Government of Vietnam or its allies. | | | | |
| Providing for a loan service of captioned films and educational media for deaf persons. | S. 2232 | EdL | Oct. 19 | 89-258 |
| Exempting from seizure under judicial process certain objects of cultural significance imported for temporary display. | S. 2273 | Jud | Oct. 19 | 89-259 |

[Illustration 41]

## EXCERPT FROM TABLE OF HOUSE BILLS, ANNUAL INDEX VOLUME CONGRESSIONAL RECORD, 1965

### HOUSE BILLS

H.R. 4742—For the relief of Keun Tak Rim and his wife, Ju Hyun Rim.
 Mr. Roybal; Committee on the Judiciary, 2465.

H.R. 4743—For the relief of Ralph Tigno Edquid.
 Mr. White of Texas; Committee on the Judiciary, 2465.—Reported with amendment (H. Rept. 1056), 24719.—Amended and passed House, 25937.—Referred to Senate Committee on the Judiciary, 26075.

H.R. 4744—For the relief of Mary H. Leon.
 Mr. Widnall; Committee on the Judiciary, 2465.

H.R. 4745—For the relief of Mrs. Horopsima Tumacan.
 Mr. Charles H. Wilson; Committee on the Judiciary, 2465.

H.R. 4746—For the relief of Grigoria Rempas.
 Mr. Yates; Committee on the Judiciary, 2465.

H.R. 4747—For the relief of Deward E. Quarles.
 Mr. Van Deerlin; Committee on the Judiciary, 2465.

H.R. 4748—For the relief of Joseph M. Hepworth.
 Mr. Van Deerlin; Committee on the Judiciary, 2465.

H.R. 4749—To amend the 1965 feed grain program to allow diverted acreage to be devoted to the production of soybeans.
 Mr. Andrews of North Dakota; Committee on Agriculture, 2521.

H.R. 4750—To provide a 2-year extension of the interest equalization tax, and for other purposes.
 Mr. Mills; Committee on Ways and Means, 2521.—Reported with amendment (H. Rept. 602), 15763.—Made special order (H. Res. 498), 19485.—Debated, amended, and passed House, 19487.—Title amended, 19499.—Referred to Senate Committee on Finance, 19641.—Reported with amendments (S. Rept. 621), 20601.—Debated, 21524, 21538.—Amended and passed Senate, 21542.—Senate insists on its amendments and asks for a conference, 21542.—Conferees appointed, 21542.—House disagrees to Senate amendments and agrees to a conference, 21873.—Conferees appointed, 21873.—Conference report (H. Rept. 988) submitted in House and agreed to, 24058.—Conference report submitted in Senate and agreed to, 24425.—Examined and signed, 25256, 25411.—Presented to the President, 25411.—Approved [Public Law 89–243], 26875.

H.R. 4751—To provide that certain lands shall be held in trust for the Lower Brule Sioux Tribe in South Dakota.
 Mr. Berry; Committee on Interior and Insular Affairs, 2521.

H.R. 4752—To amend the Internal Revenue Code of 1954 to repeal the manufacturers excise tax on household-type electric, gas, and oil appliances.
 Mr. Brademas; Committee on Ways and Means, 2521.

A Table of House and Senate Bills appears in Annual Index Volume of the Congressional Record. This is from the 1965 volume. These Tables give the legislative history of each bill introduced into Congress during the year.

It does not, however, give citations to Hearings.

## [Illustration 42]

## EXCERPT FROM THE CCH CONGRESSIONAL INDEX—1965

**Legislative History of House Bills**　　　Number 48—134

**4525**

| | |
|---|---|
| Hearing in H. | 4/27/65 |
| H. hearing available | 5/21/65 |
| Reptd., no amend., H. Rept. 343 | 5/12/65 |
| Passed H., without amend. [Voice] | |
| | 5/17/65 |
| To S. Commerce | 5/18/65 |
| Reptd., no amend., S. Rept. 380 | 6/29/65 |
| Passed S., without amend. [Voice] | |
| | 6/30/65 |
| Approved [Public Law 89-66] | 7/7/65 |

**4526**

| | |
|---|---|
| Hearing in H. | 4/27/65 |
| H. hearing available | 5/21/65 |
| Reptd., no amend., H. Rept. 346 | 5/13/65 |
| Passed H., without amend. [Voice] | |
| | 5/17/65 |
| To S. Commerce | 5/18/65 |
| Hearing in S. | 5/25/65 |
| S. hearing available | 8/4/65 |
| Reptd., no amend., S. Rept. 422 | 7/6/65 |
| Passed S., without amend. [Voice] | |
| | 7/14/65 |
| Approved [Public Law 89-89] | 7/27/65 |

**4527**

| | |
|---|---|
| Hearing in H. | 2/18/65 |
| H. hearing available | 3/22/65 |
| Reptd., with amend., H. Rept. 149 | |
| | 3/10/65 |
| Passed H., as reptd. [Voice] | 3/18/65 |
| To S. Commerce | 3/22/65 |
| Reptd., no amend., S. Rept. 148 | 4/6/65 |
| Passed S., without amend. [Voice] | |
| | 4/6/65 |
| Approved [Public Law 89-13] | 4/20/65 |

**4714**

| | |
|---|---|
| Reptd., no amend., H. Rept. 146 | 3/9/65 |
| Motion to suspend rules rejected by H. [Roll-call] | 3/15/65 |
| Passed H., without amend. [Roll-call] | |
| | 4/29/65 |
| To S. Labor and Public Welfare | 4/30/65 |
| Reptd., no amend., S. Rept. 540 | 8/5/65 |
| Passed S., without amend. [Voice] | 8/6/65 |
| Approved [Public Law 89-125] | 8/13/65 |

**4750**

| | |
|---|---|
| H. hearing available | 8/4/65 |
| Hearing in H. | 6/21/65 |
| Reptd., with amend., H. Rept. 602 | 7/7/65 |
| Passed H., as reptd. [Roll-call] | 8/5/65 |
| To S. Finance | 8/6/65 |
| Reptd., with amend., S. Rept. 621 | |
| | 8/17/65 |
| Amended on S. Floor [Voice] | 8/24/65 |
| Passed S., with amend. [Voice] | 8/24/65 |
| S. appoints conferees | 8/24/65 |
| H. appoints conferees | 8/26/65 |
| Conf. Rept. submitted to H., H. Rept. 988 | 9/14/65 |
| Conf. Rept. agreed to by H. | 9/16/65 |

This is an excerpt from the Commerce Clearing House *Congressional Index*. This is a loose service with new binders for each Congress. This Index indicates when Hearings are available but does not index debates in the Congressional Record.

In addition to the Status Tables, this service has a subject index to all bills, and other tables and information very useful in compiling a legislative history.

[Illustration 43]

## FIRST PAGE OF PUBLIC LAW 89-243

Public Law 89-243
89th Congress, H. R. 4750
October 9, 1965

### An Act

79 STAT. 954

To provide an extension of the interest equalization tax, and for other purposes.

*Be it enacted by the Senate and House of Representatives of the United States of America in Congress assembled,*

**SECTION 1. SHORT TITLE, ETC.**

(a) SHORT TITLE.—This Act may be cited as the "Interest Equalization Tax Extension Act of 1965".

(b) AMENDMENT OF 1954 CODE.—Except as otherwise expressly provided, whenever in this Act an amendment is expressed in terms of an amendment to a section or other provision, the reference is to a section or other provision of the Internal Revenue Code of 1954.

**SEC. 2. EXTENSION OF INTEREST EQUALIZATION TAX.**

Section 4911(d) is amended by striking out "December 31, 1965" and inserting in lieu thereof "July 31, 1967".

**SEC. 3. IMPOSITION OF TAX WITH RESPECT TO DEBT OBLIGATIONS HAVING MATURITY OF 1 TO 3 YEARS.**

(a) IMPOSITION OF TAX.—The following provisions are amended by striking out "3 years" each place it appears and inserting in lieu thereof "1 year"—

(1) section 4911(a);

(2) section 4914(e)(3)(D);

Interest Equalization Tax Extension Act of 1965.

78 Stat. 810.
26 USC 4911.

26 USC 4914.

26 USC 4920.

> Public Law 89-243 was introduced into the 89th Congress as H(ouse) of R(epresentative) bill number 4750.

| | |
|---|---|
| At least 1½ years, but less than 1¾ years | 1.50 percent |
| At least 1¾ years, but less than 2¼ years | 1.85 percent |
| At least 2¼ years, but less than 2¾ years | 2.30 percent |
| At least 2¾ years, but less than 3½ years | 2.75 percent". |

(c) EFFECTIVE DATE.—

(1) GENERAL RULE.—Except as provided by paragraphs (2), (3), and (4), the amendments made by subsections (a) and (b) shall apply with respect to acquisitions of debt obligations, and designations described in section 4914(e)(3)(D) or 4914(e)(3)(E)(ii) of the Internal Revenue Code of 1954, made after February 10, 1965.

(2) PREEXISTING COMMITMENTS.—Such amendments shall not apply to an acquisition—

(A) made pursuant to an obligation to acquire which on February 10, 1965—

(i) was unconditional, or

(ii) was subject only to conditions contained in a formal contract under which partial performance had occurred; or

(B) as to which on or before February 10, 1965, the acquiring United States person (or, in a case where 2 or more United States persons are making acquisitions as part of a single transaction, a majority in interest of such persons) had taken every action to signify approval of the acquisition under the procedures ordinarily employed by such person (or persons) in similar transactions and had sent or deposited

[Illustration 44]

FIRST PAGE OF H.R. 4750—89 CONGRESS, 1st SESSION

89TH CONGRESS
1ST SESSION
# H. R. 4750

---

## IN THE HOUSE OF REPRESENTATIVES

FEBRUARY 10, 1965

Mr. MILLS introduced the following bill; which was referred to the Committee on Ways and Means

---

# A BILL

To provide a two-year extension of the interest equalization tax, and for other purposes.

1    *Be it enacted by the Senate and House of Representa-*

2    *tives of the United States of America in Congress assembled,*

3    **SECTION 1. SHORT TITLE, ETC.**

4        (a) SHORT TITLE.—This Act may be cited as the

5    "Interest Equalization Tax Extension Act of 1965".

6        (b) AMENDMENT OF 1954 CODE.—Except as other-

7    wise expressly provided, whenever in this Act an amendment

8    is expressed in terms of an amendment to a section or other

9    provision, the reference shall be considered to be made to a

10   section or other provision of the Internal Revenue Code of

11   1954.

I

> H.R. 4750, after being introduced by Mr. Mills, referred to the Committee on Ways & Means.

[Illustration 45]

## FIRST PAGE OF HOUSE HEARING ON H.R. 4750

# INTEREST EQUALIZATION TAX EXTENSION ACT OF 1965

## EXECUTIVE
# HEARINGS
### BEFORE THE

## COMMITTEE ON WAYS AND MEANS
## HOUSE OF REPRESENTATIVES

### EIGHTY-NINTH CONGRESS
#### FIRST SESSION

ALONG WITH WRITTEN COMMENTS SUBMITTED TO THE
COMMITTEE ON WAYS AND MEANS

ON

# H.R. 4750

AND

TECHNICAL AMENDMENTS PROPOSED BY THE TREASURY
DEPARTMENT ON THE INTEREST EQUALIZATION
TAX ACT OF 1965

JUNE 21, 22, AND 24, 1965

Printed for the use of the Committee on Ways and Means

> The Committee to which a bill is assigned customarily holds hearings before which interested members of Congress and other invited persons testify and may submit documents in support of their testimony.
>
> The verbatim transcript of the testimony at the Hearings are usually printed.
>
> This particular volume of hearings contains 115 pages. Hearings frequently can contain several hundred pages.

U.S. GOVERNMENT PRINTING OFFICE
WASHINGTON : 1965

## [Illustration 46]
## FIRST PAGE OF HOUSE OF REPRESENTATIVES
## REPORT NO. 602 ON H.R. 4750

---

| 89TH CONGRESS | HOUSE OF REPRESENTATIVES | REPORT |
|---|---|---|
| 1st Session | | No. 602 |

### INTEREST EQUALIZATION TAX EXTENSION ACT OF 1965

---

JULY 7, 1965.—Committed to the Committee of the Whole House on the State
of the Union and ordered to be printed

---

Mr. MILLS, from the Committee on Ways and Means, submitted the
following

# REPORT

[To accompany H.R. 4750]

The Committee on Ways and Means, to whom was referred the bill (H.R. 4750) to provide a 2-year extension of the interest equalization tax, and for other purposes, having considered the same, report favorably thereon with amendments and recommend that the bill as amended do pass.

The amendments are as follows:

The amendment to the text strikes out all of the House bill and inserts in lieu thereof a substitute which appears in the reported bill in italic type.

The other amendment modifies the title of the bill to make it conform to the changes made by the amendment to the text.

### I. SUMMARY

H.R. 4750, as reported, extends the interest equalization tax from December 31, 1965, to July 31, 1967, or for 1 year and 7 months beyond its present termination date. Thus, this tax, which is designed to aid our balance-of-payments position, will be in effect for a further temporary period. This tax raises the cost to foreigners of obtaining capital in the U.S. capital market to a level more closely alined with the costs prevailing in capital markets of the other industrialized countries.

---

### ILLUSTRATION

After a Committee considers a bill referred to it, it votes either to report the bill favorably, or to table. Ordinarily, only reports favoring a bill are published.

## [Illustration 47]

## EXCERPT FROM CONGRESSIONAL RECORD

[*Congressional Record—August 3, 1965*]

[*P. 18500*]

### INTEREST EQUALIZATION TAX

Mr. DELANEY from the Committee on Rules reported the following privileged resolution (H. Res. 498, Rept. No. 719) which was referred to the House calendar and ordered to be printed:

*Resolved,* That upon the adoption of this resolution it shall be in order to move that the House resolve itself into the Committee of the Whole House on the State of the Union for the consideration of the bill (H.R. 4750) to provide a two-year extension of the interest equalizaton tax, and for other purposes. After general debate, which shall be confined to the bill and shall continue not to exceed three hours, to be equally divided and controlled by the chairman and ranking minority member of the Committee on Ways and Means, the bill shall be considered as having been read for amendment. It shall be in order to consider the substitute amendment recommended by the Committee on Ways and Means now in the bill and such substitute shall be considered as having been read for amendment. No other amendment to the bill or committee substitute shall be in order except amendments offered by direction of the Committee on Ways and Means, and said amendments shall be in order, any rule of the House to the contrary notwithstanding, but such amendments shall not be subject to amendment. At the conclusion of such consideration, the Committee shall rise and report the bill to the House, with such amendments as may have been adopted, and the previous question shall be considered as ordered on the bill and amendments thereto to final passage without intervening motion, except one motion to recommit with or without instructions.

[*August 5, 1965*]

[*P. 18757*]

### INTEREST EQUALIZATION TAX EXTENSION ACT OF 1965

Mr. DELANEY. Mr. Speaker, by direction of the Committee on Rules I call up House Resolution 498 and ask for its immediate consideration.

[*P. 18758*]

The Clerk read the resolution, as follows:

on Ways and Means now in the bill and such substitute shall be considered as having been read for amendment. No other amendment to the bill or committee substitute shall be in order except amendments offered by direction of the Committee on Ways and Means, and said amendments shall be in order, any rule of the House to the contrary notwithstanding, but such amendments shall not be subject to amendment. At the conclusion of such consideration, the Committee shall rise and report the bill to the House, with such amendments as may have been adopted, and the previous question shall be considered as ordered on the bill and amendments thereto to final passage without intervening motion, except one motion to recommit with or without instructions.

Mr. DELANEY. Mr. Speaker, I yield 30 minutes to the gentleman from California [Mr. SMITH] and pending that I yield myself such time as I may consume.

Mr. Speaker, House Resolution 498 provides for consideration of H.R. 4750, a bill to provide a 2-year extension of the interest equalization tax, and for other purposes. The resolution provides a closed rule with 3 hours of general debate, making it in order to consider the substitute amendment now in the bill.

H.R. 4750, as reported, extends the interest equalization tax from December 31, 1965, to July 31, 1967, or for 1 year and 7 months beyond its present termination date. Thus, this tax, which is designed to aid our balance-of-payments position, will be in effect for a further temporary period. This tax raises the cost to foreigners of obtaining capital in the U.S. capital market to a level more closely alined with the costs prevailing in capital markets of the other industrialized countries. The present act accomplishes this objective by imposing a tax resulting in an additional annual cost, ultimately borne by the foreign issuers or security holders, equal to approximately a 1-percent rise in interest costs. The tax was first imposed for the period July 19, 1963, through December 31, 1965.

In addition to the extension of the interest equalization tax and its application to debt obligations of 1 to 3 years' maturity, this bill also makes a series of perfecting amendments designed to meet

[box overlapping text] the en-
, 1964.
ion of

After a bill is reported out by a Committee it may be debated on the floor of the House and printed in the Congressional Record. Actually only a very small number of Public Laws are debated by the Congress.

Mr.
e as I

d and
d ex-

Reso[l]
resolut[i]
the Ho[use]
of the
Union [(H.R.]
4750) [to]
interes[t]
poses.
confine[d]
to exce[ed]
and co[n]
minori[ty]
and Means, the bill shall be considered as having been read for amendment. It shall be in order to consider the substitute amendment recommended by the Committee

Mr. SMITH of California. Mr. Speaker, as stated by the distinguished gentleman from New York [Mr. DELANEY], the rule does provide for 3

[Illustration 48]

## FIRST PAGE OF H.R. 4750, AS AMENDED BY THE HOUSE COMMITTEE

---

**Union Calendar No. 285**

89TH CONGRESS
1ST SESSION

# H. R. 4750

[Report No. 602]

---

### IN THE HOUSE OF REPRESENTATIVES

FEBRUARY 10, 1965

Mr. MILLS introduced the following bill; which was referred to the Committee on Ways and Means

JULY 7, 1965

Reported with amendments, committed to the Committee of the Whole House on the State of the Union, and ordered to be printed

[Strike out all after the enacting clause and insert the part printed in italic]

---

# A BILL

To provide a two-year extension of the interest equalization tax, and for other purposes.

1     *Be it enacted by the Senate and House of Representa-*

2 *tives of the United States of America in Congress assembled,*

3    ~~SECTION 1. SHORT TITLE, ETC.~~

4      ~~(a) SHORT TITLE.—This Act may be cited as the~~

5 ~~"Interest Equalization Tax Extension Act of 1965".~~

6      ~~(b) AMENDMENT OF 1954 CODE.—Except as other-~~

7 ~~wise expressly provided, whenever in this Act an amendment~~

8 ~~is expressed in terms of an amendment to a section or other~~

---

After the Report is issued, a new bill is printed which lines out the original language and then gives the new language of the Bill written by the Committee which incorporates the Committee's amendments.

See next Illustration.

[Illustration 48–a]

## FIFTH PAGE OF H.R. 4750, AS AMENDED

23   *SECTION 1. SHORT TITLE, ETC.*

24     *(a) SHORT TITLE.—This Act may be cited as the*

25   *"Interest Equalization Tax Extension Act of 1965".*

1     *(b) AMENDMENT OF 1954 CODE.—Except as other-*

2   *wise expressly provided, whenever in this Act an amendment*

3   *is expressed in terms of an amendment to a section or other*

4   *provision, the reference is to a section or other provision of*

5   *the Internal Revenue Code of 1954.*

6   *SEC. 2. EXTENSION OF INTEREST EQUALIZATION TAX.*

7     *Section 4911(d) is amended by striking out "December*

8   *31, 1965" and inserting in lieu thereof "July 31, 1967".*

9   *SEC. 3. IMPOSITION OF TAX WITH RESPECT TO DEBT*

10       *OBLIGATIONS HAVING MATURITY OF 1 TO 3*

11       *YEARS.*

12     *(a) IMPOSITION OF TAX.—The following provisions*

13   *are amended by striking out "3 years" each place it appears*

14   *and inserting in lieu thereof "1 year"—*

15       *(1) section 4911(a);*

16       *(2) section 4914(e)(3)(D);*

17       *(3) section 4914(e)(3)(E)(ii); and*

18       *(4) section 4920(a)(7)(B)(iv).*

19     *(b) AMOUNT OF TAX.—Section 4911(b)(2) is*

20   *amended by striking from the table the line reading*

**This page of the re-issued bill now contains the
language with the Committee's amendments.**

*At least 1½ years, but less than 1¾ years_____ 1.50 percent*
*At least 1¾ years, but less than 2¼ years_____ 1.85 percent*
*At least 2¼ years, but less than 2¾ years_____ 2.30 percent*
*At least 2¾ years, but less than 3½ years_____ 2.75 percent".*

[Illustration 49]

## FIRST PAGE OF H.R. 4750 AS AN "ACT" IN THE SENATE

89TH CONGRESS
1ST SESSION

# H. R. 4750

IN THE SENATE OF THE UNITED STATES

AUGUST 6, 1965

Read twice and referred to the Committee on Finance

# AN ACT

To provide an extension of the interest equalization tax, and for other purposes.

1　　*Be it enacted by the Senate and House of Representa-*

2　*tives of the United States of America in Congress assembled,*

3　**SECTION 1. SHORT TITLE, ETC.**

4　　　(a) SHORT TITLE.—This Act may be cited as the

5　"Interest Equalization Tax Extension Act of 1965".

6　　　(b) AMENDMENT OF 1954 CODE.—Except as other-

7　wise expressly provided, whenever in this Act an amendment

8　is expressed in terms of an amendment to a section or other

9　provision, the reference is to a section or other provision of

10　t

> After a bill passes the House, it is sent to the Senate and is now called an "Act," and referred to the appropriate Senate Committee.

[Illustration 50]

## FIRST PAGE OF SENATE REP. 621 ON H.R. 4750

# Calendar No. 604

| 89TH CONGRESS<br>*1st Session* | SENATE | REPORT<br>No. 621 |
|---|---|---|

INTEREST EQUALIZATION TAX EXTENSION ACT OF 1965

AUGUST 17, 1965.—Ordered to be printed

Mr. LONG of Louisiana, from the Committee on Finance, submitted the following

## REPORT

[To accompany H.R. 4750]

The Committee on Finance, to which was referred the bill (H.R. 4750) to provide an extension of the interest equalization tax, and for other purposes, having considered the same, reports favorably thereon with amendments and recommends that the bill as amended do pass.

### I. SUMMARY

H.R. 4750, as reported by your committee, extends the interest equalization tax from December 31, 1965, to December 31, 1967, or for 2 years beyond its present termination date. The House bill would have extended the tax for a period of 1 year and 7 months, or until July 31, 1967. Thus, this tax, which is designed to aid our balance-of-payments position, will be in effect for a further temporary period. This tax raises the cost to foreigners of obtaining capital in the U.S. capital market to a level more closely alined with the costs prevailing in capital markets of the other industrialized countries. The present act accomplishes this objective by imposing a tax resulting in an additional annual cost, ultimately borne by the foreign issuers or security holders, equal to approximately a 1-percent rise in interest costs. The tax was first imposed for the period July 19, 1963 (August 17, 1963, for listed securities), through December 31, 1965.

The interest equalization tax as initially enacted authorized the

---

After the Senate Committee considers the Act, it will, if it voted favorably, issue a report. It may also make amendments to the language of the bill as passed by the House.

Frequently, the Senate Committee will also hold Hearings and publish them. It did not do so in this instance.

[Illustration 51]

## FIRST PAGE OF H.R. 4750 AS AMENDED BY THE SENATE COMMITTEE

---

**Calendar No. 604**

89TH CONGRESS
1ST SESSION

# H. R. 4750

[Report No. 621]

### IN THE SENATE OF THE UNITED STATES

AUGUST 6, 1965
Read twice and referred to the Committee on Finance

AUGUST 17, 1965
Reported by Mr. LONG of Louisiana, with amendments

[Omit the part struck through and insert the part printed in italic]

---

# AN ACT

To provide an extension of the interest equalization tax, and for other purposes.

1    *Be it enacted by the Senate and House of Representa-*

2    *tives of the United States of America in Congress assembled,*

3    **SECTION 1. SHORT TITLE, ETC.**

4        (a) SHORT TITLE.—This Act may be cited as the

5    "Interest Equalization Tax Extension Act of 1965".

6        (b) AMENDMENT OF 1954 CODE.—Except as other-

7    wise expressly provided, whenever in this Act an amendment

8    is expressed in terms of an amendment to a section or other

9                                                                     of

10       **After the Senate issues its report, the Act is reprinted containing the Senate's committee changes.**

## [Illustration 52]

## EXCERPT FROM CONGRESSIONAL RECORD

[*August 24, 1965*]

[*P. 20725*]

### EXTENSION OF INTEREST EQUALI-ZATION TAX

Mr. MANSFIELD. In its place, I ask unanimous consent that the Senate proceed to the consideration of Calendar No. 604, H.R. 4750, the so-called interest equalization bill, which I hope the Senate will be able to dispose of this evening, if at all possible.

Mr. KUCHEL. Mr. President, has the majority leader any views on whether there may be yea-and-nay votes on that bill?

Mr. MANSFIELD. I suggest that the Senator from Florida [Mr. SMATHERS] may be able to answer that question.

Mr. SMATHERS. The equalization tax bill will be handled on the floor by the Senator from Louisiana [Mr. LONG]. He may be able to say whether yea-and-nay votes will be had on that bill. It would be my view that there is no necessity for a yea-and-nay vote. The bill was reported by the committee with only one vote against it.

Mr. LONG of Louisiana. The Senator is correct.

Mr. SMATHERS. It is merely, in essence, a continuation of the act passed 2 years ago. I do not believe there will be any need for a yea-and-nay vote.

Mr. JAVITS. Mr. President, will the Senator yield?

Mr. SMATHERS. I yield.

Mr. JAVITS. I have an amendment to offer on the bill, the effect of which would be to enable the President to suspend its operation if the balance-of-payments position of the United States does not require it to be applied.

[*P. 20726*]

I understand that the Senator in charge of the bill will give sympathetic consideration to the amendment. I do not wish any misinformation, because I do not know whether we shall be able to get together on the amendment.

As I say, I do not wish to mislead anyone. The Senator from Florida has suggested that he doubts that a yea-and-nay vote may be had. If we get into a hassle on amendments, we may not be able to get very far with the bill. I did not expect the bill to be called up until tomorrow. I would be willing to have it go over until tomorrow.

Mr. MANSFIELD. It was announced last week that it would be taken up on Tuesday. It was the intention of the leadership to do so, but there has been a delay with respect to the defense ap-propriation bill. The Senator has been on notice with respect to this bill for some time.

Mr. JAVITS. I have made no promise or commitment of any kind.

Mr. KUCHEL. How long does the majority leader contemplate having Senators stay this evening?

Mr. MANSFIELD. As long as Senators desire to remain.

Mr. KUCHEL. Is it contemplated that the Senate will conclude action on the bill?

Mr. MANSFIELD. If possible. If not, the Senate will go over until tomorrow.

The PRESIDING OFFICER. The bill will be stated by title for the information of the Senate.

The LEGISLATIVE CLERK. A bill (H.R. 4750) to provide an extension of the interest equalization tax, and for other purposes.

The PRESIDING OFFICER. Is there objection to the present consideration of the bill?

There being no objection the Senate proceeded to consider the bill, which had been reported from the Committee on Finance with amendments.

Mr. JAVITS. Mr. President, may I inquire from the Senators in charge of the bill whether they wish to proceed with its consideration or whether I shall offer my amendment. I shall be guided by their wishes.

Mr. SMATHERS. Mr. President, I say to the distinguished Senator from New York that it is my belief that the bill should be disposed of tonight. I am prepared to make a short explanation of the bill as it came from the committee with only one negative vote. With respect to the amendment of the Senator from New York I doubt whether we can live with the amendment in the form it was introduced. I, too, have an amendment along somewhat different lines I may offer if his amendment as initially introduced is accepted.

Mr. JAVITS. Lest there be any mystery about this matter, I have an amendment which relates to the power of the President to suspend by proclamation the operation of the tax. It is important because if the balance-of-payments situation does not require the application of the tax it becomes crucially important to American investors all over the world that they should not be subject to the tax merely because we have no machinery to lift it. This is a mobile situation. The amendment also would give the President the power to reimpose the tax. There is no desire to cut off Executive authority. I understood that

After the Senate report on the Act, it may be debated on the floor of the Senate.

[Illustration 53]

FIRST PAGE OF H.R. 4750 AS AMENDED BY THE SENATE

---

89TH CONGRESS
1ST SESSION

# H. R. 4750

---

## IN THE SENATE OF THE UNITED STATES

AUGUST 24, 1965

Ordered to be printed with the amendments of the Senate numbered

---

# AN ACT

To provide an extension of the interest equalization tax, and for other purposes.

1    *Be it enacted by the Senate and House of Representa-*

2 *tives of the United States of America in Congress assembled,*

3   **SECTION 1. SHORT TITLE, ETC.**

4      (a) SHORT TITLE.—This Act may be cited as the

5 "Interest Equalization Tax Extension Act of 1965".

6      (b) AMENDMENT OF 1954 CODE.—Except as other-

7 wise expressly provided, whenever in this Act an amendment

8 is expressed in terms of an amendment to a section or other

9 provision, the reference is to a section or other provision of

10

> **The Senate may adopt additional amendments to those recommended by the Committee. When it does, another printing is made of the Act, as in this instance.**

[Illustration 54]

## FIRST PAGE OF CONFERENCE REPORT ON H.R. 4750

---

| 89TH CONGRESS<br>*1st Session* | HOUSE OF REPRESENTATIVES | REPORT<br>No. 988 |

INTEREST EQUALIZATION TAX EXTENSION ACT OF 1965

---

SEPTEMBER 14, 1965.—Ordered to be printed

---

Mr. MILLS, from the committee of conference, submitted the following

## CONFERENCE REPORT

[To accompany H.R. 4750]

The committee of conference on the disagreeing votes of the two Houses on the amendments of the Senate to the bill (H.R. 4750) to provide an extension of the interest equalization tax, and for other purposes, having met, after full and free conference, have agreed to recommend and do recommend to their respective Houses as follows:

That the Senate recede from its amendment numbered 29.

That the House recede from its disagreement to the amendments of the Senate numbered 1, 3, 4, 5, 6, 7, 10, 11, 12, 13, 14, 15, 17, 18, 20, 21, 22, 23, 24, 25, 26, 27, 28, and 31, and agree to the same.

Amendment numbered 2:

That the House recede from its disagreement to the amendment of the Senate numbered 2, and agree to the same with amendments as follows:

Strike out the matter proposed to be stricken out by the Senate amendment.

Insert the matter proposed to be inserted by the Senate amendment.

On page 1 of the Senate engrossed amendments, strike out the last two lines and insert the following: *such lease, is attributable to the use*

On page 2 of the Senate engrossed amendments, strike out lines 12 through 14 and insert the following: *value of the debt obligation arising out of such lease, is attributable to the use of*

And the Senate agree to the same.

---

When the House Bill, as passed, and the Senate Bill, as passed, differ, a Joint Conference Committee is formed to adopt mutually agreeable language, and their recommendations are issued as a Conference Report. These reports are always issued as part of the House Report Series.

## [Illustration 55]

## PAGE FROM 1971 VOLUME—CONGRESSIONAL INFORMATION SERVICE (C.I.S.)

**PL92-157**

**PL92-149 RECLAMATION INVESTIGATIONS, nonreimbursable costs.**
Oct. 29, 1971. 92-1. *
●Item 575. 1 p.
85 STAT. 416.

"To provide that the cost of certain investigations by the Bureau of Reclamation shall be nonreimbursable."

Concerns investigations of potential Federal reclamation projects.

Legislative History (S. 24):
Senate Hearings: S441-40.
House Report: H443-19 (No. 92-557).
Senate Report: S443-26 (No. 92-315).
Congressional Record Vol. 117 (1971):
July 31, considered and passed Senate.
Oct. 18, considered and passed House.

**PL92-150 EXPORT ADMINISTRATION ACT, extension.**
Oct. 30, 1971. 92-1. *
●Item 575. 1 p.
85 STAT. 416.

"To extend the authority conferred by the Export Administration Act of 1969."

Extends authority until May 1, 1972.

Legislative History (S.J. Res. 167):
Senate Report: [Banking, Housing and Affairs] (No. 92-406).
Congressional Record Vol. 117 (1971):
Oct. 27, considered and passed Senate.
Oct. 28, considered and passed House, a
Oct. 29, Senate agreed to House amend

**PL92-151 TARIFF SCHEDULES, amendment.**
Nov. 5, 1971. 92-1. *
●Item 575. 2 p.
85 STAT. 417.

"To amend the Tariff Schedules of the United States with respect to the dutiable status of certain articles."

Includes duty-free treatment of certain forms of bauxite and aluminum compounds, TNT, and tinned sheets used in manufacturing maple sap evaporators.

Legislative History (H.R. 4590):
House Report: H783-8 (No. 92-240).
Senate Report: S363-9 (No. 92-268).
Congressional Record Vol. 117 (1971):
June 8, considered and passed House.
July 20, considered and passed Senate, amended.
Aug. 3, House concurred in Senate amendment with amendments.
Oct. 19, Senate agreed to House amendment with amendment.
Oct. 28, House concurred in Senate amendment.

**PL92-152 U.S.-WESTERN HEMISPHERE COUNTRIES, cooperative animal disease control.**
Nov. 5, 1971. 92-1. *
●Item 575. 1 p.
85 STAT. 418.

"To broaden and expand the powers of the Secretary of Agriculture to cooperate with Mexico,

Guatemala, El Salvador, Costa Rica, Honduras, Nicaragua, British Honduras, Panama, Colombia, and Canada to prevent or retard communicable diseases of animals, where the Secretary deems such action necessary to protect the livestock, poultry, and related industries of the United States."

Legislative History (H.R. 10458 and related bills):
House Report: H163-19 (No. 92-553).
Senate Reports: S163-24 (No. 92-388, accompanying S. 2395); S163-25 (No. 92-389, accompanying S. 2396).
Congressional Record Vol. 117 (1971):
Oct. 6, S. 2395 and S. 2396 considered and passed Senate.
Oct. 18, considered and passed House.
Oct. 27, considered and passed Senate.

**PL92-153 FOOD SERVICE PROGRAMS FOR SCHOOL CHILDREN.**
Nov. 5, 1971. 92-1. *
●Item 575. 2 p.
85 STAT. 419.

"To assure that every needy schoolchild will receive a free or reduced price lunch as required by section 9 of the National School Lunch Act."

[Senate] Hearings: S161-7; S581-4; S581-6; S581-8; S581-11.
House Report: H343-11 (No. 92-572).
Senate Report: S163-21 (No. 92-382, accompanying S.J. Res. 157).
Congressional Record Vol. 117 (1971):
Oct. 1, S.J. Res. 157 considered and passed Senate.
Oct 18, considered and passed House.
Oct 20, considered and passed Senate.

**PL92-154 CANYONLANDS NATIONAL PARK, UTAH, boundary revision.**
Nov. 12, 1971. 92-1. *
●Item 575. 2 p.
85 STAT. 421.

"To revise the boundaries of the Canyonlands National Park in the State of Utah."

Legislative History (S. 26 and related bills):
House Hearings: H441-2; H441-21. *Also see 1970 CIS/Annual: H441-22.*
Senate Hearings: S441-25. *Also see 1970 CIS/Annual: S441-17.*
House Report: H443-15 (No. 92-536, accompanying H.R. 7137).
Senate Reports: S443-16 (No. 92-155). *Also see 1970 CIS/Annual: S443-45 (No. 91-923).*
Congressional Record Vol. 117 (1971):
June 21, considered and passed Senate.
Oct. 4, considered and passed House, amended, in lieu of H.R. 7137.
Nov. 2, Senate agreed to House amendments.

**PL92-155 ARCHES NATIONAL PARK, UTAH, establishment.**
Nov. 12, 1971. 92-1. *
●Item 575. 2 p.
85 STAT. 422.

"To establish the Arches National Park in the State of Utah."

Legislative History (S. 30 and related bills):
House Document: H440-14.
House Hearings: H441-2; H441-21.
Senate Hearings: S441-25. *Also see 1970 CIS/Annual: S441-21.*
House Report: H443-14 (No. 92-535, accompanying H.R. 7136).
Senate Reports: S443-19 (No. 92-148). *Also see 1970 CIS/Annual: S443-50 (No. 91-990).*
Congressional Record Vol. 117 (1971):
June 21, considered and passed Senate.
Oct. 4, considered and passed House, amended, in lieu of H.R. 7136.
Oct. 29, Senate agreed to House amendments.

**PL92-156 ARMED FORCES, FY72 authorization.**
Nov. 17, 1971. 92-1. *
●Item 575. 8 p.
85 STAT. 423.

"To authorize appropriations during the fiscal [year 197]2 for procurement of aircraft, missiles, [naval] vessels, tracked combat vehicles, [etc.], and other weapons, and research, [developme]nt, test, and evaluation for the Armed [Forces, a]nd to authorize real estate acquisition [and cons]truction at certain installations in con[nection w]ith the Safeguard anti-ballistic missile [program, a]nd to prescribe the authorized person[nel str]ength of the Selected Reserve of each Reserve component of the Armed Forces, and for other purposes."

Includes limitations on military assistance to South Vietnam, Laos, and Thailand.

Legislative History (H.R. 8687):
House Hearings: H201-12; H201-13.
Senate Hearings: S201-11; S201-12; S201-14; S201-15; S201-16; S201-18; S201-19.
House Reports: H203-4 (No. 92-232); H203-25 (No. 92-618, Conference Report).
Senate Reports: S203-6 (No. 92-359); S203-14 (No. 92-447, Conference Report).
Congressional Record Vol. 117 (1971):
June 15-17, considered and passed House.
Sept. 10, 13, 21-24, 27-30, Oct. 1, 4-6, considered and passed Senate, amended.
Oct. 19, House considered bill and agreed to conference.
Nov. 10, House agreed to conference report.
Nov. 11, Senate agreed to conference report.
Weekly Compilation of Presidential Documents Vol. 7, No. 47:
Nov. 17, Presidential statement.

**PL92-157 HEALTH PROFESSIONS, manpower training.**
Nov. 18, 1971. 92-1. *
●Item 575. 35 p.
85 STAT. 431.

"To amend title VII of the Public Health Service Act to provide increased manpower for the health professions, and for other purposes."
The Comprehensive Health Manpower Training Act of 1971; includes provisions to: extend for

The C.I.S. started in 1969. The citations are to abstracts of the documents in the C.I.S. service.

## SECTION G.   METHOD OF CITATION

**Federal Legislative Histories**

a.   Congressional Bills

The bills introduced in Congress are cited:

H.R. 3030, 87th Cong., 1st Sess.

S. 1126, 87th Cong., 1st Sess.

b.   Congressional Reports

The reports of the U. S. Senate and House of Representative Committees are cited:

H.R.Rep.No.248, 87th Cong., 1st Sess. 17 (1961).

S.Rep.No.204, 87th Cong. 1st Sess. 8 (1961).

c.   Congressional Hearings

Cite the hearings of a Senate or House Committee as follows:

Hearings Before the Committee on Labor and Public Welfare of the United States Senate (or House of Representatives), 80th Cong., 1st Sess., pt. 1, 69 (1947).

d.   Congressional Debates

Cite to the bound volumes of the *Congressional Record* whenever possible:

99 Cong.Rec. 8669 (1953).

The daily *Congressional Record* is cited:

113 Cong.Rec. H3791 (April 10, 1967).

113 Cong.Rec. S4754 (April 10, 1967).

# Chapter 11

# STATE AND MUNICIPAL LEGISLATION

There is much similarity between the organization and publication of federal and state statutes. Presently, thirty-three states hold annual and seventeen hold biennial regular sessions. The increase of legislative activity has stimulated interest in annual sessions, and several additional states are considering them. Extraordinary or special sessions may be called by a governor or legislature, depending on constitutional authority, with the governor or the legislature determining the subject or subjects of the session.

The state legislative bodies are officially called legislatures or general assemblies. For example, in Alabama, it is designated as the legislature, and in Illinois, it is called the general assembly. Massachusetts and New Hampshire refer to it as the general court. Except for Nebraska which has a unicameral legislature, the two legislative bodies are generally identified as the senate and the house of representatives. A few states identify the house as the assembly or the house of delegates.

## SECTION A.   SESSION LAWS

All states publish the laws enacted by each legislature separately in bound or pamphlet volumes. These publications are variously identified as "acts and resolves," "statutes," "laws," and "session laws." The private, local, special or appropriations acts, and resolutions may appear in the same volume as the public laws or may be separately published. Often the laws of one or more special or extraordinary sessions are incorporated into a volume of the laws of a regular session. The popular designation of these volumes is "session laws." See illustrations 56 and 57.

The session laws of the various states are published after adjournment of the legislatures for the regular or special sessions. Most states first print the acts passed by their legislatures individually in "slip" form, similar to the federal "slip" laws, immediately after each law is enacted. Some commercial publishers publish the session laws as an advance service to supplement the state codes, which they publish, prior to the issuance of the regular current code annotated service, e. g., New York.

The session laws are generally the best evidence of state law; however, should its provisions conflict with the text of an enrolled bill (a bill officially filed with a secretary of state) the latter's language prevails. Where the law is recodified and reenacted as a code, the code is the best evidence and supersedes the session laws. As between a reenacted code and the enrolled bill, the latter's text is controlling. Attorneys rarely compare the texts of session laws or codes and enrolled bills, relying upon the accuracy of the publications. The language of unofficial codes and session laws are more frequently compared for discrepancies.

The session laws include the public, private, temporary and local acts. The state appropriation acts are also generally provided in the session laws; however, in a few states they are separately published. The compilations of state laws, discussed below, usually do not contain the private, temporary, local and appropriation acts.

---

## SECTION B.   STATE STATUTES

The public and permanent acts of the state legislatures are compiled for convenience, in single or multi-volume editions, under a logical arrangement with the obsolete and revoked laws eliminated. These statutes are variously compiled. Some are official publications, e. g., Illinois and Missouri; others are commercial ventures certified by a state official, e. g., Texas; and the remainder are unofficial private publications, e. g., Massachusetts.

The state codes are kept current by various methods, viz., annual pocket supplements, cumulative bound supplements, replacement (recompiled) volumes and pamphlet services. The official editions published by the states usually are not supplemented. In that event, the researcher must refer to the subsequent session laws for the latest changes in the statute-law or to the current legislative service of a privately published code.

### 1.   Nomenclature of Statutes

The terms applied to the types of state compilations vary from state to state.[1]

---

[1] The technical terms for the various nomenclatures of codes are:

1. *Revised Statutes.* Such statutes are compiled in the identical order as originally passed by the legislature with the temporary and repealed acts eliminated. E. g., *English Statutes Revised.*

2. *Compiled Statutes.* The acts are printed verbatim as originally enacted in a new classified order. The text is not modified; however, the repealed and temporary acts are omitted. E. g., *Ohio Revised Code.*

## 2.　Classification of Statutes

The state codes conform to some classification system in the same way as the federal statutes. By classification is meant the arrangement of statutes according to a logical plan, with or without reference to their subject matter, into some broad and general divisions.[2]

## 3.　Features Common to Most State Statutes

The characteristics common to most state statutes are given below. The student, after studying these features, should examine his state's current compilation or compilations to determine which of them are present in the local set. He should also note the features peculiar to his state's publication.

### a.　Constitutions

The constitution of the state, generally annotated and separately indexed, is included in each state code. An unannotated edition of the Federal Constitution is usually included in the state compilation. The general indexes of some state codes also cover the state constitution.

### b.　Text of Statutes

Each state code, whether it be annotated or unannotated, contains the body of operative permanent, public statutory law of the state.

### c.　Historical notes

Historical references, showing the derivation of each section of the statutes, are given on the last or succeeding line of the text of the section. Such history includes the date and citation to the law as originally enacted and dates and citations to subsequent amendments or repeals. The degree of completeness of this information varies among the codes. Some also provide reviser's notes as to the history and significance of the amendatory law.

### d.　Annotations

Annotations to judicial decisions which interpret the sections of statutes are a significant feature of most codes. The courts, through

---

3.　*Consolidated Statutes.* The text of the acts is rewritten, arranged in classified order and reenacted. The repealed and temporary acts are eliminated. E. g., New York Consolidated Law.

4.　*Codes.* The laws in force are rewritten and arranged in classified order with the addition of material having the force of law taken from judicial decrees. The repealed and temporary acts are eliminated and the revision is reenacted. A code may include all the law of the jurisdiction or relate only to a segment of the law, such as substantive or adjective law. E. g., Title 28, Judiciary and Judicial Procedure, United States Code.

2 For a more detailed discussion of statutory classification, see Pollack, Fundamentals of Legal Research, 3d ed. 1967. pp. 344–346.

judicial interpretation, drape the raw bones of legislation with muscle and flesh and breathe life into its being.  For all practical purposes, the effect of a decision may result in doctrinal change.[3]  Vague and general statutory language may be given specificity and particular meaning.[4]  Or the courts may fill legislative gaps by judicial construction.[5]

Annotations provide brief digests of the interpretative law and the names and citations to the applicable cases.  The annotations appear after the text of the pertinent sections of the statutes.  The coverage of cases usually is complete for the courts which interpret the statutes.  Generally, interpretative opinions of the appropriate attorney general also are digested.

### e.  Comparative Legislation

References to similar or identical statutes of selected states, predominantly neighboring jurisdictions, are provided by some codes. These references are especially helpful in connection with newly enacted laws on which there has been no local judicial construction and also in relation to the uniform laws now in effect.

### f.  Indexes

The state codes are indexed by subject with varying degrees of completeness.  The index is the key to the successful use of a statutory compilation.  In its absence, the code is valueless, and with a poor one, its use is markedly circumscribed.  A few states have separate indexes to each title or volume as well as a general index.  In most states the substantive and adjective laws are indexed together. In a few states, even where the substantive and adjective laws are separately published with individual indexes, there may be combined indexes of both to facilitate research, e. g., California and New York.

### g.  Forms

Some of the recent codes include not only the forms provided by statutes but also those originating through statutory requirements. The forms follow after each applicable section of the statutes, e. g., *New York Consolidated Laws Service.*

### h.  Popular Names of State Acts

As in federal legislation, state acts are sometimes identified informally by subject matter or author's name.  The state compilations generally do not list the state acts separately by their popular names;

---

[3] Dice v. Akron, C. & Y. R. Co., 342 U.S. 359, 72 S.Ct. 312, 96 L.Ed. 398 (1951).

[4] United States v. Harriss, 347 U.S. 612, 74 S.Ct. 808, 98 L.Ed. 989 (1953).

[5] In re Santourian's Estate, 125 Misc. 668, 212 N.Y.S. 116 (Surr.Ct.1925)  Contra: Oleff v. Hodapp, 129 Ohio St. 432, 195 N.E. 838 (1935).

however, the popular names, when listed, appear in their alphabetical order with other subject matter in the general indexes to the state codes. An additional source for locating a state act, when only its popular name is known, is the appropriate *Shepard's state citations*, which separately list such laws. An additional source for locating a state act, when only its popular name is known, is *Shepard's Federal and State Acts by Popular Names*, and Supplement.

i. Supplementation

State codes usually are kept current by cumulative annual pocket parts, pamphlet supplements and replacement volumes.

In most states which have unannotated codes, the codes are frequently revised rather than supplemented.

j. Tables

Various tables are included in most codes. They are called by different names but the two most common forms, regardless of their names, are those which afford cross references (1) from the uncodified sections of the laws to the corresponding sections in the codes. This table also shows the disposition made of the acts by later legislation and usually is called the Chronological Table, which applies equally to federal and state codes; and (2) from the sections of a prior compilation to the corresponding sections in a later code. It also notes the disposition made of the sections in the earlier compilation which are not included in the more recent publication. Additional miscellaneous tables also are provided by codes.

## 4. Indexes and Guides to State Legislation

There is no comprehensive indexing service providing a convenient means to locate all state statutory provisions for a topic of law.[6] There are indexes and digests of state statutes for certain selected subjects. When in need of the laws of the state on a specific subject, the following may be of use:

a. Loose-leaf services. These are described in detail in Chapter 13. Many loose-leaf services provide either full text, digests, or tables of citations to state laws on a specific subject, e. g., *CCH All-State Tax Reporter*.

b. Martindale-Hubbell Law Directory. This is an annual publication which includes a volume of "Law Digests" providing brief

[6] From 1925 to 1948, The Library of Congress published the State Law Index, on a biennial basis. A description of this set may be found at *ibid.* footnote 2 p. 350. The Aspen Systems Corporation had provided a computer-generated index to current session laws for the years 1964 to 1971. This is now defunct. (Letter from Aspen Systems Corporation of September 14, 1972, to Stanford Law Library.)

synopses of some statutory law of all of the states.   Other features
are described in Chapter 18.

c.   Digests of all current state laws on specific subjects are frequently  published  by  state  agencies,  trade  associations,  and  other
groups.   Examples are:

Corporations Manual.   Annual. 2v. United States Corporations
Co.

U. S. National Center for Air Pollution Control.   Digest of State
Air Pollution Laws.   (Annual)

d.   Other  sources.   Treatises  and  law  review  articles  will  frequently have citations to all state statutes on a specific subject.

## SECTION C.  ILLUSTRATIONS

[Illustration 56]

## A PAGE FROM THE 1969 FLORIDA SESSION LAWS

CHAPTER 69-35          LAWS OF FLORIDA 1969

### CHAPTER 69-34

House Bill No. 325

AN ACT relating to regulation of traffic on highways; amending subsection (1) of section 317.131, Florida Statutes; providing that a driver of a vehicle involved in certain accidents need not forward a report of the accident if the investigating officer has done so; providing an effective date.

*Be It Enacted by the Legislature of the State of Florida:*

Section 1. Subsection (1) of section 317.131, Florida Statutes, is amended to read:

(1) The driver of a vehicle which is in any manner involved in an accident resulting in bodily injury to or death of any person or total damage to all property to an apparent extent of fifty dollars or more shall, within five days after such accident, forward a written report of such accident to the department; provided that, when the investigating officer has made a written report of such accident, no written report need be forwarded to the department by the driver.

Section 2. This act shall take effect July 1, 1969.

Became a law without the Governor's approval.

Filed in Office Secretary of State May 24, 1969.

---

A typical state session law. Note how this Act specially refers to the section of the Florida Statutes (its codification of session laws) that it is amending.

This is most common way for states to amend their code.

[Illustration 57]

## A PAGE FROM THE 1967 PENNSYLVANIA SESSION LAWS

616     Act No. 278     1967 LAWS OF PENNSYLVANIA,

No. 278

AN ACT

SB 1054

Amending the act of May 1, 1929 (P. L. 1216), entitled "An act to define real estate brokers and real estate salesmen; and providing for the licensing, regulation, and supervision of resident and nonresident real estate brokers and real estate salesmen and their business," regulating the revocation and issuance of licenses in cases of persons guilty of certain offenses.

The General Assembly of the Commonwealth of Pennsylvania hereby enacts as follows:

Section 1. Subsections (b) and (g) of section 11 of the act of May 1, 1929 (P. L. 1216), known as the "Real Estate Brokers License Act of one thousand nine hundred and twenty-nine," amended January 18, 1952 (P. L. 2117), are amended to read:
Section 11.   *   *   *
(b) Where during the term of any license issued by the department, the licensee shall have pleaded guilty, or entered a plea of nolo contendere, or has been found guilty in a court of competent jurisdiction, in this or any other state, of forgery, embezzlement, obtaining money under false pretenses, extortion, criminal conspiracy to defraud, bribery, or other [like] offense or offenses, involving the misappropriation, larceny or burglary of money or property belonging to the Commonwealth or any of its political subdivisions or to private persons, businesses or corporations or involving obligations insured by the United States of America or any of its agen-

Another typical state session law. Note, however, how this law refers to and amends a previous session law rather than a specific section of the Pennsylvania Statutes Annotated (its codification of session laws). With only a citation to this session law, a transfer table in Purdon's Penn.Stat.Anno. must be used to find where this session law has been codified.

## [Illustration 58]

## A PAGE FROM THE INDEX TO PURDON'S PENNSYLVANIA STATUTES ANNOTATED

## REAL ESTATE BROKERS

**REAL ESTATE BROKERS (Cont'd)**
→License,
   →Discriminatory practices, revocation or suspension, 63 § 440.
   Professional education, 63 § 436.
     Schools and educational institutions, approval, 63 § 436b.
   Suspension or revocation, discriminatory practices, 63 § 440.
Misappropriation of moneys, suspension or revocation of license, 63 § 441.
Registration,
   Salesmen of limited licensee, 63 § 436a.
Residential property, transfer, credit for realty transfer tax, 72 § 3285a.
Revocation or suspension of license, discriminatory practices, 63 § 440.
Theft, suspension or revocation of license, 63 § 441.
Title insurance companies,
   Commissions, 40 § 910—30.
   Rebates, 40 § 910—31.

**REAL ESTATE BROKERS COMMISSION**
Departmental administrative commission in department of state, 71 § 62.
Professional or occupational affairs commissioner, powers and duties, 71 § 279.1 et seq.
Rules and regulations, enactment and publication, 45 § 1101 et seq.

**REAL ESTATE REGISTRY**
Boroughs, 53 § 48001 et seq.
Counties of second class, 16 § 3708.

**REAL ESTATE TAX SALE LAW**

**REASSESSMENT**
Hotel occupancy tax, see Hotel Occupancy Tax.
Sales and use tax, see Sales and Use Tax.
Taxes, buildings, counties of third to eighth classes, 16 § 1770.1.

**REBATES**
Banks, unearned charges, installment loans, 7 § 309.
Canal fares, 66 §§ 2178, 2179.
Railroad fares, 66 §§ 2178, 2179.

**REBELLION**
Firearms, carrying on public streets or property, 18 § 4628.

**REBUILT MOTOR VEHICLE**
Defined, vehicle code, 75 § 102.

**RECEIPTS**
Bail deposit, R.Cr.P. (Title 19 App.) rule 4009.
Bank deposits, 7 § 602.
   Minors, 7 § 603.
Commercial feed, inspection, samples, 3 § 58.9.
Fish law violations, penalty, 30 § 280.
Foreign insurance companies, associations or exchanges, process, 40 § 46.
Home Improvement Finance Act, 73 § 500—402.
Housing agency, auditing, 35 § 1680.207.
Money received for transmission, 7 § 607.
Motor vehicle fines and costs, delivery to defendant, 75 § 1208.
Small estates of incompetents, 50 §§ 3201, 3202.
Treasurers, boroughs, account, 53

---

Ordinarily, when doing research in state legislation, the search is started in the index volumes in the state code.

Assume problem under search is whether in Pennsylvania a real estate broker may have his license revoked for engaging in discriminatory practices.

This exhibit shows how the statute for this is located in Title 63, § 440 of Purdon's Penna. Statutes Annotated.

---

Appeal, 72 § 3291.1.
Applicability of reenacting and amending act of 1959, 72 § 3283 note.
Counties, commissions, 72 § 3287.
Credit,
   Residential property, transfer by real estate broker, 72 § 3285a.
Definitions, 72 § 3284.
Effective date, etc., 72 § 3283 note.
Exemptions, 72 § 3284.
Failure to pay, additional tax and interest, 72 § 3291.1.
Interest, failure to pay tax imposed, 72 § 3291.1.
Lien of commonwealth, 72 § 3291.2.
Local Tax Enabling Act, 53 § 6901 et seq.
Petition for redetermination, 72 § 3291.1.
Recorder of deeds, collection agent, 16 § 11011—6.
Review, board of finance and revenue, 72 § 3291.1.
Short title, 72 § 3283.

**REAPPORTIONMENT**
Congressional districts, 25 § 2199.11 et seq.

**REAR LAMP**
Defined, vehicle code, 75 § 102.

insurance guaranty association, policyholder claims, 40 §§ 1701.501, 1701.502.
Investments, prudent man rule, 20 § 821.2a.
Motor Vehicle Safety Responsibility Law, insolvency of insurer, suspension for nonpayment of judgments, 75 § 1413.
Person as including, Human Relations Act, 43 § 954.
Prudent man rule, investments, 20 § 821.2a.
Sale,
   Goods or chattels subject to rental lien, preference of claim, 68 § 322.
   Licenses, 53 § 4471—1 et seq.
Sales and use tax, collection, 72 § 7241.
   Priority of tax, 72 § 7242.
Stock,
   Holding, personal liability, 15 § 1609.
   Voting, 15 § 1506.
Transportation assistance authority, defaulted bonds, 66 § 1908.

**RECEIVING STATE**
Defined,
   Detainers, 19 § 1431.

**RECEIVING STOLEN GOODS**
Racketeering activity defined, Corrupt Organizations Act, 18 § 3923.

## [Illustration 59]

## A PAGE FROM THE PURDON'S PENNSYLVANIA STATUTES ANNOTATED

---

Ch. 13      **REAL ESTATE BROKERS**      **63 § 440**

(c) The violation of any of the provisions of this section by any licensee shall be sufficient cause for the suspension or revocation of his, her, or its license, in the discretion of the commission.

(d) No corporation or copartnership engaged in the real estate business shall include in the corporate or partnership name the name of a licensed real estate salesman, unless there shall also be included in the name of such corporation or copartnership the name of a licensed real estate ⌐                                   1410,
§ 4; |                                           1952,
Jan. 1 |     **A typical page from an annotated state**     | Dec.
15, P. | **code.**

The amendatory act of 1931 added to subsection (a) a provision for display of a sign on the outside of the place of business, and also added subsection (c).

The act of 1937 made various changes in subsections (a) and (b).

"Commission" was substituted for "department" by the 1945 amendment.

Subsection (d) was added in 1951.

Prior to the 1957 amendment no fee was required for a new license for change of location and for a new license for a salesman because of change of employer.

The act of 1959, in subsections (a) and (b), substituted "biennial" for "annual".

### Library References

Brokers ☞4.                         P.L.E. Brokers § 3.
C.J.S. Brokers § 7 et seq.
C.J.S. Licenses § 72.

### § 440.   Investigation of complaints; grounds of suspension or revocation of licenses; hearings; review

(a) The commission may, upon its own motion, and shall, promptly, upon the verified complaint in writing of any person setting forth specifically the wrongful act or acts complained of, investigate any action or business transaction of any licensed real estate broker or real estate salesman; and shall have the power temporarily to suspend or permanently to revoke licenses theretofore issued by the department, under the provisions of this act, at any time when, after due proceedings as hereinafter provided, it shall find the holder thereof to have been guilty.

(1) Of knowingly making any substantial misrepresentation; or

(2) Of knowingly making any false promise of a character likely to influence, persuade or induce; or

(3) Of a continued or flagrant course of misrepresentation, or making of false promises through agents or salesmen; or

(4) When it shall be shown that the licensee, within five years prior to the issuance of the license then in force, has pleaded guilty, entered a

[Illustration 59–a]

## A PAGE FROM THE PURDON'S PENNSYLVANIA STATUTES ANNOTATED

---

Ch. 13     **REAL ESTATE BROKERS**     **63 § 440**

(v) Every real estate broker shall keep records of all funds deposited therein, which records shall indicate clearly the date and from whom he received money, the date deposited, the dates of withdrawals, and other pertinent information concerning the transaction, and shall show clearly for whose account the money is deposited and to whom the money belongs. All such records and funds shall be subject to inspection by the commission. Such separate custodial or trust fund account shall designate the real estate broker, as trustee, and such account must provide for withdrawal of funds without previous notice.

(12) Of failure to provide his client with a fully executed copy of any sole or exclusive sales listing contract at the time of the execution thereof.

(13) Of failure to truthfully disclose information sought in the application for license.

(14) Of accepting listings on an understanding that illegal discrimination in the sale or rental of housing is to be practiced due to race, color, religious creed, ancestry or national origin of a prospective lessee or purchaser.

(15) Of giving false information for purposes of discrimination in the rental or sale of housing due to race, color, religious creed, ancestry or national origin of a prospective lessee or purchaser.

(16) Of making distinctions in location of housing or dates of availability of housing for purposes of discrimination in the rental or sale of such housing due to race, color, religious creed, ancestry or national origin of a prospective lessee or purchaser.

(17) Of violating the provisions of the act of October 27, 1955 (P.L. 744), known as the "Pennsylvania Human Relations Act,"[1] or if he deals in a discriminatory manner with any individual desiring to rent or purchase housing accommodations because of the person's race, religious creed, or national origin.

---

   **Section 440(16) prohibiting discriminatory practices by real estate brokers.**

   **While not shown in this Illustration, pocket supplement in the volume should be checked to see if this section has been amended or repealed.**

---

plicant or licensee shall so desire, the commission shall grant a hearing upon such charges, to be held on not less than ten (10) days prior notice in writing to the applicant or licensee given. At such hearing, the applicant or licensee shall be entitled to examine, either in person or by

## [Illustration 59–b]

## A PAGE FROM THE PURDON'S PENNSYLVANIA STATUTES ANNOTATED

·Ch. 13          **REAL ESTATE BROKERS**        **63 § 440**
                                                      **Note 3**

1. →

contendere, or ·has been found guilty" for "been convicted" and by adding "bribery" as an additional offense.

Subsection (a) was amended in 1957 by the addition of the words "and a copy of the lease to the lessor or lessee" to paragraph (9) and by the substitution of the present text of paragraph (11) for that as set out in a prior note. Paragraphs (12) and (13) were also added.

The 1957 amendment also modified subsection (b) by requiring hearings to be held "in Harrisburg" (deleted in 1961) rather than allowing them to be in the county of applicants or licensees business, and by increasing the maximum fee for stenographic notes from .$.25 to $.50 per folio.

Subsection (d) was also amended in 1957 by deleting a provision which limited the effective date of an order prejudicing a licensee to 30 days after notice.

The act of 1961 deleted from subsection (b) the provision (added in 1957) that hearings were to be held in Harrisburg, and substituted "with the commission" for "in the cause", following "record". This 1961 act also inserted in subsection (b) the sentences beginning: "when a matter is referred to a representative * * *" "and ending" "section 1, as amended."

The act of 1967 added paragraphs (14) to (18) to subsection (a).

### Cross References

·Cancelling certificate, license etc., see 71 P.S. § 279.2.

### 2. →Library References

Administrative Law and Procedure ·  ☞345.
Brokers ☞3.

C.J.S. Brokers § 8.
C.J.S. Public Administrative Bodies and Procedure § 80.
P.L.E. Brokers § 3.

### 3. →Notes of Decisions

·Construction and application  1
Deposits  5
Duty of broker  2
Findings of Department  4
·Grounds for suspension  3
Review  6

---

**1. Construction and application**

Paragraph (a) of this section, providing for the investigation of challenged affairs of real estate brokers and the suspension or revocation of their licen-

Brittingham, 38 D. & C.2d 342, 13 Chest. 323, 1966.

This section is penal in nature but does not contain any provision which imposes personal liability on any broker for violation of its provisions. Id.

A penal law giving commission power to suspend or revoke a broker's license will be strictly construed, in absence of any express intent in act, to deny broker right to recover commissions. Id.

The court must rule that the provi-

---

Most annotated state codes are similar to this one.

1. Notes explaining amendments
2. References to where cases on this topic may be found in Key-Number Digests
3. Annotation of cases which interpreted or cited Title 63 § 440 of the Pa.Stat.Anno.

---

penal in nature but does not contain any provision which imposes personal liability on any broker for violation of its provisions. George J. McWilliams, Inc. v.

sell his own property with secondary financing of portion of down payment and settlement costs contrary to statutes and regulations governing FHA mort-

## SECTION D.   STATE LEGISLATION:  RESEARCH PROCEDURE

When doing research in state statutory law, the important factor to keep in mind is that laws for each state are first published chronologically in sessions laws and that each state has a current code in one form or another.

### 1.   Operative State Law

If the problem relates to a state law which is in effect, consult *a current annotated code* of the state.   The Index, Topic and Definition Methods of search may be used.   Determine the possible subject headings and subheadings.   If the Index Method is used, examine the index and index supplement to the appropriate state code.   Read the text of the code section referred to in the index.   Note the historical references which follow the text of the section.   Read the annotations to the code provision and consult the latest supplement for more recent case interpretations.   When given, the references to the similar or identical statutes of other jurisdictions and their cases in point can be consulted in determining the possible interpretation of the local statute.   The listings of research aids should be examined for collateral sources.   If research aids are not noted, independently consult the pertinent local text books, local encyclopedia, *American Law Reports* and periodical literature.

*Shepard's state citations* provide additional references to cases interpreting state legislation.   This will be discussed in Chapter 14.

For the definition of words defined in a code, two procedures generally are available: check the general index or volume index (1) under "Definitions" or (2) under the topic with a subheading "Definitions".

### 2.   Inoperative State Law

Less frequently, an attorney may have a problem involving an act which has been repealed or is no longer in effect.   The text and repeal of that law, depending upon the dates, may be located in the current or an earlier annotated state code.   The annotations in the earlier compilation provide case interpretations to the inoperative section.   The other research and comparative information may be also given by the obsolete compilation.

### 3.   Popular Names of State Acts

To locate a state act when only its popular name is known, consult:

*Shepard's Federal and State Acts and Cases of Popular Names.*

The general index of the state code.

### 4.  Private, Temporary, Local and Appropriation Acts

If the law is a private, temporary, local or appropriation act, the session laws should be consulted, for such measures generally are not included in the states codes: A few states publish their appropriation acts independent of the session laws.

---

## SECTION E.  MUNICIPAL LEGISLATION: RESEARCH PUBLICATIONS

As an instrument of state policy, a municipality has such powers as the state devolves upon it.  In most states, important powers are granted municipalities by state constitutions.  The old method of legislative enactment of a special charter as the organic law of a particular municipality is still operative in a few states, but most state constitutions outlaw such special legislation.

The other three methods of organizing American municipal governments are: (1) incorporation under a uniform general law, (2) exercise of local option as to form of government under an optional charter law and (3) local framing and adoption of a so-called home rule charter.  Under (1) and (2) the pertinent general statutes in effect constitute the charter of a municipality governed by them.

### 1.  Municipal Charters

City charters are printed in various forms.  Some are annotated, some appear as pamphlets, others are included with official publications, such as compilations of city ordinances, and some are published both as pamphlets and as parts of books.

### 2.  Municipal Ordinances and Codes

Ordinances are the legislative enactments of local jurisdictions.  They are to the city what acts are to the state legislatures and the United States Congress.  Such local laws are passed generally by the municipal governing body, e. g., city council, and approved by the mayor, although there may be direct popular participation under the initiative and referendum.

In the larger cities, ordinances are first published in an official journal.  In the smaller communities, they initially may be reported in the local newspapers.  In some instances, the ordinances may be published with an annual compilation of city departmental reports.  Some states require publication of new ordinances or amendments in the local newspapers to be effective.

Municipal codes are codifications of ordinances.  They are usually classified and arranged under a logical plan and the sections are consecutively numbered.   There are various types of municipal codes; for the most part, their methods of arrangement are similar to statutes.   The publication of city codes in many communities is not as regular as federal and state compilations.   Because the city codes are often not kept current, it is frequently necessary to consult the files of the city attorney, the corporation counsel or the city clerk for the up-to-date law.   However, there is a trend towards more frequent codification and supplementation by official and unofficial publishers.

## Features Common to Most City Codes

a.   City Charters

Most city codes include the text of city charters.   They usually are unannotated.

b.   Text of Ordinances

The texts of city ordinances are the basic information contained in municipal codes.   They are rarely annotated with case digests.

c.   Topical Analyses;  Historical Notes;  Cross References

In some of the new city codes a topical analysis may precede each chapter.   The history of the sections, references to pertinent state law and notations to related provisions in the city code may be given after the text of each ordinance or in footnotes.

d.   Indexes

The codes are indexed according to various schemes.   Some index the charter and ordinances together;  some contain separate indexes to each of these units;  in a few cities, where the codes are divided into separately bound parts each part may have a detailed index and also there may be a broad general index covering all the ordinances.

e.   Tables

In some municipal codes, tables are included which show the disposition of the sections of an earlier code and the location of earlier provisions in the current compilation.

## 3.   Interpretations to Municipal Charters and Ordinances

As has been indicated, the various city codes generally do not include annotations to cases interpreting the charters and ordinances. The sources which are available for locating cases in point are limited either by the absence of written decisions over which the publisher has no control or a restricted policy as to coverage.   Notwithstanding these limitations, since they are the only available aids, their use should be neither minimized nor neglected.

a.   Shepard's State Citations

Unquestionably, the *Shepard's* citations for a state, in the absence of an annotated city code, provides the most comprehensive listing of cases construing city charters and ordinances. However, it should be remembered that a significant number of lower court decisions, interpreting city law, are rendered orally, or, if written, are not published. The location of these unreported written decisions can be ascertained, in most instances, through the assistance of the court clerks, bar association secretaries or local law librarians. But, since unreported decisions generally are not indexed, the cases in point are not readily accessible and often their disclosure entails more industry and consumes more time than the problems warrant.

### b.   State Digests

An additional aid to judicial interpretation of city ordinances is the state digest. The reported cases interpreting an ordinance are included in the state digest. It also may reveal interpretations of comparative ordinances of other cities. If there is a paucity of judicial law on the matter, such comparative consideration may prove helpful.

### c.   Shepard's Ordinance Law Annotations

Topically analyzed and arranged annotations on local subjects, covering numerous court decisions, are provided by this publication. For a fuller discussion of this set, see Chapter 14.

The *state digest* may be consulted for possible additional references to cases interpreting the local ordinances as well as for citations to decisions construing similar provisions of other cities.

---

## SECTION F.   STATE LEGISLATIVE HISTORIES

Generally, state legislatures do not publish their debates, committee reports or transcripts of hearings of legislative committees. This absence of legislative histories at the state level frequently presents uncertainties as to the meaning and the interpretations of statutory provisions when they are ambiguous or vague. However, in a few states extrinsic legislative documents serve partially to fill the need for eliciting legislative intent.

Some judges vigorously oppose the use of extrinsic aids in determining legislative intent with respect to a state statute. They hold the situation to be quite different from that which prevails in federal legislative bodies where the debates, hearings and reports are stenographically recorded or published. State legislative records, apart from the bills and the amendments thereto, are "at most a skeletonized account of the proceedings which tells practically nothing concerning the intent of the members of the Legislature except as may be gathered from their votes." [7]

Chief Justice Vanderbilt of the New Jersey Supreme Court, in a strong dissent, objected to a majority ruling that a statement attached to a state bill by its introducer assists in any way in identifying the intent of the legislature with respect to the act passed.[8]  He was of the opinion that too many extraneous and harmful factors, with no particular bearing on legislative meaning, may influence the content of such statements.  Nevertheless, he recognized that extrinsic aid "has been slowly finding its way into our judicial expressions." [9]

Despite such opposition and in the absence of recorded reports, hearings and debates, certain types of unofficial information may be useful to the researcher.  But, in weighing the information, he should recognize that the sources are unofficial.

In most states, the only official documents available are the bills as introduced into the legislature, and the Senate and House Journals. These, however, only contain a history of the voting record for a bill with no explanatory matter.  A few states [10] will, for some laws, have reports of the State Law Revision Commission or a special committee of the legislature.  If a state has an annotated code, such reports are usually cited in the notes to the appropriate statutory provision.

---

## SECTION G.  METHODS OF CITATION

### 1.  State Statutes

The statutes of the states are variously cited.  Listed below are examples of citations to the current codes of a few states.  The abbreviation "Ann.," used in connection with annotated statutes, is frequently omitted from briefs and local publications.  Also, a preference may be for the date to precede rather than follow the section number or other numerical designation.

Examples:

Ala.Code tit. 37, § 419 (1958).

Cal.Civ.Code § 1026.

---

[7] Dissenting opinion of Chief Justice Vanderbilt in Deaney v. Linen Thread Co., Inc., 19 N.J. 578, 588, 118 A.2d 28, 33 (1955).

[8] 2 Id. at 586 and 32.

[9] Ibid.

[10] For California *see* Rothe, Sources of legislative intent in California, 3 *Pacific Law Journal* 63–87 (1972); for New York, *see* Breuer, Legislative intent and extrinsic aids to statutory interpretation in New York, 1957.

Ill.Ann.Stat. c. 7, § 11 (Smith-Hurd 1954).

N.Y.Real Prop.Law § 274.

Generally, a law included in a statutory supplement is identified by the added reference (Supp. or Cum.Supp. and date), e. g., Wyo. Stat. § 9–165 (Supp.1965).

## 2.　State Session Laws

State session laws frequently are cited by chapter and section, the designations, however, differing for the various states.

Ind.Laws 1971, c. 245, § 4.

Kan.Sess.Laws 1969, c. 106, § 3.

Ky.Acts Extra Sess.1969, c. 2, § 1.

N.M.Laws 1969, c. 119 § 5.

S.C.Acts 1970, No. 935 § 7.

## SECTION H.　SUMMARY

**1.**　Session laws are published after adjournment of the state legislatures for the regular or special sessions and cover the laws enacted during that period.

**2.**　State statutes are compiled, in single or multi-volume editions, under a logical arrangement with the obsolete and revoked laws eliminated.

## 3.　Classification of Statutes

　　a.　Consecutive integers, i. e., numbering the sections consecutively by the use of whole numbers from the first section to the end of the code, e. g., 15437.

　　b.　Titles and chapters, e. g., 24–1305.

　　c.　Decimal numbers, e. g., 633.7.

## 4.　Features Common to Most State Statutes

　　a.　Constitutions.

　　　　(1)　State—usually annotated.

　　　　(2)　Federal—usually unannotated.

　　b.　Text of statutes.

　　c.　Historical notes.

　　d.　Comparative legislation.

　　e.　Annotations.

f.   Tables.

g.   Research aids.

h.   Cross references to related sections.

i.   Indexes.

j.   Forms.

k.   Popular names of state acts.

*l.*   Supplementation—cumulative annual pocket parts, pamphlet supplements and replacement volumes.

**5.   State Law Index, 1925–1948**

a.   Not cumulated; each volume is indexed separately.

b.   Not kept up-to-date.

**6.   Martindale-Hubbell Law Directory**

a.   Law Digest volume contains brief synopses of some statutory laws of all states and selected statutory laws of many foreign countries.

b.   Revised annually.

**7.   Inoperative State Law**

a.   Consult earlier annotated state code.

**8.   Popular Names of State Acts**

a.   In *Shepard's Federal and State Acts and Cases by Popular Name.*

b.   General index of the state code.

**9.   Private, Temporary, Local and Appropriation Acts**

a.   Generally, consult session laws.

**10. Municipal Charters**—variously published

**11. Municipal Ordinances** are the legislative enactments of local jurisdictions

**12. Municipal Codes** are codifications of ordinances

**13. Features Common to Most City Codes**

a.   Classified.

b.   City charters.

c.   Text of ordinances.

d.   Topical analysis; historical notes; cross references.

e.   Indexes.

f. Tables.

g. Supplementation—not always up-to-date.

h. Annotations in codes are a rarity.

## 14. Interpretations to Municipal Charters and Ordinances

a. *Shepard's State Citations.*

b. Table of State, etc. Cases in volume 14 of *U. S. Supreme Court Reports Digest* (Lawyers Co-op.).

c. State digests.

## 15. Status and History of a City Charter and Ordinances

a. Check *Shepard's State Citations.*

b. Check city code and its supplement.

# Chapter 12

# COURT PROCEDURE

This chapter is devoted to a consideration of the materials used for some phases of court procedure. It covers legislation pertaining to judicial proceedings, the rules promulgated by the courts for conducting their business, the interpretation of those rules by cases and commentaries, and the forms of instruments used in court proceedings. Other aspects of court procedure, such as the law of evidence and trial practice, which offer no significant publications problem, are omitted.

## SECTION A.  COURT RULES IN GENERAL

Duly promulgated rules of court are legislative in effect, since they control the operations of the court and the conduct of the litigants appearing before it. Court rules relate to such matters as filing of papers, assignment of cases, security for costs, and pre-trial procedures.

The purpose of court rules is threefold: (1) to aid the court in expediting and performing its business, (2) to establish uniform procedure for the conduct of the court's business, and (3) to provide parties to a suit with procedural information and instructions on matters pertaining to the judicial proceedings.

Although court rules, which are always promulgated by the courts, have features of legislative enactments, they are generally subservient to statutes since most courts are legislative in origin. Thus, where there is a conflict between a statute and the court rules, the statute, if constitutional, is supreme. However, if a constitution authorizes court rules, they prevail even though the rules may be in conflict with a statute.

Add Footnote 1.  For a general discussion of rule-making by courts see J. Weinstein, Reform of Court Rule-making Procedure.  1977.

The first law establishing the federal courts and regulating their jurisdiction and procedure was passed at the first session of the First Congress. This law is known as the Judiciary Act of 1789. Later revisions appeared in the *Revised Statutes of 1875* and as the Judicial Code of 1911, the objectives of which were to reconcile conflicting provisions of successive enactments, to consolidate the laws and to improve judicial procedure. In 1948, Congress again revised the laws relating to judicial legislation. This act, constituting new Title 28 of the *United States Code*, is entitled "Judiciary and Judicial Procedure."

In 1948, Congress also enacted the new Federal Criminal Code, Title 18 of the *United States Code*. The first criminal code was passed by Congress in 1909. Over the years, many new provisions were interspersed and added, some of which were not in the form of amendments to the Criminal Code of 1909; thus, reference to the criminal law and procedure became increasingly difficult. Besides, the law, itself, needed revaluation and further study. In 1926, the *United States Code*, containing the criminal statutes, was approved by Congress but was never enacted into law; hence, reference to the Criminal Code of 1909 was still necessary. But, finally, in 1948, a new Criminal Code was enacted by the federal legislature.

Titles 18 and 28 give to the Supreme Court of the United States rule-making authority over other federal courts. The Supreme Court, pursuant to this authority, has promulgated rules of civil and criminal procedure for use in the federal district courts and rules in admiralty, bankruptcy and copyright matters. The Supreme Court has also adopted rules for the conduct of its own business. To meet special and local needs, the individual lower federal courts are authorized to formulate rules of procedure for their use apart from those promulgated by the Supreme Court. Thus, the Courts of Appeals and District Courts have adopted individual local rules for their use, which are based upon the special requirements of each court.

## 1. Publication of Federal Court Rules

The United States Supreme Court Rules are published in pamphlet form by the Court, in scattered volumes of the United States reports (official and unofficial sets) and in the publications listed below.

The federal court rules can be classified into two general categories: (1) the individual rules of the various federal courts, and (2) the rules of general application. The publications listed below generally include both types of rules. The individual rules usually relate to the following federal courts: the Supreme Court of the United States, the Courts of Appeals, the Court of Claims, the Court of Customs and Patent Appeals, the Customs Court, the Tax Court of the United States and the Court of Military Appeals. The rules of general application cover the admiralty rules, the copyright rules, the bankruptcy rules, the federal rules of civil procedure and the federal rules of criminal procedure. The publications given below together cover all of the rules, some being more comprehensive than others.

The local federal district court rules are published separately in pamphlet format. They also are included in a single loose-leaf volume of the *Federal Rules Service* (Callaghan and Co.). The *Service* contains all the rules of the District Courts currently in force, and the rules are arranged in the alphabetical order of the states. Provision is made to keep the rules up-to-date in the *Service* as amendments and new rules are adopted. Local rules relating to admiralty, bankruptcy and criminal procedure are not included in the volume.

a.    Federal Code Annotated (U.S.C.S.–F.C.A.)

A separate annotated unit of two volumes of the *Federal Code Annotated* is devoted to the rules of the federal courts and their interpretation. Part 1 covers Rules of Civil Procedure for District Courts, and Part 2 pertains to the criminal rules and the rules of federal courts relating to practice on appeal and special proceedings. It is kept up-to-date by pocket and pamphlet supplements.

b.    U. S. Supreme Court Digest (West Pub. Co.)

Volumes 16 and 17 of this digest contain individual and general federal court rules, with Supreme Court annotations to some rules. Pocket supplements to the *Digest* keep the rules current.

c.    U. S. Supreme Court Report Digest (Lawyers Co-op. Pub. Co.)

The individual and general rules of various federal courts are included in volumes 17 and 18 of the *Digest*. Some rules are annotated with references to Supreme Court decisions interpreting them, to *American Law Reports* annotations in point and to applicable sections of the *Digest*. The volumes are kept up-to-date by pocket supplements.

d.    United States Code Annotated

Approximately 10 volumes of this set relate to individual and general federal court rules. The rules are annotated by case digests interpreting them and appear with the appropriate code titles which authorize their promulgation. To find the exact location of the various rules consult the General Index under the headings "Rules of Court," "Rules of Civil Procedure" and "Rules of Criminal Procedure."

Two volumes of individual federal court rules follow Title 28. Pocket and pamphlet supplements keep the rules and annotations current.

e.    United States Code

Individual and general federal court rules can be located in this publication by referring to its general index under the headings previously suggested in paragraph d for checking the U.S.C.A. The rules generally are found after the law authorizing them.

f.   Bender's Federal Practice Manual

This is a one-volume loose-leaf publication which includes the more common individual and general federal court rules.   Its loose-leaf format lends itself easily to the insertion of current materials. The service is also annotated.

This outline is not intended to be comprehensive, for the federal rules appear in many other publications, such as pamphlets, treatises, services, *etc.*   However, little would be gained by further exposition on those materials.   Section E, below, lists treatises and manuals which include the texts of the federal rules.

----

### SECTION C.   FULL–TEXT ANNOTATIONS TO THE FEDERAL RULES OF CIVIL AND CRIMINAL PROCEDURE

The complete texts of the court decisions which construe the Federal Rules of Civil Procedure or the Federal Rules of Criminal Procedure are included in the following publications:

1.   *Federal Rules Service* (Callaghan and Co.)

This is a most useful service to use when researching for court decisions construing the Federal Rules of Civil Procedure.   It is in four sections:

(a)  *Federal Rules Decisions.*   (First and Second Series.)   This contains the full text on all Federal court decisions construing the Federal Rules Decisions.

(b)  *Federal Rules Digest.*   This is a classified arrangement of digests of court decisions printed in (1) *supra.*

(c)  Federal Local Court Rules—see B1, *supra.*

(d)  Finding Aids volume.   This includes a Word Index to the Federal Rules of Civil Procedure and the full text of all the rules.

This volume also contains an outline on how to use this set.

### 2.   Federal Rules Decisions (cited "F.R.D.")

This unit of the *National Reporter System,* published since 1940, contains cases of the federal district courts construing the Rules of Civil and Criminal Procedure.   District court decisions interpreting the Federal Rules of Criminal Procedure have been included in this reporter since 1946.   The civil procedure cases of the district courts have been included in the publication since its inception.   The cases first appear in advance sheets and subsequently are republished in bound volumes, retaining the same volume and page numbers.   This publication began as a repository for unreported district court decisions construing the Federal Rules; hence, it does not contain any

Supreme Court or Courts of Appeals cases. The latter decisions, interpreting the Rules, appear with other appellate decisions in the *Federal Reporter, Second Series.* Supreme Court cases, interpreting the Federal Rules, are reported in the United States reports (official and unofficial) with the decisions on other subjects. F.R.D. cases are key-numbered, as are the cases in other units of the *National Reporter System.* The *Federal Rules Decisions* also includes articles on timely topics. (As was previously indicated in Section C1, above, the text of decisions of the United States Supreme Court, United States Courts of Appeals and District Courts relating to the Federal Rules also are included in the *Federal Rules Service.*)

---

### SECTION D.   DIGESTS ON FEDERAL PRACTICE

The several digests studied in Chapter 6 may be used with reference to federal practice problems. The *Modern Federal Practice Digest* is of special value in searching a federal practice problem through a digest.

---

### SECTION E.   COMMENTARIES ON FEDERAL PRACTICE

The following treatises pertain to the federal practice, covering the Judicial and Criminal Procedure Codes (Titles 28 and 18, respectively) and the Federal Rules of Civil and Criminal Procedure. These publications include comments and explanations along with the text of the statutes, the Federal Rules and forms.

1.   *Cyclopedia of Federal Procedure.* 3d ed. 1951–1966. 17 vols. with pocket supplements.

The forms are published separately as *Nichols Cyclopedia of Federal Procedure Forms.* (See below.)

2.   *Moore's Federal Practice.* 2d ed. 1955–1966. 9 vols. in 12 (Loose-leaf.)

3.   *West's Federal Practice Manual.* 1970 7 vols. with pocket supplements.

4.   *Wright's Federal Practice and Procedure.* 1969– (7 vols. published to date).

## SECTION F.  FORM–BOOKS KEYED TO THE FEDERAL RULES OF CIVIL AND CRIMINAL PROCEDURE

Model instruments or forms used in federal practice and keyed to the Federal Rules have also been published independently in the following form-books.  These forms or models of instruments can be used in federal judicial proceedings.  They contain the essential matters, proper terms or phrases and other elements necessary to make them formally correct.  They follow an accepted arrangement of the materials and are capable of being adapted to the circumstances of specific cases.  These are practice form-books.  Other form-books, discussed in Chapter 18, contain office practice instruments, such as wills, contracts, etc.

1.  *Bender's Federal Practice Forms*.  1965.  5 vols.

This is a loose-leaf publication with annotations and cross references to *Moore's Federal Practice* (2d ed.).  The forms cover the civil and criminal rules.

2.  *Nichols Cyclopedia of Federal Procedure Forms*.  1952.  3 vols.

The annotated forms cover civil and criminal procedure and some administrative agencies.  Pocket supplements keep it current.

3.  *West's Federal Forms*.  1952.  8 vols.

This set contains annotated forms for practice in the Supreme Court, the Courts of Appeals and under the Federal Rules.  Administrative agencies and miscellaneous forms also are included.  It is kept up-to-date by pocket supplements.

---

## SECTION G.  FEDERAL PRACTICE:  RESEARCH PROCEDURE

### 1.  Federal Courts

For the individual rules of the United States Supreme Court, Courts of Appeals and other federal courts (except local district courts), as well as case interpretations of those rules, consult:

    a.  Federal Code Annotated, Court Rules volumes.

    b.  United States Code Annotated.

    c.  United States Supreme Court Digest, volumes 16 and 17 (West Pub. Co.).

    d.  United States Supreme Court Reports, Digest, Court Rules, volumes 17 and 18 (Lawyers Co-op. Pub. Co.).

　　e.　Bender's Federal Practice Manual.

For additional citations to cases interpreting the rules of individual federal courts see:

　　a.　Shepard's United States Citations—for cases interpreting the United States Supreme Court Rules.

　　b.　Shepard's Federal Reporter Citations—for rules of federal courts (other than Supreme Court).

　　c.　Modern Federal Practice Digest.

Local district court rules are included in the *Federal Rules Service*. They also are published separately as pamphlets.

## 2.　Federal Rules of Civil and Criminal Procedure for the District Courts

The Federal Rules and cases interpreting them are located in:

　　a.　Federal Rules Service (Civil Procedure).

　　b.　Federal Rules Decisions.

These services contain the full texts of the opinions interpreting the rules. Case-digests construing the Federal Rules are included in the publications listed under subsections 1 and 2a, above.

Cases construing the Federal Rules are also listed in *Shepard's Federal Reporter Citations* and in the *Modern Federal Practice Digest*.

For discussions relating to the Federal Rules, case citations and the texts of the rules, consult the following treatises:

　　a.　Cyclopedia of Federal Procedure.

　　b.　Moore's Federal Practice.

　　c.　West's Federal Practice Manual.

　　d.　Wright's Federal Practice and Procedure.

## 3.　Miscellaneous Rules of General Applicability

The rules of general applicability covering the admiralty rules, the copyright rules and the bankruptcy rules are included among the publications listed under subsection 1, above.

## 4.　Forms for Practicing in the Federal Courts

See Section F *supra*. Also check the card catalog in a law library under *Civil Procedure*, or the heading *Federal Procedure* in Volume 2 of Jacobstein and Pimsleur *Law Books in Print* and its supplements.

### 5.   Additional Research Aids in Federal Practice

The following secondary aids may be helpful additional sources of information as to federal practice:

a.   Modern Federal Practice Digest, U. S. Supreme Court digests and the American Digest System—for additional case interpretations.

b.   American Law Reports—for federal annotations.

c.   Index to Legal Periodicals—for periodical articles.

---

## SECTION H.   STATE PRACTICE:  RESEARCH PUBLICATIONS

The rules of state supreme courts and other state appellate courts are generally published with the bound decisions of the courts and in the appropriate sets of the *National Reporter System*.  The backs of the volumes containing the rules are so marked, for they are not included in all volumes.  The rules are also available in pamphlet form from the clerks of the courts.

Apart from the rules adopted by individual state courts, state legislatures have enacted laws relating to civil and criminal procedure.  That legislation is published either with the substantive legislation, e. g., Pennsylvania Statutes, or separately, e. g., New York Civil Practice Acts.  The importance of simplified court procedure cannot be overstated, for it avoids delays, expense and uncertainty.  These compelling reasons have prompted the adoption of Civil Practice Acts by some states, which provide simplified procedure, e. g., Illinois Civil Practice Act.

The individual rules of the various state courts are also compiled and published with some state codes, e. g., *Florida Statutes Annotated*.  In other jurisdictions, those compilations appear as separate volumes, e. g., Michigan Court Rules.  Generally, both forms of publication include annotations to judicial interpretations of the rules.

Treatises on state civil and criminal practice have been published for a number of states.  They usually include forms.

---

## SECTION I.   STATE PRACTICE:  RESEARCH PROCEDURE

### 1.   Court Rules

To locate the text of the rules of a state court, consult:

a.   A local practice book.

b.   The court reports.

c.    The applicable unit of the *National Reporter System*.

d.    A pamphlet publication of the rules.

For references to cases interpreting the rules of specific courts refer to *a practice book* and the appropriate *Shepard's State Citations*. The *state digest* also may be examined for cases construing the rules of individual courts.

## 2. Court Practice and Procedure

Consult the pertinent *state code* or *practice manual* for legislation and judicial interpretations relating to civil and criminal practice and procedure. Discussions and forms pertaining to practice and procedure appear in appropriate treatises and manuals. The local law library can provide information as to those publications within a jurisdiction. The *local encyclopedia* is an additional source of information on state court practice. *Shepard's State Citations* and the *state digest* also may provide case references in point. The *Index to Legal Periodicals* should be consulted for articles on civil and criminal practice. The *American Law Reports* provides annotations, with state references, on court practice and procedure.

---

## SECTION J. METHODS OF CITATION

### 1. Federal Rules Decisions

A case reported in Federal Rules Decisions is cited:
Petrikin v. Chicago, R. I. & P. R. Co., 15 F.R.D. 346 (W.D.Mo. 1954).

### 2. Federal Rules Service

An illustration of a parallel citation of a case reported in the *Federal Rules Service* is:

Buckner v. Foster, 105 F.Supp. 279, 17 F.R.Serv. 14a.223, Case 5 (E.D.Mich.1952).

---

## SECTION K. SUMMARY

### 1. Purpose of court rules is:

a.    To aid the court in expediting and performing its business.

b.    To establish uniform procedure for the conduct of the court's business.

c. To provide parties to a suit with procedural information and instructions on matters pertaining to judicial proceedings.

2. **Publication of Federal Court Rules** (see Sections B1 and F1, above)

3. **Federal Rules Service**

   a. Scope

   (1) Text of decisions interpreting the Federal Rules of Civil Procedure.

   (2) Current volume is a loose-leaf service containing material which is periodically reprinted in a bound volume.

   (3) Text of Rules, commentaries, references to law review articles and local court rules.

   (4) *Federal Rules Digest* summarizes and indexes cases appearing in the bound volumes of the *Service*.

   b. Arrangement

   (1) Federal Findex System (classification scheme) of the *Service* and *Digest* is arranged by a combination of the applicable Federal Rule number and an analysis number assigned by the editors for the subordinate topic, e. g., 36a.25 relates to Rule 36a—Request for Admission, and .25—Privilege Affecting Admission of Facts (editor's topic).

4. **Federal Rules Decisions**

   a. Unit of the *National Reporter System*, published since 1940.

   b. Contains the full-text of cases of the federal district courts construing the Rules of Civil and Criminal Procedure.

   c. Cases first appear in advance sheets and subsequently are republished in bound volumes, retaining the same volume and page numbers.

   d. *Federal Rules Decisions* also includes articles on timely subjects.

   e. Key-numbered cases.

5. **Commentaries on Federal Practice** (see Section E, above)

6. **Form-books Keyed to the Federal Rules of Civil and Criminal Procedure** (see Section F, above)

7. **State Practice Publications**

   a. Rules of state supreme courts and other appellate courts are published in (1) state reports, (2) *National Reporter System*, (3) state codes and (4) individual books and pamphlets.

   b. Treatises on state civil and criminal practice.

# Chapter 13

# ADMINISTRATIVE PRACTICE

## SECTION A. FEDERAL ADMINISTRATIVE REGULATIONS AND DECISIONS

### 1. Introduction

Administrative law has been defined as:

> "[T]he law concerning the powers and procedures of administrative agencies, including especially the law governing judicial review of administrative action. An administrative agency is a governmental authority, other than a court and other than a legislative body, which affects the rights of private parties through either adjudication or rule making." [1]

The purpose of this chapter is to explain the manner in which the rules and the adjudication of federal administrative bodies are published and how they may be located.

The power of issuing regulations and of adjudication is delegated to administrative bodies by Congress.[2] The increasingly complex problems of security and economy of the last thirty-five years have brought about a tremendous proliferation of documentary output from administrative agencies. Prior to 1936, there was no procedure for the publication of administrative rulings.

Regulations are issued by administrative agencies under authority delegated to them under a federal statute, or by a Presidential Executive Order.

The type of action taken generally by federal agencies under the authority of statutes or Executive Orders may be classified as: (1) rules or regulations, (2) orders, (3) licenses, (4) advisory opinions, and (5) decisions. These are defined [3] as:

    a. "Rule" means [an] * * * agency statement of general or particular applicability and [which] has effect designed to implement, interpret, or prescribe law or policy * * *

    b. "Order" means the * * * final disposition * * * of any agency * * * matter (other than rule making) but including licensing.

---

[1] 1 Davis, Administrative Law Treatise. § 1.01. (1958).

[2] See *id.* § 201, *et seq.*, for discussion of Congressional authority to delegate legislative power to administrative agencies.

[3] 5 U.S.C. § 551 (1970).

c.  "License" includes any permit, certificate  *  *  *  or other form of permission.

d.  Advisory opinions are used for advice regarding contemplated action.  They are not binding and serve only as authoritative interpretations of statutes and regulations.

e.  Decisions are used by those federal agencies authorized by law to adjudicate controversies arising out of the violation or interpretation of statutes and administrative regulations or rules.  This function is performed by special boards of reviews, hearing examiners, and other officers through administrative decisions.

## 2.  Publication of Federal Rules and Regulations

a.  *Federal Register*.  Before 1936, there was no official source for publication of rules and regulations of federal agencies nor indeed were such agencies required to make them available to the public.  This resulted in much confusion, as there was no way of determining if a proposed action by a person or company was prohibited by some federal agency.  In fact, in one well-known instance, the federal government prosecuted a corporation for violations of an administrative regulation.  This case [4] reached the Supreme Court of the United States before the Attorney-General realized that the action was based on a regulation that had been revoked prior to the time the original action had begun.[5]

As a result of the *Panama* case, Congress passed the *Federal Register Act*, 49 *Stat*. 500, 44 U.S.C. § 301, et seq. (1970).  This provided for the publication of the *Federal Register*.  This started in 1936 and is published daily (except Saturday, Sunday and Monday, and days following holidays).  For any administrative ruling or regulation to be legally effective it must be published in the *Federal Register*.  The definition of what is considered to have general applicability and legal effect is as follows:

> "Every document issued under proper authority prescribing a penalty or a course of conduct, conferring a right, privilege, authority, or immunity, or imposing an obligation, and relevant or applicable to the general public, the members of a class, or the persons of a locality, as distinguished from names individuals or organizations  .   .   ."   (1 C.F.R. 11.2, 1971).

Thus, since 1936, the *Federal Register* contains within it every regulation having legal effect, and amendments thereto, that have been issued by any federal agency authorized by Congress of the Presi-

[4] Panama Refining Co. v. Ryan, 293 U.S. 388 (1935).

[5] 1 Davis, Administrative Law Treatise § 2.06, footnote 5.

dent to issue rules or regulations. It now consists of several hundred volumes.

Although the *Federal Register* is the source for publication of regulations, it alone is insufficient to locate the present status of a particular regulation. It is analogous to the *Statutes at Large.* Although this set contains every law ever passed by Congress, it is not useful in locating a statute on a particular subject. For this, of course, the *U. S. Code* must be consulted. In order to enable one to find federal regulations in a similar manner, the *Code of Federal Regulations* was also established. This bears the same relationship to the *Federal Register* as the U. S. Code does to the *Statutes at Large.*

b. *Code of Federal Regulations (C.F.R.)*[6] This set is a codification of the *Federal Register* wherein all regulations, and amendments thereto, in force as of the 1st of January each year, are codified and brought together by subject. It is in fifty titles similar to the arrangement of the *U. S. Code* and published in pamphlet form. Each year [7] new pamphlets are issued containing the text of regulations still in force, incorporating those promulgated during the year, and deleting those revoked.

The *C.F.R.* is divided into fifty titles, similar to those of the *U.S.C.*, and has a separate index volume. By this means, all regulations, in force, are brought by subject into one of the titles.

See Illustrations 63 and 65 for examples of the *Federal Register* and the *Code of Federal Regulations.*

c. Up-dating the *Code of Federal Regulations.* As previously indicated, the *C.F.R.* is now issued in pamphlet form with each of the fifty titles contained in separate pamphlets. Each year new pamphlets are published containing all of the regulations in force as of time of publication.

As new regulations, or amendments to existing ones, may be promulgated at any time, it is always necessary after consulting the *C.F.R.* to ascertain whether the section or part of the regulation has been amended or revoked.

This is accomplished through the use of the *Codification Guide.* This appears first in each daily issue of the *Federal Register* and in-

---

[6] For a more detailed history of the publication of the earlier editions of the Code of Federal Regulations, see Pollack, Fundamentals of Legal Research. 3d ed. 1967. p. 366–372.

[7] The Office of Federal Register has announced that beginning January, 1973.

Footnote 7. Add:

The Information Handling Service Englewood, Colorado, has prepared a chart showing the various titles of the Code of Federal Regulations issued over the years. It is an excellent graphic illustration of this often difficult to comprehend set.

dicates any part of the *C.F.R.* that has been affected by regulations in the daily issue. This guide is first cumulated monthly, and then quarterly. [See Illustration 64.]

### 3.  Publication of Presidential Administrative Documents

Although the bulk of the contents of the *Federal Register* and the *Code of Federal Regulations* results from the activities of Federal agencies operating under delegated powers from Congress, the President also has the authority to issue regulations that have legal effect. This authority is both constitutional and statutory. The publications of Presidential documents are issued in the following forms.

a.  Proclamations. While there is no legal difference between Presidential Proclamations and Executive Orders, the former is customarily used for Presidential action that has no legal effect, such as Proclamation 4689 in which the President proclaimed October, 1971 as Country Music Month. [See Illustration 60]

Another use is when a statute provides for the President to issue proclamations. [See Illustration 60–a]

(1)  Publication of Proclamations.

(a)  *Statutes at Large.*

(b)  *Federal Register.*

(c)  *C.F.R.* Title 3 and compilation volumes of Title 3.

(d)  *U. S. Code and Administrative News Service.*

(e)  *Current Public Laws and Administrative Materials.*

b.  Executive orders.[8] These are generally used by the President to direct, and govern activities of Government Officials and agencies.

(1)  Publications of Executive Orders. 3a(1) *supra,* except that they are not published in the *Statutes at Large.*

c.  Reorganization Plans. By the provisions of 5 *U.S.C.* 901 *et seq.* (1970) the President is authorized to examine the organization of all agencies and make changes that provide for the better management of the Executive branch of the Government. The President is authorized to submit proposed reorganization plans to both houses. If after 60 days neither house has passed a resolution opposed to the plan, it goes into effect.

(1)  Publication of Reorganization Plans. The President issues his proposed changed as Executive Orders. In addition to their pub-

---

[8] For a detailed study, see U. S. Congress. House Committee on Government Operations. Executive Orders and Proclamations: A Study of Use of Presidential Powers. 1957.

lication in the sources indicated at 3(a)(1) *supra*, Reorganization plans are published as approved in 5 *U.S.C.* Appendix.

d. *Weekly Compilation of Presidential Documents*

This Office of the Federal Register publication is published every Monday and contains statements, messages and other presidential materials released by the White House. It includes an Index of Contents at the front of each issue for documents in it and a quarterly cumulative Index at the back. The quarterly indexes are cumulated semi-annually. Other finding aids are: lists of laws approved by the President, nominations submitted to the Senate, and a checklist of White House releases. Similar materials are published in annual volumes, *Public Papers of the Presidents*.

### 4. U. S. Government Organization Manual

This is an annually published directory of general information about the federal government, with emphasis upon the executive branch and regulatory agencies. Each department and agency is described in concise form with citations to the statutes creating the department or agency; a description of functions and authority, names and functions of major officials; organization charts and bibliographies of major publications. Another important feature is the section that gives the history of all agencies no longer in existence and sets forth which agencies if any now have jurisdiction over the same subject matter. It is one of the most importance reference books for administrative law research. An example of its importance can be ascertained by examining the information it gives for the Civil Aeronautics Board and the Federal Aviation Administration and their predecessor agencies.

In 1 *C.F.R.* Appendix there is a guide to all of the publications with lists where information on a specific topic may be found in the various publications of federal administrative materials.

### 5. Federal Administrative Decisions

Administrative opinions are not published in the *Federal Register* or in the *Code of Federal Regulations*. However, Section 3(b) of the Administrative Procedure Act requires either the publication or the availability for public inspection of the administrative decisions rendered by the agencies. Prior to this Act, there was no requirement, except under individual acts, for the publication of administrative decisions. For the most part, the agencies now publish their opinions. In addition, some sets also have digests and indexes which permit easier integration of the subject matter of the decisions. A less frequent procedure is the publication of slip opinions and advance sheets.

A few unofficial series may include administrative and judicial opinions on special subjects, e. g., *U. S. Patents Quarterly.*

Representative examples of currently published official decisions of federal administrative tribunals are:

a. Civil Aeronautics Board. Reports, vol. 2 et seq. (1940 to date).

b. Comptroller General. Decisions, vol. 1 et seq. (1921 to date).

c. Federal Communications Commission. Reports vol. 1 et seq. (1934 to date).

d. Federal Power Commission. Opinions and Decisions, vol. 1 et seq. (1931 to date).

e. Federal Trade Commission. Decisions, vol. 1 et seq. (1915 to date).

f. National Labor Relations Board. Decisions and Orders, vol. 1 et seq. (1935 to date).

g. Securities and Exchange Commission. Decisions, vol. 1 et seq. (1934 to date).

h. Treasury Decisions, vol. 1 et seq. (1899 to date).

## SECTION B.   ILLUSTRATIONS

[Illustration 60]

## PAGE FROM TITLE 3, CODE OF FEDERAL REGULATIONS

Proc. 4089       Title 3--The President

PROCLAMATION 4089

# Country Music Month, 1971

*By the President of the United States of America*

## A Proclamation

From 1923, when Fiddlin' John Carson made the first tremendously successful country recording until today when country sounds can be heard on over 700 radio stations, the popularity of country music has been a notable part of our American culture.

Why is country music so popular? Why is the Grand Ole Opry's audience made up of people who have traveled an estimated average of 450 miles one way to be there?

The answer is simple. Country music speaks to what is tried and true for many Americans. It speaks of the common things shared by all: the happiness of a family, the pains of a broken heart, the mercy of God, and the goodness of man.

NOW, THEREFORE, I, RICHARD NIXON, President of the United States of America, ask the people of this Nation to mark the month of October, 1971, with suitable observances as Country Music Month.

IN WITNESS WHEREOF, I have hereunto set my hand this 14th day of October, in the year of our Lord nineteen hundred seventy-one, and of the Independence of the United States of America the one hundred ninety-sixth.

*Richard Nixon*

A Presidential Proclamation issued under the inherent authority of the President.

104

[Illustration 60–a]
## PAGE FROM TITLE 3, CODE OF FEDERAL REGULATIONS

Proc. 4076                    T itle 3--T he President

> **A Presidential Proclamation issued by the Presi-
> dent under Congressional authority.**

*(signature) Richard Nixon*

PROCLAMATION 4076

# Establishment of Tariff-Rate Quota
# on Certain Stainless Steel Flatware

*By the President of the United States of America*

## A Proclamation

1. WHEREAS, pursuant to the authority vested in him by the Constitution and the statutes, including section 350(a) of the Tariff Act of
1930, as amended (19 U.S.C. 1351; hereinafter referred to as "the Tariff
Act"), on October 30, 1947 the President entered into, and by Proclamation No. 2761A of December 16, 1947 (61 Stat. 1103) proclaimed, a
trade agreement with certain foreign countries designated as the General
Agreement on Tariffs and Trade (61 Stat. (pt. 5) A11; hereinafter
referred to, as supplemented from time to time, as "the General
Agreement");

2. WHEREAS the President has supplemented and modified the
General Agreement and Proclamation No. 2761A by many subsequent
agreements and proclamations, including;

(a) the Torquay Protocol of April 21, 1951 to the General Agree-
ment (3 UST (pt. 1) 615; hereinafter referred to as "the Torquay
Protocol") proclaimed by Proclamation No. 2929 of June 2, 1951 (65
Stat. C12);

(b) the Protocol of March 10, 1955 Amending the Preamble and
Parts II and III of the General Agreement (8 UST (pt. 2) 1768;
hereinafter referred to as "the 1955 Protocol") proclaimed by Proclamation No. 3513 of December 28, 1962 (77 Stat. 970, 979);

84

[Illustration 61]

## PAGE FROM TITLE 3, CODE OF FEDERAL REGULATIONS

EO 11582         Title 3--The President

2. Section 2 of that Order, placing certain positions in level V of the

**A Presidential Executive Order issued under the inherent power of the President.**

THE WHITE HOUSE,
*January 20, 1971.*

### EXECUTIVE ORDER 11582

**Observance of Holidays by Government Agencies**

By virtue of the authority vested in me as President of the United States, it is hereby ordered as follows:

SECTION 1. Except as provided in section 7, this order shall apply to all executive departments, independent agencies, and Government corporations, including their field services.

SEC. 2. As used in this order:

(a) *Holiday* means the first day of January, the third Monday of February, the last Monday of May, the fourth day of July, the first Monday of September, the second Monday of October, the fourth Monday of October, the fourth Thursday of November, the twenty-fifth day of December, or any other calendar day designated as a holiday by Federal statute or Executive order.

(b) *Workday* means those hours which comprise in sequence the employee's regular daily tour of duty within any 24-hour period, whether falling entirely within one calendar day or not.

SEC. 3. (a) Any employee whose basic workweek does not include Sunday and who would ordinarily be excused from work on a holiday falling within his basic workweek shall be excused from work on the next workday of his basic workweek whenever a holiday falls on Sunday.

(b) Any employee whose basic workweek includes Sunday and who would ordinarily be excused from work on a holiday falling within his basic workweek shall be excused from work on the next workday of his basic workweek whenever a holiday falls on a day that has been administratively scheduled as his *regular* weekly nonworkday in lieu of Sunday.

134

[Illustration 61–a]

## PAGE FROM TITLE 3, CODE OF FEDERAL REGULATIONS

Chapter II--Executive Orders                    EO 11638

*Effective Date*

SEC. 5. This order shall take effect as of the first day of the first applicable pay period beginning on or after January 1, 1972.

A Presidential Executive Order issued by President under Congressional authority.

### EXECUTIVE ORDER 11638

#### Adjusting the Rates of Monthly Basic Pay for Members of the Uniformed Services

By virtue of the authority vested in me by the laws of the United States, including the Act of December 16, 1967, and section 3 of the Economic Stabilization Act Amendments of 1971, and as President of the United States and Commander in Chief of the Armed Forces of the United States, it is hereby ordered as follows:

SECTION 1. The rates of monthly basic pay for members of the uniformed services within each pay grade are adjusted upwards as set forth in the following tables:

COMMISSIONED OFFICERS

| Pay Grade | Years of service computed under section 205 | | | | |
|---|---|---|---|---|---|
| | 2 or less | Over 2 | Over 3 | Over 4 | Over 6 |
| O-10 [1] | $2,263.50 | $2,343.30 | $2,343.30 | $2,343.30 | $2,343.30 |
| O-9 | 2,006.40 | 2,059.20 | 2,103.00 | 2,103.00 | 2,103.00 |
| O-8 | 1,817.10 | 1,871.70 | 1,916.40 | 1,916.40 | 1,916.40 |
| O-7 | 1,509.60 | 1,612.80 | 1,612.80 | 1,612.80 | 1,684.50 |
| O-6 | 1,119.00 | 1,230.00 | 1,310.10 | 1,310.10 | 1,310.10 |
| O-5 | 894.90 | 1,051.50 | 1,123.50 | 1,123.50 | 1,123.50 |
| O-4 | 754.80 | 918.30 | 980.40 | 980.40 | 997.80 |
| O-3 [2] | 701.40 | 783.90 | 837.60 | 927.30 | 971.40 |
| O-2 [2] | 611.40 | 667.80 | 802.20 | 828.90 | 846.30 |
| O-1 [2] | 530.70 | 552.60 | 667.80 | 667.80 | 667.80 |

## [Illustration 62]

## PAGE FROM ANNUAL INDEX VOLUME TO C.F.R.

**Index**

**Standards—Continued**

Pay, waiver, General Accounting Office, 4 Part 91
Poultry and products, 7 §§ 70.320—70.357
Product standards development, 15 Part 10
Property, surplus, operation by State agencies, 45 Part 14
Rabbits and products, 7 §§ 54.260—54.-277
Radio, generally, this index.
Refrigerator doors, 15 Part 260
Safety standards, generally, this index.
Small business size, 13 Part 121
State operations for surplus property, 45 Part 14
Stockyard scales, 9 §§ 201.71—201.93
Technical reports for Defense Depart-
ment
Time a
U.S. 1
Vessels,
Wine, 2
Work t
29 Pa

**State, I**
**7; 4**

Agency
gener
Aliens, g
Arms, ammunition, and implements of war, 22 Parts 121—128
Board of Appellate Review, 22 Part 7
Books, maps, newspapers, etc., 22 Part 132
Certificates of authentication, 22 Part 131
Citizens and citizenship, generally, this index.
Claims, tort, 22 Part 31
Consular services, generally, this index.
Educational exchanges, 22 Parts 61—63
Employment:
  Conduct standards, 22 Parts 10, 13
  Creditors' complaints against employees, 22 Part 12
  Equal, 22 Part 141
Foreign dignitaries protection, 22 Part 2
Foreign Service officers, 22 Parts 11, 501
Gifts and decorations from foreign governments, 22 Part 3
→ Information availability, 22 Part 6 ←
Insignia of rank, 22 Part 1
Marriages, 22 Part 52
Nationality procedures, 22 Part 50
Organization, 22 Part 5
Passports, 22 Part 51

**State, Department of—Continued**

Procurement:
  Advertising, formal, 41 Part 6-2
  Appeal regulations, 41 Part 6-60
  Authority delegations, 41 §§ 6-1.400—6-1.404-3
  Balance of payments, 41 §§ 6-6.800—6-6.806-2
  Contract clauses, 41 Part 6-7
  Examination of records, omission, 41 §§ 6-6.1000—6-6.1053
  Financing of contracts, 41 Part 6-30
  Foreign purchases, 41 Part 6-6
  Negotiation, 41 Part 6-3
  Payments, balance of, 41 Part 6-6
  Procedures, 41 Part 6-1
  Supply, sources of, 41 Part 6-5

X
Part 112
81—88
gn areas,
national

> Finding a Regulation in C.F.R. Problem: Who in the Department of State has the authority to release State Department records?
>
> STEP 1. Index to C.F.R. This Index is not easy to use as it lacks specific entries. Title 22 Part 6 should be consulted.

Engraved stationery and allied products, New York City trade area, 16 Part 37
Greeting card industry, 16 Part 244
Gummed paper, 16 Part 19
Industry trade practices, 16 Part 61
Manifold business forms industry, 16 Part 47
Sealing tape, 16 Part 19

**Statistical Reporting Service, 7, XII**

**Statistics and Statistical Services**

Children's Bureau, 42 § 206.2
Foreign trade, 15 Part 30
Freight commodity, 49 Part 1248
National Center for Health Statistics, 42 Part 3
Peanuts, 7 Part 1300
Piggyback traffic, 49 Part 1252
State educational agencies, aid for improvement of statistical services, 45 Part 140
Train order, 49 Part 233

**Stocks**

*See* Securities.

212

## [Illustration 62-a]

## PAGE FROM ANNUAL INDEX VOLUME—C.F.R.

**Index**

**Information Availability—Con.**

National Foundation on the Arts and Humanities, 45 § 1100.3
National Highway Safety Bureau, 49 § 553.7
National Labor Relations Board, 29 §§ 102.117, 102.118
National Mediation Board, 29 Part 1208
National Oceanic and Atmospheric Administration, 15 Part 903
National Transportation Safety Board, 14 Parts 400, 401
Navy, Department of, 32 Part 701
Packers and Stockyards Administration, 9 Part 204
Panama Canal Company, 35 Part 9
Patents and copyrights, 37 §§ 1.11—1.15, 201.2

**As with most indexes, references can be found under different entries.**

Securities and Exchange Commission, 17 §§ 200.80—200.81
Selective Service System, 32 Part 1670, §§ 1606.55—1606.63
Small Business Administration, 13 Part 102
Smithsonian Institution, 36 Part 504
Social Security Administration, 20 Part 401
→State, Department of, 22 Part 6
State Technical Services, Office of, 15 § 700.12
Subversive Activities Control Board, 28 Part 202
Tennessee Valley Authority, 18 § 301.1
Transportation, Department of, 49 Parts 7, 9
Treasury, Department of, 31 Parts 1, 270, 323, 351
U.S. Arms Control and Disarmament Agency, 22 Part 602
U.S. Information Agency, 22 Part 503
U.S. Tariff Commission, 19 §§ 201.5—201.6
Veterans Administration, 38 §§ 1.500—1.558
Wage and Hour Division, 29 Parts 516, 850

**Insects**

Asiatic rice borer, 7 Part 318
Bean butterfly, 7 Part 318
Bean pod borer, 7 Part 318

**Insects—Continued**

Beetles:
Cereal leaf, 7 §§ 301.84—301.84-10
Chinese rose, 7 Part 318
Japanese, 7 §§ 301.48—301.48-10
Khapra, 7 §§ 301.76—301.76-11
White fringed, 7 §§ 301.72—301.72-10
Bollworm, pink, 7 §§ 301.52—301.52-10
Cactus borer, 7 Part 318
Chafer, European, 7 §§ 301.77—301.77-10
Customs regulations, 19 §§ 12.24—12.32
European, 7 Part 319
European chafer, 7 §§ 301.77—301.77-10
European crane fly, 7 Part 331
Fire ant, 7 §§ 301.81—301.81-10
Fruit flys:
Mediterranean, 7 Part 318; § 319.56-2S
Melon, 7 Part 318; § 319.56-2S

0

e,
rt
2764
Honeybee importation, 19 § 12.32
Importation of, 19 §§ 12.29—12.32
Insecticides, 7 Parts 2762, 2764
Mango weevil, 7 Part 318
Mexican, 7 Part 320
Moths, gypsy and brown-tail, 7 §§ 301.-45—301.45-10
Pesticide chemicals, 7 Part 2763
Poisons, 7 Parts 2762, 2764
Puerto Rico, 7 Part 318
Shipping, 7 Part 330
Virgin Islands, 7 Part 318

**Insignia**

Armed forces:
Service flag and lapel button, 32 Part 57
Wearing uniform, 32 Part 53
Civil Defense, official, 32 Part 1806
4-H Club emblem, 7 Part 8
State Department, rank, 22 Part 1

**Inspector General, Agriculture, 7 XXVI**

Information availability, 7 Part 2610

**Insular Possessions and Territories**

Canal Zone Regulations, generally, this index.
Civil Service Commission, differentials and allowances payable in nonforeign areas, 5 Part 591
Customs, 19 Part 7

126

[Illustration 63]

## PAGE FROM TITLE 22 OF C.F.R.

§ 5.4            **Title 22—Foreign Relations**

Step 2. Check Part referred to by Index. This will refer to specific paragraph of Regulations.

Note that after each part, the statutory citation for the regulation is given. Citation is also to where regulation first appeared in the Federal Register.

(1) Acceptance of Gifts and Decorations from Foreign Governments. 22 CFR 3 et seq.

(2) Employee Responsibility and Conduct. 22 CFR 10 et seq.

(3) Appointment of Foreign Service Officers. 22 CFR 11 et seq.

(4) Fees for Services in the United States, fees and Charges, Foreign service. 22 CFR 21 et seq.; 22 CFR 22 et seq.

(5) Claims and Stolen Property. 22 CFR 31 et seq.

(6) Issuance of Visas. 22 CFR 41–42 et seq.

(7) Nationality and Passports. 22 CFR 50 et seq.

(8) International Educational and Cultural Exchanges. 22 CFR 61 et seq.

(9) Protection and Welfare of Americans Abroad. 22 CFR 71 et seq.

(10) Shipping and Seamen Abroad. 22 CFR 81 et seq.

(11) Other Consular Services Abroad. 22 CFR 91 et seq.

(12) Economic, Commercial and Civil Air Functions Abroad. 22 CFR 101 et seq.

(13) International Traffic in Arms. 22 CFR 121 et seq.

(14) Certificates of Authentication. 22 CFR 131 et seq.

(15) Civil Rights. 22 CFR 141 et seq.

(16) Department of State Procurement. 41 CFR 6–1 et seq.

(c) These regulations are supplemented from time to time by amendments appearing initially in the FEDERAL REGISTER.

## PART 6—AVAILABILITY OF RECORDS OF THE DEPARTMENT OF STATE

AUTHORITY: The provisions of this Part 6 issued under sec. 4, 63 Stat. 111, as amended, sec. 501, 65 Stat. 290; 22 U.S.C. 2658, 31 U.S.C. 483a, 5 U.S.C. 552, E.O. 10501; 3 CFR, 1949–1953 Comp.

SOURCE: The provisions of this Part 6 contained in Dept. Reg. 108.584, 33 F.R. 7079, May 11, 1968, unless otherwise noted.

### § 6.1   Definitions.

As used in this part, the following definitions shall apply:

(a) The term "identifiable" means, in the context of a request for a record, a reasonably specific description of the particular record sought, such as date, format, and subject matter, which will permit its location.

(b) The term "record" includes all books, papers, maps, photographs, or other documentary material, or copies thereof, regardless of physical form or characteristics, made in or received by the Department of State, and preserved as evidence of its organization, functions, policies, decisions, procedures, operations, or other activities.

### § 6.2   Availability of records.

(a) All identifiable records of the Department of State shall be made available to the public upon compliance with the procedures established in this part, except to the extent a record is determined by the Deputy Legal Advisor for Administration to be exempt from disclosure.

(b) Unclassified information, documents, and forms which have previously been provided to the public as part of the normal services of the Department of State will continue to be made available without regard to the following sections.

### § 6.3   Availability of statements of policy, interpretations, manuals, instructions.

Statements of policy, interpretations, administrative manuals (or portions thereof), opinions, orders, and instructions to staff which affect any member of the public will be made available to the public for inspection and copying in the public reading room, except to the extent they are determined by the Deputy

[Illustration 63–a]

## PAGE FROM TITLE 22 OF C.F.R.

**Chapter I—Department of State**          § 6.7

Legal Adviser to be exempt from disclosure.

§ 6.4  **Records which may be exempt from disclosure.**

---

Step 3. Read the Specific Regulation. Sec. 6.5 set forth who has authority to release State Department Records. If the cover of the pamphlet from which this illustration is taken is examined, it will be seen that it is "Revised as of Jan 1."

Hence, steps must be taken to ascertain if it has been changed since January. This is done by checking the Federal Register Codification Guide.

See next Illustration.

---

this category are records relating to the officers and employees of the Foreign Service, including efficiency records (sec. 612 of the Foreign Service Act of 1946, as amended, 22 U.S.C. 986), and the records of the Department of State or of diplomatic and consular officers of the United States pertaining to the issuance or refusal of visas or permits to enter the United States (sec. 222(f) of the Immigration and Nationality Act, 8 U.S.C. 1202(f)).

(d) *Information given in confidence.* Included in this category are records reflecting commercial and financial information, as well as other information, obtained from any person and customarily regarded as privileged and confidential by the person from whom they were obtained.

(e) *Interagency or intragency memorandums or letters.* Included in this category are records such as interagency communications and internal drafts, memorandums between officials and agencies, opinions and interpretations prepared by staff or consultants; records of the deliberations of staff personnel; and records whose premature disclosure would interfere with the achievement of the purpose for which they were being prepared.

(f) *Personnel, medical, and other files.* Included in this category are personnel and medical files and other files containing private or personnel information which, if disclosed to the public, would amount to a clearly unwarranted invasion of the privacy of any person to whom the information pertains.

(g) *Investigatory files.* Included in this category are files compiled for the enforcement of all laws, or prepared in connection with Government litigation and adjudicative proceedings, except for those portions of such files which are by law available to persons in litigation with the Department, in which case such portions will be made available to such litigants.

§ 6.5  **Authority to release and certify, or to withhold records.**

(a) Except as provided in § 6.9, authority is hereby delegated to the Chief, Records Services Division, to furnish copies of records to any person entitled thereto pursuant to these regulations, and upon request to provide certified copies thereof in accordance with Part 131 of this chapter.

(b) A determination by the Deputy Legal Adviser for Administration to deny a request to make a record available is final, and no appeal will be received by the Department of State from such a determination. This determination shall be in written form, clearly stating the basis upon which the record has been withheld.

§ 6.6  **Public reading room.**

A public reading room or area where the records described in § 6.3 shall be made available is located in the Department of State, 2201 C Street NW., Washington, D.C. The receptionist will refer the applicant to the proper room. Fees will not be charged for access by the public to this room or the records contained therein, but fees in accordance with § 6.8 will be charged for furnishing copies thereof.

§ 6.7  **Manner of requesting records.**

(a) Identifiable records may be requested by the public in person from 10 a.m. to 4 p.m., Department of State, 2201 C Street NW., Washington, D.C., where the receptionist will refer the applicant to the proper office for service and the necessary forms for making a request. Requests by mail should be addressed to the Chief, Records Services Division,

## [Illustration 64]

## PAGE FROM C.F.R. CODIFICATION GUIDE

**JANUARY–OCTOBER 1972**      **63**

| | Page |
|---|---|
| 295 | 5047, 7407, 7408, 7631, 7809, 8461, 14238, 18563, 18629, 22001 |
| 301 | 10370, 15933, 20119 |
| 303 | 10370, 15933, 20119 |
| 304 | 144, 10370 |
| 305 | 10370 |
| 306 | 10370, 15933, 20119 |
| 307 | 10370 |
| 308 | 867, 10370, 17478 |
| 311 | 10370 |
| 312 | 10370 |
| 316 | 10370 |

### 22 CFR

**Chapter I**

| | Page |
|---|---|
| 6 Heading revised | 18616 |
| 6.2 (a) revised | 18616 |
| 6.3 Revised | 18616 |
| ►6.5 Heading and (b) revised; (c) added | 18616 |
| 6.6 Amended | 18616 |
| 6.9 Revised | 18616 |
| 6.10 Added | 18617 |
| 9 Added | |
| 11.1—11.8 Revis | |
| 11.11 Revised | |
| (k) added | |
| 14 Added | |
| 21.67 (b) revised | |
| 22.1 (a) amended | |
| 41.6 (a) heading amended | |
| (e)(1) revised | |
| 41.55 (b) revised | |
| 41.65 Revised | |
| (b)(1)(ii), (b) | |
| (c) revised | |
| 41.66 (d) revised | |
| (e) Suspended | |
| 41.102 Introductory text of (b) revised; (b)(13) added | 2439 |
| (b)(12) revised | 3053 |
| 41.113 (c) revised | 14873 |
| 41.122 (e), (f), and (g) added | 9023 |
| (f)(1) amended | 11057 |
| 41.124 (e) revised | 15373 |
| 41.128 (b) revised | 15 |
| 41.134 Revised | 9024 |
| (a) revised | 11058 |
| 42.91 (a)(14)(ii)(e) revised; (a)(14)(ii)(f) removed | 14693 |
| 42.113 (c) revised | 14873 |
| 50.9 Revised | 11459 |
| 51.63 (a)(4) and (b) revised | 6053 |
| 53.2 (g) revised | 11459 |
| 63 Revised | 5940 |
| 121.01 Amended | 14694 |
| 121.14 Added | 14694 |

**Chapter II**

| | Page in F.R. |
|---|---|
| 125.11 (a)(2) and (b)(1) revised | 14694 |
| 201.01 (w) corrected | 12792 |
| 201.02 (b) corrected | 12792 |
| 201.11 (b)(4) corrected | 12792 |
| (b)(4) amended | 18192 |
| 201.13 (b)(3)(ii) corrected | 12792 |
| 201.15 (a) corrected | 12792 |
| 201.51 (d)(2)(i)(b) corrected | 12792 |
| 201.52 (c) redesignated (b); (a)(2)(iii) corrected | 12792 |
| 201.61 (e)(1) corrected | 12792 |
| 201.64 (b)(1) corrected | 12792 |
| 201.67 (a)(5)(i) and (a)(5)(i)(b) corrected | 12792 |
| 201.75 Corrected | 12792 |
| 201.80 Corrected | 12792 |
| 211.9 (c)(2) amended | 17028 |

**Chapter III**

| | Page |
|---|---|
| 301 Removed | 11066 |

**Chapter V**

| | Page |
|---|---|
| 503.6 (c)(2) revised | 11861 |

---

> **Step 4.**
>
> The Codification Guide indicates that Sec. 6.5 was revised. The text of this must now be checked in page 18616 of the 1972 Federal Register.
>
> As this Codification Guide is for Jan.-Oct., the Codification Guide in the daily issues of the Federal Register between Nov.-Dec., should also be checked for any subsequent changes.

---

| | Page |
|---|---|
| 603.2 (b) revised | 6636 |
| 603.10—603.18 Revised | 6666 |
| 603.19—603.21 Removed | 6667 |

**Chapter VIII**

| | Page |
|---|---|
| Added | 7594 |
| 801 Added | 7594 |
| 802 Added | 7594 |
| 803 Added | 7598 |
| 804 Added | 7601 |
| 805 Added | 7602 |
| 806 Added | 7603 |

**Chapter X**

| | Page |
|---|---|
| Added; incorrectly designated Ch. VII | 7312, 7883 |
| 1001 Added; incorrectly designated as 801 | 7312, 7883 |
| 1002 Added | 8375 |
| Technical correction | 9320 |

## [Illustration 65]

## PAGE FROM FEDERAL REGISTER FOR SEPTEMBER 14, 1972

18616

### RULES AND REGULATIONS

The Commissioner further concludes that the regulations should be amended to provide for residues of the drug in liver, kidney, and muscle of turkeys.

An order published in the FEDERAL REGISTER of July 11, 1972 (37 F.R. 13531) providing an amendment to § 135e.46 Clopidol included in the table published under the "Limitations" column reference to a level of "0.125 percent" of the drug. This figure is in error and should read "0.0125 percent". In addition the text in the "Limitations" column for item 5 should be clarified regarding the withdrawal of such feeds from broiler and replacement chickens before slaughter by adding, following the existing text, the phrase, "if given at the level of 0.025 percent in feed or reduce level to 0.0125 percent 5 days before slaughter."

Therefore, pursuant to provisions of the Federal Food, Drug, and Cosmetic Act (sec. 512(i), 82 Stat. 347; 21 U.S.C. 360b(1)) and under authority delegated to the Commissioner (21 CFR 2.120), Part 135e and 135g are amended as follows:

1. In Part 135e the table in § 135e.-46(e), is amended by revising the text under the "Limitations" column for item 5 to read "For broiler chickens and replacement chickens up to 16 weeks of age intended for use as caged layers; feed continuously as the sole ration; withdraw 5 days before slaughter if given at the level of 0.025 percent in feed or reduce level to 0.0125 percent 5 days before slaughter." and by adding a new item 6 as follows:

§ 135e.46  Clopidol.

\* \* \* \*

(e) Conditions of use.

COLOPIDOL IN COMPLETED FEED

| Principal ingredient | Grams per ton |
|---|---|
| \* \* \* | \* \* \* |
| 6. Clopidol..... | 113.5 or .227 (0.0125%) or 0.025%) |

Step 5.

The Federal Register, p. 18616 containing revised text of Sec. 6.6.

§ 135g.62  [Amended]

2. Part 135g is amended in § 135g.62 by changing the opening text in paragraph (b) from "In chickens:" to read "In chickens and turkeys:"

Effective date. This order shall be effective upon publication in the FEDERAL REGISTER (9–14–72).

(Sec. 512(i), 82 Stat. 347; 21 U.S.C. 360b(1))

Dated: September 6, 1972.

C. D. VAN HOUWELING,
Director,
Bureau of Veterinary Medicine.

[FR Doc.72–15563 Filed 9–13–72; 8:45 am]

## Title 22—FOREIGN RELATIONS

### Chapter I—Department of State

[Dept. Reg. 108.674]

PART 6—FREEDOM OF INFORMATION POLICY AND PROCEDURES

Availability of Records

Part 6 of Title 22 of the Code of Federal Regulations is amended as set forth below:

1. The heading of Part 6 is changed to read as set forth above.

2. Section 6.2(a) is amended to read as follows:

§ 6.2  Availability of records.

(a) All identifiable records of the Department of State shall be made available to the public upon compliance with the procedures established in this part, except to the extent that a determination is made to withhold a record exemptable under 5 U.S.C. 552(b). That determination shall be made in accordance with § 6.5(b).

\* \* \* \*

3. Section 6.3 is amended to read as follows:

§ 6.3  Availability of statements of policy, interpretations, manuals, instructions.

Statements of policy, interpretations, administrative manuals (or portions thereof), opinions, orders, and instructions to staff which affect any member of the public will be made public for inspection and copying in the public reading room, except to the extent that they are exemptable by law from disclosure and a determination to withhold is made under § 6.5(b).

4. The title of § 6.5 is changed, paragraph (b) is amended, and a new paragraph (c) is added, as follows:

§ 6.5  Authority to release and certify; authority to withhold records and appeals.

\* \* \* \*

(b) If an office of the Department of State believes that a record which has been requested under this part should not be disclosed, it shall refer the request with a copy of the record in question to the Deputy Legal Adviser for Management. The Deputy Legal Adviser for Management, in consultation with the Office of Policy and Plans of the Bureau of Public Affairs, shall determine whether the record may be exempted from disclosure and whether, if so, it should nevertheless be disclosed. This determination shall be in written form, clearly stating the basis upon which the record has been withheld, including the specific provision governing exemption under 5 U.S.C. 552(b) which has been determined to apply. That determination shall be final, subject only to review as provided in paragraph (c) of this section.

(c) Review of the determination under paragraph (b) of this section may be requested by the person who submitted the original request for a record which has been withheld. The review must be requested in writing within 30 days of the notice advising that person of the determination to withhold. The request for review should be forwarded by certified mail to the Deputy Under Secretary of State for Management, Chairman, Council on Classification Policy, Department of State, Washington, D.C. 20520, together with a copy of the written denial issued under paragraph (b) of this section. The request shall include a statement of the circumstances, reasons, or arguments advanced for insistence upon disclosure of the originally requested record. After review, the decision will be promptly communicated to the person requesting review, and will constitute the final action of the Department.

5. Section 6.6 is amended by adding a sentence at the end to read as follows:

§ 6.6  Public reading room.

\* \* \* The Chief, Records Services Division, in his discretion, may authorize persons to utilize their own portable copying equipment. Any arrangements for the use of such equipment must be consistent with security regulations of the Department of State and are subject to the availability of personnel to monitor such copying.

6. The title of § 6.9 is changed and the text is revised to read as follows:

§ 6.9  Opening of records for nonofficial research.

(a) Definition. As used in this section, "records" means records of the Department of State, including the records of U.S. posts abroad, and such other files as may be placed under the control of the Department of State.

(b) General policy. The Department will open its records on an equitable basis to all individuals engaged in nonofficial research as soon as such action may be taken without adversely affecting the national security, the maintenance of friendly relations with other nations, and the efficient operation of the Department. The opening of departmental records to nonofficial researchers will ordinarily not take place until after the records have been transferred to the custody of the National Archives and Records Service. The opening of records for nonofficial research will generally take place on the basis of large blocks of records defined by years and/or major subject categories.

(c) Open records. (1) The records of the Department, with the exceptions stated in subparagraph (2) of this paragraph, shall be automatically declassified

[Illustration 66]

## PAGE FROM TITLE 2, C.F.R.

Chapter I—Parallel Table          25 U. S. C. 2

| United States Code | Code of Federal Regulations |
|---|---|
| 22 U. S. C. 2571 | 41 CFR  Part 23–1 |
|  | Part 23–7 |
|  | Part 23–50 |
|  | Part 23–52 |
| 2572 | 41 CFR  Part 23–50 |
|  | Part 23–52 |
| 2581 | 22 CFR  Parts 601–603 |
|  | 41 CFR  Parts 23–1—23–52 |
| 2626 | 22 CFR  Part 3 |
| 2657 | 22 CFR  Part 131 |
| 2658 | 22 CFR  Parts 1–7 |
|  | Parts 11–12 |
|  | Parts 21–32 |
|  | Parts 50–52 |
|  | Part 61 |
|  | Part 63 |
|  | Part 71 |
|  | Part 91 |
|  | Part 112 |
|  | Part 131 |
|  | Part 141 |
|  | Parts 503–504 |
|  | 41 CFR  Parts 6–1—6–60 |

2

### Alternative Method of Finding C.F.R. Regulation.

When the U.S.C. citation which delegates power to issue regulations to an agency is known, this Table can be used to find C.F.R. Regulations. E. g., 22 U.S.C. 2571 is the U.S.C. citation authorizing Governmental Departments to release documents.

| | |
|---|---|
|  | Part 204 |
|  | 49 CFR  Part 551 |
| 401–404 | 49 CFR  Part 551 |
| 401 | 23 CFR  Part 204 |
| 402 | 23 CFR  Part 204 |
| 24 U. S. C. 15 | 32 CFR  Part 728 |
| 34 | 32 CFR  Part 728 |
| 37 | 32 CFR  Part 736 |
| 41 | 32 CFR  Part 574 |
| 165 | 42 CFR  Parts 301–302 |
| 177 | 42 CFR  Part 303 |
| 271 through 296 | 32 CFR  Part 553 |
| 278 | 36 CFR  Part 55 |
| 286 | 36 CFR  Part 55 |
| 321 through 329 | 45 CFR  Part 211 |
| 25 U. S. C. 2 | 25 CFR  Parts 1–11 |
|  | Parts 41–42 |
|  | Parts 43e–43f |
|  | Part 46 |
|  | Part 48 |
|  | Part 53 |
|  | Parts 88–89 |
|  | Part 104 |

## SECTION C.   LOOSE–LEAF REPORTERS OR SERVICES

The inaccessibility, complexity and bulk of federal and state administrative regulations and decisions prompted the publication of loose-leaf reporters or services by private publishers. Loose-leaf services consist of separate, perforated leaves in special binders, simplifying the insertion or substitution of new leaves. Current reports are furnished to keep the contents up-to-date and to indicate new developments. Speed of publication of the current releases is an important element, and they appear at generally uniform intervals for each reporter, i. e., weekly, biweekly or monthly. Reporters are adaptable to materials relating to the regulation of business and taxes which require frequent amendments or changes. Each service relates to a specific subject such as corporations, taxation, trade regulation, etc.

Federal and state laws are published together and the various kinds of law pertinent to the subject matter are compiled within a service or a division of a reporter. A knowledge of the scope of the services is necessary to select the appropriate one for use with a problem. Consult the library catalog or the listings of the services published, to determine whether the subject matter is covered by a service.

The first loose-leaf service appeared over fifty years ago. Since then we have seen numerous services published, covering many phases of federal and state controls. The leading publishers are the Bureau of National Affairs, Inc., Commerce Clearing House, Inc. and Prentice-Hall, Inc.

Although each service is arranged consistent with the types of materials included in it, a general pattern is usually followed in the organization of the publications. Each binder can easily hold 2,000 pages. Guide cards, with colored tabs, are used to separate the divisions of each service. Each division has a table of contents. Most services are arranged under a system of paragraph numbers which correspond to key or section numbers. The paragraph numbers are enclosed in brackets so as not to be confused with official section numbers which are also given. The material is indexed to the paragraph numbers.

The contents are generally arranged as follows:

1. *Reprint of the full text of the statutes on the topic, with significant legislative history.*

2. *Compilation of the rules and administrative and court decisions, with editorial discussion.*

3. *Subject or Topical Indexes.*

4. *Tables of Cases.*

5. *Current Reports* (these reports include supplemental, current materials and indexes).

6. A *Report Letter* is published with each release explaining the new developments on the topic and with filing instructions for the disposition of the pages included in the current release.

Where many states have statutes on a specific subject, the laws are arranged within a service by states and the same paragraph number is uniformly assigned to a given topic in each state unit. Thus, an examination of the discussions under the same paragraph number for each jurisdiction will disclose the statutory law of the states on that topic.

The following is a convenient guide in searching for information in a service:

*First*, consult the General Index (Topical or Master).

The general index may be the sole topical index to the entire service, or, as in some services, there may be a general index and each major subdivision may have a more detailed topical index.

*Second*, having obtained references to paragraphs, refer to the text by paragraph numbers.

*Third*, use the Cumulative Numerical Index or the Cross Reference Table for references to current material on the subject. Also, check the current index for additional data.

The services also include various tables (cases, analytical and citator) and finding lists.

The table of cases provide the standard information: full citation to the case and the paragraph number where the case is located in the service.

The finding list is a convenient table referring the researcher from the official sections or captions (statutes, rules, etc.) to the paragraph number in the service where the material appears. This integrates the information which is dispersed in a number of places in the service.

Citator tables are a feature of the tax services. These alphabetically list the names of decisions with their history and references to other cases which have cited them.

A recent development of the loose-leaf services is the special reporting of cases by subject. Decisions on a specific subject are compiled, either as a part of a service or as an independent publication, into bound volumes. E. g., *Commerce Clearing House, Labor Cases* and *Prentice-Hall, American Federal Tax Reports.*

*The instructional material on the use of each service, included in each, should be read before attempting to use a service.*

The basic uses of loose-leaf reporters or services can be demonstrated through the problem method.

## SECTION D.   ILLUSTRATIONS—LOOSE LEAF SERVICES

1.   **Prentice-Hall.**

67.   Page from Master Index—P. H. Federal Taxes.

68.   Pages from Volume of P.H. Federal Taxes.

69.   Page from Volume of P.H. Federal Taxes.

70.   Page from Tables Volume.

2.   **Commerce Clearing House.**

71.   Pages from CCH Labor Law Reporter—Topical Index.

72.   Page from CCH Labor Law Reporter.

73.   Case Digests in CCH Labor Law Reporter.

74.   Cumulative Index in CCH Labor Law Reporter.

75.   Case Table—CCH Labor Law Reporter.

76.   Finding Lists—CCH Labor Law Reporter.

## [Illustration 67]

## PAGE FROM MASTER INDEX OF PRENTICE–HALL FEDERAL TAXES

| 1-1-72 | **EXEMPTION—EXPENSES** | **Fed. Index—299** |
|---|---|---|

References are to Paragraph [¶] Numbers

*Exemption: (continued):*

. foreign governments and officials, income of ..30,381 et seq.; 30,391 et seq.; 30,414 et seq.
. Guamanian income of U.S. citizen affecting ..30,686(a)(b); 30,706(60); 30,707
. head of household ..3431
. individuals ..9201 et seq.
. industry-union pension plan ..19,030(15)
. insolvent banks ..39,411 et seq.
. joint return ..35,074(10)
. levy and distraint ..35,834; 35,836; 35,844
. nonresident aliens: See "Nonresident aliens, personal exemptions"
. old-age: See "Old-age exemptions"
. overstated, fraud penalty ..37,294(5)
. personal: See "Personal exemptions"
. self-employment coverage for clergymen and Christian Science practitioners ..34,013(e)
. State statutes:
. . distraint proceedings, effect on ..35,834; 35,836; 35,844(10); 41,111
. . lien for taxes ..35,775
. . transferee liability as affected by ..41,111
. states or political subdivisions ..41,490(1)
. status determination date ..9203(c); 9261—9263
. surtax purposes, corporations ..3201; 3912; 3913; 16,897; 34,463 et seq.
. . dividends received deduction ..16,560; 16,564; 34,475; 34,476; 34,490—34,495
. withholding: See "Withholding tax at source, exemption from"; "Withholding tax on wages, exemption from"

**Exhaustion:** See "Depletion"; "Depreciation"
**Exhibiting horses at fair** ..11,954(10)
**Exhibitions, foreign,** contributions to ..16,033(5)
**Existence of a "view",** collapsible corporation ..17,784

*Expenses: (continued):*

. changes in adjoining property necessitating ..11,482(55); 11,483
. chargeable to future operations ..11,286—11,326
. children ..7865
. clothing ..11,954(70)
. coal disposal: See "Coal, coal lands and coal companies, royalties"
. collecting child-support arrears ..14,752(40)
. compensation: See "Compensation"
. completed contract method ..20,261(b); 20,272; 20,300; 20,301(c)(1)
. condemnation proceedings ..16,707(20); 16,717(10)
. Congressmen's allowance ..11,375
. contingent, deductibility ..20,585; 20,590
. contributions as: See "Business expenses, contributions as"
. cost inclusion where previously deducted ..31,177(45)
. crop basis ..7162(c); 11,912; 11,919
. decedents ..28,493 et seq.
. deduction ..11,002 et seq.
. dental: See "Medical expenses"
. dependent's support ..9213(a); 9243
. dependents' care: See "Child-care expenses"
. depreciation includible as, exempt corporation ..21,013.10(40)
. development: See "Development expenditures"
. . mines: See "Minerals, mines and mining, development expenditures"
. oil and gas wells: See "Oil and gas wells, development and drilling costs"
. disallowance: See "Expenses, nondeductible"
. distraint ..35,822; 35,824; 35,871—35,877; 35,888
→ . education ..11,501—11,506; 16,312(f)
. refunds based on ..36,600(c)
. election to deduct ..33,939(15)
. election to office in athletic club ..11,239(85)

> **Using Prentice-Hall Tax Service. Problem: Can an employed student attending evening law school deduct the tuition and other expenses involved.**
>
> **Step 1. Check appropriate entries in Master Index.**

. . reimbursement, as income ..7397
. reimbursement for, as income ..7399
. stockholders:
. . to protect interests ..11,102(25); 11,334
**Expenditures for outside services** ..11,071—11,076
**Expense account allowances** ..12,062; 12,067
**Expense money, distraint of** ..35,842(35)
**Expense savings,** life insurance companies ..29,148
**Expenses:** See also "specific items
. absence of income ..11,013(15)
. accrued at death ..20,551—20,553; 28,493 et seq.
. accrued but unpaid 2 1/2 months after close of year ..16,825 et seq.
. accrued under cash basis ..20,069(10)(15)
. acquisition of subsidiaries ..16,722(25)
. administration:
. . priority in bankruptcy ..37,695(25)
. . taxes as ..37,695(25); 37,696(5)
. advertising: See "Advertising expenses"
. allocable to exempt income: See "Exempt income, expenses related to"
. alteration: See "Repairs"
. anticipated ..20,567; 20,575; 20,592
. attorney's fees: See "Attorneys' fees"
. automobile ..11,421--11,433
. . professional people ..11,426
. blocked foreign income involved ..20,293(5); 20,553(a)(4)
. building regulations ..11,482
. business: See "Business expenses"
. canvassing ..16,371(26)

. fines for violation of statutes ..11,237
. fixing-up residence to assist sale ..31,466(5); 31,748—31,750
. foreign personal holding companies ..21,517(b)(5); 21,519(e)
. foreign ships incidentally within 3-mile limit ..30,103(5)
. future:
. realty development ..31,211
. reserves ..20,575—20,585
. gift of property, applicable to ..7488; 16,014(c)
. guardianship ..16,312(j); 16,342(15)
. housing regulations ..11,485(30)
. improper deductions ..38,447
. installment sales ..16,712(30); 20,435
. . deductibility ..11,239(15)
. . real estate ..20,435
. . time for deduction ..20,379(e); 20,401
. insurance premiums: See "Insurance premiums"
. interest: See "Interest"; "Interest paid or accrued"
. investment: See "Investments, expenses"
. iron ore disposal ..16,921 et seq.
. last illness, priority of Federal taxes ..37,703(10)
. legal: See "Attorneys' fees"; "Legal expenses"
. levy and sale ..35,822; 35,824; 35,871—35,877; 35,888
. living: See "Living expenses"
. long-term contracts ..20,261(b); 20,266; 20,272; 20,300; 20,301(c)
. loose-leaf services ..11,071; 11,518; 11,520
. medical: See "Medical expenses"
. microfilming newspaper files ..16,738(25)
. minors ..7865

[Illustration 68]

## PAGE FROM VOLUME OF P–H FEDERAL TAXES

[1]                    Repairs (§ 162—¶ 11,005)                    **11,245**

(10) **Deduction allowed in full with-**          168, cert. den. 10-16-33, affirming 22
out offset on account of Director General's      BTA 302.

Step 2. Using P–H Tax Service. At the beginning of each main paragraph number, there is editorial explanation of the law or regulation. This should be read carefully.

(4 Cir.; 1933), 63 F.2d 304, 12 AFTR          on second appeal (8 Cir.), 109 F.2d
                                              1018, 24 AFTR 462.

### EXPENSES FOR EDUCATION

[¶ 11,501] Basic rules.—Generally, an individual's expenses for education (including research undertaken as part of his educational program) are deductible, even though the education may lead to a degree, if the education is undertaken for maintaining or improving skills required in his trade or business or employment, or to meet the express requirements of his employer or the requirements of applicable law or regulations imposed as a condition for his retention of his salary status or employment. Reg. § 1.162-5(a), ¶ 11,502.

Deduction for the cost of maintaining or improving skills is allowed for cost of refresher courses or courses dealing with current developments as well as academic or vocational courses. This rule applies provided the expenditures for the courses are not within the nondeductible categories contained in Reg. § 1.162-5(b)(2) or (3), Reg. § 1.162-5(c)(2). As to when an employee has undertaken education to meet the requirements of his employer or applicable law, see Reg. § 1.162-5(c)(2).

**Personal and capital expenditures.**—There are two categories of educational expenses which are personal or constitute an inseparable aggregate of personal and capital expenditures and aren't deductible even though the education maintains or improves skills required in the individual's trade or business or employment, or meets the express requirements of his employer or applicable law or regulations. Reg. § 1.162-5(b)(1).

*Minimal educational requirements.*—The first category of nondeductible educational expenses includes expenses incurred to meet the minimum educational requirements for qualification in an individual's employment or other trade or business. The minimum educational requirements are determined by considering the employer's requirements, the applicable law and regulations, and the standards of the profession, trade or business. The fact that the individual is performing service in an employment status doesn't establish that he has met the minimum requirements. However, once he has met the minimum requirements he will be treated as continuing to meet those requirements even though they are later changed. Reg. § 1.162-5(b)(2)(i).

The minimum educational requirements for qualification of a person in a position in an educational institution is the minimum level of education (in terms of aggregate college hours or degree) which under laws and regulations, in effect when the individual is first employed in such position, is normally required for persons initially being employed in such position. If there are no normal requirements, then the person will be considered as having met the requirements when he becomes a member of the faculty. Reg. § 1.162-5(b)(2)(ii)

For examples illustrating when education is required to meet minimum educational requirements, see Reg. § 1.162-5(b)(2)(iii).

Prentice-Hall, Inc.—Fed. Tax                **Reg. § 1.162-5  ¶ 11,501**

## [Illustration 68-a]

## PAGE FROM VOLUME OF P–H FEDERAL TAXES

**11,250**                    Business Expenses                    [1]

Reg. § 1.162-5(b)(2)(iii) Example (1) **Situation 4. continued**

*mum educational requirements for qualification as a secondary school teacher. Accordingly, expenditures for a fifth year of college will be deductible unless the expenditures are for education which is part of a program being pursued by A, B, or C which will lead to qualifying him in a new trade or business.*

*Example (2). D, who holds a bachelor's degree, obtains temporary employment as an instructor at University Y and undertakes graduate courses as a candidate for a graduate degree. D may become a faculty member only if he obtains a graduate degree and may continue to hold a position as instructor only so long as he shows satisfactory progress towards obtaining this graduate degree. The graduate courses taken by D constitute education required to meet the minimum educational requirements for qualification in D's trade or business and, thus, the expenditures for such courses are not deductible.*

*Example (3). E, who has completed 2 years of a normal 3-year law school course leading to a bachelor of laws degree (LL.B.), is hired by a law firm to do legal research and perform other functions on a full-time basis. As a condition to continued employment, E is required to obtain an LL.B. and pass the State bar examination. E completes his law school education by attending night law school, and he takes a bar review course in order to prepare for the State bar examination. The law courses and bar review course constitute education required to meet the minimum educational requirements for qualification in E's trade or business and, thus, the expenditures for such courses are not deductible.*

*(3)   Qualification for new trade or business.   (i) The second category of non-*

Frequently, as in this instance, the editorial explanation includes examples.

*of work. The following are examples of changes in duties which do not constitute new trades or businesses:*

*(a)   Elementary to secondary school classroom teacher.*

*(b)   Classroom teacher in one subject (such as mathematics) to classroom teacher in another subject (such as science).*

*(c)   Classroom teacher to guidance counselor.*

*(d)   Classroom teacher to principal.*

*(ii)   The application of this subparagraph to individuals other than teachers may be illustrated by the following examples:*

*Example (1). A, a self-employed individual practicing a profession other than law, for example, engineering, accounting, etc., attends law school at night and after completing his law school studies receives a bachelor of laws degree. The expenditures made by A in attending law school are nondeductible because this course of study qualifies him for a new trade or business.*

**[Footnote ¶ 11,502(1) continued]**

**Example (4).** The facts are the same as in example (3) except that, due solely to a shortage of qualified teachers, D's employer does not enforce the prescribed educational requirements in that other teachers who do not fulfill those requirements are retained in their positions. D's expenses are nevertheless deductible.

**Example (5).** E, a high school teacher of physics, in order to improve skills required by him and thus improve his effectiveness as such a teacher, takes summer school courses in nuclear physics and educational methods. E's expenses for such courses are deductible.

[Footnote continued on next page]

¶ **11,502   Reg. § 1.162-5**          LATEST DEVELOPMENTS, SEE p. 61,501

[Illustration 69]

## PAGE FROM VOLUME OF P–H FEDERAL TAXES

**11,254**     Business Expenses     **[2]**

> ### Step 3.   Using P–H Tax Service
>
> After the Editorial Explanation, Digests of all relevant court decisions and administrative rulings are given.
>
> Note in this instance the number that deal with law school education.  Note also how some are allowed, others denied.  Each has to be read in full text to determine their relevancy to the case being researched.

expenses incurred in attending law school to obtain the position of patent chemist. This was a personal expense. His job as a research chemist was not in jeopardy, nor was he required to have legal training except to obtain this other position.

> *Sandt v. Comm.* (3 Cir.; 1962), 9 AFTR 2d 1470, 303 F.2d 111, affirming ¶ 61,-181 P-H Memo TC and (Hines), ¶ 61,203 P-H Memo TC.

Deduction denied Army Captain for expenses incurred in attending university to obtain baccalaureate degree under Army Regulations No. 621-5 as amended. The expenses were personal in nature and were not undertaken pursuant to any requirement of the taxpayer's employer imposed as a condition to the retention of his status or salary. Rule equally applicable to members of all the armed forces who are subject to similar programs.

> *Rev. Rul. 61-133,* CB 1961-2, p. 35.

Education expenses of employed teacher and private tutor denied. The courses did not assist her.

> *Hartrick v. U.S.* (DC, Ohio; 1962), 9 AFTR 2d 1261, 205 F. Supp. 111.

Deduction allowed for cost of law school courses taken to improve taxpayer's efficiency as revenue agent. It was customary for fellow agents to take similar courses. It did not matter that a few weeks after taxpayer received his degree he quit his job and entered private practice.

> *Welsh v. U.S.* (DC, Ohio; 1962), 10 AFTR 2d 5713, 210 F. Supp. 597, affirmed (6 Cir.; 1964), 13 AFTR 2d 935, 329 F.2d 145.

Deduction denied revenue agent for cost of obtaining law degree. The degree qualified taxpayer for a new profession. The degree was not required by employer as a condition of continued employment.

> *James J. Engel,* ¶ 62,244 P-H Memo TC.
> *Jeffrey L. Weiler,* 54 TC 398 (No. 38).

Deduction denied IRS agent for expenses of attending night law school. Jury verdict.

> *Jaffe v. U.S.* (DC, Fla.; 1966), 18 AFTR 2d 5812.

the latter for maintenance of present employment. *Lonnie R. Lenderman,* ¶ 63,110 P-H Memo TC

Deduction denied chemical engineer for law school courses; primary purpose was to obtain a degree and practice law. *David H. Pfeffer,* ¶ 63,163 P-H Memo TC.

Education expense deduction denied teacher for graduate school courses in school administration; he was not required to take them and they were too remotely connected with his job. *Albert R. Killips,* ¶ 63,177 P-H Memo TC.

Patent trainee's primary purpose for legal education expense was keeping job and meeting employer's required condition. Allowed.

> *Williams v. U.S.* (DC, N.Y.; 1965), 15 AFTR 2d 436, 238 F. Supp. 351.

To the contrary: electrical engineer, who became patent agent, denied deduction for costs of legal education. Expense was necessary for advancement to new position, not retention of existing job.

> *Owen L. Lamb,* 46 TC 539, motion to dismiss appeal because of improper venue denied (2 Cir.; 1967), 19 AFTR 2d 964, 374 F.2d 256, appeal dismissed without discussion of this point (2 Cir.; 1968), 21 AFTR 2d 798, 390 F.2d 157.

Deduction denied realty company employee for night law school expense. Attendance was primarily to acquire new profession and not to maintain or improve skills of existing employment.

> *Gilmore C. Gulbranson,* ¶ 64,313 P-H Memo TC.
> *Gilmore C. Gulbranson,* ¶ 63,205 P-H Memo TC.
> *Gilmore C. Gulbranson,* ¶ 68,149 P-H Memo TC.
> *Huene v. U.S.* (DC, N.Y.; 1965), 16 AFTR 2d 5238, 247 F. Supp. 564.

Deduction denied patent examiner for law school expenses. 75% of patent examiners leave during or following law school courses. Education was not undertaken as condition to retain salary and job but to obtain substantial advancement.

> *John C. Martin, Jr.,* ¶ 65,188 P-H Memo

## [Illustration 70]

## PAGE FROM TABLES VOLUMES—P–H FEDERAL TAXES

| 9-7-72 | Cross Reference Table ¶ 11,504(5)—11,760 | **61,525** |

See also: Current Table—page 61,501

| From ¶ | To ¶ | |
|---|---|---|
| 11,504(5)... | | *Connelly, Robert J.*, pending CA 1 (T) |
| | | *Fleischer, Nathan*, pending CA 2 (T) |
| | | *Feistman, Eugene G.*, pending CA 9 (T) |
| | | *Kellner, Helen*, pending CA 2 (T) |
| | | *Patterson, Samuel F.*, pending CA 9(T) |
| | | *Weiman, David N.*, app dis CA 2 (G) |
| | 57,028 | *Ford:* Teacher's one year study abroad. TC, app auth CA 9 |
| | 57,087 | *Baker:* Cost of Air Force officer's college degree. TCMem |
| | 57,113 | *Gallery:* "Cooperative student's" expenses nondeductible. TC |
| | 57,153 | *Ruddy, Jr.:* Acquired new skill. TCMem, pending CA 4(T) |
| | 57,447 | *Curtin:* Qualified in new trade or business. TCMem |
| | 57,519 | *Glasgow:* Improved skills required to shepherd congregation. TC Mem, pending CA 10(G) |
| | 57,622 | *Warfsman:* Not required by employer. TCMem |
| | 60,130 | Deduction allowed for undergraduate college expenses. TCMem |
| | 72-309 | *Connelly, Jr.*, aff.: Lead to new trade. CA |
| | 72-495 | *Pharr*, aff.: Job had no bearing on education. CA |
| | 72-675 | *Fleischer*, aff.: Qualified for new employment. CA |
| 11,504(20).. | | *Weiman, David N.*, app dis CA 2 (G) |
| 11,506(5)...57,117 | | *Steinmann:* To maintain and improve skills. TCMem |
| | 57,554 | *Kirst:* Sabbatical to maintain skills. TCMem |
| 11,506(10)..57,047 | | *Denison:* Teachers' cost of cross-country trip. TCMem |

**Expenses of Professional Persons (¶ 11,511 et seq.)**

| 11,515......57,040 | *Bodley:* Qualified for new profession. TC |

---

Step 4.   Using P–H Tax Service.

Research must always be made current by checking cross-reference Volume Table. This leads to cases and rulings handed down since those printed in the main compilation volume.

---

| 11,562(5)...54,814 | Wages paid to minor child deductible if bona fide; I.T. 3767 superseded. RevRul |
|---|---|
| 11,563(20)..72-425 | *Hatt*, aff.: No other grounds. CA |
| 11,589(30)..72-534 | *Sparks Nugget, Inc.*, aff.: Excessive arm's length transaction. CA |
| 11,617(5)...57,434 | *Skyland Olds, Inc.:* Compensation reasonable. TCMem |
| 11,617(10)..57,681 | *Cozart Packing Co.:* Part-time V.P. helped business. TCMem |
| 72-354 | *Auburn & Assoc., Inc.:* Officers responsible for corporate success. DC, app not auth |
| 11,617(20)..57,454 | *Dielectric Materials Co.:* No proof of correlation. TC |
| 11,617(30)..72-311 | *East Tenn. Motor Co.*, aff.: Excessive compensation. CA |
| 72-403 | *Dietrich Mfg., Inc.:* Reasonable salary; not distribution of earnings. DC |
| 11,617(35)..54,517 | *Salem Packing Co.* (A) |
| 57,468 | *Drew:* Comp. to director for signing checks. TCMem |
| 11,620(5)...57,634 | *Andrews Distributing Co.:* Vice presidents' services as hostesses. TCMem |
| 11,620(10)..57,430 | *Office Communications Co.:* President performed clerical and secretarial duties. TCMem |
| 11,622(5)...56,628 | *Bayou Verret Land Co., Inc.*, aff.: On other grounds. CA |
| 72-322 | *Lakewood Mfg. Co.*, aff.: Insufficient proof of reasonableness. CA |
| 11,622(10)..57,454 | *Dielectric Materials Co.:* No proof of correlation. TC |
| 11,627......57,490 | *Royal Arrow Co., Inc.:* Consulting contract in package deal was severable. TCMem |
| 11,627(10)..54,941-A | *Amer. Svgs. Bk.* (A) |
| 11,628(5)...55,077 | Polak's Frutal Works, Inc. (NA) |
| 11,630(10)..72-534 | *Sparks Nugget, Inc.*, aff.: Affirmed on other grounds. CA |
| 11,637(10)..72-425 | *Hatt*, aff.: Pres. inexperienced; prior one not indicative. CA |
| 11,642(10)..57,002 | *Hudlow:* Pres. salary suddenly doubles. TCMem |
| 11,652(15)..55,328 | *Nordt, John C., Co., Inc.* (A) |
| 11,663......57,095 | *Austin State Bk.:* Board chairman's compensation unreasonable. TCMem |
| 11,693......72-534 | *Sparks Nugget, Inc.*, aff.: Affirmed on other grounds. CA |
| 11,695(5)...72-5048 | *Lehman-Mahorney, Inc.:* Bonus as net earnings percentage O.K. DC |
| 11,695(10)..57,002 | *Hudlow:* Profit-related bonus to president. TCMem |
| 11,703(5)...72-5076 | *Multnomah Plywood Corp.:* Employees with stock were paid more. DC, no auth app |
| 11,743(5)... | *Nor-Cal Adjusters*, pending CA 9 (T) |
| 11,760......57,581 | *Grant, W. T., Co.:* Wasn't issued stock. TC |

[Illustration 71]

CCH LABOR LAW REPORTER

INSTRUCTIONS ON THE USE OF THE TOPICAL INDEX

(Labor Relations, Vol. I)

---

# Topical Index

## HOW TO USE THE INDEX

*What is indexed:* Use the Topical Index where the approach to the "Labor Relations" volumes is by subject. The index is comprised of references to the compilations of law, regulations, decisions and rulings in "Labor Relations" Volumes 1, 2 and 3. New matters are indexed in the "Topical Index to New Developments," page 12,801, "Labor Relations" Volume 3.

*How it is indexed:* References are to paragraph (¶) numbers ¶ 1-2499 in Volume 1, ¶ 2500-4699 in Volume 2, and ¶ 4700-7999 in Volume 3. Each index reference leads to a paragraph covering a specific provision of law, regulations, rulings or decisions or to the "CCH Explanations" directly relating thereto. Related matters appear in neighboring paragraphs and annotations, and should also be examined.

*Arrangement:* The arrangement of this index is strictly alphabetical. Hyphenated words are treated as two words; in headings of more than one word, the first word of the heading governs the alphabetical order.

## RELATED INDEXES

The *Cumulative Index to New Developments,* beginning on page 13,001,

---

**Using CCH Labor Law Reporter.**

**Problem:**

**Can a Union insist upon an employer exerting pressure on employees to sign checkoff authorizations by telling them it is necessary to do so if they wish to continue in employment?**

**Step 1.   Consult Topical Indexes.**

**Nearly every loose leaf service, irrespective of Publisher will have pages similar to this explaining how to use the Service.   As even services from the same publisher differ in their use, these preliminary pages should always be examined with care before using a loose leaf service.**

## [Illustration 71–a]
## AN EXCERPT FROM THE TOPICAL INDEX IN THE CCH LABOR LAW REPORTER
### (Labor Relations, Vol. 1)

Following our problem through the Reporter, we look in the Index under "Check-off." We are referred to ¶ 4135.89.

```
                                            Paragraph
Charitable organizations
. NLRB jurisdiction ...................1610.505
Chauffeurs
. bargaining units ......................2627.23
Check-off ....................1415; 3560;  4600
. agency shop ...........................4600
. authorization
.. coercion of employer discrimination....
  ...................................4135.89
.. initiation fees varied ...............4140.60
. Bankruptcy Act
.. dues held by bankrupt employer....4600.71
. Copeland (Anti-Kickback) Act
.. government-financed projects........4600.74
. FLSA
.. payment to employees...............4600.72
. government-owned corporation.......4600.70
. LMRA .....................4600; 4600.05-24
.. agency shop ........................4600.12
```

Referring to editorial comment, ¶ 4135 (Illustration 72 below) and then to the reference ¶ 4135.89 (Illustration 73), we find a case in point.

[Illustration 72]

## EDITORIAL COMMENT IN CCH LABOR LAW REPORTER

### (Labor Relations, Vol. 2)

**9252**

### COERCION OF DISCRIMINATION
### [¶ 4135]

**General.**—The right of employees to engage in, or to refrain from engaging in, union activity is protected against union conduct which is calculated to bring about the kind of discriminatory treatment by employers which the NLRA makes unlawful. Unions are prohibited from causing or attempting to cause employers to discriminate against employees so as to encourage or discourage membership in a union (Section 8(b)(2)). Non-certified unions also are restricted with respect to picketing for organizational or recognition purposes (Section 8(b)(7), added by 1959 amendments, effective November 13, 1959, and discussed at ¶ 5150). Since the union under the law has no control over what workers the employer may hire, the union conduct is directed at the employer in an effort to coerce him into the union's objectives. Employers are free to hire any workers they choose regardless of whether or not they meet a union's membership requirements or other qualifications. However, an employer may, subject to certain qualifications, agree to hire through a union's offices if he so desires.

A union is guilty of causing or attempting to cause employer discrimination when it seeks some disparity of treatment among employees or applicants for employment based on union membership or activity or the lack of it. This may take the form of preference for union members or adverse treatment of nonunion employees or union members who do not cooperate with their union. A strike to force an employer to shut down a plant and transfer both workers and work to a union-represented plant was for the illegal purpose of compelling nonunion workers at the closed plant to join the union (.0672).

**Union-security contracts.**—An exception exists in the law in favor of certain types of union-security contracts—union shop and maintenance-of-membership agreements. Even under these types of agreements, union con-

> **Step 2. Read Editorial Comment.**
>
> At the beginning of the Paragraph Number referred to by the Index, there is Editorial Comment on the topic assigned to this paragraph number.

ing union membership as a condition of employment and other discriminatory practices by unions under such types of agreements are banned. If the agreement is invalid, even discharges for non-payment of dues are unlawful. See ¶ 4520.

In two separate decisions handed down at the same time, the U. S. Supreme Court has made significant determinations concerning union coercion of discrimination. In the first case, the court ruled that a provision in a union contract requiring foremen to be union members and vesting them with control over the hiring of other employees was not violative of the NLRA on its face. The high court reasoned that the contract clause was not illegal without evidence showing that union members were actually favored under its operation (.0411). However, in the court's second decision which involved

¶ 4135                                    © 1961, Commerce Clearing House, Inc.

## [Illustration 73]

## CASE-DIGESTS IN CCH LABOR LAW REPORTER

### (Labor Relations, Vol. 2)

**9286**                                    **Discrimination**

.8701 Continued existence of such contract provision is unlawful, even though employer and union have been ordered by NLRB to cease giving effect to it.

*Bell Aircraft Corp.*, (1953) 105 NLRB 755.

.8702 Contract precluding promotion of employees against whom union charges were pending was unlawful.

.88 Demotions.—In absence of union-security agreement, it was unlawful for union to demand, and for employer to grant, transfer of employee to lower-paid job because of his lack of membership in union.

*NLRB v. Peerless Quarries, Inc.*, (CA-10; 1951) 21 LABOR CASES ¶ 66,718, 193 F. (2d) 419.

.881 Compare.—Union was not guilty of

---

Step 3.  Check digests for cases in point.  Then read full text of decision.

The number to the right of the decimal point (Para. 9286.-89) refers to digests of cases and other relevant materials.

---

grant it instead to union's candidates.

*Brodsky & Son*, (1955) 114 NLRB 819.

.8741 Employee was unlawfully denied promotion as result of union pressure because he had not been union member for at least three years and not because of inexperience.

*NLRB v. Operating Engineers, Local 450*, (CA-5; 1960) 40 LC ¶ 66,716; cert. den., May 1, 1961.

.875 Causing employer to deny promotion to employee suspended from union for not participating in work stoppage, by failing to include his name on list referred to fill vacancy, as provided in union contract, is unlawful.

*Administrative Decision of NLRB General Counsel*, (1954) Case No. 1071.

.876 Employer and union did not discriminate against employee of long standing by basing promotions on departmental seniority rather than plant seniority.

*Administrative Decision of NLRB General Counsel*, (1957) Case No. F-99.

.877 Loss of promotion was not illegal where another employee was entitled to job on basis of seniority.

*Administrative Decision of NLRB General Counsel*, (1959) Case No. F-883.

*Administrative Decision of NLRB General Counsel*, (1958) Case No. F-317.

.883 Causing employer to demote employee who returned to work before end of strike and who received promotion after end of strike is unlawful.

*Bell Aircraft Corp.*, (1953) 105 NLRB 755.

.89 Checkoff Authorizations.—Causing employer to exert pressure on employees to sign checkoff authorizations by telling them it is necessary to do so if they wish to continue in employment is unlawful.

*Bayly Mfg. Co.*, (1953) 103 NLRB 1337.

.891 Union illegally caused employer to discharge employee because he refused to sign new check-off authorization for increased dues.

*American Screw Co.*, (1958) 122 NLRB 485.

.90 Right to Abandon Strike.—Union and employer jointly responsible for unlawfully forcing employees off their jobs because they had worked during strike, and for refusing to consider laid-off strike replacements for recall.

*Administrative Decision of NLRB General Counsel*, (1958) Case No. F-283.

[Illustration 74]

## AN EXCERPT FROM THE CUMULATIVE INDEX TO NEW DEVELOPMENTS IN THE CCH LABOR LAW REPORTER

(Labor Relations, Vol. 4)

---

Step 4.  Bring research up to date.

After reading the digests in the previous Illustration and noting citations to where the full text may be located, the Cumulative Index to New Materials must be checked to locate new cases handed down subsequent to those digested in the Main Volume.

---

Number 38—A91       **Cumulative Index to New Developments**       **13,409**
9–22–66

| From Compilation Paragraph (¶) No. | | To New Matter Paragraph (¶) No. |
|---|---|---|
| **4135** | .3009 Causing nonunion employee's discharge unlawful (NLRB) ........ | 20,516 |
| | .301 Charge that union coerced discharge unsupported (NLRB) .......... | 20,673 |
| | .301 Operation of union hiring hall not discriminatory (NLRB) ........ | 20,516 |
| | .301 Union's refusal to grant work clearance was not discriminatory (NLRB) ............................................................ | 20,085 |
| | .302 *Skouras Theaters Corp.* (NLRB)—Enf'd on other issue (CA–3) ........ | 11,279 |
| | .3027 Employee living in area lawfully given preference in hiring (NLRB) .. | 20,002 |
| | .303 *Plumbers, Local 2* (NLRB).—Enf'd (CA–2) .......................... | 11,234 |
| | .3009 *Operating Engineers, Local 320* (NLRB).—Enf'd (CA–5) ............. | 11,098 |
| | .3009 Union's refusal to issue work permit to job seeker unlawful (NLRB) .. | 20,396 |
| | .306 Discharge of worker resulting from denial of work permit illegal (NLRB) ............................................................. | 20,250 |
| | .3246 Refusal to hire non-union members unlawful (NLRB) ............... | 20,172 |
| | .365 Discrimination in making assignments among "casual" workers (NLRB) ............................................................. | 20,024 |
| | .874 Union caused changes in promotion list to encourage membership (NLRB) ............................................................. | 20,583 |
| | Discharge forced by employer's failure to comply with contract lawful (NLRB) ............................................................. | 20,584 |
| | Local unions not engaged in illegal conspiracy (NLRB) ................. | 20,352 |
| **4145** | .22 Reimbursement of unlawfully collected dues and fees ordered (NLRB) | 20,252 |
| | .38 NLRB's order remedying union's coercion of discrimination proper (CA–9) ............................................................. | 11,365 |
| | .83 *Plumbers, Local 2* (NLRB).—Enf'd (CA–2) ......................... | 11,234 |
| **4160** | .563 *Cunningham v. Erie R. R. Co.* (DC NY).—Aff'd (CA–2) ............. | 11,147 |
| | .9101 *Cunningham v. Erie R. R. Co.* (DC NY).—Aff'd (CA–2) ............. | 11,147 |

1——➤ (arrow pointing to "Local unions not engaged in illegal conspiracy" line)

[Illustration 75]

## HOW TO USE CASE TABLE
## CCH LABOR LAW REPORTER

(Labor Relations, Vol. 1)

# Case Table

601

**Description of Case Table.**—The LABOR LAW REPORTER consists of four units: (1) "Labor Relations," (2) "Wages—Hours," (3) "State Laws," and (4) "Union Contracts—Arbitration." Each unit, complete in itself, has its own Case Table, which lists alphabetically all court decisions and administrative rulings included in that unit. Complete information on each case is given, including references to paragraph numbers in the REPORTER at which the cases appear.

The "Labor Relations" Case Table lists all court and administrative decisions in the federal labor relations unit. Under the title of each case are shown in chronological order all rulings in the case, beginning at the trial level. Subsequent proceedings, including any appellate action, in the same case is preceded by a dash (—). See example to the right below.

Court decisions are cited to the publishers' companion series —the federal and state labor case reporter, LABOR CASES—and to other reporters. Citations to the official volumes of the National Labor Relations Board are given for NLRB decisions. Also included for NLRB decisions handed down beginning with the calendar year 1960 are citations to the publishers' series "CCH NLRB Decisions."

Paragraph references show where each case appears in the federal labor relations unit along with other authorities on the same point.

Court cases in which unions are plaintiffs and National Labor Relations Board cases in which unions are charged with unfair labor practices are grouped under the popular name of the union, as shown in the listing on page 605. Local

ABRASIVE SALVAGE CO.
(1960) 127 NLRB 381, 1960 CCH NLRB
¶ 8784

—enf in part and denied in part (CA-7
1961) 41 LC ¶ 16,712, 285 F2d 552 . . . . . . . .
. . . . . . . . . . . . . ¶ 3044.447; 3046.125; 3740.874;
3770.30; 4095.2513
ALMA MILLS: TOBIN v.
(DC SC 1950) 18 LC ¶ 65,972, 92 FSupp
728 . . . . . . . . . . . . . . . . . . . . . . . . (Wage Hour)
—aff'd as mod (CA-4 1951) 20 LC ¶ 66,630,
192 F2d 133 . . . . . . . . . . . . . . . . . (Wage Hour)
—cert denied (1952) 343 US 933
AFL v. AMERICAN SASH & DOOR CO.
(Ariz 1947) Super Ct, Maricopa Co, 13 LC
¶ 63,991
—(1947) Super Ct, Maricopa Co, 13 LC
¶ 63,995
—aff'd (1948) 14 LC ¶ 64,293, 67 Ariz 20,
189 P2d 912
—aff'd (1949) 16 LC ¶ 64,898, 335 US
538 . . . . . . . . . . . . . . . . . . . . . . . . . (State Law)
ARMSTRONG-NORWALK RUBBER CORP.
v. RUBBER WORKERS, LOCAL 283
(DC Conn 1958) 36 LC ¶ 65,001, 167 FSupp
817
—app dism'd (CA-2 1959) 37 LC ¶ 65,632,
269 F2d 618. . . . . . . . . . . . . . . . . (Contracts)

> Most loose leaf services will also have a Table of Cases. Thus, the Case Method can be used. In many instances, the Table of Cases also serves as a citator.

Contracts—Arbitration" (page 80,301)—through which may be located the paragraph numbers where the cases appear in those units.

Examples of other units of the Reporter are shown in Illustrations 108–111, below.

[Illustration 76]

## EXCERPTS FROM THE FINDING LISTS IN CCH LABOR LAW REPORTER

**461**

### Federal Law—Labor Relations

# Finding Lists

**References are to paragraph (¶) numbers**

¶ 1 to 2499 in Volume 1, Federal Labor Relations

¶ 2500 to 4699 in Volume 2, Federal Labor Relations

¶ 4700 to 8499 in Volume 3, Federal Labor Relations

## Federal Laws

### [¶ 127]

| UNITED STATES CODE | | | Title | Sec. | Par. | | Title | Sec. | Par. |
|---|---|---|---|---|---|---|---|---|---|
| Title | Sec. | Par. | 28 | 381 | 854 | | 29 | 167 | 681 |
| | | | 28 | 382 | 855 | | 29 | 168 | 682 |
| 2 | 251 | 759 | 28 | 383 | 856 | | 29 | 171 | 730 |
| 5 | 1001 | 1052 | 28 | 386 | 858 | | 29 | 172 | 731 |
| 5 | 1002 | 1053 | 28 | 387 | 859 | | 29 | 173 | 732 |
| 5 | 1003 | 1054 | 28 | 388 | 860 | | 29 | 174 | 733 |
| 5 | 1004 | 1055 | 28 | 389 | 861 | | 29 | 175 | 734 |
| 5 | 1005 | 1056 | 28 | 390 | 862 | | 29 | 176 | 735 |
| 5 | 1006 | 1057 | 28 | 1331 | 1046 | | 29 | 177 | 736 |
| 5 | 1007 | 1058 | 28 | 1332 | 1047 | | 29 | 178 | 737 |
| 5 | 1008 | 1059 | 28 | 2112 | 660 | | 29 | 179 | 738 |
| 5 | 1009 | 1060 | 29 | 52 | 857 | | 29 | 180 | 739 |
| 5 | 1010 | 1061 | 29 | 101 | 801 | | 29 | 181 | 740 |
| 5 | 1011 | 1062 | | | | | | | |

\* \* \* \* \*

Notes to Illustration 108:

1. Reference from United States Code citation to:
2. Paragraph number in the Reporter.

Most loose leaf services have Tables whereby the citation to a Code provision or administrative Regulation can be looked up and references found where they are discussed within the Service.

## SECTION E.   STATE ADMINISTRATIVE REGULATIONS AND DECISIONS

The regulations and decisions of state agencies are variously published by the states, but notwithstanding such publications, they often are not readily accessible.   In about 15 states, the state administrative rules are officially codified and kept up-to-date by supplements or releases.   The decisions of some state agencies, such as public utilities, workmen's compensation and unemployment insurance commissions, are often published.   Some state administrative rulings are privately published by loose-leaf reporters or services.

The following should be examined in connection with state administrative law.

### 1.   State Administrative Regulations

If a state has an administrative code, consult it for the rules of an administrative body.   In the absence of a code, inquiry should be directed to the pertinent agency for its regulations.   A few state administrative law topics, such as public utilities and taxation, are covered by loose-leaf services and reporters.   These services should be freely consulted.

### 2.   State Administrative Decisions

The availability of a state agency's decisions may also be determined by inquiry.   Some are *officially published*, e. g., *Wisconsin. Employment Relations Board.   Decisions.*   A few areas are treated by *loose-leaf reporters*, e. g., *C.C.H.   Unemployment Insurance Reports (Michigan).*

### 3.   Judicial Review of State Administrative Rules and Decisions

Consult the appropriate *state digest* and the *local encyclopedia* for cases which review state administrative rules and decisions.   If there is a *local treatise* on the subject, examine it for a survey of the law.   Refer to the *American Law Reports* for possible annotations. *Periodical literature* may be helpful; therefore, refer to the *Index to Legal Periodicals.*

### 4.   General State Administrative Law

Should the problem relate to matters of general administrative applicability, the secondary sources noted above should be consulted; however, for emphasis, they may bear repetition here.

Examine the following materials:

a.   State digest.

b.   Local encyclopedia.

   c.   Local treatise on administrative law.

   d.   Index to Legal Periodicals.

   e.   American Law Reports.

If the state legislature has enacted an *Administrative Procedure Act* and the problem is within the purview of that Act, the *state code* should be examined.

---

## SECTION F.  FUNCTIONAL RESEARCH

The solutions to administrative law problems, which are common to a number of agencies, may be sought through the standard federal and state secondary aids, e. g., digests of court reports, annotated reports, periodical literature, treatises, etc.  To illustrate, the *American Digest System* includes digests of federal and state judicial decisions (agency decisions are not covered) on administrative law.  With the *Fifth Decennial*, these cases have been classified under the title "Administrative Law and Procedure."  The other secondary aids can be used through the standard procedures.  *American Jurisprudence 2d* carries a discussion of the topic in volumes 1 and 2 under the title "Administrative Law."  Volume 73 of *Corpus Juris Secundum* treats these general principles under the heading "Public Administrative Bodies and Procedure."

*Pike and Fischer, Administrative Law Service* is a horizontal analysis of the general principles of administrative procedure common to the various agencies.  It does not cover the substantive rules of individual agencies which are specially applicable.

It contains the statutory text of the *Federal Administrative Procedure Act*, the *Administrative Conference Act*, and the *Administrative Practices Act*, and the rules of the various agencies.

It also reports the full text of court decisions and agencies arising out of the Acts enumerated *supra*.

---

## SECTION G.  FEDERAL ADMINISTRATIVE REGULATIONS RESEARCH PROCEDURE

### 1.  Loose-Leaf Reporters or Services

If the solution to a federal administrative problem can be found in a loose-leaf reporter or service, consult it in preference to the *Code of Federal Regulations* and *Federal Register*, for all related material is conveniently arranged between the covers of a single service.

The *Index, Topic, Case* and *Definition Methods* can be used with the various reporters. Under the *Index Method,* first consult the *general index* (topical or master). Having obtained references to pertinent paragraphs from the index, refer to those sections in the body of the service. Then consult the *Cumulative Numerical Index* or the *Cross Reference Table* for references under the appropriate paragraph number to new material on the subject contained in a current, supplemental section of the service. Also, check the *current index* for additional information.

When the researcher is familiar with the subject matter and the service, he may use the *Topic Method* of research. Under this procedure, reference to the indexes is omitted. Consult the *table of contents* of the appropriate unit of the service which lists the subject matter and paragraph numbers. Then follow the same procedure as outlined above under the *Index Method.*

Various tables, analytical and citator, are also included in the services. Consult each publication to determine the nature and scope of these aids.

The *Case Method* is the third research technique available. When a case in point is known, consult the *table of cases* of the appropriate service. This table will note the pertinent paragraphs where the case is treated in the service. After consulting these references, follow the procedure discussed above under the *Index Method.*

Frequently, the *definition of a word* is germane to the issue. It may be defined in a case or in a regulation. Consult the *general index* under the appropriate word. Then use the material as suggested above. Some loose-leaf services also separately list definitions of technical words used in the services.

## 2. The Code of Federal Regulations and the Federal Register

If the federal regulatory problem is not covered by an available loose-leaf service, consult the *Code of Federal Regulations* and the *Federal Register.* First, refer to the General Index to C.F.R. Some main entries are limited in scope and sometimes it is necessary to check the analyses in the *Code* volumes for the contents to the regulations. The Codification Guide of the appropriate cumulative issues of the later daily *Federal Registers* will identify regulatory changes subsequent to the pocket supplement.

The text of provisions in force at a specific time can be traced by using the numerical lists of sections affected (codification guides). Consult the *List of Sections Affected, 1949–1963,* for the period prior to 1964. This will indicate the changes since the 1949 addition. Refer to the "List of Sections Affected" in the appropriate revised volumes or pocket supplements for subsequent changes.

The *Topic Method* may also be used by referring to the individual volumes of the *Code*, omitting the use of the indexes. Examine the *table of contents* or analysis to the appropriate title, chapter and part. Then follow the procedure outlined in the preceding paragraph.

The words defined in the regulations are not indexed in the *Code* or *Register*. For the *definitions of words* included in the regulations, approach the problem through its subject, using the *Index* or *Topic Method*.

The *Code of Federal Regulations* and the *Federal Register* do not contain decisional law; hence, the *Case Method* is inapplicable here.

**3.  To Ascertain whether Administrative Regulations have been issued under a Federal Act**

Refer to the *Parallel tables in Title 2 of the Code of Federal Regulations* to determine whether administrative rules have been issued under the authority of a specific federal act. After consulting the applicable rule, examine the Codification Guides for any late rulings.

--------

## SECTION H.   FEDERAL ADMINISTRATIVE DECISIONS RESEARCH PROCEDURE

**1.  Agency Decisions**

The quasi-judicial decisions of a federal administrative agency, as distinguished from its regulations, are available through two sources: (1) official publications by the Government Printing Office and (2) unofficial publications by commercial publishers.

The official publications are available in most research law libraries and some public and university libraries. Indexes and digests to the decisions are generally available but they are not always up-to-date. For recent decisions, it may be necessary to check the index to each individual volume of decisions published after the latest cumulative index. Some federal agencies have advance sheets, e. g., *Federal Communications Commission Reports*.

Normally, these problems are approached by subject, except when the name of a case in point is known. Refer to the *index or digest* under the specific subject for pertinent administrative decisions. However, if this material is also included in a loose-leaf service, the research might be expedited by the use of the service.

Administrative decisions are unofficially available not only in loose-leaf services but also in serial publications on specific subjects, e. g., *U. S. Patents Quarterly*.

Judicial cases which review federal administrative decisions are found through the following publications:

(a) Serial publications on specific subjects, e. g., Trade-Mark Reporter.

(b) Modern Federal Practice Digest and Federal Digest.

(c) U. S. Supreme Court digests.

(d) American Digest System, in the absence of the preceding digests.

(e) Shepard's U. S. Citations, Shepard's Federal Reporter Citations and Shepard's U. S. Administrative Citations.

## 2. General Federal Administrative Law: Research Procedure

If the problem involves federal administrative procedure which cuts across agency lines, the following secondary aids may be helpful:

a. Consult *Pike and Fischer, Administrative Law Service*; the general encyclopedias; and administrative law treatises for discussions on the topic.

b. Check the *Index to Legal Periodicals* for law journal articles on the subject.

c. Consult the *American Law Reports*.

d. Refer to the *Modern Federal Practice Digest* and the *Federal Digest*.

e. Examine the U. S. Supreme Court digests.

f. Consult the *American Digest System*, in the absence of the preceding digests.

g. Shepardize the significant cases.

---

## SECTION I. PRESIDENTIAL PROCLAMATIONS: RESEARCH PROCEDURE

### 1. Proclamations

### a. Date or Number is Known

If the date or number of a presidential proclamation is known, its text may be located in the sources listed in Section A31, above.

### b. Subject Method

To find the text of a presidential proclamation on a specific subject, consult the *General Index to the U. S. Code and its supplements.* Look under the heading "Proclamations." Since the *U. S. Code* contains only a selected number of the proclamations, the one desired may not be found there. In that case, refer to the *indexes to the Cumulative Supplement, Compilations and Revisions after 1963 to Title 3 of the Code of Federal Regulations*. These units contain the proclamations issued since 1938. Examine the *indexes to the Statutes at Large* for proclamations prior to June, 1938. For the current proclamations, which are not published in the latest supplement to the *Code*, consult the *Federal Register* or the *U. S. Code Congressional and Administrative News*, preferably the latter.

## 2. Executive Orders: Research Procedure

### (a) Date or Number is Known

If the date or number of the executive order is known, consult the following:

1. *For earlier orders*, refer to the *Historical Record Survey's Presidential Executive Orders, vol. 1, List.*

2. *Title 3 of the Code of Federal Regulations* and the *U. S. Code Congressional and Administrative News* or the *Federal Register*.

### (b) Subject Method

The text of executive orders may be located by subject in the publications listed in Section A5, above. Volume 2 of the *Historical Records Survey* is a subject index to Executive Orders 1–8030, from 1862 through 1938. Also see Section I2, above.

### (c) Judicial Decisions Interpreting Executive Orders

For cases construing executive orders, consult the following publications:

(1) *U. S. Supreme Court Reports Digest* (Lawyers Co-op. Pub. Co.), vol. 14, pp. 412–415 and pocket supplement.

(2) *Shepard's United States Citations*. If the order appears in the *U. S. Code*, it is then listed in this citator under the appropriate title and section of the *U. S. Code*.

(3) *Shepard's State Citations*. Check the appropriate state citator under the *U. S. Code* unit.

(4) Consult the *Table of Statutes*, etc., in these publications: the *U. S. Supreme Court Reports* (L.Ed.) advance sheets; the *National Reporter System*, bound volumes and advance sheets; the *West state digests*, pamphlets supplements; some *Regional digests*, pamphlet supplements; and some *West state and Regional digests*, bound volumes.

(5) U. S. Supreme Court digests.

(6) *Modern Federal Practice Digest* and the *Federal Digest*.

## SECTION J. METHODS OF CITATION

### 1. Administrative Rules

The administrative rules and orders which appear in the *Federal Register* and *Code of Federal Regulations* are cited:

> Atomic Energy Comm.Rules of Practice § 2.701, 21 Fed.Reg. 805 (1956).

> Exec.Order No. 10655, 21 Fed.Reg. 665 (1956).

> 21 Fed.Reg. 609 (1956).

> 49 C.F.R. § 18.535 (1963).

> 49 C.F.R. § 18.535 (1963) (matured interest, dividends, and rents unpaid of express companies: uniform system of accounts established by ICC).

> 49 C.F.R. § 6.1 (Supp.1966).

Loose-leaf reporters or services are cited:

> 2 CCH Trade Reg.Rep. ¶ 6021.31.
> 4 P–H 1956 Fed.Tax Serv. ¶ 76,101.

### 2. Administrative and Court Decisions

Example citations of administrative decisions of several federal agencies are:

a. Federal Trade Commission

Eastman Kodak Co., 39 F.T.C. 154 (1944).

b. National Labor Relations Board

Standard Dry Wall Products, Inc., 91 N.L.R.B. 544 (1950).

c. Securities and Exchange Commission

Electric Bond and Share Co., 11 S.E.C. 1146 (1942).

Cases included in loose-leaf reporters or services are cited:

a. Sinkfield v. Flemming, CCH Unemp.Ins.Rep. ¶ 12,427.50 (E.D.Mich.1960).

b. Union Nat'l Bk. of Troy v. United States, 8 AFTR 2d 5133 (N.D.N.Y.1961).

Current cases first appear in the loose-leaf volumes and are later cumulated in bound or separate volumes, having distinctive titles, with the same page or paragraph numbers. In citing cases in these volumes, the publisher's name is omitted, except where it is necessary to avoid confusion between publications.

a. Coule Lines, Inc. v. United States, 10 Fed.Carr.Cas. ¶ 80,895, (E.D.La.1953).

    b.    Republic Steel Corp. v. Local 4382, United Steelworkers of Am., CIO, 7 ALAA ¶ 69,863 (1955).

---

## SECTION K.   SUMMARY

### 1.   Federal Register

    a.    Types of federal documents published in it.

    (1)   Pursuant to the Federal Register Act, see Section A1.

    (2)   Pursuant to the Federal Administrative Procedure Act, see Section A1.

    b.    Coverage is broader in scope than the *Code of Federal Regulations.*

    (1)   Presidential documents.

    (2)   Rules and regulations.

    (3)   Proposed rule making.

    (4)   Notices.

    c.    Codification Guides, listing current changes in the *Code of Federal Regulations.*

    (1)   Appear daily and are cumulated daily within the month.

    (2)   Cumulated monthly.

    d.    Classified under the 50 Titles of C.F.R.

    e.    Began publication in 1936.

    f.    Published daily (usually five days per week).

### 2.   Code of Federal Regulations

    a.    The *Federal Register* and the *Code of Federal Regulations* are *prima facie* evidence of the original regulations and are required by federal statute to be judicially noticed.

    b.    Federal Register regulations, if not revoked or if not of short duration, are subsequently published in the C.F.R. (C.F.R. regulations must be general, permanent and in force.)

    c.    C.F.R. and the daily *Register* are arranged under 50 functional titles, alphabetically grouped except for the first three titles. The titles are subdivided into chapters, subchapters, parts and sections. It is cited by section numbers which embodies the numerical designations of the superior divisions.

    d.    A single title is generally contained in a separate C.F.R. volume.

    e.    C.F.R. volumes are issued annually.

f. Title 2 of C.F.R. consists of Parallel Tables of Statutory Authorities and Rules, with references from the *U. S. Code*, which are cited as rule-making authority for administrative regulations, to the rules codified in C.F.R. Listed under U.S.C. reference.

### 3. U. S. Government Organization Manual

a. Annual handbook.

b. Describes administrative organizations required to be published in the daily *Register*.

c. Information on Congress, the federal judiciary and important agency personnel.

d. Subject index.

### 4. Official Compilations of Rules by Federal Administrative Agencies

a. A few agencies separately publish their regulations.

### 5. Presidential Proclamations

a. Text (see Section A3, above).

### 6. Executive Orders

a. Text (see Section A3b, above).

b. Indexes to executive orders (see Section A3b, above).

### 7. Weekly Compilation of Presidential Documents

a. Contains statements, messages and other Presidential materials.

### 8. Federal Administrative Decisions

a. Official and unofficial publications (see Section A5, above).

### 9. State Administrative Regulations and Decisions

a. A few states have codified their administrative rules.

b. Some states publish the decisions of administrative agencies.

### 10. Functional Research on Problems Common to a Number of Agencies

a. Use standard sources, e. g., digests, annotated reports, encyclopedias, treatises, periodical literature, etc.

b. *Pike and Fischer Administrative Law Service*.

### 11. Loose-Leaf Reporters or Services

a. Separate, perforated leaves in special binders, simplifying the insertion or substitution of new leaves.

    b.   Frequent current reports keep the contents up-to-date.

    c.   Each service relates to a specific subject.

    d.   Contents

        (1)  Text of statutes on the topic, with significant legislative history.

        (2)  Compilation of the rules and administrative and court decisions, with editorial discussion.

        (3)  Subject index.

        (4)  Table of cases.

        (5)  Current reports which include supplemental, current materials and indexes.

        (6)  Reporter letter, published with each release explaining the new developments on the topic with filing instructions.

    e.   Editorial plans

        (1)  Statutory, with contents of service determined by the sectional breakdown of the statute under analysis.

        (2)  Topical, analyzing several statutes or common law interpretations by subject.

        (3)  State treatment by units or services.

# Chapter 14

## SHEPARD'S CITATIONS

### SECTION A.  CASE CITATORS

The previous chapters were directed toward enabling one to locate court decisions relevant to a particular point of law.  In most instances, this step is preliminary toward a more concrete goal—a trial or appellate brief has to be written, or an opinion letter composed, or an article authored.  Locating cases is undertaken to find rules of law as determined from the reading of the cases, which can then be cited in another document as authority.  But before this can be done with any degree of confidence, one further step must be taken.  This is to determine that any given case that is to be relied on as authority is indeed still good authority.  The decision must be checked to make positive that it has not been reversed by a higher court, or overruled by a subsequent decision of the same court.[1]  This is accomplished by the use of *Shepard's Citations.*

These sets of law books provide a means by which any reported case (cited decision) may be checked to see when and how another court (the citing decision) has cited the first decision.  For example, assume that in the course of one's research one locates a case reported in 332 *Ill.App.* 17 (1947) that is exactly on point with the problem being researched.  As this is a decision from the Illinois Appellate Court, several possibilities may exist.

The case may have been appealed to the Illinois Supreme Court and that court may have either reversed or affirmed the appellate court decision.

In either instance, it then may have been appealed to the U. S. Supreme Court which may have reversed or affirmed it.  If this case was reversed by either the Illinois or the U. S. Supreme Court, it is no longer authority and must not be cited as if it were.

---

[1] The failure to properly "Shepardize" can lead to embarrassing situations.  One court commented on such an instance as follows: " * * * unfortunately, counsel for the defendant quoted extensively from * * * [the] Matter of Newins' Will, 29 Misc. 614, 213 N.Y.S.2d 255 that case was cited as the authority which required plaintiff herein to prove every possible and conceivable fact before a court of law will declare a marriage null and void.  The court was astounded to find that that case upon which so much reliance was placed by defendant's counsel was reversed by the Appellate Division * * * on the point in question and this reversal was affirmed by the Court of Appeals * * * ".  Rosenstiel v. Rosenstiel, 43 Misc.2d 462, 251 N.Y.S.2d 565, 578 (1964).

Another factor that must be ascertained is whether the Illinois Appellate Court itself overruled the decision in 332 *Ill.App.* 17 (assuming it had not been reversed).  This case was handed down in 1947.  It is entirely possible that more recently the Illinois Appellate Court had occasion to hear a case with a similar fact situation and decided that the earlier rule was no longer applicable and so overruled it and announced a new rule.  Again, if this did occur, 332 *Ill.App.* 17 can no longer be cited for authority.

This is determined by checking 332 *Ill.App.* 17 in the *Illinois Shepard's Citations*, or *Northeastern Shepard's Citations*.  As they list every case subsequently written in which the cited case (332 *Ill. App.* 17) was mentioned, it can be determined easily if the cited case has been reversed or overruled.

As *Shepard's Citations* presents all citing cases for a cited case, it is evident that its usefulness goes beyond only checking to see if a cited case has been reversed or overruled.  The value of a precedent for any given decision also depends to a large extent on the treatment subsequently given to it by courts deciding whether the cited case is in fact applicable to the case under consideration.  Whether a cited case has subsequently been followed, distinguished, limited, or questioned may be of vital importance in determining the present value of the cited case as a precedent.  Thus, *Shepard's* may be used to determine how a given case has been treated in subsequent decisions.

The court decisions are listed by volume and page in black letter (bold face) type.  Under the citation of the case in point subsequent decisions, which have cited the case, are listed by volume and page with letter-form abbreviations indicating the *judicial history* of the case in point and its *treatment* by subsequent decisions.  See Illustration 80.

The *history of the case* is indicated by abbreviations showing whether the case was affirmed, reversed, dismissed or modified on appeal.  Parallel citations of the cited case in the standard reports are also provided.  In like manner, the nature of the *treatment of the case* in point in subsequent decisions is indicated by abbreviations. The introductory pages of each *Shepard's Citations* explain the abbreviations used in the volume.  Some illustrative abbreviations of case citations are given below:

### History of Case [2]

a (affirmed)                    Same case below affirmed on appeal.

---

[2] These abbreviations and their descriptions are embodied in the pamphlet *How to Use Shepard's Citations*, published by Shepard's Citations, Inc.

| | |
|---|---|
| cc (connected case) | Different case from case cited but arising out of same subject matter or intimately connected therewith. |
| D (dismissed) | Appeal from same case below dismissed. |
| m (modified) | Same case below modified on appeal. |
| r (reversed) | Same case below reversed on appeal. |
| s (same case) | Same case as case cited. |
| S (superseded) | Substitution for former opinion. |

### Treatment of Case

| | |
|---|---|
| c (criticized) | Soundness of decision or reasoning in cited case criticized for reasons given. |
| d (distinguished) | Case at bar different either in law or fact from case cited for reasons given. |
| e (explained) | Statement of import of decision in cited case. Not merely a restatement of the facts. |
| f (followed) | Cited as controlling. |
| h (harmonized) | Apparent inconsistency explained and shown not to exist. |
| j (dissenting opinion) | Case cited in dissenting opinion. |
| L (limited) | Refusal to extend decision of cited case beyond precise issues involved. |
| o (overruled) | Ruling in cited case expressly overruled. |
| p (parallel) | Citing case substantially alike or identical with law or facts of cited case. |
| q (questioned) | Soundness of decision or reasoning in cited case questioned. |

There is a separate set of *Shepard's Citations* for every set of court reports. Consequently, there are fifty sets of *Shepard's*, one for each of the states; separate sets for each of the Regional Reporters of the *National Reporter System*, one set for both the *Federal Supplement* and the *Federal Reporter*, and one for the *U. S. Reports*.

As most court decisions are reported in two sets, one has to make a determination of which set of *Shepard's* is to be used in *Shepardizing* [3] a case. For example, a case reported in 332 *Ill.App.* 17 is also reported in 74 *N.E.2d* 45. It can be *Shepardized* in the *Illinois Shepard's Citations* or the *Northeastern Shepard's Citations*. When one should be selected over the other will be discussed *infra*.

### 1. State Shepard's Citations

These are to be used in connection with the state reports. As most reported decisions cover more than one point of law, *Shepard's*, through the use of superscript figures, keys each citing case to the headnotes of the cited case. For example, in the case of *City of Chicago v. Terminiello* (332 *Ill.App.* 17, 74 N.E.2d 45, 1947) the defendant was indicted for causing a breach of the peace by disrupting a public meeting. In the *Illinois Appellate* report, this decision has nine headnotes assigned, each on a different point of law. A citing case may cite *Terminiello* only for the point of law in its third headnote. In order to allow a researcher to find all citing cases which cited *Terminiello* only for the point in its third headnote, *Shepard's* adds the superscript "3" to the citing case. By this means, one can find in the *Illinois Shepard's Citations* all subsequent cases that cited *Terminiello* for that point of law.

The state *Shepard's* gives citing cases only from courts within the jurisdiction or cases that originated in a federal court within the state. Additionally, state *Shepard's* gives citations to any legal periodical published in the state (plus 11 national law reviews) that cite the cited cases. It also gives a citation to the reports of the state Attorney-General's opinion that cite the cited cases. State *Shepard's* also have a section or a separate volume arranged by the regional reporter citation. By this means, when only a state unit *Shepard's* is available, it may be *Shepardized* under the state citation, or the regional reporter citation. In both instances, citing cases are given only for the courts within the state.

### 2. Regional Shepard's Citations

In the example of *City of Chicago v. Terminiello*, that case could also be *Shepardized* in the *Northeastern Shepard's* under 74 *N.E.2d*

---

[3] The term "Shepardizing" is the trade-mark property of Shepard's Citations, Inc. and is used here with reference to its publications only and with its express consent.

45. In such instances, that volume has to be examined to determine which headnote or headnotes are of interest. In the *Northeastern Reporter*, there are six headnotes and each can be followed in citing cases in the same method as described *supra*.

In our example, if the *Illinois Shepard's* are used, all of the citing cases given are to the *Illinois Appellate* and *Illinois Reports* and Federal cases heard in Illinois. In the Northeastern *Shepard's*, all citations to the same citing case are to the *Northeastern Reporter*. The regional *Shepard's*, unlike the state *Shepard's*, also gives citations to any case throughout the *National Reporter System*. Thus, if a California case cited *City of Chicago v. Terminiello*, it can be found in the *Northeastern Shepard's* but not in the *Illinois Shepard's*. However, the regional *Shepard's* does not give citations to legal periodicals or Attorney-General's opinions.

The choice, then, of when to use a state or regional is dependent on the purpose of the research in hand. Illustrations 80 and 81 demonstrate the *Shepardizing* of the *Terminiello* case in both sets of reports.

### 3.    Federal Shepard's Citations

When a case with a *F.Supp., Fed. (F.2)*, or *U. S. Citation* is to be *Shepardized, Federal Shepard's Citations* are used for the first two, and *U. S. Shepard's Citations* for the last.

### 4.    Other Uses of Shepard's Citations

In addition to citing all cases that cite a given case, *Shepard's* also indicates when a case is cited in one of the following:

A.L.R. Annotations,

Legal periodicals.articles, (state citators only)

Restatement of the Law, (state citators only)

### 5.    Using Shepard's Citations to Find Parallel Citations

In Chapter 5 it was pointed out how, given a state report citation, the *National Reporter System* regional citations could be found through the use of the *National Reporter Blue Book*. *Shepard's* may also be used for this and, additionally, to find the state citation from the regional reporter citation. It always includes the parallel citation as the first citation under the page number the first time the case is listed. When a case has also been reported in *A.L.R.* that is also listed.

### 6.    Shepard's Citations as a Research Aid

Although *Shepard's Citations* are very useful research aids, they should not be stretched beyond their normal function.

The editors' use of the letter-form abbreviations to indicate the treatment of cases is intelligently conservative. The essence of a citing case may go beyond its expressed language. The inclusiveness of a case is not identified by the abbreviations unless its expression is clearly stated in the opinion. Therefore, a case which implicitly overrules a cited case will not be marked with the symbol "o" for "overruled." This can be determined only by a careful reading of the case. In other words, although these guides immeasurably facilitate a lawyer's research, there are no substitutes for reading and "squeezing the juices" from cases.

In addition, cases dealing with the same subject matter, which do not cite each other, are not covered by *Shepard's Citations*. Or contrariwise, since the *Shepard* editions are not selective, the citing cases may be so numerous as to create a formidable research problem. A further limitation is that *Shepard's Citations* perpetuate the inaccuracies created by judges who inappropriately cite cases. But these are minor defects which the general utility, comprehensiveness and accuracy of the citators effectively overbalance.

## SECTION B. ILLUSTRATIONS—SHEPARD CASE CITATIONS

## [Illustration 77]
## FIRST PAGE FROM 332 ILL.APP. 17

CHICAGO—FIRST DISTRICT—JUNE, 1947.    17

City of Chicago v. Terminiello, 332 Ill. App. 17.

## City of Chicago, Appellee, v. Arthur Terminiello, Appellant.

### Gen. No. 44,062.

1. CRIMES AND PUNISHMENT, § 7 *—*breach of peace, definition and test in determining.* Generally, offense of breach of peace is violation of public order or disturbance of public tranquillity by any act or conduct inciting to violence, or tending to provoke or excite others to break the peace, and each case must depend upon time, place and circumstances of the act or conduct.

2. MUNICIPAL CORPORATIONS, § 447 *—*breach of peace or diversion tending to breach of peace, evidence as establishing meeting as public.* Meeting to hear defendant speak in rented auditorium of building operated by women's club which was filled to capacity pursuant to cards of admission, admitting bearer and one friend and containing words "admission by card only," which accompanied mailed invitations stating that few extra cards were inclosed and requesting invitee to "make wise distribution of them," had necessary characteristics of public meeting so as to justify conviction under city ordinance for breach of peace or diversion tending to breach of peace, in view of surrounding circumstances. (NIEMEYER, P. J., dissenting.)

3. WITNESSES, § 171 *—*credibility as within province of jury.* In prosecution for breach of peace or diversion tending to breach of peace in violation of city ordinance arising out of speech delivered in meeting hall, whether witnesses heard what they claimed, and how much reliance could be placed upon their testimony, was clearly within province of jury, and it was not for Appellate Court to determine that jury should have believed witnesses for defendant and not those for prosecution, especially where there was little conflict upon material matters.

4. MUNICIPAL CORPORATIONS, § 447 *—*breach of peace or diversion

ten                              as
con                              ng
tha      **Headnotes of case from the Illinois Appel-**      ng
wo      **late Reports.**      ch
app                              os-
phe                              di-
tor                              om

getting into auditorium and to break up meeting, conviction of breach of peace or diversion tending to breach of peace under city ordinance was proper. (NIEMEYER, P. J., dissenting.)

5. CONSTITUTIONAL LAW, § 235 *—*freedom of speech, speech in auditorium surrounded by mob as protected by guarantee of.* Speech ap-

* See Callaghan's Illinois Digest, same topic and section number.

## [Illustration 78]

# FIRST PAGE FROM 74 N.E.2d 45

CITY OF CHICAGO v. TERMINIELLO Ill. **45**
Cite as 74 N.E.2d 45

**Headnotes from the Northeastern Reporter.**

332 Ill.App. 17
**CITY OF CHICAGO v. TERMINIELLO.**
Gen. No. 44062.

Appellate Court of Illinois. First District.
First Division.
June 25, 1947.

**1. Breach of the peace �københavn1**

In prosecution against speaker at meeting in private rented auditorium for making or aiding an improper noise, riot, disturbance, breach of peace or diversion tending to a breach of peace in violation of city ordinance, the meeting was a "public meeting" where auditorium was filled to its capacity of between 800 and 1000 and admission was by tickets which were liberally and indiscriminately distributed, and 200 to 300 ticket-holders were unable to get in, and admission was obtained by some persons not desired.

See Words and Phrases, Permanent Edition, for all other definitions of "Public Meeting".

**2. Breach of the peace ⊆8**

In prosecution against speaker at meeting for making or aiding in making an improper noise, riot, disturbance, breach of peace or diversion tending to breach of peace in violation of city ordinance, evidence was sufficient to show that speech was an appeal to fury and incitement to disorder and violence and created a diversion and breach of peace.

**3. Constitutional law ⊆274**

In prosecution against speaker for making or aiding in making an improper noise, riot, disturbance, breach of peace or diversion tending to breach of peace in violation of city ordinance, speech was not protected by constitutional guarantee of freedom of speech, where speaker was a public agitator who intentionally stirred up class prejudice, religious hatred and anti-Semitism. U.S.C.A.Const. Amends. 1, 14.

**4. Constitutional law ⊆274**

Under constitution, one may speak or write freely upon any controversial question concerning state policies, religion, politics, or any other subject, and such paramount right must be protected, and in cases of doubt, the doubt must be resolved in favor of the right, except that one is not permitted to use the constitutional privilege as instrument for abuse and incitement to violence. U.S.C.A.Const. Amends. 1, 14.

**5. Breach of the peace ⊆2**

In prosecution against speaker at meeting in private rented auditorium for making or aiding in making improper noise, riot, disturbance, breach of peace or diversion tending to breach of peace in violation of city ordinance, mob demonstration outside auditorium did not warrant speaker's appeal to fury and incitement to disorder and violence.

**6. Breach of the peace ⊆7**

In prosecution against speaker at meeting for making or aiding in making an improper noise, riot, disturbance, breach of peace or diversion tending to breach of peace in violation of city ordinance, refusal to admit pamphlets, booklets, reports, leaflets and publications of one type or another sponsored by various organizations and individuals was not error, where such items were irrelevant and could not have been used to impeach plaintiff's witnesses

[Illustration 79]

### TITLE PAGE: ILLINOIS SHEPARD'S CITATIONS

| Vol. 67 | DECEMBER, 1972 | No. 4 |
|---|---|---|

# SHEPARD'S
# ILLINOIS CITATIONS

## A COMPILATION OF CITATIONS

TO

ILLINOIS CASES REPORTED IN THE VARIOUS SERIES OF ILLINOIS
REPORTS AND IN THE NORTHEASTERN REPORTER, TO THE UNITED
STATES CONSTITUTION AND STATUTES, ILLINOIS CONSTITUTIONS,
CODES, REVISED STATUTES, LAWS, ORDINANCES, COURT
RULES AND ILLINOIS PATTERN JURY INSTRUCTIONS

## THE CITATIONS

which include affirmances, reversals, dismissals and denials of certiorari by the
Illinois Supreme Court and the United States Supreme Court and amendments,
repeals, etc. of the Illinois Constitutions, Revised Statutes, Laws and Court Rules

## APPEAR IN

ILLINOIS SUPREME COURT REPORTS
ILLINOIS APPELLATE COURT
  REPORTS
ILLINOIS COURT OF CLAIMS
  REPORTS
ILLINOIS CIRCUIT COURT REPORTS
NORTHEASTERN REPORTER (Illinois
  Cases)
UNITED STATES SUPREME COURT
  REPORTS
LAWYERS' EDITION, UNITED
  STATES SUPREME COURT
  REPORTS
SUPREME COURT REPORTER
FEDERAL CASES
FEDERAL REPORTER
FEDERAL SUPPLEMENT
FEDERAL RULES DECISIONS
ILLINOIS LAW REVIEW
NORTHWESTERN UNIVERSITY LAW
  REVIEW
UNIVERSITY OF CHICAGO LAW
  REVIEW
ILLINOIS LAW FORUM

CHICAGO-KENT LAW REVIEW
ILLINOIS BAR JOURNAL
ILLINOIS LAW BULLETIN
ILLINOIS LAW QUARTERLY
DE PAUL LAW REVIEW
CALIFORNIA LAW REVIEW
COLUMBIA LAW REVIEW
CORNELL LAW QUARTERLY
CORNELL LAW REVIEW
HARVARD LAW REVIEW
LAW AND CONTEMPORARY
  PROBLEMS
MICHIGAN LAW REVIEW
MINNESOTA LAW REVIEW
NEW YORK UNIVERSITY LAW
  REVIEW
STANFORD LAW REVIEW
TEXAS LAW REVIEW
UNIVERSITY OF PENNSYLVANIA
  LAW REVIEW
VIRGINIA LAW REVIEW
YALE LAW JOURNAL
AMERICAN BAR ASSOCIATION
  JOURNAL
LAWS OF ILLINOIS

and in annotations of

LAWYERS' EDITION, UNITED STATES SUPREME COURT REPORTS
AMERICAN LAW REPORTS

also, for Illinois cases reported prior to the Northeastern Reporter or prior to
their inclusion in the Northeastern Reporter as cited in all units of the

---

Shepardizing 332 Ill.App. 17

Each volume of Shepard's in each of its units has a title
page indicating which court reports and law reviews are
covered for citing cases.

[Illustration 80]

## PAGE FROM ILLINOIS SHEPARD'S CITATIONS—CASES

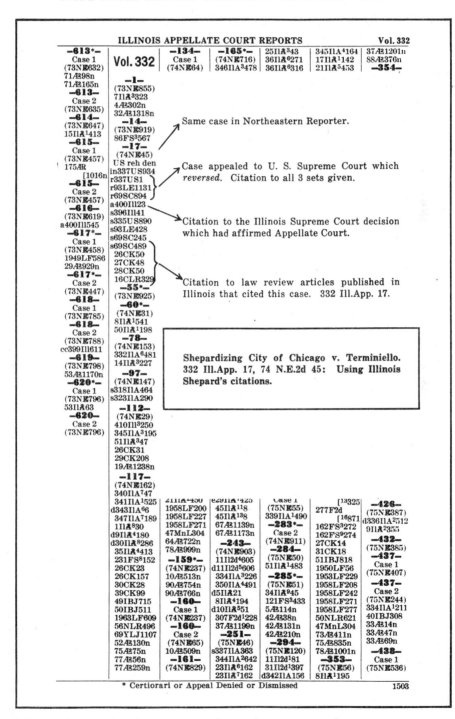

Same case in Northeastern Reporter.

Case appealed to U. S. Supreme Court which *reversed*. Citation to all 3 sets given.

Citation to the Illinois Supreme Court decision which had affirmed Appellate Court.

Citation to law review articles published in Illinois that cited this case. 332 Ill.App. 17.

Shepardizing City of Chicago v. Terminiello. 332 Ill.App. 17, 74 N.E.2d 45: Using Illinois Shepard's citations.

[Illustration 80–a]

## PAGE FROM BI–MONTHLY SUPPLEMENT TO ILLINOIS SHEPARD CITATIONS—CASE

| Vol. 331 | ILLINOIS APPELLATE COURT REPORTS | | | | | |
|---|---|---|---|---|---|---|
| **Vol. 331** | **Vol. 332** | **Vol. 333** | **Vol. 334** | **Vol. 335** | **Vol. 336** | **Vol. 337** |
| – 85 – <br> 130Ill$A^9$316 <br> 130Ill$A^{11}$316 <br> 4Ill$A^9$234 | – 112 – <br> 130Ill$A^2$303 <br><br> – 243 – <br> q3Ill$A^5$344 | – 160 – <br> Case 1 <br> 4Ill$A^1$580 <br><br> – 233 – <br> 131Ill$A^3$593 | – 59 – <br> 338FS$^1$1399 <br> 42$A_2$815n <br> 42$A_2$823n <br><br> – 253 – <br> 44$A_2$321n | – 222 – <br> 4Ill$A^1$447 <br><br> – 223 – <br> Case 1 <br> 130Ill$A^1$995 | – 56 – <br> d131Ill$A^1$373 <br><br> – 101 – <br> 131Ill$A^6$316 <br> d131Ill$A^6$526 | – 7 – <br> 4Ill$A^9$960 <br><br> – 35 – <br> 131Ill$A^6$327 <br><br> – 117 – <br> 131Ill$A^6$1085 <br> 3Ill$A^5$18 |
| – 109 – <br> Case 2 <br> d131Ill$A^1$301 | – 271 – <br> 131Ill$A^9$508 <br><br> – 301 – <br> d131Ill$A$301 | – 602 – <br> 4Ill$A^2$285 <br><br> – 617 – <br> 130Ill$A^4$843 <br> 131Ill$A^4$517 | – 313 – <br> 3Ill$A^2$442 <br><br> – 347 – <br> 4Ill$A^{12}$978 | – 293 – <br> 3Ill$A^6$948 <br><br> – 519 – <br> 131Ill$A^2$337 | – 282 – <br> 131Ill$A^3$355 <br><br> – 344 – <br> 4Ill$A^4$396 | – 369 – <br> 3Ill$A^{14}$508 <br> 5Ill$A^{14}$456 |
| – 275 – <br> 130Ill$A^1$41 <br><br> – 321 – <br> 131Ill$A^2$316 | – 335 – <br> 131Ill$A^3$67 <br><br> – 432 – <br> 4Ill$A^3$162 | | – 366 – <br> 131Ill$A^2$377 | – 570 – <br> Case 2 <br> 4Ill$A$667 | – 358 – <br> Case 1 <br> 4Ill$A^1$677 <br><br> – 541 – <br> e4Ill$A^3$795 | – 489 – <br> 5Ill$A^4$184 <br><br> – 591 – <br> 130Ill$A^1$865 <br><br> – 611 – <br> h3Ill$A^3$335 <br><br> – 649 – <br> 131Ill$A$460 <br><br> – 663 – <br> 131Ill$A^1$593 <br> 33LE$^1$229 <br> 92SC$^1$2301 |
| | – 459 – <br> 3Ill$A^5$387 <br><br> – 586 – <br> 131Ill$A$391 <br><br> – 661 – <br> Case 1 <br> 130Ill$A$427 | | | | | |

The latest bi-monthly cumulative supplement (and in some instances the monthly supplement) must always be checked. In this instance, 332 Ill.App. 17 has not been cited since the bound volume was published.

[Illustration 81]

## PAGE FROM NORTHEASTERN SHEPARD'S CITATIONS

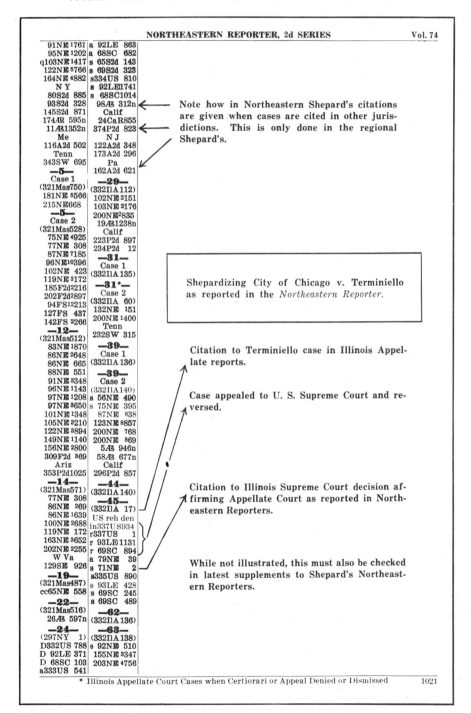

**NORTHEASTERN REPORTER, 2d SERIES**       Vol. 74

Note how in Northeastern Shepard's citations are given when cases are cited in other jurisdictions. This is only done in the regional Shepard's.

Shephardizing City of Chicago v. Terminiello as reported in the *Northeastern Reporter.*

Citation to Terminiello case in Illinois Appellate reports.

Case appealed to U. S. Supreme Court and reversed.

Citation to Illinois Supreme Court decision affirming Appellate Court as reported in Northeastern Reporters.

While not illustrated, this must also be checked in latest supplements to Shepard's Northeastern Reporters.

## [Illustration 82]

## PAGE FROM ILLINOIS SHEPARD'S CITATIONS—CASES

Vol. 327
ILLINOIS SUPREME COURT REPORTS

| | | |
|---|---|---|
| 362Ill136 | 24Il2d³368 | d260IlA²594 |
| 329IlA¹490 | 26Il2d⁸262 | 266IlA³159 |
| **—254—** | 29Il2d⁹115 | 319IlA³75 |
| (158NE442) | j290IlA⁹436 | f41F2d³3 |
| 339Ill¹524 | 326IlA³232 | 25ILR964 |
| 345Ill¹485 | 284F2d⁹665 | 108ÆR1491n |
| 281IlA⁴494 | 47IBJ218 | 108ÆR |
| 131IlA¹131 | 1953LF346 | [1499n |
| **—261—** | 70ÆR1174n | 17Æ21346n |
| (158NE568) | 70ÆR1191n | **—367—** |
| d390Ill¹194 | 132ÆR412n | (158NE698) |
| 164ÆR | **—339—** | s232IlA532 |
| [1380n | (158NE724) | 409Ill²449 |
| **—267—** | s243IlA605 | 259IlA²502 |
| (158NE476) | 346Ill²272 | 233F2d²49 |
| s235IlA417 | 357Ill196 | 98FS¹217 |
| d54IlA¹105 | 362Ill²556 | 13CK336 |
| **—269—** | d363Ill²283 | 1963LF571 |
| (158NE396) | 388Ill¹584 | 75ÆR447n |
| **—270—** | 388Ill²586 | 75ÆR1243n |
| (158NE448) | 389Ill²220 | 18Æ2190n |
| 328Ill²37 | q391Ill61 | **—381—** |
| 344Ill²562 | 250IlA623 | (158NE720) |
| 349Ill³515 | f253IlA604 | 411Ill⁴241 |
| 372Ill¹487 | 261IlA8 | 3Il2d²115 |
| 372Ill²487 | 266IlA²157 | 263IlA³278 |
| 49NLR744 | 285IlA378 | 279IlA202 |
| 56ÆR728n | 286IlA²21 | **—387—** |
| **—279—** | 300IlA²296 | (158NE703) |
| (158NE564) | 326IlA²269 | (55ÆR303) |
| 407Ill²153 | 334IlA²148 | j340IlA³328 |
| 35ILR248 | 337IlA²374 | 42ILR776 |
| 35LR257 | 41IlA²506 | 1957LF35 |
| 1950LF382 | 16IlA¹231 | 65Æ2669n |
| **—288—** | 120F2d65 | **—393—** |
| (158NE567) | 124F2d²737 | (158NE712) |
| cc322Ill597 | e138F2d¹226 | 344Ill¹482 |
| **—291—** | e138F2d¹227 | 390Ill³386 |
| (158NE570) | 153F2d²94 | 1950LF71 |
| 26ILR63 | 168F2d²16 | **—402—** |
| 1951LF17 | 171F2d836 | (158NE677) |
| **—294—** | 55FS¹826 | (56ÆR722) |
| (158NE687) | 24CK95 | 328Ill²37 |
| 328Ill²201 | 39ILR210 | 338Ill²634 |
| 328Ill⁴205 | 151ÆR40n | 344Ill¹562 |
| f341Ill¹602 | 151ÆR94n | 344Ill²562 |
| 343Ill⁴629 | 162ÆR27n | 344Ill³563 |
| 344Ill⁴376 | 162ÆR83n | 349Ill²515 |
| 348Ill⁴485 | **—346—** | 356Ill²140 |
| 358Ill²406 | (158NE709) | 357Ill²589 |
| 388Ill²427 | s242IlA654 | 361Ill¹581 |
| 294IlA⁵441 | 352Ill¹514 | f363Ill¹352 |
| 113F2d¹397 | 377Ill²58 | f363Ill²353 |
| **—305—** | 391Ill²79 | j363Ill³355 |
| (158NE729) | 305IlA¹196 | 371Ill³564 |
| 352Ill¹600 | 31IlA²433 | 379Ill³461 |
| 359Ill372 | 31IlA³433 | 406Ill²251 |
| 361Ill247 | 36IlA157 | 30CK55 |
| 375Ill³340 | 43IBJ56 | 49NLR741 |
| 375Ill³340 | 28ILR438 | **—406—** |
| 385Ill¹47 | 63ÆR1214n | (158NE692) |
| d273IlA251 | **—356—** | 327Ill³258 |
| 1CLR158 | (158NE685) | 339Ill¹527 |
| 23IBJ94 | cc332Ill422 | 346Ill⁵72 |
| **—312—** | 344Ill³372 | 395Ill²417 |
| (158NE732) | 413Ill³593 | 398Ill³37 |
| 333Ill⁹458 | d6Il2d¹598 | 264IlA¹104 |
| f337Ill⁹341 | 106ÆR990n | 271IlA154 |
| 338Ill⁸362 | 147ÆR70n | 326IlA⁵110 |
| 345Ill¹231 | 147ÆR85n | 43Æ21015n |
| d358Ill¹194 | 147ÆR96n | 43Æ21019n |
| 359Ill⁶253 | **—362—** | **—412—** |
| e368Ill⁹413 | (158NE678) | (158NE722) |
| 378Ill⁶228 | s242IlA320 | |
| 18Il2d¹286 | 330Ill642 | |

Other features of Shepard's citations.

In 340 Ill.App. 328, the point of law in 3d headnote in 327 Ill. 387 cited in dissenting opinion.

Citation to this case as reported in A.L.R.

327 Ill. 402 cited in 338 Ill. 634 for point of law in its 2nd headnote.

Point of law in 2nd headnote of 327 Ill. 402 "followed" by court in 363 Ill. 353.

Note how all citations are to Illinois reports. If the Northeastern Shepard's is consulted, only N.E. citations are given.

## SECTION C. STATUTE CITATIONS

Statutes are dealt with by *Shepard's Citations* in a manner similar to cases. The notations cover the form and operation of the law by the legislature and the courts. Its operation is identified by abbreviations denoting legislative changes (amendments, repeals, revisions, re-enactments, etc.) and judicial interpretations (constitutional, unconstitutional, invalid, etc.).

Some abbreviations used for notations in *Shepard's Citations* to statutes are given below:

### Form of Statute [4]

| | |
|---|---|
| Amend. | Amendment. |
| App. | Appropriation Act. |
| Art. | Article. |
| C or Ch. | Chapter. |
| Cl. | Clause. |
| Ex. | Extra Session. |
| Loc. | Local Acts or Laws. |
| No. | Number. |
| p. | Page. |
| Res. | Resolution. |
| Sp. | Special Session. |
| Subd. | Subdivision. |
| Subsec. | Subsection. |
| Tit. | Title. |
| § | Section. |
| ¶ | Paragraph. |

The form of statutes vary, depending on the plan adopted by a jurisdiction. The Table of Abbreviations in each unit of *Shepard's Citations* should be examined specifically to determine the local scheme.

### Operation of Statute

**Legislative**

| | |
|---|---|
| A (amended) | Statute amended. |
| Ad (added) | New section added. |
| E (extended) | Provisions of an existing statute extended in their application to a later statute, or allowance of additional time for perform- |

---

[4] Op. Cit. Note 2.

|                              | ance of duties required by a statute within a limited time. |
| L (limited)                  | Provisions of an existing statute declared not to be extended in their application to a later statute. |
| PA (proposed amendment)      | Future action necessary to confirm or reject amendment. |
| PR (proposed repeal)         | Future action necessary to confirm or reject repeal. |
| R (repealed)                 | Abrogation of an existing statute. |
| Re-en (re-enacted)           | Statute re-enacted. |
| Rn (renumbered)              | Renumbering of existing sections. |
| Rp (repealed in part)        | Abrogation of part of an existing statute. |
| Rs (repealed and superseded) | Abrogation of an existing statute, and substitution of new legislation therefor. |
| Rv (revised)                 | Statute revised. |
| S (superseded)               | Substitution of new legislation for an existing statute, not expressly abrogated. |
| Sg (supplementing)           | New matter added to an existing statute. |
| Sp (superseded in part)      | Substitution of new legislation for new part of an existing statute, not expressly abrogated. |

**Judicial**

C Constitutional.

U Unconstitutional.

V Void or invalid.

Up Unconstitutional in part.

Va Valid.

Vp Void or invalid in part.

The "Citations to Statutes" units of *Shepard's Citations* cover the following areas: citations to the United States Constitution and state constitutions; the United States Code and Acts of Congress (not included in the United States Code); the various state codes, legislative enactments and court rules; and various municipal charters and ordinances.

The information contained in the statutes units is presented in accordance with this arrangement: Statutory amendments, repeals, etc., are listed first, followed by state and federal court citations and citations in the attorneys general opinions, legal periodicals and acts of the legislature.

### 1.  Constitutions

The federal and state constitutions are covered by the *Statute Editions to Shepard's Citations*. A constitution section in a *Statute Edition* is arranged under the articles and amendments to the constitution. Citing sources are listed under these provisions. See Illustration 83.

### 2.  City Charters and Ordinances

The municipal charters and ordinances are part of the *State Citations*. Reference should be made to the citator of the state in which the city is located for citations to the city's charter or ordinances.

The section under "Municipal Charters" in the *Statute Citations* is arranged alphabetically by cities in many state editions and subdivided by topics. The unit may have a separate *Index to Municipal Charters*. The Ordinances section also may be arranged alphabetically by cities and subdivided by topics. It, too, may have a separate *Index to Ordinances*. In some citators, the citations to the ordinances of the larger cities are separately arranged. To meet editorial requirements, the citations to ordinances may be indexed by section numbers as well as topically. See Illustration 86.

3.  Shepard's Ordinance Law Annotations is a new publication, which is national in scope and is in six volumes. It contains topically analyzed and arranged annotations on local problems, covering numerous court decisions, with *National Reporter System* citations. It also includes law review references and citations to *American Law Reports annotations*. It has a fact word-index and a table of cases, arranged by state, city and county. It is kept up-to-date by annual pocket supplements.

### 4.  Court Rules

Citations to court decisions interpreting court rules are also covered by *Shepard's Citations*. The Court Rules section is arranged by courts (final, intermediate and original jurisdiction), and is subdivided by rule numbers.

## SECTION D.   ILLUSTRATIONS—STATUTE CITATIONS

[Illustration 83]

## PAGE FROM FLORIDA CONSTITUTION IN THE FLORIDA SHEPARD'S CITATIONS—STATUTES

| 1968, Art. VII | | | | FLORIDA CONSTITUTION, 1968 |
|---|---|---|---|---|

| § 1 | § 12 | § 6 | 257So2d274 | § 2 |
|---|---|---|---|---|
| 231So2d1 | 229So2d842 | 261So2d2 | 24MiL335 | 229So2d842 |
| 246So2d741 | 234So2d651 | 325F8495 | 24MiL591 | 234So2d655 |
| 261So2d1 | 235So2d1 | Subd. a | § 6 | 261So2d5 |
| Subd. a | 257So2d26 | 261So2d4 | 238So2d678 | § 6 |
| 261So2d3 | 260So2d497 | Subd. b | 239So2d628 | 257So2d273 |
| 33F1S178 | 261So2d6 | 261So2d2 | 239So2d878 | 32F1S203 |
| C410F2d | 399US213 | 33F1S116 | 23MiL349 | Subd. a |
| [1067 | 26LE530 | 33F1S178 | 24MiL578 | 223So2d37 |
| Subd. c | 90SC1996 | Subd. c | 364So6n | 33F1S178 |
| 239So2d1 | U317FS859 | 33F1S116 | Subd. a | § 7 |
| 257So2d10 | Subd. a | Subd. d | 238So2d163 | 229So2d846 |
| Subd. d | 235So2d2 | 251So2d1 | 245So2d286 | 257So2d273 |
| 239So2d3 | § 13 | 33F1S123 | 253So2d910 | Subd. b |
| 243So2d574 | 235So2d4 | Subd. e | 34F1S62 | 229So2d841 |
| 257So2d10 | § 14 | 230So2d131 | 35F1S72 | § 8 |
| § 2 | 23FLR478 | 245So2d80 | 23FLR490 | 229So2d841 |
| C410F2d | 70C70-270 | 261So2d137 | 23MiL355 | § 9 |
| [1067 | 70 p1517 | 450F2d563 | § 7 | A Nov. 4, |
| 21FLR324 | | Subd. f | 234So2d666 | [1969 |
| § 3 | Art. VIII | 224So2d688 | § 8 | (69HJR |
| 248So2d3 | 261So2d2 | 230So2d131 | Subd. a | 1851) |
| Subd. a | §§ 1-5 | 240So2d505 | 243So2d149 | 238So2d830 |
| 233So2d184 | 261So2d5 | 245So2d114 | 247So2d54 | 239So2d7 |
| § 4 | § 1 | 425F2d1142 | Subd. b | 69C69-299 |
| 240So2d884 | 245So2d113 | § 11 | 243So2d148 | 69HJR |
| 34F1S183 | 245So2d295 | Subd. 1 | § 9 | [1851 |
| 21FLR324 | 251So2d5 | ¶ f | 401US737 | 1972HJR |
| Subd. a | 23FLR660 | 239So2d635 | 28LE448 | [3576 |
| 232So2d390 | Subd. c | | 91SC1052 | Subd. a |
| 257So2d538 | 23FLR659 | Art. IX | § 10 | 1971C369 |
| § 5 | Subd. d | § 1 | 232So2d58 | 1972SJR |
| 243So2d574 | 261So2d5 | 34F1S89 | 259So2d505 | [292 |
| 1971C20 | 440F2d339 | § 3 | 23FLR651 | Subd. c |
| § 6 | 33F1S116 | 247So2d305 | § 11 | 246So2d102 |
| 222So2d424 | 21FLR324 | § 4 | 23FLR493 | ¶ 4 |
| Subd. a | 23FLR659 | Subd. b | 24MiL588 | 69C69-304 |
| 24MiL581 | Subd. e | 231So2d1 | 70 p1516 | ¶ 5 |
| § 7 | 23FLR664 | | 70HJR792 | 246So2d102 |
| 229So2d588 | Subd. f | Art. X | § 12 | 249So2d423 |
| § 9 | 251So2d1 | § 1 | 235So2d1 | 261So2d813 |
| 231So2d1 | 33F1S116 | 238So2d831 | Subd. b | § 10 |
| 246So2d738 | 1971C629 | 238So2d830 | 238So2d833 | 223So2d35 |
| 261So2d1 | | 239FS1360 | Subd. a | |

> In each Shepard's Citations state unit, there is a statute section which includes a section on the state's Constitution.
>
> This illustration is from the Florida Shepard's. Each time a section of the Florida Constitution has been cited by a Florida Court, or Federal Court sitting in Florida, the citation appears in this section of the Florida Shepard's.
>
> Note how Art. VII, section 2 and section 3 have been held Constitutional.

| 246So2d737 | Subd. a | 246So2d575 | | |
|---|---|---|---|---|
| 247So2d304 | 261So2d803 | Subd. c | § 4 | |
| 257So2d10 | 70C70-735 | 237So2d217 | 238So2d831 | |
| 261So2d6 | Subd. b | 239So2d525 | § 5 | |
| Subd. c | 244So2d536 | 254So2d777 | 243So2d575 | |
| 247So2d305 | 261So2d129 | 258So2d450 | 1971C20 | |
| 249So2d7 | 261So2d803 | 24MiL578 | | |
| 250So2d875 | § 3 | § 5 | Art. XII | |
| § 11 | 261So2d498 | 217So2d585 | 234So2d655 | |
| 245So2d863 | § 4 | 234So2d3 | 261So2d5 | |
| 246So2d102 | 261So2d5 | 247So2d41 | 69C69-230 | |
| 257So2d10 | 1971C629 | 251So2d15 | § 1 | |
| | § 5 | 252So2d826 | 32F1S203 | |
| | 261So2d5 | 254So2d777 | | |

272

[Illustration 84]

## PAGE FROM U.S. SHEPARD'S CITATIONS—STATUTES

**UNITED STATES CODE**    '70 Ed. & '71 Supp.    T. 26 § 4411

| Subd. 3 | § 4231 | 430F2d986 | § 4253 | Subsec. 3 | 88SC710 | 298FS1358 | 390F2d616 |
|---|---|---|---|---|---|---|---|
| Ad83St487 | 400F2d982 | 454F2d136 | R85St251 | 388F2d305 | 88SC717 | 5ARF185n | 391F2d230 |
| A84St1836 | 413F2d181 | 269FS274 | | 265FS68 | 89SC392 | § 4402 | 391F2d255 |

> "Shepardizing" a U. S. Code provision. This unit of Shepard's gives citations to each Court decision citing the U. S. Code. It also indicates when a code section has been amended or repealed.
>
> 1. 26 U.S.C. 4221c amended by 85 Stat. 497.
> 2. 26 U.S.C. 4251 repealed by 82 Stat. 251.
> 3. 26 U.S.C. 4401 held Constitutional in cases cited.

| | | | | | | | |
|---|---|---|---|---|---|---|---|
| A85St497 | 426F2d833 | § 4243 | § 4271 | ¶ A | 408F2d112 | § 4403 | 414F2d761 |
| 389F2d634 | 436F2d1068 | | Ad84St219 | 446F2d323 | 408F2d1017 | 390US43 | 422F2d1246 |
| § 4217 | 448F2d179 | Subsec. b | § 4272 | ¶ B | 411F2d505 | 19LE895 | 423F2d629 |
| 371F2d831 | 264FS952 | 405F2d1233 | Ad84St219 | 446F2d323 | 414F2d761 | 88SC700 | 425F2d1335 |
| § 4218 | 279FS419 | 277FS669 | § 4281 | ¶ C | 416F2d921 | 373F2d33 | 427F2d1028 |
| 296FS633 | 285FS681 | 277FS749 | Ad84St219 | 446F2d323 | 422F2d1246 | 416F2d921 | 428F2d103 |
| 329FS1273 | 293FS51 | 280FS534 | | | 423F2d629 | 446F2d1006 | 431F2d914 |
| | | | § 4282 | ¶ D | 427F2d1028 | 447F2d914 | 434F2d628 |
| Subsec. a | §§ 4232 | Subsec. c | Ad84St219 | 446F2d320 | 431F2d914 | 309FS469 | 435F2d23 |
| 371F2d832 | to 4234 | 405F2d1232 | Subd. 1 | 311FS141 | 432F2d900 | § 4404 | 437F2d737 |
| 389F2d633 | 426F2d834 | 426F2d834 | § 4291 | | 435F2d23 | 1ARF797n | 443F2d372 |
| 461F2d1268 | | Subd. 2 | A84St219 | § 4401 | 437F2d93 | § 4411 | 445F2d642 |
| 299FS1357 | § 4232 | 405F2d1233 | 371F2d442 | et seq. | 437F2d737 | et seq. | 445F2d869 |
| 329FS1274 | 426F2d834 | Subd. 3 | 449F2d906 | 401US702 | 445F2d642 | 294FS335 | 445F2d1070 |
| | 264FS953 | 405F2d1233 | 284FS503 | 28LE426 | 445F2d1070 | | 446F2d182 |
| Subsec. b | 319FS634 | Subd. 4 | 319FS419 | 91SC1165 | 446F2d1251 | § 4411 | 446F2d1251 |
| 387F2d662 | | 405F2d1233 | 325FS487 | 378F2d757 | 447F2d857 | U396F2d220 | 447F2d857 |
| Subsec. c | Subsec. b | § 4251 | § 4292 | 406F2d404 | 447F2d915 | C425F2d817 | 447F2d914 |
| 329FS1274 | 381F2d982 | | A84St219 | 406F2d1167 | 451F2d | C441F2d | 451F2d1032 |
| | 406F2d906 | Subd. 4 | | 411F2d923 | [1354 | [1337 | 456F2d153 |
| Subsec. e | 264FS952 | 405F2d1233 | § 4293 | 426F2d985 | 456F2d153 | 388US903 | 462F2d488 |
| 389F2d634 | 279FS4 | | A84St219 | 449F2d1321 | 457F2d1355 | 390US39 | 264FS395 |
| § 4220 | 319FS6 | R82St251 | § 4294 | 451F2d1028 | 462F2d488 | 390US62 | 270FS396 |
| Subsec. 1 | § 4241 | 404F2d405 | | 458F2d762 | 270FS396 | 393US963 | 276FS396 |
| 412F2d1203 | 370F2d202 | 411F2d606 | Subsec. a | 264FS182 | 280FS345 | 394US570 | 280FS345 |
| | 422F2d1059 | 449F2d906 | A84St219 | 325FS359 | 282FS635 | 395US13 | 282FS635 |
| Subsec. 2 | 430F2d986 | 319FS419 | Subsec. b | 329FS761 | 285FS148 | 396US78 | 282FS979 |
| 412F2d1203 | 430F2d1327 | 325FS487 | A83St487 | 41FRD353 | 286FS643 | 401US670 | 283FS904 |
| § 4221 | 454F2d136 | Subsec. a | § 4301 | 42FRD587 | 289FS642 | 401US715 | 285FS148 |
| 284FS287 | 269FS274 | 449F2d912 | et seq. | 17LE984s | 292FS35 | 18LE1343 | 285FS791 |
| Subsec. a | 269FS309 | 319FS419 | 265FS71 | 89 42540s | 299FS258 | 19LE889 | 286FS544 |
| Subd. 1 | 273FS756 | Subd. 1 | 266FS230 | 1ARF795n | 302FS452 | 19LE906 | 286FS643 |
| 284FS287 | 279FS587 | 319FS420 | 57ABA53 | 1ARF801n | 306FS889 | 21LE376 | 288FS57 |
| Subsec. c | 280FS534 | Subd. 2 | | 5ARF170n | 308FS518 | 22LE553 | 289FS642 |
| A85St497 | 301FS1151 | A82St92 | § 4401 | | 313FS1035 | 23LE68 | 291FS762 |
| | 207FS1081 | A82St251 | C402F2d3 | | 322FS157 | 24LE275 | 292FS35 |
| Subsec. d | Subsec. a | A83St487 | C441F2d | | 326FS960 | 28LE407 | 293FS789 |
| 399F2d883 | A84St1836 | [1337 | | 330FS596 | 28LE436 | 296FS984 |
| Subd. 5 | 405F2d1232 | | C442F2d405 | | 332FS1277 | 87SC2094 | 298FS1358 |
| A83St487 | 269FS274 | Subsec. b | C309FS469 | | 88SC697 | 299FS258 |
| Subd. 6 | 301FS1153 | A82St251 | § 4302 | 388US904 | 333FS408 | 88SC710 | 300FS1387 |
| 284FS287 | 305FS983 | A83St487 | 446F2d324 | 390US42 | 338FS273 | 89SC392 | 302FS452 |
| | 100A2739s | A84St1836 | § 4361 | 390US62 | 338FS1109 | 89SC1251 | 306FS589 |
| § 4222 | Subd. 1 | Subsec. c | 391F2d610 | 393US963 | 341FS1152 | 89SC1536 | 308FS518 |
| 390US80 | 381F2d383 | A82St92 | 301FS22 | 395US13 | 342FS833 | 90SC364 | 309FS469 |
| 19LE919 | 430F2d986 | A82St251 | § 4362 | 401US669 | 343FS1279 | 91SC1041 | 313FS1035 |
| 88SC720 | 277FS749 | | 301FS22 | 402US454 | 4ARF632n | 91SC1160 | 322FS156 |
| Subsec. d | 284FS494 | § 4252 | | 18LE1343 | Subsec. a | 369F2d106 | 322FS275 |
| A85St497 | Subd. 2 | Subsec. a | § 4371 | 19LE894 | 423F2d1207 | 372F2d698 | 326FS960 |
| | 383F2d10 | R82St251 | 265FS68 | 19LE906 | 447F2d912 | 373F2d33 | 332FS1277 |
| § 4223 | 422F2d1056 | 319FS419 | Subsec. 1 | 21LE377 | 291FS762 | 379F2d394 | 338FS341 |
| Subsec. a | § 4242 | Subsec. b | 265FS72 | 23LE69 | 1ARF795n | 379F2d946 | 338FS1109 |
| 420F2d907 | 370F2d202 | 319FS419 | Subsec. 2 | 28LE407 | | 381F2d133 | 341FS1152 |
| 284FS287 | 422F2d1059 | | 265FS72 | 29LE33 | Subsec. c | 381F2d559 | 342FS833 |
| | | | | 87SC2097 | 411F2d923 | 385F2d489 | 343FS1279 |
| | | | | 88SC697 | 291FS762 | 386F2d177 | 346FS1002 |
| | | | | | | | *Continued* |

## [Illustration 85]

## PAGE FROM MICHIGAN SHEPARD CITATIONS—STATUTES

| 119.2 | | | COMPILED LAWS OF MICHIGAN, 1948 AND SUPPLEMENT, | | | |
|---|---|---|---|---|---|---|
| **119.2** | 97NW 804 | **123.151** | **123.505** | **123.738** | 111NW 803 | **123.964** |
| 356Mch 338 | 7WR 82 | et seq. | 187FS 938 | A1964No 42 | 374Mch514 | 12McA310 |
| 97NW 129 | **123.21** | 57MLR371 | 187FS 940 | A1967No63 | 132NW682 | 162NW856 |
| **119.4** | et seq. | **123.191** | **123.506** | A1970No234 | 12McA304 | **123.965** |
| 1959AG 217 | 1959AG 217 | et seq. | 187FS 938 | **123.739** | 162NW856 | A1968No96 |
| Subd. e | **123.21** | Title | 187FS 940 | A1967No63 | '63-64AG437 | A1970No47 |
| 57MLR375 | Rs1968 | A1970No191 | **123.581** | **123.740** | 69-70AG33 | **123.991** |
| **119.7** | [No191 | **123.192** | Title | A1964No 42 | Title | 16WnL832 |
| 37DLJ48 | **123.22** | A1970No191 | A1961No205 | A1967No63 | A1967No200 | **123.1001** |
| | Rs1968 | 24McA389 | **123.583** | A1970No234 | A1969No46 | et seq. |
| **Ch. 120** | [No191 | 180NW367 | Ad1961 | **123.741** | A1970No47 | 189NW757 |
| **120.2** | 189NW760 | **123.193** | [No 205 | A1964No 42 | **123.951** | **123.1001** |
| 37DLJ 53 | **123.31** | A1970No191 | **123.641** | A1967No63 | to 123. | to 123. |
| **120.9** | et seq. | 24McA397 | et seq. | A1970No234 | 965 | 1020 |
| A1966No318 | 372Mch219 | 180NW367 | '65-66AG | **123.742** | 12WR202 | 16WnL826 |
| 37DLJ 54 | 125NW487 | **123.194** | [100 | A1964No 42 | 16WnL815 | **123.1002** |
| **120.13** | 1McA316 | 24McA397 | **123.641** | A1967No63 | **123.951** | 16WnL826 |
| A1966No318 | 136NW24 | 180NW367 | '65-66AG | A1970No234 | A1964No 41 | **123.1005** |
| 37DLJ54 | 13WR239 | **123.231** | [100 | **123.743** | A1970No47 | 16WnL826 |
| **120.13a** | **123.31** to | et seq. | **123.642** | A1964No 42 | '63-64AG437 | **123.1007** |
| 1. Ad1964No95 | [320 | 67-68AG | '65-66AG | A1967No63 | 30McA278 | 189NW758 |
| **120.14** | 11WR257 | **123.236** | [101 | A1970No234 | 186NW1 | **123.1009** |
| A1961No 10 | 372Mch222 | Ad1962No68 | **123.644** | **123.745** | **123.952** | 16WnL827 |
| A1966No318 | **123.31** | **123.241** | '65-66AG | A1964No 42 | A1964No 41 | **123.1010** |
| A1968No250 | 125NW489 | et seq. | [101 | A1967No63 | A1968No96 | 16WnL827 |
| 37DLJ54 | 1McA31 | 2. 37DLJ52 | **123.645** | **123.747** | A1969No46 | **123.1012** |
| **120.15** | 136NW | Title | A1965No362 | A1964No 42 | A1970No47 | 16WnL827 |
| A1966No318 | **123.32** | A1969No86 | | **123.754** | '63-64AG438 | 189NW758 |
| **120.16** | 372Mch219 | **123.241** | **123.7** | 3. U366Mch226 | 16WnL815 | 16WnL827 |
| (1955 | 125NW487 | to 123. | et seq | U114NW172 | **123.952a** | **123.1013** |
| No190) | **123.41** | 253 | Title | 366Mch 248 | Ad1967 | 16WnL827 |
| A1966No318 | et seq. | 16WnL818 | A1969No247 | 114NW 182 | [No200 | |
| **120.20** | 1959AG 166 | 1965No328 | **123.721** | 10WR15 | A1968No96 | **Ch. 124** |
| (1955 | '61-62AG252 | 1965No405 | to 123. | **123.763** | A1969No46 | **124.1** |
| No190) | **123.44** | **123.241** | 723 | Ad1964No42 | **123.952b** | et seq. |
| A1966No318 | '61-62AG252 | A1969No86 | 365Mch 12 | **123.771** | Ad1968No96 | 1959AG 7 |
| **120.21** | **123.51** | 16WnL818 | 112NW 225 | et seq. | **123.953** | 1959AG 169 |
| A1966No318 | et seq. | **123.247** | **123.721** | 189NW871 | A1967No200 | '61-62AG426 |
| 37DLJ54 | '63-64AG 67 | A1969No86 | A1967No290 | **123.811** | A1968No96 | 67-68AG |
| **120.24** | **123.51** to | 16WnL818 | A1969No247 | 15WnL373 | **123.954** | [320 |
| A1964No 24 | **123.54** | **123.249** | '63-64AG 66 | **123.841** | A1968No96 | **124.2** |
| A1966No318 | '61-62AG425 | A1969No86 | 15WnL297 | A1968No96 | **123.955** | 1959AG 7 |
| 1961No 10 | 1966No136 | **123.261** | **123.731** | '63-64AG336 | '63-64AG437 | 1959AG 169 |
| **120.25** | **123.51** | A1969No213 | et seq. | **123.841** | **123.955a** | '61-62AG426 |
| A1964No 96 | 11McA210 | Title | Up366Mch | A1965No115 | A1968No96 | 67-68AG |
| **120.30** | 160NW794 | A1969No213 | [227 | 373Mch 102 | '63-64AG438 | [320 |
| 37DLJ 54 | | 123.275 | | | | 124.4 |

> **"Sheppardizing" a state statute**
>
> 1. Mich.Compiled Laws 120.13a amended by 1964 Michigan session law No. 95.
>
> 2. Mich. compiled laws 123.241 et seq. cited in Univ. of Detroit Law Journal.
>
> 3. Mich. compiled laws 123.754 held unconstitutional by Michigan Supreme Court. Note citations to Michigan Reports and the Northwestern Reporter.

| **123.1** | 57MLR352 | 23McA275 | A1967No63 | **123.951** | 12McA305 | (No5)48 |
|---|---|---|---|---|---|---|
| 356Mch647 | | 178NW530 | A1970No234 | et seq. | 162NW856 | |
| | | 187FS 938 | | 364Mch 565 | 68YLJ245 | |

[Illustration 86]

## PAGE FROM ARIZONA SHEPARD'S CITATIONS—
## ORDINANCE SECTION

### INDEX TO ORDINANCES　　　　　　　　　　A-P

#### A

**Annexation**
**New Territory**
　Zoning—Interim Law .......Phoenix
**Procedure** .....................Phoenix
**Territory** .....................Benson
　　　　　　　　　Paradise Valley
　　　　　　　　　Phoenix
　　　　　　　　　Scottsdale
　　　　　　　　　Sierra Vista
　　　　　　　　　Thatcher
　　　　　　　　　Tucson

#### B

**Buildings**
**Code**
　Provisions
　　Tempe City Code '66, §8-1 et seq.
　　　　　　　　　Tucson
　Purpose .....................Phoenix
　Sign Erection—Definition ....Phoenix
　Signs—Application .........Phoenix
**Construction**
　Excavations .................Tucson
**Electrical Code**
　Fixtures—Installation—
　　Requirements ...........Tucson

#### C

**City Employees**
**Retirement**
　Regulations .................Phoenix

**Civil Service**
**Board**
　Classified Service—Rules ....Phoenix
**Employee**
　Discharge—Procedure .......Tucson
　—Procedure—Hearing .......Tucson

**Code**
**Definitions**
　Street .....................Tucson

**Courts**
**City**
　Magistrate—Duties ..........Tucson

#### D

**Disorderly Conduct**
**Prostitutes**
　Conviction .................Tucson
**Public Drunkenness** ..........Phoenix

**Disturbing the Peace**
**Intoxication**
　Fighting—Penalty ...........Miami

**Dogs**
**At Large**
　Definition .................Phoenix
**Restraint**
　Leash .....................Phoenix
**Running at Large**
　Prohibition .................Phoenix
　Restrictions .................Phoenix

#### Food
**Meat Market**
　Permit—Fees .......Maricopa County

#### H

**Housing**
**Regulations** .................Phoenix
**Unfit Habitations**
　Repair—Demolition—Notice ..Phoenix

#### J

**Jury**
**Trial**
　Offenses—City Court .........Tucson

#### L

**Lewdness**
**Indecency**
　Aiding .....................Tucson

**Licenses**
**Food Stores**
　Operation ..........Maricopa County
**Retail Food Stores**
　Fees ...............Maricopa County

**Liquor**
**Intoxicating**
　Establishments—Hours .......Tucson
　—Loitering—Hours—
　　Prohibition ..............Tucson
　Licenses—Fee ...............Tucson

#### M

**Minors**
**Loitering**
　Prohibition .................Tucson

**Misdemeanors**
**Entertainers**
　Waitresses—Topless .........Tucson

**Motor Vehicles**
**Drunken Driving** .............Phoenix

**Municipal Corporations**
**Curb Cuts**
　Driveways .................Phoenix
**Liability**
　Streets and Sidewalks—
　　Defects—Injuries .......Phoenix
　　—Defects—Notice ...........Phoenix
**Parking Lots**
　Curbing ....................Phoenix
**Street Widening**
　Condemnation ..............Phoenix

#### O

**Obscenity**

Each state unit also has a section on City Charters and Ordinances. This "Shepardizes" the charters and ordinances of the major cities within the state.

This section is followed by an index.

Thus, if one is interested in the municipal regulations of dogs in Arizona, the index indicates which cities have ordinances. The next Illustration gives citations to cases interpreting the ordinance.

[Illustration 86–a]

## PAGE FROM ARIZONA SHEPARD'S CITATIONS— ORDINANCE SECTION

**ORDINANCES**     **Phoenix**

| | | | | | | |
|---|---|---|---|---|---|---|
| **AVON-** **DALE** | **§ 60** **Personnel** Pay Plan– Adoption– | 6AzA494 433P2d811 –Rural– | **PHOENIX** | 475P2d246 12AzA123 468P2d390 | V 89Az 299 V361P2d 651 Parking | ceeds 84Az 250 326P2d 841 | 101Az448 420P2d923 Noncon- |
| **Zoning** Building Line–Set- back 86Az 379 346P2d1101 | Approval 14AzA4 480P2d27 | Lot Area 101Az448 420P2d923 Lots–Sub- standard– Acceptance | **Annexa-** **tion** New Terri- tory–Zon- ing–In- terim Law 90Az 13 | –Restric- tions 12AzA123 468P2d390 **Fences** Strength- ening Con- | Lots–Curb- ing Va93Az 260 Va379P2d [972 Street Wid- ening Con- | 100Az189 412P2d693 –Gross Proceeds –Payment –Protest 100Az189 | forming Uses– Continu- ance 6AzA494 433P2d811 –Expansion |
| | **MARI-** **COPA** **COUNTY** [1101 | –Conditions 101Az448 420P2d923 Regulations V 86Az 379 V346P2d [1101 | 363P2d607 Procedure Va83Az 98 Va317P2d [537 Territory | ments Va7AzA129 Va436P2d [641 **Fire De-** **partment** | demnation 93Az 260 379P2d 972 Occupa- tions Businesses | 412P2d693 –Gross Proceeds –Payment –Recovery 100Az189 | 102Az575 435P2d472 9AzA183 450P2d424 –Expan- sion–Per- |
| **BENSON** **Annexa-** **tion** Territory V 94Az 75 V381P2d 760 Va95Az 107 Va387P2d [807 | **Food** Meat Market –Permit V12AzA83 V467P2d923 **Licenses** | 90Az 13 363P2d 607 –Notice 14AzA576 485P2d565 –Residential 88Az 261 355P2d 900 | Va90Az 331 Va367P2d [791 92Az 61 373P2d 368 94Az 75 381P2d 760 | Salaries Va84Az 382 Va329P2d [1103 86Az 88 340P2d 997 –Appropria- tions | –License 90Az 42 365P2d 208 **Ordinances** Violation– Penalty 14AzA117 481P2d288 | 412P2d693 Cigarettes C14AzA117 C481P2d288 Liquor C14AzA117 C481P2d288 Malt | mit 13AzA472 477P2d758 C421P2d882 –Restora- tion 102Az575 435P2d472 |
| **COTTON-** **WOOD** **Zoning** Noncon- ming Uses | Food Stores– Operation 12AzA83 467P2d923 Retail Food Stores– | Rezoning– Residential –Area 15AzA149 486P2d829 | **Buildings** Code– Purpose 7AzA129 436P2d641 –Sign Erection– | 86Az 88 340P2d 997 Wage 86Az 88 340P2d 997 –Basic Wage–An- | **Sewers** Connec- tions– Avail- ability 9AzA228 | Beverages C14AzA117 C481P2d288 Room Tax– Hotels– Motels 99Az270 | Ordinances –Notice 14AzA576 485P2d565 Planned Develop- ment– |
| –Continu- ance 13AzA595 480P2d16 | Fees V12AzA83 V467P2d923 **Permits** Food Establish- ments– Regula- tions 12AzA83 | **MIAMI** **Disturb-** **ing the** **Peace** Intoxica- tion– Fighting– Penalty | Definition 12AzA595 473P2d797 –Signs– Application 12AzA595 473P2d797 **City** **Employees** Retirement –Regula- tions | nual Ad- justment 86Az 88 340P2d 997 **Housing** **Regulations** 100Az23 410P2d93 Unfit Habita- tions– | 450P2d1021 **Signs** Regulations 12AzA595 473P2d797 **Streets** Excava- tions–Dan- ger Signals –Display– Require- ment 96Az 95 | 408P2d818 **Traffic** Speed 87Az 88 348P2d 291 Stop Signs– Emergency Vehicles– Full Stop V12AzA186 V468P2d951 **Zoning** | Dwellings –Number– Determina- tion 14AzA576 485P2d565 –Project –Explana- tory Statement 14AzA576 485P2d565 |

"Shepardizing" the Phoenix ordinance regulating dogs.

| | | | | | | |
|---|---|---|---|---|---|---|
| **GLEN-** **DALE** | | | | | | Purpose 14AzA [576 485P2d [565 Variations Neighbor- hood |
| **1963** | 96Az 361 395P2d716 | | 14AzA4 480P2d27 | Drunken Driving 100Az37 | –Bonds– Revenue– Pledge | 6AZA494 433P2d811 Annexed | Welfare 14AzA576 485P2d565 |
| **As** **Amended** | **Subdivi-** **sions** Plats–Maps | **Annex-** **ation** Territory | **Disorderly** **Conduct** Public | 410P2d479 **Municipal** **Corpora-** | Va86Az 121 Va341P2d [427 | Land– County Zoning– | Prior Uses –Continu- ance –Per- |
| **Appendix B** **§ 11** **Personnel** Policy– Declara- tion | –Approval– Recorda- tion V101Az448 V420P2d923 **Waters** Reclama- | V100Az62 V411P2d168 | Drunken- ness 97Az 105 397P2d 217 103Az264 440P2d29 | tions Curb Cuts– Driveways Va93Az 260 Va379P2d [972 | **Subdivi-** **sions** Regulations –Minimum Require- | Continu- ance 101Az448 420P2d923 Districts– Commer- | mit 13AzA472 477P2d758 Regulations 90Az 13 363P2d 607 |
| 14AzA4 480P2d27 **§ 11.3** **Personnel** Positions– Classifica- tions–Com- pensation 14AzA4 480P2d27 | tion Loan 94Az 295 383P2d 748 **Zoning** Districts– Commer- cial 82Az 380 313P2d 756 –Rural 101Az375 419P2d782 | **PEORIA** **Sewers** System– Installa- tion 14AzA581 485P2d570 | **Dogs** At Large– Definition 12AzA123 468P2d390 Restraint– Leash 12AzA123 468P2d390 Running at Large– Prohibition 106Az262 | Liability– Streets and Sidewalks –Defects– Injuries V 89Az 299 V361P2d 651 –Streets and Side- walks– Defects– Notice | ments 101Az448 420P2d923 **Swimming** **Pools** Fences– Require- ments 5AzA494 428P2d439 **Taxation** Business– Gross Pro- | cial–Signs –Limita- tions 12AzA595 473P2d797 –Residen- tial 5 C 90Az 13 C363P2d 607 Lots–Sub- standard– Acceptance –Conditions | Residential –Multi Family Permitted Uses 13AzA472 477P2d758 –Single Family Vp9AzA [395 *Continued* |

See Index to Ordinances. See 1958 Bound Volume for earlier citations     355

[Illustration 87]
## PAGE FROM SHEPARD'S MUNICIPAL ORDINANCE DIGEST

# FORTUNETELLING

**EDITORIAL COMMENT.** The word "fortunetelling" evokes all kinds of images of witchcraft, sorcery, and magic. At this place, however, we are not concerned with such exotic images, but only with the prosaic matter of local regulations that attempt to see that fortunetellers do not cheat or defraud the gullible. Some cities license them, and others regulate advertising and solicitation.

§ 1. Regulating
§ 2. Prohibiting
§ 3. —Advertising
§ 4. —Soliciting
§ 5. —Where Licensed by State

§ 6. As Fraudulent Device or Practice
§ 7. Not Offense Where Defined but Not Prohibited

• • •

### § 1. Regulating

An ordinance forbidding, and providing a fine for, fortunetelling is a valid enactment in the interest of the peace, good order and safety of the community, and does not offend the right of freedom of religion.

    Mo   St Louis v Hellscher (1922) 295 Mo 293, 242 SW 652.

An ordinance making it unlawful to engage in fortunetelling is a valid exercise of delegated police power under charter authority to regulate practices detrimental to the public morals or general welfare.

    Mo   Turner v Kansas City (1945) 354 Mo 857, 191 SW2d 612.

### § 2. Prohibiting

This six volume set, published by Shepard's is actually a Digest rather than a Citator.

It is topically arranged and digests all appellate court decisions that have interpreted a city ordinance.

E. g., if research involved the power of a city to regulate Fortunetelling, this set, under that heading, will digest all cases wherein such regulation was the subject of litigation.

It is kept current by annual pocket supplements.

## [Illustration 88]
## PAGE FROM GEORGIA SHEPARD'S CITATIONS—
## COURT RULES SECTION

**GEORGIA COURT RULES**

| Supreme Court 1965 (220Ga909) | Supreme Court 1971 Revision | Court of Appeals 1971 Revision | 125GA366 1878E563 Subd. b ¶1 | Superior Court 1936 | Rules of Procedure, Pleading and Practice in Civil Actions | Rules and Regulations of the State Bar 1963 |
|---|---|---|---|---|---|---|
| **Rule 14** | (226Ga905) | (122GA885) | 124GA831 186SE323 Subd. c ¶2 | Rule 23 228Ga114 184SE158 | 1947 | (219Ga873) |
| 227Ga18 227Ga223 227Ga463 227Ga525 227Ga831 227Ga832 124GA68 183SE41 183SE384 183SE466 | **Rule 11** Subd. c Ad227Ga847 **Rule 14** 228Ga193 184SE583 Subd. a A227Ga847 | **Rule 1** et seq. 125GA204 186SE783 **Rule 8** 124GA452 184SE362 | 123GA284 123GA856 124GA515 125GA666 184SE489 188SE831 ¶3 123GA102 123GA568 125GA199 186SE781 Cl. i | Rule 41 124GA549 184SE665 Rule 84 23Mer250 | (1946p761) **Rule 1** 125GA399 188SE158 **Rule 21** 124GA825 186SE318 | **Rule 1-501** 125GA42 186SE448 **Rule 3-106** 228Ga13 125GA145 183SE749 186SE560 |
| **Rules 15 to 23** 449F2d127 **Rule 16** Subd. 2 228Ga143 184SE578 Subd. 3 227Ga248 227Ga291 227Ga430 Subd. 4 227Ga248 | 228Ga92 228Ga99 228Ga156 228Ga192 228Ga193 228Ga251 228Ga253 228Ga270 228Ga372 228Ga393 184SE156 184SE347 184SE457 184SE580 | **Rule 9** 330FS291 **Rule 10** 330FS291 **Rule 11** 126GA115 190SE88 Subd. c AdMar. 2, [1972 | 123GA856 Cl. ii 123GA856 Cl. iv 123GA102 **Rule 33** 23Mer241 Subd. f 125GA534 188SE240 **Rule 34** | | | **Rule 4-215** Subd. b 22Mer175 |

*Each state unit of Shepard's citations has a section in the Statutes Division which "Shepardizes" the Court Rules of the state Appellate Courts.*

| Supreme Court 1965 | Supreme Court 1971 | Court of Appeals 1971 | | | | |
|---|---|---|---|---|---|---|
| **Rule 18** 227Ga248 **Rule 20** 227Ga18 227Ga345 227Ga463 227Ga525 227Ga831 227Ga832 124GA68 183SE41 183SE384 183SE466 **Rule 35** 23Mer241 **Rule 45** 227Ga345 **Rule 54** 227Ga264 | Subd. a 229Ga11 189SE86 **Rule 18** Subd. c ¶2 228Ga812 229Ga65 188SE504 189SE439 **Rule 37** Subd. j A227Ga847 ¶1 228Ga675 187SE665 | 183SE41 184SE519 Subd. a A Mar. 2, [1972 124GA452 125GA541 184SE362 188SE400 23Mer327 Subd. c 125GA199 186SE780 Subd. e AdMar. 2, [1972 126GA180 126GA249 190SE139 190SE445 **Rule 16** 124GA68 124GA545 183SE41 184SE519 Subd. a 23Mer327 **Rule 18** 123GA612 | | | | |

263

## E.　OTHER UNITS OF SHEPARD'S CITATIONS

Some units of *Shepard's Citations* have additional or different features than state and *National Reporter System* regional units. These are discussed below.

### 1.　United States Citations

　　a.　(Case Edition)

**Contents:**
　　　　U. S. Reports.
　　　　L.Ed. Reports.
　　　　Supreme Court Reporter.

The full history and treatment of the Supreme Court cases appear under the official (U.S.) citation.　The Lawyers' Edition and West Reporter Edition units merely provide parallel references from their unofficial citation to the official citation.　The official entry unit of Supreme Court cases gives the unofficial parallel citations in parenthesis under the official citation.　This complete citation information is given only once, under the first reference to the cited case in the *Case Edition*.　This same procedure of providing parallel case references only under the first reference to the cited case is followed in all editions of *Shepard's Citations*.

　　b.　Statute and Department Reports Editions.

This part provides citations to all cases citing the U. S. Constitution, *U. S. Code*, and *Statutes at Large*, that have not been included in the *U. S. Code* and those cases citing U. S. Supreme Court Rules.

　　c.　United States Administrative Citations, 1967, 1 vol. and pamphlet supplements.

This publication extends the coverage of *Shepard's United States Citations*, citing administrative decisions reported in twenty-two series of reports of federal administrative departments, courts, boards and commissions.　Examples are the Securities and Exchange Commission Decisions and Reports, the Federal Trade Commission Decisions and the Federal Communications Commission Reports.　The coverage includes history (affirmed, dismissed, modified or reversed on appeal) and treatment (criticized, distinguished, followed, questioned or overruled in later administrative or court decisions).　Parallel citations and cited references in periodical articles also are noted. *Shepard's Administrative Citations* also provides direct and reverse cross reference tables which correlate decisions of agencies as reported in official government reports and in loose-leaf services and reporters.　The cross references are for decisions reported in *Federal Carrier Cases, Public Utilities Reports, Radio Regulation, Utilities*

*Law Reporter-Federal Decisions, Trade Regulation Reporter and Federal Securities Law Reporter.*

### 3.   Shepard's Federal Labor Law Citations

Shepard's Citations, Inc. has expanded its activity to include a new concept of citation service, which embodies the principle of applying the citation scheme to a subject area.   *Shepard's Federal Labor Law Citations* permits a researcher to trace any National Labor Relations Board Decision as well as any federal court labor decision through all later applications.   The coverage also includes labor decisions since 1935 (the inception of the NLRB) in U. S. Supreme Court and lower federal court reports and analyses of statutory labor provisions in the *United States Code.*

The volume divisions of the cited sources are:

a.   *Case Edition 1959:*  NLRB decisions and federal courts.

b.   *Statutes Edition 1959:*  U. S. Code.

c.   *Cross Reference Edition 1959:*  cross references from NLRB decisions and orders to Bureau of National Affairs, Commerce Clearing House and Prentice-Hall services.

d.   Supplement, 1959–1963:  cases, statutes, and cross references.

The citing sources referred to are:

a.   Reports of decisions and orders of the NLRB, all federal court reports, all state reports, all units of the *National Reporter System*, with cross references to any reports or digests of the same cases in the several loose-leaf labor law services and reports.

b.   Labor relations periodicals, such as *Labor Law Journal* and *Arbitration Journal.*

c.   Law Journals.

d.   Annotations in *U. S. Supreme Court Reports (L.Ed.)* and the *American Law Reports.*

The citations concept is applied in this service.   Thus, it provides (1) *the complete history* (affirmed, amended, dismissed, reversed or superseded) of any reported decision of the NLRB, covering both further action by the Board and action by the courts on appeal from the Board's decision, and (2) *subsequent treatment* (criticised, distinguished, explained, followed, harmonized, dissented, limited, overruled or questioned) accorded the decision by the Board and the courts.   The *Case Edition* (1959) volume covers these decisions.

### 4.   Shepard's Law Review Citations

This unit will be discussed in Chapter 14.

## SECTION F.  KEEPING SHEPARD'S CITATIONS CURRENT

As in any set of law books, there must be a method of keeping it up-to-date.  As *Shepard's Citations* are used to determine the current status of the case, the method of supplementation is of the utmost importance to *Shepard's*.  This is accomplished in this manner. Each separate *Shepard's* unit is available in at least one bound volume.  Then every two months a cumulative paper supplement is issued, covering all decisions handed down since the publication of the bound volume.  For some sets, in addition to the bi-monthly cumulative supplement, an interim monthly supplement is issued.  Some sets now have a bound volume, one or more bound supplements, and then the cumulative bi-monthly supplement.  It is extremely important before using *Shepard's* citations to ascertain that all of the volumes are at hand before using it.

*In all cases, the bound volume or volumes plus the paper supplement or supplements must be used.*

# Chapter 15

# ENCYCLOPEDIAS

The mass of primary source material has reached such voluminous proportions that aids in their use—secondary publications—have assumed significant roles in identifying and explaining the law. It is not uncommon practice for an attorney to examine such secondary materials as encyclopedias, treatises, periodical articles and annotations initially before primary publications.

The encyclopedia is a form of search-book to which the Index, Topic and Definition Methods are applicable. It contains expository statements on principles of law, topically arranged, with supporting footnote references to cases in point. On the other hand, a digest is an index to case law, giving brief, unconnected statements of courts' holdings or facts of cases which are classified by subject.

The encyclopedia is one of four narrative sources. The other three are treatises, periodical articles and annotations. Some treatises and periodical articles are critical and evaluative. The encyclopedia is noncritical in its approach; it simply states the propositions of law, with introductory topical explanations of an elementary nature.

The legal encyclopedia, because of these features, is a popular and useful research tool. However, its utility as a secondary source has been abused by both the courts and attorneys, for too often it is cited as though it were a final authoritative source rather than an expositive introduction to case authority. Yet, in fairness to them, it should be observed that this is a defensive practice resulting from the obscure maze and bulk of case law.

In many problems, it is necessary to go beyond such rudimentary research. It is not wise, in such cases, to stop one's research without reading the cited cases, for frequently cited references will not fully reflect the propositional ramifications for which they stand, or the facts will be distinguishable and separate the cited cases from the immediate problem.

This criticism should not be interpreted as being directed at the intended function of the encyclopedia. It is an excellent index and introductory guide to the law. It, therefore, is often one of the first publications consulted and it should not be denied its proper place in legal research.

There are three types of legal encyclopedias which relate to: (1) general law, (2) local law and (3) special subjects. Each is discussed below.

The general legal encyclopedia is arranged alphabetically by topics, concentrating on the common law. Federal legislation is included, relating to the topics of the encyclopedia. Some state law may be treated generally, which is wholly or partially statutory, e. g., workmen's compensation.

It includes scope-notes and analyses for determining the contents of the subject matter covered under each topic. A scope-note, which delimits and identifies the content of a topic, appears below its heading. An analysis follows the scope-note, giving a conceptual breakdown of the topic into main and subordinate categories.

Each encyclopedia has a general index, a volume index, which is arranged by topics, and a cumulative annual pocket supplement. The pocket supplement is a common pamphlet method of keeping a publication current and, depending on the publication, it may have textual, case and statutory references of recent application. The pamphlet is inserted in the back of a volume.

The general and some local encyclopedias do not have tables of cases; however, several current local encyclopedias contain this feature.

---

## SECTION A.  CURRENT GENERAL ENCYCLOPEDIAS

### 1.  Corpus Juris Secundum (cited "C.J.S.")

*Corpus Juris Secundum,* published by the West Publishing Company, is an attempt to restate the entire body of American case law from the first reported case to date. It includes both adjective and substantive law, and its publisher aims at citing all reported decisions. This revision, begun in 1936, was completed in 101 volumes and has a five-volume general index. It supersedes the text of *Corpus Juris,* its earlier edition, and the footnotes cite all reported federal and state cases rendered since the publication of the corresponding titles in *Corpus Juris.* Where there are earlier cases in point, footnote references are given to the *Corpus Juris* page and note numbers which list them; therefore, although the text of *Corpus Juris* has been superseded by the text of C.J.S., the *Corpus Juris* footnotes are still useful for references to the earlier cases. If there is no footnote reference back to *Corpus Juris,* it may be assumed that there are no earlier applicable cases. If there are no new cases on a subject and the statement in *Corpus Juris* is still the law, the original text in *Corpus Juris* is repeated, giving a few representative early case citations from *Corpus Juris.*

C.J.S. references now include citations to secondary authority, such as treatises, form-books, law journal articles and the Restatements.    Cross-references from C.J.S. titles and sections to corresponding West topics and key-numbers (section numbers) also are provided, permitting easy entry to the *American Digest System.* The West topics and key-numbers and other secondary authority sources are noted under "Library References," which precede the texts of the sections, in the C.J.S. replacement volumes published since 1961 and in the annual cumulative pocket supplements.

Thus, C.J.S. provides the complete text and recent cases and representative early cases in the absence of new ones in point.  *Corpus Juris* should be consulted only for the earlier cases when a footnote reference to it is given in C.J.S.

As previously noted, C.J.S. has a five-volume general index. Each volume also has a separate index to the topics contained in it. Where the topic is covered in more than one volume, the topic index appears in the concluding volume of the topic.

The set is kept up-to-date by replacement volumes and annual cumulative pocket supplements.  Replacement volumes appear when significant sections of the text require rewriting or when the recent pocket references become very extensive and unwieldy.  The pocket references may cover rewritten text, citations to cases rendered since the publication of the original volume and secondary sources.

Judicial and other definitions of *words and phrases* and *legal maxims* are interfiled alphabetically with the essay topics.  They also are listed in each appropriate volume preceding the index, with references to the pages containing the definitions.

*Corpus Juris Secundum* provides some discussion on federal and local statutory law, including court interpretation of these enactments.

A "Law Chart" of the topical arrangement of *Corpus Juris Secundum* is included at the beginning of the first volume of the General Index and a "List of the Titles in Corpus Juris Secundum" precedes the text of each volume of the set.  The Law Chart is a guide to the titles under seven major divisions with numerous subheads. All related titles are so grouped as to enable comparison and discrimination in their correct selection.  To use the Topical approach when you do not know the title under which your question is discussed, first select the major division in the Law Chart that covers the problem.  Then choose the pertinent subhead and the most specific title under that subhead.  The last step is to consult the text of C.J.S. under the selected title.

**2.    American Jurisprudence** (cited "Am.Jur.")

a.    *American Jurisprudence* is a 58-volume legal encyclopedia published by the Lawyers Co-operative Publishing Co., which is being revised. It, too, began publication in 1936, and superseded *Ruling Case Law*, an earlier encyclopedia.

*American Jurisprudence* is a textual statement of substantive and procedural law, arranged alphabetically under 426 titles. The difference between it and *Corpus Juris Secundum* is reflected in the differing philosophies of the two publishers. *Corpus Juris Secundum*, as previously described, cites all reported decisions in support of its textual statement of the law. *American Jurisprudence*, on the other hand, only cites selective decisions in its footnotes but does give citations to *A.L.R.* annotations. In using *American Jurisprudence*, all reported cases may be located through its footnotes and by consultation of the cited *A.L.R.* annotations. This is the reason that *American Jurisprudence* is published in 58 volumes as against the 101 volumes in *Corpus Juris Secundum*.

*American Jurisprudence* also gives in its footnotes references to treatment of a topic in *American Jurisprudence* in the other sets of the Total Client Library Service. Since *American Jurisprudence* has a detailed four-volume index, it is much more inclusive in entries than the indexes to *A.L.R.* It is frequently easier to locate an *A.L.R.* annotation by starting in the *American Jurisprudence* index, reading the section cited to, and then locate the appropriate *A.L.R.* citation in *American Jurisprudence's* footnotes.

The publishers describe *American Jurisprudence* as giving the law in breadth and *A.L.R.* as the law in depth. The former is very useful to obtain a quick answer to a problem which then may be explored in depth through the use of *A.L.R.* In use one may go directly to the volume containing the topic being researched. For example, if one is interested in the law of *Copyright*, the index volumes may be by-passed and the search started immediately by consulting the volume that contains the title *Copyright*. If the broad topic of the law under which the subject is included is not familiar to the researcher (e. g., restrictive covenants), the search should start first in the index volumes.

b. *AMERICAN JURISPRUDENCE* 2d. *American Jurisprudence* was first published in 1936, and was kept up-to-date by pocket supplements and "replaced" volumes. In 1962, the publishers decided that so much has happened in the law that a complete new edition was justified and began publication of *American Jurisprudence* 2d, and has been issuing new volumes of *American Jurisprudence* 2d at the rate of three or four per year. Currently, *American Jurisprudence* 2d is about two-thirds completed. Thus, for topics not yet covered in *American Jurisprudence* 2d, *American Jurisprudence* must be used. The section numbers in *American Jurisprudence* 2d differ from those in *American Jurisprudence*. When an entry is found in the Index to *American Jurisprudence* to a topic now in *American Jurisprudence* 2d, it is necessary to consult a table in front of each volume of *American Jurisprudence* 2d indicating where *American Jurisprudence* sections are located in *American Jurisprudence* 2d. This is a temporary measure until *American Jurisprudence* 2d is completed and its own index volumes published. *American Jurisprudence* 2d is kept up-to-date by annual cumulative pocket supplements.

In addition, Am.Jur.2d includes some new features. Greater emphasis is being placed on federal statutory law, federal procedural rules and uniform state statutory laws. The federal statutory law, germane to a topic, is covered by the encyclopedia. State statutory law is provided in general without references to the specific law of each state. Thus, the state law of drugs is viewed broadly in Am. Jur.2d, noting the impact of federal law, but the detailed statutory law on drugs of specific states is not covered. Such discussion and information are available in local encyclopedias and state codes.

2. AMJUR 2d.  The final two volumes of the General Index to AMJUR 2d came out in May, 1978.  This will greatly ease the researcher's access into this tool.

The *Desk Book* is divided into seven main categories: (1) governmental documents and historical matters, (2) the courts (the canons of judicial ethics and the business and organization of the courts), (3) lawyers and the legal profession (the canons of professional ethics, minimum requirements for admission to legal practice in the U. S. and professional data), (4) statutes and statutory material (text of the ancient statutes and tabulated statutory material—e. g., marriage laws, record of passage of Uniform and Model Acts), (5) statistical matters (financial and mathematical tables, etc.), (6) tables of law reports (abbreviations), and (7) miscellaneous information (selected legal (Latin) maxims and phrases, freely translated, etc.).

Words and phrases and definitions are interfiled alphabetically in the Volume Indexes.

c. **American Jurisprudence Proof of Facts (AM.JUR.P.O.F.)**

This set was published in 1959, and is now in 28 volumes. Its purpose is to provide lawyers with a compilation of materials that will guide the lawyer in organizing his fact material, in preparing for trial, and in the examination of witnesses. It attempts to show the elements required in presenting or defending a *prima facie* case. This is done through a text discussion of the area followed by an outline in question and answer form, demonstrating the facts discussed in the text. It is designed to assist a lawyer in obtaining information from his client, in interviewing witnesses, in preparing for the taking of depositions, in preparation of briefs, and other steps lawyers need to take in preparing a case for trial.

The set has its own index and access to it may also be obtained by references to it from *A.L.R.* and *American Jurisprudence*. It is kept up-to-date by annual pocket supplements. Each topic included in the set is usually written by an experienced lawyer.

### 4. American Jurisprudence Trials (AM.JUR.TRIALS)

This set, published in 1964, and now in 18 volumes, is essentially a treatise on trial practice. The first six volumes cover what the publishers describe as practice, strategy, and control, and include matters that are common to all types of problems. The remaining volumes are called *Model Trials* and deal with the handling of trials for a specific topic. *American Jurisprudence Trials* is written by over 250 experienced trial lawyers. As with *American Jurisprudence P.O.F.* it has its own index and is referred to in the footnotes of the other sets of the Total Library Client Service.

### 5. American Jurisprudence Pleading and Practice Forms, Annotated (AM.JUR. P & P)

This set is essentially a collection of forms designed to assist a lawyer in preparing the procedural aspects of a law suit. Other than the references in its footnotes to the other sets of the publishers, it is typical of other sets containing legal forms.

### 6. American Jurisprudence Legal Forms

This set is similar to *American Jurisprudence* P & P, but contains forms lawyers need in their practice other than pleading and practice forms.[1]

---

## SECTION B.   STATE ENCYCLOPEDIAS

Some states have encyclopedias devoted to their own laws. Six states have encyclopedias published by the Lawyers Co-operative Publishing Co./Bancroft-Whitney Co., which follow the format of *American Jurisprudence*, but cover only the law of a specific state. These are:

California Jurisprudence 2d

Florida Jurisprudence

New York Jurisprudence

---

[1] Form books will be discussed in more detail in Chapter 18, Section C.

Ohio Jurisprudence 2d

Texas Jurisprudence

Three states have encyclopedias published by the West Publishing Co. and these follow the format of *Corpus Juris Secundum*. These are:

Florida Law and Practice

Illinois Law and Practice

Michigan Law and Practice

A few other states have sets by other publishers.

The features commonly applicable to most local encyclopedias are:

1. *Scope:* case and statutory law (substantive and procedural). The cases include both state and federal courts interpreting state law.

2. *Arrangement:* alphabetically by topics.

3. *Index:* general index and individual volume indexes. In some local encyclopedias, the titles included in a volume are separately indexed in the volume.

4. *Supplementation:* cumulative annual pocket parts and replacement volumes.

5. *Table of Statutes:* shows where code sections are cited in the local encyclopedia.

6. *Words and Phrases:* definitions of words and phrases are indexed.

7. *Research aids:* references to other secondary aids, such as A.L.R. annotations, periodical articles, etc., are often provided.

## SECTION C.  ILLUSTRATIONS:  ENCYCLOPEDIAS

In Chapter six, Section A in discussing the use of the *Key-Number System* and the *American Digest System* we had the problem of finding cases dealing with the facts of the status of a person who enters a store and is injured therein.   We found cases by using the *Key Number System*.

Another approach would have been to start our search in *Corpus Juris Secundum* as shown in the following Illustrations.

89.   **Page from General Index to C.J.S.**

90.   **Page from Index to Volume 65–A, C.J.S.**

91.   **Page from Volume 65, C.J.S.**

### USING AMERICAN JURISPRUDENCE AND RELATED SETS.

PROBLEM:   How is plagiarism shown to be an infringement of copyright?

92.   **Excerpts from Index to AM.JUR.**

93.   **Page from 51 AM.JUR.2d.**

94.   **Page from Title:  Copyright and Literary Property in AM. JUR.2d.**

95.   **Page from 18 AM.JUR.2d.**

96.   **Page from Pocket Supplement.   18 AM.JUR.2d.**

97.   **Page from AM.JUR. Proof of Facts.**

98.   **Pages from volume 9, AM.JUR. Trials.**

## [Illustration 89]

## PAGE FROM GENERAL INDEX TO C.J.S.

## SHOPPING GUIDE

**SHOPPING GUIDE**

Injunctions, newspaper, publication as violation of agreement not to publish newspaper, **Injun § 84, p. 568, n. 49**

---

This page is from a volume of the General Index to C.J.S.

This is an index to the entire 100 volumes of C.J.S. and thus must be more general than specific in its entries. No entry, for example, will be found in the General Index for Customers.

If one looks under Stores and Storekeepers, a "See" reference is found to Shops and Shopkeepers. Under this heading, note sub-entry Negligence with "See" reference to Title Index to Negligence. This means that one should consult the index to the topic Negligence in the appropriate volume of C.J.S.

---

**SHOPS AND SHOPKEEPERS**—Continued

Industrial co-operative societies,
     Members' liability for debts of, **Indust Co-op § 7, p. 16, n. 33**
     Organization for purpose of operating, **Indust Co-op § 2**

Injunctions, restrictive covenant, use of premises, **Injun § 87, p. 595**

Insurance, nonoccupancy avoiding fire policy, **Ins § 556, p. 306**

Internal revenue,
     Bonded warehouses, custody, **Int Rev § 584**
     Compensation, distiller's bond to reimburse government for wages paid, **Int Rev § 574, p. 816, n. 30**

Labor and employment,
     Bailments, return of article intrusted to customer to, **Ballm § 38**
     Injuries to third persons, liability for injuries inflicted by employee, **Mast & S § 570, p. 314**
     Liability for injuries to customers, **Mast & S § 575, p. 335**

Liability insurance, excepted risks or liabilities, **Ins § 834, p. 908**

Licenses and permits,
     Power to license, municipalities, **Licen § 10, p. 489**
     Subject to license or tax, **Licen § 30, p. 584**

Limitations of actions, store account, **Lim of Act § 72, p. 1039**

Machine Shops, generally, this index

Machines, excise tax on sale or use, **Int Rev § 528**

Mechanics' liens, building within meaning of lien law, **Mech Liens § 21, p. 513**

Milk distributing plants, as, **Food § 10, n. 39**

Mortgages, land appurtenant as included, **Mtg § 188**

Motor vehicles, maintenance tax on motor vehicles used, **Motor V § 63, n. 54**

➤Negligence, see **Title Index to Negligence**

Nuisances, **Nuis § 41, p. 793; § 75, p. 822**
     Junk store, **Nuis § 75, p. 824**
     Residential zoned area, **Nuis § 41, p. 793**

Owner's liability for detective agency's extortion, **Threats § 27, p. 808, n. 48**

Pleading, statement of separate causes of action for conduct of store manager as regards need for paragraphing, **Plead § 88, p. 211, n. 33**

Purposes, restrictions, **Deeds § 165, p. 1132**

Registers, jury room, allowance in during deliberations, **Crim Law § 1369**

Repair Shops, generally, this index

Residential districts, ordinances prohibiting as denial of due process, **Const Law § 703, p. 1186**

Robbery, sufficiency of evidence, **Rob § 47, p. 495**

Segregation of goods, asportation as resulting, **Larc § 6, p. 803**

Self-service store, acceptance of goods offered for sale on shelves of, **Sales § 28, p. 641**

Snow and ice on sidewalk, duty to keep free from, **Mun Corp § 862, p. 231, n. 87**

Warrants, search of as requiring, **Searches and Seizures, § 66, p. 834**

Weapons, criminal responsibility for carrying or possessing in, **Weap § 9, p. 503**

## [Illustration 90]

## PAGE FROM INDEX TO VOLUME 65–A, C.J.S.

**NEGLIGENCE**



**This page is from the index to the topic Negligence as found in Vol. 65–A of C.J.S.**

**Note the sub-entry Customers and under it the sub-sub-entry Business visitor or invitee, 63 (119).**

**This leads one to where that matter is discussed within C.J.S.**

## [Illustration 91]

## PAGE FROM VOLUME 65, C.J.S.

### §§ 63(118)–63(119)  NEGLIGENCE        65 C. J. S.

The proprietor is liable only for his negligence;[14] and he is not liable for wrongful or negligent acts of third persons not under his control which he could not reasonably have anticipated and guarded against,[15] at least in the absence of some special relationship between him and such third persons.[16]

The proprietor may be held free from liability for acts of an employee which are not wrongful or negligent.[17]

*b. Stores*

→ **§ 63(119).  In General**

**A person who enters a store for the purpose of trade occupies the status of an invitee or business visitor.**

Library References
Negligence ⟲32(1), (2.8).

A person who enters a store for the purpose of trade occupies the status of an invitee or business visitor,[18] and in this connection it is not necessary that the person entering should have a definite purpose of making any particular purchase, but it is

This is the Reference found in the Index to the Topic Negligence in Vol. 65–A.

This is a typical page from C.J.S. Note how most of it is given over to citations supporting the statements of the text.

Note footnote 18 and the citation to McKenney v. Quality Foods, Inc., 319 P.2d 448. This is the case located using the American Digest System. See Illustration 17–a.

Also note how C.J.S. through its "Library Reference" refers to Negligence ⟲32(1), (2.8) which was also located by use of the American Digest System.

This set is kept up-to-date by pocket supplements.

Rush v. Townsend & Wall Co., 343 S.W.2d 44, 50—Gregore v. Londoff Cocktail Lounge, Inc., 314 S.W.2d 704.
N.Y.—Booth v. Sears, Roebuck & Co., 68 N.Y.S.2d 26.
Ohio.—Scott v. Allied Stores of Ohio, 122 N.E.2d 665, 96 Ohio App. 532.
Tenn.—Gargaro v. Kroger Grocery & Baking Co., 118 S.W.2d 561, 22 Tenn.App. 70.

Wis.—Radloff v. National Food Stores, Inc., 121 N.W.2d 865, 20 Wis.2d 224, rehearing denied 123 N.W.2d 570, 20 Wis.2d 224.
**Anticipation of negligence of patrons**
Proprietor of business establishment cannot usually anticipate negligence of his patrons.
La.—Alfortish v. Massachusetts Bonding & Ins. Co., App., 171 So.2d 705.
16. La.—Alfortish v. Massachusetts Bonding & Ins. Co., supra.
17. N.Y.—Greene v. Sibley, Lindsay & Curr Co., 177 N.E. 416, 257 N.Y. 190.
18. U.S.—Montgomery Ward & Co. v. Lamberson, C.C.A.Idaho, 144 F. 2d 97—Baskin v. Montgomery Ward & Co., C.C.A.N.C., 104 F.2d 531—Montgomery Ward & Co. v. Snuggins, C.C.A.Minn., 103 F.2d 458.
Rikard v. J. C. Penny Co., Columbia Division, D.C.S.C., 233 F. Supp. 133—Lucas v. City of Juneau, D.C.Alaska, 168 F.Supp. 195—Rankin v. S. S. Kresge Co., D.C.W.Va., 59 F.Supp. 613, affirmed, C.C.A., 149 F.2d 934.
Ala.—Ten Ball Novelty & Mfg. Co. v. Allen, 51 So.2d 690, 255 Ala. 418.
Cal.—Neel v. Mannings, Inc., 122 P. 2d 576, 19 C.2d 647.
Iloff v. Purity Stores, Limited, 178 C.A.2d 1, 2 Cal.Rptr. 735—McKenney v. Quality Foods, Inc., 319 P.2d 448, 156 C.A.2d 349—Lundin v. Shumate's Pharmacy, 221 P.2d 260, 98 C.A.2d 817—Sheridan v. Ravn, 204 P.2d 644, 91 C.A.2d 112—Locke v. Red River Lumber Co., 150 P.2d 506, 65 C.A.2d 322—Thompson v. B. F. Goodrich Co., 120 P.2d 693, 48 C.A.2d 723—Colombo v. Axelrad, 114 P.2d 425, 45 C.A.2d 439—Strong v. Chronicle Pub. Co., 93 P.2d 649, 34 C.A.2d 335.
Colo.—**Corpus Juris Secundum quoted in** Nettrour v. J. C. Penney Co., 360 P.2d 964, 966, 146 Colo. 150.
Conn.—Lunny v. Pepe, 165 A. 552, 116 Conn. 684.
D.C.—Custer v. Atlantic & Pacific Tea Co., Mun.App., 43 A.2d 716.
Ga.—Townley v. Rich's, Inc., 67 S.E. 2d 403, 84 Ga.App. 772—Bray v.

Barrett, 65 S.E.2d 612, 84 Ga.App. 114—Bryant v. S. H. Kress & Co., 46 S.E.2d 600, 76 Ga.App. 530.
Ill.—Olinger v. Great Atlantic & Pacific Tea Co., 167 N.E.2d 595, 26 Ill.App.2d 88, affirmed 173 N.E.2d 443, 21 Ill.2d 469—Wesbrock v. Colby, Inc., 43 N.E.2d 405, 315 Ill. App. 494—Todd v. S. S. Kresge Co., 24 N.E.2d 899, 303 Ill.App. 89.
Ind.—Clark Fruit Co. v. Stephan, 170 N.E. 558, 91 Ind.App. 152.
Iowa.—Crouch v. Pauley, 116 N.W.2d 486, 254 Iowa 14—Anderson v. Younker Bros., Inc., 89 N.W.2d 858, 249 Iowa 923—Atherton v. Hoenig's Grocery, 86 N.W.2d 252, 249 Iowa 50—Osborn v. Klaber Bros., 287 N.W. 252, 227 Iowa 105.
Kan.—Marietta v. Springer, 392 P.2d 858, 193 Kan. 266—Little v. Butner, 348 P.2d 1022, 186 Kan. 75—**Corpus Juris cited in** Thogmartin v. Koppel, 65 P.2d 571, 572, 145 Kan. 347.
Ky.—Winn-Dixie Louisville, Inc. v. Smith, 372 S.W.2d 789—Winebarger v. Fee, 205 S.W.2d 1010, 305 Ky. 814—Lyle v. Megerle, 109 S.W.2d 598, 270 Ky. 227—F. W. Woolworth Co. v. Brown, 79 S.W.2d 362, 258 Ky. 29.
La.—Burns v. Child's Properties, Inc., App., 156 So.2d 610, writ denied 159 So.2d 284, 245 La. 567—Provost v. Great Atlantic & Pacific Tea Co., App., 154 So.2d 597—Cannon v. Great Atlantic & Pacific Tea Co., App., 146 So.2d 804—Grelle v. Patecek, App., 74 So.2d 349.
Mass.—Boehm v. S. S. Kresge Co., 145 N.E.2d 691, 336 Mass. 320—Greenfield v. Freedman, 103 N.E.2d 242, 328 Mass. 272.
Mich.—Muth v. W. P. Lahey's Inc., 61 N.W.2d 619, 338 Mich. 513—Steggall v. W. T. Knepp & Co., 217 N.W. 16, 241 Mich. 260.
Miss.—Louisiana Oil Corporation v. Davis, 158 So. 792, 172 Miss. 126.
Mo.—Wilkins v. Allied Stores of Missouri, 308 S.W.2d 623—Happy v. Walz, 213 S.W.2d 410, 358 Mo. 56. Gayer v. J. C. Penney Co., App., 326 S.W.2d 413—Sullivan v. S. S. Kresge Co., 163 S.W.2d 811, 236 Mo.App. 1191—Stewart v. George

## [Illustration 92]

## EXCERPTS FROM INDEX TO AMERICAN JURISPRUDENCE

**General Index**                    1275                         **Plasterer**

**PLACE OF WORK**

**Master and Servant** (this index)

**PLACE OF WORSHIP**

**Church** (this index)

**PLACER CLAIMS**

Gas and oil, GAS & O § 46
**Mines and Minerals** (this index)

**PLAGIARISM**

→ Infringement of copyright or right in literary
    property. **Literary Property and Copy-
    right** (this index)
Libel and slander, charge as, L & S § 164

**PLAGUE**

Guaranty by owner of sufficiency of, BLDG
CONTR § 29

> There is a four vol. index to
> Am.Jur.  Under the entry "Pla-
> giarism" there is a reference to
> Literary Property.

§ 13
Statute of frauds, of improvement project
and bid as sufficient memorandum within,
STAT OF F § 335
Streets. **Highways and Streets** (this index)

\*       \*       \*

Information, rights in, LIT PROP § 17
    copyright as protecting, LIT PROP § 24
    equitable relief to protect, LIT PROP § 21
    furnishing information to subscribers as a
      publication, LIT PROP § 65
    news agency, see News, infra
→ Infringement, LIT PROP §§ 66 et seq
    actions arising out of infringements, supra
    common law and statutory copyright, LIT
      PROP § 66
    criminal act, infringement as, LIT PROP § 96
    damages for, LIT PROP §§ 102 et seq
    definition, LIT PROP § 67
    importation of piratical articles, prohibited,
      LIT PROP § 93
    impounding infringing articles, LIT PROP
      § 106
    indicia of, LIT PROP § 69
    intent as element of, LIT PROP § 66
    joint liability for, LIT PROP § 70
    patent and copyright, analogy between, LIT
      PROP § 26
    persons liable for, LIT PROP § 70
    radio broadcasting, infra
    separate publications as separate infringe-
      ments, LIT PROP § 102
    specific works, infringement as to, LIT PROP
      §§ 71 et seq
    use of designation of copyrighted articles
      or production as infringement and un-
      fair competition, TRADEM § 136
    what constitutes, LIT PROP §§ 67–69
    wilful infringement for profit, LIT PROP § 96
**Injunctions** (this index)

construction of publisher's agreement, LIT
    PROP § 86
deposit of copies, time for, LIT PROP § 59
infringements, LIT PROP § 72
    evidence of, LIT PROP § 115
publication by delivery of copies to Secre-

> Under Topic Literary Proper-
> ty in the index, note sub-entry
> Infringement, Lit.Prop. Sec. 66.
>
> This refers to the volume of
> Am.Jur. that contains the topic
> Literary Property.

copies, right of author to, LIT PROP § 13
death of writer, personal representatives
    obtaining copyright after, LIT PROP § 38
depositing letters as violating author's
    right, LIT PROP § 81
destruction of, by recipient, LIT PROP § 16
dual right of property in, LIT PROP § 14
exhibition of letters by recipient, LIT PROP
    § 16
famous persons, value in letters of, LIT
    PROP § 16
holographic manuscripts, value as, LIT PROP
    § 16
infringement by wrongful publication of,

[Illustration 93]

## PAGE FROM 51 AM.JUR.2d

§ 44           LIS PENDENS           51 Am Jur 2d

such a purchaser to intervene.[11] It would seem, for example, that the holder of an unrecorded deed to property involved in litigation should, in general, be permitted to intervene in order to protect what rights he may have, under suc[h]....[12]

I[...] [...]erty
inv[...] [...]ion,
the [...] [...]ith
res[...] [...]hts
of l[...]

Am.Jur. is in the process of being replaced by Am.Jur.2d.

Until it is totally replaced, the four-volume General Index refers to Am.Jur. The volume containing Literary Property of Am.Jur. has been replaced by Am.Jur.2d.

This shows cross-reference to the form of title now used in Am.Jur.2d.

A[...] l in
litig[...] de-
cla[...] to
init[...] the
theory that the party to the action through whom the purchaser claims represents the purchaser not only in the original action, but also in proceedings aimed at reviewing the decision rendered in the trial court.[14]

### § 44. Enforcement of judgment against pendente lite transferees.

In appropriate circumstances, a judgment that binds pendente lite transferees pursuant to the doctrine of lis pendens may require such a transferee to convey, to the successful litigant, whatever interests the transferee may have acquired on the transfer.[15]

A writ of assistance has been recognized as a proper means for ousting a pendente lite purchaser or lessee who refuses to surrender possession after the entry of a judgment against the transferor or lessor.[16] Equitable proceedings have, under some circumstances, been used to acquire possession from a pendente lite purchaser.[17] And there is precedent for holding such a purchaser in contempt of court.[18]

**11.** Mellen v Moline Malleable Iron Works, 131 US 352, 33 L Ed 178, 9 S Ct 781; White v Pond Creek Coal Co. 201 Ky 212, 256 SW 30; Roberts v Cardwell, 154 Ky 483, 157 SW 711; Adrian v Republic Finance Corp. (Mo) 286 SW 95; Brown v Neustadt, 145 Okla 140, 292 P 73; Stout v Philippi Mfg. & Mercantile Co. 41 W Va 339, 23 SE 571.

**12.** Nuckles v Tallman, 106 Kan 264, 187 P 654.

**13.** Hadley v Corey, 137 Neb 204, 288 NW 826.

**14.** Stout v Philippi Mfg. & Mercantile Co. 41 W Va 339, 23 SE 571.

**15.** Powell v Campbell, 20 Nev 232, 20 P 156; Moffatt v Shepard, 2 Pinney (Wis) 66.

**16.** Lacassagne v Chapuis, 144 US 119, 36 L Ed 368, 12 S Ct 659; Terrell v Allison, 21 Wall (US) 289, 22 L Ed 634; Howard v Kennedy, 4 Ala 592; Wetherbee v Dunn, 36 Cal 147; Oetgen v Ross, 47 Ill 142; Powell v Campbell, 20 Nev 232, 20 P 156.

**17.** Lamb v Cramer, 285 US 217, 76 L Ed 715, 52 S Ct 315.

**18.** Lamb v Cramer, supra.

W. S.

## LITERARY PROPERTY AND COPYRIGHT

### See Copyright and Literary Property

990

[Illustration 94]

PAGE FROM TITLE COPYRIGHT AND LITERARY
PROPERTY IN AM.JUR.2d

---

# COPYRIGHT AND LITERARY PROPERTY

**Scope of Topic:** This article discusses rights of authors, artists, and proprietors in their literary, artistic, or other intellectual productions—the nature, extent, creation, and termination of such rights, the remedies against those who may infringe or in any manner interfere with the owner's rights in literary property, and the protection of those rights, both under the copyright statutes and the common law, including liabilities resulting from infringement and plagiarism.

**Treated elsewhere** are matters of unfair competition involving artistic or literary property (see TRADEMARKS, TRADE NAMES, AND UNFAIR COMPETITION); agreements, assignments, or licenses which operate to effect restraints of trade or which violate trust laws (see MONOPOLIES, COMBINATIONS, AND RESTRAINTS OF TRADE); property rights in architectural plans, drawings, and designs (see 5 Am Jur 2d, ARCHITECTS § 10), in "abstract books" (see 1 Am Jur 2d, ABSTRACTS OF TITLE § 2), and in data prepared by certified public accountants (see 1 Am Jur 2d, ACCOUNTANTS § 12); subjecting copyright interest to execution (see EXECUTIONS) or to a creditor's bill (see CREDITORS' BILLS); and taxation of copyrights (see TAXATION).

✦ **Table of Parallel References see p vii.** ✦

---

> The paragraph numbers in Am.Jur.2d are different from those in Am.Jur. The General Index to Am.Jur. indicated that Infringement started at Para. 66. It now is necessary to check the Table of Parallel References to find out where Infringement is covered in Am.Jur.2d.

**299**

## [Illustration 95]

## PAGE FROM 18 AM.JUR.2d

§ 107     COPYRIGHT AND LITERARY PROPERTY     18 Am Jur 2d

if insulation from legal liability could be secured by merely refraining from making inquiry.[1]

It is to be noted that in cases of accidental omission of a copyright notice, or its omission by mistake, the liability of one who innocently infringes the copyright property by reason of such omission is limited by the statute.[2]

### § 107. Indicia—common errors or peculiarities.

Similarity of the all copyrighted work does similarity results from or have the same comi suspicion until properly priation of the labor o stitutes legal infringeme the offense was commi hand, relief will be afl any similarity of langua said that in determinii righted work and an

> **This is a typical page from Am.Jur. Note how there is more textual material than in C.J.S. This is because Am.Jur. is based on selective reporting. Further decisions can be located through A.L.R. as indicated in footnote 4.**
>
> **The text should not be relied on as final authority but rather the cases cited should always be read and analyzed.**

common knowledge of the average reader, observer, spectator, or listener, is the standard of judgment which must be used.[5]

One of the most significant evidences of infringement exists in the presence, in an alleged infringing work, of the same errors and peculiarities that are to be found in the work said to be infringed.[6]

Proof of the comparative rate of speed which may be attained by various writers or editors, while of some value in determining unfair use, is by no means conclusive—that is, it is only one of many elements to be considered.[7]

### § 108. Amount copied—impression on observer.

The question of infringement of copyright is not one of quantity but of quality and value; it depends more upon the value of the extracts than upon their length.[8] The appropriation must be of a "substantial" or "material" part

> **Note reference to English decision.**

146 F d 1983, ... (CA10)

of the facts which were narrated from those common sources. Accordingly, there may be traced throughout the work of the alleged infringer a great similarity to the outline and plan of that of the complainant, and yet there may be no piracy. <u>Pike v Nichols (Eng)</u> LR 5 Ch 251.

4. West Pub. Co. v Lawyers' Co-op. Pub. Co. (CA2) 79 F 756, 35 LRA 400.

*Annotation:* 23 ALR2d 369–372, § 42.

Piracy is obviously very difficult to determine where it appears that two authors took a common subject and depended on authors open to both of them, and where the portions of the work which were said to resemble portions of the other might have been taken from those common authors to which each was at liberty to resort; for, when once it is established that there were common sources, it would naturally be expected that there would be great similarity in the statements

5. Stanley v Columbia Broadcasting System, Inc. (Cal) 208 P2d 9, subsequent op on reh 35 Cal 2d 653, 221 P2d 73, 23 ALR2d 216.

6. Callaghan v Myers, 128 US 617, 32 L ed 547, 9 S Ct 177; W. H. Anderson Co. v Baldwin Law Pub. Co. (CA6 Ohio) 27 F2d 82; Jeweler's Circular Pub. Co. v Keystone Pub. Co. (CA2) 281 F 83, 26 ALR 571, cert den 259 US 581, 66 L ed 1074, 42 S Ct 464.

7. West Pub. Co. v Lawyers' Co-op. Pub. Co. (CA2) 79 F 756, revg judgment (CC) 64 F 360.

8. Toksvig v Bruce Pub. Co. (CA7 Wis) 181 F2d 664.

**394**

## [Illustration 96]

## PAGE FROM POCKET SUPPLEMENT—18 AM.JUR.2d

COPYRIGHT AND LITERARY PROPERTY                    § 98

p 363, n 11—
**Annotation:** 2 ALR3d 1403 (prospective assignment of renewal rights in copyright).

§ 74. Ad inte[rim ... ] ts; effect of
riodical

p 364, n 19—
Where a no[vel] ... 293, 333, Copy-
abroad in the
ad interim reg[istration]
registration of ... of assignment
refused. Hoffe[...]
396 F2d 684, c[...]
89 S Ct 235.

§ 75. Prohibi[...] ... spective assign-
                                        [r]ight).
p 365, n 5—
**Practice Aids:** 9 AM JUR TRIALS 293, 375, Copyright Infringement Litigation.

§ 77. Generally

p 367, n 2—
**Practice Aids:** 9 AM JUR TRIALS 293, 335, Copyright Infringement Litigation.

p 367, n 7—
For purposes of determining the date of publication, and for certain other purposes, a re-
production of a sound recording shall be considered to be a copy thereof. 17 USC § 26 (1971
amendment also defines sound recordings and re-
productions of sound recordings).

§ 79. What constitutes general or limited
publication

§ 81. — Delivery of lecture; performance of
drama, play, etc.

p 370, n 4—
Williams v Weisser, 273 **Cal** App 2d 726, 78
Cal Rptr 542, 38 ALR3d 761.
**Annotation:** 38 ALR3d 779, 789, § 5.

§ 85. Statutory copyright

§ 87. — Omission of copyright notice by
mistake or accident; omission or removal from copies distributed by third
person

p 376, n 6—
**Practice Aids:** 9 AM JUR TRIALS 293, 339, Copyright Infringement Litigation.

§ 89. Generally

p 377, n 1—
**Annotation:** 2 ALR3d 1403 (prospective assignment of renewal rights in copyright).
**Practice Aids:** 9 AM JUR TRIALS 293, 330, Copyright Infringement Litigation.

p 378, n 5—
The distinction between an assignment and a
license is that by an assignment the ownership
of the copyright is vested in the assignee, while
by a license the licensee acquires the privilege of
publishing, but no proprietary rights in the copyright. American Press Asso. v Daily Story Pub. Co.
(CA7 Ill) 120 F 766, app dismd 193 US 675, 48 L
ed 2d 842, 24 S Ct 852.

[18 Am Jur 2d Supp]—2

§ 90. Requisites of valid **assignment; acknowledgment**

Am.Jur.2d is kept up-to-date by annual
cumulative pocket supplements that keep current the information located in the bound volume.
   Note the references to Am.Jur. Proof of
Fact and Am.Jur.Trials.

§ 95. Motion-picture, radio, and television
rights

p 383, n 11—
The copyright owner's broad assignment of the
right "to copyright, vend, license and exhibit such
motion picture photoplays throughout the world"
includes the right to license a broadcaster to exhibit the copyrighted motion picture by a telecast
without a further grant by the copyright owner.
Bartsch v Metro-Goldwyn-Mayer, Inc. (CA2 NY)
391 F2d 150 (applying New York law), cert den
393 US 826, 21 L Ed 2d 96, 89 S Ct 86.

§ 96. Duration and termination of rights
under assignment or license

p 385—*Add paragraph following note* 6:
Where a copyright is owned by two or more
persons, their joint action is required to grant
exclusive license rights, joint action is also
required to undo what was done; consequently rescission of the contract cannot be
obtained by one co-owner alone.[6.5]

n 6.5—Denker v Twentieth Century-Fox Film Corp.
10 NY2d 339, 223 NYS2d 193, 179 NE2d 336,
3 ALR3d 1292.

§ 97. Compulsory licensing of phonograph
records and other mechanical reproduc-
tions of musical works

p 385, n 8—
17 USC § 101(e) now provides, in part, that
interchangeable parts, such as discs or tapes for
use in mechanical music-producing machines
adapted to reproduce copyrighted musical works,
shall be considered copies of the copyrighted musical
works which they serve to reproduce mechanically
for the purposes of 17 USC §§ 101, 106, and 109,
and the unauthorized manufacture, use, or sale of
such interchangeable parts shall constitute an infringement of the copyrighted work rendering the
infringer liable in accordance with all provisions
of Title 17, USC, dealing with infringements of
copyright and, in a case of wilful infringement for
profit, to criminal prosecution pursuant to 17 USC
§ 104.

§ 98. Generally

p 387, n 4—
**Practice Aids:** 20 AM JUR PROOF OF FACTS 727,
PLAGIARISM IN NARRATIVE FICTION.

17

[Illustration 97]

## PAGE FROM AM.JUR. PROOF OF FACTS

---

## PLAGIARISM IN NARRATIVE FICTION*

### I. INTRODUCTORY COMMENT

#### A. IN GENERAL

After status of law has been determined in Am. Jur.2d this set can be examined to determine the proof required to uphold an infringement action.

This article in Am.Jur. Proof of Facts could be located from the index volume to the set; or from footnote reference in Am.Jur.2d. It consists of 95 pages and sets forth in detail all the elements a lawyer needs in preparing a case for trial.

#### C. TESTS OF PLAGIARISM

---

\* Contributed by Clancy Carlile. Editing and legal material by Daniel J. Penofsky of the publisher's editorial staff.

**727**

[Illustration 97–a]

## PAGE FROM AM.JUR. PROOF OF FACTS

§ 49                         Plagiarism

Silber, Edward:  **Use of Literary Expert in Literary Piracy.**  Copyright Law Symposium Number Nine, N.Y., 1958.

White, Harold:  **Plagiarism and Imitation During the English Renaissance.** Harvard University Press, Cambridge, 1935.

Yankwich, Leon R.:  **Originality and the Law of Intellectual Property.** Copyright and Related Topics.  University of California Press, 1964.

---

## II. PROOFS WITH AUTHORITIES

**§ 49.  Proof of Similarity in Story, Plot, Characters and Expression—Testimony for Plaintiff**

**ELEMENTS OF PROOF**

Proof of the following facts and circumstances tends to show that the particular combination and arrangement of literary components found in defendant's novel were substantially and materially copied from plaintiff's novel:

— Similar or identical stories

    — subject matter

— Similar or identical themes

    — same underlying idea ⸢
      tion and purpose to th⸥

    — both stories have san⸥

— Similar or identical plots

    — incidents

    — groupings of incidents

    — causal unity between incidents and groups of incidents

    — structural devices

        — patterns

        — point of view

> **A page showing how Am. Jur. Proof of Facts points out elements of proof necessary in trial.**

[Illustration 98]

## PAGE FROM VOLUME 9, AM.JUR. TRIALS

9 AM JUR TRIALS

*Article Outline*

### I. INTRODUCTION (§§ 1–7)

> After determining the law in Am.Jur. and methods of proof in Am.Jur. P.O.F., Am.Jur. Trials, may be used to prepare for the trial of the case.
>
> This set is in 19 volumes. Each volume consists of substantial articles on different topics written by experienced trial attorneys. These articles can be located by the index to Am.Jur. Trials or by footnote references in Am.Jur.2d or Am.Jur. P.O.F.

### V. TIMING; DECLARATORY RELIEF (§§ 53–54)

### VI. PARTIES (§§ 55–61)

### VII. SELECTING THE REMEDY (§§ 62–73)

### VIII. PLEADINGS (§§ 74–80)

### IX. PRETRIAL MOTIONS (§§ 81–86)

### X. DISCOVERY (§§ 87–89)

### XI. SETTLEMENT (§§ 90–92)

### XII. TRIAL (§§ 93–112)

- A. GENERALLY (§§ 93–96)
- B. PLAINTIFF'S CASE—ESTABLISHING LIABILITY (§§ 97–102)
- C. DEFENDANT'S CASE—ESTABLISHING NONLIABILITY (§§ 103–108)
- D. PROOF OF DAMAGES (§§ 109–111)
- E. CONCLUSION OF TRIAL (§ 112)

---

### I. INTRODUCTION

- A. IN GENERAL
    - § 1. Scope of Article
    - § 2. Preliminary Background
    - § 3. — Common-Law and Statutory Copyrights Compared

**294**

**[Illustration 98–a]**

## PAGE FROM VOLUME 9, AM.JUR. TRIALS

COPYRIGHT INFRINGEMENT LITIGATION         § 47

§ 47. FACT INVESTIGATION

In investigating his client's claim of infringement,[6] with regard to the elen[  ]ertain the name of tl[  ]ing work. Either the [  A page from the article of infringe-  ]oy should then questi[  ment.  ]urce from which the [  ] that the source was plaintiff's copyrighted work. Usually, this mode of investigation is left to special investigators.

As for the element of copying, some of the circumstances from which an inference of copying may be drawn are the following:

     ☑

     ☐ 1.   The reproduction in the allegedly infringing work of errors occurring in the copyrighted work.

           Next to direct evidence, this is the most persuasive proof of copying.[7] However, where the errors are drawn from a common source in the public domain, the inference of copying is negated.[8]

     ☐ 2.   Indications that a concentrated effort was made to make various moderate distinctions between the copyrighted work and the alleged infringing work.[9]

           Subtle changes in phraseology or the manner of expressing a thought, variations in color without changing the outline of the design, inversion or substitution of words, or minor changes in melodies fall into this category.

     ☐ 3.   Reproduction of fictitious names or places or of errors that have been intentionally incorporated in the work.[10]

---

6. For methods of case investigation generally, see 1 AM JUR TRIALS, INVESTIGATING THE CIVIL CASE; GENERAL PRINCIPLES p. 357 et seq.

7. Hayden v Chalfant Press, Inc. (1960, CA9 Cal) 281 F2d 543.

8. C. S. Hammond & Co. v International College Globe, Inc. (1962, DC NY) 210 F Supp 206.

9. Joshua Meier Co. v Albany Novelty Mfg. Co. (1956, CA2 NY) 236 F2d 144.

10. R. L. Polk & Co. v Musser (1952, ED Pa) 92 US Pat Quart 124; R. R. Donnelley & Sons Co. v Haber (1942, DC NY) 43 F Supp 456.

## SECTION D.  METHODS OF CITATION

Encyclopedias may be cited by the titles.  If this procedure is followed, cite the volume, title, section number and, preferably, the appropriate footnote, since several points of laws may be discussed in the section.  Occasionally, individual volumes are replaced by revisions (called replacement volumes); therefore, to avoid confusion between the volumes, it is sound policy to note the publication date of the cited volume.

88 C.J.S., Trial § 315, n. 67 (1955).

20 Am.Jur., Evidence § 1199, n. 15 (1939).

17 Ind.L.E., Jury § 55, n. 42 (1959).

18 N.Y.Jur., Elections § 269, n. 14 (1961).

25A C.J.S., Death § 54, n. 56 (Cum.Ann.Part 1966).

54 Am.Jur., Trusts § 467 (Cum.Supp.1966).

If the subject heading is not to be given, cite to the specific page.

88 C.J.S. 834 (1955).

20 Am.Jur. 1051 (1939).

Some courts prefer both section and page references.

20 C.J.S. 45, Corporations § 1828 (1940).

The common practice, however, is to cite by title and section.

20 C.J.S. Corporations, § 1828.

1 Am.Jur.2d Administrative Law § 227.

---

## SECTION E.  SUMMARY

### 1.  Corpus Juris Secundum

    a.  *Scope*

        (1) Attempts to restate the entire body of American case law (substantive and adjective), citing all reported cases since publication of the title in *Corpus Juris*.  Where there are earlier cases in point, footnote references are given to C.J.  The text supersedes the text of C.J.

        (2) Includes some discussion of federal and state statutory law.

        (3) Definitions of words and phrases and legal maxims are interfiled alphabetically with the essay topics.

   b.  *Arrangement*

        (1) Alphabetically by titles.

        (2) "Law Chart" is an outline of the titles, with all related topics grouped together under seven major divisions.  (General Index, vol. 1.)

        (3) Scope-note—delimits and identifies the content of a title.

        (4) Analysis—appears after scope-note, giving conceptual breakdown of the topic.

   c.  *Indexes*

        (1) General Index—arranged alphabetically by broad descriptive and legal terms.

        (2) Volume Indexes—more detailed subject and fact indexes.

   d.  *Supplementation*

        (1) Cumulative (includes all preceding issues) annual pocket supplements to volumes.

        (2) Replacement volumes.

## 2.  American Jurisprudence

   a.  *Scope*

        (1) Textual statement of substantive and adjective law, with selected case references.  Supersedes *Ruling Case Law.*

        (2) Includes some discussion of federal and state statutory law.

        (3) Definitions of words and phrases are indexed in the General and Volume Indexes under "Words and Phrases."

        (4) Footnote references to A.L.R. annotations, texts and law journal articles.

   b.  *Arrangement*

        (1) Alphabetically by titles.

        (2) Scope of titles—explained in introductory statement under each article.

        (3) Analysis—topical breakdown precedes text of article.

   c.  *Indexes*

        (1) General Index—integrates material in the volume indexes;  more comprehensive;  subdivided by facts and legal phrases.

        (2) Volume Indexes—subdivided by facts and legal terms; arranged by titles in a volume and subdivided under the titles.

d. *Supplementation*

(1) Cumulative annual pocket supplements to volumes.

(2) New matter in the pocket supplements is indexed in the pocket supplements to the General Index.

## 3. American Jurisprudence 2d

a. *Scope*

(1) Textual statement of substantive and adjective law, with selected case references. Supersedes Am.Jur. as related titles are published.

(2) Greater emphasis on federal statutory laws, federal procedural rules and Uniform State Laws.

(3) State statutory law is treated broadly.

(4) Definitions of words and phrases are noted under the words and phrases which are interfiled alphabetically in a Volume Index.

(5) Footnote references to A.L.R. annotations and research aids.

(6) Table of Parallel References in each volume identifies the location of sections of the original edition in Am.Jur.2d.

(7) Table of Statutes Cited in each volume covers *United States Code*, Federal Rules of Procedure and Uniform Laws.

(8) *Desk Book.* (See Section A3, above.)

b. *Arrangement*

(1) Alphabetically by titles.

(2) A scope-note, cross references, notations to federal aspects of the law and an analysis of the section headings precede the text pertaining to a title.

c. *Indexes*

(1) General Index—to be published.

(2) Volume Indexes arranged by topics in a volume with subheadings under each topic.

d. *Supplementation*

(1) Cumulative annual pocket supplements.

(2) Replacement volumes.

e. Citations to other sets of the Total Client Library Service.

## 4. Local Encyclopedias

For an outline of the generally applicable features of local encyclopedias, see Section B, above.

# Chapter 16

## LEGAL PERIODICALS AND INDEXES

### SECTION A.  PERIODICALS

The legal periodical is an important and useful secondary authority, containing articles, frequently by specialists, on specific subjects of the law.  The articles are either critical or expository and their scholarly interpretations are relied upon frequently by American courts and lawyers.[1]

Periodicals may be classified as follows:  (1) law school periodicals, (2) periodicals published by private companies and (3) association publications.

The law school periodical has assumed a position of significance in the field of American legal research.  Many law schools sponsor legal periodicals with editorial direction stemming from the student body, guided by faculty advisors.  Most law school periodicals contain comments and notes written by students on current judicial opinions and legislative enactments.  With the end of World War II, this area of research was reactivated in the law schools which ceased their publications during the War.  Also, a number of new law school periodicals have made their appearance since 1945.

The vast majority of law school periodicals are general publications and no emphasis is placed on any specific subjects of study. A few concentrate on certain fields.  The *George Washington Law Review* and the *Georgetown Law Journal* specialize in public law. The *Tulane Law Review* is devoted in the main to comparative law. The *Texas Law Review* and the *University of Colorado Law Review* contain articles on mining law.

A new trend in law schools is to publish more than one review. The Harvard Law School, for example, publishes the *Harvard Law Review* in the traditional format and now publishes also three other periodicals, all edited by students (*Harvard Civil Rights-Civil Liberties Law Review, Harvard International Law Journal, Harvard Journal on Legislation.*)  Several other law schools now also publish

---

[1] For a discussion of the increased citation of legal periodical articles by the Supreme Court of the United States, see Newland, Legal Periodicals and the U. S. Supreme Court, 3 Midwest J.Pol.Sci. 58 (1959).

Law schools reviews have even been attacked by some members of Congress as having an insidious influence on the United States Supreme Court.  See Congressional Record 103:16160–61, (1957).

similar types of periodicals in addition to their usual law school review.

In recent years a number of significant journals were formed which cover special subjects. *The Natural Resources Journal* is published by the University of New Mexico Law School. *The Journal of Law and Economics* is sponsored by the University of Chicago Law School. The University of Louisville School of Law is responsible for the *Journal of Family Law*. The *Boston College Industrial and Commercial Law Review* includes the fields of bankruptcy, corporations, the Uniform Commercial Code, commercial law, labor relations and taxation.

Some periodicals, published by private companies, are also devoted to special subjects. *The Labor Law Journal* is a Commerce Clearing House, Inc., publication. *Corporate Practice Commentator* is one of several specialized periodicals sponsored by Callaghan & Co. *Defense Law Journal* is a product of the Allen Smith Co.

Several journals, published by law schools, devote each number to a legal subject. Each issue is called a "symposium." *Law and Contemporary Problems*, published by the Duke University School of Law, is the oldest of these publications. Other journals may intermittently devote an issue to a subject.

Association publications vary as to kind and quality. The bar association journals generally contain articles and newsworthy information of special interest to practicing attorneys. The *American Bar Association Journal* is the monthly publication of the national association. *The Practical Lawyer* is a popular magazine for the general practitioner, published by the Joint Committee on Continuing Legal Education of the American Law Institute and the American Bar Association. State and local bar associations also publish journals of local interest.

Some associations of scholarly specialists publish periodicals, e. g., *American Journal of Comparative Law*. A few federal agencies have their own bar, and the latter publish journals, e. g., *I.C.C. Practitioners' Journal*.

In passing, it should be noted that the bar associations also publish reports, committee studies, proceedings and other materials. In 1942, an *Index to State Bar Association Reports and Proceedings*, also including the American Bar Association, Association of the Bar of the City of New York, Canadian Bar Association and the New York County Lawyers' Association reports, was prepared under the auspices of the American Association of Law Libraries.

## SECTION B.  PERIODICAL INDEXES

Individual volumes of legal journals are indexed, and some periodicals have cumulative indexes to the sets; however, the need for comprehensive legal periodical indexes, covering Anglo-American journal literature, is obvious.  This need is partially met by the following comprehensive indexes:

**1.  Jones-Chipman Index to Legal Periodicals,** 1886–1937, 6 vols.

This index to English language periodicals is arranged by subject and author.  Its coverage is as follows: volume 1, prior to 1887; volume 2, 1887–1898; volume 3, 1898–1907; volume 4, 1908–1922; volume 5, 1923–1932; and volume 6, 1932–1937.  It ceased publication in 1937.

**2.  Index to Legal Periodicals,** 1908 to date

This current index to many American legal journals and substantially all British periodicals is published by The H. W. Wilson Co. in cooperation with the American Association of Law Libraries. The current numbers of the *Index to Legal Periodicals* are published monthly, except September, and are cumulated semi-annually, annually and for three-year periods.

Volumes 1–12 (1926–1961) are arranged by subject and author sections and contain book review indexes and tables of cases commented upon in the periodicals.  The subject entries give full information, including the citations to the periodical articles; however, the author entries are brief and merely refer the user to the appropriate subject section for citations to articles.

As previously indicated, the Author Section refers the user to the subjects under which articles by the author appear in the Subject Section.  The Author entry is a brief cross reference to the Subject Section.  Since volume 6 of the *Index to Legal Periodicals*, the Author Indexes include a letter in parenthesis following the subject. Articles such as "a" and "the", which introduce the title, are ignored for indexing purposes.  To illustrate the Author Section, the writings of the late Judge Charles E. Clark are noted as they appear in the Author Index to the *Index to Legal Periodicals*, 1949–1952, volume 9, as follows:

**Clark, Charles E.**
> Biography (Borchard, Moore)
>
> Book Reviews, (Atkinson, Bunn, Connecticut, Dobie, Hays, Hendel, McCormick, Michael, Nims, Vanderbilt, Virtue)

Courts IV—Connecticut

(C, F)

Eminent Domain (P)

Interpretation and Construction (S)

Judges (D)

Practice and Procedure (J, T)

Judge Clark wrote two articles on "Practice and Procedure" for law journals. The title of the first begins with the letter "J" and that of the second starts with the letter "T." Refer to the Subject Index under "Practice and Procedure." Look under "J." The first article by Judge Clark is "Judicial Council and rule-making power: dissent and protest. * * * Syracuse L.Rev. 1:346–68 Spring '50."

Note that biographies in law journals appear in the Subject Index under the main headings: "Biography: Collective" and "Biography: Individual." The units are arranged alphabetically under the names of the people written about. Thus, Judge Clark's article on Edwin Borchard in 60 Yale L.J. 1071 (1951) is cited under "Borchard, Edwin M."

Since volume 13, 1961–1964, the *Index* combines the Author and Subject Sections into one alphabetical arrangement. Biographies now are included in the combined indexes under "Biography: collective" and "Biography: individual". The Subject and Author Index (combined) is shown in Illustration 100 below.

Currently, the Index is divided into the following units: (1) Subject and Author Index, (2) Table of Cases Commented Upon, and (3) Book Review Index.

Cases which are noted or commented upon in law journals are listed by their names in the Tables of Cases Section. The listing includes references to journal notes. The case notes also are listed now in the *Index* under appropriate subjects and the subheading "Cases". Prior to October, 1963, case notes were interfiled with other headings by subjects.[2]

---

[2] The omission of the titles of case notes since October, 1963, means that the points involved in the cases can no longer be elicited through examination of the titles in the *Index*. The listing of cases under active topics in the triennial cumulations will be formidable and uninformative. For example, the annual cumulation for 1964–1965 lists 20 cases and 26 case notes under them for the topic "Municipal Corporations" without any revealing descriptions. The triennial cumulation of 1964–1967 should contain three times this number of cases under that topic. If one is interested in discussion on municipal indebtedness, then notes relating to all listed cases must be examined to learn whether any apply to that problem. This search could be both time-consuming and fruitless. See Fratcher, The Decline of the Index to Legal Periodicals, 18 J.Legal Ed. 297, 301 (1966).

Book reviews in law journals are listed under the name of the author of the book in the Book Review Index of the *Index to Legal Periodicals.* A listing under the author and the title of the book gives the name of the reviewer and the citation of the book review. For example,

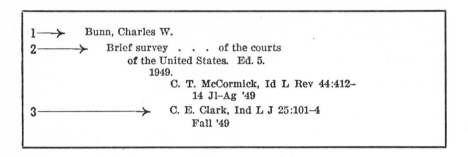

1. Author.

2. Title of book.

3. Reviewer and citation.

For book reviews published by a reviewer, consult the Author Indexes prior to 1961 under the name of the reviewer. Reference to the name of the author follows the reviewer's name. Complete citations to book reviews are given under the author's name and book title. Since 1961, there are no book-review listings under a reviewer's name.

At the beginning of each issue and cumulation, the *Index to Legal Periodicals* contains a table of Abbreviations of Periodicals Indexed and a List of Periodicals Indexed. Since 1955, a List of Subject Headings used in the *Index* is also included. These lists accentuate two significant weaknesses of the *Index:* the periodical coverage of the *Index* is limited, and its subject headings are not sufficiently subdivided and refined. The former defect results in omissions; the latter, in frequent difficulty in locating a desired article.[3]

The volumes of the *Index to Legal Periodicals* for 1908–1925 are annual publications which are not cumulated. Therefore, to locate periodical literature for the period prior to 1926, it is more convenient to use *Jones-Chipman's Index.*

---

[3] For a criticism of the editorial policy of the *Index to Legal Periodicals* see, Fratcher, The Decline of the Index to Legal Periodicals, 18 J.Legal Ed. 297 (1966). A defense of the *Index to Legal Periodicals* is presented in Drummond, The Continued Improvement of the Index to Legal Periodicals, 19 J.Legal Ed. 78 (1966).

### 3.  Index to Periodical Articles Related to Law [4]

This publication is a quarterly, listing articles of legal interest that in the opinion of the Editors are of research value. It includes all articles in English from publications throughout the world.

It is arranged by subject, with a separate index for authors and periodicals included. The last issue of each volume is cumulated. There is also a Ten-Year Cumulation for the years 1958–1968. In the future there will be a cumulated volume every five years.

### 4.  Index to Foreign Legal Periodicals

Since 1960, the Institute of Advanced Legal Studies of the University of London, in co-operation with the American Association of Law Libraries, has published an *Index to Foreign Legal Periodicals*. It covers a wide range of journals dealing with International Law (Public and Private), Comparative Law and the Municipal Law of all countries of the world other than the United States, the British Isles and nations of the British Commonwealth whose legal systems are based on the common law. It mainly complements and, to a limited extent, duplicates the *Index to Legal Periodicals*.

The *Index to Foreign Legal Periodicals* is published quarterly with annual and triennial cumulations.

Articles and book reviews of two or more pages in length are indexed in the publication.

Titles of articles are given in the language of publication, transliterated for those languages not using the Roman alphabet.

The subject headings are alphabetically arranged and reasonably follow the established headings of the *Index to Legal Periodicals*.

The publication is divided into the following units: (1) subject index; (2) geographical index; grouping, by country or region, the topics of the articles listed in the subject index; (3) book review index; and (4) author index.

As in the *Index to Legal Periodicals*, the author-index entries refer to the subject index where the notations are complete.

––––––

## SECTION C.  PERIODICAL ABRIDGMENTS

### 1.  Law Review Digest

This bi-monthly digest contains selected, condensed articles from the legal periodical literature. It began publication in November, 1950.

––––––

[4] Edited by Roy M. Mersky and J. Myron Jacobstein. Glanville Publications, Dobbs Ferry, New York.

## 2. Monthly Digest of Legal Articles

Selected legal articles from 200 periodicals are condensed and published monthly, closely following the words and style of the original writers. It began publication in 1969.

## 3. The Monthly Digest of Tax Articles

This monthly periodical presents significant current tax articles in abridged form. The publication started in October, 1950.

## 4. Commerce Clearing House, Federal Tax Articles

This monthly loose-leaf reporter of the Commerce Clearing House, Inc., which began publication in 1962, contains summaries of articles on federal (income, estate, gift and excise) taxes appearing in legal, accounting, business and related periodicals. Proceedings and papers delivered at major tax institutes are also noted. The contents are arranged by Internal Revenue Code section numbers. To find articles on federal tax problems, refer to the division entitled "Articles by Code Section," using the section number of the Internal Revenue Code. Each item is preceded by a decimal number which combines with the Code section for referencing. Descriptions of recent articles are included under Code section numbers in the division entitled "Current Articles by Code Section." To locate articles on a subject, consult the "Index by Topic" and the "Current Index by Topic." Articles are listed by author names in the "Index by Author" and the "Current Index by Author." Each basic unit has a "Current" materials or a "Current" index section. To identify the publishers of the articles, check the periodicals covered in the Reporter under the "List of Publications" division. Volume one covers the years, 1954–67, volume 2, 1968 to date.

## 5. Shepard's Law Review Citations

The edition of Shepard's started in 1968. It indicates each time a law review article has been cited by a court or in a law review since 1957. It kept up-to-date by a bi-monthly cumulative supplement.

## SECTION D.  ILLUSTRATIONS FOR LEGAL PERIODICALS

PROBLEM: Find articles, case notes, and case comments dealing with negligence action causing mental distress without physical impact.

### Illustrations

[Illustration 99]

## PAGE FROM LIST OF SUBJECT HEADINGS USED IN THE INDEX TO LEGAL PERIODICALS

LIST OF SUBJECT HEADINGS                                    xxvii

DISTRESS. See Landlord and tenant
DISTRICT and prosecuting attorneys
DIVIDENDS
DIVORCE and separation
    *See also* Alimony and maintenance; Annulment; Breach of promise; Desertion; Domestic relations; Settlements; Support of dependents
DOCTORS. See Physicians and surgeons
DOCUMENTS and records
    *See also* Court records
DOMESTIC relations
    *See also* Husband and wife; Infants; Parent and child; Support of dependents
DOMESTIC relations courts. See Family courts
DOMICILE and residence
DOUBLE jeopardy
DOUBLE taxation
    *See also* Tax treaties
DOWER and curtesy
DRAFT, Military. See Military service
DRAINAGE
    *See also* Water and watercourses
DRUGGISTS. See Pharmacists
DRUGS. See Food drug cosmetic law
DRUNKENNESS
    *See also* Blood tests
DUE process of law
DURESS
    *See also* Undue influence

EASEMENTS
    *See also* Adjoining landowners; Dedication to public use; Prescription; Rights of way
EAVESDROPPING
ECCLESIASTICAL law
    *See also* Churches
ECONOMICS
EDUCATION
    *See also* Colleges and universities; Legal education; Schools and school districts
ELECTIONS
ELECTRICITY
EMBEZZLEMENT
EMIGRATION and immigration
    *See also* Deportation
EMINENT domain
→    *See also* Dedication to public use; Expropriation and nationalization; Valuation
EMPLOYER and employee. See Master and servant
EMPLOYERS' liability. See Workmen's compensation
EMPLOYMENT. See Unemployment
ENEMY aliens
    *See also* Trading with the enemy
ENEMY property
ENFORCEMENT of judgments abroad
ENGINEERS. See Architects and engineers
ENTERTAINMENT
    *See also* Motion pictures; Sports
ENTRAPMENT
ENVIRONMENTAL control
EQUAL protection
EQUITABLE conversion
EQUITABLE remedies
EQUITABLE servitudes
EQUITY
    *See also* Discovery; Injunctions; International adjudication; Quasi-contracts; Restitution; Specific performance; Unjust enrichment

ESCHEAT
ESCROW
    *See also* Deeds
ESPIONAGE
ESTATE by entirety
    *See also* Husband and wife
ESTATE planning
    *See also* Inheritance estate and gift taxes
ESTATE tax. See Inheritance estate and gift taxes
ESTATES. See Estate planning; Inheritance

A list of subject headings used in the Index to Legal Periodicals will be found at the beginning of each volume of the Index to Legal Periodicals.

It should always be consulted first to determine which subjects are in it.

Note how "Emotional Distress" is not used as a subject heading.

In such instances, a subject heading included in the list must be chosen.

In this instance, "Negligence" seems the most useful.

bate law and practice; Trusts and trustees; Wills
EXPATRIATION
    *See also* Citizens and citizenship
EXPERT witnesses
    *See also* Field of expert (e.g., Ballistics)
EXPLOSIONS
EXPORTS and imports
    *See also* Commerce; International trade
EXPROPRIATION and nationalization
    *See also* Confiscation; Eminent domain; Government ownership
EXTORTION
EXTRADITION
EXTRATERRITORIALITY
    *See also* Diplomatic privileges and immunities

FACTORIES
    *See also* Labor law
FACTORS
FAIR employment practices. See Discrimination
FAIR trade
    *See also* Restraint of trade; Unfair competition
FAIR trial. See Due process of law; Freedom of the press
FALSE imprisonment
FALSE pretenses
FAMILY courts
FAMILY law. See Domestic relations; Husband and wife; Parent and child

[Illustration 100]

## PAGE FROM INDEX TO LEGAL PERIODICALS

### 1967–1970

---

**SUBJECT AND AUTHOR INDEX**      583

**NEGLIGENCE**—*Continued*

Down with foreseeability! Of thin skulls and rescuers. A. M. Linden. Can B Rev 47:545 D '69

Duty concept in farm accidents in Iowa: when does a wiggle become a wobble? M. G. Blackburn. Drake L Rev 18:155 My '69

Duty of reasonable care to third persons on the premises. Wash & Lee L Rev 26:128 Spring '69

Duty to act: the French experience and the New York jurisdiction. NYU Intra L Rev 23:87 Ja '68

Duty to licensees in California: in support of open adoption of restatement 2d of torts §342. G. N. Rosenkrantz. U San Francisco L Rev 2:230 Ap '68

Duty to warn extended to non-commercial vendor selling chattel "as is". Wash L Rev 43:484 D '67

Effect of Hedley Byrne. B. Coote. NZ U L Rev 2:263 Ap '67

Elimination of vicarious responsibility in regulatory offences. B. Fisse. Aust L J 42:199, 250 O-N '68

→ Emotional distress negligently inflicted upon spectator plaintiff—a suggested model for identifying protected plaintiffs based on relational interest. Utah L Rev 1969:396 Ap '69

Employer responsibility for negligent misrepresentations. Temp L Q 41:185 Winter '68

Errant golf ball: a legal hazard. G. M. Kelly. NZ L J 1968:301, 322, 346 Jl 23-Ag 20 '68

Escaping Borstal boys and the immunity of Office. C. J. Hamson. Camb L J 27:273 N '69

Evaluation of changes in the medical standard of care. Vand L Rev 23:729 My '70

Evidence—party must present sufficient evidence to place another party's physical condition in controversy as required by civil practice law and rules section 3121—party claiming physician-patient privilege has burden of showing that privilege applies and has not been waived—party who affirmatively asserts his physical condition in controversy waives privilege. Albany L Rev 34:481 Winter '70

Exercise based upon empirical data: liability for harm caused by stolen automobiles. C. J. Peck. Wis L Rev 1969:909 '69

Extension of liability to service contracts—emphasizing the furnishing of unfit blood for transfusion. S. Van Meveren. Am Bus L J 6:517 Fall '68

Factors that limit the negligence liability of a corporate executive or director. U Ill L F 1967:341 Summer '67

Failure to inform as medical malpractice. Vand L Rev 23:754 My '70

Failure to object to an irregularity. M. Newark. Crim L R 1968:310 Je '68

Failure to remove ignition key—the key to liability. SD L Rev 14:115 Winter '69

Fate of Sterling Trusts Corp. v. Postma. E. R. Alexander. Ottawa L Rev 2:441 Spring '68

Fault principle: a sketch of its development in tort law during the nineteenth century. S. J. M. Donnelly. Syracuse L Rev 18:728 Summer '67

Federal employers' liability act—a plea for reform. St Louis U L J 14:112 Fall '69

Federal medical care recovery act—the collateral source rule of damages and the relationship of the parties. H. J. Lewis jr. Ala Law 31:177 Ap '70

Foresight at sea. P. S. James. J Bus L 1968: 303 O '68

Giorgi v. Pacific Gas and Electric Co. (72 Cal Rptr 119): the "fireman's rule" in California, an anachronism? U San Francisco L Rev 4:125 O '69

Gleitman v. Cosgrove ([NJ] 227 A 2d 689]: a study of legal method. Maine L Rev 20: 143 '68

Gross negligence: excessive speed and the guest statute. U Fla L Rev 22:326 Fall '69

Gross negligence in Michigan—how gross is it? G. H. Morris. Wayne L Rev 16:457 Spring '70

Guest passenger discrimination. D. Gibson. Alberta L Rev 6:211 '68

Guest statute applicability to motor driven golf carts. Wash & Lee L Rev 25:293 Fall '68

Handling the excess coverage situation for the insurer. J. H. Locke, J. R. Austin. Ins Counsel J 36:60 Ja '69

Hard laws make bad cases—lots of them (the California guest statute) E. L. Lascher. Santa Clara Law 9:1 Fall '68

Hedley Byrne and the eager business man. M. Dean. Modern L Rev 31:322 My '68

Hedley Byrne to Rondel v. Worsley ([1967] 3 W L R 1666) P. M. North. New L J 118: 137, 148 F 8-15 '68

Hospital liability for negligence. R. L. Hanson, R. E. Stromberg. Hastings L J 21:1 N '69

Hospital operating room and the law. B. J. Ficarra. Med Tr T Q 16:13, 25 S-D '69

Impact of limitation periods on actionability in negligence. J. P. S. McLaren. Alberta L Rev 7:247 '69

> Note how each article is listed alphabetically by title. Consequently, each title must be read to determine if the article may be pertinent to the topic under search.

Informed consent to surgery—substitution of patient's subjective understanding of nature and risks of procedure for objective reasonable man test? Dick L Rev 71:675 Summer '67

Insurance—breach of a policy condition is no defense under the Georgia motor common carriers act. Ga SB J 6:225 N '69

Intent in civil assault and battery in Nebraska. Neb L Rev 46:862 Jl '67

Interspousal immunity in Indiana. Ind Legal F 3:297 Fall '69

Intrafamily immunity doctrine: the breached wall. M. M. Maliner. Forum 5:58 O '69

Invitee status in Louisiana. La L Rev 27:796 Je '67

Is criminal negligence a defensible basis for penal liability? Buffalo L Rev 16:749 Spring '68

Is the Wagon Mound good law in Canada? J. E. Côté. Can B Rev 47:292 My '69

Issue estoppel and negligence on the highway. D. S. Kelly. Aust L J 41:12, 46 My-Je '67

Judicial nullification of guest statutes. So Calif L Rev 41:884 Summer '68

Knowledge and exemption in occupier's liability. P. L. Bradbury. New L J 119:520 Je 5 '69

Land occupiers liability to business invitees for slip and fall injuries: recent developments in Iowa. Ia L Rev 54:659 F '69

Landlord-tenant—exculpatory clauses: exculpation contrary to public policy where landlord is public housing authority. Wash L Rev 44:498 Winter '69

Landlord's duty to remove snow and ice. Wash & Lee L Rev 24:319 Fall '67

Landlord's liability for ice and snow. M. R. Gareau. Ins L J 1967:661 N '67

Latent defect and customary practice. D. M Harris. Sol J 113:476 Je 20 '69

Legal approach to automobile maintenance: the law and the owner-operator. Vand L Rev 21:970 N '68

Liabilities of garages other than those arising from collisions of automobiles. B. Allen. ABA Sect Ins N&CL 1966:230 '66

Liability for accidents. J. A. Jolowicz. Camb L J 26:50 Ap '68

Liability for fire before 1880. J. I. Foote. No Ire L Q 20:141 Je '69

Liability for injuries to spectators. Osgoode Hall L J 6:305 D '68

Liability for negligence—nervous shock. J. S. Hall. New L J 117:1337 D 21 '67

Liability for negligent statements: round two. V U W L Rev 5:293 F '70

Liability for personal injuries caused by use and occupation of real estate. Montana L Rev 30:153 Spring '69

Liability for the escape of water in buildings. A. Samuels. Convey 31:247 Jl-Ag '67

Liability of a land occupier to persons injured on his premises: a survey and criticism of Kansas law. Kan L Rev 18:161 Fall '69

Liability of company directors for negligence. M. J. Trebilcock. Modern L Rev 32:499 S '69

## [Illustration 100–a]

## PAGE FROM INDEX TO LEGAL PERIODICALS, 1967–1970

584 INDEX TO LEGAL PERIODICALS 1967–1970

**NEGLIGENCE**—*Continued*

Liability of engineer for defective design. Clev St L Rev 19:184 Ja '70

Liability of officers and directors of corporations. A. L. Young. Federation Ins Coun Q 20:65 Spring '70

Liability of police officer. H. E. Greenstone. Tr Law Q 6:56 Spring-Summer '69

Liability of the unconscious defendant. J. Blalock. Trial 6:29 F-Mr '70

Liability to bystanders at accidents for mental distress. Wash & Lee L Rev 26:71 Spring '69

Limited liability. F. H. Lawson. Mo L Rev 33:537 Fall '68

Limits of foreseeability. D. B. Casson. New L J 120:157 F 12 '70

Loss of the land occupier's preferred position—abrogation of the common law classifications of trespasser, invitee, licensee. St Louis U L J 13:449 Spring '69

"Manitoba guest passenger." G. O. Jewers. Man B News 36:239 Ap '68

Mens rea, negligence and attempts. D. Stuart. Crim L R 1968:647 D '68

→ Mental distress as an actionable tortious wrong. UMKC L Rev 37:371 Summer '69

Miller vs. Dewitt (37 Ill 2d 273): and indemnification. A. P. Olschwang. Ill B J 55:988 Ag '67

Missouri abrogates the "no duty" rule as to social guests: restatement (first) adopted. Mo L Rev 35:252 Spring '70

Negligence and the infliction of emotional harm: a reappraisal of the nervous shock cases. U Chi L Rev 35:512 Spring '68

Negligence as a crime. Fac L Rev 25:141 My '67

Negligence—counting the cost. S. Cretney. New L J 119:544 Je 12 '69

Negligence—financial institution's liability to borrower's customers. Sw L J 22:869 D '68

Negligence—medical malpractice—the locality rule. De Paul L Rev 18:328 Autumn '68

Negligence on the move. H. Kalven, jr. ATL L J 33:1 '70

Negligence—parent and child—New York abrogates parent-child immunity doctrine. Notre Dame Law 44:1001 Je '69

Negligence—physicial injury caused by emotional trauma—recovery possible when plaintiff witnesses accident in which her infant daughter was killed by defendant's negligent act. Dick L Rev 73:350 Winter '69

Negligence—school bus driver held to absolute liability. Dick L Rev 73:188 Fall '68

Negligence—the end of the impact rule in Pennsylvania. Dick L Rev 74:514 Spring '70

Negligent entrustor in respondeat superior. Dick L Rev 73:696 Summer '69

Negligent notary public—employee: is his employer liable? Neb L Rev 48:503 Ja '69

Negligent operation of a police vehicle. H. S. Morrison. Clev-Mar L Rev 16:442 S '67

Negligent statements: liability of solicitors. R. G. D. Griffith. L Inst J 43:357 S '69

Negligently caused loss of consortium—a case for recognition as a cause of action in Connecticut. Conn L Rev 2:399 Winter '69-'70

Negligently caused mental distress: should recovery be allowed? SD L Rev 13:402 Spring '68

Negligently inflicted emotional shock from witnessing the death or injury of another. Ariz L Rev 10:508 Fall '68

New boundary for zone of peril. U Ill L F 1969:125 '69

Occupant's duty to warn employee of independent contractor discharged by warning the independent contractor. Sw L J 22:510 Ag '68

Occupiers' liability law. M. C. Atkinson. Tasmania U L Rev 3:82 D '68

Oil pollution of the oceans. J. C. Sweeney. Fordham L Rev 37:155 D '68

One step beyond the zone of danger limitation upon recovery for the negligent infliction of mental distress. Temp L Q 43:59 Fall '69

Origins of the lex Aquilia. D. Pugsley. L Q Rev 85:50 Ja '69

Physician's liability for torts of hospital employees. Clev-Mar L Rev 18:308 My '69

Pitfalls of plant hire. V. Powell-Smith. New L J 118:828 S 5 '68

Preparation of a hospital negligence case—frostbite resulting from malfunction of thermal cooling unit during kidney surgery. G. J. Church. Tr Law Guide 13:3 Ag '69

Present and prospective changes in California automobile negligence law. A. C. Hayton. Calif Western L Rev 5:201 Spring '69 Ins L J 1969:641 N '69

Preservation of the fault system into auto negligence cases. H. E. Greenstone. Forum 4:233 Jl '69

Proof of negligence: exclusive control and other doctrines (an exercise in semantics?) M. J. Meyer. Temp L Q 41:383 Summer '68

Proof of negligence in North Carolina. R. G. Byrd. NC L Rev 48:452 Ap '70

Proposal for a modified standard of care for

> **The practice of only listing articles under title results in articles on the same specific topic being scattered throughout the listing under the main subject heading.**

Res ipsa loquitur: the extent to which plaintiff may establish negligence. St John's L Rev 42:410 Ja '68

Res judicata and the bifurcated negligence trial. UCLA L Rev 16:203 N '68

Review of the guest act. P. W. Pretzel. Ins L J 1969:329 Je '69

Revoke the legal license to kill construction workers. H. M. Philo. De Paul L Rev 19:1 Autumn '69

Revolution in the civil law. M. Belli. Alberta L Rev 6:29 '68

Rise and gradual fall of the locality rule in medical malpractice litigation. J. R. Waltz. De Paul L Rev 18:408 Summer '69

Rondel v. Worsley ([1967] 3 W L R 1666) and criminal proceedings. P. M. North. Crim L R 1968:183 Ap '68

Rondel v. Worsley ([1967] 3 W L R 1666): immunity of the Bar. R. F. Roxburgh. L Q Rev 84:513 O '68

Rondel v. Worsley ([1967] 3 W L R 1666): the historical background. R. F. Roxburgh. L Q Rev 84:178 Ap '68

Rowland v. Christian [(Cal) 443 P 2d 561] and Washington land occupiers' liability. Gonzaga L Rev 5:235 Spring '70

Ruminations on Dixie drive it yourself versus American beverage company. W. S. Malone. La L Rev 30:363 Ap '70

Sales—breach of warranty—"danger invites rescue" doctrine applicable to situation where breach of warranty endangers a pearson so as to invite rescue by a third party who is injured. Albany L Rev 34:757 Spring '70

Scope of law: man, morals, or money? M. Barth. Wis L Rev 1967:961 Fall '67

Social guest—a legal home of his own. L. L. Finz. Tr Law Q 6:5 Fall '69

Some remarks about the element of voluntariness in offences of absolute liability. I. Patient. Crim L R 1968:23 Ja '68

Speeeder liability to pursuing police officers—a new cause of action. Syracuse L Rev 21:224 Fall '69

Split trials in negligence cases under federal rule 42 (b) J. V. Hunter, III. Forum 3:271 Jl '68

Standard of care for medical practitioners—the locality rule. SD L Rev 14:349 Spring '69

Status of visitors in the national parks located in Wyoming—federal liability under current applicable Wyoming law. Land & Water L Rev 2:447 '67

Storekeeper's liability in "rainwater" slip and fall actions. Willamette L J 5:353 Winter '69

Strange case of Mrs. Gore. F. J. Odgers. L Q Rev 86:69 Ja '70

Sudden emergency doctrine as applied in South Carolina. T. D. Wise. SC L Rev 20:408 '68

Sufficiency of debris in the plaintiff's lane of travel to prove the cause and point of impact. St Louis U L J 13:616 Summer '69

Summary judgment in automobile negligence cases: a procedural analysis and suggestions. M. D. Forkosch. Tr Law Q 5:101 Spring-Fall '68

Supervising architect: his liabilities and his remedies when a worker is injured. Nw U L Rev 64:535 S-O '69

[Illustration 101]

## PAGE FROM THE NORTHWESTERN LAW REVIEW

# Northwestern University
# LAW REVIEW

| VOLUME 56 | SEPTEMBER-OCTOBER, 1961 | NUMBER 4 |
|---|---|---|

## ANGUISH OF MIND

### Damages for Mental Suffering under Illinois Law

#### By Paul O. Proehl*

THE functions of the three classic learned professions—theology, law, and medicine—are preventive, ameliorative, and restorative, rather than productive. Unlike the architect or the engineer, whose professional efforts contribute tangibly to gross national product, a criterion of increasing importance in an increasingly materialistic age, the clergyman, the lawyer, and the doctor seek to ease, lubricate, and keep in repair the physical and social processes of life. These are vital functions, but because the worth of the end product is not capable of exact admeasurement—unlike the product [...] are often subjected t[...] gymen or doctors.

It must a[...] he legions of judges, l[...] s who are engaged acr[...] t in redistributing it—moving existing wealth from one pocket to another in the settlement of claims arising out of negligent conduct of one sort or another, and not in aid of commerce, as bankers move money. To what end?[1] We operate under an initial handicap because basically we employ the punitive principle that one hurt makes a wrong and two hurts, or simply two

A typical leading article in a typical law review.

---

* Professor of Law, Univ. of Cal. United States Foreign Service Officer, Department of State 1948–1957. Editor, LEGAL PROBLEMS OF INTERNATIONAL TRADE (1959). A.B. 1942, M.A. 1949, J.D. 1948, Univ. of Ill.; Assistant Professor of Law 1957–1959, Associate Professor of Law 1959–1961, Univ. of Ill.

[1] [T]he prevailing view is that [the state's] cumbrous and expensive machinery ought not to be set in motion unless some clear benefit is to be derived from disturbing the *status quo*. State interference is an evil, where it cannot be shown to be a good.

HOLMES, THE COMMON LAW 96 (1881).

The central problem in most torts cases is: Should the plaintiff or the defendant bear a loss? ... A loss should lie where it has happened to fall unless some affirmative public good will result from shifting it. This axiom is bottomed on a predilection against use of the power of government in the absence of some perceived likelihood of improving affairs by reordering them.

MORRIS, TORTS 9 (1953).

[Illustration 101–a]

## PAGE FROM NORTHWESTERN LAW REVIEW

486     *NORTHWESTERN UNIVERSITY LAW REVIEW*    [Vol. 56

of chagrin, humiliation, or embarrassment.[29] It is to be assumed that had such plaintiffs testified to disagreeable sensations owing to the contraction of scar tissue rather than to the more obviously "painful" sense of physical repugnance, recovery would have been had.[30] Other courts, in refusing compensation for mental disturbance claimed in connection with a physical injury and in attempting to fragment this elusive phenomenon into its "properly" compensable and non-compensable parts, have defined such element of the alleged pain and suffering of the plaintiff as "injured feelings arising in the mind,"[31] "mere humiliation or mental annoyance,"[32] "mere humiliation and grief, resulting from contemplation of a maimed and disfigured body,"[33] anguish arising from "a contemplation of what might occur,"[34] "anguish of mind, wholly sentimental, caused by loss of a child through miscarriage."[35] The effort, simply stated, seems to be to limit compensable pain and suffering to the negative, disagreeable nervous sensations exp[...] damages are today [...] suggested

This article continues on to p. 501.

Note the use of footnotes.

Most law review articles are heavily footnoted.

personal [...] of the
curious n[...] [...]oyance
and the [...] [...]l suffering" is r[...] [...] which
arises ne[...] [...]rves of
sensation[...] [...]nuation
of the o[...] [...]s. Mere
humiliat[...] [...]maimed
hands and a disfigured face do not, in a legal sense, enter into an ascertainment of the pecuniary damages one has sustained as the result of negligence. City of Decatur v. Hamilton, 89 Ill. App. 561, 569–70 (3d Dist. 1899). See also Chicago City Ry. v. Schaefer, 121 Ill. App. 334 (1st Dist. 1905).

[29] Fitzgerald v. Davis, 237 Ill. App. 488 (1st Dist. 1925) ("embarassment or chagrin"); Souleyret v. O'Gara Coal Co., 161 Ill. App. 60 (4th Dist. 1911) ("humiliation"); Knickerbocker Ice Co. v. Leyda, 128 Ill. App. 66 (2d Dist. 1906) ("annoyance and humiliation").

[30] See Fitzgerald v. Davis, *supra* note 29, at 491–92, where it was held error for counsel for the disfigured plaintiff to have argued, " 'You know what that means to a woman. Every time she goes to a party, somebody will look at the scar and folks will whisper about it.' " The court there said, "The law only prohibited the recovery of damages in such a case for mental suffering which results from embarrassment or chagrin and which suffering has no relation to physical pain." But the court went on to say that plaintiff nevertheless "might recover for disfigurement which resulted from the accident." The basis for recovery is not clear, nor is any measure of damages provided. See Chicago City Ry. v. Smith, 226 Ill. 178, 80 N.E. 716 (1907), cited in Nosko v. O'Donnell, 260 Ill. App. 544, 555 (1st Dist. 1931), as having decided affirmatively the question of damages for disfigurement, whereas *Smith* completely passed over defendant's objection that the instruction given permitted recovery for mental suffering not connected with physical injuries. In Castle v. Searles, 306 Ill. App. 304, 28 N.E.2d 619 (4th Dist. 1940), it was held that a scar is not a "permanent injury," but in Demikis v. One Cent Club, Inc., 319 Ill. App. 191, 48 N.E.2d 782 (1st Dist. 1943), the court approved an instruction which limited damages to "any permanent injury or disfigurement resulting from physical injuries."

[31] Chicago City Ry. v. Taylor, 170 Ill. 49, 48 N.E. 831 (1897).

[32] Chicago City Ry. v. Mauger, 105 Ill. App. 579 (1st Dist. 1903).

[33] Chicago & G.T. Ry. v. Spurney, 69 Ill. App. 549 (1st Dist. 1897).

[34] Illinois C.R.R. v. Cole, 165 Ill. 334, 46 N.E. 275 (1896).

[35] Duncan v. Martin's Restaurant, Inc., 347 Ill. App. 183, 106 N.E.2d 731 (1st Dist. 1952). *Contra*, Greenburg v. Stanley, 51 N.J. Super. 90, 105–06, 143 A.2d 588, 597 (1958), *modified on other grounds*, 30 N.J. 485, 153 A.2d 833 (1959): "[H]er disabilities constituted an integral situation in which the sudden, unexpected and severe physical trauma was inextricably intertwined with the emotional shock over the simultaneous fatal injury to the infant. . . ."

[Illustration 102]

## PAGE FROM THE 1969 UTAH LAW REVIEW

### Emotional Distress Negligently Inflicted upon Spectator Plaintiff — A Suggested Model for Identifying Protected Plaintiffs Based on *Relational Interest*

The rule disallowing recovery to a sympathetic plaintiff outside the zone of danger for distress suffered at seeing injury culpably inflicted upon another was challenged in *Dillon v. Legg*.[1] Defendant, driving an automobile, negligently collided with and caused the death of plaintiff Margery Dillon's small daughter Erin Lee who was lawfully crossing the road. At the moment of impact, the plaintiff and another daughter Cheryl were standing nearby. Three causes of action were brought in the district court: one for the wrongful death of Erin Lee, one for the mother's emotional distress an[...]ter, and a third for [...]'s collision with her si[...] judgment on the ple[...]al distress and dismi[...] summary judgment [...]her or not Cheryl wa[...]determina- tive of her [...]California Supreme C[...]anger and not fearing[...]vere emotional distr[...]ing the wrongfully-caused death of her child, since her emotional distress was both a foreseeable consequence of the accident and led to physical injury.

The action for recovery for emotional distress evoked by the peril of another has experienced a dichotomous history since American courts have been at odds with their British counterparts. The landmark British case of *Hambrook v. Stokes Brothers*,[3] decided in 1924, allowed a husband to recover damages occurring when his wife suffered emotional distress leading to physical injury arising from her apprehension *only* for the safety of her children and thereby overturned the apparent British rule that recovery for emotional distress would lie only when resulting from plaintiff's reasonable fear for his own safety.[4] Limiting the *Stokes* holding, a later British case[5] refused recovery to a mother who, hearing her young son scream, looked from the window of her flat and saw her young son's tricycle under the wheels of a slowly backing taxi. The opinion stated that because of the mother's extreme distance from the accident defendant could not have reasonably foreseen her injury and therefore did not owe

---

A typical law review comment. These are always written by a student editor. The purpose of a comment is to make a critical analysis of a point of law usually based on a recent decision.

Most comments are 4–5 pages in length.

---

[1] 441 P.2d 912, 69 Cal. Rptr. 72 (1968).

[3] *Id.* at 915, 69 Cal. Rptr. at 75. Contradictory evidence developed between the deposition of Mrs. Dillon, who said that at the moment of impact she saw Cheryl standing on the curb, and Cheryl's deposition, which obscured whether or not Cheryl was within the zone of danger. *Id.*

[3] [1925] 1 K.B. 141 (C.A. 1924).

[4] *Id.* at 146; Dulieu v. White & Sons, [1901] 2 K.B. 669, 673–75, 676 (dictum).

[5] King v. Phillips, [1953] 1 Q.B. 429, 437 (C.A.)

[Illustration 103]

## PAGE FROM THE STANFORD LAW REVIEW

### California Rejects Tort Action for Fear for Another

TORTS—NEGLIGENCE—DAMAGES.—Plaintiff saw defendants' negligently driven truck strike her seventeen-month-old son. In plaintiff's action to recover for mental distress and consequent physical harm,[1] the trial court sustained defendants' general demurrer to

the complaint. A judgment of dismissal was entered when plaintiff refused to amend and stated that she had felt no fear for her own safety.[2] On appeal to the California Supreme Court, *held*, Affirmed. The defendants owed no duty to plaintiff to avoid arousing injurious emotion by their negligent acts toward a third person. *Amaya v. Home Ice, Fuel & Supply Co.*, 59 Adv. Cal. 310, 379 P.2d 513 (1963) (4-to-3 decision).[3]

Virtually all United States jurisdictions which have decided cases similar t[                    ]ho was in no danger of imp[                    ]caused by fear for another.[4] [                    ] bar recovery: (1) The impa[                    ]r plaintiff has not suffered a j[                    ]s negligence;[5] (2) the fear f[                    ]n cases where

> A typical law review case note. These are written by student editors and are analyses of current cases which the editors deem significant. They are usually 1–3 pages in length.

App. 2d 232, 249 P[          ]constitute sufficient [          ]84 S.W.2d 117 (19[          ]fered since the case [          ]htmares would not [          ]9 Tenn. App. 166, [          ]type of harm suf-

2. The suprem[          ]son as an amendm[          ]Cal. 310, 314, 379 [          ]fear only for her [          ]pply Co., 59 Adv.

3. The majority included Mr. Justice White, who was appointed to hear the case in the place of Mr. Justice Tobriner, a new member of the court who disqualified himself because he had written the district court of appeal opinion, Amaya v. Home Ice, Fuel & Supply Co., 205 Adv. Cal. App. 468, 23 Cal. Rep. 131 (1st Dist. 1962). See note 11 *infra*. The dissent in the supreme court incorporated most of the district court opinion. Amaya v. Home Ice, Fuel & Supply Co., 59 Adv. Cal. 310, 335–46, 379 P.2d 513, 528–36 (1963) (dissenting opinion). Therefore, four of the present seven justices of the court presumably disagree with the decision of the present case.

4. The *Restatement of Torts* recently added a prohibition of recovery for fear for another "because of the overwhelming weight of the case law." RESTATEMENT (SECOND), TORTS, Note to Institute § 313, at 9 (Tent. Draft No. 5, 1960).

Recovery has been allowed in a few cases, which seem to be factually analogous to *Amaya*, on the basis that plaintiff was a member of a large class of people to some of whom harm from impact could be foreseen. Spearman v. McCrary, 4 Ala. App. 473, 58 So. 927 (1912) (travellers on the highway); Bowman v. Williams, 164 Md. 397, 165 Atl. 182 (1933) (owners of land adjacent to the highway); Frazee v. Western Dairy Prods., 182 Wash. 578, 47 P.2d 1037 (1935) (those on or about the highway). One case allowed recovery by holding foreseeability of physical harm unnecessary, Rasmussen v. Benson, 135 Neb. 232, 280 N.W. 890 (1938) (alternative holding), and in one case defendant had special information concerning the likelihood of harm to plaintiff and perhaps acted recklessly, Price v. Yellow Pine Paper Mill Co., 240 S.W. 588 (Tex. Civ. App. 1922). See also Hambrook v. Stokes Bros., [1925] 1 K.B. 141 (1923).

5. See, *e.g.*, Bosley v. Andrews, 393 Pa. 161, 142 A.2d 263 (1958). See generally Brody, *Negligently Inflicted Psychic Injuries: A Return to Reason*, 7 VILL. L. REV. 232 (1962); Throckmorton, *Damages for Fright*, 34 HARV. L. REV. 260 (1921).

Whether plaintiff has suffered fear for self or fear for another is immaterial in most impact jurisdictions; recovery is allowed when impact occurs and denied when it does not. See Southern Ry. v. Jackson, 146 Ga. 243, 91 S.E. 28 (1916) (memorandum opinion) (dictum); *cf.* McGee v. Vanover, 148 Ky. 737, 147 S.W. 742 (1912). *Compare* Bedenk v. St. Louis Pub. Serv. Co., 285 S.W.2d 609 (Mo. 1955), *and* Greenberg v. Stanley, 51 N.J. Super. 90, 143 A.2d 588 (App. Div. 1958), *rev'd on other grounds*, 30 N.J. 485, 153 A.2d 833 (1959), *with* Beaty v. Buckeye Fabric Finishing Co., 179 F. Supp. 688 (D. Ark. 1959), *and* Sanderson v. Northern Pac. Ry., 881 Minn. 162, 92 N.W. 542 (1902).

Plaintiff in *Amaya* suffered no physical touching.

## [Illustration 104]

## PAGE FROM TABLE OF CASES—INDEX TO LEGAL PERIODICALS, 1961–1964

808 INDEX TO LEGAL PERIODICALS 1961-1964

AMALGAMATED Clothing Workers v. Wonderland Shopping Center, Inc, 50 LRRM 2160
U Ill L F 1962:475 Fall '62
AMALGAMATED Clothing Workers. v. Wonderland Shopping Center, Inc (Mich) 122 N W 2d 785
Va L Rev 49:1571 D '63
AMALGAMATED Engineering Union v. Minister of Pensions and Nat. Ins [1963] 1 W L R 441
L Q Rev 80:160 Ap '64
AMAYA v. Home Ice, Fuel & Supply Co (Cal) 379 P 2d 513
How L J 9:87 Winter '63
ND L Rev 39:467 O '63
So Calif L Rev 36:299 '63
Stan L Rev 15:740 Jl '63
Vand L Rev 16:271 D '62
AMBROSE v. Ambrose, 21 D L R (2d) 722
Can B Rev 39:604 D '61
AMERICAN Automobile Ass'n v. U.S. 81 Sup Ct 1727
A B A J 47:1218; 48:81 D '61, Ja '62
B C Ind & Com L R 3:105 Fall '61
Chi-Kent L Rev 40:59 Ap '63
Cornell L Q 47:475 Spring '62
Ga B J 26:315 F '64
Geo Wash L Rev 30:368 D '61
NC L Rev 40:627 Ap '62
Tex L Rev 40:579 Ap '62
U Det L J 39:128 O '61
Vand L Rev 15:1024 Je '62
AMERICAN Broadcasting-Paramount Theatres v. Simpson (Ga) 126 S E 2d 873
Am U L Rev 12:222 Je '63
Ga B J 25:310 F '63
Houston L Rev 1:58 Spring '63
Marq L Rev 46:397 Winter '62-'63
Md L Rev 23:377 Fall '63
Temp L Q 36:240 Winter '63
Tul L Rev 37:147 D '62
Vand L Rev 16:472 Mr '63
Wayne L Rev 9:391 Winter '63
AMERICAN Card Co. v. H. M. H. Co (RI) 192 A 2d 150
U Pitt L Rev 25:619 Mr '64
AMERICAN Civil Liberties Union v. Board of Educ (Cal) 359 P 2d 45
Okla L Rev 14:536 N '61
AMERICAN Communications Ass'n v. U.S. 298 F 2d 648
Mich L Rev 61:978 Mr '63
AMERICAN Cyanamid Co. v. Hercules Powder Co. 211 F Supp 85
Western Res L Rev 14:607 Je '63
AMERICAN Cyanamid Co. 3 Trade Reg Rep ¶16527 (Aug.
Colum L F
NYU L Re
Stan L Re
AMERICAN I
Div. Int. U
Supp 985
Vill L Rev
AMERICAN I
Trucking Co
Okla L Re
AMERICAN F
Ins. Co (Tex
Sw L J 15
AMERICAN I
(Okla) 361 P
Ala L Rev

**When it is known that a particular case deals with a point of law under research, notes & comments in law reviews discussing the case can be located in the Table of Cases section of the Index to Legal Periodicals.**

AMERICAN Mfrs. Mut. Ins. Co. v. American Broadcasting-Paramount Theatres, 221 F Supp 848
Vill L Rev 9:492 Spring '64
AMERICAN Oil Co. v. FTC, 325 F 2d 101
BC Ind & Com L R 5:842 Spring '64
AMERICAN Pipe & Steel Corp. v. Firestone Tire & Rubber Co. 292 F 2d 640
Albany L Rev 26:111 Ja '62
Colum L Rev 61:1519 D '61
Harv L Rev 75:1656 Je '62
Mich L Rev 60:219 D '61
AMERICAN Thermos Prod. Co. v. Aladdin Indus. Inc. 207 F Supp 9
U Colo L Rev 35:295 Winter '63
AMES v. Ideal Cement Co. 235 N Y S 2d 622
NYU L Rev 38:1176 D '63
AMOS Treat & Co. v. SEC. 306 F 2d 260
Geo L J 51:186 Fall '62
Harv L Rev 76:831 F '63
ANACONDA Aluminum Co. v. Sharp (Miss) 136 S 2d 585
Miss L J 33:401 My '62
ANANDOGODA v. Queen [1962] 1 W L R 817
L Q Rev 78:467 O '62
ANASTAPLO, In re, 81 Sup Ct 978
A B A J 47:820 Ag '61
Harv L Rev 75:129 N '61
Ia L Rev 47:507 Winter '62
Ill B J 50:446 Ja '62
Notre Dame Law 37:246 D '61
Vand L Rev 15:634 Mr '62

ANDERSON v. Anderson (Ill) 187 N E 2d 746
W Va L Rev 65:309 Je '63
ANDERSON v. Bushong Pontiac Co (Pa) 171 A 2d 771
La L Rev 22:886 Je '62
ANDERSON v. Knox 297 F 2d 702
Marq L Rev 46:258 Fall '62
ANDERSON v. Martin, 84 Sup Ct 454
ABA J 50:372 Ap '64
U Pitt L Rev 25:583 Mr '64
ANDERSON v. Martin, 206 F Supp 700
Ga B J 25:416 My '63
Loyola L Rev 11:366 '62-'63
U Pa L Rev 111:827 Ap '63
ANDERSON v. Richards (Ohio) 179 N E 2d 918
U Cin L Rev 31:178 Spring '62
ANDERSON v. Sheehan-Bartling, Inc (SD) 105 N W 2d 201
S D L Rev 6:298 Fall '61
ANDERSON v. Tall Timbers Corp (Tex) 347 S W 2d 592
S T L J 6:148 Spring '62
Tex L Rev 40:409 F '62
ANDERSON, Matter of, No. 13,533 (District Court of Osage County, Kansas, March 5, 1962)
Kan L Rev 11:297 D '62
ANDREWS v. Andrews (NC) 113 S E 2d 47
NC L Rev 40:304 F '62
ANDREWS v. U.S. 83 Sup Ct 1236
ABA J 49:1008 O '63
ANGLO-AUTO Finance Co. v. James [1963] 1 W L R 1042
Modern L Rev 27:100 Ja '64
ANNAMUNTHODO v. Oilfield Workers' Trade Union [1961] 3 W L R 650
Camb L J 1962:28 Ap '62
Modern L Rev 25:86 Ja '62
ANONYMOUS v. Anonymous, 236 N Y S 2d 288
Syracuse L Rev 14:677 Summer '63
ANSCHUTZ v. Central Nat. Bank of Columbus (Neb) 112 N W 2d 545
Md L Rev 22:255 Summer '62
ANSPACH v. U.S. 305 F 2d 48
S T L J 7:69 Fall '63
ANTHONY v. International Paper Co. 289 F 2d 574
Md L Rev 22:71 Winter '62
APPLEBY v. Buck (Ky) 351 S W 2d 494
U Cin L Rev 32:127 Winter '63
APPLEMAN v. Fabert Motors, Inc (Ill) 174 N E 2d 892
U Ill L F 1961:531 Fall '61
llas (Tex) 358
2d 826
'61
Astoria Med.
Greater New
-Winter '62
Sup Ct 777
Co. v. Paull,
24
'63
N E 2d 495
ARGUS v. Michler (Mo) 349 S W 2d 389
Mo L Rev 28:320 Spring '63
ARIZONA v. California, 83 Sup Ct 1468
ABA J 49:1205 D '63
Sup Ct Rev 1963:158 '63
Utah L Rev 8:299 Winter '63-'64
ARIZONA State Bar v. Arizona Land Title and Trust Co (Ariz) 366 P 2d 1
Duke L J 1962:595 Autumn '62
ND L Rev 38:611 O '62
U Colo L Rev 35:281 Winter '63
ARIZONA State Bar v. Arizona Land Title & Trust Co (Ariz) 371 P 2d 1020
Ala L Rev 15:326 Fall '62
ARLAN'S Dep't Store, Inc. 133 NLRB No. 56
Vill L Rev 7:489 Spring '62
ARMOUR v. Freeman, 304 F 2d 404
Food Drug Cosm L J 19:196 Ap '64
ARMSTRONG v. Lloyd (Ark) 352 S W 2d 84
Ark L Rev 16:299 Spring '62
ARNOLD v. Baker (Ill) 185 N E 2d 844
W Va L Rev 65:250 Ap '63
ARO Mfg. Co. v. Convertible Top Replacement Co. 81 Sup Ct 599
B C Ind & Com L R 3:94 Fall '61
Calif L Rev 49:988 D '61
Fordham L Rev 30:373 D '61
Harv L Rev 75:242 N '61
N Y U L Rev 36:1395 N '61
Notre Dame Law 37:263 D '61
Tex L Rev 40:728 My '62
U Cin L Rev 31:61 Winter '62
U Ill L F 1961:343 Summer '61
Vill L Rev 7:149 Fall '61

## [Illustration 105]

## PAGE FROM CALIFORNIA SHEPARD'S CITATIONS

**CALIFORNIA SUPREME COURT REPORTS, 2d SERIES**          Vol. 59

| | | | | | | |
|---|---|---|---|---|---|---|
| **–227–** | d230A2d | 225A2d⁷508 | **–375–** | 11CLA725 | j63C2d⁶778 | 260A2d⁴65 | 33ChL663 |

When the citation to a case is known, Law Review articles and notes can be located in the state unit of Shepard's citations.

```
–227–        d230A2d      225A2d⁷508    –375–        11CLA725     j63C2d⁶778    260A2d⁴65    33ChL663
(28CaR865)       [¹702    230A2d⁷276   (29CaR505)    63McL772     51CaL1012    260A2d⁴656   67McL41
(379P2d321)  61C2d²464    231A2d⁷862   (379P2d937)   74YLJ1032    53CaL111     262A2d¹789   59NwL657
61C2d¹151    62C2d²647    237a2d⁷55    cc61C2d500    24Æ752s      16StnL327    259FS¹498    41Æ900s
215A2d¹726   j62C2d²678   240A2d⁷574   cc67C2d96                  9Æ866n       f226A2d²765  89Æ715s
218A2d¹639   65C2d²813    241A2d⁷525   cc325F2d573   –428–        9Æ874n       237A2d²800
239A2d¹872   68C2d²24                                                          A2d²596      –455–
241A2d¹95    240A2d²2                   When the citation to a case is known,  A2d²607      (30CaR129)
249A2d²d¹311 62C2d²64ₓ                                                         A2d²477      (380P2d817)
255A2d¹679   65C2d³81ₓ        Law Review articles and notes can be            A2d³456      s251A2d541
j228A2d⁶111  247A2d³1         located in the state unit of Shepard's          A2d³716      254A2d⁴452
237A2d⁷850   65C2d³81ₓ        citations.                                      A2d⁴201      254A2d⁴452
225A2d⁸222   247A2d⁴1ₓ                                                        A2d²765      233A2d³363
             66C2d⁵77ₓ                                                        A2d⁵226      254A2d⁴452
–234–        68C2d⁵41ₓ                                                        A2d³800      225A2d³342
(28CaR697)   62C2d⁶64ₓ                                                        2d⁴241       232A2d⁵507
(379P2d1)    62PUC51ₓ                                                         2d²274       260A2d²798
256A2d16     63PUC55ₓ                                                         2d⁴723    51CaL1001
221A2d¹491   64PUC749     j261A2d⁹459                              221A2d⁴635  216A2d⁴613
66C2d⁶379    65PUC515     244FS³317    –382–        –439–         43AG262     216A2d⁴756   –465–
236A2d⁷858                52CaL480     (29CaR657)   (30CaR1)      17HLJ557    218A2d⁴201   (30CaR135)
16HLJ163     –276–        15HLJ471     (380P2d97)   (380P2d641)               f220A2d⁴20   (380P2d823)
             (29CaR1)     16HLJ50      256A2d534    59C2d¹719     –448–       222A2d⁴27    235A2d⁴840
–241–        (379P2d481)  39JBC111     d61C2d⁶620   60C2d¹175     (30CaR18)   223A2d⁴111   68C2d²805
(28CaR714)   67C2d¹850    48MnL308     229A2d¹²58   60C2d¹311     (380P2d658) 223A2d⁴198
(379P2d18)   253FS¹711    18Æ220s      63C2d¹³261   60C2d¹744     63C2d449    d224a2d⁴287  –468–
228A2d673    f254A2d²772  64Æ100s      67C2d¹³308   d61C2d¹153    257A2d166   226A2d⁴108   (30CaR329)
d236A2d      233A2d³778                229A2d¹³58   63C2d¹706     60C2d¹383   d227A2d      (381P2d1)
       [¹169 254A2d³772   –333–        243A2d       219A2d¹763    d60C2d¹747         [²250  d224A2d
223A2d⁴341   60C2d⁵669    (29CaR13)         [¹³792  220A2d¹243    62C2d¹96    e228A2d            [¹439
f236A2d⁴382  254A2d⁴772   (379P2d493)  247A2d       227A2d¹350    62C2d¹683         [²247  249A2d¹78
51CaL720     64C2d⁵242    219A2d388         [¹³188  d229A2d       62C2d¹764    h228A2d     254A2d¹602
             j64C2d⁵256   236A2d²617   244A2d            [³58     62C2d¹796         [⁴69   256A2d¹32
–247–        254A2d⁵772   245A2d³468        [¹⁷680  237A2d¹207   64C2d¹69     228A2d²742   j257A2d¹175
(28CaR718)   d260A2d⁵70   254A2d³791   244A2d       239A2d⁷27    66C2d¹191    234A2d⁴10    d222A2d
(379P2d22)   61C2d⁶770    226A2d⁶581        [¹⁸680  241A2d¹176   67C2d⁷22     d234A2d            [²272
260A2d903    254A2d⁶772   231A2d⁶438   63C2d¹⁹261   246A2d¹109   218A2d¹201        [²64   f222A2d²737
380US198     d260A2d⁶71   232A2d⁶499   30CC282      60C2d²745    220A2d¹245   234A2d⁴666   d223A2d
13LÆ757      61C2d⁷337    18HLJ148     24Æ1413s     218A2d²227   221A2d¹723   235A2d⁴304        [²169
85SC874      64C2d⁷245    20HLJ523                  376US²487    233A2d¹180   235A2d⁴627   f229A2d²402
228A2d²632   j64C2d⁷256   40JBC250     –404–        11LÆ²860     234A2d¹42    235A2d⁴797   d229A2d
d239A2d      d260A2d⁸71   55Æ791s      (29CaR785)   84SC²892     234A2d¹488   235A2d⁴858        [²597
       [²406 d260A2d⁸71                (380P2d385)  354F2d²21    235A2d¹302   237A2d⁴621   256A2d²32
d250A2d      d260A2d⁸71   –339–        (94Æ802)     63C2d³665    e237A2d      238A2d²140   f225A2d³131
       [²566 61C2d¹⁰719   (29CaR16)    j68C2d846    65C2d³846         [⁶94   240A2d⁴493   236A2d³637
62C2d³542    d260A2d¹⁰74  (379P2d496)  65C2d³198    227A2d²215   238A2d¹218   250A2d⁴906
243A2d⁴542   65c2d¹¹507   s374US819    262A2d³589   228A2d³806   238A2d¹327   d252A2d      –475–
d239A2d      59C2d¹⁴905   s10LE1084    232A2d⁴475   237A2d⁴620   238A2d¹638         [⁴326  (30CaR333)
       [⁵411 h254A2d      s83SC1714    232A2d⁴516   d246A2d      238A2d¹678   253A2d⁴232   (381P2d5)
254A2d⁵156         [¹⁷773 cc397F2d270  232A2d⁵516        [⁷27    240A2d¹103   253A2d⁴699   cc61C2d210
f60C2d⁶719   14CLA788     60C2d⁶683    237A2d⁵646   63C2d⁴798    240A2d¹116   253A2d⁴988   243A2d119
d239A2d      54CaL96      235A2d⁶397   251A2d⁵189   226A2d⁴766   241A2d¹387   254A2d⁴326   237A2d¹813
       [⁶408 19HLJ763     249A2d⁹928   j65C2d⁶161   227A2d⁴350   242A2d¹770   254A2d⁴427   261A2d¹559
243A2d⁶540   80HLR1468    253A2d       232A2d⁶516   j235A2d⁴521  243A2d¹218   255A2d⁴692   233A2d²263
d243A2d      59NwL266          [¹⁰829  249A2d⁶636   254A2d⁴57    243A2d¹531   259A2d⁴296   233A2d²288
       [⁸806 10Æ627s      f65C2d¹³883  261A2d⁶675   j254A2d⁴58   f248A2d¹309  259A2d⁴377   237A2d²812
247A2d⁸162                66C2d¹³512   232A2d⁷517   274FS⁵188    250A2d¹79    259A2d⁴944   323F2d²596
243A2d¹539   –295–        j66C2d¹³524  279FS⁷22     63C2d⁵545    250A2d¹313   262A2d⁴288   43AG309
d243A2d      (29CaR33)    235A2d                    j63C2d⁵550   250A2d¹590   d262A2d      44AG168
       [⁹537 (379P2d513)       [¹³398  –412–        68C2d⁵428    251A2d¹596        [⁴353  40JBC37
17StnL639    66C2d¹434    j61C2d¹⁵184  (29CaR790)   d224A2d      251A2d¹616   d262A2d
20Æ367n      d231A2d²5    e60C2d¹⁶650  (380P2d390)       [²87    253A2d¹79                 –482–
20Æ372n      234A2d²307   32Æ434s      cc189A2d     231A2d²357   253A2d¹379   262A2d⁴789   (30CaR452)
             247A2d²795                             [421 f232A2d²108 j253A2d¹992 219FS²27   (381P2d188)
–257–        j68C2d³748   –367–        17HLJ581     j232A2d³111  254A2d¹22    245FS⁴397    66C2d¹931
(28CaR872)   o68C2d³748   (29CaR273)   17StnL36     235A2d⁵512   254A2d¹40    250FS¹782    220A2d¹337
(379P2d328)  225A2d³588   (379P2d761)  41NYL1102    j235A2d⁵521  254A2d¹324   291FS⁴715    e219A2d
29CC243      d231A2d³6    224A2d¹461                d239A2d      255A2d¹484   d234A2d            [²113
95Æ1410n     245A2d⁵532   240A2d¹331        [⁵703   256A2d¹635        [²64   222A2d²388
             d245A2d      243A2d¹473   239A2d⁵728   256A2d¹703   45AG72       240A2d²886
–270–              [³703  224A2d²461   242A2d⁵560   256A2d¹873   14CLA78      258A2d²61
(28CaR868)   247A2d⁵754                244A2d⁵103   257A2d⁵372   15CLA44      260A2d²468
(379P2d324)  231A2d⁶4     –370–        d246A2d      258A2d¹563   15CLA1537    e219A2d
234A2d284    d260A2d⁶691  (29CaR509)         [⁷27   259A2d²296   53CaL109           [³113
247A2d551    67C2d⁷241    (379P2d941)  260A2d¹465   d257A2d⁸87   259A2d⁴401   56CaL622     233A2d³764
262A2d11     218A2d⁷8     36Æ1146s     266FS⁵278    260A2d⁸67    259A2d¹642   17HLJ782     260A2d⁴470
59C2d¹584    219A2d⁷549                10CLA999     221FS⁵503    260A2d¹16    16StnL327    *Continued*
```

1151

[Illustration 106]

## PAGE FROM SHEPARD'S LAW REVIEW CITATIONS

**Vol. 54**                    **NORTHWESTERN UNIVERSITY LAW REVIEW**

| | | | | | | | |
|---|---|---|---|---|---|---|---|
| 15RLR503 | 56NwL348 | | **—253—** | **—525—** | | 59Ca2d307 | **—823—** |
| 16StnL830 | '65WLR | **Vol. 55** | 89NJ51 | 367US680 | **Vol. 56** | 29CaR40 | 53CaL435 |
| 47VaL571 | [417 | | 213A2d319 | 6LE1104 | | 54CaR85 | |
| **—575—** | **—803—** | **—1—** | 48CLQ47 | 81SC1705 | **—11—** | 379P2d520 | |
| 60CR965 | 314F2d903 | 17VLR112 | 49IBJ751 | 57Ca2d557 | 111PaL905 | **—525—** | |
| 45NbL72 | 203FS307 | 40WsL69 | 501BJ27 | 21CaR196 | 23PitL651 | '63WLR | |
| 36NYL116 | 246FS811 | 70YLJ348 | 501BJ838 | 370P2d996 | **—41—** | [126 | |
| 11StLJ532 | 14CM232 | **—4—** | 37MLJ57 | 32KCR | 23PitL640 | **—538—** | |
| 35WsL346 | 51MnL439 | 8CLA280 | 29MoL426 | (2)235 | **—65—** | 1962LF519 | |
| **—588—** | 37NDR37 | 76HLR987 | **—288—** | 24LLR668 | 41DLJ333 | **—547—** | |
| 226Or277 | | 14VLR467 | 37NDL501 | 41NbL186 | 41DLJ405 | 16StnL825 | |
| 13U2d70 | | 17VLR119 | **—301—** | 35TLQ35 | 24LJ628 | **—560—** | |
| 360P2d289 | | **—25—** | 381F2d299 | **—553—** | 9WnL300 | 38CBJ87 | |
| 368P2d589 | | 38DLJ581 | 3BCR117 | 114GaA377 | **—87—** | 76HLR292 | |
| 5AzL170 | | 76HLR987 | 8BCR464 | 43Msc2d | 16RLR8 | **—587—** | |
| 75HLR474 | | 36NYL565 | 10CLA41 | [233 | 17RLR387 | 4AzA427 | |
| 1961LF495 | | 114PaL213 | 38WsL494 | 44Msc2d | **—109—** | 195Kan377 | |
| 1966LF931 | | 46VaL1539 | 39WsL622 | [814 | 207FS590 | 267Min441 | |
| 17MiL505 | | 14VLR457 | **—303—** | 250S2d543 | 38DC2d67 | 261NC321 | |
| 64WVL246 | | 70YLJ346 | 245Md298 | 255S2d217 | 1965LF526 | 72NM365 | |
| **—605—** | | **—38—** | 175Neb785 | 151SE504 | 16MiL266 | 240Or74 | |
| | | | | | | 422Pa46 | |
| | | | | | | 21Wis2d | |
| | | | | | | [367 | |
| | | | | | | 220A2d874 | |
| | | | | | | 124NW322 | |
| | | | | | | 127NW170 | |
| | | | | | | 384P2d243 | |
| | | | | | | 399P2d | |
| | | | | | | [1021 | |
| | | | | | | 404P2d948 | |
| | | | | | | 420P2d999 | |
| | | | | | | 134SE668 | |
| | | | | | | 388SW864 | |
| | | | | | | 16Buf625 | |
| | | | | | | 49MnL199 | |
| | | | | | | 74YLJ74 | |
| | | | | | | **—608—** | |
| | | | | | | 380F2d899 | |
| | | | | | | 61McL25 | |

> This unit of Shepard's provides a means for "Shepardizing" law review articles cited since 1957. Through its use, one can find every time a law review article has been cited by another law review or in a court decision.
>
> For example, the article shown at Illustration 101 was cited in court decisions. This Shepard's is also kept current through a bi-monthly cumulative supplement.

| | | | | | | | |
|---|---|---|---|---|---|---|---|
| | | 15MiL342 | **—372—** | | 42DLJ107 | 59NwL200 | |
| 308F2d315 | | 111PaL153 | 67NJS141 | **—755—** | 42DLJ270 | **—630—** | |
| 229Or342 | | 531BJ329 | 14WRL297 | 42DLJ563 | 40WsL176 | | |
| 367P2d439 | | **—62—** | **—389—** | | 531BJ377 | **—662—** | |
| 40DLJ192 | | 30LCP557 | 8BCR531 | | 8VR328 | 42NCL688 | |
| 48ILR619 | | 64McL673 | 65McL | | 8VR514 | **—679—** | |
| 49MnL481 | | 51MnL867 | [1484 | | 3Wsb34 | 35FRD90 | |
| 41NCL21 | | 37NDL513 | **—419—** | | **—263—** | 41FRD34 | |
| 56NwL342 | | 60NwL647 | 356F2d342 | | 266Min224 | 73NM295 | |
| 3W&M18 | | 113PaL73 | 49CaL867 | | 123NW387 | 387P2d866 | |
| '65WLR | | 50VaL427 | 40TxL224 | | 40DLJ411 | **—688—** | |
| [417 | | 76YLJ299 | **—437—** | | **—263—** | 48CLQ709 | |
| **—711—** | | **—97—** | 350F2d138 | | 40DLJ411 | **—692—** | |
| 229Or342 | | 76YLJ53 | 28BR80 | | **—333—** | 1963DuL | |
| 367P2d439 | | **—110—** | 14CM162 | | 64Ca2d25 | [57 | |
| 40DLJ204 | | 348CL267 | 77HLR953 | | 48CaR704 | **—705—** | |
| 41DLJ52 | | **—216—** | 80HLR | | 409P2d928 | 52CaL55 | |
| 38NDL545 | | 381US485 | [1437 | | 384SW71 | 67CR614 | |
| 56NwL371 | | 14LE515 | 29LCP272 | | 39DLJ568 | 76HLR | |
| 3W&M27 | | 85SC1682 | 23LJ28 | | 40DLJ238 | [1049 | |
| '65WLR | | 4Cir246 | **—469—** | | 48ILR582 | 51KLJ653 | |
| [417 | | 229A2d561 | 103NH320 | | '65WLR | 20RLR702 | |
| **—747—** | | 43DLJ82 | 104NH510 | | [416 | 8StLJ497 | |
| 308F2d315 | | 14KLR454 | 171A2d192 | | **—391—** | 15StnL658 | |
| 334F2d545 | | 60McL170 | 190A2d419 | | 383US732 | 17StnL955 | |
| 64Ca2d27 | | 64McL203 | 72YLJ713 | | 16LE232 | **—756—** | |
| 229Or342 | | 64McL260 | **—482—** | | 86SC1142 | 14DeP35 | |
| 48CaR705 | | 42NDL691 | 303F2d742 | | **—409—** | **—777—** | |
| 367P2d439 | | 43NDR254 | 40DLJ417 | | 1963DuL | 26MdL245 | |
| 409P2d929 | | 61NwL510 | 63McL481 | | [409 | 49MnL250 | |
| 60CR903 | | 36NYL | 188LJ219 | | 57NwL1 | **—811—** | |
| 48ILR618 | | [1126 | **—505—** | | 11SDR201 | 334F2d577 | |
| 34KCR289 | | **—223—** | 43TxL278 | | **—477—** | 7BCR572 | |
| 34KCR314 | | 15VLR | '62WLR | → | 245Ca529 | 63CR263 | |
| 15MiL355 | | [1127 | [117 | | | 40WsL72 | |

## SECTION E.  INDEX TO LEGAL PERIODICALS: RESEARCH PROCEDURE

### 1.  Subject Indexes

To locate articles in legal periodicals on a specific subject, consult the Subject Indexes to the *Index to Legal Periodicals*.  For entries since 1961, the combined subject-author section to the *Index* should be consulted.  The subject headings of the *Index* are not subdivided into detailed topics; therefore, broad subject units must be scanned for articles on a particular topic.  For example, articles on promissory estoppel in contract law appear under the heading "Contracts."  To locate all the periodical writings on a specific subject from 1926 to date, each three-year cumulative volume must be examined.  For articles published after the last bound cumulation, consult the annual, semi-annual and monthly supplements.

For articles prior to 1926, see *Jones-Chipman's Index.*

### 2.  Author Indexes

When the author of an article is known and the citation is unknown or to locate articles written by an author, consult the Author Indexes to the *Index to Legal Periodicals* and the combined indexes since 1961.  The Author Indexes refer the user to the subjects under which articles by the author appear in the Subject Index.  Therefore, to find the citation or citations, examine the listings under the noted subject or subjects.  To ascertain all writings of an author, examine the appropriate Author Indexes to the cumulative volumes to 1961 and the combined indexes since 1961.

### 3.  Book Review Indexes

Citations to book reviews in legal periodicals are listed under the names of the authors of the books in the Book Review Indexes to the *Index to Legal Periodicals*.

For book reviews written by reviewers prior to 1961, consult the Author Indexes to the *Index to Legal Periodicals*.  Check under the reviewer's name and subheading "Book Reviews".  The name of the book-author is noted.  Then look under the book-author's name and the book title in the Book Review Index for the complete citation to the book review.  Since 1961, book reviews are not listed under the reviewers' names.

### 4.  Case Method

The Tables of Cases in the *Index to Legal Periodicals* list cases commented upon in the law reviews.  It does not include cases which are merely cited in articles.  To ascertain whether a discussion on a case in point has appeared in a journal, consult the pertinent index volume under the Table of Cases. Since the comments appear reasonably soon after the decisions are published, the dates of the case and the discussion are reasonably close together.

---

## SECTION F.  METHODS OF CITATION

### 1.  Leading Articles

Cite the author, title of the article, volume number, name of the law review, page number and date.  In law review footnotes, the article's title is italicized.

> Handler, Unfair Competition, 21 Iowa L.Rev. 175 (1936).

To refer to a specific page of an article, cite as follows:

> Handler, Unfair Competition, 21 Iowa L.Rev. 175, 182 (1936).

### 2.  Comments and Notes

Comments written by senior student editors in law school journals may be cited with or without the title.  Such writings are sometimes called notes.

> Comment, Public Policy and Federal Income Tax Deductions, 51 Colum.L.Rev. 752 (1951).

> Comment, 51 Colum.L.Rev. 752 (1951).

Case notes relate to a brief discussion of a recent decision.  They may be cited, without referring to the title, as follows:

> 101 U.Pa.L.Rev. 697 (1953).

### 3.  Abbreviations of Periodicals

A list of leading legal periodicals with their more frequently used abbreviations is given in Appendix A, Section C3.

---

## SECTION G.  SUMMARY

### 1.  Jones-Chipman Index to Legal Periodicals

  a.  *Scope*

   (1) Indexes English language legal periodicals published between 1886 and 1937.

   (2) It is not up-to-date but useful to find articles published prior to 1926 (beginning of the cumulative volumes to the *Index to Legal Periodicals*).

  b.  *Arrangement*

   (1) Author

   (2) Subject

## 2.   Index to Legal Periodicals

a.   *Scope and Supplementation*

(1)  Indexes numerous American and substantially all British legal periodicals from 1908 to date.

(2)  The three-year cumulative volumes began in 1926.

(3)  Current numbers are published monthly and cumulated semi-annually, annually and for a three-year period.

b.   *Arrangement*

(1)  Prior to 1961, the Subject and Author Indexes are separate; since 1961, they are combined.

(2)  Subject entries provide full information, including citations to articles.

(3)  Author entries are brief and cross-reference to the appropriate subject sections for citations to articles.

(4)  Book reviews are separately indexed.

(5)  Tables of cases commented upon in the periodicals.

(6)  Biographies appearing in journals are indexed in the Subject Index prior to 1961 and in the combined indexes since 1961. Biographies appear under the main headings: "Biography: Collective" and "Biography: Individual" and are alphabetically subdivided by the names of the individuals written about.

## 3.   Shepard's Law Review Citations

# Chapter 17

# TREATISES, RESTATEMENTS, MODEL CODES, AND UNIFORM LAWS

---

## SECTION A.  TREATISES

Each mature system of law includes opinions of legal experts as a source of the law.  A concept of American judicial law may have been derived from the textual writings of Kent or Story, who in turn may have taken it from the English or the Roman literature.  The impact of the writings of experts, such as Blackstone, Bracton, Littleton, Coke and Glanville, has been very significant in American and English case law.  This is especially noticeable in our early judicial decisions, when there were few American cases available as precedents.  Dean Pound has directed attention to the weight of influence of treatises on the formation of American law from the revolution until about 1850.[1]  However, the accretion of case law changed this.  Now judicial decisions are the more common sources cited in American opinions.  However, the diffused flow of case law has resulted in a strategic modern return to textual literature.

In the Roman law, great weight was given to the writings of legal experts.  The jurisconsults in the classical period of Roman law were unofficial experts who advised the judicial officers on pending cases.  The judges were not required to follow these opinions; yet, over the years the pre-eminence of some jurisconsults was such as to give high favor to their opinions.  Under the Emperor Augustus (31 B.C.—14 A.D.) their opinions (responsa) assumed a distinctive authority and were binding on the judges.  The jurisconsults wrote legal treatises as well as gave responses, and by the fourth century both the responsa and the treatises became primary authorities.  The writings of five pre-eminent jurists, Papinian, Paulus, Gaius, Ulpian and Modestinus, were assigned an authoritative position in the Law of Citations (426 A.D.).  Emperor Justinian gave statutory authority to his Digest (Pandicts), which consisted mainly of selections from the writings of the jurists.  The Digest assumed a pre-eminent authoritative position in the middle ages, and was favorably received in western Europe during the Renaissance, chiefly through the influence of the legal scholars who had studied its texts.[2]  The au-

---

[1] Pound, The Formative Era of American Law Ch. IV (1938).

[2] This summary is derived mainly from the brief discussion in Patterson, Jurisprudence 219 (1953).  See also, Gray, The Nature and Sources of the Law, §§ 424–434 (1909) and Paton, A Text-Book of Jurisprudence 231 (3d ed. 1964).

thoritative influence given to the writings of legal experts by the
Roman law was carried over to the civil law countries where legal
commentaries still retain much influence.

In English law, the treatise did not hold a position of such emi-
nence.  Lord Eldon once commented that a writer who had not held
a judicial office should not be cited as an authority.[3]  However, it
should not be assumed that the treatise has had no influence in England.  During the formative period, there was a dearth of judicial
precedents; therefore, great weight was given to the writings of the
early distinguished scholars.  The five great names in early English
literature are:  Glanville, Bracton, Littleton, Coke and Blackstone.
Bracton helped lay the foundations of English law, borrowing from
Roman law to fill the gaps left by the judicial decisions.  Littleton
gave to the English case law of real property a basis apart from the
Roman law.  Coke bridged the systems of medieval and modern law
and later Blackstone organized the diffused principles of case law
into a comprehensive, literate statement.

The growth of English law reports, after the time of Coke, meant
a decline in the status of the treatise.  However, as in modern America, the plethora of cases has meant its return as a guide to "the
luxuriant chaos of case law." [4]  Paton noted this development when
he observed that "In the days of Bracton the text-book was important because there were so few precedents; today it is valued because there are so many." [5]

Thus, along with other discursive treatments of the law, such as
periodical literature and encyclopedias, the treatise may be one of the
first sources consulted by the researcher.

## 1.  The Nature of Treatises

Treatises, as secondary aids, are expositions, some of which are
critical, by legal writers on case law and legislation.  Generally, legal treatises are more exhaustive in scope than encyclopedias, and
cover a broad subject or a segment of it.  However, the scope of periodical literature is usually more detailed and critical than treatises.

Although it is difficult to "type" treatises, certain distinctive
characteristics stand out which make them sufficiently identifiable
for present purposes.  These features may be classified as follows:
(1) critical, (2) interpretative and (3) expository.  This classification is intended merely to simplify and explain.  It avoids further
analytical refinement which might obfuscate where clarity is most

---

[3] Johnes v. Johnes, 3 Dow 1, 15 (1814).

[4] Paton, op. cit. at 229.

[5] Ibid.

needed. Further, it excludes those writings which have no direct bearing upon legal research, such as jurisprudence and biographies.

Critical legal treatises are uncommon publications in the United States and England; however, their number has increased in recent years. These treatises are constructively critical, expressing the views of the author as to what the law ought to be. They may also include the other two features listed above. The scholarly treatise by Wigmore on the law of *Evidence* (1940) is a good illustration of this type of publication. Another example is Gilmore's Security Interest in Personal Property. (1965).

Wigmore in this treatise skillfully supports his views as to what the law ought to be through a historical interpretation of the law, showing that a current rule had a different meaning or objective than is officially given it. He also reinforces some views by analyzing the policies behind the rules.

Sometimes writers make a critical presentation as though it were merely interpretation, thus giving it an aura of objectivity. However, the confusion which this frequently creates seems to merit a separation of the two approaches by them.

The interpretative treatise provides an analysis and interpretation of statutory or case law. In it the author does not attempt to evaluate the rules in relation to the underlying policies and concepts, for instead of emphasizing values his presentation is based primarily upon terminology and meaning. However, some writers may interstitially include their preferences. In such cases, the subtle projection may be misleading and create classification difficulties. Examples of the interpretative treatises are *Williston's Law of Contracts* (3d ed. 1957) and *Corbin on Contracts* (1950).

The summarization of statutory and judicial law is the main characteristic of expository treatises. Cooley described them as textbook digests, since their true function is that of a digest, the finding of cases. The body of the expository treatise consists primarily of synoptic essay paragraphs arranged under conventional subject headings with profuse footnote citations. At best there is a minimum of analysis or reconciliation of conflicting cases. The texts of encyclopedias are of a similar vein. The impartiality with which conflicting cases are presented with little or no comment reduces their value to that of a case-finder or general subject-refresher.

There is real danger in relying exclusively upon the expository treatise (or the encyclopedia and digest) without verifying the writer's synopsis of the cases. As Cooley has said, "Textbooks (expository—ed.) are good for what they are worth; but any lawyer who has had occasion to probe to the root of a subject has learned that it is unsafe to look to the textbook for a final statement of the law on any subject." [6]

Expository treatises are often described as practitioners' textbooks. Student textbooks may also be classified within this category, for their treatment is elementary, omitting the comprehensive, critical and interpretative features of other treatises. Some student textbooks, however, include certain of these latter characteristics, e. g., Davis, *Administrative Law Text* (1972).

The student textbooks are useful case finders; their case references are selective, being limited generally to landmark decisions. They also serve as helpful refreshers of the principles covering specific topics.

In recent years, additional sources have provided textual treatment of the law. The Practising Law Institute, a non-profit educational institution sponsored by attorneys, has provided books and portfolios of continuing legal education materials. These volumes furnish synoptic analyses of the law, practical guidance, forms and checklists, and other time-saving aids. The publications cover the following group-subjects: personal injury, estate practice, commercial and corporate practice, real estate, taxation, litigation and trial techniques, patent practice and miscellaneous fields.

The Joint Committee on Continuing Legal Education of the American Law Institute and the American Bar Association is another source of practical textual publications. Its publication series include Business Transactions Practice Handbooks, Taxation Practice and other useful subjects.

The continuing legal education groups of the states also contribute to the practical literature of the bar. Each concentrates primarily on state law. In the vanguard, is the California Continuing Education of the Bar, which in addition to its education programs for the practicing attorneys publishes handbooks which are planned to accompany the various lecture series. E. g., *California Decedents Estate Administration* (1971, California Practice Handbook No. 51).

## 2.  The Functions of Treatises

Although the various functions of treatises were described in the preceding section while dealing with their nature, it may be helpful to summarize them here. The functions are generally determined by the nature of the treatises. The functions are noted below opposite the types of treatises they implement and to which they apply.

---

[6] Cooley, Brief Making and the Use of Law Books 59 (5th ed. 1926).

| Functions | | Nature of Treatises |
|---|---|---|
| 1. Provides the views of the writer as to what the law ought to be | ⟫→ | Critical treatise |
| 2. Interpretation of statutory and case law | ⟫→ | Interpretative and Critical treatises |
| 3. Case finder | ⟫→ | Critical, Interpretative, and Expository treatises |
| 4. Presents a general view of the principles on a topic | ⟫→ | Expository treatise |

### 3. The Characteristics of Treatises

The fundamental characteristics of treatises are essentially the same. They contain the following elements:

### 1. Table of Contents

The table of contents shows the topical division of the treatise which is usually arranged by chapters and subdivisions thereof.

### 2. Table of Cases

The table of cases provides references as to where decisions discussed by the author are cited in the text.

### 3. Subject Matter

The subject matter of the text is contained in the main body of the publication.

### 4. Supplementation

The current trend is to provide pocket parts at the back of the volumes to supplement the text and indicate recent statutory and case developments.

Some current treatises are loose-leaf in format, providing for the addition of current material, usually by interfiling.

### 5. Index

The index, embodying an alphabetical arrangement of the topics, subtopics, fact and descriptive words, and cross references, is the last feature.

## SECTION B.   ILLUSTRATIONS:   TREATISES

Using treatises to find cases.

PROBLEM: Liability of one who causes emotional damage or distress by a negligent act, where the act did not result in physical contact.

### Illustrations

107.   Pages from Harper and James, Law of Torts.

108.   Page from Prosser, Handbook on the Law of Torts.

109.   Page from Osborne, Handbook on the Law of Mortgages 3rd ed.

## [Illustration 107]

## PAGE FROM VOLUME I, HARPER AND JAMES. LAW OF TORTS

---

1034               ACCIDENTS              §18.4

clude recovery for injury sustained from the jump or the fall (even where that injury comes from a wrenching of the body rather than from external contact).[15] Moreover, the rule has been found satisfied by the most trivial of impacts.[16] Altogether it has come to lack substance and invite easy circumvention by the very litigants whose fraud it was designed to guard against.[17] Little wonder then that many Anglo-American jurisdictions have come to repudiate the requirement of impact, so that it is distinctly the minority rule today.[18]

The repudiation of the impact rule, however, has not solved all problems nor ended all limitations. Many of the problems it was aimed at were real enough. In addition to the danger of false claims, the fact looms large that in many of these cases there would be no substantial injury to the vast majority of men. Plaintiff suffers (even if honestly) because of his peculiar vulnerability or idiosyncracy by way of pre-existing neurotic impairment.[19] Now the impact rule, just as it fails to weed out false claims, also fails to discriminate between stimuli which would induce serious psychic consequences in normally constituted people and those which would do so only in people already peculiarly vulnerable. It seems fairly clear that the significant distinction

> This is an example of a "critical" treatise. The lawyers are law school professors. This work, as are nearly all, has its own index.

bump against seat); Spade v. Lynn & B.R. Co., 172 Mass. 488, 52 N.E. 747 (1899) (second trial; slight blow); Porter v. Delaware L. & W.R. Co., 73 N.J.L. 405, 63 Atl. 860 (1906) (dust in eyes); Morton v. Stack, 122 Ohio St. 115, 170 N.E. 869 (1930) (inhalation of smoke); McNeice, Psychic Injury and Tort Liability in New York, 24 St. John's L. Rev. 1, 51 et seq. (1949).

[17] In an article describing and criticizing the impact rule in New York, McNeice concludes, "The only one who is defeated is the honest litigant who will not falsify, and who, if he does not come squarely within an exception, will not obtain redress for an injury which everyone agrees was foreseeable and culpably caused by another." McNeice, *supra* note 16, at 80–81.

A rule forbidding recovery for any psychic consequence of injury (even where there was impact) would afford a greater protection against tenuous proof than a rule forbidding recovery for serious physical consequences of severe emotional distress.

[18] Leading cases are Hambrook v. Stokes Bros., [1925] 1 K.B. 141; Orlo v. Connecticut Co., 128 Conn. 231, 21 A.2d 402 (1941); Chiuchiolo v. New England Wholesale Tailors, 84 N.H. 329, 150 Atl. 540 (1930). See also Smith, Relation of Emotions to Injury and Disease, 30 Va. L. Rev. 193, 206–208 (1944).

[19] On the basis of a study of 301 reported cases of this type, Smith concluded that in a substantial majority (175) of them, "The described stimulus was medically inadequate to produce injurious psychic reactions in an average person." Smith, Relation of Emotions to Injury and Disease, 30 Va. L. Rev. 193, 281, 282 (1944).

[20] Smith and Solomon, Traumatic Neuroses in Court, 30 Va. L. Rev. 87 (1943).

[Illustration 107–a]

## PAGE FROM VOLUME I, HARPER AND JAMES. LAW OF TORTS

§18.4    SCOPE OF DUTY IN NEGLIGENCE CASES    1035

problems are currently solved by resort to pervading tort principles, but some mechanical limitations linger. <u>It remains to examine and appraise the current rules.</u>

(1) Generally defendant's standard of conduct is measured by

**Explanation of Rule.**
Note the copious footnote.
This is typical of treatises.

(2) Defendant's conduct must involve foreseeable risk of harm to a class of people which includes plaintiff. This principle is one of the primary subjects of the present section. In the present context, it may come into play in two kinds of situations. Defendant's conduct may threaten unreasonable harm to plaintiff through impact (though in the event, impact is barely missed). Such cases raise no serious question on the present score.[23] In other cases, however, plaintiff is outside the zone of physical risk[24]

21 See the valuable discussion of this point in the opinion of Lord Wright in Hay or Bourhill v. Young, [1943] A.C. 92, 109, 110. Compare Braun v. Craven, 175 Ill. 401, 51 N.E. 657 (1898); Haas v. Metz, 78 Ill. App. 46 (1898). Conduct is not negligent merely because it foreseeably threatens to frighten people "unless reasonable anticipation would have shown that the fright was likely to have such [serious] consequences as to call for its avoidance." Chiuchiolo v. New England Wholesale Tailors, 84 N.H. 329, 337, 150 Atl. 540, 544 (1930). This reasoning may account for such cases as Herrick v. Evening Pub. Co., 120 Me. 138, 113 Atl. 16 (1921) (negligent insertion of false death notice). See also Toelle, The Urban Case, 27 Conn. B.J. 74 (1953); Sykes, The Urban Case: The English and Australian View, 27 id. 83 (1953). What is said here applies to conduct which is merely negligent. The hypersensitive may not be precluded from recovery for an intentional tort. Compare Gregory, Physical Consequences of Emotional Disturbance, 27 Conn. B.J. 65 (1953), with Toelle, *supra.*

22 Price v. Yellow Pine P.M. Co., 240 S.W. 588 (Tex. Civ. App. 1922) (actual notice); Chiuchiolo v. New England Wholesale Tailors, 84 N.H. 329, 150 Atl. 540 (1930) (constructive notice). If defendant's conduct will foreseeably expose a large and undeterminate number of the public to danger, he may well be held to foresee the likelihood of some peculiarly vulnerable people. Compare Gerkin v. Brown & Sehler Co., 177 Mich. 45, 143 N.W. 48 (1913); Note, 49 Mich. L. Rev. 253 (1950) (duty of care in allergy cases). See discussions in the Chiuchiolo case *supra;* in the dissenting opinion of Evatt, J., in Chester v. Waverley Corporation, 62 Commw. L. R. 1, 25, 26 (High Ct. Australia, 1939); and in Smith, Relation of Emotions to Injury and Disease, 30 Va. L. Rev. 193, 261 et seq. (1944).

23 E.g., Orlo v. Connecticut Co., 128 Conn. 231, 21 A.2d 402 (1941); Purcell v. St. Paul City Ry. Co., 48 Minn. 134, 50 N.W. 1034 (1892). The statement in the text is not meant to suggest that there should always be recovery in these cases, but simply that they do not raise a serious question as to whether plaintiff is within the class of those to whom the duty of care is owed with respect to the act or omission that threatens the impact. Compare notes 35–38 *infra.*

24 As in King v. Phillips, [1952] 2 All E.R. 459, [1952] 2 T.L.R. 277 (Q.B.D. 1953),

## [Illustration 107–b]

## PAGE FROM CUMULATIVE SUPPLEMENT, HARPER AND JAMES. LAW OF TORTS

72              ACCIDENTS              §18.4

art, The Case of the Prenatal Injury, 15 U. Fla. L. Rev. 527, at 535–538; Recent Important Cases, 31 A.T.L.A.J. 178–185 (1965); Bennett, The Liability of Manufacturers of Thalidomide to the Affected Children, 39 Australian L.J. 256, at 263–264.

Opposed to this view, and in accord with the view in the text are: Keyes v. Construction Service, Inc., 340 Mass. 633, 165 N.E.2d 912 (1960) (see Comment͏                                      6 S.W.2d 363 (Mo.                                     ); Graf v. Taggart,                 **Harper and James is kept current**          d opinion making t͏         **by a cumulative supplement keyed to**      1 72, 269 N.Y.S.2d         **the main text.**                     46 S.E.2d 425 (196͏                                      4 P.2d 16 (Okla. 19͏                                       )urrett v. Owens, 2͏                                        . L. Rev. 489 (1965); Gordon, The Unborn Plaintiff, 63 Mich. L. Rev. 579, at 591–593 (1965); Wenger, Developments in the Law of Prenatal Wrongful Death, 69 Dickinson L. Rev. 258 (1965).

Cf. also Mace v. Jung, 210 F. Supp. 706 (Alaska 1962) (no recovery for death of non-viable unborn child).

**Comment to §18.4 nn.1–2.** See also Cosgrove v. Beymer, 244 F. Supp. 824 (D. Del. 1965); Restatement of Torts Second §436A and Reporter's Notes. Id. Appendix 171–172.

→ **Comment to §18.4 n.16.** But cf. Sullivan v. H. P. Hood & Sons, Inc., 341 Mass. 216, 168 N.E.2d 80 (1960) (swallowing fecal matter of mouse in milk did not satisfy impact rule).

The rule in Spade has apparently retained its vitality in Massachusetts. See O'Dea v. Mitchell, 350 Mass. 163, 165, 213 N.E.2d 870, 872 (1966).

**Comment to §18.4 n.17.** In overruling the impact rule in New York, the court said of it: "The ultimate result is that the honest claimant is penalized for his reluctance to fashion the facts within the framework of the exceptions." Battalla v. State of New York, 10 N.Y.2d 237, 241, 219 N.Y.S.2d 34, 37, 176 N.E.2d 729, 731 (1961).

**Comment to §18.4 n.18.** More recent cases are Hopper v. United States, 244 F. Supp. 314 (D. Colo. 1965); Robb v. Pennsylvania R.R., 210 A.2d 709 (Del. 1965); Falzone v. Busch, 45 N.J. 559, 214 A.2d 12 (1965), noted in 8 Ariz. L. Rev. 181, 70 Dick. L. Rev. 247, 17 Mercer L. Rev. 482, 43 U. Det. L.J. 542, 34 U. Mo. Kan. City L. Rev. 474; Battalla v. State of New York, 10 N.Y.2d 237, 219 N.Y.S.2d 34, 176 N.E.2d 729 (1961), noted (inter alia) in 16 Ark. L. Rev. 303, 28 Bklyn. L. Rev. 180, 66 Dick. L. Rev. 239, [1962] Duke L.J. 115, 30 Ford. L. Rev. 199, 28 NACCA L.J. 33, 37 N.Y.U. L. Rev. 331, 23 Oh. S.L. Rev. 368, 36 Tul. L. Rev. 160, 39 U. Det. L.J. 137; Collã v. Mandella, 1 Wis. 2d 594, 85 N.W.2d 345, 64 A.L.R.2d 95 (1957), noted in 9 Mercer L. Rev. 377, 11 U. Fla. L. Rev. 262, [1958] Wis. L. Rev. 658; Trent v. Barrows, 397 S.W.2d 409 (Tenn. App. 1965).

See also Restatement of Torts Second §436, Appendix 166–170; Amdursky, The Interest in Mental Tranquility, 13 Buffalo L. Rev. 339 (1964), reprinted in Prac. L. Institute, Damages in Personal Injury and Wrongful Death Cases 297 (1965); annotation, 64 A.L.R.2d 100 (1959).

In addition to the articles by Professor Smith cited in this and the following notes, see Smith, Problems of Proof in Psychic Injury Cases, 14 Syr. L. Rev. 586 (1963).

Some recent decisions still adhere to the no-impact rule. Sullivan v. H. P. Hood & Sons, Inc., 341 Mass. 216, 168 N.E.2d 80 (1960); Knaub v. Gotwalt, 422 Pa. 267, 220 A.2d 646 (1966) (2 judges dissenting).

[Illustration 108]

## PAGE FROM PROSSER, HANDBOOK ON THE LAW OF TORTS. 4th ed.

---

**330**                    **LIMITED DUTY**               **Ch. 9**

running over the body,[53] and the like,[54] without such circumstances of aggravation, which now are in the majority. What all of these cases appear to have in common is an especial likelihood of genuine and serious mental distress, arising from the special circumstances, which serves as a guarantee that the claim is not spurious. There may perhaps be other such cases. Where the guarantee can be found, and the mental distress is undoubtedly real and serious, there is no essential reason to deny recovery.[55] But cases will obviously be rare in which "mental anguish," not ~~accompanied by any physical~~ harm, will be ~~so extreme as to be~~ worthy of rec~~ognition when brought about~~ by the circums~~tances.~~

*Mental Disturb~~ance with Physical Harm~~*

Where the d~~efendant's negligence causes~~ an immediate ~~physical injury, such as a~~ broken leg, none of the foregoing objections has prevented the courts from allowing compensation for purely mental elements of damage accompanying it, such as fright at the time of the injury,[57] apprehension as to its

effects,[58] nervousness,[59] or humiliation at disfigurement.[60] With a cause of action established by the physical harm, "parasitic" damages are awarded, and it is considered that there is sufficient assurance that the mental injury is not feigned.[61]

If the physical harm is not immediate, but follows subsequently as a result of the plaintiff's fright or shock—as in the case of the miscarriage which appears so frequently in these cases that it has come to typify them—[62] there is still dispute. After England had led off by denying liability,[63] a large

> This book is intended primarily for law students but is more scholarly in nature than most student treatises.
>
> It classifies as an Interpretive and Critical Treatise.

916, 173 Cal. 199,
~~o.~~ v. Brown, 1908,

~~.~~Y.2d 16, 176 N.Y.
cancer); Murray
136 ("phobic reac-
~~t~~ Corp. v. O'Neill,
2d 89 (worry over
~~s~~s); Domenico v. Kaherl, 1964, 160 Me. 182, 200 A.2d 844 (worry over unborn child); Fehely v. Senders, 1943, 170 Or. 457, 135 P.2d 283 (same). See Note, 1926, 24 Mich.L. Rev. 306.

Cf. Rome Ry. & Light Co. v. Duke, 1920, 26 Ga.App. 52, 105 S.E. 386 (mental suffering at diminished capacity for work); Templin v. Erkekedis, 1949, 119 Ind.App. 171, 84 N.E.2d 728 (virgin whose hymen was ruptured); Dulaney Inv. Co. v. Wood, Tex.Civ. App.1940, 142 S.W.2d 379 (fear of paralysis).

59. Redick v. Peterson, 1918, 99 Wash. 368, 169 P. 804.

60. Patterson v. Blatti, 1916, 133 Minn. 23, 157 N.W. 717; Erie R. Co. v. Collins, 1920, 253 U.S. 77; Main v. Grand Rapids, G. H. & M. R. Co., 1919, 207 Mich. 473, 174 N.W. 157. Contra: Diamond Rubber Co. v. Harryman, 1907, 41 Colo. 415, 92 P. 922; Camenzind v. Freeland Furniture Co., 1918, 89 Or. 158, 174 P. 139.

61. 1 Street, Foundations of Legal Liability, 1906, 470.

Co., 1928, 126 Kan. 181, 268 P. 103; Louisville & N. R. Co. v. Hull, 1902, 113 Ky. 561, 68 S.W. 433; Missouri, K. & T. R. Co. v. Hawkins, 1908, 50 Tex.Civ. App. 128, 109 S.W. 221; Hale v. Bonner, 1891, 82 Tex. 33, 17 S.W. 605.

53. St. Louis S. W. R. Co. v. White, 1936, 192 Ark. 350, 91 S.W.2d 277; Pollard v. Phelps, 1937, 56 Ga. App. 408, 193 S.E. 102; Morrow v. Southern R. Co., 1938, 213 N.C. 127, 195 S.E. 383; cf. Owens v. Liverpool Corp., [1939] 1 K.B. 394.

54. Renihan v. Wright, 1890, 125 Ind. 536, 25 N.E. 822 (misdelivery); Torres v. State, 1962, 34 Misc.2d 488, 228 N.Y.S.2d 1005 (autopsy and unauthorized burial); Lott v. State, 1962, 32 Misc.2d 296, 225 N. Y.S.2d 434 (confusion of bodies); Weingast v. State, 1964, 44 Misc.2d 824, 254 N.Y.S.2d 952 (same); Blanchard v. Brawley, La.App.1954, 75 So. 2d 891 (burning body trying to cut it out of wreck). See Note, [1960] Duke L.J. 135.

55. See Note, 1936, 21 Corn.L.Q. 166.

56. Cf. St. Louis, I. M. & S. R. Co. v. Bragg, 1901, 69 Ark. 402, 64 S.W. 226 (not a "natural" consequence).

57. Canning v. Inhabitants of Williamstown, 1848, 1 Cush., 55 Mass., 451; Baltimore & O. R. Co. v. McBride, 6 Cir. 1930, 36 F.2d 841; Easton v. United

62. "With few exceptions, recoveries have been restricted to women, and for the most part, pregnant women." Green, "Fright" Cases, 1933, 27 Ill.L.Rev. 761. Actually, this has now become something of an overstatement. Although miscarriages are still plentiful, there is also a good supply of cases of heart attacks, and the like, occurring to mere males.

63. In Victorian Railways Commissioners v. Coultas, P.C.1888, 13 App.Cas. 222. This was subsequently rejected in Dulieu v. White, [1901] 2 K.B. 669. But

## [Illustration 109]

## PAGE FROM OSBORNE, MORTGAGES, 3rd ed.

---

**182** THE OBLIGATION **Ch. 5**

### DISTINGUISHED FROM ESCROW LOAN

**115. The test in distinguishing future advances from an escrow loan is whether the mortgagee has put it out of his power to withhold payments in the future.**

In at least one jurisdiction there has been litigation to distinguish between an escrow loan and a mortgage to secure future advances. The problem arises because the full amount of the mortgage loan may be segregated and either placed in the hands of a third person under an escrow or trust agreement or retained by the mortgagee to be distributed in the future, in either case to the mortgagor or at his order in accordance with a definite [  ] fact that th[  ] money unt[  ] gage being[  ] loan of th[  ] future advances. The test is whether the mortgagee has put it out of his power to withhold the payments in the future. Where the proceeds are put in the control of an independent third person the courts have no difficulty in finding this to be the case.[90] Even when retained by a financial institution-mortgagee and the loan is either credited on the books of the mortgagee or handed over to the mortgagor and then deposited by him in the lending institution subject to agreements as to withdrawals, it has been held to be a fully present loan.[91] That the same result would be reached in the case of an individual mortgagee seems improbable.[92]

> A typical student treatise. Note use of "Black Letter Law."

### FORMS OF MORTGAGE

**116. The mortgage for future advances may assume one of two forms: A total sum stated as a present advance or the total amount left unstated but providing expressly for the advances. The former is a deceptive overstatement of the obligation but is generally upheld. The latter is held sufficiently definite not to invalidate the mortgage.**

The mortgage for future advances may be cast into one or the other of two forms. (1) It may name a certain total sum as a present loan although in truth that amount, by extrinsic agreement which may be oral, includes advances to be made later on. Or (2) it may state that it secures advances to [  ]e amounts, [  ] indefinite. [  ]l there is a [  ] is in itself, [  ]evidence of [  ] this possible fraud, which ordinarily would be hard to establish, the transaction is like the overstated present obligation already mentioned[94] but with two differences. One is that there exists the possibility of increasing the indebtedness up to the amount stated as now owing and doing so in strict accordance with the parties' agreement. The other is that this overstatement ordinarily is deliberate. The second, at least, of these two

---

**89.** See Watkins, Maryland Mortgages for Future Advances, 1940, 4 Md.L.Rev. 111, 127.

**90.** Neeb v. Atlantic Mill & Lumber Realty Co., 1939, 176 Md. 297, 5 A.2d 283; Manhattan Land Corp. v. New Baltimore Loan & Sav. Ass'n, 1921, 138 Md. 529, 114 A. 469; Western Nat. Bank v. Jenkins, 1917, 131 Md. 239, 252, 101 A. 671, 1 A.L.R. 1577; White Eagle Polish American Bldg. & Loan Ass'n v. Hart Miller Islands Co., 1934, 168 Md. 199, 204, 178 A. 214, 215.

**91.** Edelhoff v. Horner-Miller Straw-Goods Mfg. Co., 1898, 86 Md. 595, 39 A. 314; New Baltimore Loan & Savings Ass'n v. Tracey, 1923, 142 Md. 211, 120 A. 441; White Eagle Bldg. & Loan Ass'n v. Hart

**92.** See Groh v. Cohen, 1930, 158 Md. 638, 643, 149 A. 459, 461.

Similarly an elaborate and ingenious attempt to cast a mortgage for future advances under a construction loan into the form of an indemnity mortgage given by a straw man to the mortgagor was balked by the Maryland court. High Grade Brick Co. v. Amos, 1902, 95 Md. 571, 52 A. 582.

**93.** Tully v. Harloe, 1868, 35 Cal. 302, 95 Am.Dec. 102. See Glenn, Fraudulent Conveyances and References, rev. ed., § 299b. See also note 83, supra.

See also Mortgages for Future Advances: The Need for Legislation in Wisconsin, 1965 Wis.L.Rev. 175, 177; Stealey, The Mortgage for Future Advances in West Virginia, 1954, 56 W.Va.L.Rev. 107, 108, for a résumé of the forms the mortgage for future advances may take.

**94.** See supra § 108.

Miller Islands Co., Co.1934, 168 Md. 199, 204, 178 A. 214, 215.

## SECTION C. THE RESTATEMENTS OF THE LAW

In the 1920's concern was being shown by prominent American judges, lawyers and law professors over two main defects in case law—its growing uncertainty and undue complexity. Finally, in 1923, the American Law Institute was founded by a group of these leaders to overcome such weaknesses. The objectives of the Institute were focused on the reduction of the mass of legal publications which had to be consulted by the bench and bar, on the simplification of case law by a clear systematic restatement of it, and on diminishing the flow of judicial decisions. It was feared that the increasing mass of unorganized judicial opinions threatened to break down the system of articulating and developing case law.[7] Thus, the work of the Institute was directed at stating "the existing common law as developed by the courts with such care and accuracy that courts and lawyers may rely upon the Restatement as a correct statement of the law as it now stands and to express the principles of law thus stated with clarity and precision."

There are two aspects of the Restatement which delimit its scope and function and form a focal point for some criticism. First, it lacks legislative sanction. Harlan Fiske Stone foresaw the difficulty that "the mere restatement of law under private auspices would not * * * carry sufficient authority to conquer the over-powering weight of precedent."[8] His early proposal, therefore, was that some method be formulated for reconciling the doctrine of *stare decisis* with this cooperative legal scholarship "which looks beyond the particular case to the law as a whole."[9] He suggested that state legislatures be required to approve the Restatements, not as formal legislative enactments, but as aids and guides to the judiciary so they would be free to follow "the collective scholarships and expert knowledge of our profession. * * *"[10]

But this mild compromise with the codification of the common law was rejected by the Institute. Perhaps, it was feared that a legislative program would incite a controversy similar to the struggle in the nineteenth century between the utilitarians (Field and Livingston, codifiers) and the historical jurisprudents (Carter, case law advocate).

---

[7] Lewis, History of the American Law Institute and the First Restatement of the Law, in Restatement in the Courts, Permanent Edition 1 (1945).

[8] Mason, Harlan Fiske Stone Assays Social Justice, 1912–1923, 99 U.Pa.L.Rev. 887, 915 (1951).

[9] Ibid.

[10] Ibid.

Notwithstanding this absence of legislative endorsement of the Restatements, they departed from the traditionalism of the Anglo-American law, for as Judge Goodrich has indicated, the Restatements were formulated as "an authority greater than that now accorded to any legal treatise, an authority more nearly on a par with that accorded the decisions of the courts." [11] To give effect to this objective, the courts should not have gone beyond the rules articulated in the Restatements by citing the cases which formed the basis for their texts. The Restatement texts should have remained the source for the solution of each succeeding controversy. However, the traditional practice has been followed, so later judicial decisions which cited the Restatements, and not the latter, have remained as authoritative sources to be noted and obeyed. By continuing this procedure, the purpose of the Restatements has been thwarted and the compelling conditions which justified them have been aggravated rather than relieved since the Restatements function only as "an additional source of argument." [12]

Further, in 1936, Professor Yntema questioned the effectiveness of the Restatements in alleviating the evils of the common law in the absence of legislative sanction.[13] His doubt persisted, as he observed in 1949, that "the stream of materials to be consulted by the lawyer rolls on in unabated volumes." [14] In fact, he asked, " * * * where is the reported case that has lost its formal effect by reason of the Restatement or the case unreported due to its existence?" And he continued, "If there be such, and I have not heard of one, they do not affect the conclusion after a number of years that the Restatement has not relieved the public of uncertainty and expense attendant upon a system of case-law. Without formal enactment obviating the recourse in ordinary cases to the existing decisions, it could scarcely be otherwise." [15]

A second defect of the Restatements is embodied in their exclusively antecedent qualities and in the absence of prospective evaluation. Although the rules in the Restatements represent careful and scholarly historical interpretation, they do not generally reflect critical evaluation. Nor do they provide for the systematic development and modification of the law, since such responsibilities casually and loosely revert, under the Institute's program, to the courts as in the

---

[11] Goodrich, The Story of the American Law Institute, 1951, Wash.L.Q. 283, 286.

[12] Arnold, Symbols of Government 51 (1935).

[13] Yntema, What Should the American Law Institute Do? 34 Mich.L.Rev. 461 (1936).

[14] Yntema, The Jurisprudence of Codification in David Dudley Field Centenary Essays 255 (1949).

[15] Id. at 256.

past.  Although it is true that these duties were not assumed by the Restatements, their omission from the plans of the Institute narrowly constricted its operations and seriously impeded activities for the improvement of the law.  Thus, the Restatements have been described as digests, being merely statements of the law as it is,[16] for they do not satisfactorily remedy the inadequacies and defects of our legal system.

However, such differences of opinion should not detract from the valuable contribution which the Restatements have made.  As Mr. Justice Cardozo observed, "The existence of this Institute is a declaration to the world that 'laissez-faire' in law is going or has gone the way of 'laissez-faire' in economics."[17]  It represents a divergence from the main tradition of Anglo-American law, assuming the historic role of providing transition from the customary American law to a new jurisprudence.[18]

Thus, the Restatements were described by Professor Williston as dress rehearsals.  He said, "It has been the history of law in every other civilized country that after customary or common law has developed to a certain degree, or for a long period of years, and become unwieldy, a code has followed  *  *  *  Whether it be in fifty or one hundred or two hundred years, my own belief is that we shall repeat the history of other countries  *  *  *  This Restatement *  *  *  will serve as a better foundation for a code, if one should be needed, than any country has had before."[19]

And so the prologue has become the introduction to a new chapter in the activities of the American Law Institute.  It currently is in the vanguard of the codification movement in the United States, as seen by the monumental Penal Code, Uniform Commercial Code and the Model Code of Evidence which the Institute is sponsoring.

## 1.  The Features of the Restatements

The frequency with which the Restatements are cited by the courts merit their study in legal research.  From 1932 to 1950, a period of less than twenty years, the Restatements were cited 17,951 times by appellate courts.[20]  Therefore, they not only provide clear statements of the rules of the common law which are operative in the great majority of the states but also are very valuable sources for expert citations.

[16] Ibid.

[17] Cardozo, The American Law Institute in Law and Literature and Other Essays 121 (1931).

[18] Franklin, The Historic Function of the American Law Institute:  Restatement as Transitional to Codification, 47 Harv.L.Rev. 1367, 1369 (1934).

[19] Williston, Written and Unwritten Law, 17 A.B.A.J. 39, 41 (1931).

[20] Goodrich, op. cit. note 11, at 292.

A comparison of the texts of the Restatements and the laws of the several states revealed that there were surprisingly few deviations from the common law as expressed in the Restatements. It has been suggested, therefore, that there is in fact a common law which transcends state lines and prevails throughout the nation.[21] But the legal rules may at times be inaccurately and confusingly stated by the various courts. Thus, the objective of the Restatements is to clear away much of the verbal debris and bring the accepted rules to the forefront. To this extent, the Restatements are useful research aids in the law.

The Restatements cover the following subjects: agency, conflict of laws, contracts, foreign relations, judgments, property, restitution, security, torts and trusts. They are written by leading authorities working in committees. The publications appear in several drafts, are discussed at conferences and finally approved. The original intention was to have the Restatements accompanied by treatises citing and discussing the case law; however, this plan was abandoned in view of the difficulties which such group authorship presented. Further, it was decided by the Institute, with one exception (Restatement of Property), that comment or other notes to the Restatement discussing case and other authorities was not necessary since the rules articulating the existing law were the product of deliberative, precise and careful work by outstanding authorities.

However, *Annotations to the Restatements* have been prepared in some areas for individual states in which the decisions of the state courts and the Restatement's rules are compared.

It is fallacious to assume that the common law consisted of a number of universal, immutable principles, and that the function of the American Law Institute was to clarify ambiguities, correct errors and restore the law to its "pristine clarity and perfection." The Restatement generalizations, as Professor Corbin has wisely stated, "must be tested and altered and restated and abandoned in accordance with their application (or rejection) by the courts to the ever-changing problems of life." [22] This explains why the Restatements are being revised and restated and why they will be revised and restated again by a future generation. Examples of Restatement revisions are *Agency 2d*, *Torts 2d* and *Trusts 2d*. *Restatement of the Law 2d* also covers *Foreign Relations Law of the United States*.

---

[21] Goodrich, Restatement and Codification in David Dudley Field Centenary Essays 245–246 (1949).

[22] Corbin, The Judicial Process Revisited: Introduction, 71 Yale L.J. 195, 201 (1961).

The Revisions include the following new features in an Appendix:

1.   Reporter's notes.

2.   Citations to the Restatement which the courts have made since the first Restatement was published.   (These supersede the similar feature of applicable sections in the *Restatement in the Courts* and *Supplements*, which are discussed below.)

3.   Cross references to West Digest System Key Numbers and American Law Reports Annotations.

A.   *General Index to the Restatement of the Law* has also been published.   It covers the Restatements of Agency, Conflict of Laws, Contracts, Judgments, Property, Restitution, Security, Torts and Trusts.   Each Restatement also has an individual index.

In 1945, a *Restatement in the Courts*, permanent edition, 1932–1944, was published in addition to the *Restatements*, providing references to all reported decisions of federal and state appellate courts which had cited the *Restatements*.   The digested cases are listed under the applicable sections of each *Restatement*.   This is kept up-to-date by periodic bound supplement volumes.

As noted above, when a Revision or Second Restatement appears it supersedes the applicable sections of the *Restatement in the Courts* and *Supplements*, providing citations to the Restatement which the courts have made since it was first published.

## SECTION D.  ILLUSTRATIONS:  RESTATEMENTS
## OF THE LAW

PROBLEM:  Liability of one who causes emotional damage or distress by a negligent act, where the act did not involve physical contact.  (The first step of consulting the General Index to the Restatements is omitted.)

### Illustration

[Illustration 110]

## PAGE FROM RESTATEMENT OF THE LAW OF TORTS, 2d

This Section could be located by using either the Index to the Restatements, or the Index to the Restatement of Torts.

Each Section of a Restatement first states the Rule. It is then followed by the Notes of the Reporter commenting on the Rule.

### § 436 A. Negligence Resulting in Emotional Disturbance Alone

If the actor's conduct is negligent as creating an unreasonable risk of causing either bodily harm or emotional disturbance to another, and it results in such emotional disturbance alone, without bodily harm or other compensable damage, the actor is not liable for such emotional disturbance.

See Reporter's Notes.

→ Comment:

*a.* The rule stated in this Section stands in contrast to those stated in §§ 46 and 48, as to the intentional infliction of emotional distress. It is also to be contrasted with the rules stated in § 436, under which an actor who has negligently created an unreasonable risk of causing either bodily harm or emotional disturbance to another becomes subject to liability for bodily harm brought about solely by the internal operation of emotional disturbance. Under the rule stated in this Section, the negligent actor is not liable when his conduct results in the emotional disturbance alone, without the bodily harm or other compensable damage. The difference is one between the negligent automobile driver who narrowly misses a woman and frightens her into a miscarriage, and the negligent driver who merely frightens her, without more.

*b.* The reasons for the distinction, as they usually have been stated by the courts, have been three. One is that emotional disturbance which is not so severe and serious as to have physical consequences is normally in the realm of the trivial, and so falls within the maxim that the law does not concern itself with trifles. It is likely to be so temporary, so evanescent, and so relatively harmless and unimportant, that the task of compensating for it would unduly burden the courts and the defendants. The second is that in the absence of the guarantee of genuineness provided by resulting bodily harm, such emo-

See Appendix for Reporter's Notes, Court Citations, and Cross References

461

[Illustration 110–a]

## PAGE FROM RESTATEMENT OF THE LAW OF TORTS, 2d

§ 436 A          TORTS, SECOND          Ch. 16

tional disturbance may be too easily feigned, depending, as it must, very largely upon the subjective testimony of the plaintiff; and that to allow recovery for it might open too wide a door for false claimants who have suffered no real harm at all. The third is that where the defendant has been merely negligent, without any element of intent to do harm, his fault is not so great that he should be required to make good a purely mental disturbance.

*c.* The rule stated in this Section applies to all forms of emotional disturbance, including temporary fright, nervous shock, nausea, grief, rage, and humiliation. The fact that these are

After the Comments by the Reporter, Illustrations of the Rule are given.

even long continued mental disturbance, as for example in the case of repeated hysterical attacks, or mental aberration, may be classified by the courts as illness, notwithstanding their mental character. This becomes a medical or psychiatric problem, rather than one of law.

**Illustration:**

1. A negligently manufactures and places upon the market cottage cheese containing broken glass. B purchases a package of the cheese, and upon eating it finds her mouth full of glass. She is not cut or otherwise physically injured, and she succeeds in removing the glass without bodily harm; but she is frightened at the possibility that she may have swallowed some of the glass. Her fright results in nausea and nervousness lasting for one day, and in inability to sleep that night, but in no other harm. A is not liable to B.

§ **437.** Actor's Subsequent Efforts to Prevent His Negligence From Causing Harm

**If the actor's negligent conduct is a substantial factor in bringing about harm to another, the fact that after the risk has been created by his negligence the actor has exercised reasonable care to prevent it from taking**

See Appendix for Reporter's Notes, Court Citations, and Cross References

[Illustration 111]

## PAGE FROM APPENDIX VOLUME, RESTATEMENT OF THE LAW OF TORTS, 2d

---

Ch. 16                 APPENDIX                 § 436 A

§ 436 A.  Negligence Resulting in Emotional Disturbance Alone.

### REPORTER'S NOTES

This Section has been added to the first Restatement.

The general rule is well settled. See for example Tuttle v. Meyer Dairy Products Co., 75 Ohio L. Abs. 587, 138 N.E.2d 429 (App. 1956), from which Illustration 1 is taken. Also Monteleone v. Co-operative Transit Co., 128 W. Va. 340, 36 S.E.2d 475 (1945), head-aches and nervousness following broken automobile windshield, where plaintiff received a slight nick "the size of a pimple"; Espinosa v. Beverly Hospital, 114 Cal. App. 2d 232, 249 P.2d 843 (1952), emotional upset at being given the wrong baby by the hospital.

There are, however, some exceptional cases allowing recovery for emotional disturbance alone against a telegraph company which mishandles a message concerning death or illness. Seven states allow such recovery. Western Union Tel. Co. v. Cleveland, 169 Ala. 131, 53 So. 80, Ann. Cas. 1912B, 534 (1910); Mentzer v. Western Union Tel. Co., 93 Iowa 752, 62 N.W. 1, 28 L.R.A. 72, 57 Am. St. Rep. 294 (1895); Cumberland Tel. & Tel. Co. v. Quigley, 129 Ky. 788, 112 S.W. 897, 19 L.R.A. N.S. 575 (1908); Barnes v. Western Union Tel. Co., 27 Nev. 438, 76 P. 931, 65 L.R.A. 666, 103 Am. St. Rep. 776, 1 Ann. Cas. 346 (1903); Russ v. Western Union Tel. Co., 222 N.C. 504, 23 S.E.2d 681 (1943); Western Union Tel. Co. v. Potts, 120 Tenn. 37, 113 S.W. 789, 19 L.R.A. N.S. 479, 127 Am. St. Rep. 991 (1907); Western Union Tel. Co.

v. Lane, 152 S.W.2d 780 (Tex. Civ. 1941).

Four other states have statutes authorizing such recovery. Mac-

> A page from the Appendix volumes to the Restatement of the Torts 2nd. Note how the Reporter's notes cite cases upon which his text was based.

181, 58 S.E. 699, 11 L.R.A. N.S. 1149, 121 Am. St. Rep. 210 (1907); Western Union Tel. Co. v. Ferguson, 157 Ind. 64, 60 N.E. 674, 54 L.R.A. 846 (1901); West v. Western Union Tel. Co., 39 Kan. 93, 17 P. 807, 7 Am. St. Rep. 530 (1888); Francis v. Western Union Tel. Co., 58 Minn. 252, 59 N.W. 1078, 25 L.R.A. 406, 49 Am. St. Rep. 507 (1894); Western Union Tel. Co. v. Rogers, 68 Miss. 748, 9 So. 823, 13 L.R.A. 859, 24 Am. St. Rep. 300 (1891); Connell v. Western Union Tel. Co., 116 Mo. 34, 22 S.W. 345, 20 L.R.A. 172, 38 Am. St. Rep. 575 (1893); Morton v. Western Union Tel. Co., 53 Ohio St. 431, 41 N.E. 689, 32 L.R.A. 735, 53 Am. St. Rep. 648 (1895); Western Union Tel. Co. v. Foy, 32 Okla. 801, 124 P. 305, 49 L.R.A. N.S. 343, 3 N.C.C.A. 367 (1912); Connelly v. Western Union Tel. Co., 100 Va. 51, 40 S.E. 618, 56 L.R.A. 663, 93 Am. St. Rep. 919 (1902); Corcoran v.

---

Cit.—cited; fol.—followed; quot.—quoted; sup.—support.
A complete list of abbreviations faces page 1.

171

[Illustration III–a]

## PAGE FROM APPENDIX VOLUME, RESTATEMENT OF THE LAW OF TORTS, 2d

---

**§ 436 A**         TORTS, SECOND         Ch. 16

Postal Telegraph-Cable Co., 80 Wash. 570, 142 P. 29, L.R.A. 1915B, 552 (1914).

The only possible justification for a special rule in the case of telegraph companies appears to be the special responsibility to the public undertaken by the public utility. The federal rule, which controls as to interstate messages, denies recovery for mental suffering without physical consequences. Western Union Tel. Co. v. Speight, 254 U.S. 17, 41 S. Ct. 11, 65 L. Ed. 104 (1920). The majority rule is approved by the Institute, not only because of the weight of authority, but because of the absurdity of making recovery turn upon whether the message crosses a state line.

#### Cross References to

1. **Digest System Key Numbers**
   Damages ☞49

2. **A.L.R. Annotation**
   Recovery for emotional disturbance or its physical consequences, in the absence of impact or other actionable wrong. 64 A.L.R.2d 100, 108 et seq.
   Recovery by parent for distress caused parent because of personal injuries to child. 32 A.L.R.2d 1060, 1078.
   Grief and mental anguish as elements of damages for personal injury resulting in death of infant. 14 A.L.R.2d 485, 495.
   Recovery for shock or mental anguish at witnessing injury to, or fear of injury to, another. 18 A.L.R.2d 220.
   Recovery by tenant for mental anguish occasioned by wrongful eviction. 17 A.L.R.2d 936.
   Anxiety as to future disease, condition, or death therefrom, as element of da⸺, 342.
   Recovery⸺ury to or
   interf⸺
   Mental di⸺   Note reference to Key-Numbers and   on or ex-
   pulsio⸺   A.L.R. annotations. Search can be ex-
   Humiliatio⸺  panded for both additional and later  coverable
   by on⸺   cases through use of West General Di-  nexistent
   marri⸺   gest or A.L.R. Upkeep Services.
   Right to r⸺                                    sequences,
   in the⸺                                             A.L.R.2d
   100.

**§ 437. Actor's Subsequent Efforts to Prevent His Negligence From Causing Harm.**

#### REPORTER'S NOTES

Illustration 1 is based on Haverly v. State Line & S. R. Co., 135 Pa. 50, 19 A. 1013, 20 Am. St. Rep. 848 (1890); Nicholson v. Buffalo, R. & P. R. Co., 302 Pa. 41, 153 A. 128 (1930).

See also cases under division, chapter, topic, title, and subtitle that includes section under examination.

[Illustration 112]

## PAGE FROM RESTATEMENTS IN THE COURTS, 1970–1971 SUPPLEMENT

TORTS 2d § **436**

This set indicates each time a Restatement rule has been cited, and further indicates whether the court supported, or did not support, the rule.

The Restatement in the Courts and its supplements are: 1932–1944, 2 v.; 1954, 4 v.; 1965, 3 v.; 1967, 2 v.; 1968–1969, 2 v. 1970–1971, 2 v.

### § 435B. Unintended consequences of intentional invasions

N.J.Super. 1969. Cit. in sup. The plaintiff, a key employee, sued the defendants, his employers and principal stockholders in the company, for damages resulting from a false arrest and criminal charges for a crime the defendants, not the plaintiff, had committed, burning down the company's lumber yard for the insurance. The court held that the requirement of foreseeability should be abandoned in such cases as this, where principles of logic, fairness, and justice dictate that the defendant should be held liable. Seidel v. Greenberg, 108 N.J.Super. 248, 260 A.2d 863, 871, 40 A.L.R.3d 987.

### § 436. Physical harm resulting from emotional disturbance

Hawaii, 1970. Cit. in concurr. and diss. op. This was an action against the state by homeowners seeking damages for the flooding of their house, resulting from failure of a culvert to drain water from a state highway, the culvert having been blocked by beach sand. Plaintiffs alleged that the state had failed to keep the culvert free of such sand. Plaintiffs testified that the flooding of their house had left them "heartbroken" and "shocked." Judgment was for plaintiffs and included an amount for "mental anguish and suffering, inconvenience, disruption of home and family life, past and future, etc." Upon appeal, the court affirmed the judgment, except . . . as to the award for "mental anguish and suffering." In its opinion the court discussed in detail the authorities and cases involving such damages and held that the interest in freedom from negligent infliction of serious mental distress in entitled to independent legal protection, that there is a duty to refrain from the negligent infliction of serious mental distress; that whether or not the defendant is liable to the plaintiff in any particular case will be solved most justly by the application of general tort principles. The court remanded the case to the trial court to decide whether under the facts of the case, serious mental distress to plaintiffs was a reasonably foreseeable consequence of defendant's acts. The concurring and dissenting opinion rejected the position of the majority in this respect. Rodrigues v. State, 472 P.2d 509, 523.

Mich. 1970. Cit. in sup., appendix cit. in ftn. in sup.; subsec. (2) cit. in ftn. in sup., cit but dist. by diss. (and cit in ftn. by diss.) Plaintiffs alleged traumatic neurosis, emotional disturbance, and nervous upset, as well as property damage, from an explosion on their land caused by the defendant. The trial court gave a directed verdict to the defendant, except as to the property damage. The state supreme court reversed and remanded, overruling the impact rule in emotional distress cases. The dissent felt that the Restatement rule was inappropriate. Daley v. La Croix, 384 Mich. 4, 179 N.W.2d 390, 392, 394, 395, 397.

Cit.—cited; com.—comment; fol.—followed; sup.—support.
A complete list of abbreviations precedes page 1.

799

## [Illustration 113]

## PAGE FROM CALIFORNIA SHEPARD'S CITATIONS— RESTATEMENT SECTION

| RESTATEMENT OF THE LAW | | | | Torts |
|---|---|---|---|---|
| 39CaR82 | §§ 441 to | 46CaR636 | 14CaR556 | 84CaR456 | § 480 |
| 55CaR806 | 452 | 91CaR753 | 46CaR636 | 101CaR914 | 134A2d684 |
| 60CaR507 | 180A2d907 | 95CaR101 | Comment b | 102CaR803 | 286P2d377 |
| 67CaR467 | 5CaR35 | 95CaR630 | 3C3d771 | § 464 | Comment b |
| 97CaR168 | § 441 | 55CaL658 | 478P2d474 | 42C2d163 | 134A2d684 |
| 54CLR | 239A2d656 | 18HLJ616 | 91CaR754 | 7C3d180 | 283P2d81 |
| [2005 | 49CaR11 | Comment a | Comment c | 4A3d139 | 286P2d377 |
| 20HLJ437 | 21CC389 | 10A3d808 | 55C2d864 | 265P2d906 | 286P2d927 |
| 98LR65 | §§ 442 to | 89CaR273 | 362P2d349 | 496P2d1282 | 296P2d422 |
| 98LR89 | 453 | § 448 | 13CaR525 | 84CaR456 | 27SCL227 |
| § 433 | 44C2d234 | 43C2d75 | § 453 | 101CaR914 | § 481 |
| 43C2d69 | 55C2d863 | 44C2d777 | 59C2d308 | § 465 | 192A2d810 |
| 180A2d907 | 129A2d773 | 180A2d907 | 180A2d901 | 498P2d1053 | 206A2d458 |
| 235A2d783 | 133A2d112 | 199A2d145 | 260P2d280 | 102CaR805 | 251A2d385 |
| 271P2d29 | 180A2d913 | 271P2d33 | 275P2d538 | Comment b | 14CaR119 |
| 5CaR35 | 210A2d198 | 285P2d272 | 379P2d520 | 498P2d1053 | 23CaR623 |
| 45CaR647 | 237A2d170 | 5CaR35 | 5CaR31 | 102CaR805 | 59CaR387 |
| 52CLR486 | 17A3d660 | 10CaR709 | 29CaR40 | § 466 | § 482 |
| Comment d | 278P2d123 | 18CaR895 | Comment b | 42C2d163 | 192A2d810 |
| 20HLJ437 | 282P2d74 | § 449 | 43C2d73 | 7C3d180 | 234A2d609 |
| § 433B | 283P2d355 | 43C2d63 | 122A2d603 | 192A2d600 | 14CaR119 |
| 18CLA455 | 5CaR39 | 44C2d234 | 159A2d750 | 220A2d204 | 44CaR589 |
| 21StnL45 | 13CaR524 | 44C2d777 | 191A2d161 | 265P2d906 | § 483 |
| § 434 | 26CaR405 | 49C2d684 | 260P2d280 | 496P2d1282 | 68C2d583 |
| 193A2d795 | 46CaR635 | 57C2d105 | 265P2d549 | 13CaR556 | 132A2d282 |
| 241A2d526 | 95CaR101 | 67C2d242 | 271P2d31 | 33CaR764 | 220A2d178 |
| 247A2d780 | § 442 | 69C2d869 | 275P2d539 | 101CaR914 | 235A2d496 |
| 250A2d691 | 180A2d907 | 5C3d164 | 324P2d730 | Comment a | 282P2d109 |
| 276A2d219 | 237A2d169 | 122A2d603 | 12CaR297 | 7C3d180 | 440P2d509 |
| 14A3d998 | 237A2d197 | 129A2d773 | § 455 | 466P2d1282 | 33CaR715 |
| 16A3d597 | 5CaR35 | 133A2d112 | 180A2d914 | 101CaR914 | 45CaR402 |
| 14CaR557 | 46CaR634 | 159A2d749 | 5CaR40 | § 467 | 68CaR309 |
| 50CaR595 | 46CaR687 | 198A2d424 | § 457 | 43C2d544 | 34SCL405 |
| 56CaR134 | 18HLJ616 | 199A2d144 | 223A2d416 | 234A2d609 | § 485 |
| 58CaR794 | § 442A | 219A2d499 | 274A2d605 | 275P2d451 | 274P2d679 |
| 80CaR789 | | 237A2d173 | | | |
| 83CaR330 | | | | | |
| 92CaR589 | | | | | |
| 94CaR207 | | | | | |

> Nearly all state units of Shepard's Citations have a Section which "Shepardizes" the restatement for Court decisions for the state.

| | | | | |
|---|---|---|---|---|
| § 435 | | | | |
| 237A2d174 | | | | |
| 16A3d598 | | | | |
| 46CaR638 | | | | |
| 52CaR425 | | | | |
| 94CaR208 | | | | |
| 32CC57 | | 285P2d272 | 122A2d367 | § 488 |
| 52CLR476 | 30CaR8 | 294P2d131 | 274A2d604 | § 470 | 68C2d752 |
| 5HLJ3 | § 447 | 321P2d8 | 265P2d90 | 54CLR | 441P2d928 |
| 7SLR98 | 43C2d63 | 324P2d730 | 373P2d865 | [1456 | 69CaR88 |
| Comment c | 43C2d73 | 368P2d130 | 23CaR777 | § 472 | Comment b |
| 142A2d508 | 44C2d319 | 430P2d74 | 79CaR271 | 253A2d | 68C2d752 |
| 298P2d615 | 44C2d782 | 447P2d619 | Comment a | [1018 | 441P2d928 |
| § 436 | 55C2d864 | 486P2d158 | 122A2d367 | 61CaR708 | 69CaR72 |
| 247A2d795 | 3C3d770 | 10CaR709 | 265P2d90 | 95CaR269 | § 490 |
| 56CaR116 | 5C3d164 | 18CaR279 | Illustration | Comment a | 147A2d749 |
| § 436A | 159A2d749 | 18CaR530 | 1 | 95CaR269 | 306P2d34 |
| 247A2d795 | 168A2d764 | 18CaR894 | 122A2d367 | § 473 | 22AG43 |
| 56CaR116 | 180A2d907 | 33CaR284 | 265P2d90 | Comment d | Comment a |
| § 437 | 210A2d198 | 46CaR637 | Illustration | 7C3d185 | 117A2d47 |
| 67C2d242 | 237A2d171 | 50CaR598 | 2 | 192A2d600 | 129A2d555 |
| 250A2d691 | 17A3d660 | 58CaR794 | 122A2d368 | 496P2d1286 | 183A2d415 |
| 430P2d74 | 260P2d280 | 60CaR516 | 265P2d90 | 13CaR556 | 185A2d224 |
| 58CaR794 | 271P2d425 | 73CaR369 | § 463 | 101CaR918 | 255P2d39 |
| 60CaR516 | 271P2d31 | 89CaR273 | 42C2d163 | § 475 | 277P2d877 |
| §§ 439 to | 275P2d538 | 96CaR107 | 65C2d245 | 236A2d78 | 6CaR673 |
| 461 | 282P2d418 | Comment b | 7C3d180 | 45CaR766 | 8CaR223 |
| 52CLR500 | 285P2d275 | 134A2d65 | 262A2d559 | § 477 | § 491 |
| § 440 | 324P2d730 | 285P2d368 | 4A3d139 | 498P2d1051 | 274P2d679 |
| et seq. | 336P2d206 | § 452 | 265P2d906 | 102CaR803 | §§ 496A to |
| 67C2d199 | 362P2d349 | 55C2d864 | 418P2d156 | § 479 | 496G |
| 430P2d65 | 478P2d473 | 193A2d798 | 496P2d1282 | 10A3d938 | 242A2d551 |
| 55CaR807 | 486P2d158 | 237A2d171 | 498P2d1051 | 89CaR681 | 51CaR587 |
| 60CaR507 | 5CaR35 | 362P2d349 | 53CaR548 | 52CLR808 | |
| | 13CaR525 | 13CaR525 | 68CaR777 | | |
| | 26CaR405 | | | | |

## SECTION E.   UNIFORM LAWS AND MODEL CODES

### 1.   Uniform Laws

The *Restatements*, as mentioned have as their aim the restating of the common law as developed by the courts.   The movement for law reform has also focused on statutory law and the need, in many instances, for similar statutes among the states.   Towards this aim the American Bar Association passed a resolution recommending that each state and the District of Columbia adopt a law providing for the appointment of Commissioners to confer with Commissioners of other states on the subject of uniformity in legislation on certain subjects.   By 1912, all of the states, the District of Columbia, and Puerto Rico passed such a law and there was formed the *National Conference of Commissioners on Uniform State Laws*.   Its object is to "promote uniformity in state laws where uniformity is deemed desirable and practicable." [23]

The *National Conference* meets once a year and considers drafts of proposed uniform laws.   When such a law is approved, it is the duty of the Commissioners to try to convince their state legislatures to adopt it.   The *National Conference* has approved two hundred and four acts.

A complete list of acts approved by the *National Conference of Commissioners on Uniform State Laws* appears each year in Appendices in its annual *Handbook*.   These tables also list which states have adopted each uniform law.

a.   Publication of laws approved by the *National Conference of Commissioners on Uniform State Laws*.

(1)   Separate Pamphlet form.

(2)   In the annual *Handbook* of the *National Conference*.

(3)   *Uniform Laws Annotated.   Master Edition, 1969–*

This edition, published by the West Publishing Co., replaces all former editions.   To date, eight volumes have been published.   After each section of a uniform law pertinent official comment of the Commissioners is given.   This is followed by a list of Law Review Commentary and then by digests of federal and state court decisions citing the particular section of the uniform law.   It is kept up-to-date by annual pocket supplements.

### 2.   Model Codes

*The National Conference of Commissioners on Uniform State Laws* has determined that it will designate an act as a "Uniform Act".

---

[23] National Conference of Commissioners on Uniform State Laws.   Handbook. 1970. p. 314.

Section G.    Interstate Compacts.

Footnote 23.    Add:  See also U.S. Steel Corporation v.
Multistate Tax Commission.  434 U.S. --,
54 L Ed 2d. 682, 98 S. Ct. 799 (1978)

completed in 5 v.).

This is an annotated collection of texts of all treaties to which the United States was a signatory but which never went into force.

Canadian Law – Chapter 22 (FLR)

Section K (b). In 1977, a new edition was published in 661 pages.

when it has "a reasonable possibility of ultimate enactment in a substantial number of jurisdictions." [24]   Acts which do not have such possibility are designated as "Model Acts."   As a general rule, "Model Acts" embrace subject areas which do not have substantial interstate implications.

The American Law Institute also occasionally will draft and approve a model act, and will as with the *Uniform Commercial Code,* participate jointly with the *National Conference of Commissioners on Uniform Laws.*

[24] Id. at 344.

## SECTION F.   ILLUSTRATIONS:  UNIFORM LAWS

**[Illustration 114]**

## PAGE FROM VOLUME 1, UNIFORM LAWS ANNOTATED, MASTER EDITION

---

### § 2—609    UNIFORM COMMERCIAL CODE

**1. F**                                        same

> Typical Uniform Law adopted by the National Conference of Commissioners on Uniform State Laws.

contract was dependent on failure of buyer to provide cash or satisfactory security; however seller's dissatisfaction with defendant's financial standing must not be false or arbitrary. James B. Berry's Sons Co. v. Monark Gasoline & Oil Co., C.C.A.8, 1929, 32 F.2d 74 (cited in Official Comment, supra).

Where a vendor contracts to deliver goods, and allows a buyer credit for

tion of the satisfaction of the seller with the buyer's financial responsibility is to be settled by the seller before he parts with the goods; but there must be a real want of satisfaction with the buyer's financial responsibility, and the refusal to ship without payment or security must be based on that reason alone. Corn Products Refining Co. v. Fasola, 1920, 109 A. 505, 94 N.J.Law 181 (cited in Official Comment, supra).

### § 2—610.   Anticipatory Repudiation

When either party repudiates the contract with respect to a performance not yet due the loss of which will substantially impair the value of the contract to the other, the aggrieved party may

    (a) for a commercially reasonable time await performance by the repudiating party; or

    (b) resort to any remedy for breach (Section 2—703 or Section 2—711), even though he has notified the repudiating party that he would await the latter's performance and has urged retraction; and

    (c) in either case suspend his own performance or proceed in accordance with the provisions of this Article on the seller's right to identify goods to the contract notwithstanding breach or to salvage unfinished goods (Section 2—704).

⟶ **Action in Adopting Jurisdictions**

**Variations from Official Text:**

   **Kentucky.** In paragraph (b), should refer to 2—703, not to 7—703.

**|Official Comment|**

**Prior Uniform Statutory Provision:** See Sections 63(2) and 65, Uniform Sales Act.     *For text of prior provision, see Appendix in end volume.*

[Illustration 114–a]

## PAGE FROM VOLUME 1, UNIFORM LAWS ANNOTATED, MASTER EDITION

SALES       **§ 2—610**

**Purposes:** To make it clear that:

1. With the problem of insecurity taken care of by the preceding section and with provision being made in this Article as to the effect of a defective delivery under an installment contract, anticipatory repudiation centers upon an overt communication of intention or an action which renders performance impossible or demonstrates a clear determination not to continue with performance.

> After each Section the official comment of the Commissioners explaining the Section is given.

if he awaits performance beyond a commercially reasonable time he cannot recover resulting damages which he should have avoided.

2. It is not necessary for repudiation that performance be made literally and utterly impossible. Repudiation can result from action which reasonably indicates a rejection of the continuing obligation. And, a repudiation automatically results under the preceding section on insecurity when a party fails to provide adequate assurance of due future performance within thirty days after a justifiable demand therefor has been made. Under the language of this section, a demand by one or both parties for more than the contract calls for

in the way of counter-performance is not in itself a repudiation nor does it invalidate a plain expression of desire for future performance. However, when under a fair reading it amounts to a statement of intention not to perform except on conditions which go beyond the contract, it becomes a repudiation.

3. The test chosen to justify an aggrieved party's action under this section is the same as that in the section on breach in installment contracts—namely the substantial value of the contract. The most useful test of substantial value is to determine whether material inconvenience or injustice will result if the aggrieved party is forced to wait and receive an ultimate tender minus the part or aspect repudiated.

4. After repudiation, the aggrieved party may immediately resort to any remedy he chooses provided he moves in good faith (see Section 1—203). Inaction and silence by the aggrieved party may leave the matter open but it cannot be regarded as misleading the repudiating party. Therefore the aggrieved party is left free to proceed at any time with his options under this section, unless he has taken some positive action which in good faith requires notification to the other party before the remedy is pursued.

**Cross References:**

Point 1: Sections 2—609 and 2—612.

Point 2: Section 2—609.

Point 3: Section 2—612.

Point 4: Section 1—203.

1 U.L.A.–U.C.C.—26      **401**

## [Illustration 114–b]

## PAGE FROM VOLUME I, UNIFORM LAWS ANNOTATED, MASTER EDITION

### § 2—610    UNIFORM COMMERCIAL CODE

**Definitional Cross References:**

"Aggrieved party". Section 1—201.

"Contract". Section 1—201.

"Party". Section 1—201.

"Remedy". Section 1—201.

#### Cross References

Assurance of performance, see section 2—609.

Good faith, enforcement of contracts, see section 1—203.

Installment contracts, defective delivery, see section 2—612.

Letters of credit

     Anticipatory repudiation for wrongful disposition of, see section 5—115.

     Application of remedies under this section for wrongful repudiation, see section 5—115.

Recovery of damages by seller for wrongful repudiation, see section 2—708.

#### Law Review Commentaries

Anticipatory breach of contract: a comparison of the Texas law and the Uniform Commercial Code. 30 Tex. L.Rev. 744 (1952).

Remedies under law of sales in the proposed Commercial Code. Samuel Williston. 63 Harvard L.Rev. 584 (Feb. 1950).

Remedies under this title. William C. Jones. 30 Mo.L.Rev. 212 (Spring 1965).

Repudiation of a contract under the Code. Arthur Anderson. 14 DePaul L.Rev. 1 (Autumn-Winter 1964).

Sales: "from status to contract". Howard L. Hall. 1952 Wis.L.Rev. 209.

#### Library References

Sales ☞84, 98, 116, 370, 405.

C.J.S. Sales §§ 79, 98–100, 464, 520.

#### Notes of Decisions

Construction with other laws   1
Executory contracts, limitation to   2
Insolvency of parties   4
Remedies available on breach   5
Suspension of performance   3
Tender of delivery   6

time of fraud claimed as basis for rescission of contract on ground of anticipatory breach, was executed not executory. Metropolitan Distributors v. Eastern Supply Co., 1959, 21 Pa.D. & C.2d 128, 107 Pitt.L.J. 451.

#### 1. Construction with other laws

This section and sections 2—709, 2—718 and 2—719 relating to anticipatory repudiation of a sales contract, and action for price, liquidation or limitation of damages, and modification or limitation of remedy, must be read and interpreted together, and unconscionable modification or limitation of remedial provisions must be deleted. Denkin v. Sterner, 1956, 10 Pa.D. & C.2d 203, 70 York Leg.Rec. 105.

#### 2. Executory contracts, limitation to

This section and sections 2—709, Theory of an anticipatory breach cannot be invoked where contract, at

> At the end of each Section, references to additional research aids are given.
>
> Also, annotations to all court decisions citing the Section are indicated.

refusal to accept performance. Id.

[Illustration 115]

## CHART FROM 1970 HANDBOOK OF THE NATIONAL CONFERENCE OF COMMISSIONERS

RECORD OF PASSAGE OF UNIFORM A

Column headers (uniform acts):
Acknowledgment (1939) (1960); Adoption (1953) (1969); Aircraft Financial Responsibility (1954); Anatomical Gift Act (1968); Ancillary Administration of Estates (1949); Arbitration (1955); Attendance of Out of State Witnesses (1931) (1936); Certification of Questions of Law (1967); Child Custody Jurisdiction Act (1968); Civil Liability for Support (1954); Commercial Code (1951) (1957) (1962); Common Trust Fund (1938) (1952); Consumer Credit Code (1968); Consumer Sales Practices (1970); Contribution Among Tortfeasors (1955); Controlled Substances (1970); Criminal Extradition (1936); Criminal Procedure, Rules of (1952); Deceptive Trade Practices Act (1964) (1966); Declaratory Judgments (1922); Disposition of Unclaimed Property (1954) (1966); Division of Income for Tax Purpose (1957); Divorce Recognition (1947); Enforcement of Foreign Judgments (1948) (1964); Estate Tax Apportionment (1958) (1964); Evidence, Rules of (1953); Facsimile Signatures of Public Officials (1958); Federal Services Absentee Ballot (1952); Federal Tax Lien Registration (1926) (1966); Fiduciaries (1922); Foreign Money Judgments Recognition (1962); Fraudulent Conveyances (1918); Gifts to Minors (1956) (1965) (1966); Interstate Arbitration of Death Taxes (1943); Interstate Compromise of Death Taxes (1943); Interstate and International Procedure (1962); Jury Selection and Service (1970); Juvenile Court Act (1968); Land Sales Practices Act (1968); Limited Partnership (1916); Mandatory Disposition of Detainers (1958); Marriage and Divorce (1970); Military Justice (1961); Minor Student Capacity to Borrow (1969); Motor Vehicle Certificate of Title and Anti-Theft (1955); Narcotic Drug (1932) (1958); Partnership (1914); Paternity (1960)

States (rows): Alabama, Alaska, Arizona, Arkansas, California, Colorado, Connecticut, Delaware, District of Columbia, Florida, Georgia, Hawaii, Idaho, Illinois, Indiana, Iowa, Kansas, Kentucky, Louisiana, Maine, Maryland, Massachusetts, Michigan, Minnesota, Mississippi, Missouri, Montana, Nebraska, Nevada, New Hampshire, New Jersey, New Mexico, New York, North Carolina, North Dakota, Ohio, Oklahoma, Oregon, Pennsylvania, Puerto Rico, Rhode Island, South Carolina, South Dakota, Tennessee, Texas, Utah, Vermont, Virgin Islands, Virginia, Washington, West Virginia, Wisconsin, Wyoming

*Table I—UNIFORM*

> Each year the National Conference of Commissioners on Uniform State Laws publishes a Handbook. It contains, in an Appendix, a chart listing each Uniform Act and the states that have adopted it.

Total: 27 | 2 | 3 | 48 | 1 | 12 | 49 | 2 | 1 | 5 | 51 | 35 | 2 | 0 | 5 | 0 | 46 | 0 | 13 | 42 | 18 | 11 | 10 | 14 | 6 | 4 | 19 | 0 | 38 | 26 | 7 | 25 | 50 | 14 | 17 | 6 | 0 | 1 | 6 | 47 | 7 | 0 | 8 | 2 | 1 | 51 | 42 | 4

## [Illustration 116]

## TABLE FROM 1970 HANDBOOK OF NATIONAL CONFERENCE OF COMMISSIONERS

TABLE VIII

### LIST OF STATES SHOWING THE UNIFORM ACTS ADOPTED THEREIN

Note: The (*) indicates that the Uniform Act has been adopted substantially or with modifications.

ALABAMA

Act to Provide for Appointment of Commissioners (1951); Anatomical Gift Act (1969); Bills of Lading Act * (1931); Commercial Code (1965); Common Trust Fund Act (1949); Criminal Extradition Act (1931); Criminal Extradition Act Amendments (1940); Cy-Pres Act (1941); Declaratory Judgments Act (1935); Desertion and Non-Support Act (1915); Fiduciaries Act (1943); Firearms Act (1936); Gifts to Minors Act (1959) Revised, (1966); Insurers Liquidation Act (1943); Narcotic Drug Act (1935); Narcotic Drug Act as Amended (1945); Negotiable Instruments Act (1909); Photographic Copies of Business and Public Records as Evidence Act (1951); Principal and Income Act (1939); Reciprocal Enforcement of Support Act (1951), as Amended (1953); Sale of Securities Act * (1931); Sales Act and Amendments (1931); Securities Act (1959); Securities Ownership by Minors Act (1961); Simplification of Fiduciary Securities Transfers Act (1961); Simulta[                 ] Receipts Act (194[  ]   (1943); Wareho[    ] **Each year, the Handbook lists all**   [i]pts Act (1923).   **states, and indicates the Uniform Acts**

ALASKA   **adopted by each state.**

Acknowl[                                              ] Arbitration Act[                                                    ]n Act * 1957; C[                                                     ] Conditional Sales (1919); Contribution Among Tortfeasors Act (1970); Criminal Extradition Act (1960); Desertion and Non-Support Act * (1915, 1919); Division of Income for Tax Purposes Act (1959); Extradition of Persons of Unsound Mind Act (1923); Federal Tax Lien Registration Act (1933); Foreign Bank Loan Act (1960); Foreign Depositions Act (1923); Foreign Executed Wills Act (1933); Foreign Probated Wills Act of 1895; Gifts to Minors Act (1957); Insurers Liquidation Act (1966); Land Sales Practices Act (1967); Limited Partnership Act (1917); Narcotic Drug Act as Amended (1943); Narcotic Drug Act Amendments (1953); Negotiable Instruments Act (1913); Partnership Act (1917); Photographic Copies of Business and Public Records as Evidence Act (1951); Proof of Statutes Act (1923); Reciprocal Enforcement of Support Act as Amended (1953); Reciprocal Transfer Tax Act (1933); Sales Act (1913); Securities Act (1959); Simultaneous Death Act (1949); Stock Transfer Act (1913); Trust Receipts Act (1951); Vital Statistics Act (1949); Warehouse Receipts Act (1913); Total, 36.

ARIZONA

Acknowledgment Act (1943); Acknowledgment Act Amendment (1945, 1961); Act to Provide for Appointment of Commissioners (1953); Act to Secure the Attendance of Witnesses from Without a State in Criminal Proceedings (1937); Aeronautics Act *; Anatomical Gift Act (1970); Arbitration Act (1962); Bills of Lading Act (1921); Business Records as Evidence Act (1951); Commercial Code as Revised (1967); Common Trust Fund Act (1941); Conditional Sales Act (1919); Criminal Extradition Act and Amendment (1937); Declaratory Judgments Act (1927); Disposition of Unclaimed Property Act (1956); Fiduciaries Act (1951); Flag Act (1919); Foreign Depositions Act (1921); Fraudulent Conveyance Act (1919); Gifts to Minors Act (1957);

390

[Illustration 117]

## PAGE FROM THE 1970 HANDBOOK OF THE NATIONAL CONFERENCE OF COMMISSIONERS ON UNIFORM STATE LAWS

### UNIFORM LAW COMMISSIONERS' MODEL PUBLIC DEFENDER ACT *

1  SECTION 1 [*Definitions.*] In this Act, the term:
2      (1) "detain" means to have in custody or otherwise deprive
3  of freedom of action;
4      (2) "expenses," when used with reference to representation
5  under this Act, includes the expenses of investigation, other
6  preparation, and trial;
7      (3) "needy person" means a person who at the time his need

> **Model Acts are promulgated for topics where uniformity among the states is not necessary or desirable.**

14      (ii) a misdemeanor or offense any penalty for which in-
15  volves the possibility of confinement for more than 6 months
16  or a fine of more than $500; and
17      (iii) an act that, but for the age of the person involved,
18  would be a serious crime.

#### COMMENT

The term "detain" is defined in terms, drawn from *Miranda v. Arizona*,[23] that make it clear that the act in this respect is coextensive with the constitutional requirements respecting the kind of situation in which the needy person is entitled to be represented by counsel.

The term "expenses" is given a partial ("includes") rather than an exhaustive ("means") definition, because it is necessary only to make clear that preparation and trial are an integral part of adequate representation.

The term "needy person" is defined to make clear that partial need and supervening need are also included. "Undue hardship," not being susceptible to precise

---

* The National Conference of Commissioners on Uniform State Laws in the promulgation of its Uniform Acts urges, with the endorsement of the American Bar Association, their enactment in each jurisdiction. Where there is a demand for an Act covering the subject matter in a substantial number of the States, but where in the judgment of the National Conference of Commissioners on Uniform State Laws it is not a subject upon which uniformity between the States is necessary or desirable, but where it would be helpful to have legislation which would tend toward uniformity where enacted, Acts on such subjects are promulgated as Model Acts.

[23] 384 U.S. at 477

## SECTION G.   TREATISES: RESEARCH PROCEDURE

### 1.   Methods of Research

#### a.   Case Method

If the name of a leading decision in point is known, consult the *table of cases* of the treatise to ascertain whether it is discussed in the book.   If so, an examination of the cited pages in the text will reveal a discussion of the subject matter with additional cases in point.

#### b.   Index Method

Consult the *index* in the back of the book if a case in point is not known.   Select an appropriate fact or descriptive word or legal topic to use the index.   References will be to the text of the publication.

#### c.   Topic Method

The Topic Method can be used through the *table of contents*; however, its effectiveness in locating the pertinent text depends on the researcher's understanding of the structural subdivisions of the subject matter in that table.

#### d.   Definition Method

The *index* to the treatise may list words or phrases which are defined and explained in the text.

### 2.   Location of Treatises

#### a.   Card catalog.

To locate treatises on a subject, consult the *card catalog* in the law library.   The methods of using a *card catalog* are described below.

The card catalog is so made that there are ordinarily three ways of finding a book, namely:

First—Under the AUTHOR'S surname.

Second—Under the TITLE of the book, when it is distinctive.

Third—Under the SUBJECT to which the book relates.

Cards are arranged alphabetically by the first word on the top line, always disregarding "The," "A" and "An."   The labels on the outside and the guide cards inside the drawers are to aid in quickly locating the word desired.

To find whether the library has a certain book, consult the catalog as you would a dictionary or telephone directory.   In some libraries, the author and subject cards are kept in separate catalogs.

Jacobstein & Mersky, Legal Research 4th Ed. UTB—25

EXAMPLE—To find the books in the library which were written by Oliver Wendel Holmes, look for HOLMES, the surname of the author, in its alphabetical place.

The author of a publication may be an organization, governmental agency or corporation.  The main entry in the catalog is under the name of that body.

EXAMPLES:

>American Institute of Accountants
>
>U. S. Attorney General's Committee on Administrative Procedure
>
>Bureau of National Affairs

If the publication entitled "The All England Law Reports" is wanted, look for "ALL," the first word of the title not an article.

Again, to find the books on the subject COMMERCIAL LAW, look for those words, where all the cards representing the books on this subject are filed together.

Many large subjects, such as the above, are subdivided to aid in locating specific material.

Cards for books about a person follow the cards representing that person as author.

CALL NUMBER—The number at the upper left hand corner of the card constitutes the "Call Number" and directs you to the book's location on the shelves.

Cross reference cards bear no call numbers but serve to connect related subjects.  Examples—Attorneys, see Lawyers.  Damages, see also Accident Law, Negligence, Torts.

b.   For a comprehensive list of legal treatises, with book review annotations, see:

(1) *New York University, School of Law Library.  A Catalogue of the Law Collection at* New York University, ed. Julius J. Marke. 1953.  1 vol.  This is an excellent source for older treatises.

(2) Jacobstein and Pimsleur.  *Law Books in Print.*  3 vols. 1971. Supplemented by *Law Books Published,* a quarterly publication with an annual cumulation.

This publication lists legal treatises in English, which were in print as of December 31, 1970.  The set is in three volumes.  The first volume is by author and title, the second by subject and series, and the third by publisher.  Complete bibliographic information is furnished for each title.

(3) *Association of American Law Schools. Law Books Recommended for Libraries.* 1967–69 4 vols.

This set is a compilation of lists intended to provide carefully selected lists of books for law libraries. It is in six loose leaf volumes with each of the 46 topics in separate pamphlets. No. 47 is an author and subject index to the entire set. Plans are in progress to issue supplements to keep this set current.

(4) *Harvard Law School Library. Annual Legal Bibliography.* July 1, 1960 to date. Vol. 1—.

This is a subject classified list of selected United States and foreign books and periodical articles that are currently acquired by the Harvard Law Library. It covers all fields of law and is subdivided under some 40 jurisdictions. The *Annual* includes (1) an Analytical Table of Contents, subdivided into common law and civil law jurisdictions and private international and public international law, (2) subject indexes in Spanish, German and French, and (3) an Alphabetical Subject Index, covering the topics appearing in the *Annual.*

It is kept up-to-date by a *Current Legal Bibliography* which is published nine times a year, October to June. The material in the *Current* numbers of a year is cumulated into the bound *Annual* volume.

*Current Publications in Legal and Related Fields.* 1953 to date. Vol. 1—.

This mimeographed bibliography of current legal treatises and related literature is sponsored by the American Association of Law Libraries and is published by Fred B. Rothman & Co. It is issued nine times a year, viz., monthly except June, July and September, with an annual cumulation.

The cumulative issue is divided into two parts.

Each author entry is numbered. The subject index refers to the numbered author entries.

---

## SECTION H.  THE RESTATEMENTS:  RESEARCH PROCEDURE

### 1.  Index Method

Consult the *index* to the appropriate *Restatement,* e. g., *Contracts.* If the precise *Restatement* covering the problem is not known, refer to the *General Index to the Restatement of the Law.*

For cases which have cited the applicable rules of the *Restatement,* examine either (1) the *Restatement in the Courts* and its *Sup-*

*plements* or (2) if the *Restatement* has been revised, the *Appendix* to the *Second Restatement.*

The tentative drafts and the *Second Restatement's Appendix* provide annotated Reporter's notes, with interpretations and citations to leading cases.

To compare the rule in a *Restatement* with the law of a specific state, consult the *Annotations* to it for that state, if one was published. The *Annotations* provide references and discussion of the law as applied by state cases.

Also, most state units of *Shepard's Citations* have a section (usually in the pamphlet supplement) *Shepardizing* the *Restatements.*

## 2. Topic Method

The *table of contents*, rather than the index, to a specific *Restatement* can be examined to locate the appropriate rule.

As described above under the Index Method, also consult the *Restatement in the Courts*, the *1948* and *1954 Supplements* and the state *Annotations.*

## 3. Definition Method

To determine the meaning of words and phrases used in the Restatements, examine the *Glossary of Terms Defined in the Restatement* which is included in the *Restatement in the Courts.*

---

## SECTION I.  METHODS OF CITATION

### 1.  Treatises

Treatises are cited in this order: volume number (when the publication is multivolume), author, title of book, page or section, edition and date. If the citation refers to a specific page, the symbol "p." is omitted unless both page and section numbers are given. The page and section references are indicated when the section covers more than one page. Always cite the latest edition, except where the information appears only in an earlier edition.

> Finletter, The Law of Bankruptcy Reorganization 531 (1939).

> 2 Dewing, The Financial Policy of Corporations, 821 (4th ed. 1941).

> 1 Williston, Contracts § 86, p. 278 (3d ed. 1957).

Where a publication is revised and edited by a person other than the original author, the editor's name is not given.

> 1 Williston, Contracts § 86, p. 278 (3d ed. 1957).

Where the publication is the product of a corporate author, rather than a personal author, the former is listed like the latter.

Commission on Freedom of the Press, The American Radio 117 (1947).

A book with an editor but no author is cited:

2 American Law of Property § 9.8 (Casner ed. 1952).

## 2. Restatements

The Restatements of the American Law Institute are cited:

Restatement, Contracts § 347 (1932).

Restatement, Agency 2d § 303 (1958) or Restatement (Second), Agency § 303 (1958). (The latter form is preferred by *A Uniform System of Citation.*)

---

## SECTION J. SUMMARY

### 1. Treatises

  a. *Scope*

    (1) Expositions, some of which are critical, by legal writers on case law and legislation.

    (2) More exhaustive in scope than encyclopedias but periodical articles are usually more detailed and critical.

    (3) Functions

      (a) Views of the writer as to what the law ought to be—critically evaluative.

      (b) Interpretation of statutory and case law.

      (c) Case finder.

      (d) Presents a general view of the principles on a topic.

  b. *Arrangement*

Treatises usually include these features:

    (1) Table of contents.

    (2) Table of cases.

    (3) Subject matter—text.

    (4) Index.

  c. *Supplementation*

The current practice of publishers is to keep treatises current by cumulative pocket supplements. Some publications are furnished with replacement (revision) volumes.

**2.  Restatements**

   a.  *Scope*

      (1) Simplifies and restates case law on selected subjects.

      (2) Weaknesses.

         (a) Absence of legislative endorsement and sanction.

         (b) Statements treat the subject matter antecedently and not prospectively.

         (c) Inconsistency of terminology among Restatements.

   b.  *Arrangement and Supplementation*

      (1) Tentative drafts—includes Reporter's notes and case discussion.

      (2) Restatements—text.

      (3) Revisions—Restatements Second.

      (4) *Annotations*—comparison of state case law with Restatement.

      (5) *Restatement in the Courts*—digest-references to cases citing the Restatements.  Note that this information and Reporter's notes are being incorporated into Revisions.

      (6) *Glossary of Terms Defined in the Restatement*—included in the *Restatement in the Courts.*

      (7) *Supplements of 1948* and *1954*—amendments and additions to text and supplements to the *Restatement in the Courts.*

   c.  *Indexes*

      (1) *General Index*—covers the several Restatements.

      (2) Each Restatement also has an individual index.

# Chapter 18

## MISCELLANEOUS RESEARCH AIDS

---

This chapter covers various additional useful research aids: They are: (1) attorneys general opinions, (2) law dictionaries, (3) form-books, (4) appeal papers and (5) legal directories.

---

### SECTION A.  OPINIONS OF THE ATTORNEYS GENERAL

The opinions of the attorneys general have the characteristics of both primary and secondary authority.  As the legal advisor to the executive officials of the government, the attorney general renders requested legal advice to them, generally, in the form of written opinions.  Although these opinions are the official statements of an executive officer, issued in accordance with his authority, they are merely advisory statements and are not mandatory orders.  Therefore, the inquirers and other officials are not conclusively bound to follow such recommendations and conclusions.  However, the opinions are strongly persuasive and are generally followed by executive officers.  Also, they have significant influence on the courts in their deliberations.

The opinions, as a general rule, relate to:  (1) the interpretations of statutes or (2) general legal problems.  Some attorneys general limit their advice and will not render opinions as to the constitutionality of proposed legislation.

The *Opinions of the Attorneys General of the United States* first appear as advance sheets.  Subsequently, they are compiled into book form, each volume being separately indexed.  To date 41 bound volumes have been published covering the period 1789 through 1960.  Three volumes of digests of the opinions have also been published for volumes 1 through 32, 1789–1921.

The opinions of the attorneys general of the states are usually published in bound volumes.  A few states release them first in advance sheets or in mimeographed form.  Cumulative indexes are available for some sets.

Many state annotated codes include attorney-general opinions

Footnote 1.  Add:  National Association of Attorneys General.  Committee on the Office of Attorney-General.  Powers, Duties and Operations of State Attorneys General. 1977.

## SECTION B.   LAW DICTIONARIES

In the preceding discussions relating to the *Definition Method,* a number of publications, which include definitions, are given.   Among those sources are *Words and Phrases* (West Pub. Co.), encyclopedias, digests, etc.

Law dictionaries are another aid in locating the definition of words in their legal sense or use.   They are not research aids and do not restate the law, for they function merely as reference tools. Therefore, like digests, they generally are not cited as sources of the law.   However, if the meaning of a word is in dispute, the definition in a law dictionary, or a general dictionary, for that matter, may be quoted.

Law dictionaries ordinarily do not emphasize the etymology or pronunciation of words.   But *Ballentine's Dictionary* and *Cochran's Lexicon* are exceptions, for they include pronunciations.   Rawle's third revision of *Bouvier's Dictionary* is perhaps the most scholarly in its treatment of words, providing, besides the definitions, discussion on many legal topics.

The featured American and English law dictionaries are:

1.   Ballentine, Law Dictionary, with Pronunciations.   3d Ed. Rochester, N. Y., Lawyers Co-operative Publishing Co., 1969, 1 vol.

2.   Black, Law Dictionary.   4th ed. St. Paul, West Publishing Co., 1968.   1 vol.

3.   Bouvier, Law Dictionary, 3rd revision (8th ed.) by Francis Rawle.   St. Paul, West Publishing Co., 1914.   3 vols.

4.   Cochran, Law Lexicon, 4th edition by Robert A. Mace.   Cincinnati, W. H. Anderson Co., 1956.   1 vol.

5.   Jowitt, Dictionary of English Law.   London, Sweet & Maxwell, Ltd., 1959.   1 and 2 vol. eds.

6.   Mozley and Whiteley, Law Dictionary.   7th ed.   London, Butterworth, 1962.   1 vol.

7.   Wharton, Law Lexicon, 14th ed. London, Stevens and Sons, 1938.   1 vol.

Dictionaries on special subjects of interest to attorneys have also been published.   An example is *Casselman's Labor Dictionary* (1949).

Foreign language and bilingual legal dictionaries also are available when research extends to such areas.

## SECTION C.  FORM–BOOKS

Form-books are used as aids in drafting legal documents.  Since the elements of such instruments, which have been tested by the courts or found acceptable by writers, assume paramount importance, these books are standard equipment for an attorney.  Form-books, which relate to court procedure, were previously described in Chapter 12, above.  The form-books discussed here cover office instruments, such as wills and contracts.

### 1.  Annotated Form-Books

Some form-books are annotated, containing the forms of instruments, references to cases which have favorably construed the provisions, and editorial comments.  Examples are:

> American Jurisprudence, 2d ed. Legal Forms Annotated. 1971–.  With pocket supplements.

> Jones, Legal Forms Annotated. 10th ed.  1962. 3 vols.  With pocket supplements.

> Modern Legal Forms (West Pub. Co.).  1950–1965.  13 vols.  With pocket supplements.

> Nichols, Cyclopedia of Legal Forms, Annotated.  1955–1964. 10 vols. in 12.  With pocket supplements.

> Warren, Forms of Agreement.  1966.  1 vol.  Loose-leaf.

A recent development is the publication of form-books which emphasize correlative tax matters.  Examples are:

> Casey, Forms of Business Agreements with Tax Ideas, Annotated. 2d ed. 1965. 1 vol.

> Rabkin and Johnson, Current Legal Forms with Tax Analysis. 1966.  8 vols.  Loose-leaf.

### 2.  Types of Form-Books

Form-books have assumed various characteristics and relate to either general or special subjects or substantive or procedural law. Some also contain business as well as legal forms.

#### a.  General and Special Subject Form-Books

The form-books listed above are general in scope.  Illustrative form-books on special subjects are:

> Gordon, Standard Annotated Real Estate Forms.  1945. 1 vol.

> Murphy, Will Clauses Annotated: Tax Effects. 1962.  1 vol.

b.   Procedural Form-Books

Examples of form-books relating to procedure are given in Chapter 12, *Court Procedure.*

c.   Forms in Treatises

Forms are also included in treatises.   Illustrations of these publications are:

Remington, Bankruptcy Law of the United States.   5th–6th ed.
   1950–1961.   14 vols. in 15.   With pocket supplements.

Fletcher, Corporation Forms Annotated.   3d. ed.   1957–1960.   5
   vols. in 10.   With pocket supplements.   (Companion set to
   Fletcher, Cyclopedia of the Law of Private Corporations.)

d.   Forms in Directories

*Martindale-Hubbell Law Directory* includes special forms of statutory instruments for the various jurisdictions under some digests of the laws.

e.   Forms in State Codes

Some state codes include substantive and procedural forms.   Consult the general index to the code under "Forms."   Examples are:

Arkansas Statutes.   1947.   8 vols. in 19.   With pocket supplements.

Iowa Code Annotated.   1949.   60 vols. in 62.   With pocket
   supplements.

f.   Geographical Area or State Form-Books

Form-books, with emphasis on a geographical area or a state, are also available.   To illustrate:

Kentucky, Legal Forms.   Edited by F. W. Whiteside and
   others.   1963–.   6 vols.   Loose-leaf.

g.   Forms of Instructions to Juries

Forms of approved instructions to juries in criminal and civil cases are included in a number of general and local treatises.   Examples are:

Branson, The Law of Instructions to Juries in Civil and
   Criminal Cases; Rules and a Complete Collection of Approved and Annotated Forms.   3d ed.   1960–1962.   7
   vols.   With pocket supplements.

Ussery, Instructions; the Law and Approved Forms for
   Florida.   1954.   2 vols.   With pocket supplements.

## SECTION D.   APPEAL PAPERS

The printed or duplicated briefs and transcripts of the records from the lower courts, which are submitted to appellate tribunals, are significant research aids.   These papers are very useful sources, providing: (1) the theories upon which arguments hinge, (2) discussion and analysis of the law with citations to the authorities, (3) forms of preliminary motions and pleadings in the case, (4) examination and cross-examination of witnesses, (5) the instructions to the jury, (6) opinions and verdict of the trial court (the opinion may not be reported) and (7) various exhibits.   The exhibits furnish maps, charters, forms of wills, contracts, leases and other instruments.   The pleadings and examination and cross-examination of witnesses are valuable guides for trial lawyers.   The judges and lawyers pore over the charges to juries, evaluating their weaknesses and strengths.

The briefs of the appellant, appellee and amicus curiae in a case provide counsel, who has a similar case, with much of the research completed.   He has a valuable list of arguments which have, or have not, impressed the appellate court.

The briefs and records permit the analysis of the reasons for the affirmance or reversal of a case by comparing the record of the trial in the lower court with the appellate decision.   They serve, therefore, as invaluable guides for counsel in the preparation and trial of his case, and for the judge in minimizing the errors which may be granted on appeal.

The appeal papers of the Supreme Court of the United States are available in print, on microfische and on microcards in a number of the larger law libraries.   The briefs and records of appellate federal and state courts are kept in some libraries.[1]   The card catalog of the law library should be consulted to determine its holdings.   Often briefs and records can be obtained directly from counsel in the cases when they are unavailable in a library, or an extra copy may be borrowed from the clerk of the court or the state bar association.

---

## SECTION E.   LAW DIRECTORIES

Law directories provide lists of lawyers, some of which groupings are general in scope.   Others are limited to the attorneys within a region, a state, a locality or a special practice.   Lists of foreign attorneys are included in the general directories and are also special-

---

[1] See Carpentier, Appellate Records—A Beginning Union List.  62 Law Lib.J. 273.  (1969).

ly published. A few local bar associations publish lists of attorneys in their communities.

## 1. General Directories

The more important general directories are:

### a. Martindale-Hubbell Law Directory

This is an annual directory of attorneys, arranged alphabetically by state and municipality and thereunder by names of attorneys. To locate the listing of an attorney, his residence must be known. Beside the name of an attorney are given his date of birth, date of bar admission, information as to a specialty, American Bar Association membership and a confidential rating. The confidential ratings cover estimates of legal ability, recommendations and ratings for promptness in paying bills. "C" or "L," followed by a numeral, indicates the college or law school attended. Known degrees are listed following the number. An alphabetical list of colleges and law schools appears in the prefatory section.

A *Biographical Section* is devoted to information about lawyers and law firms useful in the selection of competent associate counsel or for other purposes. It also contains lists of lawyers admitted to practice before the U. S. Patent Office, lawyers of the Canadian Provinces and Territories and a selected list of foreign lawyers.

A separate volume, *Law Digests*, is the final division of this directory.

### b. The Lawyers Directory

*The Lawyers Directory* is an annual publication which lists the following:

> Part I, Leading lawyers and law firms in the United States and Canada and a list of foreign lawyers.
>
> Part II, Corporate law department counsel roster.
>
> Part III, Complete list of foreign embassies and legations in Washington, D. C., and U. S. embassies, legations and consular offices throughout the world.

### c. The American Bar, The Canadian Bar, The International Bar.

This is an annual biographical directory of ranking United States and foreign lawyers. It provides sketches of the North American law offices listed and individual biographical data. The third unit is a professional international directory of "the finest lawyers in the world."

## 2. Miscellaneous Directories

Lists, covering the lawyers within a region, a state, a community or a specialized practice, are also available.

Examples are:

Regional: Pacific Coast Legal Directory (for the states of Alaska, Arizona, California, Hawaii, Nevada, Oregon and Washington).

State: Texas Legal Directory.

Local: Brooklyn Bar Association Directory.

Special Practice: Hine's Insurance Counsel.

Foreign: The International Law List.

World Law Directory.

Academic Directories. Add two new titles: International Association of Law Libraries Directory. William Hein & Co., 1977, and Tseng, Henry P., The Law Schools of the World. William Hein & Co., 1977.

## 1. Attorneys General Opinions

a. Federal

The opinions of the United States Attorneys General may be cited:

28 Ops.Atty.Gen. 211.

or

28 Op.Atty.Gen. 211.

b. State

Examples of citations of the opinions of state attorneys general are:

1936 Ops.Atty.Gen.Ind. 191

or

1936 Ind.Ops.Atty.Gen. 191.

23 Mont.Ops.Atty.Gen. 78

or

23 Ops.Atty.Gen.Mont. 78.

## SECTION G. SUMMARY

1. **Opinions of the Attorneys General**
   a. Primary and secondary authority.
   b. Generally, they relate to
      (1) interpretations of statutes or
      (2) general legal problems.

2. **Opinions of the Attorneys General of the United States**
   a. 1789–.
   b. Advance sheets.
   c. Digest of opinions, covering volumes 1–32, 1789–1921.

3. **Opinions of the Attorneys General of the States**
   a. Usually published in bound volumes.
   b. A few states have advance sheets or release opinions initially in mimeographed form.
   c. Some states have cumulative indexes.

4. **Law Dictionaries (See Section B, above)**

5. **Form-Books (See Section C, above)**

6. **Usefulness of Appeal Papers (See Section D, above)**

7. **General Law Directories—Lists of Attorneys**
   a. Martindale-Hubbell Law Directory
      (1) Annual.
      (2) Arranged alphabetically by state and municipality and thereunder by names of attorneys. Provides basic information about attorneys and confidential ratings.
      (3) Biographical section.
      (4) Law Digests.
   b. The Lawyers Directory
      (1) Annual.
      (2) Lists leading lawyers and law firms in United States and foreign countries.
   c. The American Bar, The Canadian Bar, The International Bar.
      (1) Annual.
      (2) Biographical directory of selected American and foreign attorneys.
      (3) Selected "for known character and ability."

d.　United States Lawyers Reference Directory

This annual directory, published by the Legal Directories Publishing Co., Inc., is national in scope but selective in coverage. It is divided into the following sections: (1) a digest of courts, which is arranged alphabetically by the names of the states and includes jurisdictions, terms and personnel of all federal courts and of the state and county courts of each state, and (2) a biographical section, which is arranged alphabetically by the names of the states and subdivided by the names of cities and provides personal and professional data about individual practitioners and law firms.

## 8.　Miscellaneous Directories (See Section E2, above)

# Chapter 19

# INTERNATIONAL LAW

Research in international law is neither esoteric nor limited to the practice of the specialist. American treaties, as primary law, are frequently determinative of the rights and duties of American citizens. To illustrate this point, a Missourian may have a relative in Italy who dies leaving property. A reciprocal treaty with Italy may regulate property and inheritance rights. Therefore, the presence or absence of this treaty would have a significant effect on the rights of inheritance of this Missouri citizen. Another standard example is that of the American citizen who is injured in an airplane accident while traveling over a foreign country. His rights in this case are affected by treaty. These are not isolated illustrations, for they occur more frequently than is generally realized. It is essential, therefore, that the general practitioner have some knowledge of the sources of treaty law.

International law has been defined as

" *  *  * [A] body of rules governing the relations between states  *  *  *. Customary, as distinguished from conventional, international law is based upon the common consent of the nations extending over a period of time of sufficient duration to cause it to become crystalized into a rule of conduct. When doubt arises as to the existence or nonexistence of a rule of international law, or as to the application of a rule to a given situation, resort is usually had to such sources as pertinent treaties, pronouncements of foreign offices, statements by writers, and decisions of international tribunals and those of prize courts and other domestic courts purporting to be expressive of the law of nations." [1]

Another international law scholar has defined international law in terms of how it is made.

"When contrasted with national or 'domestic' law, we think of international law as that which is created of two or more states, whether such action is in the form of treaty-making or the formation of international customs." [2]

[1] 1 Hackworth, Digest of International Law 1 (1940).

[2] Kelsen, Principles of International Law 201 (1952).

International law as so stated is usually known as *public* international law as distinguished from *private* international law, which is defined as:

"  .   .   .   [T]hat branch of the law of municipal law which determines before the courts of what nation a particular action or suit should be brought, and by the law of what nation it should be determined." [3]

This chapter will be devoted to that of public international law and specifically to the researching of the conventional international law of the United States as represented in the treaties and other international agreements entered into between the United States and other countries.[4]

---

## SECTION A.   RESEARCH IN INTERNATIONAL LAW IN RELATION TO THE UNITED STATES

### 1.   Treaties between the United States and other countries

Texts of treaties and other international agreements.[5]

a.   1789–1950.   *Statutes at Large.*   All treaties were published in a separate part of each volume of the *Statutes at Large.*

b.   *Treaties and other International Acts Series.*   (T.I.A.S.). This series is issued in pamphlet form starting with Number 1501.[6] It contains all treaties to which the United States is a party that have been proclaimed during the calendar year, and all international agreements other than treaties to which the United States is a party that have been signed, proclaimed, or with reference to which any other final formality has been executed during each calendar year.[7] The documents are literal prints of the originals with marginal notes and footnotes.

c.   *United States Treaties and other International Acts.*   (U.S.T.) This is an annual bound publication that started in 1950 to take the

---

[3] Black Law Dictionary.   rev. 4th ed. 1968.

[4] For more information on the substantive aspects of international law, see the latest edition of Brierly, The Law of Nations, or Fenwick, International Law. 4th ed. 1965.

[5] A treaty requires confirmation by two thirds of the U. S. Senate.   An International Agreement is one that the President may enter into under his constitutional power as President or as authorized by an act of Congress.   Restatement of the Law 2nd, Foreign Relation Law of the United States § 115a.

[6] This Series replaces the Treaty Series, 1909–45, and the Executive Agreement Series, 1909–1945.

[7] 1 U.S.C. 112A (1970 ed.)

place of printing treaties in the *Statutes at Large*. It contains all of the pamphlets issued during the previous year in the *Treaty and Other International Act* Series.

By statute,[8] the treaties contain in the *Statutes at Large* and in the *United States Treaties and Other International Agreements* are evidence in all federal courts, state courts, and the courts of the Territories and insular possessions of the United States.

d. *Commerce Clearing House, Tax Treaties CCH's Tax Treaties* provide loose-leaf reporting on income and estate tax treaties between the United States and foreign countries. The reporter contains interpretative regulations, news on treaties in preparation, significant court decisions and editorial comment. A special section of the publication features *CCH Treaty Charts* which show in graphic style the contents of each treaty relating to some 200 major tax aspects.[9]

## 2. Collections of United States Treaties

U. S. Treaties have from time to time been published in separate sets. These are:

a. *Malloy's Treaties*. 4 v. (v. 3 often cited as 3 *Redman*; v. 4 as 4 *Trentwith*). This set contains all treaties, etc., between 1776 and 1937 with some annotations. Volume 4 includes an index to the set and a chronological list of treaties.

b. *Miller Treaties*. This is a more recent compilation of treaties. However, only 8 volumes covering the years 1776 and 1863 have appeared. It is doubtful if the set will continue. As yet, it has no index.

c. *U. S. Statutes at Large* (1950–51) vol. 64, pt. 3, at page B1107, et seq. Lists alphabetically, by country, all treaties that were printed in volumes 1–64.

d. A new series of *Treaties and Other International Agreements of the United States of America, 1776–1949,* is being published by the Department of State. This series covers the treaties and other international agreements published in the *Statutes at Large* during 1776–1949 and includes the English texts or, in cases where no English text was signed, the official United States Government translations. The publication begins with several volumes of multilateral treaties and other agreements, arranged chronologically according to date of signature, and will be followed by approximately 11 volumes of bilateral treaties and other agreements alphabetically grouped by the names of countries with which they were concluded. Each volume will include a brief index; however, cumulative analyti-

---

[8] Ibid.

[9] A similar service is published by Prentice-Hall.

cal indexes of the texts of both multilateral and bilateral treaties and other agreements also are envisioned. Although the compilation is annotated, its essential value rests in its collection of documentary texts. To determine the current status of a treaty or agreement, consult the latest annual edition of *Treaties in Force* and the *Department of State Bulletin* for subsequent weekly developments. This set, when completed, will be in approximately sixteen volumes.

### 3. Indexes to U. S. Treaties

a. *Treaties in Force.* This is an annual publication listing all treaties, by country and by subject, that are still in force.

b. *Sprudzs, A. Chronological Index to Multilateral Treaties in Force for the United States (as of Jan. 1, 1972).* This is a useful adjunct to Treaties in Force, which lists only multilateral treaties under subject.

c. *Department of State Bulletin.* This is a weekly publication of the Department of State. Each issue has a section entitled "Treaty Information" and gives current information on treaties. This should be used to supplement *Treaties in Force.* There is a semi-annual index to the *Department of State Bulletin* which may be used to locate current information either by subject or country.

d. *Commerce Clearing House Congressional Index.* The Constitution of the United States in Article II, Sec. 2, provides that the President shall have the power, by and with the consent of the Senate, to make treaties, provided that two-thirds of the Senate concurs. Frequently, after the President signs a treaty, there may be a considerable period of time before the Senate ratifies it. This service provides a section on treaties which is a status table for treaties pending ratification by the Senate.

### 4. Interpretations of Treaties

a. *Digests.* These are more than case digests and include excerpts from treatises, periodical articles, court decisions from various countries, and documents of the various international organizations. The various digests have been published by the Department of State and the editors have all been distinguished scholars:

Wharton's *Digest of International Law*, 3 v. 1886

Moore's *Digest of International Law*, 8 v. 1906

Hackworth's *Digest of International Law*, 8 v. 1940

Whiteman's *Digest of International Law*, 1963, to be completed in 16 v. Supplements Hackworth.

b. *Citators for Treaties.* Several methods are available for determining the subsequent legislative and judicial history of a treaty or other international agreement to which the United States is a party.

(1) *Shepard's United States Citator,* Statute volumes. Treaties entered into before 1950 may be Shepardized in the usual manner in the section for *Statutes at Large (not included in the U. S. Code).* Treaties entered into after 1950 may be Shepardized in the section for *U. S. Treaties and Other International Acts.*

(2) *Federal Code Annotated.* (USCS–FCA) There is an unnumbered volume to uncodified laws and treaties which gives annotations to all court decisions interpreting treaties.

(3) *U. S. Supreme Court Digest.* (Lawyers Co-operative ed.) v. 14 has a table of Laws cited and construed [for] Treaties and Agreements with Foreign Nations.

c. *Restatement of the Law, Second. Foreign Relations Law of the United States.* This *Restatement* was adopted by the American Law Institute in 1965. Its purpose, as stated in the introduction, is to set forth the foreign relations law of the United States, which consists of those rules the United States conceives to be established by international law and those parts of the domestic law which give effect to rules of international law.

## SECTION B. ILLUSTRATIONS: UNITED STATES TREATIES

PROBLEM: Does the United States and France have a treaty on Double Taxation in reference to estate and inheritance tax?

### Illustrations

118.  Pages from 1971 issue of Treaties in Force.

119.  Page from U. S. Shepard's citations, Statute volume.

120.  Page from Part 2, 1971 Issue of Treaties in Force.

121.  Page from U. S. Shepard's citations, Statutes volume.

122.  Page from Volume 67, No. 173 of the Department of State Bulletin.

123.  Page from Treaty Status Table—CCH Congressional Index Service.

[Illustration 118]

TITLE PAGE FROM 1971 ISSUE OF TREATIES IN FORCE

# TREATIES IN FORCE

## A List of Treaties

## and Other International Agreements

## of the United States

This publication is issued each year. It is in two sections; Part one lists all countries for which the U. S. has bilateral agreements; part two is arranged alphabetically by subject and lists all multilateral agreements to which the United States is a signatory.

This publication lists treaties and other international agreements of the United States on record in the Department of State on January 1, 1971 which had not expired by their terms or which had not been denounced by the parties, replaced or superseded by other agreements, or otherwise definitely terminated.

Compiled by the Treaty Affairs Staff,
Office of the Legal Adviser,
Department of State.

[Illustration 118–a]

## PAGE FROM 1971 ISSUE OF TREATIES IN FORCE

**FRANCE (Cont'd)**

---

### FINDING BILATERAL TREATIES

1. Use Part 1 of latest edition of Treaties in Force. All treaties which the U. S. has entered into with other countries are listed under the name of the other country.

Note citations where text of treaty may be found.

---

POSTAL MATTERS
Postal money order convention.
Signed at Washington August 19, 1931; operative February 1, 1932.

Convention relative to the exchange of parcel post.
Signed at Paris December 7 and at Washington December 30, 1935; operative August 1, 1935.
49 Stat. 3322; Post Office Department print; 171 LNTS 117.

PUBLICATIONS
Agreement relating to exchange of official publications.
Exchange of notes at Paris August 14, 1945; entered into force January 1, 1946.
60 Stat. 1944; TIAS 1579; 73 LNTS 237.

RELIEF SUPPLIES AND PACKAGES
Agreement for free entry and free inland transportation of relief supplies and packages.
Signed at Paris December 23, 1948; entered into force December 23, 1948.
62 Stat. 3587; TIAS 1873; 67 UNTS 171.

Amendments:
January 31, 1950 (1 UST 224; TIAS 2043; 67 UNTS 171).
August 3, 1950 (1 UST 597; TIAS 2107; 93 UNTS 367).
July 2 and August 5, 1952 (3 UST 5039; TIAS 2684; 181 UNTS 345).

SATELLITES
Agreement on cooperation in intercontinental testing in connection with experimental communications satellites.
Exchange of notes at Paris March 31, 1961; entered into force March 31, 1961.
12 UST 483; TIAS 4738; 409 UNTS 135.

Agreement concerning development of satellite and balloon techniques and instrumentation for the study of meteorological phenomena (Project EOLE).
Exchange of notes at Washington June 16 and 17, 1966; entered into force June 17, 1966.
17 UST 1123; TIAS 6069; 601 UNTS 113.

SMUGGLING
Convention for prevention of smuggling of intoxicating liquors.
Signed at Washington June 30, 1924; entered into force March 12, 1927.
45 Stat. 2403; TS 755; IV Trenwith 4175; 61 LNTS 415.

TAXATION
Agreement relating to relief from double income tax on shipping profits.
Exchange of notes at Washington June 11 and July 8, 1927; entered into force July 8, 1927; operative from January 1, 1921.
47 Stat. 2604; EAS 12; 114 LNTS 413.

Convention for the avoidance of double taxation and the prevention of evasion in the case of taxes on estates and inheritances, and modifying and supplementing the convention relating to income taxation signed July 25, 1939.
Signed at Paris October 18, 1946; entered into force October 17, 1949.
64 Stat. (3) B3; TIAS 1982; 140 UNTS 23.

---

Protocol modifying the convention signed October 18, 1946, for the avoidance of double taxation and the prevention of evasion in the case of taxes on estates and inheritances, and modifying and supplementing the convention relating to income taxation signed July 25, 1939.[1]
Signed at Washington May 17, 1948; entered into force October 17, 1949.
64 Stat. (3) B28; TIAS 1982; 140 UNTS 50.

---

Convention supplementing the conventions of July 25, 1939 and October 18, 1946 relating to the avoidance of double taxation, as modified and supplemented by the protocol of May 17, 1948.[1]
Signed at Washington June 22, 1956; entered into force June 13, 1957.
8 UST 843; TIAS 3844; 291 UNTS 101.

Agreement relating to relief from taxation of United States Government expenditures in France in the interests of common defense.
Exchange of notes at Paris June 13, 1952; entered into force June 13, 1952.
3 UST 4828; TIAS 2655; 181 UNTS 3.

---

[1] Provisions concerning taxes on income, on capital and tax on stock exchange transactions terminated by convention of July 28, 1967 (TIAS 6518).

[Illustration 119]

## PAGE FROM U.S. SHEPARD'S CITATIONS—STATUTE VOLUME

UNITED STATES STATUTES AT LARGE (Not in United States Code) 1946

**FINDING BILATERAL TREATIES**

After locating a treaty, it may be "Shepardized" to find subsequent amendments or other changes and to find court decisions that have cited or interpreted the treaty.

**§ 5**
70St116

**Aug. 13**
**Ch. 959**
**60 St. 1049**

329US49
91LE29
67SC171
329US684
91LE601
67SC352
329US685
91LE602
67SC364
**§ 25**
152FS953
70St547

**Aug. 13**
**Ch. 962**
**60 St. 1057**

Rs70A St1
61St798
**§§ 1 to 20**
Rs70A St1

**Aug. 14**
**Ch. 963**
**60 St. 1062**

**§ 1**
R74St726
61St214

**Aug. 14**
**Ch. 964**
**60 St. 1062**

68St526
**§ 2**
Subd. a
¶ 3
61St955
Subd. d
A61St55
61St694
Subd. f
R64St100
**§ 3**
Subsec. 44
60St1099

**Aug. 14**
**Ch. 966**
**60 St. 1082**

**Title 1**
**§ 11**
A61St694

**Aug. 14**
**61 St. 1218**

62St2144
62St2344
62St2392
62St2416
62St2441
62St2862
3UST4177
4UST1921
5UST2493

**Aug. 24**
**Ch. 210**
**60 St. 121**

79St285

**Aug. 30**
**61 St. 1236**

64St B33
3UST3922
3UST3927
4UST2058
**Protocol**
**Art. 1**
Sg1UST626
62St1654
**Art. 2**
Sg1UST626
62St1654
3UST3922
3UST3927

**Sept. 6**
**61 St. 4121**

2UST460
**Art. 8**
9UST1468
**Schedule 1**
Rs9UST [1468
**Schedule 2**
Rs9UST [1468

**Sept. 12**
**61 St. 2688**

E13UST [2266
E14UST359
158FS64
78St1248
13UST408

**Art. 1**
158FS67
¶ 1

**Art. 8**
R14UST [1022
**Art. 9**
R14UST [1022
**Art. 10**
R14UST [1022
**Art. 11**
R14UST [1022
78St1248
**Art. 12**
R14UST [1022
78St1248
¶ 1
158FS64
¶ 2
158FS64
**Art. 15**
¶ 1
A13UST409
A14UST [1023
**Art. 17**
A14UST [1022
78St1248
¶ 2
13UST410
**Schedule 1**
R14UST [1022
78St1248
**Schedule 2**
R14UST [1022
78St1248
**Notes**
Rp14UST [1022

**Sept. 13**
**61 St. 3750**

**Art. 3**
A62St1889

**Sept. 23**
**61 St. 2903**

62St3575

**Sept. 25**
**61 St. 3479**

**Arts. 23 to 31**
Rs2UST [1376
**Arts. 101 to 116**
Rs2UST [1376

**Sept. 25**
**61 St. 3524**

Rs2UST [1423

**Sept. 25**
**61 St. 3540**

Rs2UST [1458

**Sept. 30**
**61 St. 2495**

A6UST6157
**Art. 2**
A6UST6157
¶ 3
Rn ¶ 4
10UST966
¶ 3
Ad10UST [966
¶ 4
Rn ¶ 5
10UST966
**Art. 4**
¶ 2
A10UST969
¶ 3
Rs10UST [969
¶5
A10UST970
¶ 8
A10UST963
¶ 9
Rs10UST [970
¶ 10
A10UST959
¶ 14
Ad10UST [961

**Art. 5**
A6UST6157
A8UST1395
¶ 11
Ad10UST [971
**Art. 6**
A6UST6157
¶ 3
A10UST972
**Art. 11**
¶ 4
10UST961

**Oct. 1**
**61 St. 1222**

62St1659

**Oct. 7**
**61 St. 2398**

E3UST351
Sg11UST [1982
6UST3771
15UST2489
**Art. 3**
3UST352
**Art. 9**
6UST3771
**Art. 10**
6UST3771
**Art. 12**
11UST1982
**Art. 14**
11UST1982
**Art. 15**
11UST1982
**Art. 16**
11UST1982
**Art. 17**
11UST1982
**Art. 20**
11UST1982
**Art. 21**
11UST1982
**Art. 22**
11UST1982
**Art. 24**
11UST1982
**Art. 25**
11UST1982
**Art. 29**
11UST1982
**Art. 32**
11UST1982

**Oct. 9**
**62 St. 1672**

**Art. 4**
E5UST2904
5UST2906
**Art. 6**
6UST3904
**Art. 7**
6UST3904
**Art. 9**
10UST745
**Art. 11**
10UST745
**Art. 12**
10UST745
**Art. 13**
10UST745
**Art. 14**
10UST745
**Art. 15**
10UST745
**Art. 17**
10UST745
**Art. 18**
10UST745
**Art. 19**
10UST745
**Art. 20**
10UST745
**Art. 21**
10UST745
**Art. 25**
10UST745

**Oct. 18**
**64 St. B3**

Sg8UST843
**Art. 7**
Subd. a
A8UST847
**Art. 17**
A8UST848
**Protocol**
E8UST843
**Art. 1**
Subd. 3
A8UST845

**Oct. 23**
**61 St. 2876**

13UST1918

**Oct. 25**
**61 St. 1044**

A61St1073

**Oct. 30**
**62 St. 2618**

**Nov. 14**
**61 St. 2573**

5UST2165
12UST846
**Art. 2**
12UST846
**Annex**
¶ 2
A12UST847

**Nov. 16**
**61 St. 2479**

62St3023
**Annex to Air Transport Agreement**
**§ B**
A62St3023

**Nov. 20**
**61 St. 2795**

A61St3777

**Dec. 2**
**61 St. 2475**

E62St3645
Sg1UST540
109FS343
62St2283
62St3600
63St2630
63St2654
64St B84
¶ 4
A61St3614
¶ 5
A61St3614
¶ 6
Sub ¶ e
Sg1UST541
¶ 8
A61St3614
¶ 12
61St3608

**Dec. 2**
**62 St. 1716**

3UST3001

6UST645
8UST69
11UST32
14UST1690
**Art. 2**
¶ 2
1UST507
¶ 3
A10UST953
**Art. 5**
1UST507
3UST2999
6UST645
10UST331
11UST33
13UST494
¶ 1
A10UST953
¶ 3
1UST509
7UST658
10UST331
11UST33
13UST494
13UST497
14UST112
14UST1690
**Art. 7**
8UST70
**Art. 11**
3UST3003
**Schedule**
A13UST493
A13UST497
A14UST112
A14UST [1691
A15UST [2547
¶ 1
Subd. a
A11UST32
A14UST [1691
¶ 2
4UST2184
¶ 4
A4UST2181
A6UST647
¶ 4
(6UST645)
Cl. 1
A11UST33
Cl. 2
R7UST657
¶ 5
A4UST2181
Sd7UST657
A8UST2204
A11UST33
A14UST [1691
¶ 6
A1UST506
A2UST11
A3UST3001
A3UST5094
A4UST2180
A6UST647
¶ 6
(6UST645)
A10UST330
Cl. 1
A13UST498
*Continued*

See note on page 1219

1645

## [Illustration 120]

## PAGE FROM PART 2, 1971 ISSUE OF TREATIES IN FORCE

**SATELLITES** (Cont'd)

Ministry of                    Syrian Arab

---

#### FINDING MULTILATERAL TREATIES.

**PROBLEM:** Is the United States a signatory to an International Convention on Conservation of Seals.

Check in Part 2 of Treaties in Force under subject: Seals.

Note citations to where text of treaty may be located.

As additional countries become signatories, they are listed in the weekly Department of State Bulletin and then included in the next annual edition of Treaties in Force.

---

~~cations~~
Administration of Posts      Viet-Nam
 and Telecommunications 1
Ministry of Communi-         Yemen Arab
 cations                       Republic
Community of the             Yugoslavia
 Yugoslav Posts, Tele-
 graphs and Telephones 1
General Post Office 1         Zambia

---

**SEALS**

Interim convention on conservation of North Pacific fur seals.
Signed at Washington February 9, 1957; entered into force for the United States October 14, 1957.
8 UST 2283; TIAS 3948; 314 UNTS 105.
States which are parties:
Canada                       Union of Soviet
Japan                          Socialist Reps.
                             United States

Protocol amending the interim convention on conservation of North Pacific fur seals.
Done at Washington October 8, 1963; entered into force for the United States April 10, 1964.
15 UST 316; TIAS 5558; 494 UNTS 303.
States which are parties:
Canada                       Union of Soviet
Japan                          Socialist Reps.
                             United States

Extension:
September 3, 1969 (20 UST 2992; TIAS 6774).

**SHIPPING (See MARITIME**
   **MATTERS; NAVAL VESSELS;**
   **RULES OF WARFARE)**

---

5  With reservation.

[Illustration 121]

## PAGE FROM U.S. SHEPARD'S CITATIONS—STATUTES VOLUME

**UNITED STATES TREATIES AND OTHER INTERNATIONAL AGREEMENTS** Vol. 8

| | | | | | | |
|---|---|---|---|---|---|---|
| **–597–** | **Art. 3** | ¶ 7 | 10UST200 | **Art. 14** | **–1421–** | **–1633–** | First |
| 11UST388 | 12UST1045 | Rn¶8 | 10UST1033 | A10UST | 8UST869 | A13UST | Memo- |
| **–609–** | **–721–** | [12UST | 10UST1638 | [1818 | 10UST2049 | [1482 | randum of |
| 13UST288 | E8UST1392 | [2947 | 11UST2515 | **–1265–** | **–1425–** | **–1725–** | Under- |
| **–617–** | **Art. 1** | **–859–** | 12UST728 | A10UST | 10UST2081 | Sg12UST | standing |
| A12UST240 | A8UST1392 | 9UST397 | **–1063–** | [1659 | **–1427–** | [904 | § 1 |
| ¶ 4 | **Art. 2** | **–863–** | 8UST1069 | 8UST213 | 8UST821 | **–1741–** | A9UST1355 |
| A12UST240 | ¶ 1 | 12UST1195 | **–1069–** | 8UST1225 | 8UST866 | Sg11UST | E10UST159 |
| **–625–** | Cl. c | **–866–** | 8UST1063 | **Art. 6** | **–1431–** | [1405 | 9UST1003 |
| 8UST26 | A9UST1167 | A8UST1427 | **–1073–** | 13UST1770 | 8UST367 | **Art. 2** | **–1903–** |
| 8UST77 | **–738–** | 8UST821 | 8UST1063 | ¶ A | 9UST237 | ¶ 7 | 13UST2645 |
| **–637–** | A12UST155 | **–869–** | 8UST1069 | A10UST | 12UST3176 | 11UST1406 | 14UST1424 |
| 8UST279 | **Art. 4** | 10UST2050 | **–1093–** | [1659 | **–1435–** | ¶ 8 | **–1937–** |
| **–657–** | ¶ A | **–890–** | 71St454 | **Art. 8** | A11UST | 11UST1405 | 10UST2208 |
| 8UST680 | A12UST155 | 71St C51 | 10UST1425 | ¶ A | [1783 | **–1757–** | **–2021–** |
| 22UST508 | **Art. 7** | 76St1468 | 14UST1265 | A10UST | A13UST | 15UST167 | A15UST289 |
| 13UST2650 | A12UST156 | 77St972 | 14UST1489 | [1660 | [1494 | **–1767–** | **–2043–** |
| **Art. 1** | **–753–** | **–894–** | **Art. 6** | 13UST1770 | A15UST | 77St971 | 186FS300 |
| A9UST1416 | 14UST2222 | 13UST2178 | ¶ A | ¶ B | [2007 | 10UST272 | 46ABA24 |
| ¶ 1 | **–764–** | ¶ 3 | Cl. 3 | A10UST | **–1442–** | 13UST2757 | **Art. 1** |
| A9UST1417 | E10UST25 | 13UST2178 | A14UST135 | [1660 | Sg10UST | 13UST2823 | 186FS320 |
| **Art. 2** | A10UST | **Annex A** | **Art. 12** | ¶ C | [1997 | 13UST2891 | **Art. 5** |
| A9UST1417 | [1383 | A9UST1334 | 10UST87 | A10UST | **–1445–** | 15UST2590 | 288F2d375 |
| ¶ 1 | E11UST | **–899–** | 13UST416 | [1660 | A15UST | ¶ I | **Art. 6** |
| Cl. d | [1455 | 11UST2165 | ¶ A | A13UST | [1539 | 13UST2679 | ¶ 2 |
| A14UST | ¶ 6 | **Art. 8** | Cl. 1 | [1770 | **–1457–** | ¶ L | 186FS320 |
| [1066 | 10UST25 | 11UST2165 | 13UST423 | **–1289–** | 10UST1182 | 13UST2606 | **–2205–** |
| **Art. 3** | **–771–** | **–933–** | 14UST1274 | A11UST | **–1534–** | ¶ N | Sg9UST967 |
| 12UST508 | 9UST1264 | 71St C50 | ¶ C | [1872 | 8UST1629 | 13UST2679 | 13UST2068 |
| ¶ 1 | **–773–** | 76St1468 | 14UST1269 | 8UST799 | 9UST1416 | ¶ R | **Art. 1** |
| A9UST1419 | R10UST | 77St972 | **Art. 14** | 9UST1 | 21UST508 | 13UST2678 | 13UST2070 |
| ¶ 2 | [1418 | Schedule | ¶ D | 10UST1049 | **–1537–** | ¶ W | ¶ 1 |
| A9UST1419 | **–787–** | ¶ 907 | 71St454 | **–1343–** | A13UST | 76St1469 | A9UST305 |
| **Memoran-** | | | | | | | **Art. 2** |
| **dum of** | | | | | | | ¶ 1 |
| **Under-** | | | | | | | Cl. a |
| **standing** | | | | | | | A9UST1156 |
| **§ 2** | | | | | | | Cl. b |
| ¶ 1 | | | | | | | 9UST969 |
| A8UST1534 | | | | | | | Cl. c |
| A8UST1629 | | | | | | | A9UST1158 |
| A9UST1419 | | | | | | | **Art. 3** |
| **§ 3** | | | | | | | 13UST2070 |
| S10UST787 | | | | | | | **Agreed** |
| **–677–** | | | | | | | **Minute** |
| 8UST197 | | | | | | | ¶ 1 |
| 9UST1379 | **Art. 3** | [1074 | **Art. 12** | **–1363–** | Cl. e | 13UST879 | A9UST305 |
| 11UST401 | ¶ 2 | **–957–** | ¶ C | 15UST2209 | R13UST | 13UST898 | 9UST968 |
| **–680–** | Cl. d | 8UST963 | 15UST1459 | **–1367–** | [1878 | 13UST907 | 9UST1343 |
| 8UST657 | A8UST1289 | **Art. 1** | **–1225–** | A13UST | Cl. f | 13UST1037 | **–2213–** |
| **–683–** | A11UST | ¶ 3 | A13UST | [1486 | R13UST | 13UST1218 | 9UST1113 |
| Sg11UST | [1872 | 8UST963 | [1486 | **Art. 6** | [1812 | 13UST1818 | **–2283–** |
| [1982 | **–821–** | **Art. 5** | 8UST213 | A13UST | ¶ 10 | 13UST2889 | A15UST317 |
| **–691–** | 8UST866 | 11UST2382 | **Art. 4** | [1812 | Cl. b | ¶ Z | 80St1091 |
| E10UST22 | **Art. 1** | **–963–** | ¶ 3 | **Art. 8** | A13UST | **Art. 35** | **Art. 2** |
| E11UST210 | A8UST866 | 8UST957 | A13UST | A13UST | [1878 | 11UST1543 | ¶ 2 |
| 15UST1523 | A8UST1427 | **–965–** | [1486 | [1813 | Cl. d | **–1862–** | RnCl i |
| ¶ 6 | **–832–** | A13UST | **Art. 5** | **Art. 10** | A13UST | Sg11UST | [15UST317 |
| 10UST22 | A11UST | [1033 | A13UST | A13UST | [1878 | [2249 | Cl. g |
| **–697–** | [1874 | 10UST3185 | [1487 | ¶ B | **–1561–** | 10UST1730 | Ad15UST |
| A10UST | 13UST1776 | **–970–** | **Art. 11** | **Art. 12** | 10UST1620 | **Art. 1** | [317 |
| [1233 | **–835–** | 8UST721 | A13UST | A13UST | **–1567–** | A10UST | Cl. h |
| **Art. 2** | A12UST | **–973–** | [1487 | [1815 | 9UST1379 | [1733 | Ad15UST |
| ¶ 1 | [2947 | 9UST1444 | **–1245–** | **–1386–** | **–1593–** | **–1869–** | [317 |
| Cl. a | E14UST | **–979–** | A10UST | 12UST1659 | E10UST | 14UST1210 | ¶ 3 |
| A10UST | [1178 | 9UST131 | [1815 | **–1391–** | [3026 | **–1879–** | A15UST317 |
| [1233 | ¶ 4 | 9UST1073 | **Art. 4** | 8UST721 | **–1604–** | 10UST385 | **Art. 3** |
| Cl. b | A9UST1547 | 9UST1075 | ¶ A | 8UST970 | 11UST2337 | **–1885–** | A15UST318 |
| A10UST | ¶ 6 | **–993–** | A10UST | **–1395–** | **–1626–** | A9UST1003 | 80St1092 |
| [1233 | Rn¶7 | A11UST | [1815 | 10UST970 | 12UST718 | 13UST1953 | **Art. 5** |
| **–715–** | [12UST | [2532 | **Art. 7** | **–1410–** | 13UST2598 | **Art. 1** | 80St1093 |
| A9UST1025 | [2947 | A11UST | A10UST | A10UST | **–1629–** | 13UST1953 | ¶ 2 |
| 12UST1044 | ¶ 6 | [2559 | [1815 | 14UST337 | 8UST1534 | **Art. 3** | Cl. e |
| **Art. 1** | Ad12UST | 9UST1015 | **–1413–** | **–1413–** | 9UST1416 | 13UST1953 | A15UST318 |
| 12UST1045 | [2947 | 9UST1474 | | E9UST1146 | 12UST508 | 13UST1953 | Continued |

Finding Multilateral Treaties.

2. The *UST* can also be Shepardized.

While not shown in this exhibit, Shepard's will give citations to court decisions that cite the *UST*.

1729

[Illustration 122]

## PAGE FROM VOLUME 67, NO. 173 OF THE DEPARTMENT OF STATE BULLETIN

---

### TREATY INFORMATION

## Current Actions

### MULTILATERAL

**Aviation**

Convention for the suppression of unlawful acts against the safety of civil aviation. Done at Montreal September 23, 1971.[1]
*Accession deposited:* Mali, August 24, 1972.

**Fisheries**

International convention for the Northwest Atlantic fisheries. Done at Washington February 8, 1949. Entered into force July 3, 1950. TIAS 2089;

Protocol to the international convention for the Northwest Atlantic fisheries (TIAS 2089). Done at Washington June 25, 1956. Entered into force January 10, 1959. TIAS 4170;

Declaration of understanding regarding the international convention for the Northwest Atlantic fisheries (TIAS 2089). Done at Washington April 24, 1961. Entered into force June 5, 1963. TIAS 5380;

Protocol to the international convention for the Northwest Atlantic fisheries (TIAS 2089), relating to harp and hood seals. Done at Washington July 15, 1963. Entered into force April 29, 1966. TIAS 6011;

Protocol to the international convention for the Northwest Atlantic fisheries (TIAS 2089), relating to entry into force of proposals adopted by the Commission. Done at Washington November 29, 1965. Entered into force December 19, 1969. TIAS 6840;

Protocol to the international convention for the Northwest Atlantic fisheries (TIAS 2089), relating to measures of control. Done at Washington November 29, 1965. Entered into force December 19, 1969. TIAS 6841;

Protocol to the international convention for the Northwest Atlantic fisheries (TIAS 2089), relating to panel membership and to regulatory measures. Done at Washington October 1, 1969. Entered into force December 15, 1971. TIAS 7432;

Protocol to the international convention for the Northwest Atlantic fisheries (TIAS 2089), relating to amendments to the convention. Done at Washington October 6, 1970.[1]
*Adherences deposited:* Bulgaria, August 21, 1972.

**Judicial Procedures**

Convention on the taking of evidence abroad in civil or commercial matters. Done at The Hague March 18, 1970.

[1] Not in force.

*Ratifications deposited:* Norway, August 3, 1972; United States, August 8, 1972.
*Enters into force:* October 7, 1972.

**Satellite Communications System**

Agreement relating to the International Telecommunications Satellite Organization (Intelsat), with annexes. Done at Washington August 20, 1971.[1]
*Ratification deposited:* Chile, August 18, 1972.
*Accession deposited:* Saudi Arabia, August 24, 1972.

Operating agreement relating to the International Telecommunications Satellite Organization (Intelsat), with annex. Done at Washington August

The Department of State Bulletin is published weekly. Each issue has a section on Treaty Information which serves as "advance sheets" to Treaties in Force.

June 9, 1967; for the United States November 28, 1968. TIAS 6592.
*Ratification deposited:* Byelorussian Soviet Socialist Republic, July 11, 1972 (with a reservation and declaration).

**White Slave Traffic**

Agreement for the suppression of the white slave traffic, as amended by the protocol of May 4, 1949 (TIAS 2332). Signed at Paris May 18, 1904. Entered into force July 18, 1905; for the United States June 6, 1908. 35 Stat. 1979.
*Notification that it considers itself bound:* Fiji, June 12, 1972.

### BILATERAL

**Finland**

Agreement relating to the deposit by Finland of 10 percent of the value of training services furnished by the United States. Effected by exchange of notes at Helsinki August 17, 1972. Entered into force August 17, 1972; effective February 7, 1972.

**Saudi Arabia**

Agreement extending the agreement of November 9, 1963, and January 4, 1964, as amended and extended (TIAS 5659, 6071, 6413, 6555, 6998, 7265), relating to the establishment of a television system in Saudi Arabia. Effected by exchange of notes at Jidda April 24 and July 30, 1972. Entered into force July 30, 1972.

**Union of Soviet Socialist Republics**

Agreement with respect to purchases of grain by the Soviet Union in the United States and credit to be made available by the United States, with exchange of notes. Signed at Washington July 8, 1972. Entered into force July 8, 1972.

## [Illustration 123]

## PAGE FROM TREATY STATUS TABLE—CCH CONGRESSIONAL INDEX SERVICE

---

**1632**  Treaties  78 6-21-72

signed at Bogota, Colombia, on May 2, 1948, by the plenipotentiaries of the United States and other American republics.

In Foreign Relations Committee.
Reported 5/4/71
Hearing available, May 11, 1971.

**Executive O—Crimes—Genocide**

Convention on the prevention and punishment of the crime of genocide, adopted unanimously by the General Assembly of the United Nations in Paris on December 9, 1948, and signed on behalf of the United States on December 11, 1948.

In Foreign Relations Committee.
Hearing, Jan. 23, 1950.
Hearing available, May 4, 1950.
Hearing, March 10, 1971.
Reported, 5/14/71
Hearing available, May 11, 1971.

**Executive S—Labor—Right to organize**

Convention concerning Freedom of Association and Protection of the Right to Organize, adopted by the International Labor Conference at its thirty-first session, held at San Francisco June 17 to July 10, 1948.

In Foreign Relations Committee.

### Eighty-fourth Congress—Second Session

**Executive D—Crimes—Plant protection**

International plant protection convention, signed on behalf of U. S. and 36 other States at Rome from December 6, 1951, to May 1, 1952.

Injunction of secrecy removed January 12, 1956.
In Foreign Relations Committee.
Reported 6/5/72 (Exec. Rept. 92-22).
Ratified by S. [Roll Call] June 12, 1972.

### Eighty-seventh Congress—Second Session

**Executive C—Labor—International Labor Organization—Reports**

Convention concerning the partial revision of the conventions adopted by the International Labor Organization to standardize provisions regarding the preparation of reports by its governing body on the working of conventions.

Injunction of secrecy removed June 1, 1962.
In Foreign Relations Committee.

**Executive**
Conv
March 3
Injunc
In Fo

> After the President has signed a Treaty, it must be ratified by the Senate. This Table lists treaties awaiting ratification by the Senate.
>
> It is arranged by Number of Congress and gives information as to the present status of such pending treaties. Weekly supplements are issued to this Service.

York on

**Executive**
Conv
national
Injunc
In Fo

y Inter-

## SECTION C.   SOURCES OF INTERNATIONAL LAW FOR COUNTRIES OTHER THAN THE UNITED STATES

Most countries have collections of their treaties and indexes to them, but their description is beyond the scope of this book.[8]   There are, however, more general works published by international organizations which are useful when searching for information on treaties to which the United States is not a signatory.   These are briefly discussed below:

### 1.  Multinational Collections of Treaties

a.   *The Consolidated Treaties Series, 1648–1918.*   This series is a reproduced collection of world treaties in their original languages and existing translations in English or French from the foundation of the modern system of States, 1648, to the commencement of the *League of Nations Treaty Series*, 1918–1920.   It is being edited by Clive Parry and is being published by Oceana Publications, Inc., in about 100 volumes.   The publisher hopes to complete the series by about 1976.   The volumes are arranged chronologically, e. g., 1648–1652, 1653–1655.   The final volumes will contain a complete chronological list and cross indices by party and by subject.   The annotations will have limited scope, since they will not give the current status of the treaties.

b.   *League of Nations Treaty Series.*   This set covers the period of 1920 to 1946, and contains treatises of member and nonmember nations.

c.   *United Nations Treaty Series*, 1946 to date.   This set contains the text of all treaties registered with the United Nations by its member states, or filed and recorded by nonmember states or international organizations.   Each volume also includes a list of notifications of ratifications, accessions, extensions, denunciations, etc., concerning published treaties.   The *Series* is published in accordance with Article 102 of the United Nations Charter.   The texts are given in their original language with English and French translated editions.   Cumulative Indexes to the *United Nations Treaty Series* are published.   Each Cumulative Index covers from 50 to 100 volumes.

d.   *United Nations. Office of Legal Affairs. Multilateral Treaties in Respect of which the Secretary-General Performs Depositary Function.  1968.*   This is an annual publication which covers all multilateral treaties which have been concluded under the auspices of the

---

[8] For information on other countries, see Robinson, International Law and Organizations: General Sources of Information.  1967, and Bishop, International Law, cases and materials.  3d ed. 1971.  pp. xliii–xlvi.

United Nations and which have been deposited with the Secretary-General.

A loose-leaf volume (Annex) contains final clauses of the treaties deposited. It serves as a reference bank to the annual volumes.

e. *United Nations List of Treaty Collections. 1956.* This is a list of about 700 treaty collections published since the latter part of the 18th century. The compilation is arranged according to the following categories: (1) general, (2) subject, and (3) countries.

f. *Keesing's Treaties and Alliances of the World.* This single volume publication is designed to present the state of affairs with regard to groupings of States and their important treaties with each other, noting treaties in force as of early 1968. It covers several thousand agreements, mainly bilateral, which deal with trade, economic and technical aid, cultural relations and extradition.

g. *Major Peace Treaties of Modern History, 1648–1967.* This is the first comprehensive collection of peace treaties to appear in English. It consists of four volumes and is edited by Fred L. Israel. The official English translations, prepared by the British Foreign Office, were used whenever available. When such English documents were nonexistent, private translations were used. The first document in the series is the peace treaty of Westphalia, concluded in 1648, and the last document in the set is the peace settlement concluded at Tashkent in 1966 between India and Pakistan through the intercession of the Soviet Union. The treaties are chronologically arranged, with a subject index in volume 4.

h. *Pan American Union Treaty Series.* The Pan American Union, as the General Secretariat of the Organization of American States, is responsible not only for the receipt and custody of the instruments of ratification but also for the preparation and publication of the official texts of that organization.

Since 1957, these texts, in English and Spanish, have been issued by the General Legal Division as part of its Treaty Series. The Series includes Organization treaties and other significant instruments. Treaty Series No. 1 covers the Charter of the Organization of the American States, signed at the Ninth International Conference of American States, March 30–May 2, 1948.

No. 5 is a useful chart, revised at regular intervals, showing the Status of Inter-American Treaties and Conventions.

i. *Harvard Law School Library, Index to Multilateral Treaties. 1965.* This is a chronological list of multi-part international agreements from the sixteenth century (1596) through 1963, with citations to their text. A subject and regional guide is also provided. The subject analysis does not include specific sections of a treaty; nor is the current status of each treaty given.

j.  *International Legal Materials: Current Documents.*  This bimonthly publication of the American Society of International Law is a collection of current official foreign and United States documents relating to international legal affairs.  It began publication in 1962.  The documents include: (1) current materials that may not become available in more permanent collections until a later date and (2) recent materials that are not readily accessible in any other form in most law libraries.

---

## SECTION D.  INTERNATIONAL LAW:  RESEARCH PROCEDURE

Research methodology relating to treaties can be reduced to these steps: (1) identification of a problem as being within the scope of a treaty and whether a treaty covers the problem, (2) if there is a treaty in point, ascertain its present status and (3) elicit interpretations of the treaty.  The following procedure encompasses these steps.

Some individuals begin their research by checking a status table immediately to determine both the scope and the status of a treaty. Others start with a descriptive publication, such as *Whiteman's Digest*.  Still others commence their research with a treaty collection or an index.  The nature of the problem also influences research procedure.  To facilitate our explanation of methodology, we will follow a conventional procedure.

### 1.  Determination of the Existence or the Status of an American Treaty

a.  List of Treaties in Force

Check this publication first for information as to the existence and status of an American treaty.

b.  Department of State Bulletin

The current issues of the *Bulletin* provide information as to recent developments of important pending treaties.  This supplements the *List of Treaties in Force.*

c.  Malloy's Treaties and Miller's Treaties

To locate a treaty by subject between the United States and a foreign country refer to *Malloy's Treaties* (1776–1937).  If a treaty is known to exist for the period of 1776 to 1863 and its date is also roughly known, examine *Miller's Treaties.*  The absence of an index makes *Miller's Treaties* a difficult publication to use. However, its annotations are more inclusive than *Malloy's*.

    d.   Subject Index to the Treaty Series and the Executive Agreement Series, 1931

This subject index, although not up-to-date, is helpful in locating the treaties in these series prior to July, 1931. An advantage of this guide is that it indexes the content of each article of the treaties rather than the general subject matter of the treaties.

    e.   List of Treaties and Other International Agreements Contained in the United States Statutes at Large (Vol. 64, Pt. 3, Statutes at Large)

This comprehensive list, covering the American treaties prior to 1950, is useful for obtaining the *Statutes at Large* citations which then can be Shepardized. This index is arranged by the names of countries; therefore, the name of a participating country to a treaty must be known to use it. It is supplemented by the *U. S. Statutes at Large Tables of Laws Affected* and in later *Statutes at Large* volumes.

    f.   Treaties Signed But Not Yet in Force

Several lists are available for consultation as to treaties which have been signed but are not yet in force. These aids are especially useful for information as to the status of treaties submitted to the Senate for action. They are:

*Department of State's Lists of Treaties Submitted to the Senate for 1789–1934* and *1935–1944*.

The *United States Treaty Developments* [9] supplements the above lists for 1944–1950. It contains a list in Appendix I.

More recent information is available in the Treaty Section of the *Commerce Clearing House, Congressional Index* for the current session of Congress.

    g.   Additional Aids

The *Status of Inter-American Treaties and Conventions* provides information as to the status of the Pan American treaties and conventions. This is No. 5 of the Pan American Union Treaty series.

The *Harvard Law School Library, Index to Multilateral Treaties* provides citations to the text of such agreements since 1596.

---

[9] This is a loose leaf service of the Department of State that was published from 1944–1950.

C. Wiktor, Unperfected Treaties of the United States of America, 19776–1976. Oceana, 1977 – (to be completed in 5 v.).

This is an annotated collection of texts of all treaties to which the United States was a signatory but which never went into force.

## 2. Text of Treaties

a. American Treaties

The texts of American treaties are located in the following publications:

(1) Treaties and Other International Agreements. (Since 1950).

(2) Statutes at Large. (Prior to 1950).

(3) United States Treaties and other International Agreements. 1950–

(4) League of Nations Treaty Series (1920–1945) and the United Nations Treaty Series. (1946 to date).

(5) Malloy's Treaties. (1776–1937).

(6) Miller's Treaties. (1776–1863).

b. Foreign Treaties

Treaties between foreign countries may be found in a number of publications. The most exhaustive sources for such materials are the *League of Nations Treaty Series* and the *United Nations Treaty Series*. Also, check the *United Nations List of Treaty Collections* for a list of treaty collections since the 18th century.

## 3. Interpretations of Treaties

Judicial and other interpretations of treaties may be located through the following publications:

a. United States Supreme Court Reports Digest (Lawyers Co-op. Pub. Co.).

b. Federal Code Annotated, Uncodified Laws and Treaties Volume.

c. Shepard's United States Citations.

d. Shepard's State Citations.

e. Wharton's Digest.

f. Moore's Digest.

g. Hackworth's Digest.

h. Whiteman's Digest.

i. United States Department of State Bulletin.

j. United States Treaty Developments.

k. U. S. Supreme Court digests.

*l.* Modern Federal Practice Digest and the Federal Digest.

### 4.   Treaties by Popular Names

When the popular name of a treaty is known, the following publications provide references from that name to the *Statutes at Large* or *Treaties and Other International Agreements* citation:

   a.   Malloy's Treaties, Index in vol. 4 (Trenwith).

   b.   Statutes by Popular Names Table, in vol. 14 of the United States Supreme Court Reports Digest (Lawyers Co-op. Pub. Co.).

————

## SECTION E.   METHODS OF CITATION

Treaties and other international agreements are variously cited. The use of parallel citations is a common practice.

### 1.   Statutes at Large

For treaties printed in the *Statutes at Large* prior to 1950, cite as follows:

Agreement with American Republics Respecting Coffee Marketing, November 28, 1940, 55 Stat. 1143, T.S. 970.

In the above citation the date of signing by the United States follows the shortened name of the agreement.   The Treaty Series reference, "T.S.," is a duplicate citation.

### 2.   Treaties and Other International Agreements

An example of a citation to a treaty published after 1950 in *Treaties and Other International Agreements* is:

Agreement with Chile on Surplus Agricultural Commodities, March 20, 1956, 7 U.S.T. 579, T.I.A.S. 3538.

"T.I.A.S." refers to the advance publication in *Treaties and Othre International Acts Series*.

### 3.   United Nations Treaty Series

*United Nations Treaty Series* (or *League of Nations Treaty Series* "L.N.T.S.") is cited:

Agreement with Iran Concerning Civil Uses of Atomic Energy, March 5, 1957, 10 U.S.T. 733, T.I.A.S. 4207, U.N.T.S. 4898.

A parallel citation usually is provided.   The references here in order are to *Treaties and Other International Agreements, Treaties and Other International Acts Series* and the *United Nations Treaty Series.*

### 4.  Malloy's Treaties

Treaties in Malloy's (4 volumes) are cited as follows:

a.   Volumes I and II are cited: I or II Malloy.

b.   Volume III, edited by Redmond, is cited: III Redmond or III Malloy.

c.   Volume IV, edited by Trenwith, is cited: IV Trenwith or IV Malloy.

---

## SECTION F.  SUMMARY

### 1.   Treaties Between the United States and Foreign Countries are published in:

a.   Prior to 1950, *Statutes at Large*, Part 2 (with some minor variations).

b.   Since 1950, *Treaties and Other International Agreements*.

c.   *Treaties and Other International Acts Series* (functions like advance sheets or slip laws).

(1)  Replaced *Treaty Series* and *Executive Agreement Series*.

### 2.   The League of Nations Treaty Series

a.   Covers 1920–1945.

b.   Treaties of member and nonmember nations.

### 3.   The United Nations Treaty Series

a.   1946 to date—continues the *League of Nations Treaty Series*.

b.   Treaties registered with the United Nations by its members or filed by nonmember states or international organizations.

c.   English and French editions.

d.   Cumulative Indexes; each covers 50 to 100 volumes of the *Series*.

### 4.   Pan American Union Treaty Series

a.   Since 1957.

b.   Texts in English and Spanish.

c.   Instruments of ratification received by the Pan American Union for the Organization of American States.

d.   Official texts of the Organization of American States.

**5. Treaty Collections and Indexes**

  a. *Statutes at Large.*

  (1) Volume 8, covers 1776–1845.

  (2) Volume 18, Part 2, treaties in force in 1873.

  (3) Volume 7, Indian treaties, 1778–1842.

  b. *Malloy's Treaties*, 4 vols.

  (1) Covers 1776–1937.

  (2) Some annotations in volumes 1 and 2.

  (3) General Index in volume 4.

  (4) Chronological list of treaties is in volume 4.

  (5) Parallel citations to the *Treaty Series* and the *Statutes at Large.*

  (6) Arranged alphabetically by the names of the participating countries and chronologically thereunder.

  c. *Miller's Treaties*, 8 vols.

  (1) Covers 1776–1863.

  (2) No index.

  (3) Arranged chronologically.

  (4) Volume 1 is an introductory outline of the publication and contains a table of documents from 1778 through 1931.

  d. List of Treaties and Other International Agreements.

  (1) List is in volume 64, Part 3 of the *Statutes at Large* on page B1107.

  (2) Arranged alphabetically by countries.

  (3) Provides treaty series numbers, dates and *Statutes at Large* citations.

  (4) Covers treaties in volumes 1–64 of the *Statutes at Large.*

  (5) Supplemented by Treaties and Other International Agreements Table (9) in cumulative pamphlet *United States Statutes at Large Tables of Laws Affected* [*in*] *Volumes 70–74 (1956–1960).* It cites amendatory provisions of the *Statutes at Large* (volumes 70–74) which affected treaties and other international agreements. The table is updated in later volumes of the *Statutes at Large.*

  e. Harvard Law School Library, Index to Multilateral Treaties. 1965.

  (1) Chronological list of multi-party international agreements from 1596 to recent date.

  (2) Contains a subject and regional guide.

  (3) Annual supplement.

f.   United Nations List of Treaty Collections.   1956.

(1) List of some 700 treaty collections published since the latter part of the 18th century.

(2) Arrangement: (a) general, (b) subject and (c) countries.

## 6.   List of Treaties in Force

a.   Current annual publication of the State Department.

b.   Lists treaties and other international agreements of the United States which are in force.

(1) Part 1 includes bilateral treaties listed by countries and subdivided by subject under each country.

(2) Part 2 includes multilateral treaties arranged by subject, together with a list of the states which are parties to each agreement.

(3) Appendix includes a consolidated tabulation of documents affecting copyright relations of the United States.

## 7.   United States Department of State Bulletin

a.   Weekly publication.

b.   Information on the current status of important United States treaties.

## 9.   Status of Inter-American Treaties and Conventions

a.   Periodic compilation of the Pan American Union.

b.   Provides tabular information as to the status of Inter-American treaties and conventions.

## 10.   Inter-American Treaties and Conventions

a.   Information as to signatures, ratifications and deposits (Pan American Treaty Series No. 9 Revised 1961).

b.   Gives more complete information than the *Status of Inter-American Treaties and Conventions*.

## 11.   Manual of Inter-American Relations (Revised).   1956

a.   Pan-American publication which provides a systematic classification of the treaties, conventions, resolutions, declarations and recommendations adopted at Inter-American conferences and meetings.

**12. Interpretations of Treaties**

a. Volume 14 of the *U. S. Supreme Court Reports Digests* (Lawyers Co-op.). Contains citations to United States Supreme Court cases which have construed treaties.

(1) Chronological list by treaties (*Statutes at Large*).

(2) Alphabetical list by countries.

b. *Federal Code Annotated*, Uncodified Laws and Treaties Volume.

(1) Multilateral Treaties.

(2) Pan American treaties.

(3) Treaties with specific countries.

c. *Shepard's Citations.*

(1) *United States Citations*, for federal cases construing or mentioning the treaties.

(2) *State Citations*, for state cases pertaining to treaties.

d. *Wharton's Digest.*

(1) Not up-to-date.

(2) Descriptive treatment.

e. *Moore's Digest.*

(1) Representative of United States policy.

(2) Descriptive treatment.

f. *Hackworth's Digest.*

(1) Supplements *Moore's Digest.*

(2) Supports United States international law position.

(3) Descriptive treatment.

g. *Whiteman's Digest.*

(1) To be a successor to *Hackworth.*

(2) Indicates the status of developments in international law.

(3) Includes official and unofficial materials.

h. *United States Treaty Developments.*

(1) Published by the State Department, 1944–1950.

(2) Interpretations of United States treaties for 1944–1950.

(3) Status information is obsolete.

(4) Appendices include a numerical list of the several treaty series and treaty lists by subjects and regions.

i. *International Legal Materials: Current Documents.*

(1) Collection of current official foreign and United States documents relating to international legal affairs, which are otherwise unavailable.

(2) 1962 to date; bi-monthly.

j. *CCH Tax Treaties.*

(1) Loose-leaf reporter on income and estate tax treaties between the United States and foreign countries.

k. *Lists of treaties signed but not yet in force.*

(1) *Department of State's Lists of Treaties Submitted to the Senate for 1789–1934* and *1935–1944.* The lists are supplemented to 1950 in Appendix I of the *United States Treaty Developments.*

(2) *CCH Congressional Index,* Treaty Section.

l. *Treaties by popular name (see Section H4, above).*

m. *Standard digests, e. g., Modern Federal Practice Digest.*

# Chapter 20

# ENGLISH LEGAL RESEARCH

## SECTION A.  INTRODUCTION

The development of American law from England was discussed in Chapter One.  Much of the English law is still part of our legal heritage.  English cases are frequently cited as persuasive authority in American courts, and English statutory law has served as a model for many of our important laws.  No book on legal research would be complete without at least an introduction to the methods of finding English primary legal sources.  Most American law libraries have English law books in their collection and this chapter will present a brief survey of their organization and use.

## 1.  The English Legal System [1]

The United Kingdom of Great Britain and Northern Ireland does not have a single body of law universally applicable within its boundaries.  Although there has been a single parliament since 1706, Scotland has its own distinctive legal system [2] and Northern Ireland has its own Parliament [3] (as well as being represented in the Parliament at Westminster), and its own courts.  While a common court of appeals, and common opinions on broad issues have resulted in a common identity, differences in legal procedure and practice exist in Scotland and Northern Ireland.  Thus our discussion will be limited to that of England and Wales.

Perhaps the most fundamental differences between English law and the law of the United States is the lack of a written constitution in England.  This difference has been described as follows:

"Since Parliament is the supreme law-making body in the United Kingdom, Acts of Parliament are absolutely binding on all courts, taking precedence over all other sources of law; they cannot be *ultra vires* (outside the competence of —in this case Parliament) for, although the principles of natural justice (broadly speaking, rules which an ordinary,

---

[1] Much of this section is based on information obtained from The English Legal System.  Her Majesty's Stationary Office, 1968.

[2] For a discussion of Scottish law and legal sources, see Walker, The Scottish Legal System; an Introduction to Scots Law.  3d rev. ed. (1969).

[3] For an outline of the legal system of Northern Ireland and its relationship to English law, see Preliminary Note to the Title Northern Ireland in 23 Halsbury's Statutes of England.  3d ed., 808–821 (1970).

reasonable person would consider fair) have always occupied an important position in the British constitution, they have never been defined or codified in the form of guaranteed rights. Thus rights, such as the right of personal freedom, the right of freedom of discussion, and the rights of association and public meeting, which are commonly considered more or less inviolate, are not protected against change by Act of Parliament, and the courts could not uphold them if Parliament decreed otherwise. Acts of Parliament are, in fact, formal announcements of rules of conduct to be observed in the future, which remain in force until they are repealed. *The courts are not entitled to question or even discuss their validity*—being required only to interpret them according to the wording used or, if Parliament has failed to make its intentions clear, according to certain canons of interpretation." [4]

## 2. Sources of English Law

There is no code of English law, rather, the law is contained in about 3000 Acts of Parliament, thousands of statutory Instruments (Administrative law) and over 300,000 reported cases.

---

## SECTION B. STATUTES

### 1. Current Statutes

The Acts of Parliament are classified as either private and local acts, or public and general acts and are published annually in separate sets. The *Public General Acts and Measures* have been published since 1831 by the Public Printer. The same set is also available from a private publisher under the title, *Law Reports, Statutes.* Each volume contains an index and a table listing the acts alphabetically by title and chronologically. Another table shows the effect of each act upon earlier acts.

### 2. Codification of Statutes

There has not been in England a general codification of all the acts of Parliament that is comparable to the *United States Code.* There is, however, a current interest in codifying particular branches of the law, such as the criminal law and the law of Landlord and Tenant. For this purpose, a Law Reform Commission for England and Wales has been created.[5]

[4] Op. cit. at footnote 1.
[5] Id. at 28.

a. *The Statutes Revised, 3d ed.* This set is the nearest equivalent to an English statutory codification. It contains all the *Public General Laws* since 1235 which were in force in 1948. The Statute Law Commission charged by Parliament with its publication took each Act that had not been entirely repealed, and reprinted it, incorporating all amendments that added or changed the language of the Act. All of the Acts were then printed in chronological order in 32 volumes. Each year it has been supplemented by an annual volume containing amending acts.

b. *Statutes in Force, Official Revised Edition.* This is a new set which started in 1972, and when completed in 1980 will supersede the *Statutes Revised, 3d ed.*, which has become cumbersome to use as it lacks a cumulative supplement. This new set is being published in loose-leaf volumes with each Act in a separate pamphlet. It will be kept current by the issuance of a new pamphlet to replace repealed or heavily amended sets.

c. *Halsbury's Statutes of England, 3d ed.* This privately published set is an encyclopedia compilation of English statutes, in force, arranged in a classified arrangement. All acts on the same subject are brought together under one title. The third edition began in 1968 and will be completed in 40 volumes. It is kept current by annual continuation volumes and a cumulative supplement. As *Halsbury's Statutes of England* is annotated by footnotes citations to court decisions interpreting sections of each Act, it is frequently preferable to use this set in researching English statutory law. See Illustration 125.

### 3. Early English Statutes

The early English laws were published in many editions. A few sets are:

a. Statutes of the Realm, 12 vols. 1225–1713.

b. Pickering's Statutes at Large, 109 vols. 1225–1869.

c. Chitty's Statutes of Practical Utility, 6th edition, 16 vols. 1235–1910, with annual supplements to 1948.

### 4. Acts and Ordinances of the Interregnum, 1642–1640

This is a selected integration, into three volumes, of the laws enacted during the Interregnum. Volume 3 includes a Chronological Table of Acts and Ordinances, a Subject Index, and an Index of Names, Places, and Things.

## SECTION C. ENGLISH ADMINISTRATIVE LAW

The English equivalent to the rules and regulations that are published in the United States in the *Federal Register* and the *Code of Federal Regulations* is the *Statutory Instruments* (formerly called *Statutory Rules and Orders*). These are orders, rules, and regulations, known as subordinate or delegated legislation, made by a Minister of the Crown under the authority of a statute, or by-laws made by local government or other authorities exercising power conferred upon them by the Parliament.

### 1. Publication of Statutory Instruments

a. *The Statutory Rules and Orders and Statutory Instruments,* 3rd ed. This set was published in 1948 as the official English Administrative Code. It contains the administrative rules of a general applicability and permanent nature. It is kept current by annual volumes of *Statutory Instruments.*

(1) *Index to Government Orders.* This is issued biennially and serves as an index to *Statutory Instruments.* It indicates which statutory instruments are still in force. In addition to its subject index, it has a Table of Statutes which refers to the heading under which the statute is referred to in the Subject Index.

b. *Halsbury's Statutory Instruments,* 1951–52, 24 volumes. This is an unofficial compilation of statutory instruments by subject. It is published as a companion set to *Halsbury's Statutes of England.* It is kept current by the issuance of replacement volumes and a loose-leaf cumulative supplement. It is similar in format to the *Code of Federal Regulations.* It also has a separate, frequently replaced, index volume.

---

## SECTION D. COURT REPORTING

### 1. English Court Organization

Modern organization of English courts began with the *Judicature Act of 1873.* Under it and subsequent Acts, the latest being the *Courts Act, 1971,* the court organization is as follows: [6]

a. *House of Lords.* This body, in addition to its legislative function, serves as the supreme court of appeal, for the United Kingdom in civil cases, and the final court of appeal for criminal cases from England, Wales, and Northern Ireland.

---

[6] For a more detailed description and history of English courts, see Walker, The English Legal System. 2d ed. 131–137 (1969).

b. *Supreme Court of Judicature.* This Court is divided into two parts: The Court of Appeals and the High Court of Justice.

(1) *Court of Appeals.* This Court is in two divisions: civil and criminal. It hears appeals from the High Court and certain other inferior courts.

(2) *High Court.* This Court [7] now consists of three divisions: the Queen's Bench Division (including the Admiralty Court and Commercial Court), the Chancery Division, and the Family Division. In practice, each division acts as a separate court.

c. *Crown Court.* This is a new Court created by the *Courts Reform Act, 1971.*[8] This is a criminal court with unlimited jurisdiction. It assumes the jurisdiction of all criminal cases above the magistrates courts and the appellate jurisdiction of the Quarter Session courts which have now been abolished.

d. *County Courts.* These have first instance limited civil jurisdiction.

e. *Local and Special Courts.* These are mainly Magistrate courts and courts of special jurisdiction such as the Restrictive Trade Practices Court and the Labor Relation Court.

## 2. Development of English Court Reports

The history of court reporting in England is long and confusing.[9] For our purposes, we can divide the reporting of English cases into three periods.

### a. The Year Books. 1272–1535.

The Year Books are the first available law reports with the original text in "Law French." Their purpose and function are still disputed by legal historians. Other than the fact that they are the sources of modern law reporting, they serve little purpose in most legal research today other than for the study of legal history.

### b. Private Names Reporters. 1535–1865.

During this period there was no officially recognized system of court reporting. Any barrister could publish court reports and several hundred different sets were published with many covering the same period of time and the same courts with each differing in quality and accuracy. It has been the custom to refer to these reports by the name of the reporter.

---

[7] Previously to the enactment of the Courts Act, 1971, the High Court consisted of (1) Queen's Bench Division (2) Probate, Divorce, and Admiralty Division, and (3) the Chancery Division. See Courts Act, 1971–I, 115 Sol.J. 715 (1971).

[8] Ibid.

[9] Walker, op, cit. footnote 6 at 131–137.

(1) *English Reports, Full Reprint.* This is a reprint of all English cases from 1220 to 1865. When there were competing sets of the reports, the Editors included only the one that in their opinion was the most accurate. There are 176 volumes in this set, including a two-volume Table of Cases, and a chart which lists all of the named reports in alphabetical order with reference to their location in the *Full Reprint.* Most law libraries have only this set, rather than the original reports.

(2) *The Revised Reports.* The *Revised Reports* are in 149 volumes and cover the period 1785–1865. These mostly duplicate the *English Reports, Full Reprint.* Their value lies, however, in the fact that they were edited by the distinguished legal historian, Sir Frederick Pollock.

**c. The Incorporated Council of Law Reporting.** 1865–
In 1865 the Incorporated Council of Law Reporting for England and Wales was formed. While not an official body, it has a quasi-official status. The Council started in 1865 the publication of the *Law Reports* and these are the preferred set of reports.

## 3. Current Court Reports

As previously mentioned, cases reported before 1865 may be found in the *English Reports, Full Reprint* or *The Revised Reports.* Since 1865, the English cases are found in the following sets:

a. *The Law Reports.* This set reports decisions since 1865 and is selective in its reporting, covering decisions of permanent significance of the High Court. In addition to the opinions of the Judges, it also includes the legal argument presented to the court. Although originally published in twelve different series, the *Law Reports* are now published in four series: (1) Appeal Cases (includes both cases from the Court of Appeals and the House of Lords), (2) Queen's Bench, (3) Chancery, and (4) Probate, Divorce, and Admiralty.

b. *Weekly Law Reports.* This set is also published by the Incorporated Council of Law Reporting and includes all cases that will ultimately be published in the *Law Reports.* It also publishes cases not intended for publication in the *Law Reports.* Three volumes are published a year with Volume One containing the latter.

c. *Other Sets of Reports.* Although the Incorporated Council of Law Reporting assumed responsibility for systematizing court reporting, there is no prohibition of private reporting and many such sets were published. Most have now ceased publication.[10]

---

10 Ibid.

The most important of the private reports is the *All-England Law Reports*. This set started in 1936, incorporating the *Law Journal Reports* and the *Times Law Reports*. It includes the decisions of the House of Lords, the Court of Appeals, the High Court, and courts of special jurisdiction. The opinions are released in advance sheets and then in bound volumes.

d. *All-England Law Reports Reprint*. This set covers selected cases from 1558–1935 and is reprinted from the *Law Journal Reports* in 36 volumes plus an Index volume.

---

## SECTION E. DIGESTS AND ENCYCLOPEDIA

### 1. Digests

a. *The English and Empire Digest.*

This is a comprehensive digest of English cases reported from the earliest times to date, and is in 56 volumes. It includes cases from the courts of Scotland, Ireland, Canada, and other countries of the British Commonwealth and South Africa. Obsolete cases and cases of only historical interest are excluded from the publication. Cases on a topic are generally grouped in chronological order and assigned case numbers.

*The English and Empire Digest* is an annotated digest "which embodies the citator feature." Each case digest is followed by annotated notes of subsequent cases, if any, showing whether it has been approved, followed, distinguished, overruled or otherwise mentioned. Citations to each digested case are listed after the digest paragraph. Under each section of cases are references to related discussion or statutory text in *Halsbury's Laws of England* and *Halsbury's Statutes of England*. See Illustration 125. Volumes 52–54 contain a Consolidated Table of Cases, and volumes 55 and 56 include a Consolidated Index. The digest is kept up-to-date by an annual Cumulative Supplement and cumulative Continuation Volumes.

The four methods of research may be used with this digest. The indexes serve as aids to the Index Method, and the topic analyses of the parts in the front of each volume serve the Topic Method. The table of cases permits use of the digest through the Case Method. The Comprehensive Index lists definitions under "Words and Phrases," thus providing for the Definition Method.

b. *Mews' Digest of English Case Law*, 2nd edition (1924).

This digest consists of 24 volumes with ten-year cumulative and annual supplements. It covers significant early English cases and all recent cases. It also includes some decisions from the courts of

Scotland and Ireland. An *Index of Cases Judicially Noticed* is contained in volume 23 and serves as a citator. The case citator is kept up-to-date by tables of cases judicially considered, appearing in the supplements and annual volumes. The *Digest* also includes tables of statutes judicially considered. Volume 24 is the *Table of Cases.*

The two cumulative supplements to *Mews' Digest* are for the following periods:

1925–1935, 2 vols.

1936–1945, 2 vols.

Since 1946, annual supplements are published. The cases are digested and topically arranged in *Mews' Digest.*

## 2.  Encyclopedia

The standard English encyclopedia of statutory and case law is *Halsbury's Laws of England,* 3d Edition, 43 volumes. This edition began publication in 1952, and is described as the Simonds Edition in honor of the Lord High Chancellor of Great Britain. (*Halsbury's Laws of England,* which is an encyclopedia, should not be confused with *Halsbury's Statutes of England,* a previously described code.) The text in the volumes is arranged under titles, parts, sections and paragraphs, with appropriate footnote references to cases, statutes and Statutory Rules and Orders and Statutory Instruments. *Halsbury's Laws* places much emphasis on statutory law, and unlike its American counterparts, it has a Consolidated Table of Cases, which is in volume 40. Because it has a table of cases, the Case Method may be applied in using *Halsbury's Laws.* Each volume also has a table of cases discussed in it. In the volume table of cases, references to the standard English digest, *English and Empire Digest,* are provided when applicable, indicating where the case is digested. See Illustration 130.

A General Index (subject) is included in volumes 41 and 42, allowing the Index Method to be used with the publication. Each volume also has a titles index and a table of statutes cited. Volume 43 consists of a Consolidated Table of Statutes, covering a chronological table arranged by regnal years and an alphabetical list of statutes. The chronological table refers from a citation in *Halsbury's Statutes* to the page where the act is mentioned in the encyclopedia. The alphabetical list cross-references to the page of the chronological table that provides detailed references.

*Halsbury's Laws* is kept up-to-date by a (1) two-volume annual Cumulative Supplement and (2) a loose-leaf Current Service. The Cumulative Supplement, in addition to providing new matter under the *Halsbury's Laws* volumes and numbered paragraphs, contains an index to the Supplement in the second volume. A Canadian Edition also includes a Canadian Converter Supplement in its pink pages to note legislative changes and new cases subsequent to the publication of the Canadian Converter Volumes, which are discussed below. The loose-leaf Current Service updates the Cumulative Supplement. It is arranged according to a Key Number System, with a table cross-referencing from the volume and paragraph of the main publication to the Key Number under which recent annotations are noted in the Current Service. The Current Service includes such aids as a table of statutes, a table of cases and an index to its material.

The *Canadian Converter* is a complementary series of volumes of *Halsbury's Laws*, 3d edition, to bring within the reference of that publication the related Canadian case and statute law of the federal and provincial jurisdictions, except Quebec. One volume of the *Converter* is issued to every five volumes of the third edition. To use the *Converter* the researcher first consults the basic material in *Halsbury's Laws*. Having found the title and paragraph number in point, he selects the appropriate volume of the *Converter*, looking under the same title and paragraph number. If a corresponding reference appears in the *Converter*, the researcher will find federal and provincial case and statute law notations. Later references are included in the annual *Cumulative Supplement*, described above.

### 3. Current Law: Being and Complete Statement of all the Law from Every Source

This set began publication in 1947 and provides a digest of all phases of English law. It is arranged topically, and under each topic, digests cases, statutes, and statutory instruments. It consists of the following:

a. *Current Law*. A monthly pamphlet advance sheet service.

b. *Current Law Year Book*. An annual cumulation which includes (1) Table of Cases (2) Table of Statutory Instruments, and (3) Words and Phrases.

c. *Current Law Consolidation*. The *Current Law Year Books* were consolidated into a 1947–51 volume; since then, every fifth year, a cumulative Year Book is issued called the *Master Year Book*.

d. *Current Law Citator*. This will be discused in the Section on citators.

*Current Law* is also available in a Scottish edition.

## SECTION F.　CITATORS

There is no service precisely similar to *Shepard Citations* for England.　There are, however, several methods of obtaining later citations, or, as the English express it, "noting up" cases or statutes.

### 1.　Statutes

Citators for statutes are arranged in chronological order, and then for each statute, citations are given for each subsequent statute which amends or repeals the cited statute, and for each case which cited the statute.

Citators for statutes are contained in:

　　a.　*Current Law Citator,* 1947–Illustration 131.

　　b.　*All-England Reports.　Index and Noter-Up* volume.

　　c.　*Halsbury's Statutes of England.*

### 2.　Cases

　　a.　*English and Empire Digest.*　Each case in this set is assigned a case number.　After the digest of the case, citations are given to all subsequent decisions which cited the digested case.　After consulting a case in the main Digest volume, later cases citing the digested case can be found by checking the case number in the latest cumulative supplement.　See Illustrations 126 and 127.

　　b.　*All England Law Reports.　Index and Noter-Up Volume.* This has a Table of Cases judicially construed.　All cases reported since 1936 are listed alphabetically.　Under each case name, citations are given to all subsequent cases which construed the cited case.

　　c.　*Current Law Case Citator, 1948–*　This is a table of cases arranged in alphabetical order under each of which are given citations to subsequent cases which have judicially construed the cited case, and to statutes which have affected the cited case.　See Illustration 132.

### 3.　Authority of English Cases

Until 1966, the House of Lords regarded itself as strictly bound by its earlier decisions.　Once the House of Lords had rendered an opinion the rules enunciated in it could only be changed by an Act of Parliament.　In 1966 the House of Lords stated that in the future they proposed to depart from their own decisions where it appeared right to do so.[11]

[11] 1966 3 All-England Reports 77.

## SECTION G.  HOW TO FIND ENGLISH STATUTES
## AND CASES

### 1.  Statutes

a.  *Chronological Table of the Statutes* and *Index to the Statutes in Force*.  This two-volume set is issued annually and serves as the index to the *Statutes Revised, Statutes in Force,* and *The Public General Acts and Measures*.  Volume 1 contains a chronological Table of all *Public General Acts* since 1235 with references to amendments and repeals.  Volume 2 is a subject index to statutes in force.  See Illustration 124.

b.  *Halsbury's Statutes of England*.  A third edition of this set is now in process.  It will be in forty volumes and will include an index volume.  Until the Index for the 3d edition is published, it is necessary to use the Index volume to the 2nd edition.  However, as *Halsbury's Statutes of England* is arranged alphabetically by title of the Acts, the volumes of the 3d edition already published may be consulted when the title of an Act is located in the Index to the 2nd edition.  This set is kept up-to-date by annual supplement volumes and a loose-leaf supplement volume.  Its annotations to cases and *Halsbury Laws of England* makes it more advantageous to use than the official sets of statutes.  It is comparable to the *United States Code Annotated* or the *United States Code Service-F.C.A.*

### 2.  Cases

a.  *English and Empire Digest*.  This is the most comprehensive English case digest.  The following steps are involved in its use:

(1) Consult index volumes for topic(s) under research.  This will refer to volume and *case number* in main set.

(2) Consult continuation volumes for later cases.

(3) Consult Cumulative Supplement for later citations of cases found through (1) and (2).

(4) Citations are given to all sets of Court reports in which a case is reported.  Frequently, English legal writing gives only one citation for a case.  When that set is not available in the law library being used, check the Table of Cases Volume in the *English and Empire Digest* to locate other citations to the case.

b.  *All England Reports*.  The *Index and Noter-Up* volume is cumulated periodically.  The index section is a detailed subject index. It covers cases reported since 1936, and only gives citations to the *All England Reports*.

c.  *Current Law Year Book*.  Use *Master Year Book* volumes and subsequent annual volumes.  Citations are given to where cases are digested in the *Year Book*.

### 3. Other Methods of English Legal Research

It should be mentioned that it is frequently easier in starting the research for English law to commence the search, as described in the previous chapters on American law, with secondary sources. These would include:

a. *Halsbury's Laws of England.*

b. English treatises.

c. English legal periodicals. The major ones are included in the *Index to Legal Periodicals.*

———

## SECTION H. WORDS AND PHRASES

A number of the English publications include definitions of words and phrases. They are discussed in the preceding sections. In addition, several sources exclusively treat words and phrases. They are:

### 1. Stroud's Judicial Dictionary, 3d ed., 1952

This five-volume publication includes not only definitions but also tables of cases and statutes from which they are derived. It is kept current by supplementation.

A fourth edition is in process, v. 1, 1970 v. 2, 1971, have been published to date.

### 2. Burrow's Words and Phrases Judicially Defined, 1969–1970. 2d ed. by John Beechcraft

Judicial definitions are contained in this set. It consists of five volumes with current pocket supplements.

## SECTION I.   ILLUSTRATIONS

STATUTES

PROBLEM: Which English statute covers the privileges of witnesses in civil proceedings?

**124.   Page from Index to Statutes, 1235–1970.**

**125.   Pages from volume 12, Halsbury's Statutes of England, 3d ed.**

CASES

PROBLEM: Find English cases on liability of store keeper for injury to customers.

**126.   Page from Volume 36, English and Empire Digest.**

**127.   Page from 1972 Cumulative Supplement, English & Empire Digest.**

**128.   Page from 1935–56 Index Volume to the All-England Law Reports.**

**129.   Page from Index Volume to Halsbury's Laws of England, 3d ed.**

**130.   Page from 28, Halsbury's Laws of England.**

CITATORS

**131.   Page from Current Law Citator, Statute Section.**

**132.   Page from Current Law Citator, Case Section.**

## [Illustration 124]

## PAGE FROM INDEX TO STATUTES, 1235–1970

INDEX TO THE STATUTES                                       2127

**WITNESS** *cont.*

**1 General Provisions** *cont.*

Before—*cont.*

Patents Act Appeal Tribunal and Comptroller General of Patents *See* PATENTS, 8
Private Legislation Procedure (Scotland) Act Commrs. *See* PROVISIONAL ORDER, S, 2
Probate Ct. *See* SUPREME COURT, E, 6(*a*)
Solicitors Act disciplinary committee *See* SOLICITOR, E, 2(*g*)
Solicitors' Discipline (Scotland) Committee *See* SOLICITOR, S, 4(*a*)
Supreme Ct. *See* 4 *below*
Tithe Act proceedings *See* TITHES, E, 4(*d*)
tribunal of inquiry *See* INQUIRIES, I

Habeas corpus, bringing up prisoner as witness by *See* HABEAS CORPUS *And see* COUNTY
COURT, E, 5(*b*)(iv)

Mode of examination of, in every civil and criminal ct.: E NI (**a**) 1865 c.18 ss.1,3–6,8
1967 c.58 s.10,sch.3,Pt.III

Recognizances to give evidence *See* CORONER, E, 2(*b*): CRIMINAL PROCEDURE, 3(*a*)

---

**FINDING ENGLISH STATUTES.**

This volume, issued annually, indexes all English statutes
in force. This indicates that privileges of witnesses in
civil proceedings is covered in chapter 64 of an Act
passed in 1968. This citation could also be found in
the sources listed at section B of this chapter.

The next step is to locate the text of this Act.

See next Illustration.

---

to be binding if administered in form which witness declares binding *See* OATH
declaration or affirmation in lieu of *See* DECLARATION
or affirmation, form if in examination under commn., etc., in Her Majesty's dominions
beyond jurisdiction *See* EVIDENCE, 1(*d*)

Perjury, or subornation of perjury *See* PERJURY, E: PERJURY, S
prosecution of witness for, by order of ct.: NI 1851 c.100 s.19
E 1911 c.6 s.9
E 1933 c.36 s.2(2)
1964 c.43 s.5,sch.2

Unsworn evidence *See* EVIDENCE, 3
power of colonial legislatures to make ordinances for admission of: 1843 c.22

(**e**) PROTECTION

Cannot refuse to answer on ground of admitting a debt or subjecting himself to an action:
1806 c.37

Not compellable to answer question tending to criminate himself, save when defendant in
a criminal case: E NI 1851 c.99 s.3
E S 1898 c.36 s.1(*e*)(*f*)

Witness compulsorily first disclosing in civil action. destruction, etc., of will, or agent, banker,
factor, trustee, or director compulsoliry disclosing embezzlement, etc. (*see now* THEFT, E)
not liable criminally, except as to bankruptcy: NI 1861,c.96 ss.29,85
E 1914 c.59 s.166

➤ Privilege in civil proceedings—
against incrimination of self or spouse: 1968 c.64 ss.14,18
for communications made for patent proceedings: 1968 c.64 ss.15,18
abolition of certain privileges: 1968 c.64 ss.16,18
tribunals, investigations and inquiries: 1968 c.64 s.17
civil proceedings, legal proceedings, court, etc. defined: 1968 c.64 s.18

(**a**) ss.3–6,8 of this Act respectively reproduce ss.22–5 and 27 (now repealed) of the Common
Law Procedure Act 1854 c.125

(**b**) For effect to be given to orders of cts. of the Irish Free State (now Republic of Ireland)
enforcing attendance of witnesses, etc., *see* SR&O 1923/405: Rev. X, p. 298: 1923, at pp.
402–3

[Illustration 125]

## PAGE FROM HALSBURY'S STATUTES OF ENGLAND, 3rd ed.

# THE CIVIL EVIDENCE ACT 1968

### (1968 c. 64)

#### ARRANGEMENT OF SECTIONS

PART I

HEARSAY EVIDENCE

Page

The reference in the previous Illustration was to the Civil Evidence Act, 1968. This is the first page of the text from Vol. 12 of Halsbury's Statutes of England, 3d ed. The same text can also be located in the 1968 volume of The Public General Acts and Measures.

PART II

MISCELLANEOUS AND GENERAL

*Convictions, etc. as evidence in civil proceedings*

*An Act to amend the law of evidence in relation to civil proceedings, and in respect of the privilege against self-incrimination to make corresponding amendments in relation to statutory powers of inspection or investigation*

[25th October 1968]

**Northern Ireland.** This Act does not, in general, apply; see s. 20 (3), *post.*

PART I

HEARSAY EVIDENCE

### 1. Hearsay evidence to be admissible only by virtue of this Act and other statutory provisions, or by agreement

(1) In any civil proceedings a statement other than one made by a person while giving oral evidence in those proceedings shall be admissible as evidence of any fact stated therein to the extent that it is so admissible by virtue of any provision of this Part of this Act or by virtue of any other statutory provision or by agreement of the parties, but not otherwise.

(2) In this section "statutory provision" means any provision contained in, or in an instrument made under, this or any other Act, including any Act passed after this Act.

## [Illustration 125–a]

## PAGE FROM HALSBURY'S STATUTES OF ENGLAND, 3d ed.

CIVIL EVIDENCE ACT 1968, S. 7                    917

**Supplied to . . . computer.** See, further, s. 5 (5) (*a*), *ante*.

**Document . . . was produced,** etc. See, further, s. 5 (5) (*c*), *ante*.

**Sub-s. (4): For the purpose of any enactment,** etc. Corroboration is required by statute in actions for breach of promise of marriage under the Evidence Further Amendment Act 1869, s. 2, p. 846, *ante*, and in affiliation proceedings under the Affiliation Proceedings Act 1957, s. 4 (2), Vol. 1, p. 79.

As to corroboration in other cases and the treatment of uncorroborated evidence, see 15 Halsbury's Laws (3rd Edn.) 450.

**Sub-s. (4): Maker of the statement.** Cf. the note "Statement made by a person" to s. 7, *post*.

**Sub-s. (5): Wilfully.** This expression, in the words of Lord Russell of Killowen, C.J., in *R.* v. *Senior*, [1899] 1 Q.B. 283, at pp. 290, 291, "means that the act is done deliberately and intentionally, not by accident or inadvertence, but so that the mind of the person who does the act goes with it"; see also, in particular, *R.* v. *Walker* (1934), 24 Cr. App. Rep. 117; *Eaton* v. *Cobb*, [1950] 1 All E.R. 1016; and *Arrowsmith* v. *Jenkins*, [1963] 2 Q.B. 561; [1963] 2 All E.R. 210; but see *Rice* v. *Connolly*, [1966] 2 Q.B. 414; [1966] 2 All E.R. 649.

**Material.** A statement may be material on the mere ground that it renders more credible something else; cf. *R.* v. *Tyson* (1867), L.R. 1 C.C.R. 107.

**Knows.** There is authority for saying that, where a person deliberately refrains from making inquiries the results of which he might not care to have, this constitutes in law actual knowledge of the facts in question; see *Knox* v. *Boyd*, 1941 S.C. (J.) 82, at p. 86, and *Taylor's Central Garages (Exeter), Ltd.* v. *Roper* (1951), 115 J.P. 445, at pp. 449, 450, *per* Devlin, J.; and see also, in particular, *Mallon* v. *Allon*, [1964] 1 Q.B. 385; [1963] 3 All E.R. 843, at p. 394 and p. 847, respectively. However, mere neglect to ascertain what would have been found out by making reasonable enquiries is not tantamount to knowledge; see *Taylor's Central Garages (Exeter), Ltd.* v. *Roper, ubi supra, per* Devlin, J.; and cf. *London Computator, Ltd.* v. *Seymour*, [1944] 2 All E.R. 11; but see also *Mallon* v. *Allon, ubi supra*; and cf. *Wallworth* v. *Balmer*, [1965] 3 All E.R. 721.

**Indictment.** By virtue of the Criminal Law Act 1967, s. 8 (2), Vol. 21, title **Magistrates**, the offence is triable at quarter sessions.

**Fine.** There is no specific limit to the amount of the fine which may be imposed. Yet, the fine should be within the offender's capacity to pay; see, in particular, *R.* v. *Churchill (No. 2)*, [1967] 1 Q.B. 190; [1966] 2 All E.R. 215 (reversed on other grounds *sub nom. Churchill* v. *Walton*, [1967] A.C. 224; [1967] 1 All E.R. 497); and see also 25 Edw. 1 (Magna Carta) (1297), Vol. 6, p. 401, and the Bill of Rights (1688) (Sess. 2), s. 1, Vol. 6, p. 490.

**Hearsay evidence formerly admissible at common law.** For provisions as to the admissibility of certain evidence formerly admissible at common law, see s. 9, *post*.

**Definitions.** For "civil proceedings", see s. 18 (1), *post*, and for "document" and "statement", see s. 10 (1), *post*; and see as to "copy", the latter subsection.

---

Halsbury Statutes of England serves as an annotated edition. After each section there are editorial notes, citations to cases interpreting the section, and references to related statutes.

This set is kept up-to-date by a separate loose-leaf volume.

---

(*b*) evidence tending to prove that, whether before or after he made that statement, that person made (whether orally or in a document or otherwise) another statement inconsistent therewith shall be admissible for the purpose of showing that that person has contradicted himself:

Provided that nothing in this subsection shall enable evidence to be given of any matter of which, if the person in question had been called as a witness and had denied that matter in cross-examination, evidence could not have been adduced by the cross-examining party.

(2) Subsection (1) above shall apply in relation to a statement given in evidence by virtue of section 4 of this Act as it applies in relation to a statement given in evidence by virtue of section 2 of this Act, except that references to

[Illustration 126]

## PAGE FROM VOLUME 36, ENGLISH AND EMPIRE DIGEST

46                               NEGLIGENCE                          [Vol. XXXVI

Sect. 1.  *In regard to particular persons : Sub-sect.* 1, cont.]

was guilty of a breach of duty towards him in suffering the hole to be unfenced.

FINDING ENGLISH CASE LAW: ENGLISH AND EMPIRE DIGEST.

Step 1 (not shown).  Check Index Volume under appropriate headings.  This will give citation to volume, page, and case number.

Step 2.  Examine volume referred to by Index.  The number 246 is not a "key" number but the number assigned to this case in this digest.

Note how the digest of the case is more substantial than those in American digests.

Also note how citation is given to all sets where case is reported.

the horses met with an accident by stepping upon a board which broke under its weight.  Pltf. charged negligence in respect of the rotten condition of the board.  There was no evidence that deft. co. placed the board there, or knew or should have known of its presence there :—*Held :* pltf. had failed to prove any negligence of deft. co.—GUERTIN *v.* FASSETT LUMBER CO., [1931] 4 D. L. R. 916 ; O. R. 589.—CAN.

SUB-SECT. 2.  DUTY TO INVITEES

*A. Who is an Invitee*

*(a) In General*

LAW.  *See* HALSBURY'S LAWS (2nd Edn.), Vol. 23, pp. 600 *et seq.*

➤ **246. Persons entering premises of owner or occupier—For purposes of business or common interest—On invitation express or implied.**]—Upon the premises of deft., a sugar refiner, was a hole or shoot on a level with the floor, used for raising & lowering sugar to & from the different storeys of the building, & usual, necessary, & proper in the way of deft.'s business.  Whilst in use, it was necessary & proper that this hole should be unfenced.  When not in use, it was sometimes necessary, for the purpose of ventilation, that it should be open.  It was not necessary that it should, when not in use, be unfenced ; & it might at such times, without injury to the business, have been fenced by a rail.  Whether or not it was usual to fence similar places when not in actual use, did not appear.  Pltf., a journeyman gasfitter in the employ of a patentee who had fixed a patent gas regulator upon deft.'s premises, for which he was to be paid provided it effected a certain amount of saving in the consumption of gas, went upon the premises with his employer's agent for the purpose of examining the several burners, so as to test the new apparatus.  Whilst thus engaged upon an upper floor of the building, pltf., under circumstances as to which the evidence was conflicting, accidentally, &, as the jury found, without any fault or negligence on his part, fell through the hole, & was injured :—*Held :* inasmuch as pltf. was upon the premises on lawful business, in the course of fulfilling a contract in which he, or his employer & deft. both had an interest, & the hole or shoot was from its nature unreasonably dangerous to persons not usually employed upon the premises, but having a right to go there, deft.

upon the fact that the customer has come into the shop in pursuance of a tacit invitation given by the shop-keeper, with a view to business which concerns himself.  If a customer were, after buying goods, to go back to the shop in order to complain of the quality, or that the change was not right, he would be just as much there upon business which concerned the shopkeeper, & as much entitled to protection during this accessory visit, though it might not be for the shopkeeper's benefit, as during the principal visit, which was.  If, instead of going himself, the customer were to send his servant, the servant would be entitled to the same consideration as the master.  The class to which the customer belongs includes persons who go not as mere volunteers, or licensees, or guests, or servants or persons whose employment is such that danger may be considered as bargained for, but who go upon business which concerns the occupier, & upon his invitation express or implied (WILLES, J.).—INDERMAUR *v.* DAMES (1866), L. R. 1 C. P. 274 ; Har. & Ruth. 243 ; 35 L. J. C. P. 184 ; 14 L. T. 484 ; 12 Jur. N. S. 432 ; 14 W. R. 586 ; *affd.* (1867), L. R. 2 C. P. 311, Ex. Ch.

*Annotations :*—**Folld.** Smith *v.* London & St. Katharine Docks Co. (1868), L. R. 3 C. P. 326.  **Distd.** Brooks *v.* Courtney (1869), 20 L. T. 440.  **Apld.** M. S. & L. Ry. *v.* Woodcock (1871), 25 L. T. 335 ; Smith *v.* Steele (1875), L. R. 10 Q. B. 125 ; Watkins *v.* G. W. Ry. (1877), 46 L. J. Q. B. 817.  **Folld.** White *v.* France (1877), 2 C. P. D. 308.  **Apld.** Marney *v.* Scott, [1899] 1 Q. B. 986.  **Distd.** Cavalier *v.* Pope, [1906] A. C. 428.  **Apld.** Lewis *v.* Ronald (1909), 101 L. T. 534.  **Distd.** Lucy *v.* Bawden, [1914] 2 K. B. 318.  **Consd.** Norman *v.* G. W. Ry., [1915] 1 K. B. 584.  **Distd.** Maclenan *v.* Segar, [1917] 2 K. B. 325.  **Apld.** Pritchard *v.* Peto, [1917] 2 K. B. 173 ; Anchor Line (Henderson) *v.* Dundee Harbour Trustees, Ellerman Lines *v.* Dundee Harbour Trustees, Thomson, Shepherd *v.* Dundee Harbour Trustees (1922), 38 T. L. R. 299 ; Mercer *v.* S. E. & C. Ry.'s Managing Committee, [1922] 2 K. B. 549.  **Consd.** Mersey Docks & Harbour Board *v.* Procter, [1923] A. C. 253.  **Folld.** Sutcliffe *v.* Clients Investment Co., [1924] 2 K. B. 746.  **Consd.** Forbes, Abbott & Lennard *v.* G. W. Ry. (1927), 138 L. T. 286.  **Apld.** Compania Mexicana De Petroleo El Aguila *v.* Essex Transport & Trading Co. (1929), 141 L. T. 106.  **Consd.** Hillen *v.* I. C. I. (Alkali), Ltd., [1934] 1 K. B. 455 ; Howard *v.* Furness Houlder Argentine Lines, Ltd. & Brown, Ltd., [1936] 2 All E. R. 781 ; Simons *v.* Winslade, [1938] 3 All E. R. 774 ; Canter *v.* Gardner & Co., [1940] 1 All E. R. 325.  **Apld.** Horton *v.* London Graving Dock Co., [1949] 2 All E. R. 169.  **Consd.** Jacobs *v.* L. C. C., [1949] 1 All E. R. 790 ; Jennings *v.* Cole, [1949] 2 All E. R. 191 ; Denny *v.* Supplies & Transport Co. & Scruttons, Ltd. (1950), 66 (pt. 1) T. L. R. 1168.  **Apld.** London Graving Dock Co. *v.* Horton, [1951] 2 All E. R. 1.  **Consd.** Hunwick *v.* Essex Rivers Catchment Board, [1952] 1 All E. R. 765.  **Refd.**

## [Illustration 127]

## ENGLISH & EMPIRE DIGEST—CUMULATIVE SUPPLEMENT. 1972

---

539             Vol. 36—Negligence.    Cases 177—303a: *178a—*261g

### SUB-SECT. 1A. OCCUPIER

STATUTE. *See* Occupiers' Liability Act, 1957 (c. 31).

**245Aa.** *Common law duty of care—Contributory negligence.*]—ROLES *v.* NATHAN, ROLES *v.* CORNEY (1963). *See* Continuation Vol. A.

**245Ab.** —— *"Control"—What amounts to.*]—WHEAT *v.* E. LACON & Co., LTD. (1966). *See* Continuation Vol. B. *Add. Citation:*—[1966] R. A. 193. **Consd.** H. & N. Emanuel, Ltd. *v.* Greater London Council, [1971] 2 All E. R. 835. **Refd.** A. M. F. International, Ltd. *v.* Magnet Bowling, Ltd., [1968] 2 All E. R. 789; Whiting *v.* Hillingdon London B. C. (1970), 68 L. G. R. 437.

**245Ac.** —— *Occupier of structure—Structure in occupation of sub-contractor.*]—KEARNEY *v.* ERIC WALLER, LTD. (1965). *See* Continuation Vol. B. *Add. Citation:*—[1967] 1 Q. B. 29.

**245Ad.** —— *Position of trespasser.*]—PERISCINOTTI *v.* BRIGHTON WEST PIER, LTD. (1961). *See* Continuation Vol. B.

**245Ae.** —— *Injury to contractor's servant.*]—FISHER *v.* C. H. T., LTD. (1966). *See* Continuation Vol. B. *Add. Citation:*—[1966] 2 Q. B. 475. **Consd.** H. & N. Emanuel, Ltd. *v.* Greater London Council, [1971] 2 All E. R. 835. **Refd.** Wheat *v.* E. Lacon & Co., Ltd., [1966] 1 All E. R. 582.

**245Af.** —— *Injury to child.*]—MOLONEY *v.* LAMBETH LONDON B. C. (1966). *See* Continuation Vol. C.

**245Ag.** —— ——.]—WARD *v.* HERTFORDSHIRE C. C. (1970). *See* Continuation Vol. C.

**245Ah.** —— *Injury to visitor—Acceptance of risk.*]—SIMMS *v.* LEIGH RUGBY FOOTBALL CLUB, LTD. (1969). *See* Continuation Vol. C.

**245Aj.** —— *Pedestrian on railway bridge.*]—GREENHALGH *v.* BRITI...

**245Ak.** ——...
*v.* CH...
tion ...
*As to* ...

**245Al.** ——...
(1970...

***241Aa.*** *Ea...*
RYS...

**246.** Consc...
E. R...
All E...
1185,...
1 All...
E. R...
[1959...
*v.* La...
Whee...
A. M...
[1968...
Co., Ltd., [1970] 2 All E. R. 294.

**247.** *As to* (1) **Refd.** Greenhalgh *v.* British Rys. Board, [1969] 2 All E. R. 114. *Generally,* **Refd.** Hawkins *v.* Coulsdon & Purley U. D. C., [1954] 1 All E. R. 97.

**251.** **Refd.** Hawkins *v.* Coulsdon & Purley U. D. C., [1954] 1 All E. R. 97; Scruttons, Ltd. *v.* Midland Silicones, Ltd., [1962] 1 All E. R. 1; Wheat *v.* E. Lacon & Co., Ltd., [1966] 1 All E. R. 582.

**255.** **Refd.** Hawkins *v.* Coulsdon & Purley U. D. C., [1954] 1 All E. R. 97; Dyer *v.* Ilfracombe U. D. C., [1956] 1 All E. R. 581.

**260.** **Refd.** Creed *v.* McGeoch & Sons, Ltd., [1955] 3 All E. R. 123; Scruttons, Ltd. *v.* Midland Silicones, Ltd., [1962] 1 All E. R. 1; Wheat *v.* E. Lacon & Co., Ltd., [1966] 1 All E. R. 582.

**262.** *As to* (1) **Consd.** Gough *v.* National Coal Board, [1953] 2 All E. R. 1283; Bates *v.* Stone Parish Council, [1954] 3 All E. R. 38; Dyer *v.* Ilfracombe U. D. C., [1956] 1 All E. R. 581. **Apld.** Perkowski *v.* Wellington Corpn., [1958] 3 All E. R. 368. **Refd.** Cuttress *v.* Scaffolding (Great Britain), Ltd., [1953] 1 All E. R. 165; Slade *v.* Battersea & Putney Group Hospital Management Committee, [1955] 1 All E. R. 429; Videan *v.* British Transport Commission, [1963] 2 All E. R. 860. *Generally,* **Consd.** Comr. for Rys. *v.* Quinlan, [1964] 1 All E. R. 897. **Refd.** Dunster *v.* Abbott, [1953] 2 All E. R. 1573; Hawkins *v.* Coulsdon & Purley U. D. C., [1954] 1 All E. R. 97; Phipps *v.* Rochester Corpn., [1955] 1 All E. R. 129; Herrington *v.* British Rys. Board, [1971] 1 All E. R. 897.

***243a.*** *Occupier acting as guide—Special relationship.*]—HEARD *v.* NEW ZEALAND FOREST PRODUCTS, LTD. (1960).—N.Z. *See* Continuation Vol. A.

***243b.*** *When status changes.*]—STEPHENS *v.* CORCORAN (1968). —CAN. *See* Continuation Vol. C.

**275a.** *Person on railway premises.*]—BLACKMAN *v.* RAILWAY EXECUTIVE (1953). *See* Continuation Vol. A.

**283.** **Refd.** Bates *v.* Parker, [1952] 2 All E. R. 987; Hawkins *v.* Coulsdon & Purley U. D. C., [1953] 2 All E. R. 364; Wheat *v.* E. Lacon & Co., Ltd., [1966] 1 All E. R. 582.

**284.** **Consd.** Slade *v.* Battersea & Putney Group Hospital Management Committee, [1955] 1 All E. R. 429.

**284a.** *Relation visiting patient in state hospital.*]—SLADE *v.* BATTERSEA & PUTNEY GROUP HOSPITAL MANAGEMENT COMMITTEE (1955). *See* Continuation Vol. A. *Generally,* **Refd.** Slater *v.* Clay Cross Co., [1956] 2 All E. R. 625.

**286.** **Consd.** The Louis Sheid, [1958] 1 Lloyd's Rep. 606. **Refd.** Roe *v.* Ministry of Health, Woolley *v.* Same, [1954] 2 All E. R. 131; Moore *v.* R. Fox & Sons, [1956] 1 All E. R. 182; Overseas Tankship (U.K.), Ltd. *v.* Morts Dock & Engineering Co., Ltd., [1961] 1 All E. R. 404; Wheat *v.* E. Lacon & Co., Ltd., [1966] 1 All E. R. 582; Swan *v.* Salisbury Construction Co., Ltd., [1966] 2 All E. R. 138; Ludgate *v.* Lovett, [1969] 2 All E. R. 1275; S. C. M. (U.K.), Ltd. *v.* W. J. Whittall & Sons, Ltd., [1970] 2 All E. R. 417; Sir Robert McAlpine & Sons, Ltd. *v.* Minimax, Ltd., Same *v.* Same, [1970] 1 Lloyd's Rep. 397.

**287.** **Refd.** Green *v.* Fibreglass, Ltd., [1958] 2 All E. R. 521; Duncan *v.* London Borough of Lambeth, [1968] 1 All E. R. 84.

**290.** **Folld.** Hartley *v.* Mayoh, [1953] 2 All E. R. 525.

***260a.*** *Swimmer in public pool.*]—JAMES *v.* COUNCIL OF MUNICIPALITY OF KOGARTH (1961).—AUS. *See* Continuation Vol. A.

***261a.*** *Customer in steam bath.*]—BILINSKI *v.* NEHAJ (1954).

...ON *v.* WATT

...*v.* STEVENS

...*v.* DELISLE
...61).—CAN.

...L AMERICAN
...tion Vol. C.

...WEALTH OF
...ion Vol. C.

...N] PRINGLE
...*st.*

...MONWEALTH

...768. **Distd.**
...E. R. 318;

O'Reilly *v.* Imperial Chemical Industries, Ltd., [1955] 2 All E. R. 567. **Consd.** Wilson *v.* Tyneside Window Cleaning Co., [1958] 2 All E. R. 265; Roles *v.* Nathan, Roles *v.* Corney, [1963] 2 All E. R. 908; Bunker *v.* Charles Brand & Son, Ltd., [1969] 2 All E. R. 59. **Refd.** Hawkins *v.* Coulsdon & Purley U. D. C., [1954] 1 All E. R. 97; Wingrove *v.* Prestige & Co., [1954] 1 All E. R. 576; Cilia *v.* H. M. James & Sons, [1954] 2 All E. R. 9; Phipps *v.* Rochester Corpn., [1955] 1 All E. R. 129; O'Reilly *v.* I. C. I., Ltd., [1955] 3 All E. R. 382; Slater *v.* Clay Cross Co., [1956] 2 All E. R. 625; Riden *v.* A. C. Billings & Sons, [1956] 3 All E. R. 357; Davie *v.* New Merton Board Mills, Ltd., [1958] 1 All E. R. 67; Smith *v.* Austin Lifts, Ltd., [1959] 1 W. L. R. 100; Mace *v.* R. & H. Green & Silley Weir, Ltd., [1959] 1 All E. R. 655; McArdle *v.* Andmac Roofing Co., [1967] 1 All E. R. 583; S. C. M. (U.K.), Ltd. *v.* W. J. Whittall & Son, Ltd., [1970] 2 All E. R. 417.

**301.** *Duty to exercise reasonable care—To prevent damage from unusual danger—Which invitor knew or ought to have known—Danger unknown to invitee.*]—BATES *v.* PARKER (1953). *See* Continuation Vol. A. **Refd.** Smith *v.* Austin Lifts, Ltd., [1959] 1 All E. R. 81; Wigley *v.* British Vinegars, Ltd., [1961] 3 All E. R. 418.

**302.** *Generally,* **Refd.** Hawkins *v.* Coulsdon & Purley U. D. C., [1954] 1 All E. R. 97; Comr. for Rys. *v.* Quinlan, [1964] 1 All E. R. 897.

**303.** **Refd.** Braithwaite *v.* South Durham Steel Co., [1958] 3 All E. R. 161.

**303a.** *Duty to exercise reasonable care—To prevent damage from unusual danger.*]—SLADE *v.* BATTERSEA & PUTNEY GROUP HOSPITAL MANAGEMENT COMMITTEE (1955). *See* Continuation Vol A (No. 284a).

* An asterisk indicates a Scottish, Irish or Commonwealth case.

---

FINDING ENGLISH CASES: ENGLISH AND EMPIRE DIGEST.

Step 3. After examining digest in main volume, case should always be checked in the cumulative supplement for citations to later cases. This is one method of "Shepardizing" an English case.

## [Illustration 128]

## PAGE FROM 135–56 PERMANENT INDEX

364        **ALL ENGLAND LAW REPORTS**

YEAR VOL. PAGE

INTESTACY
> Succession—*Cases subject to special rules—continued.*
> > *Rights of surviving spouse—" Personal chattels "—Herd of*

---

### FINDING ENGLISH CASES: ALL-ENGLAND REPORTS

This set may be used for finding cases reported after 1936. This Illustration is from the 1935–56 Permanent Index. The subsequent Index volumes should also be consulted.

This Index only gives citations to the All-England Reports.

---

INVESTMENT
> Inducement to invest money. *See* CRIMINAL LAW.
>
> Power to trustees under settlement—*Power to invest " in or upon such investments as to them may seem fit "* [*Re* HARARI'S SETTLEMENT TRUSTS] ..   ..   ..   ..   ..   ..   Ch.D.   [1949]   1   430
>
> Unit trust scheme. *See* UNIT TRUST (Scheme).

INVESTMENT CLAUSE
> Power to vary investments. *See* TRUST AND TRUSTEE (Investments).
>
> *See also* SETTLEMENT; WILL.

INVESTMENT COMPANY
> Management expenses. *See* INCOME TAX (Repayment—*Management expenses*).
>
> Surtax. *See* SURTAX.

INVITEE
> Bailment of goods with invitor—*Goods on invitor's premises* [TINSLEY *v.* DUDLEY]   ..   ..   ..   ..   ..   ..   C.A.   [1951]   1   252
>
> Canvasser—*Injury suffered on premises of potential customer—Liability of occupier* [DUNSTER *v.* ABBOTT]   ..   ..   C.A.   [1953]   2 1572
>
> Negligence—*Children injured by scalding tea spilt from urn being carried through narrow passage—Whether danger reasonably foreseeable—Standard of care owed by occupier* [GLASGOW CORPN. *v.* MUIR]   H.L.   [1943]   2   44
>
> > *Customer at shop—Defective paving of forecourt to shop—Forecourt in occupation of landlord of shop* [JACOBS *v.* LONDON COUNTY COUNCIL]   C.A.   [1949]   1   790
> >   H.L.   [1950]   1   737
>
> > *Duty of shopkeeper—Slippery substance on floor* [TURNER *v.* ARDING & HOBBS, LTD.]..   ..   ..   ..   K.B.D.   [1949]   2   911
>
> > *Defective ladder removed from building operation—Ladder put back by unknown person—Onus on invitee to prove invitor's responsibility for or knowledge of replacement of ladder* [WOODMAN *v.* RICHARDSON AND CONCRETE, LTD.]..   ..   ..   ..   C.A.   [1937]   3   866
>
> > *Duty of occupier—Protection against unusual danger—Window cleaner—Defective window sash—Window safe for ordinary purposes* [GENERAL CLEANING CONTRACTORS, LTD. *v.* CHRISTMAS] ..   C.A.   [1952]   1   39
> >   H.L.   [1952]   2 1110
>
> > > *Protection against unusual danger—Window cleaner—Plywood panel in window—Occupier's removal of bolts—Failure to inform cleaner* [BATES *v.* PARKER]   ..   ..   Assizes   [1952]   2   987
> > >   C.A.   [1953]   1   768
>
> > > *Workman falling from staging—Workman's knowledge that staging faulty* [LONDON GRAVING DOCK CO., LTD. *v.* HORTON]   ..   ..   ..   ..   K.B.D.   [1949]   2   169
> > >   C.A.   [1950]   1   180
> > >   H.L.   [1951]   2   1
>
> > *Unusual danger—Neighbour entering premises at request of occupier to tend occupier's bedridden wife—Fall and injury to leg* [JENNINGS *v.* COLE]   ..   ..   ..   K.B.D.   [1949]   2   191
>
> > > *Person visiting railway station to meet passenger—Oily patch on platform* [STOWELL *v.* RAILWAY EXECUTIVE]   K.B.D.   [1949]   2   193

## [Illustration 129]

## PAGE FROM INDEX VOLUME, HALSBURY'S LAWS OF ENGLAND, 3d Ed.

995

**IRELAND, REPUBLIC OF**

**INVESTMENT**—*contd.*
　trustee, by—*contd.*
　　narrower-range investments—*contd.*
　　　authorised by statute, **38**, 994
　　　two groups of, **38**, 994
　　personal security, on, **38**, 989
　　powers, **38**, 993, 994
　　　variation of, **38**, 990, 991
　　preference stock, in, **38**, 1008
　　prudence, duty to exercise, **38**, 994n
　　real securities, in, **38**, 1002, 1003
　　redeemable securities, in, **38**, 1008
　　retainer of investment, **38**, 1009
　　rights offers, **38**, 1007
　　special cases, **38**, 993
　　　power, **38**, 992
　　special-range property—
　　　*meaning*, **38**, 1000

**IPSWICH**
　local court, **9**, 536
　　navigation rules, **35**, 869
　petty court of bailiffs of, **9**, 537
　public boxing and wrestling in, **37**, 51n

**IRAN**
　missionary see in, **13**, 19n

**IRAQ**
　exchange control, **27**, 112
　independence of, **5**, 546

**IRELAND**
　assurances of land for charitable purposes in, **4**, 264
　Bank of. *See* BANK OF IRELAND
　banns, publication of, in, **13**, 362

---

**FINDING ENGLISH CASES: HALSBURY'S LAWS OF ENGLAND.**

　This set is an encyclopedia of English law and should not be confused with Halsbury's Statutes of England.

　Step 1. Locate appropriate reference in Index Volume. In this instance, the topic of "invitees" will be found in Vol. 28.

---

　wider-range investments—
　　*meaning*, **38**, 993
　　advice, requirement as to, **38**, 997
　　authorised by statute, **38**, 997, 998
　　list of, **38**, 997–998
　　restrictions on, **38**, 997, 998–1000
　trustee savings banks, by, **2**, 160
　unauthorised, cestui que trust, by, **2**, 497
　　　*See also* settled land, *above*
　wife, by, in husband's name, **18**, 387

**INVESTMENT COMPANY**
　*meaning*, **20**, 550
　income tax, payment of. *See under* INCOME TAX
　surtax liability. *See* INCOME TAX (surtax)

**INVITEE**
　*meaning*, **28**, 47, 48
→　carrier of passengers, on premises of, **4**, 180
　classification of, **28**, 49
　common duty of care towards, **28**, 45
　duty at common law towards, **28**, 45
　licensee, distinguished from, **28**, 41, 48, 49
　negligence in relation to, **28**, 41, 45, 47–49
　overstaying invitation, **28**, 48
　safety of, responsibility for, **28**, 43
　theatre, public admitted as, **37**, 3, 4,
　trespasser, becoming, **28**, 53n
　visitor as, **28**, 47

**INVOICE**
　*meaning*, **34**, 171
　c.i.f. contract; requirement for. *See* C.I.F.
　　　　　　　　　　　　　　　　　　[CONTRACT
　company—
　　liquidation, notification on, **6**, 557
　　name to appear on, **6**, 429
　consular, **34**, 171
　form of, **34**, 171
　prepacked food, for, **17**, 499, 502
　provisional, effect of, **34**, 171
　warranty, as, **17**, 599

**INVOLUNTARY**
　act or omission, *meaning*, **10**, 272n

**IONIAN ISLANDS**
　registration concerning the individual, **32**, 469, 470

　admission as students in England, **3**, 7
　call to English Bar, **3**, 9n
　Bills of Sale Acts inapplicable, **3**, 257
　births, deaths, etc., admissibility of registers in
　　　　　　　　　　　　　　　[evidence, **15**, 388, 389
　British nationality—
　　retention by citizens of Eire, **1**, 537, 538, 540, 541
　　through birth or parentage before 1949, **1**, 537
　British subjects before 1949...**1**, 538, 539
　chief representative—
　　distress, privilege from, **12**, 102
　　income tax exemption, **20**, 97n, 352, 600
　　privilege, **5**, 433n; **7**, 274, 275
　　suite, persons in, **7**, 274, 275, 276
　citizens of—
　　citizenship of United Kingdom and Colonies by
　　　　　　　　　　　　[registration, **1**, 538–540
　　claim to remain British subject by, **1**, 540, 541
　　former naturalised, deprivation of citizenship of
　　　　　　　　　[United Kingdom and Colonies, **1**, 562,
　　limitation on liability for crime, **1**, 531, 532
　　persons born before 6th December, 1922 in
　　　　　　　　　[Northern Ireland held to be, **1**, 539n
　　registration as citizens of United Kingdom and
　　　　　　　　　　　　[Colonies, **1**, 550, 551
　　renunciation of citizenship of United Kingdom
　　　　　　　　　　　　[and Colonies by, **1**, 559
　　retention of British nationality by, **1**, 538, 540,
　　　　　　　　　　　　　　　　　　　　　　[541
　　treated as British subjects, **1**, 498, 531, 541
　Commonwealth, secession from, **4**, 458, 459
　company formed in, **6**, 833
　consular immunities, conferment, **7**, 275
　copyright. *See* COPYRIGHT
　death duty legislation, not applicable in, **15**, 5
　declaration of, **5**, 459
　dentists, registration in England, **26**, 86n
　diplomatic representatives, **5**, 459n
　　immunity, **5**, 433n; **7**, 7, 274
　double taxation relief—
　　income tax. *See under* INCOME TAX
　　estate duty, **15**, 61
　　legacy duty, **15**, 96
　　profits tax, **20**, 464, 650
　　succession duty, **15**, 96
　elections, right of citizens to vote, **14**, 10, 11
　extradition procedure, **16**, 579n
　foreign country, deemed not to be, **1**, 531, 537n, 538

## [Illustration 130]

## PAGE FROM v. 28, HALSBURY'S LAWS OF ENGLAND, 3d Ed.

**[Pt. 2, Sect. 1]**　　　　　　Duty of Occupier　　　　　　41

has a material interest (*l*); (3) those whom the occupier has licensed to enter the premises for their own purposes (*m*); and (4) persons who trespass upon the premises (*o*).

**36. Common law distinction between duty to invitees and duty to licensees.** At common law an invitee, using reasonable care on his part for his own safety, was entitled to expect that the occupier would on his part use reasonable care to prevent damage from unusual danger, of which he knew or ought to have known (*p*). The only duty owed by an occupier to a licensee was to warn him of concealed dangers actually known to the occupier but neither known nor obvious to the licensee (*q*). The clarity of this distinction between the duty owed to an invitee and that owed to a licensee had, however, become blurred even before the common law rules were superseded by statute (*r*). If physical facts constituting a concealed danger were known to the occupier and a reasonable man would have appreciated the risks involved, the occupier was treated as having known of the danger so as to render him liable to a licensee, and was not excused by his own failure to appreciate the risk (*s*).

**37. The statutory rules.** Statutory rules (*t*), in place of those of the common law, regulate the duty which an occupier of premises (*u*) owes to his visitors (*a*) in respect of dangers due to the state of the premises or to things done (*b*) or omitted to be done on them (*c*).

---

(*l*) Such persons are known as invitees; for the meaning of the term invitee and the distinction between invitees and licensees, see pp. 47 *et seq.*, *post*. For examples of invitees, see p. 49, *post*. There is some conflict of authority, now of little importance, whether the invitee, for his part, must share with the occupier a material interest in the purpose of the visit; see note (*g*), p. 48, *post*.

(*m*) For examples of licensees, see p. 50, *post*.

(*o*) For the limited duty owed to trespassers, see p. 53, *post*.

(*p*) *Indermaur* v. *Dames* (1866), L. R. 1 C. P. 274, at p. 288, *per* Willes, J.; affirmed (1867), L. R. 2 C. P. 311, Ex. Ch. The word "unusual" is used objectively and means such danger as is not usually found in the circumstances; it is not to be construed subjectively

---

> **FINDING ENGLISH CASES: HALSBURY'S LAWS OF ENGLAND.**
>
> This set gives a textual treatment of the law and footnote citations to cases and statutes.
>
> As it covers both cases and statutes, and has a good index, it is usually best to start the research for English law in this set. A loose-leaf volume keeps the set up-to-date and should always be consulted.

---

at pp. 330, 331; [1954] 1 All E. R. 97, at pp. 102, 103, *per* Denning, L.J.; *Slade* v. *Battersea and Putney Group Hospital Management Committee*, [1955] 1 All E. R. 429; *Slater* v. *Clay Cross Co., Ltd.*, [1956] 2 Q. B. 264, C. A.; [1956] 2 All E. R. 625; *Perkowski* v. *Wellington Corpn.*, [1959] A. C. 53, P. C., at pp. 60, 61; [1958] 3 All E. R. 368, at p. 371. As to a similar distinction in the case of trespassers, see note (*g*), p. 54, *post*.

(*t*) See the Occupiers' Liability Act, 1957 (5 & 6 Eliz. 2 c. 31), ss. 2, 3.

(*u*) The Occupiers' Liability Act, 1957 (5 & 6 Eliz. 2 c. 31), binds the Crown, except that as regards the Crown's liability in tort that Act does not bind the Crown further than the Crown is made liable in tort by the Crown Proceedings Act, 1947 (10 & 11 Geo. 6 c. 44); the last-mentioned Act and in particular *ibid.*, s. 2 (see titles Constitutional Law, Vol. 7, p. 251; Crown Proceedings, Vol. 11, pp. 4 (note (*s*)), 11), apply in relation to duties under the Occupiers' Liability Act, 1957 (5 & 6 Eliz. 2 c. 31), ss. 2–4, as statutory duties (*ibid.*, s. 6).

(*a*) At common law a reciprocal duty is owed to the occupier by the visitor (*Lomas* v. *M. Jones & Son*, [1944] K. B. 4, C. A.; [1943] 2 All E. R. 548). See also *Sybray* v. *White* (1836), 1 M. & W. 435; *Re Williams* v. *Groucott* (1863), 4 B. & S. 149; *Hawken* v. *Shearer* (1887), 56 L. J. Q. B. 284, criticised in *Hickey* v. *Tipperary County Council*, [1931] I. R. 621.

---

2*　　　　　　For notes (*b*), (*c*), see next page.

## [Illustration 131]

## PAGE FROM CURRENT LAW STATUTE CITATOR

STATUTE CITATOR 1947–67                **1893**

CAP.

### 56 & 57 Vict.—cont.

**22. Appeal (Forma Pauperis) Act, 1893.**
repealed: 12–4G.6,c.51,s.17(3)(b).

**25. Burgh Police (Scotland) Act, 1893.**
applied: 7–8E.2,c.24,s.29(7).
code 49/4801.

**26. Prison (Officers' Superannuation) Act, 1893.**
repealed: S.L.R. 1950.

**27. Land Tax Commissioners Names Act, 1893.**
repealed: S.L.R. 1964.

**29. Railway Regulation Act, 1893.**
repealed: S.L.R. 1960.

**31. Rivers Pollution Prevention Act, 1893.**

---

### CITATORS FOR ENGLISH STATUTES:

This page from the Current Law Citator illustrates how citators are arranged chronologically and then alphabetically by Title of Act. References in this Citator are to the Current Law Year Books. Other Citators listed in Section F can be used in a similar manner.

---

s. 52, amended: 2–3E.2,c.43,s.2(2).
s. 55 (1), amended: 15–6G.6&1E.2, c. 17, s.1(1).
s. 64, case 54/1590.
s. 69 (3), amended: 2–3E.2,c.43,s.10(4).
s. 74, regs. 52/1697; 58/1572.
sch. 2, para. 5, amended: 15–6G.6&1 E.2,c.17,s.1(1).

**40. Public Works Loans (No. 2) Act, 1893.**
repealed: 1964,c.9.sch.3.

**52. Burghs Gas Supply (Scotland) Act, 1893.**
repealed: 11–2G.6,c.67,sch.4.

**53. Trustee Act, 1893.**
applied: 6–7E.2,c.55,s.54(5).
s. 5 (4), repealed in part: 6–7E.2,c.11, sch.,II.
s. 21 (1), case 3882.

**61. Public Authorities Protection Act, 1893.**
case 53/2903.
repealed: 2–3E.2,c.36,s.1,sch.
s. 1, cases 751, 4154, 5759, 7599; 48/4288, 4454–4458; 49/4977, 5036; 50/4983, 5251; 51/3988, 4235, 4376; 52/2922, 4181; 53/4314; 54/3947, 3948; 55/ 1553, 1554, 3192, 3343; 56/5068, 11454; 63/4191; 64/543, 4395.
s. 3, cases 50/5071; 51/4235; 52/4274.

CAP.

### 56 & 57 Vict.—cont.

**63. Married Women's Property Act, 1893.**
article: 215 L.T. 289.
s. 2, repealed: 12–4G.6,c.78,sch.2.

**66. Rules Publication Act, 1893.**
case 9958.
repealed: 3–4E.2,c.8,sch.

**69. Savings Banks Act, 1893.**
applied: 12–4G.6,c.13.ss.11(1),13; c.47, s.48(3); 4–5E.2,c.6,s.5(10); 7–8E.2,c.6, s.15(3).
s. 5, sch. 1, repealed: 7–8E.2,c.6,sch.

**71. Sale of Goods Act, 1893.**
Repeals:
s. 22 (part), repealed: 1967,c.58,sch.3.
applied, restricted, etc.: 8–9E.2,c.65,s.7; 1964,c.53,s.27,sch:1; 1965,c.2,s.22; c. 66,ss.20,54; c.67,s.50.
articles: 14 M.L.R. 173; 1962 S.L.T. (News) 13, 137; 64 L.S.Gaz. 14.
cases 8190: 53/1801, 2979; 54/2991.
s. 1, case 67/1673.
s. 4, cases 9233, 9234, 9235; 52/3149; 53/3283; 54/2998, 2999; repealed: 2–3 E.2,c.34,s.2.
s. 7, case 9196.
s. 11, amended: 1967,c.7,s.4; cases 9244; 50/5328; 55/3656; 64/4422, 4426, 65/3530.
s. 12, article: 24 M.L.R. 690; cases 9239, 9243; 48/4840; 51/4451; 54/3000; 55/ 2495; 60/3975.
s. 13, cases 9252, 9254; 52/642; 53/3272, 3289; 67/3537.
s. 14, articles: 20 Sol. 87; 22 M.L.R. 484; cases 9189, 9190, 9196, 9244; 48/ 4844; 49/5123; 50/5328; 52/3131, 4497; 53/3268, 3269, 3272, 4620; 54/ 2979; 55/1840, 2477; 56/7940, 12882; 57/3205, 4339; 58/3034; 59/92, 4029; 60/2868, 2869; 62/2751, 2753, 3777; 65/3516, 3517; 66/10837; 67/3522.
s. 15, cases 9252: 56/8011; 60/2868.
s. 17, cases 61/626, 11181; 64/3284.
s. 18, cases 9238; 55/2841: 57/3221; 62/ 2769; 66/710, 2557, 10891.
s. 20, cases 9196, 9221.
s. 21, cases 56/7973; 57/3225; 64/1358.
s. 22, case 9232.
s. 23, case 9239.
s. 24, case 59/3384.
s. 25, cases 52/33; 53/3286; 55/3554; 57/3225; 59/2946, 2953; 65/3529.
s. 25 (2), (3), case 67/4682.
s. 26, case 58/223.
s. 28, cases 9238, 9241.
s. 30, case 62/2766.
s. 32, case 9223.
s. 34, case 53/3266.
s. 35, amended: 1967,c.7,s.4; cases 9184, 9247; 52/3152, 4499; 53/3284; 54/ 2072; 62/2750; 64/4426.
s. 38, case 58/1455.
s. 39, case 9238.
s. 43, case 57/4343.
s. 47, case 59/2946, 2953.

[Illustration 132]

## PAGE FROM CURRENT LAW CASE CITATOR

CASE CITATOR 1947–67      **TUR**

Turner, *v.* Derham [1958] Ir.Jur.Rep. 78 ............................... *Digested,* **59/2284**

—— *v.* Ford Motor Co. [1965] 1 W.L.R. 948; 109 S.J. 354; [1965] 2 All E.R. 583, C.A. ...................................................... *Digested,* 65/2277

—— *v.* Forwood [1951] W.N. 189; [1951] 1 All E.R. 746; [211 L.T. 250; 15 Conv. 183], C.A. ................................................ *Digested,* **3744**

—— *v.* Garstang Rural District Council, 109 S.J. 176; 17 P. & C.R. 218; [1965] Crim.L.R. 306, D.C. .... *Digested,* 65/**2422**: *Subsequent proceedings,* 66/11740

—— *v.* —— (1965) 64 L.G.R. 28, D.C. .. *Digested,* 66/**11740**: *Previous proceedings,* 65/2422

—— *v.* Goldsmith [1891] 1 Q.B. 544 ................................... *Applied,* 53/1298

—— *v.* Hancock (1882) 20 Ch.D. 303 ................................... *Applied,* 66/9781

—— *v.* Hatton (Bradford) [1952] 1 T.L.R. 1184; [1952] 1 All E.R. 1286; [68 L.Q.R. 445] ...................................................... *Digested,* 52/**3149**

—— *v.* Jacaranda Clubs [1953] 1 W.L.R. 961; 97 S.J. 491; [1953] 2 All E.R. 548 ............................................................ *Digested,* 53/**2766**

—— *v.* Keiller, 1950 S.L.T. 66 ........................................... *Digested,* **8442**

—— *v.* Last [1965] T.R. 249; 42 T.C. 517; 44 A.T.C. 234 ............. *Digested,* 66/**6052**

—— *v.* Liverpool Chief Constable [1965] Crim.L.R. 725; 115 L.J. 711 .. *Digested,* 65/**1746**

—— *v.* Mason (1845) 14 M. & W. 112 ........................... *Distinguished,* 59/1168

—— *v.* Metro-Goldwyn-Mayer Pictures [1950] W.N. 83; 66 T.L.R. (Pt. 1) 342; 94 S.J. 145; [1950] 1 All E.R. 449; [66 L.Q.R. 145], H.L.; reversing (1948) 92 S.J. 541, C.A.; affirming (1947) 91 S.J. 495 .. *Digested,* 5662, 5663, 5664, **5666**, 5667, 5668: *Considered,* 54/1856; 63/1998: *Applied,* 62/1749: *Referred to,* 65/2269: *Dictum not followed,* 66/7036

—— *v.* Meyers (1808) 1 Hag.Con. 414 ................................. *Applied,* 53/2865

—— *v.* Midgley [1967] 1 W.L.R. 1247; 111 S.J. 582; [1967] 3 All E.R. 601, D.C. ............................................................. *Digested,* 67/3397

—— *v.* National Coal Board (1949) 65 T.L.R. 580; [66 L.Q.R. 8], C.A. *Digested,* **6901**

—— *v.* Northern Life Assurance Co. [1953] 1 D.L.R. 427 ............. *Digested,* 53/1792

—— *v.* Stallibrass [1898] 1 Q.B. 56 .......................... *Applied,* 52/688; 66/567

—— *v.* Tavener, LVC/1757/1964 [1965] J.P.L. 684; [1965] R.V.R. 447; 11 R.R.C. 209; 195 E.G. 257; [1965] R.A. 277, Lands Tribunal .. *Digested,* 65/3325

—— *v.* Thorne and Thorne (1959) 21 D.L.R. (2d) 29 ................... *Digested,* 60/**3257**

—— *v.* Turner [1962] P. 283; [1961] 3 W.L.R. 1269; 105 S.J. 910; [1961] 3 All E.R. 944, C.A.; affirming 105 S.J. 551; [232 L.T. 241], D.C. *Digested,* 61/2906: *Applied,* 63/1053

—— *v.* —— (1964). *See* Slatter's Will Trusts, *Re.*

—— *v.* Underwood [1948] 2 K.B. 284; [1949] L.J.R. 680; 112 J.P. 272; 92 S.J. 379; [1948] 1 All E.R. 859; 46 L.G.R. 357, D.C. ........ *Digested,* 2063

—— *v.* Waterman (1961) 105 S.J. 1011 ............................... *Digested,* 61/**5840**

—— *v.* Watts (1927) 44 T.L.R. 105 ........................ *Distinguished,* 54/2866

—— *v.* —— (1928) 97 L.J.K.B. 403 ............ *Applied,* 8895: *Distinguished,* 52/1947

—— *v.* Whitehouse, LVC/540–542/1964 [1965] J.P.L. 248; [1965] R.V.R. 80; [1965] R.C.N. 50, Lands Tribunal ........................... *Digested,* 65/3325

—— *v.* Wilson, 1954 S.C. 296; 1954 S.L.T. 131 ...................... *Digested,* 54/**42**

Turner (G.) & Brothers, *Re, The Times,* February 25, 1959 .............. *Reported,* 59/**2548**

Turner (G. R.), *Ex p. See* R. *v.* Morleston and Litchurch Commissioners.

Turner & Son *v.* Owen [1956] 1 Q.B. 48; [1955] 3 W.L.R. 700; 120 J.P. 15; 99 S.J. 799; [1955] 3 All E.R. 565n.; 54 L.G.R. 69, D.C. .... *Digested,* 55/1116

Turner Bridger [ ] 1959, Lan[ ] ..................................... [Di]gested, 60/3133

Turner's Applic[ ] Lands Tr[ ] .................................... [Di]gested, 64/3123

Turner's and H[ ] Lands Tr[ ] ............................ [Dig]ested, 66/10320 [ ]/1515; 61/4269

Turner's Will T[ ] —— , *Re,* Bridg[ ] S.J. 545; [ ] ..................................... [Di]gested, **59/3005** [Di]gested, 67/**4069**

—— , *Re,* Westn[ ] [Refer]red to, 67/4077

Turney, *Re,* Tu[ ] [Di]gested, 52/**2969**

—— *v.* Hammo[ ]

Turpin *v.* Midd[ ] [ ]7/2962; 58/593

—— *v.* Turpin [Consid]ered, 65/1271: [fol]lowed, 65/1271

Turriff Construc[ ] *nom.* Cha[ ] Industrial [Tribunal] ........................................... [Di]gested, 67/**1447**

Tursi *v.* Tursi [1958] P. 54; [1957] 3 W.L.R. 573; 101 S.J. 680; [1957] 2 All E.R. 828; [20 M.L.R. 636] ........... *Digested,* 57/**518**, 1055: *Followed,* 58/**502**

> **CITATORS FOR ENGLISH CASES.**
>
> Note how cases are listed alphabetically rather than by citation as in Shepard's Citations. References in this Citator are to the Current Law Year Book.
>
> Other citators listed in Section F may be used in a similar manner.

## SECTION J.    METHODS OF CITATION

### 1.    Statutes

Prior to 1962, English statutes were cited by name, regnal year (the year of the sovereign's reign in which statute was passed) and chapter. E. g., *National Services Act, 11 & 12 Geo. 6*, c. 64. This method of citation made it necessary to consult a Table to determine the year of passage. As all legal writing on English prior to 1962 cited to regnal year, a Table of Regnal Years is set forth for convenience.

### TABLE OF REGNAL YEARS

| Sovereign | Reign Began | Sovereign | Reign Began |
|---|---|---|---|
| William I | Oct. 14, 1066 | Mary | July 6, 1553 |
| William II | Sept. 26, 1087 | Jane | July 6, 1553 |
| Henry I | Aug. 5, 1100 | Philip & Mary | July 25, 1554 |
| Stephen | Dec. 26, 1135 | Elizabeth I | Nov. 17, 1558 |
| Henry II | Dec. 19, 1154 | James I | Mar. 24, 1603 |
| Richard I | Sept. 3, 1189 | Charles I | Mar. 27, 1625 |
| John | May 27, 1199 | Charles II | Jan. 30, 1649 |
| Henry III | Oct. 28, 1216 | James II | Feb. 6, 1685 |
| Edward I | Nov. 20, 1272 | William & Mary | Feb. 13, 1689 |
| Edward II | July 8, 1307 | Anne | Mar. 8, 1702 |
| Edward III | Jan. 25, 1327 | George I | Aug. 1, 1714 |
| Richard II | June 22, 1377 | George II | June 11, 1727 |
| Henry IV | Sept. 30, 1399 | George III | Oct. 25, 1760 |
| Henry V | Mar. 21, 1413 | George IV | Jan. 29, 1820 |
| Henry VI | Sept. 1, 1422 | William IV | June 26, 1830 |
| Edward IV | Mar. 4, 1461 | Victoria | June 20, 1837 |
| Edward V | Apr. 9, 1483 | Edward VII | Jan. 22, 1901 |
| Richard III | June 26, 1483 | George V | May 6, 1910 |
| Henry VII | Aug. 22, 1485 | Edward VIII | Jan. 20, 1936 |
| Henry VIII | Apr. 22, 1509 | George VI | Dec. 11, 1936 |
| Edward VI | Jan. 28, 1547 | Elizabeth II | Feb. 6, 1952 |

This method of citation was changed by the Acts of Parliament Numbering and Citation Act, 1962. Under it, citation is to the name of the Act and calendar year. Since 1898, each Act of Parliament has a section indicating the title of the Act under which it is to be cited. E. g., Section 87 of *Highways Acts of 1971* is entitled *Short Title, Citations, and Commencement and Extent*.

## 2. Cases

a. Prior to 1865

The favored citation to English cases prior to 1865 is to give the original report and the parallel reference in the *English Reports, Full Reprint.*

How v. Lacy, 1 Taunt. 119, 127 Eng.Rep. 777 (C.P.1808).

b. 1865 to date

The *Law Reports* citation is given if the case appears therein.

Blackpool Corp. v. Locker, [1948] 1 K.B. 349.

Galloway v. Galloway, [1954] P. 312 (C.A.).

A case in the *All England Law Reports* is cited:

Harding v. Price, [1948] 1 All E.R. 284 (K.B.).

## 3. Administrative Regulations

*Statutory Rules and Orders* (Revised 1948) are cited to the annual volume which preceded the revision:

(1919) Stat.Rules & Orders 53 (No. 1517) or S.R. & O.1919 (No. 1517) 53.

Since 1948, the series is identified as *Statutory Instruments.* Cite by year, number, volume and page.

(1950) 2 Stat.Instr. 478 (No. 1556) or

S.I.1950 (No. 1556) 2, p. 478.

# Chapter 21

# A GENERAL SUMMARY OF RESEARCH
# PROCEDURE

For convenience in formalizing research procedure, we classify general legal problems, requiring solution through research, into four divisions: (1) constitutional law, (2) statute law, (3) case law (common law) and (4) administrative law. In this connection, we do not concern ourselves with international law, which we studied in Chapter 19, for the solutions to its problems are not found in the systematically related use of general legal publications.

Each of these units is generally subdivided into federal, state and local law. As you will observe in your practice, some problems cross over divisions, relate to more than one area and concurrently may refer to federal, state or local laws within a single division. To illustrate, a controversy may pertain to the interpretation of a state statute and its constitutionality, thus fitting into categories one and two, above. Also, the constitutional issue may have both federal and state ramifications. It follows, therefore, that legal problems cannot be neatly compartmentalized, for concepts often are interconnected and merge into multiple issues.

Notwithstanding this interrelationship of legal issues, we will simplify the presentation by evaluating each as a separate, independent unit. The publications, applicable to the solution of problems in each area, will be listed in accordance with a systematic scheme of research methodology.

As we noted in Chapter 3, when we began our study of legal research, secondary expository publications, such as encyclopedias, treatises, periodical articles and annotations, have assumed significant roles in identifying and explaining the law. Therefore, we begin our research, generally, through the use of these publications. The second step is to examine the primary sources. This is followed by a perusal of their interpretative publications. The final verification step requires the use of *Shepard's Citations*. Of course, there are some variations to this procedure which will be disclosed as we study each function.

## SECTION A.  CONSTITUTIONAL LAW PROBLEM

### 1.  Federal Constitution

   a.   General Background

For a general discussion on a federal constitutional law question, consult a general legal encyclopedia (*Corpus Juris Secundum* or *American Jurisprudence 2d*).   More critical and detailed studies may be found in the periodical literature by examining the *Index to Legal Periodicals*.   A recent treatise may be consulted to explore the area. Several other interpretative sources are given in Chapter 8.

Examine the *American Law Reports* and the *United States Supreme Court Reports* (L.Ed.) for possible annotations.

   b.   Text and Interpretation

If the matter is a recognizable federal constitutional problem, consult the following sources:

For the text of the Constitution and its interpretation see:

*United States Code Annotated.*

*Federal Code Annotated.*—U.S.C.S.

*Constitution of the United States* (Library of Congress ed. 1964).

   c.   *Shepard's Citations*

Shepardize:  (1) several important cases and (2) the applicable provision of the Constitution in *Shepard's United States Citations* and the provision in the appropriate *Shepard's State Citations*.   Use *Shepard's Federal Reporter Citations* when given an intermediate or lower court decision.   Numerous case citations under a provision of the Constitution in *Shepard's United States Citations* may make the Constitution section in *Shepard's* unwieldly and unusable.

   d.   Additional Cases

Check a United States Supreme Court digest, the *Modern Federal Practice Digest* and the *Federal Digest*, or the *American Digest System* for additional and judicial interpretations.

   e.   Intent

In the absence of adequate judicial interpretation or to re-examine the meaning given to the Constitution by its framers, the following historical source materials should be studied.

The Madison Papers.

Elliott's Debates.

The Federalist.

The Documentary History of the Constitution, 1786–1870.

Documents Illustrative of the Formation of the Union of the American States.

## 2. State Constitution

### a. General Background

For a discussion of a state constitution, consult a local encyclopedia, if one is published for the state, e. g., *Texas Jurisprudence 2d* and *Illinois Law and Practice*. In the absence of a local encyclopedia, a general encyclopedia (C.J.S. or Am.Jur.2d) may provide a helpful general discussion of the question. An *American Law Reports* annotation or a periodical article also may treat the constitutional issue.

### b. Text and Interpretation

The text and case interpretations of a state constitution are included in the appropriate annotated state code.

Additional cases may be located through the state digest.

### c. *Shepard's Citations*

Shepardize: (1) several leading cases and (2) the provision of the state constitution in the appropriate *Shepard's State Citations*.

### d. Additional Cases

For cases of other states, consult the *American Digest System.*

The *Index Digest of State Constitutions*, 2d edition, cites comparative state constitutions. Through these references, the annotated constitutions of other states may be examined, evaluated and compared. This procedure is useful in citing persuasive decisions from another state whose provision was copied or where the provision, situation and setting are comparable or where there is a dearth of judicial interpretation of the provision by your state courts.

Comparative constitutional study also may be engaged by Shepardizing cases under their *Reporter* citations in the appropriate *Shepard's Reporter Citations*.

### e. Intent

Examine the proceedings, reports and other documents relating to state constitutional conventions for the meaning given the provision by its draftsmen.

---

## SECTION B. STATUTE PROBLEM

## 1. Federal Statute

### a. General Background

Treatises are available for a number of federal statutory laws, e. g., *Callman, Law of Unfair Competition, Trademarks and Monopolies*, 3rd ed. 1969, 5 vols. They provide not only background but also detailed subject information. Thus they are valuable not only for their informational content but also as case finders.

Annotations in the *American Law Reports* and the *United States Supreme Court Reports* (L.Ed.) and periodical literature are additional useful secondary aids.

Am.Jur.2d and C.J.S. also provide statutory information.

### b.   Text and Interpretation

For the text and interpretation of a federal statute which is in force, use the *United States Code Annotated* or the *Federal Code Annotated.* The amendatory history of the act is included in these annotated codes.

For the legislative history (intent of the draftsmen) of the act, consult the Congressional bills, reports, hearings and debates.

### c.   *Shepard's Citations*

Shepardize: (1) the provision (*United States Code* or *Statutes at Large*) for the history and the treatment of the act and (2) several significant cases in *Shepard's United States Citations.* Consult *Shepard's Federal Reporter Citations* to Shepardize intermediate and lower federal court cases.

State court decisions which cite federal statutes are listed in *Shepard's State Citations.*

### d.   Additional Cases

When there are meager case interpretations, examine the United States Supreme Court digests, the *Modern Federal Practice Digest* and the *Federal Digest,* or the *American Digest System.*

If it is a federal procedure or practice problem, the *Modern Federal Practice Digest* should be consulted (see Chapter 12).

## 2.   State Statute

### a.   General Background

The local encyclopedia is helpful in providing information and interpretations to a state statute. Local treatises and periodical articles, having more detailed bearing on the act, are equally useful references.

Where there is no local encyclopedia, Am.Jur.2d and C.J.S. may give general information on some topics.

Annotations in the *American Law Reports* cover statutory law of the several states.

### b.   Text and Interpretation

Unannotated state codes provide the text of the statutes.

Annotated state codes give both the text of the statutes and case interpretations.

The codes provide the amendatory history of the state acts. For legislative histories, consult the official and unofficial sources (see Chapter 11).

c. *Shepard's Citations*

Shepardize: (1) the provision of the state statute and (2) several important cases in the applicable *Shepard's State Citations.*

d. Additional Cases

For additional cases interpreting the statute, examine the state digest.

If there is a dearth of statutory interpretation in the state, consult the annotated codes of other states for other states' interpretations. Such interpretation can be very persuasive. Some codes list comparative legislation of representative and neighboring states.

## 3. Local

a. Text and Interpretation

The text of city ordinances are included in city codes. Generally, city codes are not annotated.

The appropriate state digest is useful in providing interpretations to the city ordinance, but the problem must be approached by subject or topic.

In the absence of a current city code, check the ordinances in the office of the city counsel, city clerk or other local official whose duties include the maintenance of a current file of city laws.

b. *Shepard's Citations*

Shepardize: (1) the provision of the city code and (2) several significant cases, if existing, in the applicable *Shepard's State Citations.*

---

## SECTION C.   CASE LAW PROBLEM

## 1.   General Background

When the problem is not covered by a constitution or a statute, then the answer must be sought in the judicial decisions of a state.

As noted in Section A2, above, the local encyclopedia is a good source for a discussion of the topic. In the absence of a local encyclopedia, *American Jurisprudence 2d* or *Corpus Juris Secundum* may be consulted for an exposition on the case law.

*American Jurisprudence 2d* may give specific references to *American Law Reports* annotations, eliminating the use of A.L.R. indexes.

In some fields of the law, the researcher might begin with a local treatise or periodical article.

## 2. Interpretation

References to state court cases may be found in the appropriate state digest.

## 3. Shepard's Citations

Shepardize several of the significant cases in *Shepard's State Citations.*

## 4. Additional Cases

Other state digests, the regional digests and the *American Digest System* provide judicial decisions of other states on the point of law.

*Shepard's Reporter Citations* gives additional references to cases from other states which have cited an applicable state case.

---

## SECTION D. ADMINISTRATIVE LAW PROBLEM

## 1. Federal Administrative Law

### a.  General Background

*Corpus Juris Secundum* or *American Jurisprudence 2d* discuss federal administrative law. *Pike and Fischer, Administrative Law,* treatises (e. g., *Davis, Administrative Law*) and periodical literature provide more detailed studies of administrative law.

Annotations on the subject are included in the *American Law Reports* and the *United States Supreme Court Reports* (L.Ed.).

### b.  Text and Interpretation

The text of federal administrative regulations are contained in: (1) loose-leaf services and (2) the *Code of Federal Regulations* and the *Federal Register.*

The decisions of federal administrative agencies are included in: (1) loose-leaf services and (2) agency reports.

Interpretative sources of federal administrative law are: (1) loose-leaf services, (2) U. S. Supreme Court digests and (3) the *Modern Federal Practice Digest* and the *Federal Digest.*

c.  *Shepard's Citations*

Cases of certain agencies may be Shepardized in *Shepard's United States Administrative Citations.*

Court cases on federal administrative law are Shepardized in *Shepard's United States Citations* and *Shepard's Federal Reporter Citations.*

## 2.  State Administrative Law

a.   General Background

Refer to a local encyclopedia for a discussion of state administrative law.

Other secondary aids, such as local treatises, periodical articles and *American Law Reports* annotations, also are helpful sources.

b.   Text and Interpretation

If a state has a current administrative code, check it for state regulatory material.  In the absence of an administrative code, inquiry should be directed to the appropriate agency for its regulations.

If a loose-leaf service covers the state law, it can be consulted for agency rules and decisions.

The accessibility of agency decisions should be determined by inquiry.

Interpretative cases are covered by the state digest.

c.  *Shepard's Citations*

Shepardize applicable court cases in *Shepard's State Citations.*

d.   Additional Cases

Court decisions of other states relating to a comparable administrative law problem may be located in (1) other state digests, (2) regional digests, and (3) the *American Digest System.*

*Shepard's Reporter Citations* also provides citations to cases of other states which cited a state court decision in point.

## 3.  Local Administrative Law

a.   Text and Interpretation

If available, city administrative regulations generally are published separately as pamphlets for each body.  Information regarding these rules, such as regulatory and licensing provisions, should be obtained directly from the local administrative department.

Cases pertaining to local administrative law are included in the state digest.

b.  *Shepard's Citations*

Shepardize cases on the problem by using *Shepard's State Citations.*

## SECTION E.  CHART ON LEGAL RESEARCH PROCEDURE

The outline of research procedure, presented in the preceding sections, is summarized graphically in the following chart:

**CHART ON LEGAL RESEARCH PROCEDURE**

| RESEARCH PROBLEM | GENERAL BACKGROUND | MORE CRITICAL & DETAILED STUDIES | ANNOTATIONS | TEXT OF LAW | LEGISLATIVE HISTORY | INTERPRETATION | SHEPARDIZING | ADDITIONAL CASES |
|---|---|---|---|---|---|---|---|---|
| **CONSTITUTIONAL LAW** | | | | | | | | |
| 1. Federal | 1. C.J.S. 2. Am. Jur.2d | 1. Treatises 2. Periodicals: Index Leg. P. | A.L.R. L.Ed. | 1. U.S.C.A. 2. F.C.A. 3. L. C. Const. | Citations: U.S.C.A., F.C.A., Shep.U.S., U.S.C., Stat. at L. Intent: Mad. Papers, Federalist, etc. | 1. U.S.C.A. 2. F.C.A. | 1. Provisions: U.S., State Cases: U.S., Fed., State 2. Cases: U.S., Fed., State | 1. U.S.Sup.Ct.digs. 2. Mod. Fed. P. Dig. & Fed. Dig. 3. Am. Dig. |
| 2. State | 1. Local Ency. 2. C.J.S. or Am. Jur.2d | 1. Periodicals: Index Leg. P. | A.L.R. | State Code | State Const. Conv. 1. Proceedings 2. Reports, etc. | 1. Annot. State Code 2. State Dig. | 1. Provisions: State Cit. 2. Cases: State Cit. | 1. Am. Dig. 2. Index Dig. of State Const. 2d ed. 3. Shepard's Reporter Clts. |
| **STATUTORY LAW** | | | | | | | | |
| 1. Federal | (C.J.S. or Am. Jur.2d) | 1. Treatises 2. Periodicals | A.L.R. L.Ed. | 1. U.S.C.A. 2. F.C.A. | Citations: U.S.C.A., F.C.A., Shep.U.S. Intent: Cong. Bills, Reps., Hear., Debates | 1. U.S.C.A. 2. F.C.A. | Prov. & Cases: U.S. Cases: Fed. Prov.: State | 1. U.S.Sup.Ct.Digs. 2. Mod.Fed.Prac.Dig. & Fed.Dig. |
| 2. State | Loc. Ency. (C.J.S. or Am. Jur.2d) | 1. Treatises 2. Periodicals | A.L.R. | State Code | Citations: State Code Intent: Official & Unofficial Sources | Annot. State Code | Prov. & Cases: State Cit. | 1. State Dig. 2. Comparative Leg. In State Code. |
| 3. Local | | | | Mun. Code | | State Dig. | Prov. & Cases: State Cit. | |

## CHART ON
## LEGAL RESEARCH PROCEDURE
### (Continued)

| RESEARCH PROBLEM | GENERAL BACKGROUND | MORE CRITICAL & DETAILED STUDIES | ANNOTATIONS | TEXT OF LAW | LEGISLATIVE HISTORY | INTERPRETATION | SHEPARDIZING | ADDITIONAL CASES |
|---|---|---|---|---|---|---|---|---|
| CASE LAW: STATE | 1. Loc. Ency. 2. C.J.S. or Am.Jur.2d | 1. Treatises 2. Periodicals | A.L.R. | | | State Dig. | State Cit. | 1. Am. Dig. 2. Other state digs. 3. Shepard's Reporter Cits. |
| ADMINISTRATIVE LAW 1. Federal | C.J.S. or Am.Jur.2d | 1. Pike & Fischer 2. Treatises 3. Periodicals | A.L.R. L.Ed. | 1. Loose-Leaf Serv.: Rules & Decs. 2. C.F.R. & Fed. Reg.: Rules 3. Agency Reps.: Decs. | | 1. Loose-Leaf Services 2. U.S.Sup.Ct. digs. 3. Mod.Fed.P. Dig. & Fed. Dig. | Agency Cases: U.S.Admin. Cit. Court Cases: U.S. and Fed. | |
| 2. State | Loc.Ency. | 1. Treatises 2. Periodicals | A.L.R. | 1. Ad. Code, if pub. 2. Loose-Leaf Serv.: Rules & Decs. 3. Agency: Rules & Decs. | | State Dig. | Cases: State Cit. | 1. Am. Dig. 2. Other state digs. 3. Shepard's Reporter Cits. |
| 3. Local | | | | 1. Local Adm. Dept. 2. Pamph. | | State Dig. | Cases: State Cit. | |

## SECTION F.  EXTENSIVENESS OF RESEARCH

There is no uniform rule as to how extensive the research should be in solving a legal problem.  This is influenced by extraneous factors, such as the limitations of time, compensation, etc.; the nature of the problem; the legal measures being adopted; and the research habits and attitudes of the attorney.

The preceding discussion in this chapter exhaustively outlines the methods of legal research; however, such complete procedure is not always necessary.  Carrying a problem through all the sources might be needless, unwarranted or repetitious.  Common sense, therefore, has a significant bearing on research procedure.

The following simplified procedure should suffice in a significant number of research situations for *most states*.  Opinions may differ as to the best order of using the publications; however, they are presented here in logical progression and the arrangement reflects some advantageous practices.  Of course, in certain circumstances, the sequence can be modified to advantage.

1.  Refer to *American Jurisprudence 2d* or *Corpus Juris Secundum* for general discussions on constitutional or common law problems.  If the state has a local encyclopedia, initially consult it in all situations.  *American Jurisprudence 2d* may give specific citations to annotations in the *American Law Reports,* eliminating the use of the indexes to A.L.R.  When appropriate, check L.Ed. annotations.  In some areas of the law, the researcher might begin with a *treatise* or *periodical article*.

2.  Examine the *annotated constitutions* or *statutes* and/or the *digest*.

3.  Read and analyze the cases found.

4.  Shepardize several of the best representative cases favoring your position and all decisions in opposition.  With a federal constitutional or federal statutory problem, the pertinent sections of the instrument should be examined in *Shepard's U. S.* and *Shepard's State Citations*.  If it is a state statutory matter, examine the statute section in *Shepard's State Citations*, and Shepardize several important cases.

Should the research stop here?  Obviously, there is no arbitrary answer covering all situations.  It has been suggested that if this research elicits several cases, and no opposing decisions, with at least one recent and one state Supreme Court case, that might be adequate.[1]  If not, the secondary aids outlined under the preceding comprehen-

---

[1] Emery, A Streamlined Briefing Technique 30 (1955).

sive procedures should be consulted until the researcher is satisfied that he has adequately covered or exhausted the problem.

But it should be emphasized that for most problems, the researcher follows a simple procedure.   In some situations, merely a spot-check of a *single* publication will suffice, e. g., a general encyclopedia.   In most cases, duplicate sources are not examined, i. e., Am.Jur.2d and C.J.S., the researcher being satisfied to rely on a single source if it provides a satisfactory answer.   It must always be remembered that a lawyer's stock in trade is *time*; therefore, he should wisely use it.   The sophisticated lawyer learns his legal research as much for the knowledge of what can be omitted as for what and how materials are used to solve legal problems.

\*

# Appendix A

## CITATION FEATURES AND ABBREVIATIONS USED IN LEGAL WRITING

No attempt was made in relation to the preceding chapters to provide exhaustive citation information covering all phases of legal writing. Only the more common forms which the lawyer encounters were outlined. For more detailed and discursive treatment of citations see Price, *A Practical Manual of Standard Legal Citations*, 2d ed., 1958, and *A Uniform System of Citation*, 11th ed., 1967.

Several supplemental aids in citing are given in this Appendix A:

Section A.   Order of Citations

Section B.   Signals

Section C.   Forms of Abbreviations

---

## SECTION A.   ORDER OF CITATIONS

Since the objective of citations is to persuade and inform the reader, the most important authority should be cited first, followed by the less important in descending order. Thus, primary authority is cited before secondary materials. Within the framework of primary authority, statutes should precede judicial interpretations. Cases should be cited in this order:

1.   United States Supreme Court cases.

2.   United States Court of Appeals cases.

3.   United States District Court cases.

4.   State court cases in the alphabetical order of states.

5.   English and other foreign cases.

Within each of the above divisions, the citations should be in reverse chronological order, first giving the most recent cases.

In the absence of circumstances suggesting an arrangement determined by the intrinsic worth of the writings or the reputation of authors, secondary authorities should be listed in the following order:

1.   Treatises, arranged alphabetically by names of the authors.

2.   Leading articles, arranged alphabetically by names of the authors.

3.   Comments and notes, arranged alphabetically by names of the journals. Some law reviews cite their own journal first, followed by the others in alphabetical order.

## SECTION B.  SIGNALS

To conserve space and save time, a system of standardized signals, identifying the distinctions and gradations of authorities and arguments, has been developed.  This scheme of using symbols to indicate supporting, contrary and other positions relating to propositions is particularly popular in law review writing.  However, the usage of the symbols has too frequently been indiscriminate and careless, with resulting misunderstanding and confusion as to their meanings.  An explanation of the designations may help clarify these discrepancies and at the same time be informative.

### 1.  No Signal

If a holding is squarely in point or a statute directly supports the proposition, a signal is not used.  The reference is a standard citation without a symbol.

> Westlake Mercantile Finance Corp. v. Merritt, 204 Cal. 673, 269
> Pac. 620 (1928).

### 2.  "Accord"

"Accord" is used to indicate substantial support of a proposition although the holding may be distinguishable in some respects.  "Accord" is italicized in law reviews.

> Workman v. Wright, 33 Ohio St. 405 (1878); accord, Shinew
> v. First National Bank, 84 Ohio St. 297, 95 N.E. 881 (1911).

> Accord, Justice v. Stonecipher, 267 Ill. 448, 108 N.E. 722 (1915).

### 3.  "Alternative Holding"

"Alternative Holding" is used to identify a case decided on two or more independent principles either of which can be interpreted as a holding.

> Schechter Poultry Corp. v. United States, 295 U.S. 495 (1935)
> (alternative holding).

### 4.  "Contra"

"Contra" indicates a square holding against the proposition.  "Contra" is italicized in law reviews.

> Westlake Mercantile Finance Corp. v. Merritt, 204 Cal. 673, 269
> Pac. 620 (1928).  Contra, Heller v. Cuddy, 172 Minn. 126,
> 214 N.W. 924 (1927).

> Contra, Johnson v. Bradstreet Co., 77 Ga. 172, 4 Am.St.Rep. 77
> (1886).

### 5.  "Cf."

"Cf." is used for a case which is parallel to the proposition but contains materially different facts.  "Cf." is italicized in law reviews.

> Fonseca v. Cunard S. S. Co., 153 Mass. 553, 27 N.E. 665 (1891);
> cf. Murray v. Cunard S. S. Co., 235 N.Y. 162, 139 N.E. 226
> (1923).

> Cf. Wisconsin v. Minnesota Mining & Mfg. Co., 311 U.S. 452
> (1940).

**6. "See"**

*"See"* (in italics) is used to indicate a dictum which supports the proposition. A dictum page citation should be given for both the official and unofficial reports.

> *See* Shattuck v. Shattuck, 67 Ariz. 122, 130, 192 P.2d 229, 234 (1948).

**7. "See"**

"See" (in Roman type) is used in a non-signal sense to introduce secondary authority which supports the proposition.

> See Scott, Collateral Estoppel by Judgment, 56 Harv.L.Rev. 1, 15 (1942).

**8. "But see"**

*"But see"* (in italics) indicates a dictum which is opposed to the proposition. Dicta pages should be cited.

> But *see* United States v. Wong Kim Ark, 169 U.S. 649, 703 (1898).

**9. "But see"**

"But see" (in Roman type) is used in a non-signal sense to introduce secondary authority which opposes the proposition. Specific pages should be cited.

> But see Slocombe, The Psychology of Safety, 20 Personnel J. 42, 105 (1941).

**10. "But cf."**

"But cf." is used to indicate a contrary holding in a case with substantially different facts. "But cf." is italicized in law reviews.

> But cf. Easton v. Medema, 246 Mich. 130, 224 N.W. 636 (1929).

**11. "Semble"**

If the holding of a case is not clear, use "semble" following the citation.

> Rushmore v. Manhattan Screw and Stamping Works, 163 Fed. 939 (2d Cir.1908) semble.

**12. Dissenting or Concurring Opinion**

To cite a dissenting or a concurring opinion, introduce the citation with "see" and follow with a parenthetical explanation.

> See Winters v. New York, 333 U.S. 507, 520 (1947) (dissenting opinion).

**13. "Compare * * * with * * *"**

"Compare * * * with * * *" is used to compare one case with another, rather than the specific texts. The words "compare" and "with" are italicized in law reviews.

> Compare McPhee v. People, 108 Colo. 530, 120 P.2d 814 (1941), with Stewart v. United States, 300 Fed. 769 (8th Cir. 1924).

**14. "E. g."**

The support of a proposition by numerous holdings or dicta may be illustrated by a selective citation of one or a few cases preceded by *"E. g." "E. g."* is italicized, even when it precedes secondary authority, and it always is followed by a comma. Another signal may precede it to indicate a distinction with an example where there are many cases in point.

> *E. g.*, Eichten v. Central Minn. Cooperative Power Ass'n., 224 Minn. 180, 28 N.W.2d 862 (1947).

> *See, e. g.*, Toledo Newspaper Co. v. United States, 247 U.S. 402 (1918).

**15. "Accord," "see" and "cf."**

The rules do not require that these signals, which support the proposition, be set off by new sentences. They are generally preceded by a semicolon when used with a string of citations.

> Kasanovich v. George, 348 Pa. 199, 34 A.2d 523 (1943); **cf.** Potter v. Gillmore, 282 Mass. 49, 184 N.E. 373 (1933).

**16. "Contra," "But see" and "But cf."**

These signals, indicating opposition to the proposition, are always introduced by new sentences.

> Westlake Mercantile Finance Corp. v. Merritt, 204 Cal. 673, 269 Pac. 620 (1928). Contra, Heller v. Cuddy, 172 Minn. 126, 214 N.W. 924 (1927).

**17. Repetitive Citations**

Short-cut techniques have been developed and practiced in scholarly writings to avoid repeating citations. These devices are usually inapplicable to brief writing and in that connection their use is not recommended. However, to understand their application in treatises, law reviews and footnoted briefs, these terms are described below.

**a. "Supra"**

This word identifies a case or publication previously cited on the same or preceding page. It should not be used if more than one page intervenes between the citations. It is always italicized.

> Ladd v. Weiskopf, *supra.*

If the case or other publication has been previously cited in the same footnote, a dictum or another reference may be indicated as follows:

> Attorney General v. Taggart, *supra* at 369, 29 Atl. at 1031.

> Hening, *supra* at 310.

Reference to a complete footnote is made as follows:

> See note 5, *supra.*

**b. "Ibid." "Id."**

Where a reference to a citation is immediately repeated with the same volume and page numbers, the successive designation should read only: *Ibid.* It is always italicized.

If the successive citation is to a different page of the same case or publication, cite as follows: *Id.* at 43. If the case is cited unofficially, too, the reference is: *Id.* at 43, 25 N.E.2d at 310. *"Id."* is italicized. Section references are noted: *Id.* § 1431.

Where the publication, such as Williston, Contracts, contains more than one volume, repeat the volume number. 2 *Id.* § 1095.

c. Repeating Titles

To avoid repeating titles of books and periodical articles, the following abbreviations are suggested:

If a text has been cited previously within reasonable footnote range, use *"op. cit. supra.",* preceded by the author's name and followed by the previous footnote reference and the page number.

Finletter, *op. cit. supra* note 12, at 535.

5 Fletcher, *op. cit. supra* note 9 § 2169.

Where reference is to a section number, the word "at" is omitted as shown in the second example above.

*"Op. cit. supra"* should be used only when the omission of the title effects some saving in space and when the second reference is not too far removed from the first.

Periodical articles, previously cited, may be referred to as illustrated below.

Seavey, *supra* note 4, at 384.

**18. Summary**

The meanings and descriptive elements of signals are recapitulated below in tabular form.

| Type of Signal Used | | Elements in the Publication Cited |
|---|---|---|
| No signal | Supports proposition | Same facts |
| Accord | Supports proposition | Some differences in facts |
| Contra | Opposes proposition | Same facts |
| Cf. | Supports proposition | Substantially different facts |
| But cf. | Opposes proposition | Substantially different facts |
| See | Supporting dictum | |
| But see | Opposing dictum | |

## SECTION C.  FORMS OF ABBREVIATIONS

1. **Case Names**
    a.  The significant words in the name of a case should not be abbreviated.

> Miami Transportation Co. v. United States, not Miami Trans.
>> Co. v. United States.

    b.  "United States" is not abbreviated in the name of a case.  See example above.

    c.  Case names may be condensed by:
        (1) Omission of words which are not essential

"State of," "City of" are omitted except when necessary to avoid confusion.

"Inc." may be omitted from the name of a party which includes "Co." Miami Transportation Co., not Miami Transportation Co., Inc.

> Allard v. Board of Education, not Allard v. Board of Education
>> Madison County Township Rural School District.

        (2) Abbreviations

"Railroad Company" and "Railway Company" are usually abbreviated "R. R." and "Ry.," respectively.

> Erie R. R. Co. v. Garman.

> Leis v. Cleveland Ry. Co.

"Corporation," "Company" and "Association" are abbreviated in the titles of cases.  Meredith v. Realty Associates Securities Corp.; Suttle v. Reich Bros. Construction Co.; Hazel Park Taxpayers Assn. v. Royal Oak.

The lengthy names of railroads are often abbreviated by giving the first word in full and the initial letters of the remainder.  Bowman v. Chicago & N. W. Ry. Co.

The ampersand, &, is used for "and" in corporate or firm names.

Law reviews generally compress an administrative agency's name when it is a party to the suit.

> FTC v. Bunte Bros., Inc.

> FPC v. Hope Natural Gas Co.

The given names of individuals are omitted in the titles of cases; however, corporate and firm names bearing personal names are not condensed.

> Marshall Field & Co. v. Esch.

> C. W. Blakeslee & Sons v. United States.

2. **Words Not Abbreviated**
    The following words are not abbreviated, except when used locally in some briefs and other restricted publications: Alaska, Hawaii, Idaho, Iowa, Ohio and Utah.  However, the preference is to avoid such contractions, even locally.

## 3. Popular Abbreviations

| | |
|---|---|
| Abbott's Appeal Decisions | Abb.App.Dec. |
| Abbott's New Cases | Abb.N.Cas. |
| Abbott's Practice Reports | Abb.Pr. |
| Academy of Political Science Proceedings | Acad.Pol.Sci.Proc. |
| Acta Juridica | Acta Jur. |
| Adelaide Law Review | Adelaide L.Rev. |
| Administrative Law | Ad.L. |
| Administrative Law, Second Series | Ad.L.2d |
| Administrative Law Review | Ad.L.Rev. |
| Advance California Appellate Reports | A.C.A. |
| Advance California Reports | A.C. |
| Advocate, The | Advocate |
| Agriculture Decisions | Agri.Dec. |
| Akron Law Review | Akron L.Rev. |
| Alabama Appellate Court Reports | Ala.App. |
| Alabama Court of Appeals Reports | Ala.App. |
| Alabama Law Review | Ala.L.Rev. |
| Alabama Lawyer, The | Ala.Law. |
| Alabama Reports | Ala. |
| Alabama State Bar Foundation Bulletin | Ala.St.B.Found.Bull. |
| Alaska Bar Journal | Alaska B.J. |
| Alaska Law Journal | Alaska L.J. |
| Alaska Reports | Alaska |
| Albany Law Review | Albany L.Rev. |
| Alberta Law Quarterly | Alta.L.Q. |
| Alberta Law Reports | Alta. |
| Alberta Law Review | Alta.L.Rev. |
| All England Law Reports | All E.R. |
| All India Criminal Decisions | All India Crim.Dec. |
| All India Reporter | All India Rptr. |
| All Pakistan Legal Decisions | All Pak.Leg.Dec. |
| Allen | Allen |
| American Academy of Matrimonial Lawyers Journal | Am.Acad.Matri.Law. J. |
| American and English Annotated Cases | Am. & Eng.Ann.Cas. |
| American Bankruptcy Law Journal | Am.Bankr.L.J. |
| American Bankruptcy Reports | Am.Bankr.R. |
| American Bankruptcy Reports, New Series | Am.Bankr.R. (N.S.) |
| American Bankruptcy Review | Am.Bankr.Rev. |
| American Bar Association Journal | A.B.A.J. |
| American Bar Association Reports | A.B.A.Rep. |
| American Business Law Journal | Am.Bus.L.J. |
| American Criminal Law Quarterly | Am.Crim.L.Q. |
| American Criminal Law Review | Am.Crim.L.Rev. |
| American Decisions | Am.Dec. |
| American Federal Tax Reports | Am.Fed.Tax R. |
| American Federal Tax Reports, Second Series | Am.Fed.Tax R.2d |
| American Journal of Comparative Law | Am.J.Comp.L. |

American Journal of Criminal Law --------------- Am.J.Crim.L.
American Journal of International Law ---------- Am.J.Int'l L.
American Journal of Jurisprudence --------------- Am.J.Jurisprud.
American Journal of Legal History --------------- Am.J.Legal Hist.
American Jurisprudence --------------------------- Am.Jur.
American Jurisprudence, Second Series ------------ Am.Jur.2d
American Labor Arbitration Awards (P-H) -------- P-H Am.Lab.Arb.
                                                  Awards
American Labor Cases (P-H) ---------------------- P-H Am.Lab.Cas.
American Labor Legislation Review --------------- Am.Lab.Leg.Rev.
American Law Register --------------------------- Am.L.Reg.
American Law Register, New Series --------------- Am.L.Reg., (N.S.)
American Law Register, Old Series --------------- Am.L.Reg., (O.S.)
American Law Reports ---------------------------- A.L.R.
American Law Reports, Second Series ------------- A.L.R.2d
American Law Reports, Third Series -------------- A.L.R.3d
American Law Reports Federal -------------------- A.L.R.Fed.
American Maritime Cases ------------------------- A.M.C.
American Political Science Review --------------- Am.Pol.Sci.Rev.
American Reports -------------------------------- Am.R.
American State Reports -------------------------- Am.St.R.
American Trial Lawyers Law Journal ------------- Am.Trial Law.L.J.
American University Law Review ----------------- Am.U.L.Rev.
Annals of the American Academy of Political and So-
  cial Science ---------------------------------- Annals
Annotated Tax Cases ---------------------------- Ann.Tax.Cas.
Annual Digest and Reports of International Law
  Cases ----------------------------------------- Ann.Dig.
Antitrust Law and Economics Review ------------- Antitrust L. & Econ.
                                                  Rev.
Antitrust Law Journal -------------------------- Antitrust L.J.
Appeals Cases, District of Columbia ------------- App.D.C.
Appellate Division Reports, N. Y. Supreme Court ---- App.Div.
Appellate Division Reports, N. Y. Supreme Court,
  Second Series --------------------------------- App.Div.2d
Arbitration Journal, New Series ----------------- Arb.J. (N.S.)
Arbitration Journal, Old Series ----------------- Arb.J. (O.S.)
Arbitration Law; A Digest of Court Decisions ------ Arb.L.Dig.
Arizona Bar Journal ---------------------------- Ariz.B.J.
Arizona Law Review ---------------------------- Ariz.L.Rev.
Arizona Reports -------------------------------- Ariz.
Arkansas Law Review --------------------------- Ark.L.Rev.
Arkansas Lawyer, The -------------------------- Ark.Law.
Arkansas Reports ------------------------------- Ark.
Atlantic Reporter ------------------------------ A.
Atlantic Reporter, Second Series ---------------- A.2d
Atomic Energy Law Journal --------------------- Atomic Energy L.J.
Atomic Energy Law Reporter (CCH) ------------- CCH Atom.En.L.Rep.
Attorney General ------------------------------- Att'y Gen.
Attorney General's Opinions, United States --------- Op.Att'y Gen.

Attorney General's Reports, United States --------- Att'y Gen.Rep.
Auckland University Law Review ---------------- Auck.U.L.Rev.
Australian Argus Law Reports ---------------- Austl.Argus L.R.
Australian Bankruptcy Cases ----------------- Aust.Bankr.Cas.
Australian Commercial Journal ---------------- Austl.Com.J.
Australian Journal of Forensic Sciences --------- Austl.J.For.Sci.
Australian Law Journal ---------------------- Austl.L.J.
Australian Law Journal Reports ---------------- Austl.L.J.Rep.
Australian Tax Decisions ------------------- Austl.Tax.
Australian Yearbook of International Law -------- Austl.Y.B.Int'l L.
Automobile Cases ----------------------- Auto.Cas.
Automobile Cases, Second Series --------------- Auto.Cas.2d
Aviation Cases ------------------------- Av.Cas.
Aviation Law Reporter (CCH) ---------------- Av.L.Rep.
B. Monroe ----------------------------- B.Mon.
Banking Law Journal --------------------- Banking L.J.
Bankruptcy Law Reporter (CCH) -------------- Bankr.L.Rep.
Barbour's Supreme Court Reports -------------- Barb.
Baylor Law Review ---------------------- Baylor L.Rev.
Bill of Rights Journal ------------------- Bill of Rights J.
Binney ------------------------------- Binn.
Black -------------------------------- Black
Black Law Journal ---------------------- Black L.J.
Blue Sky Law Reporter (CCH) --------------- Blue Sky L.Rep.
Board of Review (Army) ------------------ B.R. (Army)
Board of Review and Judicial Council of the Army -- B.R.-J.C. (Army)
Board of Tax Appeals Report ---------------- B.T.A.
Boston Bar Journal --------------------- Boston B.J.
Boston College Industrial and Commercial Law     B.C.Ind. & Com.L.
   Review ----------------------------- Rev.
Boston University Law Review ---------------- B.U.L.Rev.
Boyce -------------------------------- Boyce
Brief, The ---------------------------- Brief
British Columbia Law Reports --------------- B.C.
British Journal of Criminology --------------- Brit.J.Criminol.
British Tax Review --------------------- Brit.Tax Rev.
British Year Book of International Law ---------- Brit.Y.B.Int'l L.
Brooklyn Law Review -------------------- Brooklyn L.Rev.
Buffalo Law Review --------------------- Buffalo L.Rev.
Bulletin of the Copyright Society of the U. S. A. ---- Bull.Copyright Soc'y
Bulletin of the United States Trademark Association, Trademark Bull. (N.
   New Series -------------------------- S.)
Bush -------------------------------- Bush
Business Lawyer, The -------------------- Bus.Law.
Cahiers de Droit, Les ------------------- Cahiers de Droit
Caines' Cases ------------------------- Cai.Cas.
Caines' Reports ----------------------- Cai.R.
Calcutta Weekly Notes ------------------- Calcutta W.N.
California Appellate Reports ---------------- Cal.App.

| | |
|---|---|
| California Appellate Reports, Second Series | Cal.App.2d |
| California Jurisprudence | Cal.Jur. |
| California Jurisprudence, Second Edition | Cal.Jur.2d |
| California Law Review | Calif.L.Rev. |
| California Reporter | Cal.Rptr. |
| California Reports | Cal. |
| California Reports, Second Series | Cal.2d |
| California Western International Law Journal | Calif.W.Int'l L.J. |
| California Western Law Review | Calif.W.L.Rev. |
| Call | Call |
| Cambridge Law Journal | Camb.L.J. |
| Cameron's Privy Council Decisions | Cam. |
| Cameron's Supreme Court Cases | Cameron |
| Canada Exchequer Court Reports | Can.Exch. |
| Canada Law Reports, Exchequer | Can.Exch. |
| Canada Law Reports, Supreme Court | Can.S.Ct. |
| Canada Supreme Court Reports | Can.S.Ct. |
| Canada Tax Appeal Board Cases | Can.Tax App.Bd. |
| Canada Tax Cases | ( ) C.T.C. |
| Canada Tax Cases Annotated | Can.Tax Cas.Ann. |
| Canadian Bankruptcy Reports Annotated | Can.Bankr.Ann. |
| Canadian Bankruptcy Reports Annotated, New Series | Can.Bankr.Ann. (N. S.) |
| Canadian Bar Association Journal | Can.B.A.J. |
| Canadian Bar Journal | Can.B.J. |
| Canadian Bar Review | Can.B.Rev. |
| Canadian Commercial Law Reports | Can.Com.R. |
| Canadian Criminal Cases Annotated | Can.Crim.Cas.Ann. |
| Canadian Criminal Cases, New Series | Can.Crim.Cas. (N.S.) |
| Canadian Labour Law Cases | C.L.L.C. |
| Canadian Patent Reporter | C.P.R. |
| Canadian Railway and Transport Cases | Can.Ry. & T.Cas. |
| Canadian Railway Cases | Can.Ry.Cas. |
| Canadian Reports, Appeal Cases | Can.App. |
| Cartwright's Constitutional Cases (Can.) | Cart.B.N.A. |
| Case & Comment | Case & Com. |
| Case Western Reserve Journal of International Law | Case W.Res.J.Int'l L. |
| Case Western Reserve Law Review | Case W.Res.L.Rev. |
| Cassels' Practice Cases (Can.) | Cass.Prac.Cas. |
| Cassels' Supreme Court Decisions | Cass.S.C. |
| Catholic Lawyer, The | Catholic Law. |
| Catholic University of America Law Review | Catholic U.L.Rev. |
| Central Law Journal | Cent.L.J. |
| Chicago-Kent Law Review | Chi.-Kent L.Rev. |
| Cincinnati Law Review | Cin.L.Rev. |
| Civil Aeronautics Authority Reports | C.A.A. |
| Civil Aeronautics Board Reports | C.A.B. |
| Civil Liberties Docket | Civ.Lib.Dock. |
| Civil Liberties Reporter | Civ.Lib.Rptr. |

Clarke and Scully's Drainage Cases (Ont.) --------- C. & S.
Cleveland Bar Association Journal --------------- Clev.Bar Ass'n J.
Cleveland State Law Review --------------------- Clev.St.L.Rev.
Cleveland-Marshall Law Review ----------------- Clev.-Mar.L.Rev.
Code of Federal Regulations -------------------- C.F.R.
Coldwell ------------------------------------- Cold.
Coleman & Caines' Cases ----------------------- Cole. & Cai.Cas.
Coleman's Cases ------------------------------ Cole.Cas.
Colorado Court of Appeals Reports ------------- Colo.App.
Colorado Reports ----------------------------- Colo.
Columbia Human Rights Law Review ------------ Colum.Human Rights
                                       L.Rev.
Columbia Journal of Law and Social Problems ------- Colum.J.L. & Soc.
                                       Prob.
Columbia Journal of Transnational Law ---------- Colum.J.Transnat'l L.
Columbia Law Review -------------------------- Colum.L.Rev.
Columbia Society of International Law Bulletin ---- Colum.Soc'y Int'l L.
                                       Bull.
Columbia Survey of Human Rights Law ---------- Colum.Survey Human
                                       Rights L.
Commerce Clearing House ---------------------- CCH
Commercial and Municipal Law Reporter --------- Com. & Mun.L.Rep.
Commercial Cases ----------------------------- Com.Cas.
Commercial Law Journal ----------------------- Com.L.J.
Commissioner of Patents, Decisions-------------- Dec.Com.Pat.
Common Market Law Reports -------------------- Comm.Mkt.L.R.
Common Market Law Review -------------------- Comm.Mkt.L.Rev.
Common Market Reporter (CCH) ---------------- CCH Comm.Mkt.Rep.
Common Pleas Reporter ------------------------ Pa.C.P.
Commonwealth Arbitration Reports ------------- Commw.Art.
Commonwealth Law Reports -------------------- Commw.L.R.
Comparative and International Law Journal of      Comp. & Int'l L.J.S.
    South Africa --------------------------------- Afr.
Comparative Juridical Review -------------------- Comp.Jurid.Rev.
Comptroller General Decisions ------------------- Comp.Gen.
Comptroller of Treasury Decisions --------------- Comp.Dec.
Comstock ------------------------------------- Comst.
Conditional Sale-Chattel Mortgage (CCH) --------- Condit.Sale-Chat.
                                       Mort.Rep.
Congressional Digest -------------------------- Cong.Dig.
Congressional Record -------------------------- Cong.Rec.
Connecticut Bar Journal ----------------------- Conn.B.J.
Connecticut Law Review ----------------------- Conn.L.Rev.
Connecticut Reports --------------------------- Conn.
Connecticut Supplement ------------------------ Conn.Supp.
Constitution --------------------------------- Const.
Conveyancer & Property Lawyer (New Series) ------ Convey. (N.S.)
Cornell International Law Journal --------------- Cornell Int'l L.J.
Cornell Law Quarterly ------------------------- Cornell L.Q.

| | |
|---|---|
| Cornell Law Review | Cornell L.Rev. |
| Corporate Practice Commentator | 'Corp.Pract.Comment. |
| Corporate Reorganizations | Corp.Reorg. |
| Corporation (P-H) | P-H Corp. |
| Corporation Journal | Corp.J. |
| Corpus Juris | C.J. |
| Corpus Juris Secundum | C.J.S. |
| Court of Appeals for District of Columbia | D.C.Cir. |
| Court of Claims | Ct.Cl. |
| Court of Customs and Patents Appeals Reports | C.C.P.A. |
| Court of Customs Appeals Reports | Ct.Cust.App. |
| Court of Military Appeals (U. S.) | U.S.C.M.A. |
| Court Review | Ct.Rev. |
| Court Martial Reports | C.M.R. |
| Court-Martial Reports of the Judge Advocate General of the Air Force | C.M.R. (Air Force) |
| Coutlea's Supreme Court Cases | Coutlea |
| Cowen | Cow. |
| Cox's Criminal Cases | Cox Crim.Cas. |
| Cranch | Cranch |
| Creighton Law Review | Creighton L.Rev. |
| Crime and Delinquency | Crime & Delin'cy |
| Criminal Appeal Reports | Crim.App. |
| Criminal Law Bulletin | Crim.L.Bull. |
| Criminal Law Journal Reports | India Crim.L.J.R. |
| Criminal Law Quarterly | Crim.L.Q. |
| Criminal Law Reporter | Crim.L.Rptr. |
| Criminal Reports (Canada) | Can.Crim. |
| Criminal Reports, New Series | Crim.Rep. (N.S.) |
| Criminal Law Review (England) | Crim.L.Rev. (Engl.) |
| Criminal Law Review (Manhattan) | Crim.L.Rev. |
| Criminology | Criminology |
| Cumberland-Samford Law Review | Cum.-Sam.L.Rev. |
| Cumulative Bulletin | Cu.Bull. |
| Current Law | Current L. |
| Current Law Yearbook | Current L.Y.B. |
| Current Legal Problems | Current Legal Prob. |
| Current Medicine for Attorneys | Current Med. |
| Cushing | Cush. |
| Customs Court Reports | Cust.Ct. |
| Dakota Reports (Territorial) | Dak. |
| Dallas | Dall. |
| Daly | Daly |
| Decalogue Journal | Decalogue J. |
| Decisiones de Puerto Rico | D.P.R. |
| Defense Law Journal | Defense L.J. |
| Delaware Chancery Reports | Del.Ch. |
| Delaware County Reports | Del.County |
| Delaware Reports | Del. |

Demarest's Surrogate Courts Reports ............... Dem.
Denio ......................................................... Denio
Denver Journal of International Law and Policy .... Denver J.Int'l L. & Policy
Denver Law Journal ..................................... Denver L.J.
Department of State Bulletin, United States ........ Dep't State Bull.
DePaul Law Review ..................................... DePaul L.Rev.
Detroit Law Review ..................................... Det.L.Rev.
Dickinson Law Review .................................. Dick.L.Rev.
Dicta ......................................................... Dicta
District Court, District of Columbia ................. D.D.C.
District of Columbia Bar Journal ..................... D.C.B.J.
District of Columbia, Court of Appeals Cases ...... D.C.Cir.
Dominion Law Reports .................................. D.L.R.
Dominion Law Reports, 1912–1922 ................. D.L.R.
Dominion Law Reports, 1923–1955 ................. [   ] D.L.R.
Dominion Law Reports, Second Series .............. D.L.R.2d
Dominion Law Reports (Third Series), 1969–Present . D.L.R.3d
Dominion Tax Cases ..................................... D.T.C.
Drake Law Review ........................................ Drake L.Rev.
Draper (Ont.) .............................................. Draper
Drug Abuse Law Review ................................ Drug Abuse L.Rev.
Dublin University Law Review ......................... Dublin U.L.Rev.
Duke Law Journal ........................................ Duke L.J.
Duquesne University Law Review ..................... Duquesne U.L.Rev.
Duvall ....................................................... Duv.
East Africa Law Reports ............................... E.Afr.L.R.
Eastern Law Reporter ................................... E.L.R.
Eastern School Law Review ............................ E.School L.Rev.
Ecology Law Quarterly .................................. Ecology L.Q.
English Historical Review .............................. Engl.Hist.Rev.
English Reports—Full Reprint ........................ Eng.Rep.
Environment Law Review ............................... Env.L.Rev.
Environmental Law ...................................... Env.L.
Environmental Law Reporter .......................... Env.L.Rptr.
Environmental Reporter Cases ........................ ERC
Estate Planning (P-H) .................................. P-H Est.Plan.
European Treaty Series .................................. Europ.T.S.
Exchequer Court Reports (Canada) 1923–present .. (   ) Ex.C.R.
Exchequer Reports of Canada ......................... Can.Exch.
Executive Agreement Series, United States ......... E.A.S.
Executive Order ........................................... Exec.Order
Faculty of Law Review (Toronto) .................... Fac.L.Rev.
Family Law Quarterly ................................... Family L.Q.
Federal Banking Law Reporter (CCH) .............. CCH Fed.Banking L. Rep.

Federal Bar Journal ...................................... Fed.B.J.
Federal Carriers Cases (CCH) ........................ F.Carr.Cas.
Federal Carriers Reporter (CCH) .................... Fed.Carr.Rep.

| | |
|---|---|
| Federal Cases | Fed.Cas. |
| Federal Communications Bar Journal | Fed.Com.B.J. |
| Federal Communications Commission Reports | F.C.C. |
| Federal Estate and Gift Tax Reporter (CCH) | Fed.Est. & Gift Tax Rep. |
| Federal Law Reports | Fed.L.Rep. |
| Federal Law Review | Fed.L.Rev. |
| Federal Power Commission Reports | F.P.C. |
| Federal Register | Fed.Reg. |
| Federal Reporter | F. |
| Federal Reporter, Second Series | F.2d |
| Federal Rules Decisions | F.R.D. |
| Federal Rules Service | Fed.Rules Serv. |
| Federal Rules Service, Second Series | Fed.Rules Serv.2d |
| Federal Securities Law Reporter (CCH) | CCH Fed.Sec.L.Rep. |
| Federal Supplement | F.Supp. |
| Federal Taxes (P-H) | P-H Fed.Taxes |
| Federal Trade Commission Decisions | F.T.C. |
| Federal Wage and Hour (P-H) | P-H Fed.Wage & Hour |
| Federation of Insurance Counsel Quarterly | Fed'n Ins. Counsel Q. |
| Fire and Casualty Cases (CCH) | Fire & Casualty Cas. |
| Florida Bar Journal | Fla.B.J. |
| Florida Law Journal | Fla.L.J. |
| Florida Reports | Fla. |
| Florida Supplement | Fla.Supp. |
| Food Drug Cosmetic Law Journal | Food Drug Cosm.L.J. |
| Food Drug Cosmetic Law Reporter (CCH) | F.D.Cosm.L.Rep. |
| Fordham Law Review | Ford.L.Rev. |
| Fordham Urban Law Journal | Ford.Urban L.J. |
| Forum, The | Forum |
| Fox's Patent, Trade Mark, Design and Copyright Cases | Fox Pat.C. |
| Gazette Law Reports | Gaz.L.R. |
| George Washington Law Review | Geo.Wash.L.Rev. |
| Georgetown Law Journal | Geo.L.J. |
| Georgia Appeals Reports | Ga.App. |
| Georgia Business Lawyer | Ga.Bus.Law. |
| Georgia Journal of International & Comparative Law | Ga.J.Int'l & Comp.L. |
| Georgia Law Review | Ga.L.Rev. |
| Georgia Reports | Ga. |
| Georgia State Bar Journal | Ga.St.B.J. |
| Gilmer | Gilm. |
| Golden Gate Law Review | Golden Gate L.Rev. |
| Gonzaga Law Review | Gonzaga L.Rev. |
| Government Contracts Reporter (CCH) | Gov't Cont.Rep. |
| Grattan | Gratt. |
| Gray | Gray |

| | |
|---|---|
| Greene | Greene |
| Guild Practitioner | Guild Prac. |
| Harrington | Harr. |
| Harrington, W. W. | W.W.Harr. |
| Harrison & Hodgins' Municipal Reports (Ont.) | Harr. & Hodg. |
| Harvard Business Review | Harv.Bus.Rev. |
| Harvard Civil Rights—Civil Liberties Law Review | Harv.Civ.Rights-Civ.Lib.L.Rev. |
| Harvard International Law Journal | Harv.Int'l L.J. |
| Harvard Journal on Legislation | Harv.J.Legis. |
| Harvard Law Review | Harv.L.Rev. |
| Hastings Law Journal | Hastings L.J. |
| Hazzard & Warburton's Reports (P.E.I.) | P.E.I. |
| Hawaii Bar Journal | Hawaii B.J. |
| Hawaii Reports | Hawaii |
| Haywood | Hay. |
| Head | Head |
| Heiskell | Heisk. |
| Hempstead's Circuit Court Reports | Hemp. |
| Hening and Munford | Hen. & M. |
| Hill | Hill |
| Houston | Houst. |
| Houston Law Review | Houst.L.Rev. |
| Howard | How. |
| Howard Law Journal | How.L.J. |
| Howard's Practice | How.Pr. |
| Howard's Practice, New Series | How.Pr. (N.S.) |
| Humphrey | Humph. |
| Hun | Hun |
| Hunters Torrens Cases | Hunt.Torrens |
| I.C.C. Practitioners' Journal | I.C.C.Prac.J. |
| Idaho Law Review | Idaho L.Rev. |
| Idaho Reports | Idaho |
| Idea | Idea |
| Illinois Appellate Court Reports | Ill.App. |
| Illinois Appellate Court Reports, Second Series | Ill.App.2d |
| Illinois Bar Journal | Ill.B.J. |
| Illinois Circuit Court | Ill.Cir. |
| Illinois Continuing Legal Education | Ill.Cont.Legal Ed. |
| Illinois Court of Claims Reports | Ill.Ct.Cl. |
| Illinois Law Review | Ill.L.Rev. |
| Illinois Reports | Ill. |
| Immigration and Nationality Decisions | I. & N.Dec. |
| Immigration Bar Bulletin | Immig.B.Bull. |
| India Supreme Court Reports | India S.Ct. |
| Indian Cases | Indian Cas. |
| Indian Law Reports, (e. g) | Indian L.R. (e. g.) |
| Allahabad Series | Allahabad Ser. |
| Indian Rulings | Indian Rul. |

Indian Territory Reports ----------------------------------------- Indian Terr.
Indiana Appellate Reports --------------------------- Ind.App.
Indiana Law Journal ----------------------------- Ind.L.J.
Indiana Law Review ----------------------------- Ind.L.Rev.
Indiana Legal Forum ----------------------------- Ind.Legal F.
Indiana Reports --------------------------------- Ind.
Industrial and Labor Relations Review ------------- Ind. & Lab.Rel.Rev.
Industrial Law Review --------------------------- Indus.L.Rev.
Industrial Relations, American Labor Arbitration     P-H Ind.Rel., Lab.
  (P-H) --------------------------------------------------- Arb.
Industrial Relations: Journal of Economy and So-     Ind.Rel.J.Econ. &
  ciety --------------------------------------------------- Soc.
Industrial Relations, Union Contracts and Collective   P-H  Ind.Rel., Union
  Bargaining (P-H) ----------------------------- Conts.
Inheritance, Estate, and Gift Tax Reporter (CCH) --CCH Inh.Est. & Gift
                                                    Tax Rep.
Insurance Counsel Journal ----------------------- Ins.Counsel J.
Insurance Law Journal --------------------------- Ins.L.J.
Insurance Law Reporter (CCH) ------------------- Ins.L.Rep.
Insurance Law Reporter (Can.) ------------------- I.L.R.
Inter-American Law Review ----------------------- Inter-Am.L.Rev.
Interior Department Decisions -------------------- Interior Dec.
Internal Revenue Bulletin ------------------------ Int.Rev.Bull.
Internal Revenue Code of 1954 ------------------- Int.Rev.Code of 1954
International Affairs ----------------------------- Int'l Aff.
International and Comparative Law Quarterly ------ Int'l & Comp.L.Q.
International Arbitration Journal ----------------- Int'l Arb.J.
International Court of Justice Reports ------------ I.C.J.
International Journal ----------------------------- Int'l J.
International Journal of Politics ----------------- Int'l J.Pol.
International Law Quarterly ---------------------- Int'l L.Q.
International Law Reports ------------------------ I.L.R.
International Lawyer, The ------------------------ Int'l Law.
International Legal Materials --------------------- Int'l Legal Materials
Interstate Commerce Commission, Motor Carrier
  Cases ------------------------------------------- M.C.C.
Interstate Commerce Commission Reports ----------- I.C.C.
Interstate Commerce Commission, Valuation
  Reports ----------------------------------------- Val.R. (I.C.C.)
Interstate Oil Compact Commission Bulletin -------- I.O.C.C.Bull.
Intramural Law Review --------------------------- Intramural L.Rev.
Iowa Law Review -------------------------------- Iowa L.Rev.
Iowa Reports ----------------------------------- Iowa
Irish Jurist ------------------------------------- Ir.Jur.
Irish Law Times Reports ------------------------- Ir.L.T.R.
Irish Reports ----------------------------------- Ir.R.
Irish Reports, Common Law Series ---------------- Ir.R.C.L.
Israel Law Review ------------------------------- Israel L.Rev.
JAG Bulletin (USAF) --------------------------- JAG Bull.

JAG Journal ---------------------------------------------JAG J.

John Marshall Journal of Practice and Procedure ----John Mar.J.Prac. &
                                          Proc.

John Marshall Law Journal ------------------------- John Marshall L.J.

John Marshall Law Quarterly --------------------- John Mar.L.Q.

Johnson's Cases -----------------------------------Johns.Cas.

Johnson's Chancery Reports ----------------------Johns.Ch.

Johnson's Reports ------------------------------- Johns.

Journal of Accountancy --------------------------J.Accountancy

Journal of Air Law and Commerce ----------------J.Air L. & Com.

Journal of Business Law ------------------------- J.Bus.L.

Journal of Comparative Legislation and Interna-   JComp.Leg & Int'l L.
    tional Law, Third Series ----------------------- (3d Series)

Journal of Criminal Law (England) ---------------J.Crim.L. (Eng.)

Journal of Criminal Law, Criminology and Police
    Science --------------------------------------J.Crim.L.C. & P.S.

Journal of Family Law --------------------------J.Fam.L.

Journal of Forensic Medicine ---------------------J.For.Med.

Journal of Forensic Sciences ----------------------J.For.Sci.

Journal of International Law and Economics -------J.Int'l L. & Econ.

Journal of International Law and Politics -----------J.Int'l L. & Pol.

Journal of Land & Public Utility Economics -------- J.Land & P.U.Econ.

Journal of Law and Economic Development ---------J.Law & Econ.Dev.

Journal of Law and Economics --------------------J.Law & Econ.

Journal of Law Reform --------------------------J.Law Reform

Journal of Legal Education ----------------------J.Legal Ed.

Journal of Maritime Law & Commerce ------------ J.Mar.Law & Com.

Journal of Planning and Property Law -------------J.Plan. & Prop.L.

Journal of Public Law ---------------------------J.Pub.L.

Journal of Taxation ----------------------------J.Tax.

Journal of the American Judicature Society ---------J.Am.Jud.Soc'y

Journal of the American Medical Association ------J.A.M.A.

Journal of the American Society of Chartered Life
    Underwriters --------------------------------J.Am.Soc'y C.L.U.

Journal of the Association of Law Teachers ---------J.Ass'n L. Teachers

Journal of the Bar Association of the State of
    Kansas --------------------------------------J.B.Ass'n St.Kan.

Journal of the Canadian Bar Association ----------J.Can.B.Ass'n

Journal of the Forensic Science Society -----------J.For.Sci.Soc'y

Journal of the Law Society of Scotland ------------J.L.Soc'y

Journal of the Missouri Bar ---------------------J.Mo.Bar

Journal of the National Association of Referees in
    Bankruptcy (Referees' Journal) ----------------Ref.J.

Journal of the Patent Office Society --------------J.Pat.Off.Soc'y

Journal of the Society of Public Teachers of Law --- J.Soc'y Pub.Teachers
                                         L.

Journal of the State Bar of California -------------J.St.Bar Calif.

Journal of Urban Law --------------------------J.Urban L.

Journal of World Trade Law ---------------------J.World Trade L.

Judge Advocate Journal, The --------------------- Judge Advoc.J.
Judge's Journal --------------------------------- Judge's J.
Juridical Review -------------------------------- Jurid.Rev.
Jurimetrics Journal ----------------------------- Jurimetrics J.
Justice of the Peace ---------------------------- J.P.
Justice of the Peace and Local Government Review -- Just.P.
Justiciary Cases -------------------------------- Just.Cas.
Justinian -------------------------------------- Justinian
Juvenile Court Journal -------------------------- Juv.Ct.J.
Kansas Bar Association Journal ------------------ Kan.B.Ass'n J.
Kansas Reports --------------------------------- Kan.
Kentucky Commentator --------------------------- Ky.Comment'r
Kentucky Law Journal --------------------------- Ky.L.J.
Kentucky Law Reporter -------------------------- Ky.L.Rptr.
Kentucky Reports ------------------------------- Ky.
Kentucky State Bar Journal --------------------- Ky.St.B.J.
Kenya Law Reports ----------------------------- Kenya L.R.
Kernan --------------------------------------- Kern.
King's Counsel --------------------------------- K. Counsel
Knapp, Privy Council --------------------------- Kn.P.C.
Knight's Industrial Reports --------------------- Knight's Ind.
Labor Arbitration Awards (CCH) ----------------- CCH Lab.Arb.Awards
Labor Arbitration Reports (BNA) ---------------- Lab.Arb.
Labor Cases (CCH) ----------------------------- CCH Lab.Cas.
Labor Law Journal ----------------------------- Lab.L.J.
Labor Law Reporter (CCH) ---------------------- CCH Lab.L.Rep.
Labor Relations Reference Manual (BNA) --------- L.R.R.M.
Labor Relations Reporter (BNA) ----------------- Lab.Rel.Rep.
Labour Arbitration Cases ----------------------- L.A.C.
Land and Water Law Review --------------------- Land & Water L.Rev.
Lansing's Supreme Court ------------------------ Lans.
Law and Contemporary Problems ----------------- Law & Contemp.Prob.
Law and Policy in International Business --------- Law & Pol'y Int'l
                                                 Bus.
Law and Society Review ------------------------- Law & Soc'y Rev.
Law and the Social Order Arizona State Law
  Journal ------------------------------------- Law & Soc.Ord.
Law Commentary -------------------------------- L.Comment'y
Law Guardian ---------------------------------- L.Guard.
Law in Transition Quarterly -------------------- L.Trans.Q.
Law Institute Journal -------------------------- L.Inst.J.
Law Institute Journal of Victoria --------------- L.Inst.J.Vict.
Law Journal New Series Chancery ---------------- L.J.Ch.
Law Journal New Series Common Law, Magistrates
  Cases (discontinued) ------------------------- L.J.Mag.
Law Journal New Series Exchequer --------------- L.J.Ex.
Law Journal New Series House of Lords ---------- L.J.H.L.
Law Journal New Series Privy Council ----------- L.J.P.C.
Law Journal New Series Queen's Bench (or King's
  Bench) -------------------------------------- L.J.Q.B. or L.J.K.B.

Law Journal Old Series (1822–1830) ---------------- L.J.O.S.
Law Journal Reports, (e. g.) King's Bench, New     (e. g.) L.J.K.B. (N.
    Series ------------------------------------------ S.)
Law Notes -------------------------------------------- Law Notes
Law Quarterly Review --------------------------------- L.Q.Rev.
Law Reports ------------------------------------------ L.R.
Law Reports Appeal Cases, Second Series ----------- App.Cas.
Law Reports Appeal Cases, Third Series ------------ A.C.
Law Reports Chancery --------------------------------- L.R.Ch.
Law Reports Chancery Division, Second Series ------ Ch.D.
Law Reports Chancery Division, Third Series -------- Ch.
Law Reports Common Pleas --------------------------- L.R.C.P.
Law Reports Common Pleas Division to 1880 -------- C.P.D.
Law Reports Equity ---------------------------------- L.R.Eq.
Law Reports Exchequer ------------------------------- L.R.Ex.
Law Reports Exchequer Division to 1880 ------------ Ex.D.
Law Reports House of Lords --------------------------- L.R.H.L.
Law Reports, Indian Appeals ------------------------- L.R.Indian App.
Law Reports, Ireland -------------------------------- L.R.Ir.
Law Reports King's Bench, Third Series ------------ K.B.
Law Reports Probate and Divorce ------------------- L.R.P. & D.
Law Reports Probate, Divorce & Admiralty Division,
    Second Series ---------------------------------- P.D.
Law Reports Probate, Divorce & Admiralty Division,
    Third Series ----------------------------------- P.
Law Reports Queen's Bench --------------------------- L.R.Q.B.
Law Reports Queen's Bench Division, Second Series -- Q.B.D.
Law Reports Queen's Bench, Third Series ----------- Q.B.
Law Reports Weekly Law Reports -------------------- W.L.R.
Law Society Gazette --------------------------------- Law Soc'y Gaz.
Law Society Journal (New South Wales) ----------- Law Soc'y J.
Law Times, New Series (Eng.) ----------------------- L.T. (N.S.)
Law Times, Old Series (Eng.) ----------------------- L.T. (O.S.)
Law Times Reports, New Series --------------------- L.T.R. (N.S.)
Lawyer and Banker and Central Law Journal -------- Lawyer & Banker
Lawyers' Edition, U. S. Supreme Court Reports ------ L.Ed.
Lawyers' Edition, U. S. Supreme Court Reports,
    Second Series ---------------------------------- L.Ed.2d
Lawyers' Medical Journal --------------------------- Lawyers' Med.J.
Lawyers Reports Annotated -------------------------- L.R.A.
Lawyers Reports Annotated, 1915a–1918F ---------- (e. g.) 1917E L.R.A.
                                              405
Lawyers Reports Annotated, New Series ----------- L.R.A. (N.S.)
League of Nations Official Journal ----------------- League of Nations
                                            Off.J.
League of Nations Treaty Series -------------------- L.N.T.S.
Lefroy and Cassels' Practice Cases (Ont.) ----------- L. & C.
Leigh ------------------------------------------------ Leigh
Life (Health & Accident) Cases (CCH) ------------- Life Cas.

Life (Health & Accident) Cases, Second Series
   (CCH) ------------------------------------------ Life Cas.2d
Lincoln Law Review ----------------------------- Lincoln L.Rev.
Lloyd's List Law Reports ----------------------- LL.Rep.
Lloyd's List Law Reports Admiralty ------------- Lloyd's Rep.
Local Government and Magisterial Reports --------- Local Gov't
Local Government Reports of Australia ------------ Local Gov't R.Austl.
Louisiana Annual Reports ------------------------ La.Ann.
Louisiana Bar Journal --------------------------- La.B.J.
Louisiana Courts of Appeal Reports -------------- La.App.
Louisiana Law Review ---------------------------- La.L.Rev.
Louisiana Supreme Court Reports ----------------- La.
Louisville Lawyer ------------------------------- Louisville Law.
Lower Canadian Reports -------------------------- Low.Can.R.
Loyola Digest ----------------------------------- Loyola Dig.
Loyola Law Review ------------------------------- Loyola L.Rev.
Loyola University of Chicago Law Journal --------- Loyola U.Chi.L.J.
Loyola University of Los Angeles Law Review ----- Loyola U.L.A.L.Rev.
MacArthur --------------------------------------- MacArth.
MacArthur and Mackey ---------------------------- McArth. & M.
McCahon ----------------------------------------- McCahon
McGill Law Journal ------------------------------ McGill L.J.
Mackey ------------------------------------------ Mackey
Magisterial Cases ------------------------------- Mag.Cas.
Maine Law Review -------------------------------- Maine L.Rev.
Maine Reports ----------------------------------- Me.
Manitoba Bar News ------------------------------- Man.B.News
Manitoba Law Journal ---------------------------- Man.L.J.
Manitoba Law Reports ---------------------------- Man.
Manning's Unreported Cases ---------------------- Mann.Unrep.Cas.
Marijuana Review, The --------------------------- Marijuana Rev.
Maritime Law Cases, New Series ------------------ Mar.L.Cas. (N.S.)
Maritime Provinces Reports ---------------------- Mar.Prov.
Marquette Law Review ---------------------------- Marq.L.Rev.
Martin Mining Cases ----------------------------- Martin Mining
Marvel ------------------------------------------ Marv.
Maryland Bar Journal ---------------------------- Md.B.J.
Maryland Law Review ----------------------------- Md.L.Rev.
Maryland Reports -------------------------------- Md.
Massachusetts Appellate Decisions --------------- Mass.App.Dec.
Massachusetts Appellate Division Reports -------- Mass.App.Div.
Massachusetts Law Quarterly --------------------- Mass.L.Q.
Massachusetts Reports --------------------------- Mass.
Medical Trial Technique Quarterly --------------- Med.Trial Tech.Q.
Medicine, Science and the Law ------------------- Med.Sci. & L.
Medico-Legal Journal ---------------------------- Med.-Legal J.
Melanesian Law Journal (Papua and New Guinea) -- Melanesian L.J.
Melbourne University Law Review ----------------- Melb.U.L.Rev.
Memphis State University Law Review ------------- Memphis St.U.L.Rev.

| | |
|---|---|
| Mercer Law Review | Mercer L.Rev. |
| Metcalf | Met. |
| Miami Law Quarterly | Miami L.Q. |
| Michigan Law Review | Mich.L.Rev. |
| Michigan Reports | Mich. |
| Michigan State Bar Journal | Mich.St.B.J. |
| Military Law Review | Mil.L.Rev. |
| Mills | Mills |
| Minnesota Continuing Legal Education | Minn.Cont.Legal Ed. |
| Minnesota Law Review | Minn.L.Rev. |
| Minnesota Reports | Minn. |
| Mississippi Law Journal | Miss.L.J. |
| Mississippi Reports | Miss. |
| Missouri Appeal Reports | Mo.App. |
| Missouri Bar Journal | Mo.B.J. |
| Missouri Law Review | Mo.L.Rev. |
| Missouri Reports | Mo. |
| Modern Law Review | Mod.L.Rev. |
| Monroe, B. | B.Mon. |
| Monroe, T. B. | T.B.Mon. |
| Montana Law Review | Mont.L.Rev. |
| Montana Reports | Mont. |
| Montreal Law Reports (Queen's Bench) | M.L.R. (Q.B.) |
| Montreal Law Reports (Superior Court) | M.L.R. (S.C.) |
| Moore, New Series, Privy Council | Moo.P.C. (N.S.) |
| Moore, Privy Council | Moo.P.C. |
| Motor Carrier Cases, Interstate Commerce Commission | M.C.C. |
| Munford | Munf. |
| Municipal Attorney | Mun.Att'y |
| Municipal Law Court Decisions | Mun.L.Ct.Dec. |
| Municipal Law Journal | Mun.L.J. |
| Municipal Ordinance Review | Mun.Ord.Rev. |
| NACCA Law Journal | NACCA L.J. |
| Narcotics Control Digest | Narcotics Control Dig. |
| National Civic Review | Nat'l Civic Rev. |
| National Labor Relations Board Decisions | N.L.R.B. |
| National Legal Magazine | Nat'l Legal Mag. |
| National Municipal Review | Nat'l Mun.Rev. |
| National Railroad Adjustment Board Awards | [e. g.] N.R.A.B. (4th Div.) |
| National School Law Reporter | Nat'l School L.Rptr. |
| National Tax Journal | Nat'l Tax J. |
| Natural Law Forum | Natural L.F. |
| Natural Resources Journal | Natural Resources J. |
| Nebraska Law Review | Neb.L.Rev. |
| Nebraska Reports | Neb. |
| Nebraska State Bar Journal | Neb.St.B.J. |

Negligence & Compensation Cases Annotated _____ Negl. & Comp.Cas.
Ann.

Negligence & Compensation Cases Annotated, New     Negl. & Comp.Cas.
Series _____ Ann. (N.S.)

Negligence & Compensation Cases Annotated, Third   Negl. & Comp.Cas.
Series _____ Ann.3d

Negligence Cases (CCH) _____ Negl.Cas.

Negligence Cases, Second Series (CCH) _____ Negl.Cas.2d

New Brunswick Equity Reports _____ N.B.Eq.

New Brunswick Reports _____ N.B.

New England Law Review _____ N.Eng.L.Rev.

New Hampshire Bar Journal _____ N.H.B.J.

New Hampshire Reports _____ N.H.

New Jersey Equity Reports _____ N.J.Eq.

New Jersey Law _____ N.J.L.

New Jersey Law Journal _____ N.J.L.J.

New Jersey Law Reports _____ N.J.Law

New Jersey Miscellaneous Reports _____ N.J.Misc.

New Jersey Reports _____ N.J.

New Jersey State Bar Journal _____ N.J.St.B.J.

New Jersey Superior Court and County Courts
Reports _____ N.J.Super.

New Jersey Superior Court Reports _____ N.J.Super.

New Jersey Supreme Court Reports _____ N.J.

New Law Journal _____ New L.J.

New Mexico Law Review _____ N.Mex.L.Rev.

New Mexico Reports _____ N.M.

New South Wales State Reports _____ N.S.W.

New York Civil Procedure _____ N.Y.Civ.Proc.

New York Civil Procedure, New Series _____ N.Y.Civ.Proc. (N.S.)

New York Continuing Legal Education _____ N.Y.Cont.Legal Ed.

New York County Lawyers Association Bar           N.Y. County Law.
Bulletin _____ Ass'n B.Bull.

New York Court of Appeals Reports _____ N.Y.

New York Criminal Reports _____ N.Y.Crim.

New York Department Reports _____ N.Y.Dep't R.

New York Jurisprudence _____ N.Y.Jur.

New York Law Forum _____ N.Y.L.F.

New York Law Journal _____ N.Y.L.J.

New York Miscellaneous Reports _____ N.Y.Misc.

New York Miscellaneous, Second Series _____ N.Y.Misc.2d

New York State Bar Journal _____ N.Y.St.B.J.

New York Supplement _____ N.Y.S.

New York Supplement, Second Series _____ N.Y.S.2d

New York Supreme Court, Appellate Division
Reports _____ App.Div.

New York Supreme Court, Appellate Division Reports,
Second Series _____ App.Div.2d

New York University Conference on Charitable      N.Y.U.Conf.Char-
Foundations Proceedings _____ itable

New York University Conference on Labor ......... N.Y.U.Conf.Lab.
New York University Institute on Federal Taxation -- (e. g.) N.Y.U.7th
                                                       Inst. on Fed.Tax.
New York University Intramural Law Review ...... N.Y.U.Intra.L.Rev.
New York University Journal of International     N.Y.U.J.Int'l Law &
   Law and Politics ------------------------------ Pol.
New York University Law Center Bulletin ......... N.Y.U.L.Center Bull.
New York University Law Quarterly Review ....... N.Y.U.L.Q.Rev.
New York University Law Review ................. N.Y.U.L.Rev.
New York University Review of Law and Social    N.Y.U.Rev.Law &
   Change ----------------------------------------- Soc.C.
New Zealand Law Journal ..................... N.Z.L.J.
New Zealand Law Reports ..................... N.Z.L.R.
New Zealand Universities Law Review ............ N.Z.U.L.Rev.
Nevada Reports ----------------------------------- Nev.
Nevada State Bar Journal ..................... Nev.St.B.J.
Newfoundland Reports ............................ Nfld.R.
Newfoundland Supreme Court Decisions ........... Newf.S.Ct.
Nigeria Law Reports .......................... Nigeria L.R.
NOLPE School Law Journal ..................... NOLPE School L.J.
North Atlantic Regional Business Law Rev. ....... N.Atlantic Reg.Bus.
                                                       L.Rev.
North Carolina Central Law Journal .............. N.C.Cent.L.J.
North Carolina Law Review ..................... N.C.L.Rev.
North Carolina Reports ....................... N.C.
North Central School Law Review ............... N.Cent.School L.Rev.
North Dakota Law Review ..................... N.D.L.Rev.
North Dakota Reports ......................... N.D.
North Eastern Reporter ....................... N.E.
North Eastern Reporter, Second Series ......... N.E.2d
North West Territories Law Reports ............. N.W.T.L.R.
North Western Reporter ------------------------- N.W.
North Western Reporter, Second Series ......... N.W.2d
Northern Ireland Law Reports ................. N.Ir.L.R.
Northern Ireland Legal Quarterly ............... N.Ir.L.Q.
Northumberland Legal Journal ................... Northumb.Legal J.
Northwest Territories Supreme Court Reports ...... N.W.Terr.
Northwestern University Law Review ............. Nw.U.L.Rev.
Notre Dame Lawyer ........................... Notre Dame Law.
Nova Scotia Reports .......................... N.S.R.
Office of Contract Settlement Decisions ............ O.C.S.
Official Gazette. United States Patent Office ....... O.G.Pat.Off.
Ohio Appellate Reports ....................... Ohio App.
Ohio Appellate Reports, Second Series ........... Ohio App.2d
Ohio Circuit Court Reports ..................... Ohio C.C.R.
Ohio Circuit Court Reports, New Series ........... Ohio C.C.R. (N.S.)
Ohio Circuit Decisions ....................... Ohio C.Dec.
Ohio Courts of Appeals Reports .................. Ohio Ct.App.
Ohio Decisions ----------------------------------- Ohio Dec.
Ohio Decisions, Reprint ........................ Ohio Dec.Reprint

Ohio Jurisprudence --------------------------------------------- Ohio Jur.
Ohio Jurisprudence, Second Series ------------------ Ohio Jur.2d
Ohio Law Abstract --------------------------------- Ohio L.Abs.
Ohio Miscellaneous Reports ------------------------- Ohio Misc.
Ohio Nisi Prius Reports ---------------------------- Ohio N.P.
Ohio Nisi Prius Reports, New Series --------------- Ohio N.P. (N.S.)
Ohio Opinions ------------------------------------- Ohio Op.
Ohio Opinions, Second Series --------------------- Ohio Op.2d
Ohio Reports -------------------------------------- Ohio
Ohio State Law Journal --------------------------- Ohio St.L.J.
Ohio State Reports ------------------------------- Ohio St.
Ohio State Reports, Second Series ---------------- Ohio St.2d
Ohio Supplement ---------------------------------- Ohio Supp.
Oil & Gas Compact Bulletin ----------------------- Oil & Gas Compact
      Bull.
Oil and Gas Institute ---------------------------- Oil & Gas Inst.
Oil and Gas Journal ------------------------------ Oil & Gas J.
Oil and Gas Reporter ----------------------------- Oil & Gas Rptr.
Oil and Gas Tax Quarterly ------------------------ Oil & Gas Tax Q.
Oklahoma Bar Association Journal ----------------- Okla.B.Ass'n J.
Oklahoma Criminal Reports ------------------------ Okla.Crim.
Oklahoma Law Review ------------------------------ Okla.L.Rev.
Oklahoma Reports --------------------------------- Okla.
Ontario Appeal Reports --------------------------- O.A.R.
Ontario Election Cases --------------------------- Ont.Elec.
Ontario Labour Relations Board Monthly Report ---- [  ] November
      Monthly Report (O.
      L.R.B.)
Ontario Law Reports, 1901–1930 ------------------- O.L.R.
Ontario Reports, 1882–1900 ----------------------- O.R.
Ontario Reports, 1931 to present ----------------- [  ] O.R.
Ontario Weekly Notes, 1909–1932 ------------------ O.W.N.
Ontario Weekly Notes, 1933–1962 ------------------ [  ] O.W.N.
Ontario Weekly Reporter -------------------------- O.W.R.
Opinions of the Attorney General, United States --- Op.Att'y Gen.
Oregon Law Review -------------------------------- Ore.L.Rev.
Oregon Reports ----------------------------------- Ore.
Oregon State Bar Bulletin ------------------------ Ore.St.B.Bull.
Osgoode Hall Law Journal ------------------------- Osgoode Hall L.J.
Otago Law Review --------------------------------- Otago L.Rev.
Ottawa Law Review -------------------------------- Ottawa L.Rev.
Pacific Coast Law Journal ------------------------ P.Coast L.J.
Pacific Law Journal ------------------------------ Pacific L.J.
Pacific Reporter --------------------------------- P.
Pacific Reporter, Second Series ------------------ P.2d
Pakistan Law Reports, (e. g.) Lahore Series ------ [e. g.] Pak.L.R.La-
      hore Ser.
Pan-American Treaty Series ----------------------- Pan-Am.T.S.
Papua and New Guinea Law Reports ----------------- Papua & N.G.

Patent and Trade Mark Review `------------------` Pat. & T.M.Rev.
Patent Law Review `---------------------------` Pat.L.Rev.
Patent, Trademark & Copyright Journal `----------` Pat.T.M. & Copy.J.
Patents, Decisions of Commissioner and of U. S.
    Courts `-----------------------------------` Dec.Com.Pat.
Pennewill `------------------------------------` Penne.
Pennsylvania Bar Association Quarterly `-----------` Pa.B.Ass'n Q.
Pennsylvania Bar Brief `----------------------------` Pa.B.Brief
Pennsylvania County Court Reports `------------------` Pa.County Ct.
Pennsylvania District and County Reports `----------` Pa.D. & C.
Pennsylvania District and County Reports, Second
    Series `-----------------------------------` Pa.D. & C.2d
Pennsylvania District Reports `----------------------` Pa.Dist.
Pennsylvania Fiduciary Reporter `-----------------` Pa.Fid.
Pennsylvania Miscellaneous Reports `----------------` Pa.Misc.
Pennsylvania State Reports `--------------------------` Pa.
Pennsylvania Superior Court Reports `--------------` Pa.Super.
Penrose and Watts `----------------------------------` Pen. & W.
Personal Finance Law Quarterly Report `-----------` Pers.Finance L.Q.
Personal Injury Commentator `-------------------` Pers.Inj.Comment'r
Peters `-------------------------------------------` Pet.
Pickering `------------------------------------------` Pick.
Pinney `-----------------------------------------` Pin.
Pittsburgh Legal Journal `-------------------------` Pitt.L.J.
Planning and Compensation Reports `----------------` Plan. & Comp.
Planning, Zoning & Eminent Domain Institute `------` Plan., Zoning & E.D.
    Inst.
Police Law Quarterly `-----------------------------` Police L.Q.
Political Science Quarterly `----------------------` Pol.Sci.Q.
Pollution Abstracts `--------------------------------` Pollution Abs.
Portia Law Journal `--------------------------------` Portia L.J.
Portland University Law Review `------------------` Portland U.L.Rev.
Practical Lawyer `---------------------------------` Prac.Law.
Practice Reports (Ont.) `----------------------------` P.R.
Prentice-Hall `--------------------------------------` P-H
Price's Mining Commissioner's Cases (Ont.) `--------` Price
Prince Edward Island `-----------------------------` Pr.Edw.Isl.
Prison Law Reporter `-------------------------------` Prison L.Rptr.
Probate and Property `-----------------------------` Prob. & Prop.
Property and Compensation Reports `----------------` Prop. & Comp.
Public Contract Law Journal `----------------------` Pub. Contract L.J.
Public Employee Relations Reports `----------------` Pub.Employee Rel.
    Rep.
Public Land and Resources Law Digest `------------` Pub.Land & Res.L.
    Dig.
Public Law `------------------------------------` Pub.L.
Public Utilities Fortnightly `----------------------` Pub.Util.Fort.
Public Utilities Reports `-----------------------------` P.U.R.
Public Utilities Reports, New Series `--------------` P.U.R. (N.S.)
Public Utilities Reports, Third Series `-------------` P.U.R.3d

Publishing, Entertainment, Advertising and Allied
   Fields Law Quarterly --------------------------------- PEAL
Puerto Rico, Decisiones de ------------------------- D.P.R.
Puerto Rico Federal Reports ----------------------- P.R.F.
Puerto Rico Reports -------------------------------- P.R.R.
Pyke's Reports, King's Bench (Que.) -------------- Pyke
Quebec Law Reports -------------------------------- Que.L.R.
Quebec Official Reports (King's Bench or Queen's   [  ] Que.K.B. or
   Bench) 1941 to present --------------------------- [  ] Que.Q.B.
Quebec Official Reports (Queen's Bench or King's  Que.Q.B. or Que.K.
   Bench) 1892–1941 ------------------------------- B.
Quebec Official Reports (Superior Court) 1892–
   1941 --------------------------------------------- Que.S.C.
Quebec Offical Reports (Superior Court) 1942–
   present ------------------------------------------ [  ] Que.S.C.
Quebec Practice Reports --------------------------- Que.Prac.
Quebec Rapports Judiciares Officiels (Banc de la
   Reine); Cour supérieure ------------------------ Que.B.R.;  Que.C.S.
Quebec Revised Reports ---------------------------- R.J.R.O.
Queen's Bench, Manitoba temp. Wood, by Armour -- Armour
Queen's Law Journal ------------------------------- Q.L.J.
Queensland Justice of the Peace Reports ---------- Queensl.J.P.Rep.
Queensland Reports --------------------------------- Queensl.
Queensland State Reports -------------------------- Queensl.St.Rep.
Race Relations Law Reporter ---------------------- Race Rel.L.Rep.
Race Relations Law Survey ------------------------ Race Rel.L.Survey
Radio Regulation Reporter ------------------------ P & F Radio Reg.
Ramsay's Appeal Cases (Que.) -------------------- R.A.C.
Randolph ----------------------------------------- Rand.
Rawle -------------------------------------------- Rawle
Real Estate Law Report --------------------------- Real Est.L.Rep.
Real Estate Review -------------------------------- Real Est.Rev.
Real Property, Probate and Trust Journal ---------- Real Prop.Prob. &
   Trust J.

Record of the Association of the Bar of the City of
   New York ---------------------------------------- Record of N.Y.C.B.A.
Referees' Journal (Journal of National Association
   of Referees in Bankruptcy) --------------------- Ref.J.
Religion and the Public Order --------------------- Rel. & Pub.Order
Reports of Family Law ----------------------------- Rep.Fam.L.
Reports of Patent Cases --------------------------- R.P.C.
Reports of Patent, Design and Trade Mark Cases ---- Pat.Cas.
Reports of Restrictive Practices Cases ------------ Restric.Prac.
Reports of Tax Cases ------------------------------ Tax Cas.
Res Ipsa Loquitur --------------------------------- Res Ipsa
Review of Securities Regulation, The ------------- Rev.Sec.Reg.
Review of Selected Code Legislation --------------- Rev.Sel.Code Leg.
Revised Reports ----------------------------------- Rev.R.
Revised Statutes ---------------------------------- Rev.Stat.

Revista de Derecho del Colegio de Abogados de Puerto  
    Rico ------------------------------------------------- Rev.C.Abo.P.R.  
Revista de Derecho Puertorriqueño ----------------- Rev.D.P.R.  
Revista Juridica de la Universidad de Puerto Rico ---- Rev.Jur.U.P.R.  
Revue de Notariat ---------------------------------- Rev.Not.  
Revue du Barreau ---------------------------------- Rev.Bar.  
Revue Juridique Themis, La ----------------------- Themis  
Revue Legale ------------------------------------- Rev.Legale  
Rhode Island Bar Journal -------------------------- R.I.B.J.  
Rhode Island Reports ------------------------------ R.I.  
Rights --------------------------------------------- Rights  
Robinson ------------------------------------------ Rob.  
Rocky Mountain Law Review ---------------------- Rocky Mt.L.Rev.  
Rocky Mountain Mineral Law Institute ------------ Rocky Mt.Min.L.Inst.  
Rocky Mountain Mineral Law Review ------------- Rocky Mt.Mineral L.  
    Rev.  
Russell's Election Cases (Nova Scotia) ------------- Rus.  
Russell's Equity Decisions (Nova Scotia) ----------- R.E.D.  
Rutgers Journal of Computers and the Law --------- Rutgers J. Computers  
    & Law  
Rutgers Law Review ------------------------------- Rutgers L.Rev.  
Rutgers-Camden Law Journal --------------------- Rutgers-Camden L.J.  
St. John's Law Review ----------------------------- St. John's L.Rev.  
St. Louis Law Review ------------------------------ St. Louis L.Rev.  
Saint Louis University Law Journal ---------------- St. Louis U.L.J.  
St. Mary's Law Journal ---------------------------- St. Mary's L.J.  
San Diego Law Review ----------------------------- San Diego L.Rev.  
San Francisco Law Journal ------------------------- S.F.L.J.  
Santa Clara Lawyer ------------------------------- Santa Clara Law.  
Saskatchewan Law Reports ------------------------ Sask.  
Saskatchewan Law Review ------------------------- Sask.L.Rev.  
Scottish Court of Session Cases ------------------- Sess.Cas.  
Scottish Law Review and Sheriff Court Reports ------ Scot.L.Rev.  
Scots Law Times Reports -------------------------- Scots L.T.R.  
Search and Seizure Bulletin ----------------------- Search & Seizure  
Securities and Exchange Commission Decisions and  
    Reports --------------------------------------- S.E.C.  
Securities Law Review ----------------------------- Sec.L.Rev.  
Securities Regulation & Law Report --------------- BNA Sec.Reg.  
Securities Regulation and Transfer Report --------- Sec.Reg. & Trans.  
Selden's Notes ------------------------------------ Seld.  
Selective Service Law Reporter -------------------- Sel.Serv.L.Rptr.  
Sergeant and Rawle ------------------------------- S. & R.  
Session Laws -------------------------------------- Sess.Laws  
Seton Hall Law Review ---------------------------- Seton Hall L.Rev.  
Sex Problems Court Digest, The ------------------- Sex Prob.Ct.Dig.  
Shingle ------------------------------------------- Shingle  
Smedes and Marshall ------------------------------ S. & M.  
Sneed -------------------------------------------- Sneed

Social Security Taxes (P-H) ------------------------- P-H Soc.Sec.Taxes
Solicitor ------------------------------------------ Sol.
Solicitors' Journal -------------------------------- Sol.J.
Somerset Legal Journal ----------------------------- Som.L.J.
South African Law Journal -------------------------- S.Afr.L.J.
South African Law Reports -------------------------- S.Afr.L.R.
South African Law Reports Appellate ---------------- S.Afr.L.R.App.
South African Tax Cases ---------------------------- S.Afr.Tax Cas.
South Australia State Reports ---------------------- S.Austl.
South Australian Law Reports ----------------------- S.Austl.L.R.
South Carolina Law Quarterly ----------------------- S.C.L.Q.
South Carolina Law Review -------------------------- S.C.L.Rev.
South Carolina Reports ----------------------------- S.C.
South Dakota Law Review ---------------------------- S.D.L.Rev.
South Dakota Reports ------------------------------- S.D.
South Dakota State Bar Journal --------------------- S.D.St.B.J.
South Eastern Reporter ----------------------------- S.E.
South Eastern Reporter, Second Series -------------- S.E.2d
South Texas Law Journal ---------------------------- S.Tex.L.J.
South Western Reporter ----------------------------- S.W.
South Western Reporter, Second Series -------------- S.W.2d
Southern California Law Review --------------------- S.Cal.L.Rev.
Southern Reporter ---------------------------------- So.
Southern Reporter, Second Series ------------------- So.2d
Southwestern Law Journal --------------------------- Sw.L.J.
Southwestern University Law Review ----------------- Sw.U.L.Rev.
Standard Federal Tax Reporter (CCH) ---------------- CCH Stand.Fed.Tax
                                                     Rep.
Stanford Journal of International Studies ---------- Stan.J.Int'l Stud.
Stanford Law Review -------------------------------- Stan.L.Rev.
State and Local Taxes (P-H) ------------------------ P-H State & Local
                                                     Taxes
State Government ----------------------------------- State Gov't
State Tax Cases Reporter (CCH) --------------------- CCH State Tax Cas.
                                                     Rep.
State Tax Review (CCH) ----------------------------- CCH State Tax Rev.
Statutes at Large ---------------------------------- Stat.
Stewart's Vice-Admiralty Reports (N.S.) ------------ Stewart
Stockton's Vice-Admiralty Reports (N.B.) ----------- Stockton
Storey --------------------------------------------- Storey
Student Lawyer ------------------------------------- Student Law.
Student Lawyer Journal ----------------------------- Student Law.J.
Suffolk University Law Review ---------------------- Suffolk U.L.Rev.
Supreme Court Reporter ----------------------------- S.Ct.
Supreme Court Reports (Canada) 1876–1922 ----------- S.C.R.
Supreme Court Reports (Canada) 1923–present -------- [ ] S.C.R.
Supreme Court Review ------------------------------- S.Ct.Rev.
Sydney Law Review ---------------------------------- Sydney L.Rev.
Syracuse Law Review -------------------------------- Syracuse L.Rev.

| | |
|---|---|
| T. B. Monroe | T.B.Mon. |
| Tasmania University Law Review | Tasm.U.L.Rev. |
| Tasmanian Law Reports | Tasm.L.R. |
| Tasmanian State Reports | Tasm. |
| Tax Administrators News | Tax.Adm'rs News |
| Tax Adviser, The | Tax Adviser |
| Tax Appeal Board Cases | Tax A.B.C. |
| Tax Cases | Tax Cas. |
| Tax Counselor's Quarterly | Tax Counselor's Q. |
| Tax Court Memorandum Decisions (CCH) | CCH Tax Ct.Mem. |
| Tax Court Memorandum Decisions (P-H) | P-H Tax Ct.Mem. |
| Tax Court of the United States Reports | T.C. |
| Tax Court Reporter (CCH) | CCH Tax Ct.Rep. |
| Tax Court Reports and Memorandum Decisions (P-H) | P-H Tax Ct.Rep. & Mem.Dec. |
| Tax Law Review | Tax L.Rev. |
| Tax Lawyer, The | Tax Law. |
| Tax Management Memorandum (BNA) | TMM |
| Taxation Reports | Tax.R. |
| Taxes, the Tax Magazine | Taxes |
| Temple Law Quarterly | Temp.L.Q. |
| Tennessee Appeals Reports | Tenn.App. |
| Tennessee Appellate Bulletin | Tenn.App.Bull. |
| Tennessee Chancery Reports | Tenn.Ch. |
| Tennessee Law Review | Tenn.L.Rev. |
| Tennessee Reports | Tenn. |
| Territories Law Reports (N.W.T.) | Terr.L.R. |
| Terry | Terry |
| Texas Bar Journal | Tex.B.J. |
| Texas Civil Appeals Reports | Tex.Civ.App. |
| Texas Court of Appeals Reports | Tex.Ct.App.R. |
| Texas Criminal Reports | Tex.Crim. |
| Texas International Law Forum | Tex.Int'l L.F. |
| Texas International Law Journal | Tex.Int'l L.J. |
| Texas Jurisprudence | Tex.Jur. |
| Texas Jurisprudence, Second Series | Tex.Jur.2d |
| Texas Law Review | Texas L.Rev. |
| Texas Reports | Tex. |
| Texas Southern University Law Review | Tex.So.U.L.Rev. |
| Texas Supreme Court Reporter | Tex.S.Ct. |
| Texas Tech Law Review | Tex.Tech L.Rev. |
| Times Law Reports | T.L.R. |
| Title News | Title News |
| Trade Cases (CCH) | Trade Cas. |
| Trade Regulation Reporter (CCH) | Trade Reg.Rep. |
| Trade-Mark Bulletin | Trademark Bull. |
| Trade-Mark Bulletin, New Series | Trademark Bull (n.s.) |
| Trade-Mark Reporter | Trademark Rptr. |
| Transportation Law Journal | Transp.L.J. |

| | |
|---|---|
| Transvaal and Witswatersrand Reports | Trans. & Wit. |
| Treasury Decisions | T.D. |
| Treaties and Other International Act Series, United States | T.I.A.S. |
| Treaty Series, United States | T.S. |
| Trial | Trial |
| Trial Lawyers' Quarterly | Trial Law.Q. |
| Trueman's Equity Cases (New Brunswick) | Trueman Eq. |
| Trust Bulletin | Trust Bull. |
| Trust Territory Reports | Trust Terr. |
| Trusts and Estates | Trusts & Estates |
| Tucker and Clephane | Tuck. & Cl. |
| Tulane Law Review | Tul.L.Rev. |
| Tulane Tax Institute | Tul.Tax.Inst. |
| Tulsa Law Journal | Tulsa L.J. |
| U.C.L.A. Intramural Law Review | U.C.L.A.Intra.L.Rev. |
| U.C.L.A. Law Review | U.C.L.A.L.Rev. |
| U.C.L.A.-Alaska Law Review | U.C.L.A.-Alaska L. Rev. |
| Unauthorized Practice News | Un.Prac.News |
| Unemployment Insurance Reporter (CCH) | Unempl.Ins.Rep. |
| Uniform Commercial Code Law Letter | U.C.C.Law Letter |
| Uniform Commercial Code Reporting Service | U.C.C.Rep.Serv. |
| United Nations Treaty Series | U.N.T.S. |
| United States Air Force JAG Law Review | JAG L.Rev. |
| United States and Canadian Aviation Reports | U.S. & Can.Av. |
| United States Attorneys General's Opinions | Op.Att'y Gen. |
| United States Attorneys General's Reports | Att'y Gen.Rep. |
| United States Aviation Reports | U.S.Av. |
| United States Civil Aeronautics Board Reports | C.A.B. |
| United States Code | U.S.C. |
| United States Code Annotated | U.S.C.A. |
| United States Code Congressional and Administrative News | U.S.Code Cong. & Ad. News |
| United States Code Service | U.S.C.S. |
| United States Code, Supplement | U.S.C. (Supp.) |
| United States Comptroller General Decisions | Comp.Gen. |
| United States Comptroller of Treasury Decisions | Comp.Dec. |
| United States Court of Customs Appeals Reports | Ct.Cust.App. |
| United States Court of Military Appeals | U.S.C.M.A. |
| United States Department of State Bulletin | Dep't State Bull. |
| United States Federal Communications Commission Reports | F.C.C. |
| United States Federal Power Commission Reports | F.P.C. |
| United States Federal Trade Commission Decisions | F.T.C. |
| United States Interior Department Decisions | Interior Dec. |
| United States Internal Revenue Bulletin | Int.Rev.Bull. |
| United States Internal Revenue Code of 1954 | Int.Rev.Code of 1954 |
| United States Internal Revenue Cumulative Bulletin | Cum.Bull. |

United States Interstate Commerce Commission,
Motor Carrier Cases ----------------------------- M.C.C.
United States Interstate Commerce Commission
Reports -------------------------------------- I.C.C.
United States Interstate Commerce Commission Valu-
ation Reports ---------------------------------- Val.R. (I.C.C.)
United States Law Week (B.N.A.) ----------------- U.S.L.W.
United States National Labor Relations Board
Decisions ------------------------------------- N.L.R.B.
United States Office of Contract Settlement
Decisions ------------------------------------- O.C.S.
United States Patent Quarterly -------------------- U.S.P.Q.
United States Securities and Exchange Commission -- S.E.C.
United States Supreme Court Reporter (West) ------ S.Ct.
United States Supreme Court Reports -------------- U.S.
United States Supreme Court Reports (Lawyers'
Edition) -------------------------------------- L.Ed.
United States Supreme Court Reports (Lawyers'
Edition Second Series) ------------------------- L.Ed.2d
United States Tax Cases (CCH) ------------------- U.S.Tax Cas.
United States Tax Court Reports ------------------ T.C.
United States Treasury Decisions ----------------- T.D.
United States Treaties and Other International
Agreements ----------------------------------- U.S.T.
United States Treaty Developments ---------------- U.S.T.D.
United States Treaty Series --------------------- T.S.
University of British Columbia Law Review --------- U.B.C.L.Rev.
University of California at Davis Law Review ------ U.C.D.L.Rev.
University of Chicago Law Review ----------------- U.Chi.L.Rev.
University of Chicago Law School Record ----------- U.Chi.L.Rec.
University of Cincinnati Law Review --------------- U.Cin.L.Rev.
University of Colorado Law Review ---------------- U.Colo.L.Rev.
University of Detroit Law Journal ---------------- U.Det.L.J.
University of Florida Law Review ----------------- U.Fla.L.Rev.
University of Illinois Law Forum ------------------ U.Ill.L.F.
University of Kansas City Law Review ------------- U.Kan.City L.Rev.
University of Kansas Law Review ----------------- Kan.L.Rev.
University of Miami Law Review ------------------ U.Miami L.Rev.
University of Michigan Journal of Law Reform ------ U.Mich.J.Law
                                                   Reform
University of Missouri at Kansas City Law Review -- U.Mo.K.C.L.Rev.
University of Missouri Bulletin Law Series -------- U.Mo.Bull.L.Ser.
University of New Brunswick Law Journal -------- U.N.B.L.J.
University of Pennsylvania Law Review ----------- U.Pa.L.Rev.
University of Pittsburgh Law Review ------------- U.Pitt.L.Rev.
University of Queensland Law Journal ------------ U.Queens.L.J.
University of Richmond Law Review -------------- U.Rich.L.Rev.
University of San Fernando Valley Law Review ------ U.San Fernando V.L.
                                                   Rev.

University of San Francisco Law Review ----------- U.San Fran.L.Rev.
University of South Carolina Governmental Review -- U.S.C. Govt'l Rev.
University of Southern California Tax Institute ---- [e. g.] U.So.Cal.1955
                                                        Tax Inst.
University of Tasmania Law Review (or Tasmania
   University Law Review) ----------------------- U.Tasm.L.Rev.
University of Toledo Law Review ---------------- U.Toledo L.Rev.
University of Toronto Law Journal ---------------- U.Toronto L.J.
University of Toronto School of Law Review ------- U.Tor.L.Rev.
University of Washington Law Review ------------ U.Wash.L.Rev.
University of West Los Angeles School of Law,
   Law Review ------------------------------------- U.W.L.A.Rev.
University of Western Australia Law Review ------- U.W.Austl.L.Rev.
University of Windsor Law Review --------------- U.Windsor L.Rev.
Upper Canada Chambers Reports ---------------- Ch.R.
Upper Canada Chancery Chambers Reports ------- Chy.Chrs.
Upper Canada Chancery Reports, by Grant --------- Gr.
Upper Canada Common Pleas --------------------- U.C.C.P.
Upper Canada Error & Appeal Reports, by Grant ---- E. & A.
Upper Canada King's Bench Reports, by Taylor ------ Taylor
Upper Canada Queen's Bench, Old Series ----------- U.C.Q.B. (O.S.)
Upper Canada, Queen's Bench Reports ------------- U.C.Q.B.
Urban Law Annual ------------------------------- Urban Law Ann.
Urban Lawyer, The ------------------------------ Urban Law.
Utah Law Review -------------------------------- Utah L.Rev.
Utah Reports ----------------------------------- Utah
Utah Reports, 2d Series -------------------------- Utah 2d
Utilities Law Reporter (CCH) -------------------- Util.L.Rep.
Valparaiso University Law Review ---------------- Val.U.L.Rev.
Valuation Reports, Interstate Commerce
   Commission --------------------------------------- Val.R. (ICC)
Vanderbilt Journal of Transnational Law ----------- Vand.J.Transnat'l L.
Vanderbilt Law Review -------------------------- Vand.L.Rev.
Vermont Reports -------------------------------- Vt.
Victoria University Law Review ------------------ Vict.U.L.Rev.
Victoria University of Wellington Law Review ------ Vict.U.Well.L.Rev.
Victorian Law Reports --------------------------- Vict.L.R.
Victorian Reports ------------------------------- Vict.
Villanova Law Review --------------------------- Vill.L.Rev.
Virgin Islands Bar Journal ----------------------- V.I.B.J.
Virgin Islands Reports -------------------------- V.I.
Virginia Bar News ------------------------------ Va.Bar News
Virginia Cases (criminal) ----------------------- Va.Cas.
Virginia Journal of International Law ------------- Va.J.Int'l L.
Virginia Law Register, New Series --------------- Va.L.Reg. (N.S.)
Virginia Law Review ---------------------------- Va.L.Rev.
Virginia Reports -------------------------------- Va.
W. W. Harrington ------------------------------- W.W.Harr.
Wage and Hour Cases (BNA) -------------------- Wage & Hour Cas.

Wake Forest Intramural Law Review ------------- Wake For.Intra.L. Rev.

Wake Forest Law Review ---------------------- Wake For.L.Rev.

Wallace ----------------------------------------- Wall.

Washburn Law Journal --------------------------- Washburn L.J.

Washington and Lee Law Review ----------------- Wash. & Lee L.Rev.

Washington Law Review -------------------------- Wash.L.Rev.

Washington Reports ----------------------------- Wash.

Washington Reports, Second Series -------------- Wash.2d

Washington Territory Reports ------------------- Wash.Terr.

Washington University Law Quarterly ----------- Wash.U.L.Q.

Watts ------------------------------------------- Watts

Watts and Sargeant ----------------------------- W. & S.

Wayne Law Review ------------------------------- Wayne L.Rev.

Weekly Law Reports ----------------------------- W.L.R.

Weekly Notes ----------------------------------- W.N.

Weekly Reports --------------------------------- W.R.

Welfare Law Bulletin --------------------------- Welfare L.Bull.

Welfare Law News ------------------------------- Welfare L.News

Wendell ----------------------------------------- Wend.

West African Court of Appeal Reports ----------- W.Afr.App.

West Coast Reporter ---------------------------- W.Coast Rptr.

West Virginia Law Review ----------------------- W.Va.L.Rev.

West Virginia Reports -------------------------- W.Va.

Western Australia Industrial Gazette ----------- W.Austl.Ind.Gaz.

Western Australia Justice of the Peace --------- W.Austl.J.P.

Western Australian Law Reports ----------------- W.Austl.L.R.

Western Australian Reports --------------------- West.Austl.

Western Law Reporter --------------------------- West.L.R.

Western Law Review ----------------------------- West.L.Rev.

Western Law Times and Reports ------------------ W.L.T.

Western Ontario Law Review --------------------- W.Ont.L.Rev.

Western Reserve Law Review --------------------- W.Res.L.Rev.

Western School Law Review ---------------------- West.School L.Rev.

Western Weekly Reports ------------------------- W.W.R.

Western Weekly Reports, New Series 1951–1955 ---- W.W.R. (N.S.)

Westmoreland County Law Journal ---------------- Wes.C.L.J.

Wharton ----------------------------------------- Whart.

Wheaton ----------------------------------------- Wheat.

Willamette Law Journal ------------------------- Willamette L.J.

William & Mary Law Review ---------------------- Wm. & Mary L.Rev.

Wisconsin Law Review --------------------------- Wis.L.Rev.

Wisconsin Reports ------------------------------ Wis.

Wisconsin Student Bar Journal ------------------ Wisc.Stud.B.J.

Women Lawyer's Journal ------------------------- Women Law.J.

Women's Rights Law Reporter -------------------- Women's Rights L. Rptr.

Wyoming Law Journal ---------------------------- Wyo.L.J.

Wyoming Reports -------------------------------- Wyo.

# Appendix B

## CONVERSION TABLE OF ABBREVIATIONS

### A

| | |
|---|---|
| A. | Atlantic Reporter |
| A.2d | Atlantic Reporter, Second Series |
| A. & E. | Adolphus & Ellis Queen's Bench (Eng.) |
| A. & E.Ann. Cas. | American & English Annotated Cases |
| A. & E.Anno. | Same |
| A. & E.Cas. | Same |
| A. & E.Corp. Cas. | American & English Corporation Cases |
| A. & E.Corp. Cas.(N.S.) | Same, New Series |
| A. & E.Enc. L. & Pr. | American & English Encyclopedia of Law and Practice |
| A. & E.Ency. | American & English Encyclopedia of Law |
| A. & E.Ency. Law | Same |
| A. & E.P. & P. | American & English Pleading and Practice |
| A. & E.R.Cas. | American & English Railroad Cases |
| A. & E.R.Cas. (N.S.) | Same, New Series |
| A. & E.R.R. Cas. | American & English Railroad Cases |
| A. & E.R.R. Cas. (N.S.) | Same, New Series |
| A.B. | Anonymous Reports at end of Benloe, or Bendloe (1661) (Eng.) |
| A.B.A.J. | American Bar Association Journal |
| A.B.A.Jour. | Same |
| A.B.A.Rep. | American Bar Association Reports |
| A.B.C.Newsl. | International Association of Accident Boards and Commissions Newsletter |
| A.B.F. Research Reptr. | American Bar Foundation Research Reporter |
| A.C. | Law Reports Appeal Cases (Eng.) |
| | Law Reports Appeal Cases (Eng.) Third Series |
| | Appeal Cases (Can.) |
| | Advance California Reports |

| | |
|---|---|
| A.C.A. | Advance California Appellate Reports |
| A.C.L.U.Leg. Action Bull. | American Civil Liberties Union Legislative Action Bulletin |
| A.C.R. | American Criminal Reports |
| A.D. | American Decisions |
| AFTR | American Federal Tax Reports |
| A.I.D. | Accident/Injury/Damages |
| A.K.Marsh. | A. K. Marshall (Ky.) |
| A.L.I. | American Law Institute |
| A.L.R. | American Law Reports |
| A.L.R.2d | Same, Second Series |
| A.L.R.3d | Same, Third Series |
| A.L.R.Fed. | American Law Reports Federal |
| A.L.Rec. | American Law Record |
| A.L.Reg. (N.S.) | American Law Register, New Series |
| A.L.Reg. (O.S.) | American Law Register, Old Series |
| A.M. & O. | Armstrong, Macartney & Ogle Nisi Prius (Ir.) |
| A.M.C. | American Maritime Cases |
| A.O.C.Newsl. | Administrative Office of the Courts Newsletter |
| A.R.C. | American Ruling Cases |
| A.R.M. | Appeals & Review Memorandum Committee (I.R.Bull.) |
| A.R.R. | Appeals & Review Recommendation (I.R.Bull.) |
| A.S.A.Newsl. | Association for the Study of Abortion Newsletter |
| A.S.R. | American State Reports |
| A.T. | Alcohol Tax Unit (I.R.Bull.) |
| A.T.L.A.J. | American Trial Lawyers Association Journal |
| Ab.N. | Abstracts, Treasury Decisions, New Series |
| Abb. | Abbott (U.S.) |
| Abb.Adm. | Abbott's Admiralty (U.S.) |
| Abb.App.Dec. | Abbott's Appeal Decisions (N.Y.) |
| Abb.Dec. | Abbott's Decisions (N.Y.) |

| | | | |
|---|---|---|---|
| Abb.Dict. | Abbott's Dictionary | Albany L.Rev. | Same |
| Abb.N.Cas. | Abbott's New Cases (N.Y.) | Alc. & N. | Alcock & Napier King's Bench (Ir.) |
| Abb.Prac. | Abbott's Practice (N.Y.) | Alc.Reg.Cas. | Alcock Registry Cases (Ir.) |
| Abb.Prac.N.S. | Same, New Series | | |
| Abb.R.P.S. | Abbott's Real Property Statutes (Wn.) | Ald. | Alden's Condensed Reports (Pa.) |
| A'Beck.Res. Judgm. | A'Beckett's Reserved Judgments (Victoria) | Aleyn | Aleyn, King's Bench (Eng.) |
| Abs. | Abstracts, Treasury Decisions Ohio Law Abstract | Alison Pr. | Alison Practice (Sc.) |
| | | All E.R. | All England Law Reports |
| Acad.Pol. Sci.Proc. | Academy of Political Science Proceedings | All India Crim.Dec. | All India Criminal Decisions |
| | | All India Rptr. | All India Reporter |
| Act. | Acton Prize Cases Privy Council (Eng.) | All Pak. Leg.Dec. | All Pakistan Legal Decisions |
| Acta Cancelariae | English Chancery Reports | Allen | Allen (Mass.) |
| | | Allen N.B. | Allen, New Brunswick |
| Acta Jur. | Acta Juridica | Allinson | Allinson, Pa.Superior District Courts |
| Acton | Acton Prize Cases Privy Council (Eng.) | Alta. | Alberta Law Reports |
| Ad. & El. | Adolphus & Ellis Queen's Bench (Eng.) | Alta.L. | Alberta Law |
| | | Alta.L.Q. | Alberta Law Quarterly |
| Ad. & El. (N.S.) | Same, New Series | Alta.L.Rev. | Alberta Law Review |
| Ad.L. | Administrative Law | Am. & E.Corp. Cas. | American & English Corporation Cases |
| Ad.L.2d | Same, Second Series | | |
| Ad.L.Rev. | Administrative Law Review | Am. & E.Corp. Cas. (N.S.) | Same, New Series |
| Adams | Adams (Me.) Adams (N.H.) | Am. & E.R. Cas. | American & English Railroad Cases |
| Add. | Addison (Pa.) | Am. & E.R. Cas. (N.S.) | Same, New Series |
| Add.Eccl.Rep. | Addams' Ecclesiastical Reports (Eng.) | Am. & Eng. Ann.Cas. | American & English Annotated Cases |
| Add.Penn. | Addison (Pa.) | Am. & Eng. Eq.D. | American & English Decisions in Equity |
| Add.Rep. | Same | | |
| Adelaide L.Rev. | Adelaide Law Review | Am. & Eng. Pat.Cas. | American & English Patent Cases |
| Adm. & Ecc. | Admiralty & Ecclesiastical (Eng.) | Am.Acad. Matri.Law. J. | American Academy of Matrimonial Lawyers Journal |
| Advocate | The Advocate | | |
| Agri.Dec. | Agriculture Decisions | Am.B.R. (N.S.) | American Bankruptcy Reports, New Series |
| Aik. | Aikens (Vt.) | | |
| Air L.Rev. | Air Law Review | Am.Bankr.L.J. | American Bankruptcy Law Journal |
| Akron L.Rev. | Akron Law Review | | |
| Ala. | Alabama | Am.Bankr. Reg. | American Bankruptcy Register (U.S.) |
| Ala.App. | Alabama Court of Appeals | | |
| Ala.L.Rev. | Alabama Law Review | Am.Bankr. Rep. | American Bankruptcy Reports |
| Ala.Law. | The Alabama Lawyer | | |
| Ala.Sel.Cas. | Alabama Select Cases | Am.Bankr. Rev. | American Bankruptcy Review |
| Ala.St.B. Found.Bull. | Alabama State Bar Foundation Bulletin | Am.Bus.L.J. | American Business Law Journal |
| Alaska | Alaska Reports | | |
| Alaska B.J. | Alaska Bar Journal | Am.Corp.Cas. | American Corporation Cases |
| Alaska L.J. | Alaska Law Journal | Am.Cr. | American Criminal Reports |
| Alb.L.J. | Albany Law Journal | | |
| Alb.L.Q. | Alberta Law Quarterly | Am.Crim.L.Q. | American Criminal Law Quarterly |
| Alb.L.R. | Alberta Law Reports | Am.Crim. L.Rev. | American Criminal Law Review |
| Alb.L.Rev. | Albany Law Review | | |

| | |
|---|---|
| Am.Dec. | American Decisions |
| Am.Elect.Cas. | American Electrical Cases |
| Am.Fed. Tax R. | American Federal Tax Reports |
| Am.Fed. Tax R.2d | Same, Second Series |
| Am.Hist.Rev. | American Historical Review |
| Am.Insolv. Rep. | American Insolvency Reports |
| Am.J.Comp.L. | American Journal of Comparative Law |
| Am.J.Crim.L. | American Journal of Criminal Law |
| Am.J.Int.L. | American Journal of International Law |
| Am.J. Jurisprud. | American Journal of Jurisprudence |
| Am.J.Legal Hist. | American Journal of Legal History |
| Am.Jur. | American Jurisprudence American Jurist |
| Am.Jur.2d | American Jurisprudence, Second Series |
| Am.L.Ins. | American Law Institute |
| Am.L.J. | American Law Journal (Pa.) |
| Am.L.J. (N.S.) | Same, New Series |
| Am.L.Rec. | American Law Record (Ohio) |
| Am.L.Reg. | American Law Register |
| Am.L.Reg. (N.S.) | Same, New Series |
| Am.L.Reg. (O.S.) | Same, Old Series |
| Am.L.Rev. | American Law Review |
| Am.L.School Rev. | American Law School Review |
| Am.L.T. Bankr. | American Law Times Bankruptcy Reports |
| Am.Lab.Leg. Rev. | American Labor Legislation Review |
| Am.Law Rec. | American Law Record |
| Am.Law Reg. | American Law Register |
| Am.Negl.Cas. | American Negligence Cases |
| Am.Negl.Rep. | American Negligence Reports |
| Am.Pol. Sci.Rev. | American Political Science Review |
| Am.Pr.Rep. | American Practice Reports (D.C.) |
| Am.Prob. | American Probate Reports |
| Am.Prob. (N.S.) | Same, New Series |
| Am.R. | American Reports |
| Am.R. & Corp. | American Railroad Corporation |
| Am.R.Rep. | American Railway Reports |

| | |
|---|---|
| Am.Railw.Cas. | American Railway Cases (Smith & Bates) |
| Am.Rep. | American Reports |
| Am.Ry.Rep. | American Railway Reports |
| Am.St.R. | American State Reports |
| Am.St.R.D. | American Street Railway Decisions |
| Am.St.Rep. | American State Reports |
| Am.Tr.M.Cas. | American Trademark Cases (Cox) |
| Am.Trial Law.L.J. | American Trial Lawyers Law Journal |
| Am.U.Intra.L. Rev. | American University Intramural Law Review |
| Am.U.L. Rev. | American University Law Review |
| Amb. | Ambler, Chancery (Eng.) |
| Ames | Ames (R.I.) Ames (Minn.) |
| Ames K. & B. | Ames, Knowles & Bradley (R.I.) |
| An.B. | Anonymous Reports at end of Benloe, or Bendloe (1661) (Eng.) |
| And. | Anderson Common Pleas (Eng.) |
| Andr. | Andrews King's Bench (Eng.) |
| Ang. | Angell (R.I.) |
| Ang. & Dur. | Angell & Durfee (R.I.) |
| Ann. | Annaly's Hardwicke King's Bench (Eng.) |
| Ann.Cas. | American Annotated Cases |
| Ann.Dig. | Annual Digest and Reports of International Law Cases |
| Ann.Tax Cas. | Annotated Tax Cases |
| Annals | Annals of the American Academy of Political and Social Science |
| Annaly | Annaly's Hardwicke King's Bench (Eng.) |
| Anst. | Ansthruther, Exchequer (Eng.) |
| Anth.N.P. | Anthon's Nisi Prius (N.Y.) |
| Antitrust L. & Econ. Rev. | Antitrust Law and Economics Review |
| Antitrust L.J. | Antitrust Law Journal |
| App. | Appleton (Me.) |
| App.Cas. | Law Reports Appeal Cases (Eng.) |
| App.Cas.2d | Same, Second Series |
| App.D.C. | Appeal Cases (D.C.) |
| App.Div. | Appellate Division (N.Y.) |
| App.Div.2d | Same, Second Series |

| | | | |
|---|---|---|---|
| App.N.Z. | Appeal Reports (New Zealand) | Atk. | Atkyns Chancery (Eng.) |
| App.R.N.Z. | Same, Second Series | Atl. | Atlantic Reporter |
| App.Rep.Ont. | Ontario Appeal Reports | Atomic Energy L.J. | Atomic Energy Law Journal |
| Arb.J. | Arbitration Journal | Att'y Gen. | Attorney General |
| Arb.J. (N.S.) | Same, New Series | Att'y Gen.Rep. | United States Attorneys General's Reports |
| Arb.J. (O.S.) | Same, Old Series | | |
| Arb.L.Dig. | Arbitration Law; A Digest of Court Decisions | Atty.Gen. | Attorney General |
| | | Atwater | Atwater (Minn.) |
| Archer | Archer (Fla.) | Auck.U.L.Rev. | Auckland University Law Review |
| Archer & H. | Archer & Hogue (Fla.) | | |
| Argus L.R. | Argus Law Reports (Aust.) | Aust.Jur. | Australian Jurist |
| | | Aust.L.T. | Australian Law Times |
| Ariz. | Arizona | | |
| Ariz.B.J. | Arizona Bar Journal | Austl.Argus L.R. | Australian Argus Law Reports |
| Ariz.L.Rev. | Arizona Law Review | | |
| Ark. | Arkansas | Austl.Bankr. Cas. | Australian Bankruptcy Cases |
| Ark.Just. | Arkley's Justiciary (Sc.) | | |
| Ark.L.J. | Arkansas Law Journal | Austl.Com.J. | Australian Commercial Journal |
| Ark.L.Rev. | Arkansas Law Review | | |
| Ark.Law. | The Arkansas Lawyer | Austl.J. For.Sci. | Australian Journal of Forensic Sciences |
| Armour | Queen's Bench, Manitoba Temp. Wood, by Armour | | |
| | | Austl.L.J. | Australian Law Journal |
| Arms.Con. Elec. | Armstrong's Contested Elections (N.Y.) | Austl.L.J. Rep. | Australian Law Journal Reports |
| Arn. | Arnold Common Pleas (Eng.) | Austl.Tax | Australian Tax Decisions |
| | | Austl.Y.B. Int'l L. | Australian Yearbook of International Law |
| Arn. & H. | Arnold & Hodges Queen's Bench (Eng.) | Austr.C.L.R. | Commonwealth Law Reports, Australia |
| Arnold | Arnold Common Pleas (Eng.) | Auto.Cas. | Automobile Cases |
| | | Auto.Cas.2d | Same, Second Series |
| Ashm. | Ashmead (Pa.) | Av.Cas. | Aviation Cases |
| Aspin. | Aspinall's Maritime Cases (Eng.) | Av.L.Rep. | Aviation Law Reporter (CCH) |

# B

| | | | |
|---|---|---|---|
| B. | Weekly Law Bulletin | B. & F. | Broderip & Freemantle's Ecclesiastical (Eng.) |
| B. & A. | Barnewall & Alderson, King's Bench (Eng.) | | |
| B. & Ad. | Barnewall & Adolphus King's Bench (Eng.) | B. & H.Cr. Cas. | Bennet & Heard's Criminal Cases (Eng.) |
| B. & Ald. | Barnewall & Alderson, King's Bench (Eng.) | B. & H.Crim. Cas. | Same |
| B. & Arn. | Barron & Arnold Election Cases (Eng.) | B. & Macn. | Brown & Macnamara Railway Cases (Eng.) |
| B. & Aust. | Barron & Austin Election Cases (Eng.) | | |
| B. & B. | Ball & Beatty's Chancery (Ir.) Broderip & Bingham Common Pleas (Eng.) | B. & P. | Bosanquet & Puller, Common Pleas (Eng.) |
| | | B. & P.N.R. | Bosanquet & Puller's New Reports (Eng.) |
| B. & C. | Barnewall & Cresswell's King's Bench (Eng.) | B. & S. | Best & Smith, Queen's Bench (Eng.) |
| B. & C.R. | Reports of Bankruptcy & Companies Winding up Cases (Eng.) | B.C. | British Columbia |
| | | B.C.C. | Bail Court Cases (Eng.) |
| B. & D. | Benloe & Dalison Common Pleas (Eng.) | B.C.Ind. & Com.L.Rev. | Boston College Industrial and Commercial Law Review |

| | | | |
|---|---|---|---|
| B.C.R | Bail Court Cases (Eng.) | Bar. & Arn. | Barron & Arnold, Election Cases (Eng.) |
| B.D. & O. | Blackham, Dundas & Osborne, Nisi Prius (Ir.) | Bar. & Aust. | Barron & Austin, Election Cases (Eng.) |
| B.Mon. | B. Monroe (Ky.) | Barb. | Barber (Ark.) Barbour (N.Y.) |
| BNA | Bureau of National Affairs | Barb.Ch. | Barbour's Chancery (N.Y.) |
| BNA Sec.Reg. | Securities Regulation & Law Report | Barber | Barber (N.Y.) |
| B.R. (Army) | Board of Review (Army) | Barn. | Barnardiston, King's Bench (Eng.) |
| B.R.C. | British Ruling Cases | | |
| B.R.–J.C. (Army) | Board of Review and Judicial Council of the Army | Barn. & Ad. | Barnewall & Adolphus, King's Bench (Eng.) |
| B.T.A. | Board of Tax Appeals Reports | Barn. & Ald. | Barnewall & Alderson, King's Bench (Eng.) |
| B.U.L.Rev. | Boston University Law Review | Barn. & C. | Barnewall & Cresswell, King's Bench (Eng.) |
| B.W.C.C. | Butterworth's Workmen's Compensation Cases (Eng.) | Barn. & Cress. | Same |
| | | Barn.Ch. | Barnardiston Chancery (Eng.) |
| Bac.Abr. | Bacon's Abridgment (Eng.) | Barnes | Barnes Practice Cases (Eng.) |
| Bag. & Har. | Bagley & Harman (Cal.) | Barnes' Notes | Barnes' Notes (Eng.) |
| Bagl. | Bagley (Cal.) | Barnet | Barnet's Reports, Common Pleas (Eng.) |
| Bagl. & H. | Bagley & Harman (Cal.) | | |
| Bail Ct.Cas. | Bail Court Cases (Lowndes & Maxwell) (Eng.) | Barr | Barr (Pa.) |
| | | Barr.Ch.Pr. | Barroll Chancery Practice (Md.) |
| Bail.Eq. | Bailey's Equity (S.C.) | Barr.MSS. | Barradall Manuscript Reports (Va.) |
| Baild. | Baildon's Select Cases in Chancery (Eng.) | Bart.Elec. Cas. | Bartlett's Election Cases |
| Bailey | Bailey's Law (S.C.) | | |
| Bal.Ann. Codes | Ballinger's Annotated Codes & Statutes (Wash.) | Bates Ch. | Bates Chancery (Del.) |
| | | Batty | Batty, King's Bench (Ir.) |
| Baldw. | Baldwin (U.S.) | Baxt. | Baxter (Tenn.) |
| Balf.Pr. | Balfour's Practice (Sc.) | Bay | Bay (Mo.) Bay (S.C.) |
| Ball & B. | Ball & Beatty Chancery (Ir.) | Baylor L. Rev. | Baylor Law Review |
| Balt.L.T. | Baltimore Law Transcript | | |
| Ban. & A. | Banning & Arden Patent Cases (U.S.) | Beasl. | Beasley (N.J.) |
| | | Beav. | Beavan Rolls Court (Eng.) |
| Bank. & Ins.R. | Bankruptcy & Insolvency Reports (Eng.) | | |
| Bank.Cas. | Banking Cases | Beav. & W. Ry.Cas. | Beavan & Walford's Railway & Canal Cases (Eng.) |
| Bank.Ct.Rep. | Bankrupt Court Reports | | |
| Bank.L.J. | Banking Law Journal | Beav.R. & C. Cas. | Beavan, Railway & Canal Cases (Eng.) |
| Banking L.J. | Same | | |
| Bankr.L.Rep. | Bankruptcy Law Reporter (CCH) | Beaw.Lex Mer. | Beawes Lex Mercatoria (Eng.) |
| Bankr.Reg. | National Bankruptcy Register (N.Y.) | Bee | Bee's Admiralty U.S. District Court (S.C.) |
| Banks | Banks (Kan.) | | |
| Bann. | Bannister's Common Pleas (Eng.) | Bee Adm. | Bee's (U.S.) |
| | | Bee C.C.R. | Bee's Crown Cases Reserved (Eng.) |
| Bann. & A. | Banning & Arden, Patent Cases (U.S.) | Bell. | Bellewe, King's Bench (Eng.) |
| Bann. & Ard. | Same | | |

| | | | |
|---|---|---|---|
| Bell App.Cas. | Bell's Appeal Cases, House of Lords (Sc.) | Bing. | Bingham New Cases Common Pleas (Eng.) |
| Bell C.C. | Bell's Crown Cases Reserved (Eng.) | Binn. | Binney (Pa.) |
| | | Biss. | Bissell (U.S.) |
| Bell Cas. | Bell's Cases (Sc.) | Bitt.Rep. in Ch. | Bittleson's Reports, Queen's Bench (Eng.) |
| Bell.Cas.t.H. VIII | Bellewe, King's Bench, temp. Henry VIII (Eng.) | | |
| | | Bitt.W. & P. | Bittleson, Wise & Parnell Practice Cases (Eng.) |
| Bell.Cas.t.R.II | Same, temp. Richard II (Eng.) | Bk. | Black (U.S.) |
| Bell Comm. | Bell's Commentaries (Eng.) | Bl. | William Blackstone's King's Bench (Eng.) |
| Bell Cr.C. | Bell's Crown Cases Reserved (Eng.) | Bl.H. | Henry Blackstone's Common Pleas (Eng.) |
| Bell H.L. | Bell's Appeal Cases, House of Lords (Sc.) | Bl.W. | William Blackstone's King's Bench (Eng.) |
| Bell P.C. | Bell's Parliament Cases (Sc.) | Bla. | Same |
| Bell Sc.Cas. | Bell's Scotch Court of Sessions Cases | Bla.H. | Henry Blackstone's Common Pleas (Eng.) |
| Bell Ses.Cas. | Same | Bla.W. | William Blackstone's King's Bench (Eng.) |
| Bellewe | Bellewe, King's Bench (Eng.) | | |
| Ben. | Benedict (U.S. District Court) | Black | Black (Ind.) Black (U.S.) |
| Ben. & H.L.C. | Bennett & Heard Leading Criminal Cases (Eng.) | Black L.J. | Black Law Journal |
| | | Black. | William Blackstone's King's Bench (Eng.) |
| Bendl. | Bendloe's English Common Pleas | Black.Cond. | Blackwell's Condensed Reports (Ill.) |
| Bened. | Benedict (U.S. District Court) | Black.Cond. Rep. | Same |
| Benl. | Benloe's Common Pleas (Eng.) Benloe's King's Bench (Eng.) | Black.D. & O. | Blackham, Dundas & Osborne Nisi Prius (Ir.) |
| Benl. & D. | Benloe & Dalison Common Pleas (Eng.) | Black.H. | Henry Blackstone's Common Pleas (Eng.) |
| Benl. & Dal. | Benloe & Dalison Common Pleas (Eng.) | Black.Jus. | Blackerby's Justices' Cases (Eng.) |
| Benl.K.B. | Benloe's King's Bench (Eng.) | Blackf. | Blackford (Ind.) |
| Benl.Old | Benloe Old English Common Pleas | Blackst.R. | William Blackstone's King's Bench (Eng.) |
| Benn. | Bennett (Cal.) Bennett (Dakota) Bennett (Mo.) | Blackw.Cond. | Blackwell's Condensed Reports (Ill.) |
| | | Blair Co. | Blair County (Pa). |
| Bent. | Bentley's Chancery (Ir.) | Blake | Blake (Mont.) |
| Berry | Berry (Mo.) | Blake & H. | Blake & Hedge (Mont.) |
| Bibb | Bibb (Ky.) | | |
| Bibl.Cott. | Cotton MSS. | Bland | Bland's Chancery (Md.) |
| Bick. | Bicknell (Nev.) | Blatchf. | Blatchford (U.S.) |
| Bick. & H. | Bickness & Hawley (Nev.) | Blatchf. & H. | Blatchford & Howland (U.S. District Court) |
| Big.Ov.Cas. | Bigelow's Overruled Cases | Blatchf.Prize Cas. | Blatchford's Prize Cases (U.S.) |
| | | Bleckley | Bleckley (Ga.) |
| Bill of Rights J. | Bill of Rights Journal | Bli. | Bligh House of Lords (Eng.) |

| | | | |
|---|---|---|---|
| Bli. (N.S.) | Same, New Series | Brantly | Brantly (Md.) |
| Bligh | Same | Brayt. | Brayton (Vt.) |
| Bligh (N.S.) | Same, New Series | Breese | Breese (Ill.) |
| Bliss | Bliss Delaware County (Pa.) | Brev. | Brevard (S.C.) |
| | | Brew. | Brewer (Md.) |
| Blue Sky L.Rep. | Blue Sky Law Reporter (CCH) | | Brewster (Pa.) |
| | | Brews. | Brewster (Pa.) |
| Bluett | Bluett's Isle of Man Cases | Bridg. | J. Bridgmore, Common Pleas (Eng.) |
| Bond | Bond (U.S.) | | |
| Book of Judg. | Book of Judgments (Eng.) | Bridg.J. | Sir J. Bridgman, Common Pleas (Eng.) |
| Boor. | Booraem (Calif.) | | |
| Bos. | Bosworth, Superior Court (N.Y.) | Bridg.O. | Sir Orlando Bridgman, Common Pleas (Eng.) |
| Bos. & P. | Bosanquet & Puller, Common Pleas (Eng.) | | |
| | | Brief | The Brief |
| Bos. & P.N.R. | Bosanquet & Puller's New Reports Common Pleas (Eng.) | Brightly | Brightly (Pa.) |
| | | Brightly El. Cas. | Brightly's Leading Election Cases (Pa.) |
| Bos. & Pul. | Bosanquet & Puller, Common Pleas (Eng.) | Brisb. | Brisbin (Minn.) |
| Bos.Pol.Rep. | Boston Police Reports | Brit.J. Criminol. | British Journal of Criminology |
| Bost.L.R. | Boston Law Reporter | Brit.Cr.Cas. | British Crown Cases |
| Boston B.J. | Boston Bar Journal | Brit.Tax Rev. | British Tax Review |
| Bosw. | Bosworth, Superior Court (N.Y.) | Brit.Y.B. Int'l L. | British Year Book of International Law |
| | Boswell (Sc.) | | |
| Bott Poor Law Cas. | Bott's Poor Laws Settlement Cases (Eng.) | Bro. & F. | Broderick & Freemantle's Ecclesiastical (Eng.) |
| Bott's Set. Cas. | Same | Bro. & Fr. | Same |
| Bould. | Bouldin (Ala.) | Bro. & Lush. | Browning & Lushington's Admiralty (Eng.) |
| Bouv. | Bouvier Law Dictionary | Br.Eccl | Brown's Ecclesiastical (Eng.) |
| Bov.Pat.Cas. | Bovill's Patent Cases | | |
| Boyce | Boyce (Del.) | Bro.Just. | Brown's Justiciary (Sc.) |
| Br. & B. | Broderip & Bingham, Common Pleas (Eng.) | Brock. | Brockenbrough (U.S.) |
| | | Brock. & Hol. Cas. | Brockenbrough & Holmes Cases (Va.) |
| Br. & Col. | British & Colonial Prize Cases | Brock.Cas. | Brockenbrough's Cases (Va.) |
| Br. & F.Ecc. | Broderick & Freemantle's Ecclesiastical Cases (Eng.) | Brod. & F.Ecc. Cas. | Broderick & Freemantle's Ecclesiastical Cases (Eng.) |
| Br. & Gold. | Brownlow & Goldesborough's Common Pleas (Eng.) | Brod. & Fr. Ecc.Cas. | Same |
| | | Brodix Am. & El.Pat.Cas. | Brodix American & English Patent Cases |
| Br. & L. | Brownlow & Lushington's Admiralty Cases (Eng.) | Brook Abr. | Brook's Abridgment (Eng.) |
| Br. & Lush. | Same | Brooklyn L.Rev. | Brooklyn Law Review |
| Br.N.C. | Brooks New Cases, King's Bench (Eng.) | Brook N.Cas. | Brook's New Cases, King's Bench (Eng.) |
| Br.N.Cas. | Same | | |
| Bract. | Bracton De Legibus et consuetudinibus Angliae (Eng.) | Brooks | Brooks (Mich.) |
| | | Brown | Brown (Miss.) |
| Bradf. | Bradford (Iowa) | | Brown (Mo.) |
| Bradf.Surr. | Bradford's Surrogate Court (N.Y.) | | Brown (Neb.) |
| Bradl. | Bradley (R.I.) | Brown & MacN. | Brown & MacNamara, Railway Cases (Eng.) |
| Bradw. | Bradwell (Ill.) | | |
| Brame | Brame (Miss.) | | |
| Branch | Branch (Fla.) | Brown & R. | Brown & Rader (Mo.) |

| | | | |
|---|---|---|---|
| Brown A. & R. | Brown's United States District Court Admiralty & Revenue Cases | Buck.Dec. | Buckner's Decisions (Freeman's Chancery) (Miss.) |
| Brown Adm. | Brown's Admiralty (U.S.) | Buffalo L.Rev. | Buffalo Law Review |
| Brown Ch. | Brown's Chancery (Eng.) | Bull. | Weekly Law Bulletin |
| Brown Dict. | Brown's Law Dictionary | Bull. | |
| Brown Ecc. | Brown's Ecclesiastical (Eng.) | Bull. Copyright Soc'y | Bulletin of the Copyright Society of the U.S.A. |
| Brown N.P. | Brown's Nisi Prius (Mich.) | Buller N.P. | Buller's Nisi Prius (Eng.) |
| Brown Parl. Cas. | Brown's House of Lords Cases (Eng.) | Bulstr. | Bulstrode (London) King's Bench (Eng.) |
| Brown P.C. | Same | | |
| Brown. & L. | Browning & Lushington, Admiralty (Eng.) | Bunb. | Bunbury Exchequer (Eng.) |
| Browne | Browne (Mass.) | Burf. | Burford (Okla.) |
| | Browne Common Pleas (Pa.) | Burgess | Burgess (Ohio) |
| | | Burk | Burk (Va.) |
| Browne & G. | Browne & Gray (Mass.) | Burlesque Rep. | Skillman's New York Police Reports |
| Browne & H. | Browne & Hemingway (Miss.) | Burnett | Burnett (Ore.) |
| Browne Bank Cas. | Browne's National Bank Cases | | Burnett (Wis.) |
| Brownl. & G. | Brownlow & Goldesborough, Common Pleas (Eng.) | Burr. | Burrow, King's Bench (Eng.) |
| Bruce | Bruce (Sc.) | Burr.S.Cases | Burrow's Settlement Cases (Eng.) |
| Brunn.Coll. Cas. | Brunner's Collected Cases (U.S.) | Burr.t.M. | Burrow's Reports, temp. Mansfield (Eng.) |
| Bt. | Benedicts (U.S.) | | |
| Buck | Buck Bankrupt Cases (Eng.) | Bus.Law. | The Business Lawyer |
| | Buck (Mont.) | Busb.Eq. | Busby Equity (N.C.) |
| Buck. | Bucknill's Cooke's Cases of Practice Common Pleas (Eng.) | Busb.L. | Busbee Law (N.C.) |
| | | Bush | Bush (Ky.) |
| | | Buxton | Buxton (N.C.) |

# C

| | | | |
|---|---|---|---|
| C. | Cowen (N.Y.) | C. & E. | Cababe & Ellis Queen's Bench (Eng.) |
| C. & A. | Cooke & Alcock King's Bench and Exchequer (Ir.) | C. & F. | Clark & Finnelly House of Lords (Eng.) |
| C. & C. | Case and Comment | C. & J. | Crompton & Jervis Exchequer (Eng.) |
| | Colemand & Caines Cases (N.Y.) | C. & K. | Carrington & Kirwan Nisi Prius (Eng.) |
| C. & D. | Corbett & Daniel's Election Cases (Eng.) | C. & L. | Connor & Lawson's Chancery (Ir.) |
| | Crawford & Dix's Abridged Cases (Ir.) | C. & L.C.C. | Caines & Leigh Crown Cases (Eng.) |
| C. & D.A.C. | Crawford & Dix's Abridged Cases (Ir.) | C. & M. | Carrington & Marshman's Nisi Prius (Eng.) |
| C. & D.C.C. | Crawford & Dix's Circuit Cases (Ir.) | | Crompton & Meeson's Exchequer (Eng.) |
| | Crawford & Dix's Criminal Cases (Ir.) | C. & Marsh. | Carrington & Marshman's Nisi Prius (Eng.) |

| | |
|---|---|
| C. & N. | Cameron & Norwood's North Carolina Conference |
| C. & P. | Carrington & Payne's Nisi Prius (Eng.) |
| | Craig & Phillips Chancery (Eng.) |
| C. & R. | Cockburn & Rowe's Election Cases |
| C. & S. | Clarke & Scully's Drainage Cases (Ont.) |
| C.A.A. | Civil Aeronautics Authority Reports |
| C.A.B. | Civil Aeronautics Board Reports |
| C.A.D. | Customs Appeals Decisions |
| C.B. | Cumulative Bulletin (Internal Revenue) |
| | Common Bench (Manning, Granger & Scott) (Eng.) |
| C.B. (N.S.) | Common Bench (Manning, Granger & Scott), New Series (Eng.) |
| C.B.R. | Canadian Bankruptcy Reports |
| C.C. | Ohio Circuit Court Reports |
| C.C. (N.S.) | Ohio Circuit Court Reports, New Series |
| C.C.A. | Circuit Court of Appeals (U.S.) |
| C.C.C. | Canadian Criminal Cases, 1893–1962 |
| [  ] C.C.C. | Canadian Criminal Cases, 1963– |
| CCF | Federal Contract Cases, CCH |
| CCH | Commerce Clearing House |
| CCH Atom. En.L.Rep. | Atomic Energy Law Reporter (CCH) |
| CCH Comm. Mkt.Rep. | Common Market Reporter (CCH) |
| CCH Fed. Banking L. Rep. | Federal Banking Law Reporter (CCH) |
| CCH Fed.Sec. L.Rep. | Federal Securities Law Reporter (CCH) |
| CCH Inh.Est. & Gift Tax Rep. | Inheritance, Estate, and Gift Tax Reporter (CCH) |
| CCH Lab.Arb. Awards | Labor Arbitration Awards (CCH) |
| CCH Lab.Cas. | Labor Cases (CCH) |
| CCH Lab.L. Rep. | Labor Law Reporter (CCH) |
| CCH Stand. Fed.Tax Rep. | Standard Federal Tax Reporter (CCH) |
| CCH State Tax Cas. Rep. | State Tax Cases Reporter (CCH) |
| CCH State Tax Rev. | State Tax Review (CCH) |
| CCH Tax Ct.Mem. | Tax Court Memorandum Decisions (CCH) |
| CCH Tax Ct.Rep. | Tax Court Reporter (CCH) |
| C.C.P.A. | Court of Customs & Patent Appeals (U.S.) |
| | Court of Customs & Patent Appeals Reports |
| C.C.Supp. | City Court Reports Supplement (N.Y.) |
| C.D. | U. S. Customs Court Decisions |
| | Commissioner of Patents |
| | Ohio Circuit Decisions |
| C.E.Gr. | C. E. Greene's Equity (N.J.) |
| C.E.Greene | Same |
| C.F.R. | Code of Federal Regulations |
| C.J. | Corpus Juris |
| C.J.Ann. | Corpus Juris Annotations |
| C.J.S. | Corpus Juris Secundum |
| C.L.Chambers | Chambers' Common Law (Upper Can.) |
| C.L.L.C. | Canadian Labour Law Cases |
| C.L.R. | Common Law Reports (Eng.) |
| | Common Law Reports (Aust.) |
| C.L.Rec. | Cleveland Law Record |
| C.L.Reg. | Cleveland Law Register |
| C.L.Rep. | Cleveland Law Reporter |
| C.M. & R. | Crompton, Meeson & Roscoe Exchequer (Eng.) |
| C.M.R. | Court-Martial Reports |
| C.M.R. (Air Force) | Court-Martial Reports of the Judge Advocate General of the Air Force |
| C.P.Coop. | C. P. Cooper Chancery (Eng.) |
| C.P.D. | Law Reports Common Pleas Division (Eng.) (1865–1880) |
| C.P.R. | Canadian Patent Reporter |
| C.P.Rep. | Common Pleas Reporter (Pa.) |
| C.R. | Criminal Reports (Canada) |
| C.R.A.C. | Canadian Reports, Appeal Cases |
| C.R.C. | Canadian Railway Cases |
| C.R.T.C. | Canadian Railway & Transport Cases |
| C.Rob. | Christopher Robinson's Admiralty (Eng.) |

| | | | |
|---|---|---|---|
| C.S.C.R. | Cincinnati Superior Court Reporter | Cam. & N. | Cameron & Norwood's Conference (N.C.) |
| C.S.T. | Capital Stock Tax Division (I.R.Bull.) | Cam.Cas. | Cameron's Cases (Can.) |
| | | Camb.L.J. | Cambridge Law Journal |
| C.T. | Carriers Taxing Ruling (I.R.Bull.) | Cameron | Cameron's Supreme Court Cases |
| [ ] C.T.C. | Canada Tax Cases | Cameron Pr. | Cameron's Practice (Can.) |
| C.W.Dud. | C. W. Dudley's Law or Equity (S.C.) | Camp | Camp (N.D.) |
| C.W.Dudl.Eq. | C. W. Dudley's Equity (S.C.) | Campb. | Campbell (Neb.) |
| | | | Campbell's Nisi Prius (Eng.) |
| Cab. & E. | Cababe & Ellis Queen's Bench (Eng.) | Campb.L.G. | Campbell's Legal Gazette (Pa.) |
| Cahiers | Les Cahiers de Droit | Can.App.Cas. | Canadian Appeal Cases |
| Cai. | Caines (N.Y.) | Can.B.A.J. | Canadian Bar Association Journal |
| Cai.Cas. | Caines' Cases | | |
| Cai.R. | Caines' Reports | Can.B.J. | Canadian Bar Journal |
| Cal. | California | Can.B.R. | Canadian Bar Review |
| Cal.2d | California, Second Series | Can.B.Rev. | Same |
| Cal.App. | California Appellate | Can.Bankr. Ann. | Canadian Bankruptcy Reports Annotated |
| Cal.App.2d | California Appellate, Second Series | Can.Bankr. Ann. (N.S.) | Same, New Series |
| Cal.App.Dec. | California Appellate Decisions | Can.Com.R. | Canadian Commercial Law Reports |
| Cal.Dec. | California Decisions | Can.Cr.Cas. | Canadian Criminal Cases |
| Cal.Ind.Acci. Dec. | California Industrial Accidents Decision | Can.Crim. | Criminal Reports (Can.) |
| Cal.Jur. | California Jurisprudence | Can.Crim. Cas. (N.S.) | Canadian Criminal Cases, New Series |
| Cal.Jur.2d | California Jurisprudence, Second Edition | Can.Crim. Cas.Ann. | Canadian Crimnial Cases Annotated |
| Cal.Leg.Rec. | California Legal Record | Can.Exch. | Canadian Exchequer |
| Cal.Prac. | California Practice | Can.J. Correction | Canadian Journal of Correction |
| Cal.Rptr. | California Reporter (West) | Can.L.J. | Canada Law Journal |
| Cal.S.B.J. | California State Bar Journal | Can.L.J. (N.S.) | Same, New Series |
| Cal.Unrep. Cas. | California Unreported Cases | Can.L.T.Occ. N. | Canadian Law Times Occasional Notes |
| Calcutta W.N. | Calcutta Weekly Notes | Can.Mun.J. | Canadian Municipal Journal |
| Cald. | Caldecott's Magistrate's and Settlement Cases (Eng.) | Can.R.Cas. | Canadian Railway Cases |
| | | Can.Ry.Cas. | Same |
| | Caldwell (W.Va.) | Can.S.C. | Canada Supreme Court |
| Cald.J.P. | Caldecott's Magistrate's and Settlement Cases (Eng.) | Can.S.Ct. | Canada Supreme Court Reports |
| Cald.M.Cas. | Same | Can.Tax App.Bd. | Canada Tax Appeal Board Cases |
| Cald.Mag.Cas. | Same | Cas.Tax Cas.Ann. | Canada Tax Cases Annotated |
| Cald.S.C. | Same | | |
| Cald.Sett.Cas. | Same | Cane & L. | Cane & Leigh's Crown Cases Reserved (Eng.) |
| Calif.L.Rev. | California Law Review | | |
| Calif.W.Int'l L.J. | California Western International Law Journal | Car. & K. | Carrington & Kirwan, Nisi Prius (Eng.) |
| Calif.Western L.Rev. | California Western Law Review | Car. & P. | Carrington & Payne, Nisi Prius (Eng.) |
| Call | Call (Va.) | Car.H. & A. | Carrow, Hamerton & Allen (Eng.) |
| Calthr. | Calthrop (Eng.) | Carp. | Carpenter (Cal.) |
| Cam. | Cameron's Privy Council Decisions | Carp.P.C. | Carpmael Patent Cases (Eng.) |

| | | | |
|---|---|---|---|
| Cart.B.N.A. | Cartwright's Constitutional Cases (Can.) | Ch.R. | Upper Canada Chambers Reports |
| Carter | Carter (Ind.) | Ch.R.M. | R. M. Charlton (Ga.) |
| | Carter Common Pleas (Eng.) | Ch.Rep. | Chancery Reports (Eng.) |
| Carth. | Carthew King's Bench (Eng.) | | Chancery Reports (Ir.) |
| Cartwr.Cas. | Cartwright's Cases (Can.) | Ch.Sent. | Chancery Sentinel (N.Y.) |
| Cary | Cary Chancery (Eng.) | Ch.T.U.P. | T.U.P. Charlton (Ga.) |
| Cas.C.L. | Cases in Crown Law (Eng.) | Cha.App. | Chancery Appeal Cases English Law Reports |
| Cas.t.Hardw. | Cases temp. Hardwicke King's Bench (Eng.) | Chamb.Rep. | Chancery Chambers (Ont.) |
| Cas.t.Holt | Cases temp. Holt, King's Bench (Eng.) | Chandl. | Chandler (N.H.) |
| | | | Chandler (Wis.) |
| Cas.t.King | Cases temp. King, Chancery (Eng.) | Chaney | Chaney (Mich.) |
| | | Charley Pr. Cas. | Charley's Practice Cases (Eng.) |
| Cas.t.Northington | Cases temp. Northington, Chancery Reports (Eng.) | Charlt. | Charlton, R.M. (Ga.) |
| | | | Charlton, T.U.P. (Ga.) |
| | | Chase | Chase (U.S.) |
| Cas.t.Talb. | Cases temp. Talbot, Chancery (Eng.) | Chest.Co. | Chester County (Pa.) |
| | | Chev.Ch. | Cheve's Chancery (S.C.) |
| Cas.t.Wm. III | Cases temp. William III (Eng.) | Chev.Eq. | Same |
| | | Cheves | Cheves Law (S.C.) |
| Cas.Tak. & Adj. | Cases Taken and Adjudged (Reports in Chancery, First Edition) (Eng.) | Chi.-Kent L.Rev. | Chicago-Kent Law Review |
| | | Chi.Leg.N. | Chicago Legal News (Ill.) |
| Case & Com. | Case & Comment | Chic.L.T. | Chicago Law Times |
| Case W.Res.J. Int'l L. | Case Western Reserve Journal of International Law | Chicago L.B. | Chicago Law Bulletin |
| | | Chicago L.J. | Chicago Law Journal |
| | | Chicago L.Rec. | Chicago Law Record |
| | | Chip. | Chipman (N.Bruns.) |
| Case W.Res. L.Rev. | Case Western Reserve Law Review | | Chipman (Vt.) |
| Casey | Casey (Pa.) | Chit. | Chitty's Bail Court (Eng.) |
| Cass.Prac. Cas. | Cassels' Practice Cases (Can.) | Chit.B.C. | Same |
| | | Chitt. | Same |
| Cass.S.C. | Cassels' Supreme Court Decisions | Choyce Cas.Ch. | Choyce's Cases in Chancery (Eng.) |
| Cates | Cates (Tenn.) | Chr.Rep. | Chamber Reports (Upper Can.) |
| Catholic Law. | The Catholic Lawyer | Chr.Rob. | Christopher Robinson's Admiralty (Eng.) |
| Catholic U.L. Rev. | Catholic University of America Law Review | Chy.Chrs. | Upper Canada Chancery Chambers Reports |
| Cent.Dig. | Century Digest | Cin.L.Rev. | Cincinnati Law Review |
| Centr.L.J. | Central Law Journal | Cin.Law Bull. | Weekly Law Bulletin (Ohio) |
| Ch. | Law Reports, Chancery (Eng.) | Cin.Mun.Dec. | Cincinnati Municipal Decisions |
| | Law Reports Chancery Division, Third Series | Cin.R. | Cincinnati Superior Court Reporter |
| Ch.Cal. | Calendar of Proceedings in Chancery (Eng.) | Cin.S.C.R. | Same |
| Ch.Cas. | Cases in Chancery (Eng.) | Cin.S.C.Rep. | Same |
| Ch.Chamb. | Chancery Chambers (Upper Can.) | Cinc.L.Bul. | Same |
| | | Cinc.Sup.Ct. Rep. | Same |
| Ch.Col.Op. | Chalmer's Colonial Opinions | | |
| Ch.D. | Law Reports, Chancery Division (Eng.) | Cincinnati Law Bull. | Weekly Law Bulletin (Ohio) |
| Ch.D.2d | Same, Second Series | Cir.Ct.Dec. | Ohio Circuit Court Decisions |
| Ch.Prec. | Precedents in Chancery | | |

| | | | |
|---|---|---|---|
| City Ct.R. | City Court Reports (N.Y.) | Co.Ct.Rep. | Pennsylvania County Court Reports |
| City Ct.R. Supp. | City Court Reports Supplements (N.Y.) | Co.Inst. | Coke's Institutes (Eng.) |
| City Hall Rec. | City Hall Recorder (N.Y.) | Co.Litt. | Coke on Littleton (Eng.) |
| City Hall Rep. | City Hall Reporter, Lomas (N.Y.) | Co.Mass.Pr. | Colby Mass. Practice |
| | | Co.P.C. | Coke Pleas of the Crown (Eng.) |
| Civ.Lib.Dock. | Civil Liberties Docket | | |
| Civ.Lib.Rptr. | Civil Liberties Reporter | Cobb | Cobb (Ala.) |
| Civ.Proc.R. | Civil Procedure Reports (N.Y.) | | Cobb (Ga.) |
| | | Cochr. | Cochran (Nova Scotia) |
| Cl. & F. | Clark & Finnelly, House of Lords (Eng.) | | Cochrane (N.D.) |
| Clark | Clark (Ala.) | Cockb. & R. | Cockburn & Rowe's Election Cases (Eng.) |
| | Clark (Pa.) | | |
| Clark & F. | Clark & Finnelly, House of Lords (Eng.) | Cocke | Cocke (Ala.) |
| | | | Cocke (Fla.) |
| Clark & F. (N.S.) | Same, New Series | Code Rep. | Code Reporter (N.Y.) |
| | | Code Rep. (N.S.) | Code Reporter, New Series (N.Y.) |
| Clark App. | Clark Appeal Cases House of Lords (Eng.) | Coff.Prob. | Coffey's Probate (Cal.) |
| | | Coke | Coke King's Bench (Eng.) |
| Clark Col.Law | Clark Colonial Law | Col. | Coleman (Ala.) |
| Clarke | Clarke (Iowa) | Col. & C.Cas. | Coleman & Caine's Cases (N.Y.) |
| | Clarke (Mich.) | | |
| Clarke & S. Dr.Cas. | Clarke & Scully's Drainage Cases (Ont.) | Col.Cas. | Coleman's Cases (N.Y.) |
| | | Col.L.Rev. | Columbia Law Review |
| Clarke Ch. | Clarke Chancery (N.Y.) | Cold. | Coldwell |
| Clayt. | Clayton's Reports York Assizes (Eng.) | Coldw. | Coldwell (Tenn.) |
| | | Cole | Cole (Ala.) |
| Clemens | Clemens (Kan.) | | Cole (Iowa) |
| Clev.Bar Ass'n J. | Cleveland Bar Association Journal | Cole. & Cai. Cas. | Coleman & Caines' Cases |
| Clev.St. L.Rev. | Cleveland State Law Review | Cole.Cas. | Coleman's Cases |
| | | Coll. | Collyer's Chancery (Eng.) |
| Cleve.L.Rec. | Cleveland Law Record (Ohio) | Coll. & E. Bank. | Collier's & Eaton's American Bankruptcy Reports |
| Cleve.L.Reg. | Cleveland Law Register (Ohio) | Colles | Colles Cases in Parliament (Eng.) |
| Cleve.L.Rep. | Cleveland Law Reporter (Ohio) | Colo. | Colorado |
| Cleve.Law R. | Cleveland Law Reporter (Ohio) | Colo.App. | Colorado Appeals |
| | | Colo.Law Rep. | Colorado Law Reporter |
| Cleve.Law Rec. | Cleveland Law Record (Ohio) | Coltm. | Coltman Registration Appeal Cases (Eng.) |
| Cleve.Law Reg. | Cleveland Law Register (Ohio) | Colq. | Colquit (Modern) (Eng.) |
| Clev.-Mar.L. Rev. | Cleveland-Marshall Law Review | Colum. Human Rights L.Rev. | Columbia Human Rights Law Review |
| Cliff. | Clifford (U.S.) | | |
| Clif.South.El. Cas. | Clifford, Southwick Election Cases | Colum.J. Transnat'l Law | Columbia Journal of Transnational Law |
| Clk's Mag. | Clerk's Magazine (London) | Colum.L.Rev. | Columbia Law Review |
| | Clerk's Magazine (R.I.) | Colum.Soc'y Int'l L.Bull. | Columbia Society of International Law Bulletin |
| | Clerk's Magazine (Upper Can.) | Colum. Survey Human Rights L. | Columbia Survey of Human Rights Law |
| Co.Ct.Cas. | County Court Cases (Eng.) | | |
| Co.Ct.Ch. | County Court Chronicle (Eng.) | | |

| | | | |
|---|---|---|---|
| Com. & Mun. L.Rep. | Commercial & Municipal Law Reporter | Convey. (N.S.) | Conveyancer & Property Lawyer, New Series |
| Com.**B.** | Common Bench (Manning, Granger & Scott) (Eng.) | Cook Vice-Adm. | Cook's Vice-Admiralty (Lower Can.) |
| Com.Cas. | Commercial Cases Since 1895 (Eng.) | Cooke | Cooke Cases of Practice, Common Pleas (Eng.) |
| Com.Dec. | Commissioners' Decisions (Patent) | | Cooke (Tenn.) |
| Com.L. | Commercial Law (Can.) | Cooke & A. | Cooke & Alcock King's Bench (Ir.) |
| Com.L.J. | Commercial Law Journal | Cooley | Cooley (Mich.) |
| Com.P.Reptr. | Common Pleas Reporter (Scranton) | Coop. | Cooper (Fla.) |
| Comb. | Comberbach, King's Bench (Eng.) | | Cooper's Chancery (Eng.) |
| | | | Cooper's Chancery (Tenn.) |
| Comb.B. (N.S.) | Common Bench (Manning, Granger & Scott) (Eng.) | Coop.C. & P. R. | Cooper's Chancery Practice Reporter (U.S.) |
| Comm.Mkt. L.R. | Common Market Law Reports | Coop.Pr.Cas. | Cooper's Practice Cases (Eng.) |
| Comm.Mkt. L.Rev. | Common Market Law Review | Coop.t.Brough. | Cooper's Cases temp. Brougham Chancery (Eng.) |
| Commw.Arb. | Commonwealth Arbitration Reports | Coop.t.Cott. | Cooper's Cases temp. Cottenham Chancery (Eng.) |
| Commw.L.R. | Commonwealth Law Reports | Coop.t.Eldon | Cooper's Reports temp. Eldon Chancery (Eng.) |
| Comp. & Int'l L.J.S.Afr. | Comparative and International Law Journal of South Africa | Cope | Cope (Cal.) |
| Comp.Dec. | U. S. Comptroller of Treasury Decisions | Copp Min.Dec. | Copp's Mining Decisions (U.S.) |
| Comp.Gen. | U. S. Comptroller General Decisions | Corb. & D. | Corbett & Daniels Election Cases (Eng.) |
| Comp. Jurid.Rev. | Comparative Juridical Review | Cornell Int'l L.J. | Cornell International Law Journal |
| Comptr.Treas. Dec. | U. S. Comptroller of Treasury Decisions | Cornell L.Q. | Cornell Law Quarterly |
| Comst. | Comstock Appeals (N.Y.) | Cornell L.Rev. | Cornell Law Review |
| Comyns | Comyns King's Bench and Common Pleas (Eng.) | Corp.J. | Corporation Journal |
| | | Corp.Pract. Comment. | Corporate Practice Commentator |
| Comyns Dig. | Comyns Digest (Eng.) | Corp.Reorg. | Corporate Reorganizations |
| Con.B.J. | Connecticut Bar Journal | | |
| Condit. Sale-Chat. Mort.Rep. | Conditional Sale-Chattel Mortgage (CCH) | Corp.Reorg. & Am.Bank. Rev. | Corporate Reorganization & American Bankruptcy Review |
| Conf. | Conference Reports (N.C.) | Coup. | Couper's Justiciary (Sc.) |
| Cong.Dig. | Congressional Digest | Court. & MacL. | Courtenay & MacLean (Sc.) |
| Cong.Rec. | Congressional Record (U.S.) | Coutlea | Coutlea's Supreme Court Cases |
| Conn. | Connecticut | Cow. | Cowen (N.Y.) |
| Conn.B.J. | Connecticut Bar Journal | Cow.Cr. | Cowen's Criminal (N.Y.) |
| Conn.L.Rev. | Connecticut Law Review | Cowp. | Cowper King's Bench (Eng.) |
| Conn.Supp. | Connecticut Supplement | | |
| Conn.Surr. | Connolly's Surrogate (N.Y.) | Cowp.Cas. | Cowper's Cases (Chancery) (Eng.) |
| Conov. | Conover (Wis.) | Cox | Cox (Ark.) |
| Const. | Constitution | Cox & Atk. | Cox & Atkinson Registration Appeals (Eng.) |
| Const.Rep. | Constitutional Reports (S.C). | Cox Am.T. Cas. | Cox's American Trademark Cases |
| Convey. | Conveyancer | | |

| | | | |
|---|---|---|---|
| Cox C.C. | Cox's Criminal Cases (Eng.) | Critch. | Critchfield (Ohio St.) |
| | | Cro. | Croke's King's Bench (Eng.) |
| Cox Ch. | Cox's Chancery (Eng.) | | |
| Cox Crim.Cas. | Cox's Criminal Cases | Cro.Car. | Croke temp. Charles I (Eng.) |
| Cox Eq. | Cox's Equity | | |
| Cox J.S.Cas. | Cox's Joint Stock Cases (Eng.) | Cro.Eliz. | Croke temp. Elizabeth (Eng.) |
| | | Cro.Jac. | Croke temp. James I King's Bench (Eng.) |
| Coxe | Coxe (N.J.) | | |
| Cr. & M. | Crompton & Meeson, Exchequer (Eng.) | | |
| | | Cromp. | Star Chamber Cases (Eng.) |
| Cr. & Ph. | Craig & Phillips Chancery (Eng.) | Cromp. & J. | Crompton & Jervis Exchequer (Eng.) |
| Cr.App. | Criminal Appeals (Eng.) | Cromp. & M. | Crompton & Meeson Exchequer (Eng.) |
| Cr.Cas.Res. | Crown Cases Reserved, Law Reports (Eng.) | | |
| | | Cromp.M. & R. | Crompton, Meeson & Roscoe, Exchequer (Eng.) |
| Crabbe | Crabbe (U.S.) | | |
| Craig & Ph. | Craig & Phillips Chancery (Eng.) | Crosw.Pat. Cas. | Croswell's Collection of Patent Cases (U.S.) |
| Cranch | Cranch (U.S.) | | |
| Cranch C.C. | Cranch's Circuit Court (U.S.) | Crounse | Crounse (Neb.) |
| | | Crumrine | Crumrine (Pa.) |
| Cranch Pat. Dec. | Cranch's Patent Decisions (U.S.) | Ct.Cl. | Court of Claims (U.S.) |
| | | Ct.Cust. & Pat.App. | Court of Customs & Patent Appeals |
| Crane | Crane (Mont.) | | |
| Craw. | Crawford (Ark.) | Ct.Cust.App. | Court of Customs Appeals (U.S.) |
| Crawf. & D. Abr.Cas. | Crawford & Dix's Abridged Cases (Ir.) | | |
| | | Ct.Rev. | Court Review |
| | | Cum.Bull. | Cumulative Bulletin |
| Crawf. & Dix | Crawford & Dix Circuit Cases (Ir.) | Cum.-San. L.Rev. | Cumberland-Sanford Law Review |
| | Crawford & Dix Criminal Cases (Ir.) | Cummins | Cummins (Idaho) |
| Creighton L.Rev. | Creighton Law Review | Cunn. | Cunningham King's Bench (Eng.) |
| Crim.App. | Criminal Appeal Reports | Cur.Leg. Thought | Current Legal Thought |
| Crim.App. Rep. | Cohen's Criminal Appeals Reports (Eng.) | | |
| | | Current L. | Current Law |
| Crim.L.Bull. | Criminal Law Bulletin | Current L.Y.B. | Current Law Yearbook |
| Crim.L.Mag. | Criminal Law Magazine (N.J.) | | |
| | | Current Legal Prob. | Current Legal Problems |
| Crim.L.Q. | Criminal Law Quarterly | | |
| Crim.L.Rec. | Criminal Law Recorder | Current Med. | Current Medicine for Attorneys |
| Crim.L.Rep. | Criminal Law Reporter | | |
| Crim.L.Rev. | Criminal Law Review (Manhattan) | Curry | Curry (La.) |
| | | Curt. | Curtis Circuit Court (U.S.) |
| Crim.L.Rev. (Eng.) | Criminal Law Review (Eng.) | Curt.Eccl. | Curtis Ecclesiastical (Eng.) |
| Crim.L.Rptr. | Criminal Law Reporter | | |
| Crim.Rep. (N.S.) | Criminal Reports, New Series | Cush. | Cushing (Mass.) |
| | | Cust.App. | United States Customs Appeals |
| Crime & Delin'cy | Crime & Delinquency | | |
| Criminology | Criminology Croke's King Bench | Cust.Ct. | Custom Court Reports (U.S.) |
| Cripp Ch.Cas. | Cripp's Church & Clergy Cases | Cyc. | Cyclopedia of Law & Procedure |

# D

| | | | |
|---|---|---|---|
| D. | Disney (Ohio) | D.C.Cir. | District of Columbia Court of Appeals Cases |
| | Ohio Decisions | | |
| D. & B. | Dearsley & Bell's Crown Cases (Eng.) | D.Chip. | D. Chipman (Vt.) |
| | | D.Chipm. | Same |
| D. & B.C.C. | Same | D.D.C. | District Court, District of Columbia |
| D. & C. | Dow & Clark's Parliamentary Cases (Eng.) | | |
| | | D.Dec. | Dix's School Decisions (N.Y.) |
| | Deacon & Chitty's Bankruptcy Cases (Eng.) | D.L.R. | Dominion Law Reports (Can.) 1912–1922 |
| D. & Ch. | Same | | |
| D. & Chit. | Same | [ ] D.L.R. | Same, 1923–1955 |
| D. & E. | Dwinford & East's King's Bench Term Reports (Eng.) | D.L.R.2d | Same, Second Series |
| | | D.L.R.3d | Same, Third Series, 1969–present |
| D. & J. | De Gex & Jones' Chancery (Eng.) | D.P.R. | Decisiones de Puerto Rico |
| D. & J.B. | De Gex & Jones Bankruptcy (Eng.) | D.Rep. | Ohio Decisions Reprint |
| | | D.Repr. | Same |
| D. & L. | Dowling & Lowndes Bail Court (Eng.) | D.T.C. | Dominion Tax Cases |
| | | Dak. | Dakota |
| D. & M. | Davison & Merivale's Queen's Bench (Eng.) | Dak.L.Rev. | Dakota Law Review |
| | | Dal.C.P. | Dalison's Common Pleas (Eng.) |
| D. & P. | Denison & Pearce's Crown Cases (Eng.) | | |
| | | Dale | Dale (Okla.) |
| D. & R. | Dowling & Ryland's King's Bench (Eng.) | Dale Ecc. | Dale's Ecclesiastical (Eng.) |
| D. & R.M.C. | Dowling & Ryland's Magistrates' Cases (Eng.) | Dale Eccl. | Same |
| D. & R.Mag. Cas. | Same | Dale Leg.Rit. | Dale's Legal Ritual (Eng.) |
| | | Dall. | Dallam's Decisions |
| D. & R.N.P. | Dowling & Ryland's Nisi Prius Cases (Eng.) | | Dallas (Pa.) |
| | | | Dallas (U.S.) |
| D. & R.N.P.C. | Same | Dall. in Keil. | Dallison in Keilway's King's Bench (Eng.) |
| D. & S. | Drewry & Smale's Chancery (Eng.) | Dalr. | Dalrymple's Decisions (Sc.) |
| | Deane & Swabey's Ecclesiastical (Eng.) | Daly | Daly (N.Y.) |
| D. & Sm. | Drewry & Smale's Chancery (Eng.) | Dan. | Daniell's Exchequer & Equity (Eng.) |
| D. & Sw. | Deane & Swabey Ecclesiastical (Eng.) | Dana | Dana (Ky.) |
| | | Dane Abr. | Dane's Abridgment (Eng.) |
| D. & W. | Drewry & Walsh's Chancery (Ir.) | Dann | Dann (Ariz.) |
| | Drewry & Warren's Chancery (Ir.) | | Dann (Cal.) |
| | | Dann. | Danner (Ala.) |
| D. & War. | Drewry & Warren's Chancery (Ir.) | Dans. & L. | Danson & Lloyd's Mercantile Cases (Eng.) |
| D.B. | Domesday Book | Dans. & Lld. | Same |
| D.B. & M. | Dunlop, Bell & Murray (Sc.) | D'Anv.Abr. | D'Anver's Abridgment (Eng.) |
| D.C. | Treasury Department Circular (I.R.Bull.) | Dass.Ed. | Dassler's Edition, Kansas Reports |
| | District of Columbia | Dauph.Co. | Dauphin County (Pa.) |
| D.C.A. | Dorion's Queen's Bench (Can.) | Dav. & M. | Davison & Merivale Queen's Bench (Eng.) |
| D.C.App. | District of Columbia Appeals | Dav. & Mer. | Same |
| | | Daveis | Daveis (Ware) (U.S.) |
| D.C.B.J. | District of Columbia Bar Journal | Davies or Davis | Davis King's Bench (Ir.) |

| | | | |
|---|---|---|---|
| Davis | Daveis (Ware) (U.S.) | De G.J. & S. | De Gex, Jones & Smith, Chancery (Eng.) |
| | Davis (Hawaii) | De G.M. & G. | De Gex, Macnaughten & |
| | Davis King's Bench (Ir.) | | Gordon, Chancery |
| Davys | Davys King's Bench | | (Eng.) |
| Day | Day (Conn.) | De Gex | De Gex Bankruptcy |
| Dayton | 3 Ohio Miscellaneous Decisions | | (Eng.) |
| Dayton T.R. | Same | Del. | Delaware |
| Dayton Term Rep. | Iddings' Term Reports (Ohio) | Del.Ch. | Delaware Chancery |
| | | Del.Co. | Delaware County (Pa.) |
| Dea. | Deady, U. S. Circuit & District Courts (Cal. & Ore.) | Del.County | Delaware County Reports |
| | | Del.Cr.Cas. | Delaware Criminal Cases |
| | | Dem. | Demarest's Surrogate (N. Y.) |
| Dea. & Chit. | Same | Dem.Surr. | Same |
| Dea. & Sw. | Deane & Swabey's Ecclesiastical (Eng.) | Den. | Denio (N.Y.) |
| | | | Denis (La.) |
| | Deane & Swabey's Probate & Divorce (Eng.) | Den. & P. | Denison & Pearce's Crown Cases (Eng.) |
| Deac. | Deacon, Bankruptcy (Eng.) | Den. & P.C.C. | Same |
| Deac. & C. | Deacon & Chitty, Bankruptcy (Eng.) | Den.C.C. | Denison's Crown Cases (Eng.) |
| Deac. & Chit. | Same | Den.L.J. | Denver Law Journal |
| Deacon & C. | Same | Den.L.N. | Denver Legal News |
| Deacon, Bankr.Cas. | Deacon, Bankruptcy (Eng.) | Denio | Denio (N.Y.) |
| | | Denis | Denis (La.) |
| Deady | Deady, U. S. Circuit and District Courts (Cal. & Ore.) | Denver J. Int'l L. & Policy | Denver Journal of International Law and Policy |
| Deane | Deane (Vt.) | Denver L.J. | Denver Law Journal |
| | Deane (& Swabey's) Probate & Divorce (Eng.) | De Paul L. Rev. | De Paul Law Review |
| Deane & S. Eccl.Rep. | Deane & Swabey's Ecclesiastical (Eng.) | Dept.State Bull. | Department of State Bulletin, United States |
| Deane & Sw. | Same | Des. | Dessaussure's Equity (S. C.) |
| Deane Ecc. | Same | | |
| Deane Ecc. Rep. | Same | Desaus.Eq. | Same |
| Dears. | Dearsley & Bell Crown Cases (Eng.) | Dess. | Same |
| | | Dessaus. | Same |
| Dears. & B. | Same | Det.L.Rev. | Detroit Law Review |
| Dears. & B. C.C. | Same | Det.Leg.N. | Detroit Legal News |
| | | Detroit L.Rev. | Detroit Law Review |
| Dears.C.C. | Same | Dev. | Devereux's Equity (N.C.) |
| Deas & A. | Deas & Anderson (Sc.) | | Devereux's Law (N.C.) |
| Deas & And. | Same | | Devereux's U. S. Court of Claims |
| Dec.Com.Pat. | Decisions of Commissioner of Patents | Dev. & B. | Devereux & Battle's Equity (N.C.) |
| Dec.Dig. | Decennial Digest | | Devereux & Battle's Law (N.C.) |
| Dec.Rep. | Ohio Decisions Reprint | | |
| Dec.U.S. Compt.Gen. | Decisions of U. S. Comptroller General | Dev.Ct.Cl. | Devereux's Court of Claims (U.S.) |
| Decalogue | Decalogue Journal | Dew. | Dewey (Kan.) |
| Defense L.J. | Defense Law Journal | De Witt | De Witt (Ohio) |
| De G. & J. | De Gex & Jones, Chancery (Eng.) | Di. | Dyer's King's Bench (Eng.) |
| De G. & Sm. | De Gex & Smale, Chancery (Eng.) | Dice | Dice (Ind.) |
| | | Dick. | Dickens' Chancery (Eng.) |
| De G.F. & J. | De Gex, Fisher & Jones, Chancery (Eng.) | | Dickinson's Equity (N.J.) |

| | |
|---|---|
| Dick.L.Rev. | Dickinson Law Review |
| Dicta | Dicta of Denver Bar Association |
| Dill. | Dillon, Circuit Court (U.S.) |
| Dirl.Dec. | Direlton's Decisions (Sc.) |
| Disn. | Disney (Ohio) |
| Disney | Same |
| Dod. | Dodson's Admiralty (Eng.) |
| Dod.Adm. | Same |
| Dods. | Same |
| Dom.L.R. | Dominion Law Reports (Can.) |
| Donaker | Donaker (Ind.) |
| Donn. | Donnelly's Chancery (Eng.) |
| | Donnelly's Irish Land Cases |
| Donnelly | Same |
| Dorion | Dorion (Lower Can.) |
| Doug. | Douglas (Mich.) |
| | Douglas' King's Bench (Eng.) |
| Dougl. | Douglas (Mich.) |
| Dougl.El.Cas. | Douglas Election Cases (Eng.) |
| Dougl.K.B. | Douglas' King's Bench (Eng.) |
| Dow | Dow's House of Lords (Parliamentary) Cases (Eng.) |
| Dow. | Dowling's Practice Cases (Eng.) |
| Dow & Cl. | Dow & Clark's House of Lords Cases (Eng.) |
| Dow. & L. | Dowling & Lowndes' Bail Court (Eng.) |
| Dowl. & Lownd. | Dowling & Lowndes' Practice Cases (Eng.) |
| Dowl. & R. | Dowling & Ryland's King's Bench (Eng.) |
| | Dowling & Ryland's Queen's Bench & Magistrates' Cases (Eng.) |
| Dowl.P.C. (N.S.) | Dowling Practice Cases, New Series (Eng.) |
| Dowl.Pr.Cas. | Dowling Practice Cases (Eng.) |

| | |
|---|---|
| Down. & Lud. | Downton & Luder's Election Cases (Eng.) |
| Drake L.Rev. | Drake Law Review |
| Draper | Draper (Upper Can.) |
| Drew | Drew (Fla.) |
| Drew. | Drewry's Chancery (Eng.) |
| Drew. & S. | Drewry & Smale's Chancery (Eng.) |
| Drinkw. | Drinkwater Common Pleas (Eng.) |
| Drug Abuse L.Rev. | Drug Abuse Law Review |
| Drury | Drury's Chancery (Ir.) |
| Dublin U.L. Rev. | Dublin University Law Review |
| Dudl. | Dudley (Ga.) |
| | Dudley's Equity (S.C.) |
| | Dudley's Law (S.C.) |
| Duer | Duer's Superior Court (N Y.) |
| Duke B.A.J. | Duke Bar Association Journal |
| Duke L.J. | Duke Law Journal |
| Duke's Charitable Uses | Duke's Charitable Uses (Eng.) |
| Dunc.Ent.Cas. | Duncan Entail Cases (Sc.) |
| Dunc.N.P. | Duncombe Nisi Prius |
| Dunl. | Dunlop, Bell & Murray (Sc.) |
| Dunl.B. & M. | Same |
| Dunlop | Dunlop (Sc.) |
| Dunn. | Dunning's King's Bench (Eng.) |
| Duquesne U.L.Rev. | Duquesne University Law Review |
| Durf. | Durfee (R.I.) |
| Durfee | Same |
| Durie | Durie (Sc.) |
| Durn. & E. | Durnford & East's King's Bench (Term Reports) (Eng.) |
| Dutch. | Dutcher's Law (N.J.) |
| Duv. | Duval's Supreme Court (Can.) |
| | Duval's Reports (Can.) |
| Dy. | Dyer's King's Bench (Eng.) |
| Dyer | Same |

# E

| | |
|---|---|
| E. | East's King's Bench (Eng.) |
| E. & A. | Spink's Ecclesiastical & Admiralty (Eng.) |
| | Upper Canada Error & Appeal Reports, Grant |
| E. & B. | Ellis & Blackburn's Queen's Bench (Eng.) |

| | |
|---|---|
| E. & E. | Ellis & Ellis' Queen's Bench (Eng.) |
| E. & I. | English & Irish Appeals, House of Lords (Eng.) |
| E.A.S. | Executive Agreement Series, United States |
| E.Afr.L.R. | East Africa Law Reports |

| | | | |
|---|---|---|---|
| E.B. & E. | Ellis, Blackburn & Ellis' Queen's Bench (Eng.) | Edw.Adm. | Edward's Admiralty (Eng.) |
| E.B. & S. | Ellis, Best & Smith's Queen's Bench (Eng.) | Edw.Ch. | Edward's Chancery (N.Y.) |
| E.C. | English Chancery | Edw.Lead.Dec. | Edward's Leading Decisions in Admiralty |
| E.C.L. | English Common Law | | |
| E.D.S. | E. D. Smith (N.Y.) | Edw.Pr.Cas. | Edward's Prize Cases (Eng.Admiralty) |
| E.D.Smith | Same | | |
| E.E. | English Exchequer | Edw.Pr.Ct. Cas. | Edward's Prerogative Court Cases |
| E.E.R. | English Ecclesiastical Reports | Efird | Efird (S.C.) |
| E.G.L. | Encyclopedia of Georgia Law | El. | Elchie's Decisions (Sc.) |
| | | El. & B. | Ellis & Blackburn's Queen's Bench (Eng.) |
| E.L. & Eq. | English Law & Equity Reports | El. & Bl. | Same |
| E.L.R. | Eastern Law Reporter (Can.) | El. & El. | Ellis & Ellis, Queen's Bench (Eng.) |
| E.R. | East's King's Bench (Eng.) | El.B. & E. | Ellis, Blackburn & Ellis' Queen's Bench (Eng.) |
| E.R.C. | English Ruling Cases | El.B. & El. | Same |
| | Environmental Reporter Cases | El.B. & S. | Ellis, Best & Smith's Queen's Bench (Eng.) |
| E.School L.Rev. | Eastern School Law Review | El.Bl. & El. | Ellis, Blackburn & Ellis' Queen's Bench (Eng.) |
| E.T. | Estate Tax Division (I.R. Bull.) | El.Cas. | Election Cases |
| | | Elchies' | Elchies' Decisions (Sc.) |
| Ea. | East's King's Bench (Eng.) | Elect.Cas. (N.Y.) | Election Cases, Armstrong, New York |
| Eag. & Y. | Eagle & Young's Tithe Cases (Eng.) | Elect.Rep. | Election Reports, Ontario |
| Eag.T. | Eagle's Commutation of Tithes (Eng.) | Ell. & Bl. | Ellis & Blackburn's Queen's Bench (Eng.) |
| East | East's King's Bench (Eng.) | Ell.Bl. & Ell. | Ellis, Blackburn & Ellis' Queen's Bench (Eng.) |
| | Eastern Reporter (U.S.) | Els.W.Bl. | Elsley's Edition of Wm. Blackstone's King's Bench (Eng.) |
| East P.C. | East's Pleas of the Crown (Eng.) | Em.App. | Emergency Court of Appeals (U.S.) |
| East.L.R. | Eastern Law Reporter (Can.) | Enc.Pl. & Pr. | Encyclopedia of Pleading & Practice |
| East.Rep. | Eastern Reporter (U.S.) | Enc.U.S.Sup. Ct.Rep. | Encyclopedia of United States Supreme Court Reports |
| East.T. | Eastern Term (Eng.) | | |
| Ebersole | Ebersole (Iowa) | | |
| Eccl. & Adm. | Spink's Ecclesiastical & Admiralty (Upper Can.) | Eng. | English (Ark.) |
| Eccl.R. | Ecclesiastical Reports (Eng.) | Eng.Adm. | English Admiralty |
| | | Eng.Adm.R. | Same |
| Eccl.Rep. | Same | Eng.C.C. | English Crown Cases |
| Ecology L.Q. | Ecology Law Quarterly | Eng.C.L. | English Common-Law Reports |
| Ed. | Eden's Chancery (Eng.) | | |
| Ed.Ch. | Edward's Chancery (N.Y.) | Eng.Ch. | English Chancery Condensed English Chancery |
| Eden | Eden's Chancery (Eng.) | | |
| Edg. | Edgar (Sc.) | Eng.Com.L.R. | English Common-Law Reports |
| Edinb.L.J. | Edinburgh Law Journal | | |
| Edm.Sel.Cas. | Edmond's Select Cases (N.Y.) | Eng.Cr.Cas. | English Crown Cases |
| | | Eng.Ecc.R. | English Ecclesiastical Reports |
| Edw. | Edwards (Mo.) | | |
| | Edward's Chancery (N.Y.) | Eng.Eccl. | Same |
| Edw.Abr. | Edward's Abridgment Privy Council | Eng.Exch. | English Exchequer |
| | | Eng.Hist.Rev. | English Historical Review |
| | Edward's Abridgment Prerogative Court Cases | Eng.Ir.App. | Law Reports English & Irish Appeals |

| | | | |
|---|---|---|---|
| Eng.Judg. | English Judges (Sc.) | Esp. | Espinasse's Nisi Prius (Eng.) |
| Eng.L. & Eq. | English Law & Equity Reports | Esp.N.P. | Same |
| Eng.L. & Eq.R. | Same | Euer | Euer Doctrina Placitandi (Eng.) |
| Eng.Rep. | English Reports, Full Reprint | | |
| Eng.Rep.R. | Same | Europ.T.S. | European Treaty Series |
| Eng.Ry. & C. Cas. | English Railway and Canal Cases | Evans | Evans, Washington Territory Reports |
| Eng.Sc.Ecc. | English & Scotch Ecclesiastical Reports | Ex. | Exchequer Reports (Eng.) |
| Env.L. | Environmental Law | Ex.C.R. | Exchequer Court Reports (Can.) (1923–present) |
| Env.L.Rev. | Environmental Law Review | Ex.D. | Law Reports Exchequer Division (Eng.) (To 1880) |
| Env.L.Rptr. | Environmental Law Reporter | | |
| Eq.Cas.Abr. | Equity Cases Abridged (Eng.) | Ex.Div. | Same |
| Eq.Rep. | Harper's Equity (S.C.) | Exch. | Exchequer (Welsby, Hurlstone & Gordon) (Eng.) |
| Equity Rep. | Equity Reports (Gilbert) (Eng.) | | Exchequer (Sc.) |
| | Harper's Equity (S.C.) | Exch.Can. | Exchequer Reports (Can.) |
| | English Chancery Appeals | Exch.Cas. | Exchequer Cases (Sc.) |
| Err. & App. | Error & Appeals (Upper Can.) | Exch.Rep. | Exchequer Reports |
| | | Exec.Order | Executive Order |
| Ersk. | Erskine (U.S.C.C. in 35 Ga.) | Eyre | Eyre's King's Bench (Eng.) |

# F

| | | | |
|---|---|---|---|
| F. | Federal Reporter (U.S.) | F.Supp. | Federal Supplement |
| F.2d | Same, Second Series | F.T.C. | Federal Trade Commission Decisions |
| F. & F. | Foster & Finlanson Nisi Prius (Eng.) | Fac.L.Rev. | Faculty of Law Review (Toronto) |
| F.A.D. | Federal Anti-Trust Decisions | | |
| | | Fairf. | Fairfield (Me.) |
| F.B.C. | Fonblanque's Bankruptcy Cases (Eng.) | Falc. | Falconer's Court of Sessions Cases (Sc.) |
| FBILEB | F.B.I. Law Enforcement Bull. | Falc. & F. | Falconer & Fitzherbert's Election Cases (Eng.) |
| F.C. | Faculty Collection of Decisions (Sc.) | Family L.Q. | Family Law Quarterly |
| | | Far. | Farresley's King's Bench (Eng.) |
| F.C.A. | Federal Code Annotated | | |
| F.C.C. | Federal Communication Commission Reports | Fed. | Federal Reporter (U.S.) |
| | | Fed.B.A.J. | Federal Bar Association Journal |
| F.Carr.Cas. | Federal Carriers Cases (CCH) | | |
| | | Fed.B.J. | Federal Bar Journal |
| F. (Ct.Sess.) | Fraser's Court of Sessions Cases (Sc.) | Fed.Carr.Rep. | Federal Carriers Reporter (CCH) |
| F.D.Cosm.L. Rep. | Food, Drug, Cosmetic Law Reporter (CCH) | Fed.Cas. | Federal Cases (U.S.) |
| | | Fed.Comm.B.J. | Federal Communications Bar Journal |
| F.H.L. | Fraser, House of Lords (Sc.) | | |
| | | Fed.Est. & Gift Tax Rep. | Federal Estate and Gift Tax Reporter (CCH) |
| F.L.P. | Florida Law and Practice | | |
| F.P.C. | Federal Power Commission Decisions | Fed.Juror | Federal Juror |
| | | Fed.L.Rep. | Federal Law Reports |
| FR | Federal Register | Fed.L.Rev. | Federal Law Review |
| F.R.D. | Federal Rules Decisions | Fed.Reg. | Federal Register |

| | |
|---|---|
| Fed.Rules Serv. | Federal Rules Service |
| Fed.Rules Serv.2d | Same, Second Series |
| Fed'n Ins. Counsel Q. | Federation of Insurance Counsel Quarterly |
| Ferg.Cons. | Fergusson's Consistory (Divorce) (Sc.) |
| Fergusson | Fergusson (of Kilkeran) (Sc.) |
| Finch | Finch's Chancery (Eng.) |
| Fire & Casualty Cas. | Fire and Casualty Cases (CCH) |
| Fish.Pat.Cas. | Fisher's Patent Cases (U.S.) |
| Fish.Pat.R. | Fisher's Patent Reports (U.S.) |
| Fish.Prize Cas. | Fisher's Prize Cases (U.S.) |
| Fitzh. | Fitzherbert's Abridgment (Eng.) |
| Fitzh.N.Br. | Fitzherbert's Natura Brevium (Eng.) |
| Fla. | Florida |
| Fla. & K. | Flanagan & Kelly, Rolls (Ir.) |
| Fla.B.J. | Florida Bar Journal |
| Fla.Jur. | Florida Jurisprudence |
| Fla.L.J. | Florida Law Journal |
| Fla.Supp. | Florida Supplement |
| Flan. & Kel. | Flanagan & Kelly, Rolls (Ir.) |
| Flipp. | Flippin (U.S.) |
| Fogg | Fogg (N.H.) |
| Fonbl. | Fonblanque's Bankruptcy (Eng.) |
| Food Drug Cosm.L.J. | Food, Drug, Cosmetic Law Journal |
| Forbes | Forbes (Sc.) |

| | |
|---|---|
| Ford.L.Rev. | Fordham Law Review |
| Ford.Urban L.J. | Fordham Urban Law Journal |
| Fordham L.Rev. | Fordham Law Review |
| Form. | Forman (Ill.) |
| Forr. | Forrest's Exchequer (Eng.) |
| Forrester | Forrester's Chancery Cases temp. Talbot (Eng.) |
| Fort.L.J. | Fortnightly Law Journal |
| Fortesc. | Fortescue's King's Bench (Eng.) |
| Forum | The Forum |
| Fost. | Foster's Crown Cases (Eng.) |
| | Foster (Hawaii) |
| | Foster's Legal Chronicle Reports (Pa.) |
| | Foster (N.H.) |
| Fount.Dec. | Fountainhall's Decisions (Sc.) |
| Fox | Fox's Registration Cases (Eng.) |
| | Fox's Decisions (Me.) |
| Fox & S. | Fox & Smith's King's Bench (Ir.) |
| Fox Pat.C. | Fox's Patent, Trade Mark, Design and Copyright Cases |
| France | France (Colo.) |
| Fraser | Fraser, Court of Session Cases (Sc.) |
| Freem. | Freeman (Ill.) |
| Freem.Ch. | Freeman's Chancery (Miss.) |
| Freem.K.B. | Freeman's King's Bench (Eng.) |
| French | French (N.H.) |
| Fuller | Fuller (Mich.) |

# G

| | |
|---|---|
| G. & D. | Gale & Davison's Queen's Bench (Eng.) |
| G. & G. | Goldsmith & Guthrie (Mo.) |
| G. & J. | Gill & Johnson (Md.) |
| | Glyn & Jameson's Bankruptcy (Eng.) |
| G. & R. | Geldert & Russell (N.S.) |
| GA | Decisions of General Appraisers (U.S.) |
| G.C.M. | General Counsel's Memorandum (I.R.Bull.) |

| | |
|---|---|
| G.Coop. | G. Cooper's Chancery (Eng.) |
| G.S.R. | Gongwer's State Reports (Ohio) |
| Ga. | Georgia |
| Ga.App. | Georgia Appeals |
| Ga.B.J. | Georgia Bar Journal |
| Ga.Bus.Law. | Georgia Business Lawyer |
| Ga.Dec. | Georgia Decisions |
| Ga.J.Int'l & Comp.L. | Georgia Journal of International & Comparative Law |
| Ga.L.J. | Georgia Law Journal |
| Ga.L.Rep. | Georgia Law Reports |

| | | | |
|---|---|---|---|
| Ga.L.Rev. | Georgia Law Review | Glanv.El.Cas. | Glanville's Election Cases (Eng.) |
| Ga.St.B.J. | Georgia State Bar Journal | Glasc. | Glascock (Ir.) |
| Ga.Supp. | Georgia Supplement (Lester) | Glenn | Glenn (Louisiana Annual) |
| | | Glyn & J. | Glyn & Jameson's Bankruptcy Cases (Eng.) |
| Galb. | Galbraith (Fla.) | | |
| Galb. & M. | Galbraith & Meek (Fla.) | | |
| Gale | Gale's Exchequer (Eng.) | Glyn & Jam. | Same |
| Gale & D. | Gale & Davison's Queen's Bench (Eng.) | Godb. | Godbolt's King's Bench (Eng.) |
| | | Goebel | Goebel's Probate (Ohio) |
| Gale & Dav. | Same | Gold. & G. | Goldsmith & Guthrie (Mo.) |
| Gall. | Gallison (U.S. Circuit Court) | | |
| Gard.N.Y. Reptr. | Gardenier's New York Reporter | Golden Gate L.Rev. | Golden Gate Law Review |
| Garden. | Gardenhire (Mo.) | Gonzaga L.Rev. | Gonzaga Law Review |
| Gaz. | Weekly Law Gazette (U.S.) | Gottschall | Gottschall (Ohio) |
| Gaz.L.R. | Gazette Law Reports | Gouldsb. | Gouldsborough's King's Bench (Eng.) |
| Geld. & M. | Geldart & Maddock's Chancery (Eng.) | Gov't Cont. Rep. | Government Contracts Reporter (CCH) |
| Geld. & O. | Geldert & Oxley (N.S.) | | |
| Geo.L.J. | Georgetown Law Journal | Gow | Gow's Nisi Prius (Eng.) |
| Geo.Wash.L. Rev. | George Washington Law Review | Gr. | Grant, Upper Canada Chancery Reports |
| George | George (Miss.) | Granger | Granger (Ohio) |
| Gibb.Surr. | Gibbon's Surrogate (N.Y.) | Grant | Grant's Cases (Pa.) |
| Gibbs | Gibbs (Mich.) | Grant Err. & App. | Grant's Error & Appeal (Upper Can.) |
| Giff. | Giffard's Chancery (Eng.) | | |
| Giff. & H. | Giffard & Hemming's Chancery (Eng.) | Gratt. | Grattan (Va.) |
| | | Gray | Gray (Mass.) |
| Gil. | Gilman (Ill.) | | Gray (N.C.) |
| Gilb. | Gilbert's Chancery (Eng.) | Green | Green Equity (N.J.) |
| Gilb.C.P. | Gilbert's Common Pleas (Eng.) | | Green Law (N.J.) |
| | | | Green (Okla.) |
| Gilb.Cas. | Gilbert's Cases, Law & Equity (Eng.) | | Green (R.I.) |
| | | Green Cr. | Green's Criminal Law (Eng.) |
| Gilb.Exch. | Gilbert's Exchequer (Eng.) | Greene | Greene (Iowa) |
| Gildr. | Gildersleeve (N.Mex.) | | Greene's Annotated Cases (N.Y.) |
| Gilf. | Gilfillan (Minn.) | | |
| Gill | Gill (Md.) | Greenl. | Greenleaf (Me.) |
| Gill & J. | Gill & Johnson (Md.) | Greenl.Ov.Cas. | Greenleaf's Overruled Cases |
| Gill & Johns. | Same | | |
| Gilm. | Gilmer (Va.) | Grein.Pr. | Greiner Louisiana Practice |
| Gilm. & Falc. | Gilmour & Falconer (Sc.) | Griffith | Griffith (Ind.) |
| Gilp. | Gilpin (U.S.) | Gris. | Griswold (Ohio) |
| Gl. & J. | Glyn & Jameson's Bankruptcy Cases (Eng.) | Griswold | Same |
| | | Guild Prac. | Guild Practitioner |
| Glanv. | Glanville De Legibus et Consuetudinibus Angliae (Eng.) | Guthrie | Guthrie (Mo.) |
| | | Gwill.T.Cas. | Gwillim's Tithe Cases (Eng.) |

# H

| | | | |
|---|---|---|---|
| H. | Handy (Ohio) | | Hale's Common Law (Eng.) |
| H. & B. | Hudson & Brooke's King's Bench (Ir.) | Hale P.C. | Hale's Pleas of the Crown (Eng.) |
| H. & C. | Hurlstone & Coltman's Exchequer (Eng.) | Hall | Hall (N.H.) |
| | | | Hall's Superior Court (N.Y.) |
| H. & D. | Hill & Denio, Lalor's Supplement (N.Y.) | Hall & Tw. | Hall & Twell's Chancery (Eng.) |
| H. & G. | Harris & Gill (Md.) | Hall. | Hallett (Colo.) |
| | Hurlstone & Gordon's Exchequer (Eng.) | Halst. | Halsted's Equity (N.J.) |
| H. & H. | Harrison & Hodgin's Municipal Reports (Upper Can.) | | Halsted's Law (N.J.) |
| | | Ham. | Hammond (Ga.) |
| | Horn & Hurlstone's Exchequer (Eng.) | | Hammond (Ohio) |
| H. & J. | Harris & Johnson (Md.) | Ham. & J. | Hammond & Jackson (Ga.) |
| | Hayes & Jones' Exchequer (Ir.) | Ham.A. & O. | Hamerton, Allen & Otter, New Session Cases (Eng.) |
| H. & J.Ir. | Same | Hamlin | Hamlin (Me.) |
| H. & M. | Hening & Munford (Va.) | Hammond | Hammond (Ohio) |
| | Hemming & Miller's Vice-Chancery (Eng.) | Han. | Handy (Ohio) |
| H. & M.Ch. | Hemming & Miller's Vice-Chancery (Eng.) | Han.N.B. | Hannay's Reports (New Brunswick) |
| H. & McH. | Harris & McHenry (Md.) | Hand | Hand (N.Y.) |
| H. & N. | Hurlstone & Norman's Exchequer (Eng.) | Handy | Handy (Ohio) |
| | | Hans. | Hansbrough (Va.) |
| H. & R. | Harrison & Rutherford's Common Pleas (Eng.) | Har. | Harrington (Del.) |
| | | | Harrington's Chancery (Mich.) |
| H. & S. | Harris & Simrall (Miss.) | | Harrison (La.) |
| H. & T. | Hall & Twell's Chancery (Eng.) | | Harrison's Chancery (Mich.) |
| H. & W. | Harrison & Wollaston's King's Bench (Eng.) | Harc. | Harcarse, Decisions (Sc.) |
| | Hurlstone & Walmsley's Exchequer (Eng.) | Hard. | Hardesty Term Reports (Del.) |
| H.Bl. | Henry Blackstone's Common Pleas (Eng.) | Hardes. | Same |
| | | Hardin | Hardin (Ky.) |
| H.L.Cas. | House of Lords Cases (Eng.) | Hardres | Hardres' Exchequer (Eng.) |
| H.W.Gr. | H. W. Green's Equity (N.J.) | Hare | Hare's Vice-Chancery (Eng.) |
| Ha. | Hare's Vice-Chancery (Eng.) | Hare & W. | American Leading Cases, Hare & Wallace |
| Ha. & Tw. | Hall & Twell's Chancery (Eng.) | Harg. | Hargrove (N.C.) |
| Had. | Hadley (N.H.) | Harp. | Harper's Equity (S.C.) |
| Hadd. | Haddington MSS Reports (Sc.) | | Harper's Law (S.C.) |
| | | Harper | Harper's Conspiracy Cases (Md.) |
| Hadl. | Hadley (N.H.) | Harr. | Harrington |
| Hagan | Hagan (Utah) | Harr. | Harrison (Ind.) |
| Hagans | Hagans (W.Va.) | | Harrison (N.J.) |
| Hagg.Adm. | Haggard's Admiralty (Eng.) | Harr. & H. | Harrison & Hodgins' Municipal Reports (Upper Can.) |
| Hagn. & M. | Hagner & Miller (Md.) | | |
| Hailes Dec. | Haile's Decisions (Sc.) | Harr. & Hodg. | Same |
| Hale | Hale (Cal.) | Harr. & J. | Harris & Johnson (Md.) |

| | | | |
|---|---|---|---|
| Harr. & M. | Harris & McHenry (Md.) | Hempst. | Hempstead (U.S.) |
| Harr. & R. | Harrison & Rutherford's | Hen. & M. | Hening & Munford (Va.) |
| | Common Pleas (Eng.) | Hepb. | Hepburn (Colo.) |
| Harr. & W. | Harrison & Wollaston's | Het. | Hetley's Common Pleas |
| | King's Bench | | (Eng.) |
| | (Eng.) | Hibb. | Hibbard (N.H.) |
| Harr.Ch. | Harrison's Chancery | Hight | Hight (Iowa) |
| | (Eng.) | Hil.T. | Hilary Term (Eng.) |
| Harris | Harris (Pa.) | Hill | Hill (Ill.) |
| Harris & G. | Harris & Gill (Md.) | | Hill (N.Y.) |
| Harris & S. | Harris & Simrall (Miss.) | | Hill's Equity (S.C.) |
| Hart. | Hartley (Tex.) | | Hill's Law (S.C.) |
| Hart. & H. | Hartley & Hartley (Tex.) | Hill & D. | Hill & Denio (N.Y.) |
| Harv.Bus.Rev. | Harvard Business Review | Hillyer | Hillyer (Cal.) |
| Harv.Civ. | Harvard Civil Rights– | Hilt. | Hilton (N.Y.) |
| Rights–Civ. | Civil Liberties Law | Hines | Hines (Ky.) |
| Lib.L.Rev. | Review | Hob. | Hobart's Common Pleas & |
| Harv.Int'l | Harvard International | | Chancery (Eng.) |
| L.J. | Law Journal | Hobart | Hobart's King's |
| Harv.J.Legis. | Harvard Journal on | | Bench (Eng.) |
| | Legislation | Hod. | Hodges' Common Pleas |
| Harv.L.Rev. | Harvard Law Review | | (Eng.) |
| Hasb. | Hasbrouck (Idaho) | Hodg.El. | Hodgin's Election (Upper |
| Hask. | Haskell (U.S. Mine) | | Can.) |
| | (Fox's Decisions) | Hodges | Hodges' Common Pleas |
| Hast. | Hastings (Me.) | | (Eng.) |
| Hastings L.J. | Hastings Law Journal | Hoffm. | Hoffman's Chancery |
| Havil. | Haviland (Prince Edward | | (N.Y.) |
| | Island) | | Hoffman's Land Cases |
| Hawaii | Hawaii Reports | | (U.S.) |
| Hawaii B.J. | Hawaii Bar Journal | Hog. | Hogan's Rolls Court (Ir.) |
| Hawk. | Hawkins' Louisiana | Hogue | Hogue (Fla.) |
| | Annual | Holl. | Hollingshead (Minn.) |
| Hawk.P.C. | Hawkins' Pleas of the | Holmes | Holmes (Ore.) |
| | Crown | | Holmes (U.S.) |
| Hawks | Hawks (N.C.) | Holt Adm. | Holt's Admiralty Cases |
| Hawl. | Hawley (Nev.) | | (Eng.) |
| Hay & H. | Hay & Hazelton (U.S.) | Holt Eq. | Holt's Equity Vice-Chan- |
| Hay & M. | Hay & Marriott's Admiral- | | cery (Eng.) |
| | ty (Eng.) | Holt K.B. | Holt's King's Bench |
| Hay. | Haywood | | (Eng.) |
| Hayes | Hayes' Exchequer (Ir.) | Holt N.P. | Holt's Nisi Prius (Eng.) |
| | Hayes (Sc.) | Home | Home MSS. Decisions, |
| Hayes & J. | Hayes & Jones' Exchequer | | Court of Sessions (Sc.) |
| | (Ir.) | Hook. | Hooker (Conn.) |
| Hayw. | Haywood (N.C.) | Hope Dec. | Hope's Decisions (Sc.) |
| | Haywood (Tenn.) | Hopk. | Hopkins' Chancery (N.Y.) |
| Haz.Reg. | Hazard's Register (Pa.) | Hopk.Dec. | Hopkinson's Admiralty |
| Head | Head (Tenn.) | | Decisions (Pa.) |
| Heath | Heath (Me.) | Hopw. & C. | Hopwood & Coltman's |
| Hedges | Hedges (Mont.) | | Registration Appeal Cas- |
| Heisk. | Heiskell (Tenn.) | | es (Eng.) |
| Helm | Helm (Nev.) | Hopw. & P. | Hopwood & Philbrick's |
| Hem. & M. | Heming & Miller's | | Registration Appeal Cas- |
| | Vice-Chancery | | es (Eng.) |
| | (Eng.) | Horner | Horner (S.D.) |
| Heming. | Hemingway (Miss.) | Horw.Y.B. | (Horwood) Year Book of |
| Hemp. | Hempstead's Circuit | | Edward I |
| | Court Reports | Hosea | Hosea (Ohio) |
| | | Hoskins | Hoskins (N.D.) |

| | | | |
|---|---|---|---|
| Houghton | Houghton (Ala.) | How.St.Tr. | Howell's State Trials (Eng.) |
| Houst. | Houston (Del.) | | |
| Houst.Cr. | Houston Criminal Cases (Del.) | Howard L.J. | Howard Law Journal |
| | | Hubb. | Hubbard (Me.) |
| Houst.L.Rev. | Houston Law Review | Hud. & B. | Hudson & Brooke's King's Bench (Ir.) |
| Hov. | Hovenden's Supplement, Vesey's Chancery (Eng.) | | |
| | | Hughes | Hughes (Ky.) |
| How. | Howard (Miss.) | | Hughes (U.S.) |
| | Howard (U.S. Supreme Court) | Hume | Hume's Decisions (Sc.) |
| | Howell (Nev.) | Humph. | Humphrey |
| How. & Beat. | Howell & Beatty (Nev.) | Humphr. | Humphrey's (Tenn.) |
| How. & N. | Howell & Norcross (Nev.) | | |
| How.A.Cas. | Howard's Appeal Cases (N.Y.) | Hun | Hun (N.Y.) |
| | | Hunt.Torrens | Hunter's Torrens Cases |
| How.Ch. | Howard's Chancery (Ir.) | Hurl. & G. | Hurlstone & Gordon's Exchequer (Eng.) |
| How.L.J. | Howard Law Journal | | |
| How.N.P. | Howell's Nisi Prius (Mich.) | Hurl. & W. | Hurlstone & Walmsley's Exchequer (Eng.) |
| | | Hutch. | Hutcheson (Ala.) |
| How.Pr. | Howard's Practice (N.Y.) | Hutt. | Hutton's Common Pleas (Eng.) |
| How.Pr. (N.S.) | Same, New Series | | |

# I

| | | | |
|---|---|---|---|
| 1. & N.Dec. | Immigration and Nationality Decisions | Idding | Same |
| | | Iddings T.R. D. | Same |
| ICC | Interstate Commerce Commission | | |
| | | Idea | Idea |
| I.C.C.Pract.J. | Interstate Commerce Commission Practitioners' Journal | Ill. | Illinois |
| | | Ill.App. | Illinois Appellate Court |
| | | Ill.App.2d | Same, Second Series |
| I.C.J. | International Court of Justice Reports | Ill.B.J. | Illinois Bar Journal |
| | | Ill.Cir. | Illinois Circuit Court |
| I.C.J.Y.B. | Yearbook of the International Court of Justice | Ill.Cont.L.Ed. | Illinois Continuing Legal Education |
| I.D. | Interior Department Decisions, Public Land (Since v. 53) | Ill.Cont. Legal Ed. | Same |
| I.L.E. | Indiana Law Encyclopedia | Ill.Ct.Cl. | Illinois Court of Claims Reports |
| I.L.P. | Illinois Law and Practice | | |
| I.L.R. | Insurance Law Reporter (Can.) | Ill.L.B. | Illinois Law Bulletin |
| | | Ill.L.Q. | Illinois Law Quarterly |
| | International Law Reports | Ill.L.Rev. | Illinois Law Review |
| I.O.C.C.Bull. | Interstate Oil Compact Commission Bulletin | Immig.B.Bull. | Immigration Bar Bulletin |
| | | Ind. | Indiana |
| I.R. | Internal Revenue Decisions | Ind. & Lab. Rel.Rev. | Industrial and Labor Relations Review |
| I.R.B. | Internal Revenue Bulletin | Ind.App. | Indiana Appellate Court Reports |
| I.R.C. | Internal Revenue Code | | |
| IT | Internal Revenue Bulletin | Ind.L.J. | Indiana Law Journal |
| I.T.R. | Irish Term Reports (Ridgeway) | Ind.L.Rev. | Indiana Law Review |
| Idaho | Idaho Reports | Ind.Legal F. | Indiana Legal Forum |
| Idaho L.Rev. | Idaho Law Review | Ind.Rel.J. Econ. & Soc. | Industrial Relations: Journal of Economy and Society |
| Idd.T.R. | Idding's Term Reports (Dayton, Ohio) | | |

| | |
|---|---|
| Ind.S.C. | Indiana Superior Court |
| India Crim. L.J.R. | Criminal Law Journal Reports |
| India S.Ct. | India Supreme Court Reports |
| Indian Cas. | Indian Cases |
| Indian L.R. [e.g.] Allahabad Ser. | Indian Law Reports [e.g.] Allahabad Series |
| Indian Rul. | Indian Rulings |
| Indian Terr. | Indian Territory Reports |
| Indus.L.Rev. | Industrial Law Review |
| Ins.Counsel J. | Insurance Counsel Journal |
| Ins.L.J. | Insurance Law Journal (Pa.) |
| Ins.L.Rep. | Insurance Law Reporter (CCH) |
| Int.Arb.J. | International Arbitration Journal |
| Int.Jurid. Assn.Bull. | International Juridical Association Bulletin |
| Int.Rev.Bull. | Internal Revenue Bulletin |
| Int.Rev. Code | Internal Revenue Code |
| Int.Rev.Code of 1954 | Internal Revenue Code of 1954 |
| Int.Rev.Rec. | Internal Revenue Record |
| Inter-Am.L. Rev. | Inter-American Law Review |
| Interior Dec. | United States Interior Department Decisions |
| Int'l & Comp. L.Q. | International and Comparative Law Quarterly |
| Int'l Aff. | International Affairs |
| Int'l Arb.J. | International Arbitration Journal |
| Int'l J. | International Journal |
| Int'l J.Pol. | International Journal of Politics |
| Int'l L.Q. | International Law Quarterly |
| Int'l Law. | The International Lawyer |
| Int'l Legal Materials | International Legal Materials |
| Intramural L.Rev. | Intramural Law Review |
| Iowa | Iowa Reports |
| Iowa L.B. | Iowa Law Bulletin |
| Iowa L.Rev. | Iowa Law Review |
| Ir. | Law Reports (Ir.) |
| Ir.C.L. | Irish Common Law |
| Ir.Ch. | Irish Chancery |
| Ir.Cir. | Irish Circuit Reports |
| Ir.Eccl. | Irish Ecclesiastical Reports |
| Ir.Eq. | Irish Equity |
| Ir.Jur. | Irish Jurist |
| Ir.L. & Eq. | Irish Law & Equity |
| Ir.L.T.R. | Irish Law Times Reports |
| Ir.R. | Irish Reports |
| Ir.R.C.L. | Irish Reports Common Law |
| Ir.R.Eq. | Irish Reports Equity |
| Ired. | Iredell's Law (N.C.) |
| Ired.Eq. | Iredell's Equity (N.C.) |
| Irv.Just. | Irvine's Justiciary (Sc.) |
| Israel L.Rev. | Israel Law Review |

# J

| | |
|---|---|
| J. & C. | Jones & Cary's Exchequer (Ir.) |
| J. & H. | Johnson & Hemming's Chancery (Eng.) |
| J. & L. | Jones & La Touche's Chancery (Ir.) |
| J. & La T. | Same |
| J. & S. | Jones & Spencer's Superior Court (N.Y.) |
| J. & W. | Jacob & Walker's Chancery (Eng.) |
| JAG Bull. | JAG Bulletin (USAF) |
| JAG J. | JAG Journal |
| JAG L.Rev. | United States Air Force JAG Law Review |
| J.A.M.A. | Journal of the American Medical Association |
| J.Accountancy | Journal of Accountancy |
| J.Air L. & Com. | Journal of Air Law and Commerce |
| J.Am.Jud. Soc'y | Journal of the American Judicature Society |
| J.Am.Soc'y C.L.U. | Journal of the American Society of Chartered Life Underwriters |
| J.Ass'n L. Teachers | Journal of the Association of Law Teachers |
| J.B.Ass'n St.Kan. | Journal of the Bar Association of the State of Kansas |
| J.B.Moore | J. B. Moore's Common Pleas (Eng.) |
| J.Bridg. | Sir John Bridgman's Common Pleas (Eng.) |
| J.Bridgm. | Same |
| J.Bus.L. | Journal of Business Law |
| J.C. | Johnson's Cases (N.Y.) |
| J.C.R. | Johnson's Chancery (N.Y.) |
| J.Can.B.Ass'n | Journal of the Canadian Bar Association |
| | Johnson's Chancery (N.Y.) |

| | | | |
|---|---|---|---|
| J.Ch. | Johnson's Chancery (N.Y.) | Jack.Tex.App. | Jackson's Texas Appeals |
| | | James | James' Reports (Nova Scotia) |
| J.Comp.Leg. & Int'l L.3d | Journal of Comparative Legislation and International Law, Third Series | James. & Mont. | Jameson & Montagu's Bankruptcy (Eng.) |
| J.Crim.L. (Eng.) | Journal of Criminal Law (Eng.) | Jebb | Jebb's Crown Cases (Ir.) |
| | | Jebb & B. | Jebb & Bourke's Queen's Bench (Ir.) |
| J.Crim.L. & Criminology | Journal of Criminal Law and Criminology | Jebb & S. | Jebb & Symes' Queen's Bench (Ir.) |
| J.Crim.L., C. & P.S. | Journal of Criminal Law, Criminology and Police Science | Jebb & Sym. | Same |
| | | Jebb C.C. | Jebb's Crown Cases (Ir.) |
| J.Fam.L. | Journal of Family Law | Jeff. | Jefferson (Va.) |
| J.For.Med. | Journal of Forensic Medicine | Jenk. | Jenkins' Exchequer (Eng.) |
| J.For.Sci. | Journal of Forensic Sciences | Jenk.Cent. | Same |
| | | Jenks | Jenks' (N.H.) |
| J.For.Sci. Soc'y | Journal of the Forensic Science Society | Jenn. | Jennison (Mich.) |
| J.Int'l L. & Econ. | Journal of International Law and Economics | Jo. & La T. | Jones & La Touche's Chancery (Ir.) |
| J.Int'l L. & Pol. | Journal of International Law and Politics | John. | Johnson (N.Y.) Johnson's Vice-Chancery (Eng.) |
| J.J.Mar. | J. J. Marshall (Ky.) | | |
| J.J.Marsh. (Ky.) | Same | John Mar.J. Prac. & Proc. | John Marshall Journal of Practice and Procedure |
| J.L.Soc'y | Journal of the Law Society of Scotland | John Marsh. L.J. | John Marshall Law Journal |
| J.Land & P.U.Econ. | Journal of Land and Public Utility Economics | John Marsh. L.Q. | John Marshall Law Quarterly |
| J.Law & Econ. | Journal of Law and Economics | Johns. | Johnson (N.Y.) Johnson's Vice-Chancery (Eng.) |
| J.Law & Econ.Dev. | Journal of Law and Economic Development | Johns. & H. | Johnson & Hemming's Chancery (Eng.) |
| J.Law Reform | Journal of Law Reform | Johns. & Hem. | Same |
| J.Legal Ed. | Journal of Legal Education | Johns.Cas. | Johnson's Cases (N.Y.) |
| J.Legal Educ. | Journal of Legal Education | Johns.Ch. | Johnson's Chancery Decisions (Md.) Johnson's Chancery (N.Y.) |
| J.Mar.Law & Com. | Journal of Maritime Law and Commerce | | |
| J.Mo.Bar | Journal of the Missouri Bar | Johns.Ct.Err. | Johnson's Court of Errors (N.Y.) |
| J.P. | Justice of the Peace (Eng.) | Johns.Dec. | Johnson's Chancery Decisions (Md.) |
| J.P.Sm. | J. P. Smith's King's Bench (Eng.) | Johns.N.Z. | Johnson's New Zealand Reports |
| J.Pat.Off. Soc'y | Journal of the Patent Office Society | Johns.U.S. | Johnson's U. S. Circuit Court Decisions |
| J.Pub.L. | Journal of Public Law | Jon. & L. | Jones & La Touche's Chancery (Ir.) |
| J.R. | Johnson (N.Y.) | | |
| J.Radio L. | Journal of Radio Law | Jon. & La T. | Same |
| J.S.Gr. (N.J.) | J. S. Green (N.J.) | Jones | Jones (Ala.) (Mo.) (Pa.) |
| Jac. | Jacob's Chancery (Eng.) | | Jones' Exchequer (Ir.) |
| Jac. & W. | Jacob & Walker's Chancery (Eng.) | | Jones' Law or Equity Jones, T., King's Bench (Eng.) |
| Jac. & Walk. | Same | | Jones' Reports (Upper Can.) |
| Jac.L.Dict. | Jacob's Law Dictionary | | |
| Jack. | Jackson (Ga.) | | Jones, W., King's Bench (Eng.) |
| Jack. & L. | Jackson & Lumpkin (Ga.) | | |

| | | | |
|---|---|---|---|
| Jones & C. | Jones & Cary's Exchequer (Ir.) | Judd | Judd (Hawaii) |
| Jones & L. | Jones & La Touche's Chancery (Ir.) | Judge Advoc.J. | The Judge Advocate Journal |
| Jones & La T. | Same | Judge's J. | Judge's Journal |
| Jones & McM. (Pa.) | Jones & McMurtrie (Pa.) | Judicature | Journal of the American Judicature Society |
| Jones & S. | Jones & Spencer's Superior Court (N.Y.) | Jur. | Jurist (Eng.) |
| | | Jur. (N.S.) | Jurist, New Series |
| | | Jurid.Rev. | Juridical Review |
| Jones & Spen. | Same | Jurimetrics J. | Jurimetrics Journal |
| Jones, B. & W. (Mo.) | Jones, Barclay & Whittelsey (Mo.) | Just.Cas. | Justiciary Cases |
| | | Just.L.R. | Justice's Law Reporter (Pa.) |
| Josephs | Josephs (Mo.) | Just.P. | Justice of the Peace and Local Government Review |
| Jud.Rep. | Judicial Repository (N.Y.) | | |
| | | Justinian | Justinian |
| Jud.Repos. | Same | Juv.Ct.J. | Juvenile Court Journal |

# K

| | | | |
|---|---|---|---|
| K. & G. | Keane & Grant's Registration Appeal Cases (Eng.) | Keen | Keen's Rolls Court (Eng.) |
| | | Keil. | Keilway's King's Bench (Eng.) |
| K. & Gr. | Same | Kel.C.C. | Kelyng's Crown Cases (Eng.) |
| K. & G.R.C. | Same | | |
| K.B. | Law Reports King's Bench (Eng.) | Kel.W. | Kelyng's Chancery (Eng.) |
| K.Counsel | King's Counsel | Kellen | Kellen (Mass.) |
| Kames Dec. | Kames' Decisions (Sc.) | Kelly | Kelly (Ga.) |
| Kames Elucid. | Kames' Elucidation (Sc.) | Kelly & C. | Kelly & Cobb (Ga.) |
| Kames Rem. Dec. | Kames' Remarkable Decisions (Sc.) | Kenan | Kenan (N.C.) |
| | | Keny. | Kenyon (Lord) King's Bench (Eng.) |
| Kames Sel. Dec. | Kames' Select Decisions (Sc.) | | |
| Kan. | Kansas | | Kenyon, Notes (Hammer) |
| Kan.App. | Kansas Appeals | Keny.Ch. | Kenyon's Chancery (Eng.) |
| Kan.B.Ass'n J. | Kansas Bar Association Journal | Kenya L.R. | Kenya Law Reports |
| | | Kern | Kern (Md.) |
| Kan.C.L.Rep. | Kansas City Law Reporter | Kern. | Kernan (N.Y.) |
| | | Kerr | Kerr (Ind.) |
| Kan.City L.Rev. | Kansas City Law Review | | Kerr (N.B.) |
| | | | Kerr's Civil Procedure (N.Y.) |
| Kan.L.Rev. | University of Kansas Law Review | Keyes | Keyes (N.Y.) |
| Kan.St.L.J. | Kansas State Law Journal | Kilk. | Kilkerran's Decisions (Sc.) |
| Kansas L.J. | Kansas Law Journal | Kilkerran | Same |
| Kay | Kay's Vice-Chancery (Eng.) | King | King's Civil Practice Cases (Colo.) |
| Kay & J. | Kay & Johnson's Chancery (Eng.) | | King's Louisiana Annual |
| Ke. | Keen's Rolls Court (Eng.) | Kirby | Kirby (Conn.) |
| Keane & G. R.C. | Keane & Grant's Registration Appeal Cases (Eng.) | Kn.P.C. | Knapp's Privy Council (Eng.) |
| | | Knapp | Knapp's Privy Council (Eng.) |
| Keane & Gr. | Same | Knapp & O. | Knapp & Ombler's Election Cases (Eng.) |
| Keb. | Keble's King's Bench (Eng.) | | |

| | | | |
|---|---|---|---|
| Knight's Ind. | Knight's Industrial Reports | Ky. | Kentucky |
| Knowles | Knowles (R.I.) | Ky.Comment'r | Kentucky Commentator |
| Knox | Knox (N.S.W.) | Ky.Dec. | Kentucky Decisions |
| Knox & F. | Knox & Fitzhardinge (N.S.W.) | Ky.L.J. | Kentucky Law Journal |
| Kreider | Kreider (Wash.) | Ky.L.R. | Kentucky Law Reporter |
| Kress | Kress (Pa.) | Ky.L.Rptr. | Same |
| Kulp | Kulp (Pa.) | Ky.Op. | Kentucky Opinions |
| | | Ky.St.B.J. | Kentucky State Bar Journal |

# L

| | | | |
|---|---|---|---|
| L. & B.Bull. | Weekly Law and Bank Bulletin (Ohio) | L.J.Ch. (O.S.) | Law Journal Chancery, Old Series (Eng.) |
| L. & C. | Leigh & Cave's Crown Cases Reserved (Eng.) | L.J.Eccl. | Law Journal Ecclesiastical (Eng.) |
| L. & C. | Lefroy and Cassels' Practice Cases (Ont.) | L.J.Exch. | Law Journal Exchequer, New Series (Eng.) |
| L. & E. | English Law & Equity Reports (Boston) | L.J.Exch. (O.S.) | Law Journal Exchequer, Old Series (Eng.) |
| L. & E.Rep. | Law & Equity Reporter (N.Y.) | L.J.H.L. | Law Journal House of Lords, New Series |
| L. & M. | Lowndes & Maxwell, Bail Cases (Eng.) | L.J.K.B. | Law Journal King's Bench New Series (Eng.) |
| L.A.C. | Labour Arbitration Cases | L.J.K.B. (O.S.) | Law Journal King's Bench Old Series (Eng.) |
| L. in Trans.Q. | Law in Transition Quarterly | L.J.M.C. | Law Journal Magistrate Cases New Series (Eng.) |
| L.C. | Lower Canada | L.J.M.C. (O.S.) | Law Journal Magistrate Cases Old Series (Eng.) |
| L.C.D. | Ohio Decisions (Ohio Lower Decisions) | | |
| L.C.Jur. | Lower Canada Jurist | L.J.Mag. | Law Journal New Series Common Law, Magistrates Cases (discontinued) |
| L.C.L.J. | Lower Canada Law Journal | | |
| L.C.Rep.S.Qu. | Lower Canada Reports Seignorial Questions | L.J.N.C. | Law Journal Notes of Cases (Eng.) |
| L.Comment'y | Law Commentary | L.J.O.S. | Law Journal, Old Series (1822–1830) |
| L.D. | Land Office Decisions (U.S.) | L.J.P. & M. | Law Journal Probate & Matrimonial (Eng.) |
| L.Ed. | Lawyers' Edition, U. S. Supreme Court Reports | L.J.P.C. | Law Journal Privy Council (Eng.) |
| L.Ed.2d | Same, Second Series | L.J.P.C. (N.S.) | Same, New Series |
| L.G. | Law Glossary | L.J.P.D. & Adm. | Law Journal Probate, Divorce & Admiralty (Eng.) |
| L.Guard. | Law Guardian | | |
| L.Inst.J. | Law Institute Journal | | |
| L.Inst.J. Vict. | Law Institute Journal of Victoria | L.J.Q.B. | Law Journal Queen's Bench New Series (Eng.) |
| L.J.Adm. | Law Journal Admiralty (Eng.) | | |
| L.J.Bankr. | Law Journal Bankruptcy (Eng.) | L.M. & P. | Lowndes, Maxwell & Pollock's Bail Cases (Eng.) |
| L.J.C.P. | Law Journal Common Pleas New Series (Eng.) | L.N.T.S. | League of Nations Treaty Series |
| L.J.C.P. (O.S.) | Law Journal Common Pleas Old Series (Eng.) | L.Q.Rev. | Law Quarterly Review |
| L.J.Ch. | Law Journal Chancery, New Series (Eng.) | L.R. | Law Recorder (Ir.) |
| | | | Law Reports (Eng.) |
| | | | Ohio Law Reporter |

| | |
|---|---|
| L.R.A. | Lawyers' Reports Annotated (U.S.) |
| L.R.A. & E. | Law Reports Admiralty & Ecclesiastical (Eng.) |
| L.R.A. (N.S.) | Lawyers' Reports Annotated, New Series |
| L.R.App.Cas. | Law Reports House of Lords Appeal Cases (Eng.) |
| L.R.C.C. | Law Reports Crown Cases (Eng.) |
| L.R.C.C.R. | Law Reports Crown Cases Reserved (Eng.) |
| L.R.C.P. | Law Reports Common Pleas Cases (Eng.) |
| L.R.C.P.D. | Law Reports Common Pleas Division (Eng.) |
| L.R.Ch. | Law Reports Chancery Appeal Cases (Eng.) |
| L.R.Ch.D. | Law Reports Chancery Division (Eng.) |
| L.R.Eq. | Law Reports Equity Cases (Eng.) |
| L.R.Exch. | Law Reports Exchequer Cases (Eng.) |
| L.R.Exch.D. | Law Reports Exchequer Division (Eng.) |
| L.R.H.L. | Law Reports House of Lords (English & Irish Appeal Cases) |
| L.R.H.L.Sc. | Law Reports, House of Lords (Scotch Appeal Cases) |
| L.R.Indian App. | Law Reports, Indian Appeals (Eng.) |
| L.R.Ir. | Law Reports (Ir.) |
| L.R. (N.S.) | Irish Law Recorder, New Series |
| L.R.N.S.W. | Law Reports New South Wales |
| L.R.P.C. | Law Reports Privy Council (Eng.) |
| L.R.P. & D. | Law Reports Probate & Divorce (Eng.) |
| L.R.Q.B. | Law Reports Queen's Bench (Eng.) |
| L.R.Q.B.Div. | Law Reports, Queen's Bench Division (Eng.) |
| L.R.R. | Labor Relations Reporter |
| L.R.R.M. | Labor Relations Reference Manual (BNA) |
| L.R.S.A. | Law Reports, South Australia |
| L.S.G. | Law Society Gazette (Eng.) |
| L.T. | Law Times (Pa.) |
| L.T. (N.S.) | Law Times, New Series (Eng.) |
| L.T. (O.S.) | Law Times, Old Series (Eng.) |
| L.T.R. (N.S.) | Law Times Reports, New Series (Eng.) |
| L.T.Rep.N.S. | Law Times Reports, New Series (Eng.) |
| L.Trans.Q. | Law in Transition Quarterly |
| La. | Louisiana |
| La.Ann. | Louisiana Annual |
| La.App. | Louisiana Appeals |
| La.App. (Orleans) | Court of Appeal, Parish of Orleans |
| La.B.J. | Louisiana Bar Journal |
| La.L.J. | Louisiana Law Journal |
| La.L.Rev. | Louisiana Law Review |
| La.T.R. | Martin's Louisiana Term Reports |
| Lab. | Labatt's District Court (Cal.) |
| Lab.Arb. | Labor Arbitration Reports (BNA) |
| Lab.L.J. | Labor Law Journal |
| Lab.Rel.Rep. | Labor Relations Reporter |
| Lack.Jur. | Lackawanna Jurist (Pa.) |
| Lack.Leg.N. | Lackawanna Legal News (Pa.) |
| Lack.Leg.Rec. | Lackawanna Legal Record (Pa.) |
| Ladd | Ladd (N.H.) |
| Lalor | Lalor's Supplement to Hill & Denio (N.Y.) |
| Lamar | Lamar (Fla.) |
| Lamb | Lamb (Wis.) |
| Lanc.Bar | Lancaster Bar (Pa.) |
| Lanc.L.Rev. | Lancaster Law Review (Pa.) |
| Land & Water L. Rev. | Land and Water Law Review |
| Land Dec. | Land Decisions (U.S.) |
| Lane | Lane's Exchequer (Eng.) |
| Lans. | Lansing (Mich.) |
| Latch | Latch's King's Bench (Eng.) |
| Lath. | Lathrop (Mass.) |
| Law & Bk. Bull. | Weekly Law and Bank Bulletin (Ohio) |
| Law & Contemp.Prob. | Law and Contemporary Problems |
| Law & Pol'y Int'l Bus. | Law and Policy in International Business |
| Law & Soc. Ord. | Law and the Social Order Arizona State Law Journal |
| Law & Soc'y Rev. | Law and Society Review |
| Law Cases | Law Cases, Wm. I to Rich. I (Eng.) (Placita Anglo-Normannica) |
| Law Lib.J. | Law Library Journal |

| | | | |
|---|---|---|---|
| Law Notes | Law Notes | Lewis | Lewis (Mo.) (Nev.) |
| Law Rep. | Law Reports (Eng.) (1865–1875) | | Lewis' Kentucky Law Reporter |
| | Law Reporter (Mass.) | Ley | Ley King's Bench, Common Pleas, Excheq-uer, Court of Wards and Court of Star Chamber (Eng.) |
| Law Rep. (N.S.) | Law Reports, New Series (N.Y.) | | |
| Law Soc'y Gaz. | Law Society Gazette | | |
| Law Soc'y J. | Law Society Journal (New South Wales) | Life Cas. | Life (Health & Accident) Cases (CCH) |
| Lawr. | Lawrence (Ohio) | Life Cas.2d | Same, Second Series |
| Lawrence | Same | Lincoln L.Rev. | Lincoln Law Review |
| Lawyer & Banker | Lawyer and Banker and Central Law Journal | Ll. & G.t.Pl. | Lloyd & Goold temp. Plunkett, Chancery (Ir.) |
| Lawyer's Med.J. | Lawyers' Medical Journal | | |
| Ld.Raym. | Lord Raymond's King's Bench (Eng). | Ll. & G.t.S. | Lloyd & Goold temp. Sugden, Chancery (Ir.) |
| Lea | Lea (Tenn.) | Ll. & W. | Lloyd & Welsby Mercan-tile Cases (Eng.) |
| Leach C.C. | Leach's Crown Cases, King's Bench (Eng.) | Ll.L.Rep. | Lloyd's List Reports (Eng.) |
| League of Nations Off.J. | League of Nations Official Journal | Lloyd's Rep. | Lloyd's List Law Reports Admiralty |
| Lee | Lee (Calif.) | Local Gov't | Local Government and Magisterial Reports |
| Lee Eccl. | Lee's Ecclesiastical (Eng.) | Local Gov't R.Austl. | Local Government Reports of Australia |
| Lee t.Hardw. | Lee temp. Hardwicke, King's Bench (Eng.) | Lock.Rev.Cas. | Lockwood's Reversed Cases (N.Y.) |
| Leese | Leese (Neb.) | Lofft | Lofft's King's Bench (Eng.) |
| Leg. & Ins.R. | Legal & Insurance Reporter (Pa.) | Long & R. | Long & Russell's Election Cases (Mass.) |
| Leg.Chron. | Legal Chronicle (Pa.) | Longf. & T. | Longfield & Townsend's Exchequer (Ir.) |
| Leg.Gaz. | Legal Gazette Reports (Pa.) | | |
| Leg.Int. | Legal Intelligencer (Pa.) | Louisville Law. | Louisville Lawyer |
| Leg.Op. | Legal Opinions (Pa.) | Low.Can.R. | Lower Canadian Reports |
| Leg.Rec. | Legal Record (Pa.) | Lowell | Lowell (U.S.) |
| Leg.Rep. | Legal Reporter (Tenn.) | Lower Ct.Dec. | Lower Court Decisions (Ohio) |
| Leg.Rev. | Legal Review (Eng.) | Loyola Dig. | Loyola Digest |
| Lehigh Co. L.J. | Lehigh County Law Journal (Pa.) | Loyola L.Rev. | Loyola Law Review |
| Lehigh Val. L.R. | Lehigh Valley Law Reporter (Pa.) | Loyola U. Chi.L.J. | Loyola University of Chicago Law Journal |
| Leigh | Leigh (Pa.) | Loyola U.L. A.L.Rev. | Loyola University of Los Angeles Law Review |
| Leigh & C. | Leigh & Cave's Crown Cases (Eng.) | | |
| Leigh & C. C.C. | Same | Ludd. | Ludden (Me.) |
| Leo. | Leonard, King's Bench, Common Pleas, Exchequer (Eng.) | Lump. | Lumpkin (Ga.) |
| | | Lush. | Lushington's Admiralty (Eng.) |
| Leon. | Same | Lutw. | Lutwyche's Common Pleas (Eng.) |
| Lester | Lester (Ga.) | | |
| Lester & B. | Lester & Butler's Supplement (Ga.) | Lutw.Reg.Cas. | Lutwyche's Registration Cases (Eng.) |
| Lev. | Leving, King's Bench, Common Pleas (Eng.) | Luz.L.J. | Luzerne Law Journal (Pa.) |
| Lew.C.C. | Lewin's Crown Cases (Eng.) | Luz.L.T. | Luzerne Law Times (Pa.) |

| | | | |
|---|---|---|---|
| Luz.Leg.Obs. | Luzerne Legal Observer (Pa.) | Lynd. | Lyndwoode, Provinciale (Eng.) |
| Luz.Leg.Reg. | Luzerne Legal Register (Pa.) | Lyne | Lyne's Chancery (Ir.) |

# M

| | | | |
|---|---|---|---|
| M. & A. | Montague & Ayrton's Bankruptcy (Eng.) | M. & W.Cas. | Mining & Water Cases (Annotated) |
| M. & Ayr. | Same | M. & Y. | Martin & Yerger (Tenn.) |
| M. & B. | Montague & Bligh's Bankruptcy (Eng.) | M.C.C. | Mixed Claims Commission |
| M. & C. | Montague & Chitty's Bankruptcy (Eng.) | | Motor Carriers' Cases (I.C.C.) |
| | Mylne & Craig's Chancery (Eng.) | M.C.J. | Michigan Civil Jurisprudence |
| M. & Cht. Bankr. | Montague & Chitty's Bankruptcy (Eng.) | M.D. | Master's Decisions (Patents) |
| M. & G. | Maddock & Geldhart's Chancery (Eng.) | M.L.E. | Maryland Law Encyclopedia |
| | Manning & Granger's Common Pleas (Eng.) | M.L.P. | Michigan Law and Practice |
| M. & Gel. | Maddock & Geldhart's Chancery (Eng.) | M.L.R. (Q.B.) | Montreal Law Reports (Queen's Bench) |
| M. & Gord. | Macnaghten & Gordon's Chancery (Eng.) | M.L.R. (S.C.) | Montreal Law Reports (Superior Court) |
| M. & H. | Murphy & Hurlstone's Exchequer (Eng.) | M.P.R. | Maritime Province Reports |
| M. & K. | Mylne & Keen's Chancery (Eng.) | Mac. | Macnaghten's Chancery (Eng.) |
| M. & M. | Moody & Malkin's Nisi Prius (Eng.) | Mac. & G. | Macnaghten & Gordon's Chancery (Eng.) |
| M. & McA. | Montague & McArthur's Bankruptcy (Eng.) | Mac. & Rob. | Maclean & Robinson's Appeals, House of Lords (Sc.) |
| M. & P. | Moore & Payne's Common Pleas & Exchequer (Eng.) | McAll. | MacAllister (U.S.) |
| | | MacAr. | McArthur's District of Columbia |
| M. & R. | Maclean & Robinson's Appeal Cases (Sc.) | | MacArthur's Patent Cases |
| | Manning & Ryland's King's Bench (Eng.) | MacAr. & M. | MacArthur & Mackey's District of Columbia Supreme Court |
| | Moody & Robinson's Nisi Prius (Eng.) | MacAr. & Mackey | Same |
| M. & R.M.C. | Manning & Ryland's Magistrates' Cases, King's Bench (Eng.) | MacAr.Pat. Cas. | MacArthur's Patent Cases (D.C.) |
| M. & Rob. | Moody & Robinson's Nisi Prius (Eng.) | MacArth. | MacArthur (D.C.) |
| | | | MacArthur's Patent Cases (D.C.) |
| M. & S. | Manning & Scott's Common Pleas (Eng.) | MacArth. & M. | MacArthur & Mackey (D.C.) |
| | Maule & Selwyn's King's Bench (Eng.) | McBride | McBride (Mo.) |
| | | McC. | McCahon (Kan.) |
| | Moore & Scott's Common Pleas (Eng.) | McCah. | Same |
| | | McCarter | McCarter's Chancery (N.J.) |
| M. & Scott | Same | McCartney | McCartney's Civil Procedure (N.Y.) |
| M. & W. | Meeson & Welsby's Exchequer (Eng.) | McClell. | McClelland's Exchequer (Eng.) |

| | | | |
|---|---|---|---|
| McClell. & Y. | McClelland & Younge's Exchequer (Eng.) | Man.Gr. & S. | Same |
| McCook | McCook (Ohio) | Man.L.J. | Manitoba Law Journal |
| McCord | McCord's Chancery (S.C.) | Man.t.Wood | Manitoba temp. Wood |
| McCork. | McCorkle. (N.C.) | Man.Unrep. Cas. | Manning's Unreported Cases (La.) |
| McCrary | McCrary (U.S.) | Mann. | Manning (Mich.) |
| MacFarl. | MacFarlane, Jury Court (Sc.) | Mann. & G. | Manning & Granger's Common Pleas (Eng.) |
| McG. | McGloin (La.) | | |
| McGill L.J. | McGill Law Journal | Mansf. | Mansfield (Ark.) |
| Mackey | Mackey | Manson | Manson's Bankruptcy (Eng.) |
| MacL. | MacLean, U. S. Circuit Court | Mar.L.Cas. (N.S.) | Maritime Law Cases, New Series |
| MacL. & R. | Maclean & Robinson's House of Lords (Eng.) | Mar.Prov. | Maritime Provinces Reports |
| McLean | McLean (U.S.) | March | March's King's Bench (Eng.) |
| McMul. | McMullan's Chancery (S.C.) | Marijuana Rev. | The Marijuana Review |
| | McMullan's Law (S.C.) | Mark's & Sayre's | Mark's & Sayre's (Ala.) |
| Macn. & G. | Macnaghten & Gordon's Chancery (Eng.) | Marq.L.Rev. | Marquette Law Review |
| Macph. | Macpherson, Court of Sessions (Sc.) | Mars.Adm. | Marsden's Admiralty (Eng.) |
| Macph.L. & B. | Macpherson, Lee & Bell (Sc.) | Marsh. | Marshall, A. K. (Ky.) |
| | | | Marshall, J. J. (Ky.) |
| Macph.S. & L. | Macpherson, Shireff & Lee (Sc.) | | Marshall (U.S.) |
| | | | Marshall (Utah) |
| Macq. | Macqueen's Scotch Appeal Cases | | Marshall's Common Pleas (Eng.) |
| Macr. | Macrory's Patent Cases (Eng.) | Mart. & Y. | Martin & Yerger (Tenn.) |
| | | Martin | Martin (Ga.) (Ind.) (La.) (U.S.) |
| McWillie | McWillie (Miss.) | | |
| Madd. | Maddock (Mont.) | . | Martin's Decisions (Law) (N.C.) |
| | Maddock's Chancery (Eng.) | Martin Mining | Martin Mining Cases |
| Madd. & B. | Maddock & Back (Mont.) | | Martin's New Series (La.) |
| Madd.Ch.Pr. | Maddock's Chancery Practice (Eng.) | Marv. | Marvel (Del.) |
| | | Mason | Mason (U.S.) |
| Mag. | Magruder (Md.) | Mass. | Massachusetts |
| Mag.Cas. | Magisterial Cases | Mass.App.Dec. | Massachusetts Appellate Decisions |
| Maine L.Rev. | Maine Law Review | Mass.App.Div. | Massachusetts Appellate Division Reports |
| Malloy | Malloy's Chancery (Ir.) | | |
| Malone | Malone's Heiskell (Tenn.) | Mass.L.Q. | Massachusetts Law Quarterly |
| Man. | Manitoba Law | Mathews | Mathews (W.Va.) |
| | Manning (Mich.) | Matson | Matson (Conn.) |
| Man. & G. | Manning & Granger's Common Pleas (Eng.) | Md. | Maryland |
| | | Md.B.J. | Maryland Bar Journal |
| Man. & Ry. Mag. | Manning & Ryland's Magistrates' Cases (Eng.) | Md.Ch. | Maryland Chancery |
| | | Md.L.Rec. | Maryland Law Record |
| Man. & S. | Manning & Scott's Common Bench (Old Series) (Eng.) | Md.L.Rep. | Maryland Law Reporter |
| | | Md.L.Rev. | Maryland Law Review |
| | | Me. | Maine |
| Man.B.News | Manitoba Bar News | Means | Means (Kan.) |
| Man.G. & S. | Manning, Granger & Scott's Common Bench (Eng.) | Med.-Legal J. | Medico-Legal Journal |
| | | Med.Sci. & L. | Medicine, Science and the Law |

| | | | |
|---|---|---|---|
| Med.Trial Tech.Q. | Medical Trial Technique Quarterly | Mo. | Missouri |
| Medd. | Meddaugh (Mich.) | Mo.A.R. | Missouri Appellate Reporter |
| Meg. | Megone Company Cases (Eng.) | Mo.App. | Missouri Appeals |
| Meigs | Meigs (Tenn.) | Mo.B.J. | Missouri Bar Journal |
| Melanesian L.J. | Melanesian Law Journal (Papua and New Guinea) | Mo.Dec. | Missouri Decisions |
| | | Mo.L.Rev. | Missouri Law Review |
| | | Moak | Moak (Eng.) |
| Melb.U.L. Rev. | Melbourne University Law Review | Mod. | Modern (Eng.) |
| Memp.L.J. | Memphis Law Journal (Tenn.) | Mod.L.Rev. | Modern Law Review |
| | | Mod.Pract. Comm. | Modern Practice Commentator |
| Memphis St. U.L.Rev. | Memphis State University Law Review | Moll. | Molloy's Chancery (Ir.) |
| Menken | Menken's Civil Procedure (N.Y.) | Mon. | Monroe, B. or T. B. (Ky.) |
| | | Mont. | Montana Reports |
| Mercer Law Rev. | Mercer Law Review | Mont. & Ayr. | Montagu & Ayrton's Bankruptcy (Eng.) |
| Meriv. | Merivale's Chancery (Eng.) | Mont. & M. | Montagu & McArthur's Bankruptcy (Eng.) |
| Met. | Metcalf | Mont.L.Rev. | Montana Law Review |
| Metc. | Metcalf (Mass.) (R.I.) (Ky.) | Mont.Super. | Montreal Law Reports (Superior Court) |
| Miami L.Q. | Miami Law Quarterly | Month.L.J. | Monthly Journal of Law (Wash.) |
| Mich. | Michigan | | |
| Mich.L.Rev. | Michigan Law Review | Month.L.Mag. | Monthly Law Magazine (London) |
| Mich.N.P. | Michigan Nisi Prius | Month.L.Rep. | Monthly Law Reporter (Boston) Monthly Law Reports (Can.) |
| Mich.St.B.J. | Michigan State Bar Journal | | |
| Mich.T. | Michaelmas Term (Eng.) | Month.L.Rev. | Monthly Law Review |
| Michie's Jur. | Michie's Jurisprudence of Va. and W.Va. | Month.Leg. Exam. | Monthly Legal Examiner (N.Y.) |
| Mil.L.Rev. | Military Law Review | Month.West. Jur. | Monthly Western Journal (Bloomington) |
| Miles | Miles (Pa.) Miles' Philadelphia District Court | Montr.Cond. Rep. | Montreal Condensed Reports |
| Mill. | Miller (Law) (Md.) | Montr.Leg.N. | Montreal Legal News |
| Mill Const. | Mill's Constitutional Reports (S.C.) | Montr.Q.B. | Montreal Law Reports Queen's Bench |
| Mill.Dec. | Miller's Decisions (U.S.) | Moo.C.C. | Moody's Crown Cases Reserved (Eng.) |
| Mills | Mills (N.Y. Surrogate) | | |
| Milw. | Milward's Ecclesiastical (Ir.) | Moo.P.C. | Moore, Privy Council |
| Min. | Minor (Ala.) | Moo.P.C. (N.S.) | Moore, New Series, Privy Council |
| Minn. | Minnesota | | |
| Minn.Cont. L.Ed. | Minnesota Continuing Legal Education | Mood. & Mack. | Moody & Mackin's Nisi Prius (Eng.) |
| Minn.Cont. Legal Ed. | Same | Mood. & Malk. | Moody & Malkin's Nisi Prius (Eng.) |
| Minn.L.Rev. | Minnesota Law Review | Mood. & Rob. | Moody & Robinson's Nisi Prius (Eng.) |
| Misc. | Miscellaneous (N.Y.) | | |
| Misc.Dec. | 3 Ohio Miscellaneous Decisions | Moody Cr.C. | Moody's Crown Cases Reserved (Eng.) |
| Miss. | Mississippi | Moon | Moon (Ind.) |
| Miss.Dec. | Mississippi Decisions (Jackson) | Moore | Moore (Ala.) (Ark.) (Tex.) |
| Miss.L.J. | Mississippi Law Journal | Moore & S. | Moore & Scott's Common Pleas (Eng.) |
| Miss.St.Cas. | Mississippi State Cases | | |
| Mister | Mister (Mo.) | Moore & W. | Moore & Walker (Tex.) |

| | | | |
|---|---|---|---|
| Moore C.P. | Moore's Common Pleas (Eng.) | Mun.Ord.Rev. | Municipal Ordinance Review |
| Moore Indian App. | Moore's Indian Appeals (Eng.) | Mun.Rep. | Municipal Reports, Canada |
| Moore K.B. | Moore's King's Bench (Eng.) | Munf. | Munford (Va.) |
| Moore P.C.C. | Moore's Privy Council Cases (Eng.) | Munic. & P.L. | Municipal & Parish Law Cases (Eng.) |
| Morg. | Morgan's Chancery Acts & Orders (Eng.) | Mur. | Murray's New South Wales Reports |
| Morr. | Morrill's Bankruptcy Cases (Eng.) | | Murray's Scotch Jury Court Reports |
| | Morris (Cal.) (Iowa) (Miss.) | Mur. & H. | Murphy & Hurlstone's Exchequer (Eng.) |
| Morr.St.Cas. | Morris State Cases (Miss.) | Mur. & Hurl. | Same |
| | | Murph. | Murphy (N.C.) |
| Morr.Trans. | Morrison's Transcript U. S. Supreme Court Decisions | Murph. & H. | Murphy & Hurlstone's Exchequer (Eng.) |
| | | Murr. | Murray's Scotch Jury Court Reports |
| Morris. | Morrissett's (Ala.) | | |
| Morrow | Morrow (Ore.) | Murr.Over. Cas. | Murray's Overruled Cases |
| Morse Exch. Rep. | Morse's Exchequer Reports (Can.) | Myer Fed.Dec. | Myer's Federal Decisions |
| Mosely | Mosely's Chancery (Eng.) | Myl. & C. | Mylne & Craig's Chancery (Eng.) |
| Moult.Ch. | Moulton's Chancery Practice (N.Y.) | Myl. & Cr. | Same |
| Mun. | Munford (Va.) | Myl. & K. | Mylne & Keen's Chancery (Eng.) |
| Mun.Att'y | Municipal Attorney | | |
| Mun.Corp.Cas. | Municipal Corporation Cases | Mylne & K. | Same |
| Mun.L.Ct.Dec. | Municipal Law Court Decisions | Myr. | Myrick's Probate (Cal.) |
| | | Myr.Prob. | Same |
| Mun.L.J. | Municipal Law Journal | Myrick (Cal.) | Same |

# N

| | | | |
|---|---|---|---|
| NACCA L.J. | NACCA Law Journal | N.Benl. | New Benloe, King's Bench (Eng.) |
| NOLPE School L.J. | NOLPE School Law Journal | N.C. | North Carolina |
| | | N.C.C. | New Chancery Cases (Eng.) |
| N. & H. | Nott & Huntington's U. S. Court of Claims | N.C.C.A. | Negligence & Compensation Cases Annotated |
| N. & M. | Neville & Manning's King's Bench (Eng.) | N.C.Cent. L.J. | North Carolina Central Law Journal |
| | | N.C.Conf. | North Carolina Conference Reports |
| N. & Mc. | Nott & McCord (S.C.) | | |
| N. & McC. | Same | N.C.L.Rev. | North Carolina Law Review |
| N. & Macn. | Nevile & Macnamara Railway & Canal Cases (Eng.) | N.C.T.Rep. | North Carolina Term Reports |
| N. & P. | Nevile & Perry's King's Bench (Eng.) | N.Cent. School L.Rev. | North Central School Law Review |
| N.Atlantic Reg.Bus. L.Rev. | North Atlantic Regional Business Law Review | N.Chipm. | North Chipman (Vt.) |
| | | N.D. | North Dakota |
| N.B. | New Brunswick | N.D.L.Rev. | North Dakota Law Review |
| N.B.Eq. | New Brunswick Equity | | |
| N.B.Rep. | New Brunswick Reports | N.E. | Northeastern Reporter |

| | | | |
|---|---|---|---|
| N.E.2d | Northeastern Reporter, Second Series | N.Y.App.Div. | New York Supreme Court Appellate Division Reports |
| N.Eng.L.Rev. | New England Law Review | N.Y.Cas.Err. | New York Cases in Error (Claim Cases) |
| N.H. | New Hampshire | | |
| N.H.B.J. | New Hampshire Bar Journal | N.Y.Ch.Sent. | Chancery Sentinel (N.Y.) |
| N.Ir.L.Q. | Northern Ireland Legal Quarterly | N.Y.City Ct. | New York City Court |
| | | N.Y.City Ct. Supp. | New York City Court Supplement |
| N.Ir.L.R. | Northern Ireland Law Reports | N.Y.City H. Rec. | New York City Hall Recorder |
| N.J. | New Jersey | N.Y.Civ.Pro. | New York Civil Procedure |
| | New Jersey Reports | | |
| N.J.Eq. | New Jersey Equity | N.Y.Civ.Pro. R. (N.S.) | Same, New Series |
| N.J.L. | New Jersey Law | | |
| N.J.L.J. | New Jersey Law Journal | N.Y.Civ.Proc. | New York Civil Procedure |
| N.J.L.Rev. | New Jersey Law Review | N.Y.Civ.Proc. (N.S.) | Same, New Series |
| N.J.Law | New Jersey Law Reports | | |
| N.J.Misc. | New Jersey Miscellaneous Reports | N.Y. Code Rep. | New York Code Reporter |
| N.J.St.B.J. | New Jersey State Bar Journal | N.Y.Code Rep. (N.S.) | New York Code Reports, New Series |
| N.J.Super. | New Jersey Superior Court and County Court Reports | N.Y.Cond. | New York Condensed Reports |
| | | N.Y.Cont. L.Ed. | New York Continuing Legal Education |
| N.L.R.B. | National Labor Relations Board Reports | N.Y.Cont. Legal Ed. | Same |
| N.M. | New Mexico | | |
| N.Mex.L.Rev. | New Mexico Law Review | N.Y.County Law.Ass'n B.Bull. | New York County Lawyers Association Bar Bulletin |
| N.P. | Ohio Nisi Prius Reports | | |
| N.P. (N.S.) | Ohio Nisi Prius Reports, New Series | N.Y.Cr. | New York Criminal |
| | | N.Y.Crim. | New York Criminal Reports |
| N.P. & G.T. Rep. | Nisi Prius & General Term Reports (Ohio) | N.Y.Daily L.Gaz. | New York Daily Law Gazette |
| [e.g.] N.R.A.B. (4th Div.) | National Railroad Adjustment Board Awards | N.Y.Daily L.Reg. | New York Daily Law Register |
| | | N.Y.Dep't R. | New York Department Reports |
| N.S. | Nova Scotia | | |
| N.S.Dec. | Nova Scotia Decisions | N.Y.Elec.Cas. | New York Election Cases |
| N.S.R. | Nova Scotia Reports | | |
| N.S.W. | New South Wales State Reports | N.Y.Jur. | New York Jurisprudence New York Jurist |
| N.S.W.St.R. | New South Wales State Reports | N.Y.L.Cas. | New York Leading Cases |
| N.S.Wales | New South Wales | N.Y.L.F. | New York Law Forum |
| N.S.Wales L. | New South Wales Law | N.Y.L.J. | New York Law Journal |
| N.S.Wales L.R.Eq. | New South Wales Law Reports Equity | N.Y.L.Rec. | New York Law Record |
| | | N.Y.L.Rev. | New York Law Review |
| N.W. | Northwestern Reporter | N.Y.Leg.N. | New York Legal News |
| N.W.2d | Same, Second Series | N.L.Leg. Obs. | New York Legal Observer |
| N.W.T.L.R. | North West Territories Law Reports | | |
| N.W.Terr. | Northwest Territories Supreme Court Reports | N.Y.Misc. | New York Miscellaneous Reports |
| N.Y. | New York | N.Y.Misc.2d | Same, Second Series |
| N.Y.Anno. Cas. | New York Annotated Cases | N.Y.Month.L. Bul. | New York Monthly Law Bulletin |
| N.Y.Anno. Dig. | New York Annotated Digest | N.Y.Month.L. Rep. | New York Monthly Law Reports |

| | | | | |
|---|---|---|---|---|
| N.Y.Mun.Gaz. | New York Municipal Gazette | | Nat'l Tax J. | National Tax Journal |
| | | | Natural L.F. | Natural Law Forum |
| N.Y.P.R. | New York Practice Reports | | Natural Resources J. | Natural Resources Journal |
| N.Y.Pr.Rep. | Same | | Neb. | Nebraska |
| N.Y.Rec. | New York Record | | Neb. (Unoff.) | Nebraska Unofficial Reports |
| N.Y.S. | New York Supplement | | | |
| N.Y.S.2d | Same, Second Series | | Neb.L.Bul. | Nebraska Law Bulletin |
| N.Y.St. | New York State Reporter | | Neb.L.Rev. | Nebraska Law Review |
| N.Y.St.B.J. | New York State Bar Journal | | Neb.St.B.J. | Nebraska State Bar Journal |
| N.Y.Super. | New York Superior Court | | Negl. & Comp.Cas. Ann. | Negligence & Compensation Cases Annotated |
| N.Y.Supp. | New York Supplement | | | |
| N.Y.U.Conf. Charitable | New York University Conference on Charitable Foundations Proceedings | | Negl. & Comp.Cas. Ann. (N.S.) | Same, New Series |
| N.Y.U.Conf. Lab. | New York University Conference on Labor | | Negl. & Comp.Cas. Ann.3d | Same, Third Series |
| [e.g.] N.Y.U. Inst.on Fed.Tax. | New York University Institute on Federal Taxation | | Negl.Cas. | Negligence Cases (CCH) |
| N.Y.U.Intra.L. Rev. | New York Intramural Law Review | | Negl.Cas.2d | Same, Second Series |
| | | | Negro.Cas. | Bloomfield's Manumission (N.J.) |
| N.Y.U.J.Int'l Law & Pol. | New York University Journal of International Law and Politics | | Nels. | Nelson's Chancery (Eng.) |
| | | | Nels.Abr. | Nelson's Abridgment (Eng.) |
| N.Y.U.L. Center Bull. | New York University Law Center Bulletin | | Nev. | Nevada |
| N.Y.U.L.Q. Rev. | New York University Law Quarterly Review | | Nev. & P. | Neville & Perry's King's Bench (Eng.) |
| N.Y.U.L.Rev. | New York University Law Review | | Nev.St.Bar J. | Nevada State Bar Journal |
| | | | Nev.St.Bar J. | Same |
| N.Y.U.Rev. Law & Soc. C. | New York University Review of Law and Social Change | | New L.J. | New Law Journal |
| | | | New Rep. | New Reports in All Courts (Eng.) |
| N.Y.Wkly.Dig. | New York Weekly Digest | | New Sess.Cas. | New Session Cases (Eng.) |
| N.Z.L.J. | New Zealand Law Journal | | New Zeal.L. | New Zealand Law |
| N.Z.L.R. | New Zealand Law Reports | | New. | Newell (Ill.) |
| N.Z.U.L.Rev. | New Zealand Universities Law Review | | Newb.Adm. | Newberry's Admiralty (U.S.) |
| Napt. | Napton (Mo.) | | | |
| Napton | Same | | Newf.S.Ct. | Newfoundland Supreme Court Decisions |
| Narcotics Control Dig. | Narcotics Control Digest | | Newfoundl. | Newfoundland |
| | | | Nfld.R. | Newfoundland Reports |
| Nat.Bankr. Reg. | National Bankruptcy Register (U.S.) | | Nigeria L.R. | Nigeria Law Reports |
| Nat.Corp.Rep. | National Corporation Reporter | | Nolan | Nolan, Magistrates' Cases (Eng.) |
| | | | Norc. | Norcross (Nev.) |
| Nat.L.Rep. | National Law Reporter | | Norris | Norris (Pa.) |
| Nat.Munic. Rev. | National Municipal Review | | North | North (Ill.) |
| Nat.Reg. | National Register (By Mead) | | North & G. | North & Guthrie (Mo.) |
| | | | North. | Northington's Chancery (Eng.) |
| Nat'l Civic Rev. | National Civic Review | | | |
| Nat'l Legal Mag. | National Legal Magazine | | North.Co. | Northampton County Legal News (Pa.) |
| Nat'l Mun. Rev. | National Municipal Review | | Northumb.Co. Leg.News | Northumberland County Legal News (Pa.) |
| Nat'l School L.Rptr. | National School Law Reporter | | Northumb. Legal J. | Northumberland Legal Journal |

| | | | |
|---|---|---|---|
| Notes of Cas. | Notes of Cases (Eng.) | Noy | Noy, King's Bench (Eng.) |
| Notre Dame Law. | Notre Dame Lawyer | Nw.U.L.Rev. | Northwestern University Law Review |

# O

| | | | |
|---|---|---|---|
| O. | Ohio, Oklahoma, Oregon | O.N.P. (N.S.) | Same, New Series |
| O.A. | Ohio Appellate | O.O. | Ohio Opinions |
| O.A.R. | Same | O.R. | Ontario Reports, 1882–1900 |
| | Ontario Appeal Reports | [ ] O.R. | Same, 1931 to present |
| O.App. | Ohio Appellate | O.S. | Ohio State Reports |
| O.B. & F.N.Z. | Olliver, Bell & Fitzgerald's New Zealand Reports | O.S.C.D. | Ohio Supreme Court Decisions (Unreported Cases) |
| O.Ben. | Old Benloe, Common Pleas (Eng.) | O.S.L.J. | Ohio State Law Journal |
| O.Benl. | Same | O.S.U. | Ohio Supreme Court Decisions (Unreported Cases) |
| O.Bridgm. | Orlando Bridgman, Common Pleas (Eng.) | O.St. | Ohio State Reports |
| O.C.A. | Ohio Courts of Appeals Reports | O.Su. | Ohio Supplement |
| O.C.C. | Ohio Circuit Court Decisions | O.W.N. | Ontario Weekly Notes, 1909–1932 |
| | Ohio Circuit Court Reports | [ ] O.W.N. | Same, 1933–1962 |
| | | O.W.R. | Ontario Weekly Reporter |
| O.C.C. (N.S.) | Ohio Circuit Court Reports, New Series | Odeneal | Odeneal (Ore.) |
| | | Off.Brev. | Officina Brevium |
| O.C.D. | Ohio Circuit Decisions | Off.Gaz. | Official Gazette (U.S.) Patent Office |
| O.C.S. | Office of Contract Settlement Decisions | Officer | Officer (Minn.) |
| O.D. | Office Decisions (I.R. Bull.) | Ogd. | Ogden (La.) |
| | Ohio Decisions | Oh. | Ohio Reports (1821–1852) |
| O.D.C.C. | Ohio Circuit Decisions | Oh.A. | Ohio Court of Appeals |
| O.D.N.P. | Ohio Decisions | Oh.Cir.Ct. | Ohio Circuit Court |
| O.Dec.Rep. | Ohio Decisions Reprint | Oh.Cir.Ct. (N.S.) | Same, New Series |
| O.E.M. | Office of Emergency Management | Oh.Cir.Dec. | Ohio Circuit Decisions |
| O.F.D. | Ohio Federal Decisions | Oh.Dec. | Ohio Decisions |
| O.G. | Official Gazette (U.S.) Patent Office | Oh.Dec. (Reprint) | Ohio Decisions (Reprint) |
| O.G.Pat.Off. | Same | Oh.F.Dec. | Ohio Federal Decisions |
| O.L.A. | Ohio Law Abstract | Oh.Jur. | Ohio Jurisprudence |
| O.L.B. | Weekly Law Bulletin (Ohio) | Oh.L.Bul. | Ohio Law Bulletin |
| O.L.D. | Ohio (Lower) Decisions | Oh.L.Ct.D. | Ohio Lower Court Decisions |
| O.L.J. | Ohio Law Journal | Oh.L.J. | Ohio Law Journal |
| O.L.Jour. | Same | Oh.L.Rep. | Ohio Law Reporter |
| O.L.N. | Ohio Legal News | Oh.Leg.N. | Ohio Legal News |
| O.L.R. | Ohio Law Reporter | Oh.N.P. | Ohio Nisi Prius |
| | Ontario Law Reports, 1901–1930 | Oh.N.P. (N.S.) | Same, New Series |
| | | Oh.Prob. | Ohio Probate |
| O.L.R.B. | Ontario Labour Relations Board Monthly Report | Oh.S. & C.P. | Ohio Superior & Common Pleas Decisions |
| O.L.Rep. | Ohio Law Reporter | Oh.S.C.D. | Ohio Supreme Court Decisions (Unreported Cases) |
| O.Legal News | Ohio Legal News | | |
| O.Lower D. | Ohio (Lower) Decisions | | |
| O.N.P. | Ohio Nisi Prius | Oh.St. | Ohio State Reports |

| | | | |
|---|---|---|---|
| Ohio | Ohio Reports (1821–1852) | Ohio R.Cond. | Ohio Reports Condensed |
| Ohio App. | Ohio Appellate Reports | Ohio S. & C.P. Dec. | Ohio Decisions |
| Ohio App.2d | Same, Second Series | | |
| Ohio Bar | Ohio State Bar Association Reports | Ohio S.U. | Ohio Supreme Court Decisions (Unreported Cases) |
| Ohio C.A. | Ohio Courts of Appeals Reports | Ohio St. | Ohio State Reports |
| Ohio C.C. | Ohio Circuit Court Reports | Ohio St.2d | Same, Second Series |
| | | Ohio St.L.J. | Ohio State Law Journal |
| Ohio C.C.R. | Same | Ohio St. (N.S.) | Ohio State Reports, Annotated |
| Ohio C.C.R. (N.S.) | Same, New Series | Ohio Sup. & C.P.Dec. | Ohio Decisions |
| Ohio C.Dec. | Ohio Circuit Decisions | | |
| Ohio Cir.Ct. | Ohio Circuit Court Decisions | Ohio Supp. | Ohio Supplement |
| Ohio Cir.Ct. (N.S.) | Ohio Circuit Court Reports, New Series | Ohio Unrep. Jud.Dec. | Pollack's Ohio Unreported Judicial Decisions Prior to 1823 |
| Ohio Cir.Ct.R. | Ohio Circuit Court Reports | Ohio Unrept. Cas. | Ohio Supreme Court Decisions (Unreported Cases) |
| Ohio Cir.Ct.R. (N.S.) | Same, New Series | Oil & Gas Compact Bull. | Oil and Gas Compact Bulletin |
| Ohio Ct.App. | Ohio Courts of Appeals Reports | Oil & Gas Inst. | Oil and Gas Institute |
| Ohio Dec. | Ohio Decisions | Oil & Gas J. | Oil and Gas Journal |
| Ohio Dec. Repr. | Ohio Decisions Reprint | Oil & Gas Rptr. | Oil and Gas Reporter |
| Ohio F.Dec. | Ohio Federal Decisions | Oil & Gas Tax Q. | Oil and Gas Tax Quarterly |
| Ohio Fed.Dec. | Same | Okla. | Oklahoma |
| Ohio Jur. | Ohio Jurisprudence | Okla.B. Ass'n J. | Oklahoma Bar Association Journal |
| Ohio Jur.2d | Same, Second Edition | | |
| Ohio L.Abs. | Ohio Law Abstract | Okla.Cr. | Oklahoma Criminal |
| Ohio L.B. | Weekly Law Bulletin (Ohio) | Okla.Crim. | Oklahoma Criminal Reports |
| Ohio L.J. | Ohio Law Journal | Okla.L.J. | Oklahoma Law Journal |
| Ohio L.R. | Ohio Law Reporter | Okla.L.Rev. | Oklahoma Law Review |
| Ohio Law Abst. | Ohio Law Abstract | Okla.S.B.J. | Oklahoma State Bar Journal |
| Ohio Law Bull. | Weekly Law Bulletin (Ohio) | Olcott | Olcott (U.S.) |
| | | Oliv.B. & L. | Oliver, Beavan & Lefroy (Eng. Ry. & Canal Cases) |
| Ohio Law J. | Ohio Law Journal | | |
| Ohio Law R. | Ohio Law Reporter | Olliv.B. & F. | Olliver, Bell & Fitzgerald (New Zealand) |
| Ohio Leg.N. | Ohio Legal News | | |
| Ohio Legal N. | Same | O'M. & H.El. Cas. | O'Malley & Hardcastle, Election Cases (Eng.) |
| Ohio Lower Dec. | Ohio (Lower) Decisions | | |
| | | Ont. | Ontario Reports |
| Ohio Misc. | Ohio Miscellaneous Reports | Ont.A. | Ontario Appeals |
| | | Ont.El.Cas. | Ontario Election Cases |
| Ohio Misc.Dec. | 3 Ohio Miscellaneous Decisions | Ont.Elec. | Same |
| | | Ont.L. | Ontario Law |
| Ohio N.P. | Ohio Nisi Prius Reports | Ont.L.J. | Ontario Law Journal |
| Ohio N.P. (N.S.) | Same, New Series | Ont.L.J. (N.S.) | Same, New Series |
| Ohio, N.S. | Ohio Reports, Annotated | Ont.L.R. | Ontario Law Reports |
| Ohio Op. | Ohio Opinions | Ont.Pr. | Ontario Practice |
| Ohio Op.2d | Same, Second Series | Ont.W.N. | Ontario Weekly Notes |
| | | Ont.W.R. | Ontario Weekly Reporter |
| Ohio Prob. | Goebel's Ohio Probate Reports | Op. | Opinions of Attorneys General (U.S.) |

| | |
|---|---|
| Op.Att'y Gen. | Opinions of the Attorney General, United States |
| Op.Sol.Dept. | Opinions of the Solicitor, U. S. Department of Labor |
| Ops.Atty.Gen. | Opinions of Attorneys General (U.S.) |
| Or. | Oregon |
| Ore. | Same |
| Ore.L.Rev. | Oregon Law Review |
| Ore.St.B.Bull. | Oregon State Bar Bulletin |
| Orleans' App. | Orleans' Appeals (La.) |
| Orleans Tr. | Orleans Term Reports (La.) |
| Ormond | Ormond (Ala.) |
| Osgoode Hall L.J. | Osgoode Hall Law Journal |
| Otago L.Rev. | Otago Law Review |
| Ottawa L.Rev. | Ottawa Law Review |
| Otto | Otto (U.S.) |
| Out. | Outerbridge (Pa.) |
| Outerbridge | Same |
| Over. | Overton (Tenn.) |
| Overt. | Same |
| Overton | Same |
| Ow. | Owen's King's Bench & Common Pleas (Eng.) |
| Owen | Same |
| Oxley | Young's Vice Admiralty Decisions (Nova Scotia) (By Oxley) |

# P

| | |
|---|---|
| P. | Pacific Reporter |
| | Pickering (Mass.) |
| | Probate |
| | Law Reports Probate, Divorce & Admiralty Division, Third Series |
| P.2d | Pacific Reporter, Second Series |
| P. & B. | Pugsley & Burbridge's Reports, New Brunswick |
| P. & C. | Prideaux & Cole's New Sessions Cases (Eng.) |
| P. & D. | Perry & Davison's Queen's Bench (Eng.) |
| P. & F. Radio Reg. | Radio Regulation Reporter |
| P. & H. | Patton & Heath (Va.) |
| P. & K. | Perry & Knapp Election Cases (Eng.) |
| P. & W. | Penrose & Watts (Pa.) |
| P.C. | Price Control Cases (CCH) |
| P.Coast L.J. | Pacific Coast Law Journal |
| P.D. | Law Reports Probate, Divorce & Admiralty Division, Second Series Division |
| | Pension and Bounty (U.S. Dept. of Interior) |
| P.Div. | Law Reports, Probate Division (Eng.) |
| PEAL | Publishing, Entertainment, Advertising and Allied Fields Law Quarterly |
| P.E.I. | Haszard & Warburton's Reports (P.E.I.) |
| P.F.Smith | P. F. Smith (Pa.) |
| P–H | Prentice-Hall |
| P–H Am.Lab. Arb.Awards | American Labor Arbitration Awards (P–H) |
| P–H Am.Lab. Cas. | American Labor Cases (P–H) |
| P–H Corp. | Corporation (P–H) |
| P–H Est.Plan. | Estate Planning (P–H) |
| P–H Fed. Taxes | Federal Taxes (P–H) |
| P–H Fed.Wage & Hour | Federal Wage and Hour (P–H) |
| P–H Ind.Rel., Lab.Arb. | Industrial Relations, American Labor Arbitration (P–H) |
| P–H Ind.Rel., Union Conts. | Industrial Relations, Union Contracts and Collective Bargaining (P–H) |
| P–H Soc.Sec. Taxes | Social Security Taxes (P–H) |
| P–H State & Local Taxes | State and Local Taxes (P–H) |
| P–H Tax Ct.Mem. | Tax Court Memorandum Decisions (P–H) |
| P–H Tax Ct.Rep. & Mem.Dec. | Tax Court Reported and Memorandum Decisions (P–H) |
| P.L.E. | Pennsylvania Law Encyclopedia |
| P.Jr. & H. | Patton, Jr., & Heath (Va.) |
| P.R. | Parliamentary Reports |
| | Probate Reports |
| | Practice Reports (Ont.) |
| | Puerto Rico Supreme Court Reports |
| P.R. & D.El. Cas. | Power, Rodwell & Dew's Election Cases (Eng.) |
| P.R.F. | Puerto Rico Federal Reports |
| P.R.R. | Puerto Rico Reports |
| P.T. | Processing Tax Division (I.R.Bull.) |

| | | | |
|---|---|---|---|
| P.U.Fort. | Public Utilities Fort-nightly | Pasch. | Paschal (Tex.) |
| P.U.R. | Public Utilities Reports | Pat. & T.M. Rev. | Patent & Trade Mark Review |
| P.U.R. (N.S.) | Same, New Series | Pat. & Tr.Mk. Rev. | Same |
| P.U.R.3d | Same, Third Series | Pat.Cas. | Reports of Patent, Design and Trade Mark Cases |
| P.Wms. | Peere-Williams Chancery (Eng.) | Pat.L.Rev. | Patent Law Review |
| Pa. | Pennsylvania | Pat.Off.Rep. | Patent Office Reports |
| Pa.B.Ass'n Q. | Pennsylvania Bar Association Quarterly | Pat.T.M. & Copy.J. | Patent, Trademark & Copyright Journal |
| Pa.B.Brief | Pennsylvania Bar Brief | Pater.Ap.Cas. | Paterson's Appeal Cases (Sc.) |
| Pa.C.P. | Common Pleas Reporter | Paton App. Cas. | Paton's Appeal Cases (Can.) |
| Pa.C.Pl. | Penn. Common Pleas | | |
| Pa.Cas. | Penn. Supreme Court Cases (Sadler) | Patt. & H. | Patton & Heath (Va.) |
| Pa.Co.Ct. | Penn. County Court | Peab.L.Rev. | Peabody Law Review |
| Pa.D. & C. | Penn. District & County Reporter | Peake N.P. | Peake's Nisi Prius (Eng.) |
| | | Peake N.P. Add.Cas. | Peake, Additional Cases Nisi Prius (Eng.) |
| Pa.D. & C.2d | Same, Second Series | Pearce C.C. | Pearce's (Dearsley's) Crown Cases (Eng.) |
| Pa.Dist. | Penn. District Reporter | | |
| Pa.Fid. | Pennsylvania Fiduciary Reporter | Pearson | Pearson, Common Pleas (Pa.) |
| Pa.L.J. | Penn. Law Journal | Peck | Peck (Ill.) |
| Pa.L.J.R. | Clark's Penn. Law Journal Reports | | Peck (Tenn.) |
| Pa.L.Rec. | Penn. Law Record | Peck.El.Cas. | Peckwell's Election Cases (Eng.) |
| Pa.Misc. | Pennsylvania Miscellaneous Reports | Peeples | Peeples (Ga.) |
| Pa.State | Penn. State Reports | Peeples & Stevens | Peeples & Stevens (Ga.) |
| Pa.Super. | Penn. Superior Court Reporter | Peere Williams | Peere Williams' Chancery (Eng.) |
| Pac. | Pacific Reporter | Peere Wms. | Same |
| Pacific L.J. | Pacific Law Journal | Pen. | Pennington's Law (N.J.) |
| Paige | Paige's Chancery (N.Y.) | Pen. & W. | Penrose and Watts |
| Paine | Paine (U.S.) | Penn.B.A.Q. | Penn.Bar Association (Quarterly) |
| [e.g.] Pak.L. R.Lahore Ser. | Pakistan Law Reports, [e.g.] Lahore Series | Penn.Del. | Pennewill (Del.) |
| Palm. | Palmer (N.H.) (Vt.) | Pennyp. | Pennypacker (Pa.) |
| | Palmer, King's Bench & Common Pleas (Eng.) | Pennyp.Col. Cas. | Pennypacker's Colonial Cases |
| Pan-Am.T.S. | Pan-American Treaty Series | Penr. & W. | Penrose & Watts (Pa.) |
| Papua & N.G. | Papua and New Guinea Law Reports | Perry & K. | Perry & Knapp's Election Cases (Eng.) |
| Papy | Papy (Fla.) | Pers.Finance L.Q. | Personal Finance Law Quarterly Report |
| Park. | Parker's Exchequer (Eng.) | Pers.Inj. Comment'r | Personal Injury Commentator |
| Park.Cr. | Parker's Criminal Reports (N.Y.) | Pet. | Peters |
| Park.Cr.Cas. | Same | Pet.Ab. | Petersdorf's Abridgment |
| Park.Ins. | Parker's Insurance | Pet.Adm. | Peters' Admiralty (U.S.) |
| Parker | Parker (N.H.) | | |
| Parker Cr. Cas. | Parker's Criminal Reports (N.Y.) | Pet.Br. | Petit (Or Little) Brook (Brooke) New Cases King's Bench (Eng.) |
| Pars.Dec. | Parson's Decisions (Mass.) | Pet.C.C. | Peters' Circuit Court (U.S.) |
| Pars.Eq.Cas. | Parsons' Select Equity Cases (Pa.) | Peters | Peters (U.S.) |

| | |
|---|---|
| Pheney Rep. | Pheney's New Term Reports. See Harrison & Wollaston (Eng.) |
| Phil. | Phillips' (Ill.) |
| | Phillips' Chancery (Eng.) |
| | Phillips' Equity (N.C.) |
| | Phillips' Law (N.C.) |
| Phil.El.Cas. | Phillips Election Cases (Eng.) |
| Phil.L.J. | Philippine Law Journal |
| Phila. | Philadelphia (Pa.) |
| Phillim. | Phillimore Ecclesiastical (Eng.) |
| Pick. | Pickering (Mass.) |
| Pickle | Pickle (Tenn.) |
| Pig. & R. | Pigott & Rodwell's Registration Cases (Eng.) |
| Pike | Pike (Ark.) |
| Pin. | Pinney (Wis.) |
| Pinn. | Pinney (Wis.) |
| Pitt.L.J. | Pittsburgh Legal Journal |
| Pitts.Leg.J. (N.S.) | Pittsburgh Legal Journal, New Series (Pa.) |
| Pitts.Rep. | Pittsburgh Reports (Pa.) |
| Pittsb. | Pittsburgh (Pa.) |
| Pittsb.Leg.L. | Pittsburgh Legal Journal (Pa.) |
| Pittsb.R. (Pa.) | Pittsburgh Reporter (Pa.) |
| Pl.Ang.-Norm. | Placita Anglo-Normannica Cases (Bigelow) |
| Plan. & Comp. | Planning and Compensation Reports |
| Plan., Zoning & E.D.Inst. | Planning, Zoning & Eminent Domain Institute |
| Plowd. | Plowden, King's Bench (Eng.) |
| Pol. | Pollack's Ohio Unreported Judicial Decisions Prior to 1823 |
| | Pollexfen, King's Bench (Eng.) |
| Pollexf. | Same |
| Pol.Sci.Q. | Political Science Quarterly |
| Police L.Q. | Police Law Quarterly |
| Pollution Abs. | Pollution Abstracts |
| Pomeroy | Pomeroy (Cal.) |
| Poph. | Popham, King's Bench & Common Pleas & Chancery (Eng.) |
| Port. | Porter (Ala.) (Ind.) |
| Portia L.J. | Portia Law Journal |
| Portland U.L. Rev. | Portland University Law Review |

| | |
|---|---|
| Porto Rico Fed. | Porto Rico Federal |
| Posey | Posey (Tex.) |
| Posey Unrep. Cas. | Posey's Unreported Commissioner Cases (Texas) |
| Post | Post (Mich.) (Mo.) |
| Potter | Potter (Wyo.) |
| Pow.Surr. | Power's Surrogate (N.Y.) |
| Pr. | Price (Exchequer) (Eng.) |
| Pr.Edw.Isl. | Prince Edward Island |
| Pr.Reg.B.C. | Practical Register, Bail Court (Eng.) |
| Pr.Reg.C.P. | Practical Register Common Pleas (Eng.) |
| Pr.Reg.Ch. | Practical Register Chancery (Eng.) |
| Pr.Rep. | Practice Reports (Eng.) |
| | Practice Reports (Upper Can.) |
| Pract.Law. | Practical Lawyer |
| Prec.Ch. | Precedents in Chancery (Eng.) |
| Price | Price (Exchequer) (Eng.) |
| | Price's Mining Commissioner's Cases (Ont.) |
| Price Pr.Cas. | Price's Notes of Practice Cases (Eng.) |
| Prick. | Prickett (Idaho) |
| Prin.Dec. | Printed Decisions (Sneed's) (Ky.) |
| Prison L. Rptr. | Prison Law Reporter |
| Prob. & Prop. | Probate and Property |
| Prob.Rep. | Probate Reports (Ohio) |
| Prop. & Comp. | Property and Compensation Reports |
| Prouty | Prouty (Vt.) |
| Pub.Contract L.J. | Public Contract Law Journal |
| Pub.Employee Rel.Rep. | Public Employee Relations Reports |
| Pub.L. | Public Law |
| Pub.Land & Res.L.Dig. | Public Land and Resources Law Digest |
| Pub.Util.Fort. | Public Utilities Fortnightly |
| Pugs. | Pugsley (New Brunswick) |
| Pugs. & B. | Pugsley & Burbridge (New Brunswick) |
| Pugs. & T. | Pugsley & Trueman (New Brunswick) |
| Puls. | Pulsifer (Me.) |
| Pulsifer | Same |
| Pyke | Pyke (Lower Can.) |
| | Pyke's Reports, King's Bench (Que.) |

# Q

| | | | |
|---|---|---|---|
| Q.B. | Law Reports, Queen's Bench, Third Series | Que.Q.B. or Que.K.B. | Quebec Official Reports (Queen's Bench or King's Bench) 1892–1941 |
| Q.B.D. | Law Reports, Queen's Bench Division, Second Series | Que.Rev.Jud. | Quebec Revised Judicial |
| Q.B.L.C. | Queen's Bench (Lower Canada) | Que.S.C. | Quebec Official Reports (Superior Court) 1892–1941 |
| Q.B.U.C. | Queen's Bench (Upper Canada) | [ ] Que.S.C. | Same, 1942 to present |
| Q.L. | Quebec Law | Que.Super. | Quebec Reports Superior Court |
| Q.L.J. | Queen's Law Journal | Queensl. | Queensland Reports |
| Q.L.R. | Quebec Law Reports | Queensl.J.P. | Queensland Justice of the Peace |
| Que.B.R.; Que.C.S. | Quebec Rapports Judicaires Officiels (Banc de la Reine; Cour supérieure) | Queensl.J.P. Rep. | Queensland Justice of the Peace Reports |
| [ ] Que.K.B. or [ ] Que. Q.B. | Quebec Official Reports (King's Bench or Queen's Bench) 1941 to present | Queensl.L. | Queensland Law |
| | | Queensl.L.J. | Queensland Law Journal |
| | | Queensl.S.C.R. | Queensland Supreme Court Reports |
| Que.L. | Quebec Law | Queensl.St. Rep. | Queensland State Reports |
| Que.L.R. | Quebec Law Reports | | |
| Que.Pr. | Quebec Practice | Queensl.W.N. | Queensland Weekly Notes |
| Que.Prac. | Quebec Practice Reports | Quincy | Quincy (Mass.) |

# R

| | | | |
|---|---|---|---|
| R. | Rawle (Pa.) | R.L.B. | U. S. Railroad Labor Board Decisions |
| | The Reports, Coke's King's Bench (Eng.) | R.M.C.C. | Ryan & Moody's Crown Cases (Eng.) |
| R. & C. | Russell & Chesley (Nova Scotia) | R.M.C.C.R. | Same |
| R. & Can.Cas. | Railway & Canal Cases (Eng.) | R.M.Charlt. | R. M. Charlton (Ga.) |
| R. & Can.Tr. Cas. | Railway & Canal Traffic Cases (Eng.) | R.P.C. | Reports of Patent Cases |
| | | R.P. & W. | (Rawle) Penrose & Watt (Pa.) |
| R. & M. | Russell & Mylne's Chancery (Eng.) | R.P.W. | Same |
| R. & M.C.C. | Ryan & Moody's Crown Cases (Eng.) | R.R. | Revised Reports (Eng.) |
| | | Race Rel.L. Rep. | Race Relations Law Reporter |
| R. & R. | Russell & Ryan Crown Cases (Eng.) | Race Rel.L. Survey | Race Relations Law Survey |
| R. 1 Cro. | Croke, Elizabeth | | |
| R. 2 Cro. | Croke, James I. | Rader | Rader (Mo.) |
| R. 3 Cro. | Croke, Charles I. | Rand | Rand (Ohio) |
| R.A.C. | Ramsay's Appeal Cases (Que.) | Rand. | Randolph (Kan.) (Va.) |
| | | | Randall (Ohio) |
| R.C.L. | Ruling Case Law | Rand.Ann. | Randolph Annual (La.) |
| R.E.D. | Russell's Equity Decisions (Nova Scotia) | Raney | Raney (Fla.) |
| R.I. | Rhode Island | Rawle | Rawle (Pa.) |
| R.I.B.J. | Rhode Island Bar Journal | Raym. | Raymond (Iowa) |
| R.J.R.Q. | Quebec Revised Reports | Real Est. L.Rep. | Real Estate Law Report |
| R.L. & S. | Ridgeway, Lapp & Schoales, King's Bench (Ir.) | Real Est.Rev. | Real Estate Review |
| | | Real Prop. Prob. & Trust J. | Real Property, Probate and Trust Journal |
| R.L. & W. | Robert, Leaming & Wallis County Court (Eng.) | | |

| | | | |
|---|---|---|---|
| Reap.Dec. | U. S. Customs Court Reappraisement Dec. (From Treas. Dec. & C.D.) | Rev.Not. | Revue de Notariat |
| | | Rev.R. | Revised Reports (Eng.) |
| | | Rev.Rep. | Revised Reports (Eng.) |
| Record of N.Y.C.B.A. | Record of the Association of the Bar of the City of New York | Rev.Sec.Reg. | Review of Securities Regulation |
| | | Rev.Sel. Code Leg. | Review of Selected Code Legislation |
| Redf. & B. | Redfield & Bigelow's Leading Cases (Eng.) | Rev.Stat. | Revised Statutes |
| | | Revised Rep. | Revised Reports (Eng.) |
| Redf.Surr. | Redfield's Surrogate (N.Y.) | Reyn. | Reynolds (Miss.) |
| | | Rice | Rice's Equity (S.C.) |
| Reding. | Redington (Me.) | | Rice's Law (S.C.) |
| Reese | Reese, Heiskell's (Tenn.) | Rich. | Richardson (N.H.) |
| Reeve Eng.L. | Reeve's English Law | | Richardson's Equity (S.C.) |
| Ref.J. | Referees' Journal (Journal of National Association of Referees in Bankruptcy) | | Richardson's Law (S.C.) |
| | | Rich. & H. | Richardson & Hook's Street Railway Decisions |
| | | Rich. & W. | Richardson & Woodbury (N.H.) |
| Rel. & Pub. Order | Religion and the Public Order | Rich.C.P. | Richardson's Practice, Common Pleas (Eng.) |
| Remy | Remy (Ind.) | Rich.Ct.Cl. | Richardson's Court of Claims |
| Rep.Atty.Gen. | Attorneys General's Reports (U.S.) | Ridg.Ap. | Ridgeway's Appeals Parliament Cases (Ir.) |
| Rep.Pat.Cas. | Reports of Patent Cases (Eng.) | Ridg.App. | Same |
| Rep.Pat.Des. & Tr.Cas. | Reports of Patents Designs & Trademark Cases | Ridg.L. & S. | Ridgeway, Lapp & Schoales' King's Bench (Ir.) |
| Reports | Reports Coke's King's Bench (Eng.) | Ridg.P.C. | Ridgeway's Parliamentary Cases (Ir.) |
| Reprint | English Reports, Full Reprint | Ridg.t.Hardw. | Ridgeway temp. Hardwicke, Chancery, King's Bench |
| Rept.t.Finch | Cases temp. Finch (Chancery) (Eng.) | | |
| Rept.t.Holt | Cases temp. Holt (King's Bench) (Eng.) | Ried. | Riedell (N.H.) |
| Res Ipsa | Res Ipsa Loquitur | Rights | Rights |
| Res. & Eq. Judgm. | Reserved & Equity Judgments (N.S.Wales) | Riley | Riley (W.Va.) |
| | | | Riley's Equity (S.C.) |
| Restric. Prac. | Reports of Restrictive Practices Cases | | Riley's Law (S.C.) |
| | | Ritchie | Ritchie's Equity (Can.) |
| Rettie | Rettie, Crawford & Melville's Session Cases (Sc.) | Rob. | Robard (Mo.) |
| | | | Robard Conscript Cases (Tex.) |
| Rev.Bar. | Revue du Barreau | | Robert's Louisiana Annual |
| Rev.C.Abo.Pr. | Revista de Derecho del Colegio de Abogados de Puerto Rico | | Robertson (Hawaii) |
| | | | Robertson's Marine Court (N.Y.) |
| Rev.Crit. | Revue Critique (Can.) | | Robertson's Superior Court (N.Y.) |
| Rev.D.P.R. | Revista de Derecho Puertorriqueno | | Robinson (Calif.) (Colo.) (La.) (Nev.) (Upper Can.) (Va.) |
| Rev.de Legis | Revue de Legislation (Can.) | | |
| Rev.Jur. U.P.R. | Revista Juridica de la Universidad de Puerto Rico | | Robinson's (La.) Annual |
| | | Rob. & J. | Robard & Jackson (Tex.) |
| Rev.Leg. | Revue Legale (Can.) | | Robertson & Jacob's Marine Court (N.Y.) |
| Rev.Leg. (N.S.) | Same, New Series | Rob.Adm. | Robinson, Admiralty (Eng.) |
| Rev.Leg. (O.S.) | Same, Old Series | Rob.Eccl. | Robertson's Ecclesiastical (Eng.) |
| Rev.Legale | Revue Legale | | |

| | |
|---|---|
| Rob.L. & W. | Robert, Leaming & Wallis' County Court (Eng.) |
| Robb Pat.Cas. | Robb's Patent Cases (U.S.) |
| Robert.App. Cas. | Robertson's Appeal Cases (Sc.) |
| Robin.App.Cas. | Robinson's Appeal Cases (House of Lords) (Sc.) |
| Rocky Mt.L. Rev. | Rocky Mountain Law Review |
| Rocky Mt.Min. L.Inst. | Rocky Mountain Mineral Law Institute |
| Rocky Mt. Miner.L.Rev. | Rocky Mountain Mineral Law Review |
| Rodm. | Rodman (Ky.) |
| Rogers | Rogers (La.) Annual |
| Roll. | Rolle (King's Bench) (Eng.) |
| Rolle | Same |
| Rolle Abr. | Rolle's Abridgment (Eng.) |
| Rom.Cas. | Romilly's Notes of Cases (Eng.) |
| Root | Root (Conn.) |
| Rose | Rose Bankruptcy (Eng.) |
| Rose's Notes (U.S.) | Rose's Notes on U. S. Reports |
| Ross Lead.Cas. | Ross Leading Cases (Eng.) |
| Rot.Chart. | Rotulus Chartarum (The Charter Roll) |
| Rot.Claus. | Rotuli Clause (The Close Roll) |
| Rot.Parl. | Rotulae Parliamentarum |
| Rot.Pat. | Rotuli Patenes |
| Rot.Plac. | Rotuli Placitorum |
| Rotuli Curiae Reg. | Rotuli Curiae Regis (Eng.) |
| Rowe | Rowe, Parliament & Military Cases (Eng.) |
| Rowell | Rowell (Vt.) |

| | |
|---|---|
| Rowell El.Cas. | Rowell Election Cases (U.S.) |
| Rucker | Rucker (W.Va.) |
| Ruff. & H. | Ruffin & Hawks (N.C.) |
| Runn. | Runnell (Iowa) |
| Rus. | Russell's Election Cases (Nova Scotia) |
| Rus. & C.Eq. Cas. | Russell & Chesley's Equity Cases (N.S.) |
| Russ. & Geld. | Russell & Geldert (N.S.) |
| Russ. & M. | Russell & Mylne Chancery (Eng.) |
| Russ. & Ry. | Russell & Ryan Crown Cases (Eng.) |
| Russ.El.Cas. | Russell's Election Reports (Can.) |
| | Russell's Election Cases (Mass.) |
| Russ.Eq.Cas. | Russell's Equity Cases (N.S.) |
| Russ.t.Eld. | Russell's Chancery temp. Eldon (Eng.) |
| Russell | Russell's Chancery (Eng.) |
| Rutgers J. Computers & Law | Rutgers Journal of Computers and the Law |
| Rutgers L.Rev. | Rutgers Law Review |
| Rutgers U.L. Rev. | Rutgers University Law Review |
| Rutgers-Camden L.J. | Rutgers-Camden Law Journal |
| Ry. & M. | Ryan & Moody's Nisi Prius (Eng.) |
| Ry.M.C.C. | Ryan & Moody Crown Cases (Eng.) |
| Ryan & M. | Ryan & Moody's Nisi Prius (Eng.) |
| Ryde | Ryde's Rating Appeals (Eng.) |

# S

| | |
|---|---|
| S. | Shaw, Dunlop & Bell (Sc.) |
| | Shaw's Appeal Cases, House of Lords (Sc.) |
| | Southern Reporter |
| S. & B. | Smith & Batty's King's Bench (Ir.) |
| S. & C. | Saunders & Cole's Bail Court (Eng.) |
| S. & C.P.Dec. | Ohio Decisions |
| S. & D. | Shaw, Dunlop & Bell's 1st Series (Sc.) |
| S. & L. | Schoales & Lefroy's Chancery (Ir.) |
| S. & M. | Smedes & Maclean's Appeal Cases, House of Lords (Sc.) |
| | Smedes & Marshall (Miss.) |

| | |
|---|---|
| S. & M.Ch. | Smedes & Marshall's Chancery (Miss.) |
| S. & Mar. | Smedes & Marshall (Miss.) |
| S. & Mar.Ch. | Smedes & Marshall's Chancery (Miss.) |
| S. & R. | Sergeant & Rawle (Pa.) |
| S. & S. | Sausse & Scully's Rolls Court (Ir.) |
| | Simons & Stuart's Vice-Chancery (Eng.) |
| S. & Sc. | Sausse & Scully's Rolls Court (Ir.) |
| S. & Sm. | Searle & Smith's Probate & Divorce Cases (Eng.) |
| S. & T. | Swabey & Tristram's Probate & Divorce Cases (Eng.) |

| | | | |
|---|---|---|---|
| S.Afr.L.J. | South African Law Journal | St. John's L.Rev. | St. John's Law Review |
| S.Afr.L.R. | South African Law Reports | St. Louis L.Rev. | St. Louis Law Review |
| S.Afr.L.R. App. | South African Law Reports Appellate | St. Louis U.L.J. | St. Louis University Law Journal |
| S.Afr.Tax Cas. | South African Tax Cases | St. Mary's L.J. | St. Mary's Law Journal |
| S.Aust.L. | South Australian Law | Sal. | Salinger (Iowa) |
| S.Austl. | South Australia State Reports | Salk. | Salkeld King's Bench Common Pleas & Exchequer (Eng.) |
| S.Austl.L.R. | South Australian Law Reports | San Diego L.Rev. | San Diego Law Review |
| S.B.J. | State Bar Journal (Cal.) | San Fran.L.J. | San Francisco Law Journal |
| S.C. | Court of Session Cases (Sc.) | | |
| | South Carolina | Sand.I.Rep. | Sandwich Islands Reports (See Robertson's Reports) (Hawaii) |
| S.C.Cas. | Supreme Court Cases (Cameron's) (Can.) | | |
| S.C.Eq. | South Carolina Equity | Sandf. | Sandford's Superior Court (N.Y.) |
| S.C.L.Q. | South Carolina Law Quarterly | Sandf.Ch. | Sandford Chancery (N.Y.) |
| S.C.L.Rev. | South Carolina Law Review | Sanf. | Sanford (Ala.) |
| | | Santa Clara Law. | Santa Clara Lawyer |
| S.C.R. | Supreme Court Reports (Canada) 1876–1922 | Sar.Ch.Sen. | Saratoga Chancery Sentinel |
| [ ]S.C.R. | Same, 1923 to present | Sask. | Saskatchewan Law Reports |
| S.Cal.L.Rev. | Southern California Law Review | Sask.L. | Saskatchewan Law |
| S.Calif.Law Rev. | Southern California Law Review | Sask.L.Rev. | Saskatchewan Law Review |
| S.Ct. | Supreme Court Reporter (U.S.) | Sau. & Sc. | Sausee & Scully, Rolls Court (Ir.) |
| S.Ct.Rev. | Supreme Court Review | Sauls. | Saulsbury (Del.) |
| S.D. | South Dakota | Saund. | Saunders King's Bench (Eng.) |
| S.D.L.Rev. | South Dakota Law Review | | |
| S.D.St.B.J. | South Dakota State Bar Journal | Saund. & Cole | Saunders & Cole, Bail Court (Eng.) |
| S.E. | South Eastern Reporter | Sav. | Savile, Common Pleas & Exchequer (Eng.) |
| S.E.2d | Same, Second Series | | |
| S.E.C. | U. S. Security and Exchange Commission Decisions | Sawy. | Sawyer Circuit Court (U.S.) |
| | | Sax. | Saxton's Chancery (N.J.) |
| S.F.L.J | San Francisco Law Journal | Say. | Sayer, King's Bench (Eng.) |
| S.L.C. | Stuart's Appeal Cases (Lower Can.) | Sc.Sess.Cas. | Scotch Court of Sessions Cases |
| S.M. | Solicitor's Memorandum (Treasury) (I.R.Bull.) | Scam. | Scammon (Ill.) |
| S.R. | Solicitor's Recommendation (I.R.Bull.) | Sch. & Lef. | Schoales & Lefroy, Equity (Ir.) |
| S.S.T. | Social Security Tax Ruling (I.R.Bull.) | Scher. | Scherer's Miscellaneous Reports (N.Y.) |
| S.T. | Sales Tax Division (I.R. Bull.) | Schm.L.J. | Schmidt's Law Journal (New Orleans) |
| S.Tex.L.J. | South Texas Law Journal | Schuyl.L.Rec. | Schuylkill Legal Record (Pa.) |
| S.W. | South Western Reporter | | |
| S.W.2d | Same, Second Series | Scot.Jur. | Scottish Jurist |
| S.W.L.J. | South Western Law Journal (Nashville) | Scot.L.J. | Scottish Law Journal |
| | | Scot.L.M. | Scottish Law Magazine |
| Sadler | Sadler's Cases (Pa.) | Scot.L.Rep. | Scottish Law Reporter |

| | | | |
|---|---|---|---|
| Scot.L.Rev. | Scottish Law Review and Sheriff Court Reports | Shaw, D. & B. | Shaw, Dunlop & Bell's Court of Sessions (1st Series) (Sc.) |
| Scot.L.T. | Scottish Law Times | | Shaw, Dunlop & Bell's Session Cases (Sc.) |
| Scots L.T.R. | Scots Law Times Reports | | |
| Scott | Scott Common Pleas (Eng.) | Shaw, D. & B. Supp. | Shaw, Dunlop, & Bell's Supplement, House of Lords Decisions (Sc.) |
| Scott N.R. | Scott's New Reports, Common Pleas (Eng.) | Shaw Dec. | Shaw's Decisions in Scotch Court of Sessions (1st Series) |
| Scr.L.T. | Scranton Law Times (Pa.) | | |
| Search and Seizure | Search and Seizure Bulletin | Shaw, Dunl. & B. | Shaw, Dunlop & Bell's Sessions Cases (Sc.) |
| Sec.L.Rev. | Securities Law Review | Shaw, W. & C. | Shaw, Wilson & Courtnay, House of Lords |
| Sec.Reg. & Trans. | Securities Regulation and Transfer Report | Shep. | Shepherd (Ala.) Shepley (Me.) |
| Sel.Cas. | Yates' Select Cases (N.Y.) | | |
| Sel.Cas.Ch. | Select Cases in Chancery (Eng.) | Shep.Abr. | Sheppard's Abridgment |
| | | Shep.Sel.Cas. | Shepherd's Select Cases (Ala.) |
| Sel.Serv.L. Rptr. | Selective Service Law Reporter | Sher.Ct.Rep. | Sheriff Court Reports (Sc.) |
| Seld. | Selden's Notes (N.Y.) | Shingle | Shingle |
| Selden | Selden's N. Y. Court of Appeals | Shipp | Shipp (N.C.) |
| Selw.N.P. | Selwyn's Nisi Prius (Eng.) | Shirl. | Shirley (N.H.) |
| Serg. & R. | Sergeant & Rawle (Pa.) | Shirl.L.C. | Shirley's Leading Crown Cases (Eng.) |
| Sess.Ca. | Sessions Cases King's Bench (Eng.) | Show. | Shower King's Bench (Eng.) |
| Sess.Cas. | Court of Sessions Cases (Sc.) | Show.P.C. | Shower's Parliamentary Cases (Eng.) |
| | Sessions Cases King's Bench (Eng.) | Sick. | Sickel's Court of Appeals (Eng.) |
| Sess.Laws | Session Laws | Sid. | Siderfin King's Bench (Eng.) |
| Seton Hall L. Rev. | Seton Hall Law Review | Sil. | Silver Tax Division (I.R. Bull.) |
| Sex Prob.Ct. Dig. | Sex Problems Court Digest | Silv.A. | Silvernail's Appeals (N.Y.) |
| Shad. | Shadford's Victoria Reports | Silv.Sup. | Silvernail's Supreme Court (N.Y.) |
| Shan. | Shannon (Tenn.) | Silv.Unrep. | Silvernail's Unreported Cases (N.Y.) |
| Shand | Shand (S.C.) | Sim. | Simmon's (Wis.) |
| Shand Pr. | Shand, Practice, Court of Sessions (Sc.) | | Simon's Vice-Chancery (Eng.) |
| Shaw | Shaw (Vt.) | Sim. (N.S.) | Simon's Vice-Chancery, New Series (Eng.) |
| | Shaw Appeal Cases, English House of Lords From Scotland | Sim. & C. | Simmons & Conover (Wis.) |
| | Shaw, Scotch Justiciary Cases | Sim. & St. | Simons & Stuart's Vice-Chancery (Eng.) |
| | Shaw, Scotch Teind Reports, Court of Sessions | Skill.Pol.Rep. | Skillman's N. Y. Police Reports |
| Shaw & D. | Shaw & Dunlop (Sc.) | | |
| Shaw & Dunl. | Same | Skin. | Skinner (King's Bench) (Eng.) |
| Shaw & M. | Shaw & McLean Appeals, House of Lords (Sc.) | Skink. | Skinker (Mo.) |
| Shaw & Macl. | Same | Sm. & M. | Smedes & Marshall (Miss.) |
| Shaw App. | Shaw Appeal Cases (Sc.) | | |
| Shaw Crim. Cas. | Shaw's Criminal Cases, Justiciary Court (Sc.) | Sm. & M.Ch. | Smedes & Marshall, Chancery (Miss.) |

| | | | |
|---|---|---|---|
| Smale & G. | Smale & Gifford's Vice-Chancery (Eng.) | Sol.J. | Solicitor's Journal (Eng.) |
| Smith | Smith (Calif.) (Dak.) (Eng.) (Ind.) (Me.) (Mo.) (N.H.) (Wis.) | Sol.Op. | Solicitor's Opinions (I.R. Bull.) |
| | Smith, E. B. (Ill.) | Somerset L.J. | Somerset Legal Journal |
| | Smith, E. D. Common Pleas (N.Y.) | Southard | Southard (N.J.) |
| | Smith, E. H. Court of Appeals (N.Y.) | Southwestern L.J. | Southwestern Law Journal |
| | Smith, E. P. Court of Appeals (N.Y.) | Spaulding | Spaulding (Me.) |
| | Smith, P. F. (Pa.) | Spear | Spear's Law (S.C.) |
| Smith & B. | Smith & Batty, King's Bench (Ir.) | Spear Ch. | Spear's (or Speer) Chancery (S.C.) |
| Smith & B.R.C. | Smith & Bates, American Railway Cases | Spear Eq. | Spear's Equity (S.C.) |
| Smith & G. | Smith & Guthrie (Mo.) | Speer | See Spear |
| Smith & H. | Smith & Heiskell (Tenn.) | Spenc. | Spencer (Minn.) |
| Smith C.C.M. | Smith Circuit Courts-Martial (Me.) | | Spencer Law (N.J.) |
| Smith Cond. | Smith's Condensed Alabama Reports | Spencer | Spencer Law (N.J.) |
| Smith K.B. | Smith's King's Bench (Eng.) | Spinks | Spinks Ecclesiastical and Admiralty (Eng.) |
| Smith L.J. | Smith's Law Journal | Spinks Eccl. & Adm. | Same |
| Smith Lead. Cas. | Smith's Leading Cases (Eng.) | Spoon. | Spooner (Wis.) |
| Smith Reg. Cas. | Smith's Registration Cases (Eng.) | Spooner | Same |
| Smy. | Smythe Common Pleas (Ir.) | Spott. | Spottiswoode (Sc.) |
| | | Spott.C.L. Rep. | Spottiswoode's Common Law |
| Smythe | Same | Spottis. | Spottiswoode (Sc.) |
| Sneed | Sneed (Tenn.) | Spottis.C.L. & Eq.Rep. | Common Law & Equity Reports published by Spottiswoode |
| | Sneed's Decisions (Ky.) | | |
| Sneed Dec. | Sneed's Kentucky Decisions | Spottis.Eq. | Spottiswoode's Equity (Sc.) |
| Sneedy Ky. | Same | Sprague | Sprague (U. S. District Court Admiralty) |
| Snow | Snow (Utah) | St.Rep. | State Reporter |
| So. | Southern Reporter | St.Rep.N.S.W. | State Reports (New South Wales) |
| So.2d | Same, Second Series | | |
| So.Calif.L. Rev. | Southern California Law Review | Stafford | Stafford (Vt.) |
| So.Car.Const. | South Carolina Constitutional Reports | Stair | Stair (Sc.) |
| | | Stan.J.Int'l Stud. | Stanford Journal of International Studies |
| So.Car.L.J. | South Carolina Law Journal | Stan.L.Rev. | Stanford Law Review |
| | | Stan.Pa.Prac. | Standard Pennsylvania Practice |
| So.L.J. | Southern Law Journal (Nashville) | Stant. | Stanton (Ohio) |
| | | Stanton | Same |
| So.L.Q. | Southern Law Quarterly | Star Ch.Cas. | Star Chamber Cases (Eng.) |
| So.L.Rev. | Southern Law Review (Nashville) | Stark. | Starkie's Nisi Prius (Eng.) |
| | Southern Law Review (St. Louis) | Stat. | Statutes at Large (U.S.) |
| | | Stat. at L. | Same |
| So.L.Rev. (N.S.) | Southern Law Review, New Series (St. Louis) | State Gov't | State Government |
| | | State Tr. | State Trials (Eng.) |
| So.Law T. | Southern Law Times | Stath.Abr. | Statham's Abridgment |
| So.Tex.L.J. | South Texas Law Journal | Stev. & G. | Stevens & Graham (Ga.) |
| Sol. | Solicitor | Stew. | Stewart (Ala.) (S.D.) |
| | | | Stewart's Reports (N.S.) |

| | | | |
|---|---|---|---|
| Stew. & P. | Stewart & Porter (Ala.) | Style | Style, King's Bench, Rolle & Glyn's Decisions (Eng.) |
| Stew.Admr. | Stewart's Admiralty (N.S.) | | |
| Stew.Eq. | Stewart's Equity (N.J.) | Suffolk U.L. Rev. | Suffolk University Law Review |
| Stewart | Stewart's Vice-Admiralty Reports (N.S.) | Summerfield | Summerfield (Nev.) |
| Stiles | Stiles (Iowa) | Sumn. | Sumner Circuit Court (U.S.) |
| Still.Eccl.Cas. | Stillingfleet's Ecclesiastical Cases (Eng.) | Sup. & C.P. Dec. | Ohio Decisions |
| Stiness | Stiness (R.I.) | Sup.Ct. | Superior Ct. (Pa.) |
| Stockett | Stockett (Md.) | Sup.Ct.Rep. | Supreme Court Reporter (U.S.) |
| Stockt. | Stockton's Equity (N.J.) | | |
| Stockt.Vice-Adm. | Stockton's Vice-Admiralty (N.B.) | Susq.Leg. Chron. | Susquehanna Legal Chronical (Pa.) |
| Stockton | Same | Sw.L.J. | Southwestern Law Journal |
| Storey | Storey | Sw.U.L.Rev. | Southwestern University Law Review |
| Story | Story (U.S.) | | |
| Story Eq.Jur. | Story on Equity Jurisprudence | Swab. | Swabey's Admiralty (Eng.) |
| Str. | Strange's King's Bench (Eng.) | Swab. & Tr. | Swabey & Tristram, Probate & Divorce (Eng.) |
| Stra. | Same | Swan | Swan (Tenn.) |
| Strahan | Strahan (Ore.) | Swanst. | Swanston Chancery (Eng.) |
| Stratton | Stratton (Ore.) | | |
| Stringf. | Stringfellow (Mo.) | Sween. | Sweeney's Superior Court (N.Y.) |
| Strob. | Strobhart's Law (S.C.) | | |
| Strob.Eq. | Strobhart's Equity (S.C.) | Swin. | Swinton's Registration Appeal Cases (Sc.) |
| Stu.M. & P. | Stuart, Milne & Peddie (Sc.) | | |
| Stu.Mil. & Ped. | Same | Sydney L. Rev. | Sydney Law Review |
| Stuart | Stuart's King's Bench (Lower Can.) | Syme | Syme's Justiciary Cases (Sc.) |
| Stuart Vice-Adm. | Stuart's Vice-Admiralty (Lower Can.) | Syn.Ser. | Synopsis Series of Treasury Decisions (U.S.) |
| Student Law. | Student Lawyer | | |
| Student Law. J. | Student Lawyer Journal | Syracuse L. Rev. | Syracuse Law Review |

# T

| | | | |
|---|---|---|---|
| T. | Tappan's Reports (Ohio) | T.B.M. | Tax Board Memorandum (I.R.Bull.) |
| | Tobacco Division (I.R.Bull.) | T.B.Mon. | T. B. Monroe (Ky.) |
| T. & C. | Thompson & Cook N. Y. Supreme Court Reports | T.B.R. | Advisory Tax Board Recommendation (I.R.Bull.) |
| T. & G. | Tyrwhitt & Granger's Exchequer (Eng.) | T.C. | Tax Court of the United States Reports |
| T. & M. | Temple & Mew's Crown Cases (Eng.) | T.D. | Treasury Decisions |
| | | t.Holt | Same as Modern Cases (Eng.) |
| T. & P. | Turner & Phillips' Chancery (Eng.) | T.I.A.S. | Treaties and Other International Acts Series (U.S.) |
| T. & R. | Turner & Russell's Chancery (Eng.) | | |
| T.B. & M. | Tracewell, Bowers & Mitchell, Comptroller's Decisions (U.S.) | T.Jones | Thomas Jones, King's Bench and Common Pleas (Eng.) |

| | | | |
|---|---|---|---|
| T.L.R. | Times Law Reports (Eng.) | Taylor | Same |
| T.M.Bull. | Trade Mark Bulletin (U.S.) | Taylor U.C. | Taylor, King's Bench (Ont.) |
| T.M.Bull. (N.S.) | Same, New Series | Temp. & M. | Temple & Mew Crown Cases (Eng.) |
| T.M.M. | Tax Management Memorandum (BNA) | Temp.Geo.II | Cases in Chancery temp. Geo. II. (Eng.) |
| T.M.Rep. | Trade Mark Reporter | Temp.L.Q. | Temple Law Quarterly |
| T.N.E.C. | Temporary National Economic Committee | Temp.Wood | Manitoba Reports temp. Wood (Can.) |
| T.R. | Term Reports, King's Bench (Durnford & East) (Eng.) | Temple & M. | Temple & Mew Crown Cases (Eng.) |
| | | Temple L.Q. | Temple Law Quarterly |
| T.Raym. | Thomas Raymond, King's Bench (Eng.) | Tenn. | Tennessee |
| | | Tenn.App. | Tennessee Appeals |
| T.S. | Treaty Series (U.S.) | Tenn.App. Bull. | Tennessee Appellate Bulletin |
| T.U.P.Charlt. | T. U. P. Charlton (Ga.) | Tenn.C.C.A. | Tennessee Court of Civil Appeals |
| Tait | Tait's Manuscript Decisions (Sc.) | | |
| Tal. | Cases temp. Talbot, Chancery (Eng.) | Tenn.Cas. | Shannon's Tennessee Cases |
| Talb. | Same | Tenn.Ch. | Tennessee Chancery, Cooper |
| Tam. | Tamlyn (Rolls Court) (Eng.) | Tenn.Ch.App. | Tennessee Chancery Appeals |
| Taml. | Same | Tenn.Civ.App. | Tennessee Court of Civil Appeals |
| Tamlyn | Tamlyn's Chancery (Eng.) | | |
| Tamlyn Ch. | Same | Tenn.L.Rev. | Tennessee Law Review |
| Taney | Taney, Circuit Court (U.S.) | Tenn.Leg.Rep. | Tennessee Legal Reporter |
| | | Term | Term Reports, King's Bench (See Durnford & East) (Eng.) |
| Tann. | Tanner (Ind.) | | |
| Tanner | Same | | |
| Tapp. | Tappan's Reports (Ohio) | Term N.C. | Term Reports, North Carolina (Taylor) |
| Tappan | Same | Term R. | Term Reports, King's Bench (See Durnford and East) (Eng.) |
| Tasm. | Tasmanian State Reports | | |
| Tasm.L.R. | Tasmania Law Reports | | |
| Tasm.U.L. Rev. | Tasmania University Law Review | Term Rep. | Same |
| | | Terr. | Terrell (Tex.) |
| Taun. | Taunton, Common Pleas (Eng.) | Terr. & Wal. | Terrell & Walker (Tex.) |
| Taunt. | Same | Terr.L.R. | Territories' Law Reports N. W. |
| Tax A.B.C. | Canada Tax Appeal Board Cases | | |
| Tax Adm'rs News | Tax Administrators News | Terry | Terry |
| | | Tex. | Texas |
| Tax Advisor | The Tax Advisor | Tex.A.Civ. Cas. | White & Wilson's Civil Cases (Tex.) |
| Tax Cas. | Tax Cases (Eng.) | | |
| Tax Counselor's Q. | Tax Counselor's Quarterly | Tex.A.Civ. Cas. (Wilson) | Texas Court of Appeal Civil Cases |
| Tax L.Rep. | Tax Law Reporter | | |
| Tax L.Rev. | Tax Law Review | Tex.App. | Texas Civil Appeals Cases |
| Tax Law. | The Tax Lawyer | | |
| Tax Mag. | Tax Magazine | | Texas Court of Appeals Cases |
| Tax.R. | Taxation Reports | | |
| Taxes | Taxes, The Tax Magazine | Tex.B.J. | Texas Bar Journal |
| Tay. | Taylor's Carolina Reports (N.C.) | Tex.Civ.App. | Texas Civil Appeals |
| | | Tex.Civ.Rep. | Same |
| | Taylor's King's Bench (Can.) | Tex.Com.App. | Texas Commission Appeals |
| | Taylor's Term Reports (N.C.) | Tex.Cr.App. | Texas Criminal Appeals |
| | | Tex.Cr.R. | Same |

| | | | |
|---|---|---|---|
| Tex.Crim. | Texas Criminal Reports | Trade Reg. Rep. | Trade Regulation Reporter (CCH) |
| Tex.Ct.App. R. | Texas Court of Appeals Reports | Trade Reg. Rev. | Trade Regulation Review |
| Tex.Dec. | Texas Decisions | Trademark Bull. | Trade-Mark Bulletin |
| Tex.Int.L. Forum | Texas International Law Forum | Trademark Bull.(N.S.) | Same, New Series |
| Tex.Int'l L.F. | Same | Trademark Rptr. | Trade-Mark Reporter |
| Tex.Int'l L.J. | Texas International Law | | |
| Tex.Jur. | Texas Jurisprudence | Trans. & Wit. | Transvaal & Witswatersrand Reports |
| Tex.Jur.2d | Same, Second Series | Transc.A. | Transcript Appeals (N.Y.) |
| Tex.L.J. | Texas Law Journal | Transp.L.J. | Transportation Law Journal |
| Tex.L.Rev. | Texas Law Review | | |
| Tex.S.Ct. | Texas Supreme Court Reporter | Tread.Const. | Treadway's Constitutional Rep. (S.C.) |
| Tex.So.U.L. Rev. | Texas Southern University Law Review | Treas.Dec. | Treasury Decisions (U.S.) |
| Tex.Supp. | Texas Supplement | Trem.P.C. | Tremaine, Pleas of Crown |
| Tex.Tech L. Rev. | Texas Tech Law Review | Trial | Trial |
| Tex.Unrep. Cas. | (Posey's) Unreported Cases (Tex.) | Trial Law. Guide | Trial Lawyer's Guide |
| Texas L.Rev. | Texas Law Review | Trial Law.Q. | Trial Lawyers' Quarterly |
| Th. & C. | Thompson & Cook's N. Y. Supreme Court | Trin.T. | Trinity Term (Eng.) |
| | | Tripp | Tripp (Dak.Terr.) |
| Thatcher Cr. | Thatcher's Criminal Cases (Mass.) | Tru. | Trueman's Equity Cases (N.B.) |
| Thayer | Thayer (Ore.) | Tru.Railw. Rep. | Truman, American Railway Reports |
| Themis | La Revue Juridique Themis | Truem.Eq. Cas. | Trueman's Equity Cases (N.B.) |
| Thom. | Thomson's Reports (Nova Scotia) | Trust Bull. | Trust Bulletin |
| Thomas & Fr. | Thomas & Franklin Chancery (Md.) | Trust Terr. | Trust Territory Reports |
| Thomp. | Thompson (Cal.) | Trusts & Estates | Trusts and Estates |
| Thomp.Tenn. Cas. | Thompson's Unreported Tennessee Cases | Tuck. | Tucker (Mass.) |
| Thompson & C. | Thompson & Cook New York Supreme Court | Tuck. & C. | Tucker & Clephane (D.C.) |
| | | Tuck.Dist. of Col. | Tucker's Appeals (D.C.) |
| Thomson | Thomson's Reports (Nova Scotia) | Tuck.Sel.Cas. | Tucker's Select Cases (Newf.) |
| Thor. | Thorington (Ala.) | Tuck.Surr. | Tucker's Surrogate (N.Y.) |
| Thorpe | Thorpe's Louisiana Annual | Tul.L.Rev. | Tulane Law Review |
| Tiff. | Tiffany Court Appeals (N.Y.) | Tul.Tax Inst. | Tulane Tax Institute |
| | | Tulane L.Rev. | Tulane Law Review |
| Tiffany | Same | Tulsa L.J. | Tulsa Law Journal |
| Till. | Tillman (Ala.) | Tupp.App. | Tupper's Appeal Reports (Ont.) |
| Tillman | Same | Turn. | Turner (Ark.) |
| Tinw. | Tinwald (Sc.) | | Turner (Ky.) |
| Title News | Title News | | Turner & Russell's Chancery (Eng.) |
| Tobey | Tobey (R.I.) | Turn. & P. | Turner & Phillips' Chancery (Eng.) |
| Toth. | Tothill's Chancery (Eng.) | Turn. & Ph. | Same |
| Tr. & H.Pr. | Troubat & Haly's Practice (Pa.) | Turn. & R. | Turner & Russell's Chancery (Eng.) |
| Trace. & M. | Tracefell & Mitchell (Comptroller's Decisions) (U.S.) | Turn. & Rus. | Same |
| | | Turn. & Russ. | Same |
| Trade Cas. | Trade Cases (CCH) | Tutt. | Tuttle (Cal.) |

| | | | |
|---|---|---|---|
| Tutt. & C. | Tuttle & Carpenter (Cal.) | Tyrw. | Tyrwhitt Exchequer (Eng.) |
| Tutt. & Carp. | Same | | |
| Tyler | Tyler (Vt.) | Tyrw. & G. | Tyrwhitt & Granger Exchequer (Eng.) |
| Tyng | Tyng (Mass.) | | |

# U

| | | | |
|---|---|---|---|
| U.B.C.L.Rev. | University of British Columbia Law Review | U.C.L.A.— Alaska L. Rev. | U.C.L.A.—Alaska Law Review |
| U.C. | Upper Canada | U.C.L.J. | Upper Canada Law Journal |
| U.C. (O.S.) | Upper Canada Queen's Bench Reports, Old Series | U.C.L.J. (N.S.) | Same, New Series |
| U.C.App. | Upper Canada Appeal Reports | U.C.P.R. | Upper Canada Practice Reports |
| U.C.App. Rep. | Same | U.C.Pr. | Same |
| U.C.C.Law Letter | Uniform Commercial Code Law Letter | U.C.Q.B. | Upper Canada Queen's Bench Reports |
| U.C.C.P. | Upper Canada Common Pleas Reports | U.C.Q.B. (O.S.) | Same, Old Series |
| U.C.C.P.D. | Upper Canada Common Pleas Division Reports (Ont.) | U.C.R. | Upper Canada Queen's Bench Reports |
| | | U.C.Rep. | Upper Canada Reports |
| U.C.C.Rep. Serv. | Uniform Commercial Code Reporting Service | U.Chi.L.Rec. | University of Chicago Law School Record |
| U.C.Ch. | Upper Canada Chancery Reports | U.Chi.L.Rev. | University of Chicago Law Review |
| U.C.Ch. Rep. | Same | U.Cin.L.Rev. | University of Cincinnati Law Review |
| U.C.Cham. | Upper Canada Chamber Reports | U.Colo.L. Rev. | University of Colorado Law Review |
| U.C.Chamb. Rep. | Same | U.Det.L.J. | University of Detroit Law Journal |
| U.C.Chan. | Upper Canada Chancery Reports | U.Fla.L.Rev. | University of Florida Law Review |
| U.C.D.L.Rev. | University of California at Davis Law Review | U.Ill.L.F. | University of Illinois Law Forum |
| U.C.E. & A. | Upper Canada Error & Appeals Reports | U.Ill.L.Forum | University of Illinois Law Forum |
| U.C.Err. & App. | Same | U.Kan.City L.Rev. | University of Kansas City Law Review |
| U.C.I.S. | Benefit Series, Unemployment Compensation Interpretation Service | U.Miami L. Rev. | University of Miami Law Review |
| | | U.Mich.J.Law Reform | University of Michigan Journal of Law Reform |
| | Federal Series, Unemployment Compensation Interpretation Service | U.Mo.Bull.L. Ser. | University of Missouri Bulletin Law Series |
| | | U.Mo.K.C. L.Rev. | University of Missouri at Kansas City Law Review |
| | State Series, Unemployment Compensation Interpretation Service | U.N.B.L.J. | University of New Brunswick Law Journal |
| U.C.Jur. | Upper Canada Jurist | U.N.T.S. | United Nations Treaty Series |
| U.C.K.B. | Upper Canada King's Bench Reports, Old Series | U.Newark L.Rev. | University of Newark Law Review |
| U.C.L.A. Intra.L.Rev. | U.C.L.A. Intramural Law Review | U.Pa.L.Rev. | University of Pennsylvania Law Review |
| U.C.L.A. L.Rev. | U.C.L.A. Law Review | U.Pitt.L.Rev. | University of Pittsburgh Law Review |

| | | | |
|---|---|---|---|
| U.Queens.L.J. | University of Queensland Law Journal | U.S.T. | United States Treaties and Other International Agreements |
| U.Rich.L.Rev. | University of Richmond Law Review | U.S.T.D. | United States Treaty Development |
| U.S. | United States Reports | | |
| U.S. & Can. Av. | United States and Canadian Aviation Reports | U.S.Tax Cas. | United States Tax Cases (CCH) |
| U.S.App. | United States Appeals | U.S.V.A.A.D. | U. S. Veterans Administration Administrator's Decisions |
| U.S.Av.R. | Aviation Reports (U.S.) | | |
| U.S.Aviation | Same | | |
| U.S.C. | United States Code | U.S.V.B.D.D. | U. S. Veterans Bureau Directors Decisions |
| U.S.C. (Supp.) | United States Code, Supplement | U.San.Fernando V.L.Rev. | University of San Fernando Valley Law Review |
| U.S.C.A. | U. S. Code Annotated | | |
| U.S.C.Govt'l Rev. | University of South Carolina Governmental Review | U.San.Fran. L.Rev. | University of San Francisco Law Review |
| U.S.C.M.A. | United States Court of Military Appeals | [e.g.] U.So.Cal. 1955 Tax Inst. | University of Southern California Tax Institute |
| U.S.C.S. | United States Code Service | U.Tasm.L. Rev. | University of Tasmania Law Review (or Tasmania University Law Review) |
| U.S.Code Cong. & Ad.News | United States Code Congressional & Administrative News | | |
| U.S.Ct.Cl. | United States Court of Claims Reports | U.Toledo L. Rev. | University of Toledo Law Review |
| U.S.D.C. | United States District Court | U.Tor.L.Rev. | University of Toronto School of Law Review |
| U.S.I.C.C.V.R. | U. S. Interstate Commerce Commission Valuation Reports | U.Toronto L.J. | University of Toronto Law Journal |
| U.S.Jur. | United States Jurist (D.C.) | U.W.Austl.L. Rev. | University of Western Australia Law Review |
| U.S.L.Ed. | United States Supreme Court Reports, Lawyers' Edition | U.W.L.A.L. Rev. | University of West Los Angeles School of Law, Law Review |
| U.S.L.J. | United States Law Journal | U.Wash.L. Rev. | University of Washington Law Review |
| U.S.L.Mag. | United States Law Magazine | U.Windsor L.Rev. | University of Windsor Law Review |
| U.S.L.Week | United States Law Week | Udal | Fiji Law Reports (Fiji) |
| U.S.Law.Ed. | United States Supreme Court Reports, Lawyers' Edition | Un.Prac. News | Unauthorized Practice News |
| U.S.M.C. | U. S. Maritime Commission | Unempl.Ins. Rep. | Unemployment Insurance Reporter (CCH) |
| U.S.P.Q. | United States Patent Quarterly | Unof. | Unofficial Reports |
| | | Urban Law Ann. | Urban Law Annual |
| U.S.S.B. | U. S. Shipping Board | Urban Law. | Urban Lawyer |
| U.S.S.C.Rep. | United States Supreme Court Reports | Utah | Utah |
| | | Utah 2d | Same, Second Series |
| U.S.Sup.Ct. Rep. | United States Supreme Court Reporter (West) | Utah L.Rev. | Utah Law Review |
| | | Util.L.Rep. | Utilities Law Reporter (CCH) |

# V

| | | | |
|---|---|---|---|
| V.C.Rep. | Vice Chancellor's Reports (Eng.) | Vern. & S. | Vernor & Scriven, King's Bench (Ir.) |
| V.I. | Virgin Islands Reports | Vern. & Sc. | Same |
| V.I.B.J. | Virgin Islands Bar Journal | Vern. & Scr. | Same |
| | | Vern. & Scriv. | Same |
| V.R. | Valuation Reports, Interstate Commerce Commission | Vern.Ch. | Vernon's Chancery (Eng.) |
| | | Ves. | Vesey Chancery Reports (Eng.) |
| Va. | Virginia | | Vesey, Senior, Chancery (Eng.) |
| Va.Bar News | Virginia Bar News | | |
| Va.Cas. | Virginia Cases | Ves. & B. | Vesey & Beames' (Eng.) |
| Va.Ch.Dec. | Chancery Decisions (Va.) | Ves. & Bea. | Same |
| Va.Dec. | Virginia Decisions | Ves. & Beam. | Same |
| Va.J.Int'l L. | Virginia Journal of International Law | Ves.Jr. | Vesey, Junior, Chancery (Eng.) |
| Va.L.J. | Virginia Law Journal | | |
| Va.L.Reg. | Virginia Law Register | Ves.Jun. | Same |
| Va.L.Reg. (N.S.) | Same, New Series | Ves.Jun.Supp. | Vesey, Junior, Supplement, Chancery (Eng.) |
| Va.L.Rev. | Virginia Law Review | Ves.Sen. | Vesey, Senior, Chancery (Eng.) |
| Va.R. | Virginia Reports (Gilmer) | Ves.Sr. | Same |
| Val.R. (I.C.C.) | Interstate Commerce Commission Valuation Reports | Ves.Supp. | Vesey, Senior, Supplement, Chancery (Eng.) |
| | | Vez. | Vezey, Same as Vesey |
| Val.U.L.Rev. | Valparaiso University Law Review | Vict. | Victoria |
| | | Vict.Admr. | Victorian Admiralty |
| Van K. | Van Koughnett's Common Pleas (Upper Can.) | Vict.Eq. | Victorian Equity |
| | | Vict.L. | Victorian Law |
| Van Ness Prize Cas. | Van Ness Prize Cases (U.S.) | Vict.L.R. | Victorian Law Reports |
| Vand.J. Transnat'l L. | Vanderbilt Journal of Transnational Law | Vict.L.R.Min. | Victorian Law Mining Reports |
| | | Vict.L.T. | Victorian Law Times |
| Vand.L.Rev. | Vanderbilt Law Review | Vict.Rev. | Victorian Review |
| Vaug. | Vaughan Common Pleas (Eng.) | Vict.St.Tr. | Victorian State Trials |
| | | Vict.U.L.Rev. | Victoria University Law Review |
| Vaugh. | Same | | |
| Vaughan | Same | Vict.U.Well. L.Rev. | Victoria University of Wellington Law Review |
| Vaux | Vaux Decisions (Pa.) Vaux Recorder's Decisions (Pa.) | Vil. & Br. | Vilas & Bryant's Ed. Reports (Wis.) |
| Ve. | Vesey Chancery Reports (Eng.) | Vilas | Vilas' N. Y. Criminal Reports |
| | Vesey, Senior, Chancery (Eng.) | Vill.L.Rev. | Villanova Law Review |
| | | Vin.Abr. | Viner's Abridgment (Eng.) |
| Ve. & B. | Vesey & Beames Chancery (Eng.) | Vin.Supp. | Viner's Abridgment Supplement (Eng.) |
| Veaz. | Veazey (Vt.) | Vir. | Virgin (Me.) |
| Veazey | Same | Virgin | Same |
| Vent. | Ventris King's Bench (Eng.) | Virgin Is. | Virgin Islands |
| | Ventris Common Pleas (Eng.) | Vr. | Vroom's Law Reports (N.J.) |
| Ventr. | Ventris King's Bench (Eng.) | Vroom | Same |
| | | Vroom (G.D.W.) | Vroom, G. D. W. (N.J.) |
| Ver. | Vermont | Vroom (P.D.) | Vroom, P. D. (N.J.) |
| Vern. | Vernon's Cases (Eng.) | Vt. | Vermont |

# W

| | | | |
|---|---|---|---|
| W. | Watts (Pa.) | W.L.Gaz. | Same |
| | Wandell (N.Y.) | W.L.J. | Western Law Journal |
| | Wheaton's Supreme Court (U.S.) | W.L.Jour. | Weekly Law Journal |
| | | W.L.M. | Western Law Monthly (Ohio) |
| | Wright (Ohio) | | |
| W.A'B. & W. | Webb, A'Beckett & Williams (Victoria) | W.L.R. | Weekly Law Reports (Eng.) |
| W. & C. | Wilson & Courtenay's Appeal Cases | | Western Law Reporter |
| W. & M. | Woodbury & Minot Circuit Court (U.S.) | W.L.T. | Western Law Times and Reports |
| | | W.N. | Weekly Notes (Eng.) |
| W. & S. | Watts & Sergeant (Pa.) | W.Ont.L.Rev. | Western Ontario Law Review |
| | Wilson & Shaw's Appeal Cases (Sc.) | W.R. | Weekly Reports |
| W. & W. | White & Webb's Victorian Reports | W.Res.L. Rev. | Western Reserve Law Review |
| W. & W.Vict. | Wyatt & Webb's Victorian Reports | W.Rob. | William Robinson's Admiralty (Eng.) |
| | | W.Va. | West Virginia |
| W.Afr.App. | West African Court of Appeal Reports | W.Va.L.Q. | West Virginia Law Quarterly |
| W.Austl.Ind. Gaz. | Western Australia Industrial Gazette | W.Va.L.Rev. | West Virginia Law Review |
| W.Austl.J.P. | Western Australia Justice of the Peace | W.W. & D. | Willmore, Wollaston & Davison, Queen's Bench (Eng.) |
| W.Austl.L.R. | Western Australia Law Reports | W.W. & H. | Willmore, Wollaston & Hodges' Queen's Bench (Eng.) |
| W.Bl. | Sir William Blackstone's King's Bench & Common Pleas (Eng.) | | |
| | | W.W.Harr. | W. W. Harrington (Del.) |
| W.Bla. | Same | W.W.R. | Western Weekly Report (Can.) |
| W.C.C. | Washington's Circuit Court (U.S.) | | |
| | | W.W.R. (N.S.) | Same, New Series, 1951–1955 |
| | Workmen's Compensation Cases | Wa. | Watts (Pa.) |
| W.C.Ins.Rep. | Workmen's Compensation & Insurance Reports | | Wage and Hour Reporter |
| | | Wage & Hour Cas. | Wage and Hour Cases (BNA) |
| W.C.Rep. | Workmen's Compensation Reports | Wage & Hour Rep. | Wage & Hour Reporter |
| W.Coast Rep. | West Coast Reporter | | |
| W.H. & G. | Welsby, Hurlstone & Gordon's Exchequer (Eng.) | Wake For. L.Rev. | Wake Forest Law Review |
| | | Wake Forest Intra.L.Rev. | Wake Forest Intramural Law Review |
| W.H.Cases | Wage & Hour Cases | | |
| W.H.Man. | Wages & Hours Manual | Wal.By L. | Wallis, Irish Chancery (By Lyne) |
| W.H.R. | Wage & Hour Reporter | | |
| W.Jo. | William Jones King's Bench, Common Pleas, House of Lords and Exchequer (Eng.) | Wal.Jr. | Wallace Junior (U.S.) |
| | | Walk. | Walker (Ala.) (Miss.) (Pa.) (Tex.) |
| W.Jones | Same | | |
| W.Kel. | William Kellynge, King's Bench & Chancery (Eng.) | Walk.Ch. | Walker's Chancery (Mich.) |
| | | Walk.Ch.Cas. | Same |
| W.L.B. | Weekly Law Bulletin (Ohio) | Wall. | Wallace (U.S.) (Philadelphia) |
| W.L.G. | Weekly Law Gazette (Ohio) | Wall.C.C. | Wallace Circuit Court (U.S.) |
| | | Wall.Jr. | Wallace Junior (U.S.) |

| | | | | |
|---|---|---|---|---|
| Wall.Rep. | Wallace's Supreme Court Reports (U.S.) | Week.L.Gaz. | Weekly Law Gazette (Ohio) |
| | Wallace, The Reporters | Week.L.Rec. | Weekly Law Record |
| Wall.Sr. | Wallace Senior (U.S.) | Week.Law Bull. | Weekly Law Bulletin (Ohio) |
| Wallis | Wallis' Chancery (Ir.) | | |
| Wallis by L. | Wallis, Irish Chancery (By Lyne) | Week.Law Gaz. | Weekly Law Gazette (Ohio) |
| Walsh | Walsh's Registry Cases (Ir.) | Week.Notes Cas. | Weekly Notes of Cases (London) |
| Ward. | Warden (Ohio) | | Weekly Notes of Cases (Pa.) |
| Ward. & Sm. | Warden & Smith (Ohio) | Week.Rep. | Weekly Reporter (Eng.) |
| Warden's Law & Bk.Bull. | Weekly Law & Bank Bulletin (Ohio) | Week.Trans. Rep. | Weekly Transcript Reports (N.Y.) |
| Ware | Ware, District Court (U.S.) | Weekly L.R. | Weekly Law Reports (Eng.) |
| Wash. | Washington | Welfare L. Bull. | Welfare Law Bulletin |
| | Washington Reports (Va.) | Welfare L. News | Welfare Law News |
| Wash.2d | Washington Reports, Second Series | Welsb.H. & G. | Welsby, Hurlstone & Gordon's Exchequer (Eng.) |
| Wash. & Haz. P.E.I. | Washburton & Hazard's Reports (Prince Edward Island) | Welsby H. & G. | Same |
| Wash. & Lee L.Rev. | Washington & Lee Law Review | Welsh | Welsh's Registry Cases (Ir.) |
| Wash.C.C. | Washington Circuit Court (U.S.) | Wend. | Wendell (N.Y.) |
| Wash.L.Rep. | Washington Law Reporter (D.C.) | Wenz. | Wenzell (Minn.) |
| Wash.L.Rev. | Washington Law Review | Wes.C.L.J. | Westmoreland County Law Journal |
| Wash.Terr. | Washington Territory | West | West's Chancery (Eng.) |
| Wash.Terr. (N.S.) | Same, New Series | West Ch. | West's Chancery (Eng.) |
| Wash.Ty. | Washington Territory | West Va. | West Virginia |
| Wash.U.L.Q. | Washington University Law Quarterly | West. | Weston (Vt.) |
| Washb. | Washburn (Vt.) | West.Austl. | Western Australian Reports |
| Washburn L.J. | Washburn Law Journal | West.Jur. | Western Jurist (Des Moines) |
| Watts | Watts (Pa.) (W.Va.) | West.L.Gaz. | Western Law Gazette (Ohio) |
| Watts & S. | Watts & Sergeant (Pa.) | West.L.J. | Western Law Journal |
| Watts & Ser. | Same | West.L.M. | Western Law Monthly (Ohio) |
| Watts & Serg. | Same | West.L.Mo. | Same |
| Wayne L.Rev. | Wayne Law Review | West.L.Month. | Same |
| Webb | Webb (Kans.) (Tex.) | West.L.R. | Western Law Reporter (Can.) |
| | Webb's Civil Appeals (Tex.) | West.L.Rev. | Western Law Review |
| Webb & D. | Webb & Duval (Tex.) | West.Law J. | Western Law Journal |
| Webb & Duval | Same | West.Law M. | Western Law Monthly (Ohio) |
| Webb, A'B. & W. | Webb, A'Beckett & Williams Reports (Aust.) | West.R. | Western Reporter |
| | | West.School L.Rev. | Western School Law Review |
| Webs.Pat.Cas. | Webster's Patent Cases (Eng.) | West t.Hardw. | West temp. Hardwicke, Chancery (Eng.) |
| Week.Cin.L.B. | Weekly Law Bulletin (Ohio) | West.Week. Rep. | Western Weekly Reports (Can.) |
| Week.Dig. | Weekly Digest (N.Y.) | | |
| Week.Jur. | Weekly Jurist (Ill.) | | |

| | | | |
|---|---|---|---|
| West.Wkly. | Western Weekly (Can.) | Willes | Willes, King's Bench & Common Pleas (Eng.) |
| Western Res. L.Rev. | Western Reserve Law Review | Williams | Williams (Mass.) (Utah) (Vt.) |
| Westm. | Statute of Westminster (Eng.) | | Peere-Williams' English Chancery Reports |
| Westm.L.J. | Westmoreland Law Journal (Pa.) | Williams & Bruce Ad.Pr. | Williams & Bruce's Admiralty Practice |
| Wethey | Wethey's Queen's Bench (Upper Can.) | Williams P. | Peere-Williams' English Chancery Reports |
| Whart. | Wharton (Pa.) | Williams-Peere | Same |
| Whart.Law Dict. | Wharton's Law Lexicon | Willm.W. & D. | Willmore, Wollaston & Davison's Queen's Bench (Eng.) |
| Whart.St.Tr. | Wharton's State Trials (U.S.) | | |
| Wheat. | Wheaton (U.S.) | Willm.W. & H. | Willmore, Wollaston & Hodges' Queen's Bench (Eng.) |
| Wheel. | Wheeler's Criminal Cases (N.Y.) | | |
| | Wheelock (Tex.) | Willson | Willson Civil Cases (Tex.) |
| Wheeler Abr. | Wheeler's Abridgment | | |
| Wheeler C.C. | Wheeler's Criminal Cases (N.Y.) | Willson, Civ. Cas.Ct.App. | Same |
| Whit.Pat.Cas. | Whitman's Patent Cases (U.S.) | Wilm. | Wilmot's Notes (Eng.) |
| White | White (W.Va.) (Tex.) | Wils. | Wilson (Cal.) (Minn.) (Ore.) |
| | White's Justiciary Cases (Sc.) | | Wilson (Superior Court) (Ind.) |
| White & T. Lead. Cas.Eq. | White & Tudor's Leading Cases in Equity (Eng.) | | Wilson's King's Bench & Common Pleas (Eng.) |
| White & W. | White & Wilson (Tex.) | Wils. & S. | Wilson & Shaw (House of Lords) (Sc.) |
| Whitm.Lib. Cas. | Whitman's Libel Cases (Mass.) | | |
| Whitt. | Whittlesey (Mo.) | Wils.Ch. | Wilson's Chancery (Eng.) |
| Wight | Wight's Election Cases (Sc.) | Wils.C.P. | Wilson's Common Pleas (Eng.) |
| Wight. | Wightwick, Exchequer (Eng.) | Wils.Exch. | Wilson's Exchequer (Eng.) |
| Wightw. | Wightwick, Exchequer (Eng.) | Wils.K.B. | Wilson's King's Bench (Eng.) |
| Wilc. | Wilcox (Ohio) | Wils.P.C. | Wilson's Privy Council (Eng.) |
| Wilc.Cond. | Wilcox Condensed Ohio Reports | Winch | Winch, Common Pleas (Eng.) |
| Wilcox | Wilcox (Ohio) | | |
| | Wilcox (Pa.) | Winst. | Winston (N.C.) |
| Wilcox Cond. | Wilcox Condensed Ohio Reports | Wis. | Wisconsin |
| Wilk. | Wilkinson (Aust.) | Wis.L.N. | Wisconsin Legal News |
| | Wilkinson Court of Appeals and Civil Appeals (Tex.) | Wis.L.Rev. | Wisconsin Law Review |
| | | Wisc.Stud. B.J. | Wisconsin Student Bar Journal |
| Will. | Williams (Mass.) | Withrow | Withrow (Iowa) |
| | Willson (Tex.) | Wkly.Dig. | Weekly Digest (N.Y.) |
| Will.L.J. | Willamette Law Journal | Wkly.L.Bul. | Weekly Law Bulletin (Ohio) |
| Will., Woll. & Dav. | Willmore, Wollaston & Davison Queen's Bench (Eng.) | Wkly.L.Gaz. | Weekly Law Gazette (Ohio) |
| Will.Woll. & H. | Willmore, Wollaston & Hodges' Queen's Bench (Eng.) | Wkly.Law Bull. | Weekly Law Bulletin (Ohio) |
| Will.Woll. & Hodg. | Same | | |

| | | | |
|---|---|---|---|
| Wkly.N.C. | Weekly Notes of Cases (Pa.) | Women's Rights L. Rptr. | Women's Rights Law Reporter |
| Wkly.Rep. | Weekly Reporter (Eng.) | Wood. | Woodbury & Minot, Circuit Court (U.S.) |
| Wm. & Mary L.Rev. | William & Mary Law Review | Wood. & M. | Same |
| Wol. | Wolcott's Chancery (Del.) | Woodb. & M. | Same |
| | Wollaston's English Bail Court Reports (Eng.) | Woods | Woods Circuit Court (U.S.) |
| Wolf. & B. | Wolferstan & Bristow's Election Cases (Eng.) | Woodw. | Woodward's Decisions (Pa.) |
| Wolf. & D. | Wolferstan & Dew's Election Cases (Eng.) | Woolw. | Woolworth (Neb.) |
| | | | Woolworth Circuit Court (U.S.) |
| Woll. | Wollaston's English Bail Court Reports | Wright | Wright (Ohio) (Pa.) |
| Woll.P.C. | Same | Wy. & W. | Wyatt & Webb (Vict.) |
| Women Law. J. | Women Lawyer's Journal | Wy., W. & A'Beck. | Wyatt, Webb & A'Beckett (Vict.) |
| Women Lawyer's J. | Same | Wyo. | Wyoming |
| | | Wyo.L.J. | Wyoming Law Journal |
| | | Wythe | Wythe's Chancery (Va.) |

# Y

| | | | |
|---|---|---|---|
| Y. | Yeates' (Pa.) | Yearb. | Year Book, King's Bench (Eng.) |
| Y. & C. | Younge & Collyer's Chancery (Eng.) | Yearb.P.7, Hen.VI | Year Books, Part 7, Henry VI |
| Y. & C.C.C. | Same | Yeates | Yeates (Pa.) |
| Y. & J. | Younge & Jervis' Exchequer (Eng.) | Yel. | Yelverton, King's Bench (Eng.) |
| Y.A.D. | Young's Admiralty Decisions (Nova Scotia) | Yelv. | Same |
| Y.B. | Year Book, King's Bench, etc. (Eng.) | Yerg. | Yerger (Tenn.) |
| | | York Leg.Rec. | York Legal Record (Pa.) |
| Y.B. (Rolls Series) | Year Books Rolls Series (Eng.) | Yorke Ass. | Yorke Assizes (Clayton) |
| Y.B. (Sel. Soc.) | Year Books (Selden Society) (Eng.) | You. | Younge's Exchequer (Eng.) |
| Y.B.Ed.I | Year Books, Edward I | You. & Coll. Ch. | Younge & Collyer's Exchequer (Eng.) |
| Y.B.Eur. Conv. on Human Rights | Yearbook of the European Convention on Human Rights | You. & Coll. Ex. | Same |
| | | You. & Jerv. | Younge & Jervis Exchequer (Eng.) |
| Y.B.Int'l L. Comm'n | Yearbook of the International Law Commission | Young | Young (Minn.) |
| | | Young Adm. | Young Admiralty (N.S.) |
| Y.B.P.1, Edw.II | Year Books, Part 1, Edward II | Young Adm. Dec. | Same |
| Y.B.S.C. | Year Books, Selected Cases | Young Naut. Dict. | Young's Nautical Dictionary |
| Yale L.J. | Yale Law Journal | Younge | Younge's Exchequer (Eng.) |
| Yale Rev.Law & Soc.Act'n | Yale Review of Law and Social Action | Younge & C.Ch. Cas. | Younge & Collyer's Chancery or Exchequer Equity (Eng.) |
| Yates Sel.Cas. | Yates' Select Cases (N.Y.) | Younge & C. Exch. | Younge & Collyer's Exchequer Equity (Eng.) |
| Yea. | Yeates (Pa.) | | |

| | | | |
|---|---|---|---|
| Younge & Coll. Ex. | Same | Younge & Je. | Same |
| Younge & J. | Younge & Jervis Exchequer (Eng.) | Younge Exch. | Younge Exchequer (Eng.) |
| | | Younge M.L. Cas. | Younge Maritime Law Cases (Eng.) |

# Z

| | |
|---|---|
| Zab. | Zabriskie (N.J.) |
| Zane | Zane (Utah) |

# INDEX

References are to Pages

Italic type indicates Titles of Publications

**CITATION, METHODS OF**—Cont'd

Encyclopedias, 329.

English, 447–448.

Federal legislative histories, 206.

*Federal Rules Decisions*, 236.

*Federal Rules Service*, 236.

Federal statutes, 174–175.

Internal Revenue Code, 175.

Legal periodicals, 57–58.

Public law, 174.

Restatements, 389.

State session laws, 225.

State statutes, 224–225.

*Statutes at Large*, 175.

Treaties, 418.

Treatises, 388.

*United States Code*, 175.

*United States Revised Statutes*, 175.

**CITATORS.**

Definition of, 281.

English, 433.

   Illustrations of, 445–446.

*Shepard's Citations*, 281–308.

**CITED CASE, 282.**

**CITING CASE, 282.**

**CITY CHARTERS, ORDINANCES, CODES.**

See Legislation, Municipal.

**CIVIL PRACTICE.**

See Court Procedure.

*COCHRAN, LAW LEXICON*, 392.

*CODE OF FEDERAL REGULATIONS*, 240–241.

Executive orders, 241.

General index, 241.

Index method, 273.

Presidential proclamations, 241.

Research procedure, 272–273.

Topic method, 273.

**CODES.**

   See also Legislation.

Defined, 208–209.

**COMMERCE CLEARING HOUSE, INC.**

*Congressional Index*, 185, 403.

*Federal Tax Articles*, 338.

*Legislative Reporting Service*, 342.

*Tax Treaties*, 402.

*United States Supreme Court Bulletin*, 37.

**COMMON LAW, 1–2.**

**COMPILED STATUTES.**

Defined, 208–209.

**CONCURRING OPINION, 17.**

*CONGRESSIONAL RECORD*, 182, 183–184.

*Daily Digest*, 183, 186.

Index to, 184.

**CONSOLIDATED STATUTES.**

Defined, 208–209.

*CONSOLIDATED TREATIES SERIES*, 413.

**CONSTITUTIONAL LAW.**

Federal, research procedure, summary of, 450.

State, research procedure, summary of, 451.

**CONSTITUTIONS, 133–148.**

Citation, methods of, 146–147.

Comparative information, 144–146.

Federal,

   Amending, 138–139.

   Historical sources, 134.

   Illustrations of, 140–141.

   Judicial interpretation of, 135–137.

   Publications, 133.

Foreign, 146.

Research procedure, 133.

Shepardizing, 297.

   Illustrations of, 299–300.

State, research procedure, 143–144.

Summary, 148.

Treatises, 138.

*CONSTITUTIONS OF THE STATES AND THE UNITED STATES*, 145.

*CONSTITUTIONS OF THE UNITED STATES*, 146.

*COOLEY, CONSTITUTIONAL LIMITATIONS*, 138.

*CORPUS JURIS*, 310.

*CORPUS JURIS SECUNDUM*, 310–311.

Citation of, 329.

Definitions, 311.

Illustrations, Use of, 317–319.

Law chart, 311.

Summary, 329–330.

**COURT CASES.**

Briefs of counsel, synopsis of, 17.

Counsel, names of, 17.

Decision,

   Date of, 15.

   With judgment or decree, 18.

Facts, statement of, 8.

Opinion, 9–10.

Prefatory statement, 15.

Syllabus, 15–16.

Title of, 14.

**PRIMARY AUTHORITY, 6.**
Federal, 4.
Sources of, 2.
State, 4.

**PRIVATE LAW.**
Defined, 150.
Inoperative, 173.

**PUBLIC LAW.**
Citation, method of, 174.
Defined, 150.
Illustrations of, 154.

**RATIO DECIDENDI, 18.**

**RECORDS AND BRIEFS, 395.**

**REGIONAL DIGESTS, 79.**

**REGNAL YEARS.**
English table of, 447.

*REMINGTON, BANKRUPTCY LAW OF THE UNITED STATES,* 394.

*RESTATEMENTS OF THE LAW,* 364–375.
Annotations to, 367.
Citation, methods of, 389.
Cited, frequency, 366.
Codification movement, influence of, on, 364.
Defects, 365–366.
Evaluation of the law, absence of, 365.
Features of, 366–368.
General index, 368.
Illustrations, Use of, 369–374.
Index method, 387.
Legislative endorsement, absence of, 365.
Research procedure, 387–388.
*Restatement in the Courts,* 368.
Revisions, 368.
Shepardizing, Illustrations of, 375.
Summary, 390.
Supplements, 368.
Topic method, 388.

*REVISED REPORTS,* 429.

**REVISED STATUTES.**
Defined, 208.

*REVISED STATUTES.*
See *United States Revised Statutes.*

*SCHWARTZ, A COMMENTARY ON THE CONSTITUTION OF THE UNITED STATES,* 138.

**SCOPE–NOTE.**
Explained, 310.

*SCOTT AND BEAMAN, INDEX ANALYSIS OF FEDERAL STATUTES,* 170.

**SEARCH BOOKS.**
See Books of Search.

**SECONDARY AUTHORITY.**
Sources of, 2–3.

**SECONDARY SOURCES.**
Explanation of, 6.

**SESSION LAWS.**
Citation, methods of, 225.
Description of, 207–208.
Illustrations of, 213–219.

*SHEPARD'S CITATIONS.*
*Administrative,* 307.
As research aid, 285–286.
Cases,
  Abbreviation, 282–283.
  History of, 282.
  Illustrations, Use of, 287–294.
  Units of, 284.
Charters, 297.
Constitutions, 297.
  Illustration, 299.
Court rules, 297.
  Illustration of, 305.
Features of, Illustration of, 294.
Federal, 285.
Keeping current, 308.
*Labor Law,* 307.
*Law Review Citations,* 307.
*Ordinance Law Annotations,* 297.
  Illustration of, 304.
Ordinances, 297.
  Illustrations of, 302–303.
  Index to, 297.
Parallel citations from, 285.
Regional units, Discussion of, 284.
State units, Discussion of, 284.
Statutes,
  Abbreviations, 295–296.
  Illustration of, 201.
Treatment of, 283.
United States,
  Contents of, 306–307.
  Illustration of, 305.
Uses of, 285.

*SHEPARD'S FEDERAL ACTS BY POPULAR NAMES,* 173, 178.

*SHEPARD'S FEDERAL LABOR LAW CITATIONS,* 307.

*SHEPARD'S LAW REVIEW CITATIONS,* 328.

**SLIP LAW, 151, 207.**

**SLIP OPINION, 20.**

**SOURCES.**
Law, 1.
State, 3.

END OF VOLUME

—. "La No-Violencia y el Perdon Revolucionario." In *Estudios Vascos de Criminología* (pp. 269–74). Mensajero, Bilbao, 1982.

tain, Antonio; Larrea, Maria Angeles; and Mieza, Rafael Maria. "Fuentes del Derecho Penal Vasco (Siglos XI–XVI)." *Gran Enciclopedia Vasca.* Mensajero, Bilbao, 1980.

an, Harold. *The Interaction of Law and Religion.* Abingdon Press, Nashville, 1974.

ndo, Pedro. "Algunos Modos Pasionales del Vasco." In *Estudios Vascos de Criminología* (pp. 63–64). Mensajero, Bilbao, 1982.

n, E.R. *History of Egypt under the Ptolemaic Dynasty.* Methuen, London, 1927.

, The, Revised Standard Version. Fontana Books, London, 1952.

erman, Elias Joseph. *Chronology of the Ancient World.* Cornell University Press, New York, 1968.

rdi, Arnaldo. *Diritto Greco Antico.* Giuffrè, Varesse, 1982.

, Franz. *El Arte Primitivo.* Fondo de Cultura Economica, Mexico, 1947.

la, Ida. *Herencia de Sumeria* (translated from the original by Leonardo Castañeda). Museo de las Culturas, Mexico, 1967.

, Albert de. *Met de "Mercator" naar de Stille Zuidsee. Reisdagboek van een Kadet.* Tweede uitgave, De Sikkel, Antwerpen, 1944.

—. *Croisière du "Mercator" au Pacific* (translated from the Dutch by Richard Lavaque). Imp. L. Vaumelle, Gent, Belgique, 1985.

le, Derk, and Morris, Clarence. *Law in Imperial China* (Taiwan ed.) 1971.

er, Robert, and Smith, Gertrude. *The Administration of Justice from Homer to Aristitle* (2 vol.). AMS Press, New York, 1970.

, Sukumar, and Varma, Paripurnanand. "Philosophical significance of Ancient Indian Penology." *Journal of Indian Philosophy,* Vol. 10, # 1, March 1982 (pp. 61–100).

on, E. *O Codigo de Hammurabi.* Imp. "Vozes," Petropolis, Brasil, 1976.

ra, C.M. *Classical Greece.* Time-Life International, Nederland, N.V., 1966.

lwood, Robert J. *The Near East and the Foundation of Civilization.* Eugene, Oregon, 1962.

iello, V. "Diritto Penale Romano." *Novissimo Digesto Italiano,* Vol. V, Torino, 1960 (pp. 960–66).

sted, James Henry. *A History of Egypt* (2nd ed.) Scribner, New York, 1923.

eault, J. "Proces contre les Cadavres dans l'Ancient Droit." *Revue Historique du Droit Français et Etranger,* Vol. 1 (pp. 619–22).

nt, John. *A History of Israel.* SCM Press, London, 1962.

nowski, J. *The Ascent of Man.* Little, Brown, Boston, 1973.

vn, Jose David. "India." In *Biblioteca Universal de Life en Espanol,* Offset Multicolor, S.A. Mexico, D.F. 1961.

, Sir Peter (Te Rangi Hiroa). *The Vikings of the Sunrise.* Fred A. Stokes, New York, 1938.

—. *The Coming of the Maori* (2nd ed.). Maori Purposes Fund Board, Whitecomb and Tombs, Wellington, 1966.

, A.R. *Persia and the Greeks.* Edward Arnold, London, 1962.

on, John. *The Collection of the Qur'an.* Cambridge University Press, Cambridge, 1977.

*familicus*—no violent criminal behavior occurred. The natives were kind and peaceful; they all had work to do, and all of them tried to help us as much as they could.

Regarding the killing of Dutrou Bornier, according to what I heard from the most important natives on the island, he was the victim of a plot. The natives, tired of his abuses and excesses, decided to kill him. Pieces of straw, one of which was short, were offered to all participants in the plot. The one who drew the short piece of straw was to be the executioner. However, I was never told who he was.

When I visited Pitcairn Island, there were only ninety inhabitants, all of them of mixed ethnic origin (English and Tahitians) and direct descendants of the mutineers of the *Bounty*. During the two days we spent there, the natives received us with great kindness. When we inquired about certain types of behavior, such as stealing or homicide, the people were very surprised; they could not recall any incidents of such a nature, despite being the descendants of the *Bounty*'s mutineers. I found only one young man of an unbalanced character; he was the only one on the island that was not working. He would wander from place to place, trying to catch birds with a catapult, but he was not of a violent character. He did not disturb the other islanders, and they did not disturb him. In short, it was a perfect arrangement.

# Bibliography

Adamson Hoebel, E. *The Law of Primitive Man*. Atheneum,

Adler, Morris. *El Mundo del Talmud*. Editorial Paidos, Buen

Aldred, Cyril. *The Egyptians*. Thames and Hudson, London,

Alexiou, Stylianos. *La Civilization Minoènne*. Spiros Alexiou
no date.

*Anales de la Universidad de Chile*, 161–162, November 1
(totally devoted to the publication of papers on Easter Islan
Gonzalo Figueroa G.H., Claudio Cristino, and others).

Atkins, Harry. *A History of Ethiopia*. Central Press, Addis A

Ayarragaray, Carlos A. *La Justicia en la Biblia y el Talm*
Abeledo, Buenos Aires, 1948.

Babini, Rosa de. *Los Siglos de la Historia*. Fondo de Cultura
1960.

Bamberger, B.J. *La Biblia: Un Enfoque Judío Moderno*. Edi
Aires, 1963.

Barandarian, Jose Miguel de. "Ciertos Delitos en el Pais Vasco
*de Criminología* (pp. 35–42) Mensajero, Bilbao, Spain.

Baron, Salo Wittmayer. *A Social and Religious History of the J*
Jewish Publication Society of America, Philadelphia, 195

Barrera Carrasco, Carlos de la. "Informe del Estado Actual
Control de la Lepra en la Isla de Pascua" (a typed docum
1978.

Beaglehole, John Cawte. "The Development of New Zealand
*of World History* (UNESCO), Vol. II, # 1, Librairie des M

Bengtson, Hermann (ed.). *The Greeks and the Persians*. (trar
man by J. Conway). Weidenfeld and Nicolson, London,

Beristain, Antonio (ed.). *Estudios Vascos de Criminología*. Mer

———. "Las Violencias y las No-Violencias en Euskadi." In
*Criminología* (pp. 43–55). Mensajero, Bilbao, 1982.

———. "El Fuero de San Sebastian y su Continuación en el D
In *Estudios Vascos de Criminología* (pp. 103–58). Mensa

———. "La Violencia como Desafío en España y en el Pais
In *Estudios Vascos de Criminología* (pp. 201–67). Mensa

Bury, J.B.; Cook, S.A.; and Adcock, F.E. (eds.). *The Persian Empire and the West,* The Cambridge Ancient History, Vol. IV. Cambridge University Press, Cambridge, 1969.

Calhoun, George M. *The Growth of Criminal Law in Ancient Greece.* University of California Press, Berkeley, 1927.

Cameron, George C. *History of Early Iran.* University of Chicago Press, Chicago, 1969.

Campion, Arturo. *Fuero General de Navarra Euskariana. Algo de Historia.* Impr. Garcia Estafeta, Pamplona, Spain, 1915.

Caro Baroja, Julio. "Otro Trago Amargo." In *Estudios Vascos de Criminología* (pp. 65–75). Mensajero, Bilbao, Spain, 1982.

Casson, Lionel. *Ancient Egypt.* Time-Life International, Nederland, N.V., 1966.

Castex, Louis. "L'Aviation Chiliènne prend position a l'Ile de Pâques." *Le Figaro,* Paris, 14 September 1964.

————. *Iles: Relais du Ciel.* Allon, Paris, 1965.

————. *Les Secrets de l'Ile de Pâques.* Hachette, Paris, 1966.

Celaya Ibarra, Adrian. "El Derecho Foral, los Grandes Delitos y los Grandes Castigos." In *Estudios Vascos de Criminología* (pp. 159–68). Mensajero, Bilbao, Spain, 1982.

Chang, Dae H. *Criminology: A Cross-Cultural Perspective* (2 vols.). Carolina Academic Press, Durham, N.C., 1976.

Chauvet, Stephen. *L'Ile de Pâques et ses Mystères.* Edition Tel, Paris, 1935.

————. "Outils anciens et de formes inédites (en obsidienne eclatêe) ressortisant a la civilisation de la Pièrre Polie de l'Ile de Pâques." *Bulletin de la Société Préhistorique Française,* # 7–8, 1935 (pp. 1–4).

Childe, Gordon. *De la Préhistoire à la Histoire* (translated from the original English by Andre Mansat and Jean Barthalen). Gallimard, Paris, 1963.

Ch'U, T'ung-tau. *Law and Society in Traditional China.* Rainbow-Bridge Books, Taiwan, 1961.

Clark, Grahame. *Prehistoria Universal* (translated from the original English by Juan A. Haster). Editorial Universitaria, Santiago, Chile, 1971.

Clark, Kenneth. *Civilization.* British Broadcasting Corporation and John Murray, London, 1971.

Cohn, Haim H. "The Penology of the Talmud." *Israel Law Review,* Vol. 5, # 1, January 1970 (pp. 53–74).

————. *Jewish Law in Ancient and Modern Israel.* KATV Publishing House, Jerusalem, 1971.

————. "Victimology and Ancient Law." Opening Lecture, First International Symposium on Victimology, Jerusalem, 1976.

Corporacion Venezolana de Guayana. "Las Relaciones Culturales." *Informe Anual,* 1969.

Costa, Fausto. *El Delito y la Pena en la Historia de la Filosofía* (translated from the original Italian by Mariano Ruiz Funes). Union Tipográfica Editorial Hispano-Americana, Mexico, 1953.

Coulson, Noel J. *A History of Islamic Law.* University Press, Edinburgh, 1964.

————. "Law and Religion in Contemporary Islam." *Hastings Law Journal,* Vol. 29, # 6, July 1978, University of California Press, San Francisco.

Culican, William. *The Medes and the Persians.* Praeger, New York, 1965.

Danforth, Kenneth C. *Journey into China.* National Geographical Society, Washington, D.C., 1976.

Dart, Raymond A., and Craig, Dennis. *Adventures with the Missing Link.* Viking Press, Harpers, New York, 1959.

Davaras, Costis. *The Palace of Knossos.* Editorial Hannibal, Athens, no date.

Davidson, Basil. *African Kingdoms.* Time-Life International, Nederland, N.V., 1967.

Deimel, A. *Codex Hammurabi.* Scripta Pontificci, Istituti Biblici, Roma, 1930.

Diamond, A.S. *Primitive Law, Past and Present.* Methuen, London, 1971.

Diamond, Stanley (ed.). *Primitive Views of the World.* Columbia University Press, New York, 1964.

Doresse, Jean. *Ethiopia. Ancient Cities and Temples* (2nd ed.). Elek Books, London, 1967.

Drapkin, Israel. "Contribution to the Demographic Study of Easter Island." Bernice P. Bishop Museum, Occasional Papers, Vol. XI, # 12, Honolulu, Hawaii, 1935a.

———. "Contribución al Estudio Antropológico y Demográfico de los Pascuences." *Bulletin de la Société des Americanistes de Paris* (New Séries), Vol. XXVII (pp. 265–302), Paris, 1935b.

———. "Contribution a l'Étude Démographique de l'Ile de Pâques." *Bulletin de la Société de Americanistes de Belgique,* # 18 (pp. 137–58), Bruxelles, December 1935c.

———. "L'Etat Sanitaire de l'Ile de Pâques." *Bulletin de l'Office International d'Hygiène Publique,* Tome XXVIII, Fasc. IV, #4 (pp. 723–8), Paris, April 1936a.

———. "La Lèpre à l'Ile de Pâques." Deliberatious Congressus Dermatologorum Internationalis IX-i, Tome II, Institutum Typographicum "Patria," Budapest, 1936b.

———. "Takatore. La Mancha Mongólica en los Pascuences." *Revista Chilena de Historia y Geografía,* Tomo LXXXII (pp. 145–55), Santiago, Chile, July 1937.

———. "Corrections in Israel." In Wickes and Cooper (eds.) *International Corrections.* Lexington Books, Lexington, Mass., 1979.

———. "Prolegómenos al Estudio del Derecho Penal en China Imperial." *Anuario de Derecho Penal y Ciencias Penales* (pp. 581–97), Madrid, 1982.

Driver, G.R., and Miles, J.C. *The Assyrian Laws.* Oxford University Press, Oxford, 1935.

Durant, Will. *La Civilización de la India* (traducción de C.A. Jordana) Editorial Sudamericana, Buenos Aires, 1952.

Dussau Alvelo, Adolfo. "Breves Comentarios sobre la Lepra y su Tratamiento en la Isla de Pascua" (typed report). Santiago, Chile, 1941.

Eastman, Max. "What Plato Says." In *Great Lives, Great Deeds* (pp. 99–104). London, 1965.

Eban, Abba. *My People: The History of the Jews* (Taiwan ed.) no date.

———. *Heritage. Civilization and the Jews.* Steimatzky, Tel Aviv, 1985.

Eberhard, Wolfram. *A History of China* (4th ed.) University of California Press, Berkeley, 1977.

Edwards, Rafael. *La Isla de Pascue: Consideraciones acerca de sus visitas en Julio 1916 y Jnion 1917.* Imprenta San Jose, Santiago, Chile, 1918.

Eilers, W. "Die Gesetzstele Chammurabis." *Der Alte Orient,* Vol. XXXI, # 3–4, 1932.

Eldine, M.A. Charaf: "Le Talion en Droit Egyptien et Musulman." *Revue de Sciences Criminelles et de Droit Pénal Comparé* (Nouvelle Série,) # 2 April–June 1975 (pp. 393–401).

Enoki, K. "Les Origines de l'Empire du Japon dans leurs Rapport avec l'Histoire Général de l'Extrême Orient." *Cahiers d'Histoire Mondiale* (UNESCO), Vol. II, # 1 (pp. 26–37) Librairie des Méridiens, Paris, 1954.

Espinosa B., and Marcial, R. "Estudios Botánicos." *Boletin del Museo Nacional de Historia Natural,* Tomo XX, (pp. 27–34). Santiago, Chile, 1942.

Farmer, Sarah S. *Tonga and the Friendly Islands,* Mission History Series # 2. Kaila Press, Canberra, 1976.

Farrow, John. *Damien the Leper.* Image Books, New York, December 1962.

Ferdon, E.N., Jr. "Easter Island Exchange Systems." *Southwestern Journal of Anthropology,* Vol. 14, 1958 (pp. 135–51).

Ferri, Enrico. *Les Criminels dans l'Art et la Literature.* Alcan, Paris, 1897.

Ferrini, Contardo. *Diritto Penale Romano.* U. Hoepli, Milano, 1899.

Fisher, H.A.L. *A History of Europe* (2 vols.). Collins, Fontana Library, London, 1969.

Forte, David F. "Comparative Criminal Law Enforcement: Islam. In *Encyclopedia of Crime and Justice* (Vol. 1, pp. 193–200). Free Press, New York, 1983.

Freeman, Derek. *Margaret Mead and Samoa.* Penguin Books, London, 1984.

Freud, Sigmund. *Totem and Taboo.* Pelican Books, London, 1938.

Frye, Richard N. *The Heritage of Persia.* World, Cleveland, Ohio, 1963.

Galindez Suarez, J.G. *La Legislación Penal en Vizcaya* (con la transcripción, como apéndice, del "Quaderno Penal de 1342" y del "Quarderno de Hermandad de 1394"). Bilbao, Spain, 1934.

Galvin, Deborah M. "Hebraic Law." Unpublished seminar work, University of Pennsylvania, Fall 1972.

Garcio-Gallo, Alfonso. *Manual de Historia del Derecho Espanol* (2 vols., 6th rev. ed.). Artes Graficas y Ediciones, Madrid, 1975.

Gardiner, Sir Alan H. *Egypt of the Pharaohs.* Clarendon Press, Oxford, 1961.

Ghurye, G.S. *The Scheduled Tribes* (3rd ed.). Popular Prakashan, Bombay, 1963.

Gibb, Sir Hamilton Alexander Rosskeen. "An Interpretation of Islamic History." *Journal of World History* (UNESCO), Vol. I. # 1, July 1953 (pp. 39–62).

———. *Mohammedanism: An Historical Survey.* Mentor Books, New York, 1955.

Gioffredi, Carlo. *I Principi del Diritto Penale Romano.* Giappichelli, Torino, 1970.

Glanville, Stephen Ranulph Kingdon (ed.). *The Legacy of Egypt.* Clarendon Press, Oxford, 1942.

Goldin, H.E. *Hebrew Criminal Law and Procedure.* Twayne, New York 1952.

Goldin, Judah. *The Living Talmud.* University of Chicago Press, Chicago, 1957.

Gosita, Arif. "The Relevance of a Life Philosophy for a Nation towards Developing Community Responsibility in Prevention of Victimization and Victim Assistance: Some Notes." Unpublished paper presented at the Fifth International Symposium of Victimology, Zagreb, 1985.

Granet, Marcel. *Chinese Civilization* (translated from the original French by Kathleen E. Innes and Mabel R. Brailsford). Meridian Books, Cleveland, Ohio, 1964.

Greenberg, Moshe. "The Biblical Conception of Asylum." *Journal of Biblical Literature.* Vol. LXXVIII, Part II, 1959 (pp. 125–32).

————."Some Postulates of Biblical Criminal Law." in J. Goldin (ed.), *The Jewish Expression* (pp. 5–28). Bantam Books, New York, 1970.

Grun, Bernard. *The Timetables of History*. Simon and Schuster, New York, 1975.

Haberman, Clyde. "Pacific Islands take Micro-Steps toward Home Rule." *New York Times,* November 17, 1985.

Hadas, Moses. *Imperial Rome*. Time-Life International, Nederland N.V., 1966.

Hagen, Anders. *Rock Carvings in Norway*. Johan Grundt Tanum Forlag, Oslo, 1971.

Hallie, Philip. *The Paradox of Cruelty*. Wesleyan University Press, Middletown, Conn., 1969.

Hamblin, Dora Jane. *The Etruscans*. Time-Life International, Nederland N.V., 1977.

Harrison, A.R.W. *The Law of Athens* (2 vols.). Oxford University Press, Oxford, 1971.

Hartman, Louis F., and Dilella, Alexander A. *The Anchor Bible*. Doubleday, New York, 1978.

Haruo, Abe, assisted by B.J. George, Jr. "The Accused and Society: Therapeutic and Preventive Aspects of Criminal Justice in Japan." In *Law in Japan: The Legal Order in a Changing Society,* ed. Arthur Taylor von Mehren, pp. 324–63. Harvard University Press, Cambridge, Mass. 1963.

Hattori, Takaaki, assisted by Richard Rabinowitz. "The Legal Profession in Japan: Its Historical Development and Present State." In *Law in Japan: The Legal Order in a Changing Society,* ed. Arthur von Mehren, pp. 111–52. Harvard University Press, Cambridge, Mass. 1963.

Hatzfeld, Jean: *Histoire de la Grèce Ancienne*. Payot, Paris, 1950.

Heyerdahl, Thor. *L'Expédition du Kon-Tiki* (translated from the Norwegian by Marguerite Gay and Gerd de Mautort). Albin Michel, Paris, 1951.

————.*American Indians in the Pacific: The Theory behind the "Kon-Tiki Expedition." Allen and Unwin, London, 1952.*

————. *Aku-Aku: Le Secret de l'Ile de Pâques* (translated from the Norwegian by Marguerite Gay and Gerd de Mautort). Albin Michel, Paris, 1958.

————. *The Art of Easter Island*. Allen and Unwin, London, 1976.

————. "The Heterogeneity of Small Sculptures on Easter Island before 1886." *Asian Perspectives,* XXII (1), 1979 (pp. 13–31).

Hicks, Jim. *The Persians*. Time-Life International, USA edition, 1975.

Hoorebeeck, Albert van. "Chronologie de l'Ile de Paques." *Kadath, Chroniques de Civilisations Disparues,* # 22, Bruxelles, Mars–Avril 1977a (pp. 3–12).

————. "Insondable Ile de Pâques," a series of articles in *La Libre Belgique,* Brussels, August 8, 9, 10, 11 and 12, 1977b.

————. *La Vérité sur l'Ile de Pâques*. Pierrette d'Antoine, Le Havre, 1979.

Horowitz, George. *The Spirit of the Jewish Law*. Central, New York, 1963.

Hough, Richard. *Captain Bligh and Mister Christian*. Cassell, London, 1980.

Hrozni, F. *Code Hittite Provenant de l'Asie Mineure*. Paris, 1922.

Ihering, Rudolf von. *Der Geist des Roemischen Recht* (10th ed.). Breitkopf und Härtel, Leipzig, 1968.

Ishii, Ryosuke. "Keibatsu no Rekishi (Nippon)." In *History of Punishment (Japan)*. 1952.

Jackson, Bernard S. *Theft in Early Jewish Law.* Clarendon Press, Oxford, 1972.

Jacobsen, Thorkild. "An Ancient Mesopotamian Trial of Homicide. A Sumerian Trial of a Case of Murder." Anacleta Biblica 12, *Studia Biblica et Orentalia,* Vol. III. (pp. 130–50). Oriens Antiquus, Pontificio Istituto Biblico, Roma, 1959.

Jimenez de Asua, Luis. *Tratado de Derecho Penal* (5 vols.). Editorial Losada, Buenos Aires, 1950.

Judd, Gerrit P., IV. *Hawaii: An Informal History.* Collier Books, Macmillan, New York, 1967.

*Justice in Japan.* Supreme Court of Japan, Tokyo, 1975.

Kara, Mustafa. "The Philosophy of Punishment in Islamic Law." Doctoral dissertation, Claremont Graduate School. Ann Arbor, Mich., University Microfilms, 1980.

Kaster, Heinrich L. *Breve Historia del Cercano Oriente* (translated by J.J. Thomas). El Ateneo, Buenos Aires, 1961.

Kenyon, Katheleen. *Archaeology in the Holy Land.* Ernest Benn, London, 1971.

Khadduri, Majid. *Islamic Jurisprudence.* John Hopkins Press, Baltimore, 1961.

Knoche, Walter. *Die Osterinsel.* Concepción, Chile, 1925.

Kramer, Samuel Noah. "A Father and His Perverse Son: The First Example of Juvenile Delinquency in the Recorded History of Man." *National Probation and Parole Association Journal,* Vol. 3, # 2, April 1957 (pp. 169–73).

———. *History Begins at Sumer.* Doubleday, New York, 1959.

———. *The Sumerians: Their History, Culture and Character.* University of Chicago Press, Chicago, 1963.

———. *Cradle of Civilization.* Time-Life International, Amsterdam, 1968.

———. *Sumerian Mythology.* University of Pennsylvania Press, Philadelphia, 1972.

Kunkel, Wolfgang. *An Introduction to Roman Legal and Constitutional History* (translated by J.M. Kelley). Oxford University Press, Oxford, 1973.

———. *Historia del Derecho Romano* (translated from the 4th German edition by Juan Miquel). Editorial Ariel, Barcelona, 1982.

*L'Art du Japon Eternel* (avec Introduction de Sazo Idemitsu). Musée du Petit Palais de la Ville de Paris, 1981.

Lavachery, Henri. "La Mission Franco-Belge dans l'Ile de Pâques (July 1934–April 1935). Bref Aperçu de ses Travaux." *Bulletin des Musées Royaux d'Art et d'Histoire,* Troisième Série, VII Année, # 3, May-June 1935 (pp. 50–63).

———. *Ile de Paquês.* Bernard Grasset, Paris, 1935.

———. "Construction à l'Etude de l'Archeologie de l'Ile de Pitcairn. *Bulletin de la Société des Americanistes de Belgique,* # 19, Bruxelles, March 1936.

———. "Mission Franco-Belge a l'Ile de Pâques (July 1934–April 1935)." XVI Congres Internationale d'Anthropologie, Bruxelles, 1935. Imprimerie Médical et Scientifique, Bruxelles, 1936b.

———. "Sculptures Modernes de l'Ile de Pâques." *Outre-Mer, Revue Générale de Colonisation,* Année 1937, 4éme. Trimestre. Librairie Larose, Paris (pp. 1–14).

———. "Une Figure en Pierre de l'Ile de Pâques." *Bulletin des Musées Royaux d'Art et d'Histoire,* # 3, Bruxelles, June 1938 (pp. 55–61).

———. *Les Petrogliphes de l'Ile de Pâques,* Première Parti (texte), Deuxième Parti (Planches). De Sikkel, Anvers, 1939.

————. "Vie des Polynesiens." Collection Lebègue, 6ème. Série, No. 70, Bruxelles, 1946.

————. "Notes sur l'Art Plastique de l'Ile de Pâques." In *Melanges Georges Smets* (pp. 481–95). Librairie Encyclopedique, Bruxelles, 1952.

————. "Thor Heyerdahl et le Pacific." *Journal de la Société des Océanistes,* Tome XXI, # 21, Musée de l'Homme, Paris, December 1965 (pp. 151–9).

Lawrence, George. *Indian Art.* Tudor, New York, 1963.

Leakey, R.E., and Lewin, R. *Origins.* Macdonald and Jane's, London, 1977.

Lebon, Gustavo. *Las Primeras Civilizaciones.* M. Aguilar, Madrid, no date.

Lecuona, Manuel de. "El Derecho Penal en el Fuero: Fuentes." In *Estudios Vascos de Criminología* pp. 169–77. Mensajero, Bilbao, Spain, 1982.

Le Senne, Rene. *Traité de Caractérologie.* Presses Universitaires de France, Paris, 1963.

Levine, Donald N. *Wax and Gold: Tradition and Innovation in Ethiopia.* University of Chicago Press, Chicago, 1965.

Lissner, Ivar. *The Living Past: 7,000 Years of Civilization* (translated from the German by J. Maxwell Brownjohn-Oxon). Putnam, New York, 1957.

Logiadou-Platonos, Sosso. *Crète.* Methioulakis, Athens, no date.

Lopez-Rey, Manuel. *Crime: An Analytical Appraisal.* Routledge and Kegan Paul, London, 1970.

Lorenz, Konrad Z. *On Aggression* (translated from the original German by Marjorie Latzke). Bantam, New York, 1970.

Ma, Herbert H.P. "Law and Morality: Some Reflections on the Chinese Experience, Past and Present." *Philosophy East and West,* Vol. 21, # 4, October 1971 (pp. 443–60).

Mackey, The Rev. Virginia. *Punishment in the Scripture and Tradition of Judaism, Christianity and Islam.* National Interreligious Task Force on Criminal Justice, New York, 1983.

MacMillan Brown, J. *The Riddle of the Pacific.* T. Fischer and Unwin, London, 1924.

Maine, Sir Henry Summer. *Ancient Law: Its Connection with the Early History of Society and Its Relations to Modern Ideas* (11th ed.). John Murray, London, 1887.

Malinowsky, Bronislaw. *Crime and Custom in Savage Society.* Trubner, London, 1940.

————. "El Crimen Primitivo y su Castigo." *Criminología, Gobierno del Estado de Mexico,* Ano 1, # 5, Editorial Tollocan, Toluca, Mexico, April 17, 1978, (pp. 55–101).

Mariani, Fosco. "The Enchanted Castle of 'Safe' Myths." In *This is Japan,* # 16 (pp. 112–17). Asahi Shimbum, Tokyo, 1969.

Masaki, Akira. *Reminiscences of a Japanese Penologist.* Japan Criminal Policy Association, Tokyo, 1964.

Maziere, Francois. *Fantastique Ile de Pâques.* Robert Laffont, Paris, 1965.

McNeill, William H., and Robinson Waldman, Marilyn (eds.). *The Islamic World,* Readings in World History, Vol. 6. Oxford University Press, New York, 1973.

McNeill, William H., and Sedlar, Jean W. (eds.). *The Origins of Civilization,* Readings in World History, Vol. 1. Oxford University Press, New York, 1968.

———. *The Ancient Near East,* Readings in World History, Vol. 2. Oxford University Press, New York, 1968.

———. *The Classical Mediterranean World,* Readings in World History, Vol. 3. Oxford University Press, New York, 1969.

———. *Classical India,* Readings in World History, Vol. 4. Oxford University Press, New York, 1969.

———. *Classical China,* Readings in World History, Vol. 5. Oxford University Press, New York, 1977.

———. *China, India and Japan: The Middle Period,* Readings in World History, Vol. 7. Oxford University Press, New York, 1971.

Mead, Margaret. *Coming of Age in Samoa.* Penguin Books, London, 1981a.

———. *Growing Up in New Guinea.* Penguin Books, London, 1981b.

Metraux, Alfred. *Introduction a la Connaissance de l'Ile de Pâques. A propos d'une Exposition.* Musée d'Ethnographie du Trocadero, Paris, 1935.

———. *La Isla de Pascua* (translated from the original French by J.J. Arreola). Fondo de Cultura Económica, Mexico, 1950.

———. *Voodoo in Haiti.* Deutsch, London, 1959.

Middendorff, Wolf. *Estudios de Criminología Histórica,* Estudios de Psicología Criminal, Vol. XIV (translated from the original German by José Belloch Zimmerman). Espasa-Calpe, Madrid, 1976.

Mommsen, Teodoro. *El Derecho Penal Romano* (translated from the original German by P. Dorado, 2 vols.). La España Moderna, Madrid, no date.

Montagu, Ashley. "Give Those Neanderthals a Break." Letter to the Editor in July 14, 1985, *The New York Times.* Copyright © 1985 by The New York Times Company. Reprinted by permission.

Montgomery, James A. *The International Christian Commentary: The Book of Daniel.* Clark, Edinburgh, 1950.

Morris, Desmond. *The Naked Ape: A Zoological Study of Human Behavior.* J. Cape, London, 1968.

Moulin, Raoul Jean. *Prehistoric Painting.* Heron Books, London, 1965.

Mueller, Gerhard O.W. "Tort, Crime and the Primitive." *Journal of Criminal Law, Criminology and Police Science,* Vol. 46 (pp. 303–32).

Mulloy, William, and Figueroa G.H., Gonzalo. *The A Kivi-Vai Teka Complex and its Relationship to Easter Island Prehistory,* Asian and Pacific Archaeology Series #8. Social Science Research Institute, University of Hawaii at Manoa, 1978.

Munro, George. *Rapa Nui, Te Pito o Te Henua.* Publicaciones y Ediciones, Santiago, Chile, 1985.

Negenman, Jean. *Univers de la Bible: Atlas du Proche-Orient Biblique* (translated by R.P. Jacques Potin, O.P.). Elzevir-Sequoia, Bruxelles, 1971.

Neusner, Jacob. *History of the Jews in Babylonia* (5 vols.). New York, 1965–70.

Noda, Yosiyuki. *Introduction to Japanese Law* (translated and edited by Arthur H. Angelo). University of Tokyo Press, Tokyo, 1977.

Nogrady, Georges L. (ed.). *Microbiology of Easter Island* (Vol. 1). Published by the editor, Montreal, 1974.

Nordhoff, Charles, and Hall, James Norman. *The Mutiny of the Bounty.* Heritage Press, 1947.

————. *The Hurricane*. Triangle Books, New York, 1944.

Nordman, P.I. *Tahiti*. Fernand Nathan, Paris, 1938.

Noveck, Simon (ed.). *Great Jewish Personalities in Ancient and Medieval Times*. Farrar, Straus and Cudahy, New York, 1959.

Oda, Susumu. "A Historical-Criminological Study of the Offenders of the Tokugawa Era (1600–1867) in Japan." *Acta Criminologiae et Medicinae Legalis Japonica*, Vol. 41, # 2, April 1975 (pp. 97–101).

Ogrizek, Doré. *La Grèce*. Editions Odé, Paris, 1953.

Olmstead, Albert ten Eyck. *History of the Persian Empire*. University of Chicago Press, Chicago, 1948.

Pacini, Dante. *Filosofia da Ciência Criminal*, ed. J. Di Giorgio. Rio de Janeiro, J. Di Gregorio, 1983.

Palacio Sanchez-Izquierdo, Jose Ricardo. "Informe acerca del Decreto-Ley del 26 de Agosto de 1975 sobre Prevención del Terrorismo." In *Estudios Vascos de Criminología* (pp. 275–90). Mensajero, Bilbao, Spain, 1982.

Parmelee, Maurice. *Criminology*. Macmillan, New York, 1918.

Patar, D.P., and Khan, M.Z. "A Preliminary Monograph on the Problem of Dacoity in Buldenkhand and the Chambal Valley." Unpublished paper, Department of Criminology and Forensic Science, University of Saugar, India, 1974.

Peretz, Don; Moench, Richard U.; and Mohsen, Safia K. *Islam: Legacy of the Past, Challenge of the Future*. North River Press, New York, 1983.

Perham, Margery. *The Government of Ethiopia*. Faber and Faber, London, 1947.

Philips, Anthony. *Ancient Israel's Criminal Law*. Basil Blackwell, Oxford, 1970.

Pinatel, Jean. "Esquisse de la Pensée Criminologique dans la Grèce Antique." *Revue de Science Criminelle et de Droit Pénal Comparé*, Nouvelle Série, # 3, July–September 1974 (pp. 645–54).

————. "Trois Moments de l'Histoire de la Pensée Criminologique: Rome, le Christianisme et la Renaissance." *Revue de Science Criminelle et de Droit Pénal Comparé*, Nouvelle Série, # 3, July–September 1978 (pp. 687–92).

————. "Introducción." In *Estudios Vascos de Criminología* (pp. 19–26). Mensajero, Bilbao, Spain, 1982.

Pirenne, Jacques. *Histoire des Institutions et du Droit Privé de l'Ancient Egypt*. Edition de la Fondation Egyptologique Reine Elizabeth, Bruxelles, 1932–35.

Plato. *The Republic* (translated with an introduction by Desmond Lee, 2nd rev. ed.). Penguin Books, London, 1974.

Pontius, Anneliese A. "Easter Island Stone Giants: A Neuro-Psychiatric View." *Perceptual and Motor Skills*, Vol. 28, 1969 (pp. 207–12).

Porteous, J. Douglas. *The Modernization of Easter Island*, Western Geographical Series, Vol. 19. University of Victoria, British Columbia, Canada, 1981.

Postgate, Nicholas. *The First Empires*. Elsevier-Phaidon, Turnhout, Belgium, 1977.

Potok, Chaim. *Wanderings: History of the Jews*. Knopf, New York, 1983.

Prins, Adolfo. *Criminalidad y Represión* (translated from the original French by Manuel Nuñez de Arenas). Revista de Legislación y Jurisprudencia, Madrid, 1911.

Pritchard, James. *Ancient Near Eastern Texts*. Princeton University Press, Princeton, NJ, 1969.

Ramirez O., Julio T. *Navegando a Rapa Nui.* Impr. San Francisco, Padre Las Casas, Chile, 1935.

Rebollo Paz, Ana Maria M. de. *Historia de la Civilización y de las Instituciones* (2 vols., 2nd ed.). Cathedra, Buenos Aires, 1971.

Reni, David. *World Legal Systems in the World Today.* 1972.

*Rock-Painting in Africa.* South African Archaeological Society, Rustica Press, Cape Town, no date.

Rodriguez Devesa, Jose Maria. *Derecho Penal: Parte General* (5th ed.). Madrid, 1976.

Rodriguez R., Roberto; Matthei S., Oscar; and Quezada M., Max. *Flora Arbórea de Chile.* Editorial de la Universidad de Concepción, Chile, 1983.

Rosenberg, Shalom. *Breve Historia de Jerusalen.* Biblioteca Popular Judía, Congreso Judio Mundial, Buenos Aires, 1967.

Rosenthal, Erwin I.J. *Judaism and Islam.* Thomas Yoseloff, New York, 1961.

Rothman, David I. *The Discovery of the Asylum.* Little, Brown, Boston, 1971.

Rousselet, Marcel. *Histoire de la Justice.* Presses Universitaires de France, Paris, 1948.

Routledge, Scoresby. *The Mystery of Easter Island: The Story of an Expedition.* Sifton, Praed and Co., London, 1919.

Rowland, Benjamin. *The Ajanta Caves.* A Mentor-UNESCO Art Book, Milan, Italy, 1963.

Rukang, Wu. Information published in the *Jerusalem Post,* 6 April 1980, based on reports from Reuters and Agence France Press.

Rutter, Owen. *The Court-Martial of the "Bounty" Mutineers.* William Hodge, London, 1931.

Sachar, Abram Leon. *A History of the Jews.* Knopf, New York, 1943.

Saggs, H.W.F. *The Greatness That Was Babylon.* Hawthorn Books, London, 1966.

St. Clair, D. *Drum and Candle.* Macdonald, London, 1971.

Sakellarakis, J.A. *Heraklion Museum.* Ekdotike Athenon, Athens, 1982.

Saleilles, Raymond. *The Individualization of Punishment.* Little, Brown, Boston, 1913.

Santalucia, B. "Pena Criminale (Diritto Romano)." In *Encyclopedia del Diritto,* Vol. XXXII (pp. 734–9). Milano, 1982.

Schacht, Joseph. *An Introduction to Islamic Law.* Oxford University Press, Oxford, 1964.

Schafer, Stephen. *Introduction to Criminology.* Reston, Reston, Va., 1976.

Schisas, F.M. *Offences Against the State in Roman Law.* London, 1926.

Schmökel, Hartmut. *El País de los Sumerios* (translated by Dr. Guillermo Koehle). Editorial Universitaria de Buenos Aires, 1965.

Schulberg, Lucille. *Historic India.* Time-Life International, Netherland N.V., 1968.

Sciacca, Federico. *Historia de la Filosofía.* Miracle Editor, Barcelona, 1954.

Scott, Ralph W. *A New Look at Biblical Crime.* Nelson-Hall, Chicago, 1979.

Seiroku, Noma. *The Arts of Japan* (2 vols.). Kodansa International, Tokyo, 1967 and 1968.

Senderey, Moises. *Breve Historia del Pueblo de Israel* (2 vols.). Editorial Yehuda, Buenos Aires, 1959.

Sethna, J.M.J. *Society and the Criminal.* Tripathi, Bombay, 1971.

Shapiro, A.L. "The Physical Relationships of the Easter Islanders." In *Ethnology of*

*Easter Island,* ed. Alfred Metraux. Bernice P. Bishop Museum Bulletin # 160. Honolulu, Hawaii, 1940.

Shibuya, Nobuhisa. *The History of Japanese Punishments* (published in Japanese), 1963.

Shoro, Shimada. *Asia: Rekishi to Ho (Asia-History and Law),* 1963.

Sjöberg, Åke W. "Der Vater und sein missratener Sohn." *Journal of Cuneiform Studies,* Vol. XXV, # 3, Cambridge, Mass., July 1973 (pp. 105–69).

Smith, William Stevenson. *Ancient Egypt.* Greenwich, Boston, 1960.

Speiser, E.A. (ed.). *At the Dawn of Civilization.* Rutgers University Press, New Brunswick, N.J., 1964.

Steele, F.R. "The Code of Lipit-Ishtar." *American Journal of Archaeology,* Vols. 51 and 52, pp. 158 ff. and 425 ff., respectively, 1947 and 1948.

Steinmetz, Sebald Rudolf. *Ethnologische Studien zur ersten Entwicklung der Strafe* (2 vols.). Leiden, 1894.

Stevens, Roger. *The Land of the Great Sophy* (2nd ed.). Metheun, London, 1971.

Stewart, Desmond. *Early Islam.* Time-Life International, Nederland N.V., 1968.

———. "The Effect of Islamic Legislation on Crime and Punishment in Saudi Arabia." *Proceedings of the Symposium held in Ryadh (9–13 October, 1976).* Translated, edited and printed in collaboration with the U.N. Social Defense Research Institute (UNSDRI), Rome, 1980.

Strachan-Davidson, James Leigh. *Problems of the Roman Criminal Law* (2 vols.). Clarendon Press, Oxford, 1912.

Su, Jyun-hsyong. "On Traditional Legal Thought and its Political Consequences in China." *National Taiwan University Law Journal,* Vol. 2, # 1, October 1972 (pp. 49–73).

Taft, Donald. *Criminology* (3rd ed.). Macmillan, New York, 1956.

Tanaka, Shuyu. *Sekai Hoshi Gaisetsu (Outline of the World History of Laws).* 1950.

Taylor, A.G. "Medical Expedition to Easter Island." *Royal Canadian Dental Corps Quarterly,* Vol. 6, # 12, 1965 (pp. 15–25).

Telechea Idigoras, J. Ignacio. "La Criminología frente al Pasado Vasco." In *Estudios Vascos de Criminología* (pp. 179–84). Mensajero, Bilbao, Spain, 1982.

Thoma, Clemens. "The Death Penalty and Torture in the Jewish Tradition." In Bockle and Pohier (eds.), *The Death Penalty and Torture.* Seabury Press, New York, 1979.

Thomas, Hugh. *La Guerra Civil Española.* Ediciones Ruedo Ibérico, Paris, 1962.

Thomson, John. *China: The Land and Its People.* John Warner, Hong Kong, 1977.

Thomson, W.J. (Paymaster). *Te Pito te Henua or Easter Island.* Report of the National Museum under the Direction of the Smithsonian Institution for the year ending June 30, 1889. Washington, D.C., 1891.

Thonissen, Jean Joseph. "Etudes sur l'Histoire du Droit Criminel des Peuples Anciens." *Bulletins de l'Academie Royale de Belgique,* 2ème. Série, Vol. 22, Bruxelles, 1866.

Thot, Ladislao. "Ciencia Penitenciaria." *Revista de Identificación y Ciencias Penales,* Facultad de Ciencias Jurídicas y Sociales, Universidad Nacional de La Plata, Argentina, Vol. 32, September 1937.

———. "Historia de las Antiguas Instituciones de Derecho Penal. (Arqueología Criminal)." *Revista de Identificación y Ciencias Penales,* Facultad de Ciencias Jurídicas y Sociales, Universidad Nacional de La Plata, Argentina, Vol. 43, December 1939.

Tseng, Beauson. "Origins of a Great Culture." *Free China Review,* December 1973 (pp. 17–21).

Tuchman, Barbara W. *Practicing History.* Knopf, New York, 1981.

Tylor, Edward B. *Researchers into the Early History of Mankind.* Phoenix Books, University of Chicago Press, Chicago, 1964.

Uematsu, Tadashi. "Trends of the Revision of the Penal Code in Japan." *Hitotsubashi Journal of Law and Politics,* Vol. 3, April 1964.

Valdeavellano, Luis G. de. "El Desarrollo del Derecho en la Peninsual Ibérica hasta alrededor del año 1300." *Cahiers d'Histoire Mondiale,* Vol. III, No. 4, UNESCO, Neuchâtel, 1957 (pp. 833–53).

Varma, Sri Paripurnanand. *Pathology of Crime and Delinquency.* Sahitya Bhawan Agra, 1972.

———. *Suicide in India and Abroad.* Sahitya Bhawan, Agra, 1976.

———. *Sex Offences in India and Abroad.* B.R. Publishing, Delhi, 1979.

Vasyayana. *Kama Sutra: The Hindu Art of Love* (translated from the original Sanskrit by S.C. Upadhyaya). Bombay, 1963.

Vold, George B. *Theoretical Criminology.* Oxford University Press, New York, 1958.

Von Aster, Ernst. *Historia de la Filosofia.* Zig-Zag, Santiago, Chile, 1949.

Wang, Dominique T.C. *Les Sources du Droit Japonais.* Librairie Droz, Genève, 1978.

Watanabe, Yozo, assisted by Max Rheinstein. "The Family and the Law: The Individualistic Premise and Modern Japanese Family Law." In Arthur Taylor von Mehren, *Law in Japan. The Legal Order in a Changing Society* (pp. 364–98). Harvard University Press, Cambridge, Mass., 1963.

Weigel, James, Jr. *Mythology for the Modern Reader.* Centennial Press, Lincoln, Neb. 1974.

Wiet, Gaston. "L'Empire Neo-Byzantine des Omeyyades et l'Empire Neo-Sassanide des Abbassides." *Cahiers d'Histoire Mondiale,* UNESCO, Vol. I, – 1, July 1953 (pp. 63–71).

Willetts, William. *Foundations of Chinese Art* (Taiwan ed.). 1967.

Williams, John Alden (ed.). *Islam.* George Braziller, New York, 1962.

Wu, John C.H. "Joy in Chinese Philosophy." *Free China Review,* January 1974 (pp. 13–24).

Yaron, Reuven. *The Laws of Eshnunna.* Magnes Press, Hebrew University of Jerusalem, 1969.

Yokoyama, Minoru. "How Have Prisons Been Used in Japan?" Unpublished paper presented at the World Congress of the International Sociological Association, Mexico City, 18 August 1982.

Zepos, Pan J. *Greek Law.* Three lectures delivered at Cambridge and Oxford in 1946. A. Sideris, Athens, 1949.

Zilboorg, Gregory, in collaboration with George W. Henry. *A History of Medical Psychology.* Norton, New York, 1941.

# Index

# About the Author

Israel Drapkin, M.D., is Professor Emeritus of Criminology, Faculty of Law, The Hebrew University of Jerusalem, since 1974. Formerly, he was the director of the Institute of Criminology of Chile (1936–1959), and Professor at the University of Chile (1950–1959). He was the United Nations Expert in Israel (1957), and at the Asia and Far East Institute for the Prevention of Crime and Treatment of Offenders—UNAFEI (1965 and 1968). He has been visiting professor at the University of Pennsylvania (Philadelphia) and the American University (Washington, D.C.).